Employee Benefits Answer Book

Third Edition

Cynthia M. Combe, Esq.
Gerald J. Talbot, Esq.

THE PANEL ANSWER BOOK SERIES

A PANEL PUBLICATION
ASPEN PUBLISHERS, INC.

Copyright © 1994

by
PANEL PUBLISHERS
A division of Aspen Publishers, Inc.
A Wolters Kluwer Company

36 West 44th Street
Suite 1316
New York, NY 10036
(212) 790-2000

ISBN 1-56706-044-7

Printed in the United States of America

About Panel Publishers

Panel derives its name from a panel of business professionals who organized in 1964 to publish authoritative, timely books, information services, and journals written by specialists to assist accountants, tax practitioners, attorneys, and other business professionals; human resources, compensation and benefits, and pension and profit-sharing professionals; and owners of small to medium-sized businesses. Our mission is to provide practical, solution-based, "how-to" information to business professionals.

Available in the Panel Answer Book Series:

The Pension Answer Book
COBRA Handbook
ERISA Fiduciary Answer Book
401 (K) Answer Book
Executive Compensation Answer Book
Employment Law Answer Book
Health Insurance Answer Book
Individual Retirement Account Answer Book
Nonqualified Deferred Compensation Answer Book

PANEL PUBLISHERS
A division of Aspen Publishers, Inc.
Practical Solutions for Business Professionals

Preface

In this past year, welfare benefits have been heavily scrutinized and regulated. In addition, President Clinton's proposed Health Security Act has focused attention on preservation of health care coverage and on the content and funding of health care benefits. In particular, the scope and complexity of the laws governing group health plans have increased dramatically. The Omnibus Budget Reconciliation Bill of 1993 (OBRA '93) effected several important changes, a number of which have a significant impact on group health plans and not all of which have been well-publicized. Among them are:

- **Retiree Medical Plans:** Buried in the middle of OBRA '93 was a three-word change to the Social Security Act that makes retiree medical plans secondary to Medicare for 18 months for individuals of any age who are entitled to Medicare due to end-stage renal disease.

- **QMCSOs:** Group health plans must adopt a procedure for determining whether a court order is a qualified medical child support order (QMCSO), distribute the procedure to the alternate payees listed in the court order and, if the plan administrator determines that a court order is a valid QMCSO, honor the QMCSO and pay group health plan benefits to the alternate payees specified in the QMCSO.

- **Pediatric Vaccines:** The level of group health plan coverage in effect on May 1, 1993 for pediatric vaccines has "vested" and cannot be cut back.

- **Adopted Children:** Group health plans must cover adopted children and children placed for adoption, whether or not the adoption is final, on the same terms and conditions as other children but without the application of any preexisting condition limitations.

- **Data Reporting:** Employers will be required to make detailed annual reports concerning group health plan participants to a newly established Medicare and Medicaid Coverage Data Bank.

- **Disability-Based Distinctions:** The EEOC's new Interim Final Rule under the Americans With Disabilities Act of 1990 restricts the use of disability-based benefit limits in group health plans except under very limited circumstances.

- **Family Leave:** The Family and Medical Leave Act of 1993 (FMLA) and the DOL's Interim Final Rule implementing the FMLA impose complex new requirements regarding unpaid family leave, substitution of paid leave for unpaid leave, continuation of health benefit coverage during leave, and resumption of all benefit coverage upon return from leave.

- **Employer Deduction for Group Health Plan Expenses:** The employer's Code Section 162 deduction will be lost unless the employer complies with new Code Section 162(n) regarding payment of New York hospital rates.

These and countless other changes are detailed in this revised and expanded Third Edition of the *Employee Benefits Answer Book*. We have also revised the COBRA chapter in response to reader request to expand the treatment of gross misconduct, late notice of qualifying events, and divorce. In addition, for your ease of reference, we have also broken out separate chapters on retiree medical benefits, on accounting for nonpension retirement and postemployment benefits, and on the Americans With Disabilities Act of 1990, the Family Leave Act of 1993, and the Age Discrimination in Employment Act of 1967.

Lastly, as the manuscript for this edition was at the printer, the text of President Clinton's long-awaited Health Security Act was released. We are pleased to be able to include a special appendix to the Third Edition summarizing the main features of the Health Security Act for your reference in the exciting debate to come.

> Cynthia M. Combe
> Gerard J. Talbot
> January 1994

How to Use This Book

The Third Edition of the *Employee Benefits Answer Book* is designed for professionals who need quick and authoritative answers to help them decide whether to institute or continue medical, group term life, cafeteria plans, or other employee welfare benefit plans, how to choose the plans most suited to their needs, and how to comply with the morass of federal requirements. This book uses simple, straightforward language and avoids technical jargon where possible. Citations of authority are provided as research aids for those who need to pursue particular items in greater detail.

The question-and-answer format, with its breadth of coverage and plain-language explanations, effectively conveys the complex and essential subject matter of employee welfare benefit plans to the subscriber.

Numbering System: The questions are numbered consecutively within each chapter (e.g., 2:1, 2:2, etc.).

Detailed List of Questions: The detailed List of Questions that follows the Table of Contents in the front of the book helps the reader locate the areas of immediate interest. This list is comparable to a detailed table of contents, providing both the question number and the page on which the answer appears.

Glossary of Terms: Because the employee welfare benefits area is replete with technical terms that have specific legal meanings, a special glossary of terms is provided following the question-and-answer portion of the book. Expressions not defined elsewhere, and abbreviations used throughout the book, are defined in the glossary, which is arranged in alphabetical order.

Index: An index is provided as a further aid to locating specific information. Key words included in the glossary are used in the index as well. All references in the index are to question numbers.

Use of Abbreviations: Because of the breadth of subject area, a number of terms and statutory references are abbreviated throughout the *Employee Benefits Answer Book*. Among the most common of these shorthand references are:

IRC—The Internal Revenue Code of 1986

ERISA—The Employee Retirement Income Security Act of 1974, as amended

IRS—The Internal Revenue Service

DOL—The U.S. Department of Labor

COBRA—The Consolidated Omnibus Budget Reconciliation Act of 1985

For explanations of other abbreviations, consult the Glossary.

About the Authors

Cynthia M. Combe is president of the Scarsdale, New York firm of Combe Benefits, Inc., an employee benefits consulting company. Ms. Combe previously served as Special Counsel-Benefits with the law firm of Rosenman & Colin in New York. Before joining Rosenman & Colin, she was an associate and group consultant with William M. Mercer, Incorporated. Ms. Combe also has served as an ERISA attorney at the New York law firm LeBoeuf, Lamb, Leiby & MacRae and at JC Penney Company, Inc. A frequent lecturer on various benefit topics, including ERISA and managed care, tax issues in medical plan design, COBRA, HMOs, and retiree benefits, Ms. Combe has chaired the Practising Law Institute's seminar on "Employee Welfare Benefit Plans" and is past chairman of its seminar "Managed Health Care: Legal and Operational Issues" and is a member of the Institute's Employee Benefits Law Advisory Committee. Ms. Combe's professional memberships include the American Bar Association's Business Law Section, the Tax Section, and Torts and Insurance Section; The National Health Lawyers Association; and the Association of the Bar of the City of New York. Ms. Combe is the co-author of Panel Publishers' *Employee Benefits Answer Book Special Supplement on COBRA*.

Gerard J. Talbot, Esq. is currently a practicing attorney in New York City. For many years he was Vice-President and Tax Counsel of the Metropolitan Life Insurance Company. He has over 30 years of legal experience in tax and employee benefits matters and has been a frequent writer and speaker on tax and employee benefits issues. Mr. Talbot has been chairman of the Tax Section of the Association of Life Insurance Counsel, a member of the Employee Benefits Committee of the Tax Section of the American Bar Association, and a member of the Program Committee of the Tax Foundation. He also served as Metropolitan Life's official representative to the ERISA Industry Committee and was a member and past chairman of the Fiduciary Task Force of the American Council of Life Insurance. Mr. Talbot also has been a member of the Tax Executives Institute and has served on the ACLI-HIAA Joint Task Force on Retiree Health Benefits, the ACLI Pension Committee, the HIAA Tax Committee, and the ABA Insurance Committee. Mr. Talbot received his law degree from Fordham Law School, where he was an editor of the law review, and holds a master of laws in taxation degree from New York University School of Law.

Acknowledgments. The authors wish to thank our editor, Ellen Ros, for her incisive and careful work on this extensive revision. We are also grateful to Susan Holt, developmental editor, for her assistance on this project. We also thank the entire staff at Panel Publishers for their extremely hard work in getting this manuscript through production.

As always, we are especially indebted to Richard Kravitz, Publisher, for his vision and commitment to excellence in employee benefit publications.

Lastly, we want to thank our families. Cynthia Combe thanks her husband Carter for his patience and support and her seven-year-old son Paul for his "help," and Gerard Talbot thanks his wife Marguerite for her encouragement and understanding.

Contents

Contents

List of Questions

Requirements for Plan Document

Reporting and Disclosure

Penalties and Enforcement

Effect of the Proposed Clinton Health Plan

Chapter 3 Medical Plans Generally

Basic Concepts

Legal Parameters of Benefit Design

Qualified Medical Child Support Orders

Medicare and Medicaid Coverage Data Bank Reporting Requirement

Code Section 105(h) Nondiscrimination Rules

Employee Assistance Programs

Effect of the Proposed Clinton Health Plan

Chapter 4 Retiree Medical Benefits

Basic Concepts

Funding Options

Chapter 5 Health Maintenance Organizations

Basic Concepts

Chapter 6 COBRA Requirements for Continuation of Coverage under Group Health Plans

Chapter 7 Cafeteria Plans

Chapter 8   Dependent Care Assistance, Educational Assistance, and Group Legal Services

I

Qualified Scholarships and Tuition Reductions

Chapter 9   Group Long-Term Care Insurance

Basic Concepts

Chapter 10 Disability Income Plans

Basic Concepts

Tax Treatment of Employers

Tax Treatment of Employees

Tax Treatment of Self-Employed Persons and Subchapter S Corporation Shareholder-Employees

Chapter 11 Group Term Life Insurance Plans

"Group of Employees" Requirement

Policy Carried Directly or Indirectly by the Employer

Benefit Formula Precluding Individual Selection

Nondiscrimination Rules

Other Plan Design Limitations

Tax Treatment of Employer Contributions

Income Tax Treatment of Coverage Provided to Employees

Chapter 12 Death Benefits Other Than Employee Group Term Life Insurance

Dependent Group Term Life Insurance

Uninsured Death Benefits

Split-Dollar Life Insurance

Chapter 13   Fringe Benefits

Introduction

No-Additional-Cost Services

Cars and Other Vehicles

Employee Gifts and Achievement Awards

Chapter 14 Vacation and Severance Pay Plans

Vacation Pay Plans

Severance Pay Plans

"Golden Parachute" Payments

Chapter 15   Family and Medical Leave

Basic Concepts

Covered Employers

Chapter 16 Age Discrimination in Employment Act (ADEA) of 1967

Using Retirement Benefits to Reduce Other Benefits

Chapter 18 Other Federal Laws

Labor Laws and Collective Bargaining

Worker Adjustment and Retraining Notification Act of 1988 (WARN)

Retiree Benefits of Bankrupt Companies

Veterans Health Care Amendments of 1986

Welfare Benefit Fund Rules

Financing Welfare Benefits with Life Insurance

Chapter 20   Financial Accounting Rules for Nonpension Retiree and Postemployment Benefits

Chapter 1

Introduction

Employee welfare benefits are a major component of the compensation package provided by employers to their employees. In recent years, as the cost of these benefits has risen, employers, their counsel, and employee benefit professionals have devoted more and more of their resources to the establishment and administration of these plans and to maintaining legal compliance with a variety of statutory requirements. This chapter introduces the reasons for having welfare benefit plans and the regulatory environment in which these plans must exist.

Q 1:1   What are employee welfare benefits?

In addition to the employee's salary or hourly wage, many employers provide fringe benefits to their employees. These benefits fall into two general categories: retirement benefits, such as pension plans and profit-sharing plans, and welfare benefits. Welfare benefits generally protect an employee during his or her active working years and include benefits such as medical coverage, life insurance, disability income protection, vacation pay, and severance pay. Often, the employer also will supplement the active employee protection with some welfare benefit protection during retirement, such as retiree medical coverage.

Q 1:2 Why do employers provide employee welfare benefits?

Employers provide their employees with employee welfare benefits for a variety of reasons:

1. To achieve and maintain a competitive edge in the job market, particularly in the employer's specific industry or geographic location;

2. To provide employees with security and peace of mind to help enhance their job performance;

3. To retain employees who possess valuable knowledge, skills, and experience;

4. To provide owners or management with needed benefits, which are then extended to the rank-and-file employees (usually as a result of tax requirements); and

5. To provide an additional means of compensating employees on a tax-favored basis without inflating salaries.

Q 1:3 Why are they important to employees?

Employee welfare benefits are important to employees for a number of reasons.

1. The employer often pays all or a major part of the cost of the coverage. For some benefits, such as medical benefits, the difference that an employer contribution makes can be quite significant and may be the only way that employees can obtain the coverage.

2. If employees are required to contribute, coverage under the various plans is often less expensive than if the employee purchased it individually, because the employer can take advantage of group rates.

3. Employer-provided welfare benefits generally are entitled to tax benefits that the employee would be unable to obtain on his or her own.

4. Employer-provided welfare benefits provide financial protection for the employee, his or her family, and beneficiaries against various adverse contingencies, such as:

—Temporary loss of income due to disability (short- and long-term disability plans),

—Catastrophic expenses (medical plans),

—Loss of the ability to perform the activities of daily living (long-term care insurance plans), and

—Death of the employee (life insurance and business travel accident insurance).

5. Employees feel that the employer-provider is concerned about their welfare.

Q 1:4   What federal laws govern these plans?

A myriad of federal laws govern employee welfare benefit plans, because they are often seized upon as a means of accomplishing Congress's social policy goals. Some of the major federal laws affecting these plans are:

- Employee Retirement Income Security Act of 1974 (ERISA)
- Internal Revenue Code (IRC Code)
- Consolidated Omnibus Budget Reconciliation Act of 1985 (COBRA)
- Health Maintenance Organization Act of 1973 (HMO Act)
- Age Discrimination in Employment Act of 1967 (ADEA)
- Civil Rights Act of 1964, in particular, Title VII
- Americans with Disabilities Act of 1990 (ADA)
- Family and Medical Leave Act of 1993 (FMLA)

Numerous other federal laws also govern employee welfare benefits, to a greater or lesser extent. The result is a maze of requirements that must be met to have a plan that complies with applicable laws.

Q 1:5   Do any of these federal laws force the employer to offer a plan?

No, no federal law requires an employer to offer an employee welfare benefit plan. (Mandatory employer contributions under the

Social Security Federal Insurance Contribution Act (FICA) for Medicare and Social Security disability benefits are rarely viewed as benefits provided by the employer.) All of the federal laws discussed in this book do, however, place strings, requirements, conditions, and limitations on plans that the employer may voluntarily offer.

Q 1:6   What mechanisms does the IRC use to influence the scope and content of employee welfare benefit plans?

By far the most popular method for influencing employer-provided welfare benefit plans is congressional tinkering with the Internal Revenue Code (IRC). The IRC offers unique opportunities to target aspects of a single type of benefit plan or a class of benefit plans, because the Internal Revenue Service (IRS) often is authorized to restrict or deny favorable tax treatment without the necessity of commencing a lawsuit first. Congress can create a powerful economic push toward desired employer behavior by incorporating financial incentives or disincentives into the IRC. Typically, one of four techniques is used:

1. Allowing or restricting the deductibility of employer contributions to plans,
2. Exempting from taxation or taxing the value of coverage provided to employees,
3. Exempting from taxation or taxing the benefits received from the plan by the employee or beneficiary, and
4. Imposing excise taxes on the employer for undesirable practices.

These methods are often used to ensure that the plan's eligibility provisions and covered benefits do not discriminate in favor of highly compensated employees. They are also used to encourage employers to extend plan coverage to a significant portion of rank-and-file employees and, more recently, to adopted children and children placed for adoption. Occasionally, these methods are used to virtually force coverage of benefits deemed socially desirable, such as continuation of medical plan coverage for a period of time after termination of employment, death, or divorce (COBRA excise tax), coverage of specific medical conditions, such as end-stage renal disease (Code

Section 5000 excise tax), or coverage of pediatric vaccines. Occasionally, these techniques are used in combination to achieve the maximum desired behavior.

Q 1:7   How do other federal laws influence the scope and content of employee welfare benefit plans?

Other federal laws generally fall into two categories: those that seek to regulate employee benefit plans directly, and those that do so more indirectly. For example, the federal HMO Act directly requires employers to offer certain health maintenance organizations as alternatives to their voluntary medical plans; new Section 609 of ERISA requires group health plans to cover adopted children and freezes the level of pediatric vaccine coverage; and COBRA and the Family and Medical Leave Act of 1993 require that the right to continue group health plan coverage be granted in certain circumstances. Other federal laws prohibit broad categories of specified behavior, such as discrimination based on age, sex, race, color, religion, national origin, or disability, within specified contexts, such as in hiring, firing, and wage and compensation practices. For example, Title VII of the Civil Rights Act prohibits, among other things, discrimination on the basis of sex in a wide variety of employment contexts, including employer-provided fringe benefit plans.

These laws use a variety of tools to force desired social behavior. The statutes may impose civil fines for violations, and criminal sanctions for intentional wrongdoing, allow private individuals to bring lawsuits, or empower governmental agencies to impose fines and penalties or to bring enforcement proceedings.

Q 1:8   What federal agencies have jurisdiction over employee welfare benefit plans?

A wide range of federal agencies have jurisdiction over specific aspects of employee welfare benefit plans. The agencies with major responsibilities in the employee welfare benefit plan area include:

- The IRS, the agency responsible for administration of the IRC provisions governing various types of welfare benefit plans;

- The U.S. Department of Labor (DOL), the agency responsible for administration of ERISA, the FMLA, and other federal labor laws;

- The Equal Employment Opportunity Commission (EEOC), the agency responsible for administering the Civil Rights Act of 1964, ADEA, and the ADA; and

- The U.S. Department of Health and Human Services (DHHS), the agency responsible for administering the federal HMO Act and FICA, the Social Security Act, including the provisions affecting employer-provided medical plan treatment of Medicare-eligible individuals.

Q 1:9 How does the existence of governmental welfare benefit programs affect the design of employee welfare benefit plans?

Employee welfare benefit plans frequently are structured to take into account the benefits available to employees under various kinds of governmental welfare benefit programs. Thus, an employee benefit plan may integrate its benefits with the governmental benefits (sometimes resulting in reduced benefits from the employer's plan) so that the employees do not receive more total benefits than is considered appropriate.

In recent years, the federal government has become more sensitive to employer attempts to achieve savings in this manner, and statutory changes have limited or forbidden integration in certain areas, particularly in the area of Medicare and Medicaid benefits.

Q 1:10 How do state laws influence the scope and content of employee welfare benefit plans?

Federal law (ERISA) generally preempts all state laws affecting employee welfare benefit plans. However, an exception is provided for insured plans, which remain subject to extensive state insurance laws and regulations. Accordingly, a multistate employer may find it difficult, if not impossible, to maintain a uniform nationwide welfare benefit plan unless the plan is uninsured.

States continue to aggressively attempt regulation of the scope and content of employee welfare benefit plans (requiring, for example, substance abuse coverage, hospice care, coverage of divorced spouses, and coverage of the services of various licensed professionals such as podiatrists, chiropractors, and midwives) and to broadly define when a plan is "insured" and, thus, subject to state insurance laws. As a result, the cases on whether ERISA preempts state law continue to proliferate.

More recently, states have aggressively sought waivers of ERISA preemption of innovative new state health programs or hospital rate laws. Such waivers will impede the ability of multistate employers to maintain a uniform benefit program for all of their employees. Although no state-specific waivers of ERISA preemption have been enacted yet, the State of New York won a tax penalty to enforce its hospital rate law, as enacted in the Omnibus Budget Reconciliation Act of 1993.

Q 1:11   Can pension plans provide welfare benefits?

The principal purpose of pension plans is to provide retirement benefits. However, the IRC permits a pension or profit-sharing plan to provide medical and life insurance benefits that are incidental to the retirement benefits.

Chapter 2

The Regulatory Scheme—The Employee Retirement Income Security Act of 1974 (ERISA)

Although ERISA is perhaps more frequently viewed in a retirement plan context and, in general, regulates retirement plans more heavily than welfare benefit plans, ERISA provides very significant protections for participants in employee welfare benefit plans and their beneficiaries. To this end, ERISA imposes a variety of reporting and disclosure requirements on administrators of welfare benefit plans. These requirements mandate that certain financial and other plan information be reported to the Internal Revenue Service (IRS) and the Department of Labor (DOL) and disclosed to plan participants and their beneficiaries. ERISA also mandates standards of conduct, responsibility, and obligation for fiduciaries of employee benefit plans, and provides appropriate remedies, sanctions, and access to the federal courts when these responsibilities have been breached. ERISA also prevents the application of state laws to welfare benefit plans in many instances. This chapter describes the ERISA rules that pertain to welfare benefit plans only; pension plan rules are beyond the scope of this book.

Basic Concepts and Definitions

Q 2:1   Which welfare benefit plans are subject to ERISA?

ERISA generally covers most employee welfare benefit plans established or maintained by any of the following:

- Any employer engaged in interstate commerce or in any industry or activity affecting interstate commerce [ERISA §§ 3(5), 3(11), 3(12), 4(a)(1)];
- One or more employee organizations representing employees engaged in interstate commerce or in any industry or activity affecting interstate commerce [ERISA §§ 3(4), 3(11), 3(12), 4(a)(2)4(a)(3); DOL Adv Op 90-11A (Apr 25, 1990)]; or
- Jointly by both of the above. [ERISA § 41(a)(3)]

It was held in one U.S. district court case that where an employer had 2 employees and was engaged in a business that did not affect interstate commerce, the employer's welfare benefit plan was not subject to ERISA. [Sheffield v Allstate Life Ins Co, 756 F Supp 309 (SD Tex 1991)]

Q 2:2   Is there a minimum number of employees required for ERISA coverage?

No. ERISA covers employers of any size and employee benefit plans of any size.

Q 2:3   Is a plan covering only one employee subject to ERISA?

Yes, it can be. If the interstate commerce requirement is satisfied by the employer, then a plan maintained by the employer for only one employee can constitute an ERISA plan. Note, however, that an employee benefit plan covering only a self-employed individual and his or her spouse is excluded from ERISA coverage (see Question 2:7).

Q 2:4   Can an individual pre-employment agreement constitute an ERISA plan?

This is a developing area of the law. In the past, courts have generally taken the position that individual employment contracts are not ERISA plans. [See Lackey v Whitehall Corp, 704 F Supp 201 (D Kan 1988); McQueen v Salida Coca-Cola Bottling Co, 652 F Supp 1471 (D Colo 1987)] However, a series of employment contracts providing "golden parachute" payments upon a change in control has been held to constitute an ERISA severance pay plan. [Purser v Enron Corp, 10 EBC (BNA) 1561 (WD Pa 1988)] DOL Advisory Opinion 91-20A [(July 2, 1991)] examined a severance arrangement entered into by an employer as consideration for an individual's acceptance of employment as general counsel and the accompanying move across the country. The DOL concluded that, even though the severance arrangement covered only one individual, it was a severance pay plan governed by ERISA.

Q 2:5   Can an individual post-employment agreement constitute an ERISA plan?

The Court of Appeals for the Eleventh Circuit has held that a letter agreement between an employer and a general manager who agreed to retire in return for certain payments and benefits, including medical insurance, was an ERISA plan. [Williams v Wright, 927 F 2d 1540 (11th Cir 1991)]

Q 2:6   Does ERISA cover employee benefit plans even if they are employee-pay-all plans?

Yes, it can. Whether ERISA applies is a question of fact. As discussed in Question 2:1, a plan is governed by ERISA if it is established or maintained by an employer, an employee organization, or both. The DOL has issued a regulation for determining when a group or group-type insurance arrangement may be excluded from ERISA. [DOL Reg § 2510.3-1(j)] Group or group-type programs that an insurer offers to employees or members of an employee organization will be excluded from ERISA coverage if the following four requirements are met:

1. The employer or employee organization does not make any contributions;

2. Participation in the program is completely voluntary for employees or members;

3. The employer's or employee organization's sole functions with respect to the program are, *without endorsing the program,* (a) to permit the insurer to publicize the program to employees or members, (b) to collect premiums through payroll deductions or dues checkoffs, and (c) to remit the premiums to the insurer; and

4. The employer or employee organization receives no consideration (in the form of cash or otherwise) in connection with the program other than reasonable compensation, excluding any profit, for administrative services actually rendered in connection with payroll deductions or dues checkoffs.

The Court of Appeals for the Fifth Circuit has considered how limited the employer's involvement in an employee-pay-all group insurance plan must be to fall within the above regulatory exemption. The employer in question provided accidental death and dismemberment insurance to its employees on an employee-pay-all basis, and participation by employees was voluntary. The employer collected and remitted premiums to the insurance company, hired an employee benefits administrator to forward employee claims to the insurance company, presented the plan as a supplement to the rest of its benefit program, and distributed to employees a descriptive benefit booklet with the employer's own name and logo on it. The booklet encouraged employees to give participation in the plan careful consideration because it could be a valuable supplement to their existing coverages.

The appellate court concluded that the employer endorsed the plan and that its involvement in the plan was not limited to the activities specified in the regulation. It also found that, apart from the regulation, the employer clearly intended to establish an ERISA plan. The court also determined that the employer had "established" an ERISA plan because there was a meaningful degree of employer participation in the creation and administration of the plan. [Hansen v Continental Ins Co, 940 F 2d 971 (5th Cir 1991)]

Q 2:7   Which welfare benefit plans are not subject to ERISA?

The following types of employee welfare benefit plans are not covered by ERISA:

- *Government plans.* Plans maintained by federal, state, and local governments or agencies thereof for their employees. [ERISA §§ 4(b)(1), 3(32)]
- *Church plans.* Certain plans maintained by tax-exempt churches for their employees. [ERISA §§ 4(b)(2), 3(33)]
- *Plans required by state law.* Plans maintained *solely* for the purpose of complying with applicable workers' compensation laws or unemployment compensation or disability insurance laws. [ERISA § 4(b)(3)]
- *Foreign plans.* Plans maintained outside of the United States primarily for the benefit of persons substantially all of whom are nonresident aliens. [ERISA § 4(b)(4)] The DOL has ruled that a plan of a foreign corporation under which slightly less than 10 percent of the participants were U.S. citizens or residents qualified as a foreign plan and therefore was exempt from ERISA. [DOL Adv Op 82-38A (Aug 2, 1982)]

- *Plans that cover only self-employed individuals.* Plans that cover no "common-law employees" are not subject to ERISA. Although the definition of a common-law employee is too complex to explain in detail here, one ground rule is that a common-law employee is someone who works under the control of another person or legal entity such as a corporation. A plan covering only a self-employed individual, such as a sole proprietor or partners in a partnership and their spouses, is not an ERISA plan. [Meredith v Time Ins Co, 16 EBC (BNA) 1296 (5th Cir 1993] In addition, DOL regulations indicate that a plan covering only an individual and his or her spouse who are the sole owners of a corporation, whether or not the individual's spouse is a common-law employee of the corporation, is not treated as an ERISA plan. [DOL Reg §§ 2510.3-3(b), 2510.3-3(c)]

Certain other exclusions apply to welfare benefit plans that are subject to ERISA. For example, welfare benefit plans are generally subject to much simpler reporting and disclosure requirements than pension plans and are entirely exempt from the participation, vesting, benefit accrual, and funding requirements of ERISA that apply to pension plans. [ERISA §§ 101, 105, 201(1), 301(a)(1)] In the case of a so-called top-hat welfare benefit plan, almost all of the ERISA provisions are not applicable, either by statute or by regulation (see Qs 2:8 and 2:9).

Q 2:8   What is a top-hat welfare benefit plan?

A welfare benefit plan is considered a top-hat welfare benefit plan under the following conditions:

1. The plan is maintained by an employer primarily for the purpose of providing benefits for a select group of management or highly compensated employees, and
2. The benefits of the plan are provided:
   a. Solely from the employer's general assets,
   b. Solely from insurance contracts, the premiums for which are paid from the employer's general assets, issued by an insurance company or similar organization qualified to do business in any state, or

c. From a combination of (a) and (b).

Such a top-hat welfare benefit plan is exempt by regulation from all of the reporting and disclosure requirements of ERISA, except for the requirement to provide plan documents to the secretary of labor upon request. [ERISA § 104(a)(3); DOL Reg § 2520.104-24; compare DOL Reg. § 2520.104-23 for top-hat pension plans]

Q 2:9 Can a top-hat welfare benefit plan cover some employees who are not part of a select group of management or highly compensated employees?

Apparently not. The DOL takes the position that the word "primarily" (see Q 2:8) refers to the employer's purpose of providing benefits, and not to the group of employees covered. Thus, it appears that to qualify for the regulatory exemption, the top-hat plan must be solely for the benefit of a select group of management or highly compensated employees. [DOL Adv Op 90-14A (May 8, 1990)]

While there are no DOL regulations defining what constitutes a "select group of management or highly compensated employees," the DOL has indicated informally that it views the group as smaller than the "highly compensated" classification used by IRS in the tax-qualified pension plan context.

Q 2:10 Who is the plan sponsor?

Under ERISA, the plan sponsor is:

- The employer, if the plan is established or maintained by a single employer;
- The employee organization, if the plan is established or maintained by an employee organization; or
- The association, committee, joint board of trustees, or other similar group of representatives of the parties that establish or maintain the plan, if the plan is established or maintained by two or more employers or jointly by one or more employers and one or more employee organizations.

[ERISA § 3(16)(B)]

Q 2:11   Who is the plan administrator?

Under ERISA, the plan administrator is either:

- The person who the plan instrument specifically designates as plan administrator; or
- In the absence of such a designation, the plan sponsor.

[ERISA 3(16)(A)]

Q 2:12   What constitutes a welfare benefit plan for purposes of ERISA?

For purposes of ERISA, an employee welfare benefit plan is any plan, fund, or program established or maintained by an employer, employee organization, or both, to the extent established or maintained for the purpose of providing participants or their beneficiaries, through the purchase of insurance or otherwise, any or all of the following:

- Medical, surgical, or hospital care or benefits;
- Benefits in the event of sickness, accident, disability, death, or unemployment;
- Vacation benefits;
- Apprenticeship or other training programs;
- Day care centers;
- Scholarship funds;
- Prepaid legal services; or
- Any benefit (other than pensions at retirement or death and insurance to provide such pensions) described in Section 302(c) of the Labor Management Relations Act (LMRA) of 1947. These include severance benefits and financial assistance for employee housing.

[ERISA § 3(1); DOL Reg § 2510.3-1(a)(2)]

DOL Advisory Opinion 91-25A (July 2, 1991) states that a dependent care spending account plan that was established by an employer solely to permit employees to contribute on a pre-tax basis for reimbursement of dependent care service provider expenses was not an employee welfare benefit plan subject to ERISA, because the plan allowed employees to choose the service providers and the plan did not provide particular day care centers.

Q 2:13   Is an employee assistance plan (EAP) an ERISA progam?

Yes, it can be. If the EAP offers more than referrals to health care providers and actually either provides or reimburses medical care services, it is an ERISA plan. An EAP that provided no initial evaluation or counselling, no reimbursement for services, and was limited to referrals only has been determined not to be an ERISA plan. [DOL Adv Op 91-26A (July 19, 1991)] (See Qs 3:108–3:115.)

Q 2:14   Are there employee benefit practices and programs that are not considered employee welfare benefit plans under ERISA?

Yes. DOL regulations specify certain practices and programs providing benefits to employees that are not considered welfare benefit plans subject to ERISA. These include the following:

- *Payroll practices.* The payment of an employee's normal compensation in full or in part out of the employer's general assets for periods when the employee is physically or mentally unable to work—that is, unfunded, short-term disability plans. [DOL Adv Op 93-20A (July 16, 1993); McGraw v FD Services, Inc, No 2-92-2788-18 (DS Carolina, January 18, 1992)] It appears that if a disability program provides more than an employee's normal compensation or is funded in any way—that is, is provided through insurance or by a union welfare fund—the program will be a welfare benefit plan subject to ERISA. [DOL Reg §§ 2510.3-1(b)(1), 2510.3-1(b)(2); Abella v WA Foote Memorial Hospital, Inc, 740 F 2d 4 (6th Cir. 1984); DOL Adv Op. 85-23A (Apr. 16, 1985)]

- *Group or group-type employee-pay-all insurance programs.* (See Q 2:6.)

- *Unfunded scholarship programs.* Including tuition and educational expense refund programs, under which payments are made solely from the employer's or employee organization's general assets. [DOL Reg § 2510.3-1(k)]

- *On-premises facilities.* Including recreation, dining, first-aid, or other facilities (other than day care centers) maintained on the premises of the employer or employee organization for use by employees or members of the employee organization. [DOL Reg § 2510.3-1(c)]

- *Holiday gifts and remembrance funds.* Small gifts, such as turkeys, given by employers to employees at Christmas or other holidays or programs that provide remembrances such as flowers or a small gift for sickness, death, or termination of employment of employees or members of their families. [DOL Reg §§ 2510.3-1(d), 2510.3-1(g)]

Q 2:15   When does a "practice" constitute a "plan" for the purposes of ERISA?

This issue has been the subject of case law developments in recent years. A one-time, lump-sum payment triggered by a single event (such as a single payment of severance pay upon a plant closing) has been held insufficient to create a plan. However, an employer commitment to pay benefits systematically on a regular, ongoing basis does constitute an ERISA plan if such a commitment relies on a uniform administrative scheme, including a set of standard procedures for the processing of claims and the payment of benefits. [Fort Halifax Packing Co, Inc v Coyne, 482 US 1 (1987)]

Funded practices, such as funded vacation pay and severance pay programs, are welfare benefit plans subject to ERISA. [Mackey v Lanier Collection Agency & Serv, Inc, 486 US 825 (1988); DOL Adv Op 89-06A (Apr 7, 1989)]

Vacation pay plans that are unfunded are exempt from ERISA as "payroll practices." [Massachusetts v Morash, 490 US 107 (1989)] However, under DOL regulations, unfunded severance pay plans are generally considered welfare benefit plans and, in certain circumstances, may be considered pension plans for ERISA purposes. See Chapter 14 for a more detailed discussion of vacation and severance pay plans. [ERISA § 3(2)(B); DOL Reg §§ 2510.3-1(a)(3), 2510.3-2(b); DOL Adv Op 83-47A (Sept 13, 1983)]

Q 2:16   When does an individual become a plan participant in a welfare benefit plan for ERISA purposes?

For purposes of ERISA, an individual becomes a participant in a welfare benefit plan on the earliest of the following dates:

- The date designated by the plan as the date on which the individual begins participation in the plan;
- The date on which the individual becomes eligible for a benefit under the plan, subject only to the occurrence of the contingency for which the benefit is provided; or
- The date on which the individual makes a voluntary or mandatory contribution to the plan.

[DOL Reg § 2510.3-3(d)(l)(i)]

Q 2:17   When does an individual stop being a participant in a welfare benefit plan for ERISA purposes?

For purposes of ERISA, an individual ceases to be a participant in a welfare benefit plan on the earliest date on which he or she becomes ineligible to receive any plan benefit, even if the contingency for which the benefit is provided occurs, and is not designated by the plan as a participant. [DOL Reg § 2510.3-3(d)(2)(i)]

Q 2:18   How does ERISA regulate the structure or design of a welfare benefit plan?

A welfare benefit plan covered by ERISA must meet the following legal requirements:

1. The plan must be in writing and contain specified information (see Qs 2:19–2:23).

2. The assets of the plan must be held in trust by one or more trustees, unless certain exemptions are satisfied (see Qs 2:68–2:73).

3. The plan must establish, maintain, and inform participants and beneficiaries of the procedure for presenting claims for benefits, the basis for claim denials, and the procedure for appealing denials of claims. The appeal procedure must afford a reasonable opportunity for a full and fair review by the appropriate named fiduciary (see Qs 2:97–2:112).

4. The plan must contain whatever benefit provisions may be required under ERISA. ERISA now contains several substantive ERISA benefit requirement applicable to employee welfare benefit plans meeting ERISA's separate definition of "group health plan." First, under the Consolidated Omnibus Budget Reconciliation Act of 1985 (COBRA) continuation of group health plan coverage rights must be provided. (See Chapter 6 for a discussion of COBRA.) Second, new Section 609 of ERISA, added by the Omnibus Budget Reconciliation Act of 1993 (OBRA '93), imposes additional coverage requirements on group health plans, including required coverage of adopted children and children placed for adoption and pediatric vaccines, and the requirement that group health plans honor qualified medical child support orders (QMCSOs). These requirements are discussed in detail in Chapter 3.

[ERISA §§ 402, 403, 503, 601, 609]

Case law has attempted to impose a "federal" standard for coordination of benefits under self-insured ERISA plans. A federal district court in Michigan examined the coordination of benefit provisions under two employer-provided medical plans that were self-insured, voiding a provision under one of them as violating of Title VII of the federal Civil Rights Act of 1964 because it was gender-based. [Reinforcing Iron Workers Health and Welfare Fund v Michigan Bell Tel Co, 12 EBC (BNA) 2580 (ED Mich 1990); see also PM Group Life Ins Co v Western Growers Assurance Trust, 953 F 2d 543 (9th Cir 1992)] (See Qs 3:33–3:45 for further information on coordination of benefits under health plans.)

Requirements for Plan Document

Q 2:19 What provisions must the written plan document contain?

The written plan document required by ERISA must contain the following information:

1. A designation (by name or pursuant to a procedure contained in the plan) of one or more fiduciaries (see Qs 2:25–2:31) with authority to control and manage the operation and administration of the plan;
2. A procedure for establishing and carrying out a funding policy and method consistent with the objectives of the plan and with ERISA requirements (but see Q 2:23);
3. A description of any procedure for allocating responsibilities for plan operation and administration;
4. A procedure for amending the plan and for identifying those persons with authority to amend the plan;
5. A statement of the basis on which payments are made to the plan (such as by contributions from the employer or from employees, or both); and
6. A statement of the basis on which the plan makes payments (for example, the covered benefits under the plan), including the elective COBRA continuation of group health plan coverage benefits specifically mandated by ERISA.

[ERISA §§ 402(a), 402(b)]

Q 2:20 Does an ERISA plan exist even if there is no written plan document?

Yes, if the plan's benefits include one or more of the benefits governed by ERISA, an ERISA plan exists. No written plan document or funding mechanism need exist for there to be a plan for ERISA purposes. A plan administrator's failure or refusal to put a plan in writing is merely a violation of ERISA and does not avoid coverage of the plan by ERISA. [Blau v Del Monte Corp, 748 F 2d 1348 (9th Cir 1984); Adams v Avondale Indust, Inc, 905 F 2d 943 (6th Cir 1990)]

When an employer had an unwritten severance pay policy for executives, which entitled terminated executives to a year's salary and coverage in the employer's benefit plans, it was held that an ERISA plan existed and a terminated executive was entitled to benefits under the unwritten plan. [Warner v JP Stevens & Co, Inc., No 90-2720 (5th Cir June 26, 1991), opinion not designated for publication, cited in CCH Pension Plan Guide, ¶ 23,840K]

Q 2:21   May the plan document contain other provisions?

The plan document may, but is not required to, include provisions to the effect that:

1. Any person or group may serve in more than one fiduciary capacity concerning the plan;

2. A fiduciary may employ one or more persons to render advice with regard to any responsibility the fiduciary has under the plan; and

3. A named fiduciary (defined in Qs 2:19, 2:25, 2:26) with respect to the control and management of the plan may appoint one or more investment managers to manage any assets of the plan.

[ERISA § 402(c)]

Q 2:22   Must benefits under an ERISA welfare benefit plan be definitely determinable?

This is a developing area of the law as far as welfare benefit plans are concerned. It appears that if the plan document specifically reserves the right to determine eligibility for benefits, or for the amount of benefits, on a case-by-case basis, such a plan provision will be recognized. In contrast to the rules governing ERISA pension plans, there appears to be no requirement that welfare benefits be fixed and determinable. [Hamilton v Air Jamaica, Ltd, 945 F 2d 74 (3rd Cir 1991); see also Petrella v NL Industries, Inc, 529 F Supp 1357 (D NJ 1982)] (Note that the proposed tax regulations under Former Section 89 of the Internal Revenue Code ("Code") would have added a requirement that benefits be definitely determinable.)

Q 2:23   If benefits are paid out of the employer's general assets, must the plan document contain a funding policy and procedure?

No. If the welfare benefit plan is unfunded, the plan need not provide such a procedure. [ERISA § 301(a)(1); DOL Reg § 2509.75-5, Q&A FR-5] (See Chapter 19 for a further discussion of funding.)

Q 2:24   Does ERISA supersede and preempt state laws affecting welfare benefit plans?

Generally, yes, it does. ERISA broadly preempts all state laws that "relate" to employee welfare benefit plans subject to ERISA. [ERISA § 514(a)] The preemption of state laws includes state regulations, administrative interpretations, court decisions, and other state actions. [ERISA § 514(c)(1)] ERISA contains a "saving clause" that saves certain state laws from preemption. Additionally, certain Medicaid provisions, a Hawaii health benefit law, and certain medical child support orders issued pursuant to state law are exempted from ERISA's general preemption of state law. (See "ERISA Preemption of State Laws" Qs 2:137–2:150.)

Fiduciaries

Q 2:25   Who is a plan fiduciary?

Under ERISA, any person (including an individual, partnership, joint venture, corporation, or the like, as defined in ERISA Section 3(9)) is a fiduciary with respect to an employee welfare benefit plan to the extent that the person:

- Exercises any discretionary authority or control over plan management, or exercises any authority or control (whether or not it is discretionary) over management or disposition of plan assets;

- Renders investment advice for a fee or other compensation, direct or indirect, for any plan money or other plan property; or

- Has any discretionary authority or responsibility for plan administration.

Only persons who perform one or more of the functions described above are plan fiduciaries. Thus, persons who have no authority or control over plan assets but who perform only administrative or nondiscretionary functions for a plan are not considered fiduciaries (see Q 2:28). [ERISA § 3(21)(A); DOL Reg § 2509.75-8, Q&A D-2]

Planning Pointer. Under the above definition, a plan's fiduciaries ordinarily would include the plan's trustees, the plan administrator, the plan's investment manager, the members of the plan's investment committee, and the person who selects these individuals. Since a person's status as a fiduciary depends on his or her function rather than title, a person may be a fiduciary even if he or she does not hold a titled position with respect to a plan if he or she has authority or exercises the responsibility described above. [DOL Reg §§ 2509.75-8, Q&As D-3, D-4, and FR-17, 2509.75-5, and 2510.3-21]

Q 2:26   What is a named fiduciary?

Every plan covered under ERISA must specifically designate in the plan document at least one named fiduciary, identified by office (that is, title or position) or identified by name, who has the responsibility for the plan's operation and administration. This requirement enables employees and other interested parties to determine who is responsible for operating the plan. [ERISA § 402(a); DOL Reg §§ 2509.75-8, Q&A FR-12, 2510.3-21]

Employer. The employer can designate itself as the named fiduciary. [DOL Reg § 2509.75-5, Q&A FR-3] A corporate employer may designate itself as the named fiduciary in order to shield its officers, employees, directors, and the like from personal liability. The Court of Appeals for the Third Circuit noted that a corporation always exercises discretionary authority, control, or responsibility through its employees. However, when the plan names the corporation as a fiduciary, an officer of the corporation who exercises discretion on behalf of that corporation is not a fiduciary under ERISA unless it can be shown that the officer has an individual discretionary role as to plan administration. For example, if the corporation delegates some of its fiduciary responsibilities under the plan to an officer, then the officer would be an ERISA fiduciary. [Confer v Custom Eng'g Co, 952 F 2d 34 (3rd Cir 1991)]

Plan Committees and Joint Boards. The plan committee is the named fiduciary if the plan document (1) provides that a plan committee has the authority to control and manage the operation and administration of the plan and (2) specifies who constitutes the committee, either by position or by naming individuals to the committee. A plan document may split these functions between two or more plan committees, such as an administrative committee and an investment committee. Similarly, in a union-negotiated employee welfare benefit plan, if the joint board on which employees and employers are equally represented is expressly given such authority, the persons designated as members of the joint board are named fiduciaries. [ERISA § 402(a); DOL Reg § 2509.75-5, Q&As FR-1, FR-2]

Q 2:27   Are members of the employer's board of directors fiduciaries?

Yes, they are, if the plan is established and maintained by the employer. The board members will be fiduciaries only to the extent that they perform fiduciary duties. If they select plan fiduciaries pursuant to authorization contained in the plan, they retain residual fiduciary responsibility for the prudent selection and retention of those individuals. If the directors are named fiduciaries in the plan document, their liability can be limited by allocating fiduciary responsibilities and delegating them according to procedures contained in the plan. However, they are still subject to cofiduciary liability. [ERISA § 405; DOL Reg. § 2509.75-8, Q&As D-4, FR-16]

Q 2:28   Is someone who performs purely ministerial functions a fiduciary?

No, a person who lacks the power to make any decisions about plan policy, interpretations, practices, or procedures and who performs certain administrative functions for an ERISA plan within a framework of policies, interpretations, rules, practices, and procedures made by others is not a fiduciary.

The administrative functions that are covered by this protective blanket are:

- Applying the rules for determining eligibility for participation or benefits;
- Calculating service and compensation credits for benefits;
- Preparing employee communications material;
- Maintaining participants' service and employment records;
- Preparing reports required by government agencies;
- Calculating benefits;
- Orienting new participants and advising participants of their rights and options under the plan;
- Collecting and applying contributions as provided in the plan;
- Preparing reports concerning participants' benefits;
- Processing claims; and
- Making recommendations to others about decisions with respect to plan administration.

[DOL Reg § 2509.75-8, Q&A D-2]

Planning Pointer. Even if individuals perform only ministerial duties and have none of the responsibilities listed in Question 2:25, they nonetheless may have to be bonded if they handle funds or other property of the plan. (See the discussion of bonding at Questions 2:90 through 2:96.)

Q 2:29 Is an attorney, accountant, actuary, or consultant generally a fiduciary?

No, an attorney, accountant, actuary, or consultant (other than an investment advisor to the plan) who renders legal, accounting, actuarial, or consulting services to an employee welfare benefit plan will not be a fiduciary unless he or she also:

- Exercises discretionary authority or control over plan management;

- Exercises authority or control over management or disposition of plan assets;
- Renders investment advice for plan assets for a direct or indirect fee; or
- Possesses any discretionary authority or responsibility in plan administration.

[DOL Reg § 2509.75-5, Q&A D-1]

Planning Pointer. If an advisor makes plan decisions on behalf of a client, instead of merely presenting alternatives for the client's decision, this exercise of discretion could make the advisor a fiduciary.

Q 2:30   Need a plan have a specific number of fiduciaries?

No, plans are not required to have a specific number of fiduciaries. However, at least one named fiduciary must serve as plan administrator and there must be an appropriate named fiduciary for appeals of denied claims. If plan assets must be held in trust (see Qs 2:68–2:72), there must be at least one trustee. [DOL Reg § 2509.75-8, Q&A FR-12]

Q 2:31   May fiduciary duties be allocated among fiduciaries and delegated by fiduciaries to others?

Yes, they may, but only pursuant to authority contained in the plan. Delegation of the authority or discretion to manage or control plan assets is strictly circumscribed. Additionally, even a permissible allocation or delegation does not relieve a fiduciary of cofiduciary duties (see Q 2:82). [ERISA § 403(a), 405(b)(1), 405(b)(3)(B), 405(c), 405(d); DOL Reg § 2509.75-8, Q&As FR-13–FR-17]

Fiduciary Responsibility

Q 2:32   What standards must an ERISA fiduciary satisfy in discharging duties under the plan?

A fiduciary must adhere to four general rules of conduct in discharging the fiduciary's plan duties:

1. The exclusive benefit rule;
2. The prudent man rule;
3. The diversification rule; and
4. The adherence-to-plan-documents rule.

[ERISA § 404(a)]

Q 2:33 What is the exclusive benefit rule to which a fiduciary must conform?

ERISA's exclusive benefit rule requires a fiduciary to discharge his or her fiduciary duties with respect to a plan (1) solely in the interest of the participants and beneficiaries and (2) for the exclusive purpose of providing benefits to participants and their beneficiaries and defraying reasonable administrative expenses. [ERISA § 404(a)] Generally, this means that plan assets must never inure to the benefit of the employer. [ERISA § 403(c)]

Q 2:34 What is the prudent man rule to which a fiduciary must conform?

ERISA's prudent man rule requires a fiduciary to act with the same care, skill, prudence, and diligence that a prudent person acting in a like capacity and familiar with such matters would use in the conduct of an enterprise of the same character and aims under the same circumstances. [ERISA § 404(a)(1)(B)]

Q 2:35 What is the diversification rule with which a fiduciary must comply?

An ERISA fiduciary with investment responsibilities must diversify the investments of the plan to minimize the risk of large losses unless, under the circumstances, it is clearly prudent not to do so. [ERISA § 404(a)(1)(C)]

The conference report issued under ERISA states that plans may invest all of their assets in a single bank or other pooled investment fund that has diversified investments within the pooled fund. The conference report indicates that same rule is applied to investments in a mutual fund. Also, the conference report states that, generally, a plan can be invested wholly in insurance or annuity contracts without violating the diversification rules because the insurance company's assets are usually invested in a diversified manner. [H Rpt 93-1280, 93d Cong, 2d Sess at 305 (1974)]

Q 2:36   How must fiduciaries adhere to the plan documents?

ERISA fiduciaries are directed to discharge their duties in accordance with the documents and instruments governing the plan. For welfare benefit plans, they may do this only to the extent that the documents and instruments do not contravene ERISA Title I concerning reporting and disclosures, fiduciary responsibility, prohibited transactions, and the like. [ERISA § 404(a)(1)(D)]

Furthermore, ERISA restricts the manner in which the plan document may be used to limit the liability of fiduciaries. Provisions contained in a plan document, instrument, or agreement that attempt to relieve fiduciaries from responsibility or liability—other than an express allocation or delegation of responsibility that is permitted under ERISA (see Qs 2:31, 2:83)—are void as against public policy. [ERISA §§ 403(a), 405(b)(l), 405(b)(3)(B), 405(c), 405(d), 410(a)]

Q 2:37   What consequences may ensue if no written plan document exists?

A number of risks are present if the plan administrator fails to perform its fiduciary responsibility by preparing a written plan document. The chief risk incurred by maintaining an unwritten ERISA plan is that a court may disagree with the employer's characterization of what benefits the plan covers or excludes and rule against the employer and in favor of the employee(s) on coverage issues. This can be quite costly for the employer.

Q 2:38   Are there consequences if employees try to circumvent coverage limitations contained in a plan document, such as a copayment requirement?

At least one case has upheld an insurance company's right to deny plan benefits altogether when a health care provider agreed not to charge the plan participant the 20 percent copayment that the participant otherwise would have had to pay under the plan, in effect accepting the insurance company's reimbursement as full payment. The court in that case upheld complete denial of the claim. [Kennedy v Connecticut Gen Life Ins Co., 924 F 2d 698 (7th Cir 1991)]

Plan Development: Adoption, Amendment, and Termination

Q 2:39   When an employer adopts a new employee welfare benefit plan, is the adoption of the plan a fiduciary function?

No, it is not. Employers are free to offer welfare benefit plans, and the decision to have one is purely a management decision. The employer is under no duty to act solely in the interests of employees and potential plan participants and beneficiaries when determining whether to have a plan or what the content of the plan will be. [Belade v ITT Corp, 909 F 2d 736 (2d Cir 1990); Moore v Metropolitan Life Ins Co, 856 F 2d 488 (2d Cir 1988)]

Q 2:40   Is an employer's decision to amend an existing employee welfare benefit plan a fiduciary function?

No, under ERISA, decisions regarding what benefits are to be included in a welfare benefit plan and whether to increase or decrease welfare benefit plan benefits are corporate management decisions, not fiduciary decisions. An employer that is under no obligation to offer a plan at all also is under no obligation to offer any particular level of benefits under a voluntarily provided plan (other than those mandated by law for the particular type of plan at issue). [Chervin v Sulzer Bingham Pumps, Inc, 1992 US App Lexis 12627 (9th Cir)]

However, and most importantly, an employer's ability to change a benefit plan will be affected if it fails to clearly and unambiguously reserve the right to alter or diminish benefits under the plan or engages in a course of conduct that a court may find to have effectively guaranteed a particular level of benefits. [Schalk v

Teledyne, Inc, 751 F Supp 1261 (WD Mich, 1990); Alexander v Primerica Holdings Inc, 967 F 2d 90 (3rd Cir 1992)]

Furthermore, the employer may have contractually agreed to maintain a particular level of benefits, such as in a collectively bargained plan, and may be unable later to unilaterally alter benefits without subjecting itself to a charge of engaging in an unfair labor practice.

Q 2:41 Is an employer's decision to cut back or to terminate an employee welfare benefit plan a fiduciary function?

No, the mere determination to do so is not a fiduciary function. [Moore v Metropolitan Life Ins Co, 856 F 2d 488 (2d Cir 1988); Musto v American Gen Corp, 861 F 2d 897 (6th Cir 1988)] Note, however, that the employer may be precluded from doing so by past communications and actions or by a collective bargaining agreement. [See Senn v United Dominion Industries Inc., 951 F 2d 806 (7th Cir 1992)] A U.S. appellate court has held that an employer can modify its ERISA plan benefits even though treatment for specific conditions has already begun. [Owens v Storehouse, Inc, 984 F 2d 394 (11th Cir 1993)]

Q 2:42 Can a written plan document be amended orally?

No, it cannot. Oral amendments are not effective to modify the written terms of an ERISA plan. Where a company announced that its new medical plan would not cover motorcycle accidents, but the plan document failed to exclude them, the Court of Appeals for the Third Circuit held that the employer's oral statements were not plan amendments and that the employer's attempted retroactive amendment of the plan to correct the omission was not effective to exclude the employee's claims. The court affirmed a lower court's holding that the employer displayed bad faith by backdating the plan to deprive the employee of benefits. The court also held that a formal plan amendment could be prospective only. [Confer v Custom Eng'g Co, 952 F 2d 41 (3rd Cir 1991); see also Hozier v Midwest Fasteners, Inc, 908 F 2d 1155 (3rd Cir 1990)]

A developing area of the law concerns whether oral verification of the existence of medical insurance coverage takes priority over the actual terms of the plan (if different), such as when a hospital calls the employer's insurance carrier to verify coverage prior to admission or treatment. At least one court has held that the plan document's exclusions will apply even if an erroneous oral verification of coverage was previously made, and that the plan is not estopped from denying coverage. [Rodrigue v Western and Southern Life Ins Co, 948 F 2d 969 (5th Cir 1991); see also Owens v Storehouse, Inc, 984 F 2d 394 (11th Cir 1993)] However, a health care provider, as an assignee of an employee's claims, was permitted to sue the employer's insurance carrier for coverage based upon on the insurance carrier's oral verification of coverage despite the prior cancellation of the employee's coverage. [Psychiatric Inst of Washington, DC, Inc v Connecticut Gen Life Ins Co, 780 F Supp 24 (D DC 1992)]

Q 2:43 Can an employer amend an ERISA welfare benefit plan to cut back benefits after expenses have been incurred?

No, generally not. The Court of Appeals for the Third Circuit has held that an employer that intended to exclude coverage for motorcycle accidents under its medical plan but failed to do so cannot retroactively amend the plan to deprive employees of benefits. [Confer v Custom Eng'g Co, 952 F 2d 41 (3rd Cir 1991)]

Q 2:44 Can an employer amend an ERISA welfare benefit plan to cut back benefits even though the medical condition already exists?

The Supreme Court has stated that "ERISA does not mandate that employers provide any particular benefits, and does not itself proscribe discrimination in the provision of employee benefits." [Shaw v Delta Airlines, Inc, 463 US 85 (1983)]

Accordingly, it appears that, so long as the employer has expressly reserved the right to cut back benefits, ERISA permits an employer to do so prospectively.

Note. ERISA now contains several substantive welfare benefit requirements affecting group health plans, including Section 601 to

608 COBRA coverage requirements, Section 609 coverage requirements concerning pediatric vaccines and adopted and pre-adoptive children, and Section 514 requirements regarding Medicaid-eligible individuals. These provisions, which are discussed in detail in Chapter 3, must be borne in mind when considering any plan amendment or cutback.

Except for the ERISA requirements above noted, the right to prospectively cut back benefits would include expenses incurred in the future for conditions that are first manifested or for which the employee first sought treatment prior to the date of the plan amendment. State insurance laws that fall outside of ERISA's preemption provisions may preclude reduction of particular insured benefits. However, general state labor laws prohibiting employment discrimination in the terms, conditions, and privileges of employment would probably be preempted from applying to ERISA welfare benefit plans.

The employer's right *under ERISA* to prospectively reduce coverage for particular conditions is highlighted in ERISA cases dealing with Acquired Immune Deficiency Syndrome (AIDS). The Court of Appeals for the Fifth Circuit has upheld an employer's adoption of a $5,000 cap under its self-insured medical plan for lifetime benefits for AIDS, notwithstanding that the plan's lifetime limit for other conditions was $1,000,000. The court rejected the employee's claim of retaliation, noting that employer adopted the restriction as a cost-saving measure. The court held that ERISA does not provide a vested right to medical benefits and that employers may reserve the right to amend or modify the terms of the plan:

> Proof of defendant's specific intent to discriminate among plan beneficiaries on grounds not proscribed by Section 510 [of ERISA] does not enable [plaintiff] to avoid summary judgment. ERISA does not broadly prevent an employer from "discriminating" in the creation, alteration or termination of employee benefits plans; thus, evidence of such intentional discrimination cannot alone sustain a claim under Section 510. That section does not prohibit welfare plan discrimination between or among categories of diseases. Section 510 does not mandate that if some, or most, or virtually all catastrophic illnesses are covered, AIDS (or any other particular catastrophic illness) must be among them. It does not prohibit an employer from electing not to cover or continue

to cover AIDS, while covering or continuing to cover other catastrophic illnesses, even though the employer's decision in this respect may stem from some "prejudice" against AIDS or its victims generally. The same, of course, is true of any other disease and its victims. [McGann v H & H Music Co, 946 F 2d 401 (5th Cir 1991); see also, Owens v Storehouse, Inc, 984 F 2d 394 (11th Cir 1993)]

Even though ERISA may allow flexibility of benefit design, ERISA does not preempt other federal laws. Accordingly, other federal laws prohibiting discrimination on the basis of age, sex, race, national origin, religion, or disability could constrict the employer's flexibility of plan design. (see Chapters 15 through 18). For example, a provision limiting or denying health benefits because of AIDS now appears to violate the federal Americans with Disabilities Act of 1990 (ADA) (see Q. 17:9).

Q 2:45   Can an employer implement plan cutbacks before "official" plan amendments have been adopted?

This practice could backfire on an employer. In one case, an employer's human resources department circulated a description of new, reduced benefits to management, and the plan was administered in accordance with that description. However, several terminated employees successfully sued for the previous, higher level of severance benefits because no written plan amendment had been adopted before the benefit cutbacks were implemented. [Hozier v Midwest Fasteners Inc, 908 F 2d 1155 (3rd Cir 1990)]

Q 2:46   Is the employer responsible if the written description of the plan's benefits contains an error?

An employer may be held to the obligation described in the erroneous document. An employer that intended to exclude coverage for motorcycle accidents under its medical plan but failed to do so was not permitted to retroactively amend the plan to deprive employees of benefits. [Confer v Custom Eng'g Co, 952 F 2d 41 (3rd Cir 1991)] A handbook that erroneously listed higher severance pay benefits than the company intended due to a printer's error was held to be an enforceable ERISA written plan. [Hamilton v Air Jamaica,

Ltd, 945 F 2d 74 (3rd Cir 1991) (denying the employee's claim based upon another provision in the handbook)]

> **Planning Pointer.** While the cases cited above involve a simple mistake, coverage may be granted for failure to "tie up all the loose ends" in benefit documents. In view of the case law developments concerning ERISA plan documents, summary plan descriptions, and other employee communications, it is advisable to review carefully all such documents from a legal standpoint prior to implementing or publishing them. Prevention is key here. Once the document is out, employees may rely on it to their detriment or, if they are unhappy with a denial of benefit coverage, may be able to exploit loopholes in a lawsuit. When an insurance contract is involved, the cases indicate that a separate plan document may be advisable, and it is extremely important that the summary plan description fairly disclose all material terms, conditions, limitations, and exclusions contained in the insurance contract.

Because the awards in some cases have been extremely high relative to the cost of simple "preventive planning," it is advisable to periodically do an ERISA legal review to plug up all the loopholes highlighted by (or newly created by) case law developments. Such reviews may save a company from an embarrassing and expensive court case resulting in judgment for the employee on a point that easily could have been anticipated and dealt with in the planning stage. And, as highlighted by *Hamiltion,* even if benefit communications are being handled by an outside consulting firm or printer, the employer should review the printer's proof to help catch any inadvertent errors.

Plan Assets

Q 2:47   What are plan assets?

There is no ERISA definition of the term "plan assets." In the ordinary sense of the words, plan assets are those amounts set aside in trust or otherwise in order to provide plan benefits and to pay for plan expenses. Plan assets generally are derived from employer and employee contributions and from investment earnings on such contributions.

Q 2:48   Why is it important to know if there are plan assets?

If there are plan assets under the plan, they must be maintained and administered in accordance with the fiduciary responsibility and prohibited transaction rules of ERISA (see Q 2:32–2:37, 2:73–2:78)

Q 2:49   Does an unfunded welfare benefit plan have plan assets?

No. If the welfare benefit plan is truly unfunded—that is, the welfare benefits are paid solely from the general assets of the employer—there are no plan assets.

Q 2:50   Are funds held in trust for the payment of benefits (and expenses) under a welfare benefit plan considered to be plan assets?

Yes, generally they are. However, the DOL recently ruled that funds held in an employer's revocable trust and subject to the claims of the employer's creditors, to be used by the employer as a discretionary source of employer premiums, are not plan assets. [DOL Op Ltr 93-14A (May 5, 1993)]

Q 2:51   Is an insurance policy purchased by an employer or plan trustee for the purpose of providing plan benefits a plan asset?

Yes, generally it is. [ERISA § 401(b)(2)] However, corporate-owned life insurance or stop-loss insurance purchased to finance plan benefits, if structured properly, should not be treated as a plan asset (see Qs 19:96–19:102).

The DOL issued an advisory opinion [Adv Op 92-02A, Jan 17, 1992] clarifying that a stop-loss policy (see Q 19:14) purchased directly by the employer, under which the proceeds are payable into the general assets of the employer and subject to the claims of the general creditors of the employer, does not constitute a plan asset.

The advisory opinion specified that no representation would be made to plan participants or beneficiaries that the policy would provide plan benefits or be security for payment of plan benefits. In addition, the plan benefits would not be limited or controlled in any manner by the amount of stop-loss insurance proceeds received by the employer. The advisory opinion concluded that, because the policy would not be an asset of the plan and would not provide benefits under the plan, it need not be reported (on Schedule A) or submitted with the annual report Form 5500 the IRS. [Kyle Railways, Inc v Pacific Admin Serv Inc, 16 EBC 2032 (9th Cir 1993)]

Q 2:52 If the ERISA plan invests in another entity, such as a corporation or partnership, do the underlying assets of the other entity constitute plan assets?

Generally, when a plan invests in another entity, the plan's assets include its investment in the other entity but do not, solely because of such investment, include any of the underlying assets of the other entity.

However, if the plan's investment is an "equity interest" in an entity that is neither a publicly offered security nor a registered investment company (such as a mutual fund), the plan's investment includes the equity interest and an undivided interest in the underlying assets of the other entity, unless:

- The entity is an operating company, or
- Equity participation in the entity by benefit plan investors is not significant.

[DOL Reg § 2510.3-101(a)]

Q 2:53 What is an equity interest?

An equity interest is any interest in an entity other than an investment that is treated as indebtedness under applicable local law and that has no substantial equity features. An equity interest includes a profits interest in a partnership, an undivided ownership interest in property, and a beneficial interest in a trust. [DOL Reg § 2510.3-101(b)(1)]

Q 2:54 What is an operating company?

An operating company is an entity that is primarily engaged, directly or through a majority-owned subsidiary or subsidiaries, in the production or sale of a product or service other than the investment of capital. For example, if a plan invests in the stock of an automobile manufacturer, the stock held by the plan will be plan assets, but the assets (plants, equipment) owned by the automobile manufacturer will not be, because the automobile manufacturer is an operating company. [DOL Reg § 2510.32-101(c)(1)]

If an entity does not qualify as an operating company under the above definition, it may still qualify as an operating company if it meets a detailed definition in the DOL regulations for either a venture capital operating company or a real estate operating company. [DOL Reg §§ 2510.3-101(c)(1), 2510.3-101(d), 2510.3-101(e)]

Q 2:55 When is equity participation by benefit plan investors in an entity not "significant," so that the underlying assets of the entity will not be considered plan assets?

Equity participation in an entity by benefit plan investors is significant on any date if, immediately after the most recent acquisition, 25 percent or more of the value of any class of equity interests in the entity is held by benefit plan investors. Thus, it is necessary to keep equity participation of benefit plan investors below the 25 percent level in order for the assets of the entity not to be considered plan assets (assuming the entity is not an operating company). For this purpose, a benefit plan investor includes not only ERISA plans but non-ERISA employee benefit plans such as governmental plans and individual retirement accounts and annuities (IRAs) [DOL Reg § 2510.3-101(f)]

Q 2:56   If an employer or plan trustee purchases an insurance contract to provide welfare plan benefits, are the underlying assets of the insurance company considered plan assets?

Generally, no. ERISA provides that, in the case of a plan to which a guaranteed benefit policy is issued, the assets of the plan include the policy, but not the underlying assets of the insurance company. The term "guaranteed benefit policy" is defined for this purpose as an insurance policy or contract to the extent that it provides benefits whose amount is guaranteed by the insurance company. The term's definition does not include amounts held in the insurance company's separate account (other than any of the insurance company's own funds held in the separate account, that is, separate account surplus). [ERISA § 401(b)(2)] Insurance policies purchased to provide employee welfare benefits (for example, group term life, medical, disability) generally meet the definition of a guaranteed benefit policy, and thus the insurance company's underlying assets (other than employee benefit plan assets held in a separate account) are not deemed to be plan assets. [Mack Boring and Parts v Meeker Sharkey Moffitt, 930 F 2d 267 (3rd Cir 1991)] However, the term "guaranteed benefit policy" recently was narrowly interpreted to find that funds held in an insurer's general account under a pension policy could be plan assets. [Harris Trust & Sav Bank v John Hancock Mut Life Ins Co, 970 F 2d 1138, 15 EBC 1993 (2d Cir 1992)] The U.S. Supreme Court has agreed to hear the Harris Trust case and the DOL has filed a brief supporting the life insurance company's position. [113 S Ct 1576 (1993)]

Q 2:57   What is the insurance company's "separate account"?

A "separate account" is a designated pool of investment assets maintained by an insurance company pursuant to policies under which the policyholders have agreed to have part or all of the contributions under the policies invested in the separate account. Generally, the benefits provided under the policies will vary depending wholly or partially on the investment experience of the separate account. A separate account may be established for one customer or for a number of customers (this latter type is known as a pooled separate account).

Generally, insurers maintain a number of separate accounts, some as pooled accounts and some as single-customer accounts. Each separate account ordinarily will be established with a specific type of investment portfolio involved—for example, a common stock account, a bond account, or a real estate account.

Separate account contracts of insurance companies are issued primarily for the purpose of funding pension and savings plans. However, they can be used in the welfare benefit plan area, and have been used as a funding vehicle for reserves maintained to provide postretirement group life and medical benefits.

Q 2:58   Are the assets held in an insurance company's separate account in which an ERISA welfare benefit plan participates considered plan assets under ERISA?

Yes, they are. The only exceptions are the following:

1. If the insurance company has its own funds in the separate account (that is, separate account surplus), such funds are not plan assets [ERISA § 401(b)(2)(B)]; and

2. If the insurance company maintains the separate account solely in connection with fixed contractual obligations of the insurance company, under which the amounts payable or credited to the plan and to any participant or beneficiary of the plan are not affected in any manner by the investment performance of the separate account, the funds in the separate account are not plan assets. [DOL Reg § 2510.3-101(h)(1)(iii)]

For example, a plan may have a guaranteed interest contract (called a GIC) that guarantees a fixed rate of interest, such as 8 percent. The insurance company may set up a separate account on its books that holds bonds providing it with an investment return of at least 8 percent. As long as the plan has the fixed obligation of the insurance company and does not have to rely on the investment return of the bonds in the separate account, the bonds in the separate account are not considered plan assets.

Q 2:59 **Are insurance company assets not held for the benefit of separate account policies deemed to be plan assets because the insurance company insures welfare plan benefits?**

Generally not. Such assets are referred to as "general account" assets. An insurer's general account assets consist of all the assets held by the insurer to meet all of its policy and contractual liabilities (other than separate account assets held for liabilities to separate account policyholders) and all other liabilities, as well as the insurer's capital and surplus funds.

As discussed in Question 2:56, ERISA provides that, in the case of a guaranteed benefit policy, the assets underlying the policy (that is, all the insurer's general account assets) are not deemed to be plan assets. Furthermore, DOL regulations provide that, if an insurance company issues a policy of insurance to a plan and places the consideration for such policy in its general account, the assets in the general account will not be considered plan assets. Therefore, a subsequent transaction involving the general account between a party in interest to the plan and the insurance company will not, solely because the plan has been issued under a policy of insurance, be a prohibited transaction under ERISA. [DOL Reg § 2509.75-2(b)]

Example. Employer A buys a group term life insurance policy covering its employees from Insurance Company Y. In an unrelated transaction, Y grants a loan to A from its general account assets. Since the general account assets are not plan assets, no prohibited transaction has occurred. However, if Y were to condition the granting of the loan to A on the placing or retention of the group life insurance policy coverage with Y, a prohibited transaction would occur. [DOL Reg § 2509.75-2(c)]

Q 2:60 **Are employee contributions to a welfare benefit plan considered to be plan assets?**

Yes, they are. [DOL Reg § 2510.3-102] See Questions 2:69 through 2:72 for a discussion of when employee contributions must be held in trust.

Trustees and Investment Managers

Q 2:61   Must a trustee consent to being named or appointed?

Yes, the trustee must expressly accept the appointment or nomination in order for ERISA responsibility to attach. [ERISA § 403(a)]

Q 2:62   What responsibility does ERISA impose on a plan trustee?

Except for certain carefully drawn exceptions, the plan trustee or trustees have exclusive authority and discretion to manage and control the assets of the plan. This makes them ERISA fiduciaries. [ERISA § 403(a)] Although trustees are appointed by plan sponsors, ERISA imposes upon them a duty of undivided loyalty to the trust fund beneficiaries, that is, the employees and their dependents. [See NLRB v Amax Coal Co, 453 US 322 (1981)]

Q 2:63   How is responsibility shared when there are multiple trustees?

When two or more trustees hold plan assets, the trustees must jointly manage and control the assets of the plan unless the trust instrument specifically provides otherwise. Additionally, each trustee must use reasonable care to prevent a cotrustee from committing a breach of fiduciary duty (see Q 2:82). [ERISA § 405(b)]

Q 2:64   What if the plan assets are held in more than one trust?

A trustee generally is responsible only for acts and omissions concerning the assets that the particular trustee holds in trust. [ERISA § 405(b)(3)]

Q 2:65   Can a plan delegate investment authority over plan assets?

Yes, investment authority can be delegated—under strictly limited circumstances. Investment authority over plan assets may be delegated to a qualified investment manager (as defined in Question

2:66) if the plan expressly gives the named fiduciary responsible for control and management of plan assets the power to appoint an investment manager or managers to manage (including the power to acquire or dispose of) plan assets. In this case, the trustee or trustees generally are not liable for the acts or omissions of the investment manager and are not under an obligation to invest or otherwise to manage any plan assets that are subject to the management of the investment manager. [ERISA §§ 402(c)(3), 403(a)(2), 405(d)(1)]

Q 2:66 What are the requirements for an investment manager?

An investment manager must be a person registered under the Investment Advisors Act of 1940; a bank or trust company; or an insurance company qualified under the laws of more than one state to manage, acquire, or dispose of plan assets.

Additionally, the investment manager must acknowledge in writing that it is a fiduciary with respect to the plan. [ERISA § 3(38)]

Q 2:67 May trustees follow instructions from named plan fiduciaries?

Yes, they may, at least under limited circumstances. The plan document must expressly provide that the trustee is subject to the direction of a named fiduciary who is not a trustee. In that case, the investment manager is subject to any "proper" directions that the nontrustee named fiduciary makes, as long as those instructions are in accordance with the terms of the plan and are not otherwise contrary to ERISA. [ERISA § 403(a)(1)]

Trust Requirement

Q 2:68 Must plan assets always be in trust?

The assets of ERISA plans must be held in trust unless they consist of insurance contracts or policies issued by an insurance company qualified to do business in a state; or are held by an insurance company. [ERISA §§ 403(a), 403(b)]

Q 2:69 Are employee contributions always plan assets that must be held in trust?

Yes, plan assets include amounts (other than union dues) that a participant or beneficiary pays to an employer, or amounts that a participant has withheld from his or her wages by an employer, for contribution to the plan. These amounts must be held in trust (unless they are held by an insurance company). [DOL Reg § 2510.3-102]

Q 2:70 Are there any exemptions from the trust requirement for employee contributions?

Yes, there are. The general rule is that employee contributions that become plan assets are subject to ERISA's trust requirement. [DOL Reg § 2510.3-102] The DOL has stated that it would consider the appropriateness of an exemption from the trust requirement for certain welfare benefit plans that could show that employee contributions constituted reimbursement to the employer for monies expended in premium payments or benefits. [Preamble to Final Plan Asset Reg, 53 Fed Reg 17628 (May 17, 1988)] It has also suspended enforcement of the trust requirement for employee contributions which are applied only to the payment of premiums for certain insured welfare benefit plans until the adoption of final regulations providing relief from the trust and reporting and disclosure requirements of Title I of ERISA. [ERISA Tech Rel 92-01, 57 Fed Reg 23272 (June 2, 1992) as modified by DOL News Rel 93-363 (Aug 27, 1993)]

Q 2:71 When must employee contributions be placed in trust?

Employee contributions must be placed in trust as of the earliest date on which they can reasonably be segregated from the employer's general assets. This period may in no event exceed 90 days from the date on which the contributions:

- Are received by the employer (if the participant or beneficiary pays them to the employer); or
- Would otherwise have been payable to the participant in cash (if the amounts are withheld by an employer from a participant's wages).

It is important to note that the 90-day limit is an outside limit on when employee contributions must be deposited in trust, not a safe harbor provision. [DOL Reg § 2510.3-102]

> **Planning Pointer.** The point at which employee contributions to ERISA welfare benefit plans become "plan assets" that must be deposited in trust will vary by employer, because of differing pay periods and the complexity of the payroll systems.

Q 2:72 Are elective contributions to cafeteria plans treated as employee contributions for purposes of the trust requirement?

The DOL has not adopted the tax concept of treating employee contributions made pursuant to elective salary reduction as employer contributions (see Q 7:44). Accordingly, the DOL's final regulation on the trust requirement for employee contributions to ERISA welfare benefit plans, which contains no specific mention of cafeteria plans, apparently would require elective salary reduction contributions to medical flexible spending accounts under cafeteria plans to be held in trust. The DOL has confirmed this interpretation but suspended enforcement while it considers whether to grant a class exemption or individual exemptions from the trust requirement in these circumstances. The suspension is effective until the adoption of final regulations providing relief from the ERISA Title I trust and reporting and disclosure requirements. However, participant contributions may only be used for the payment of plan benefits and reasonable administrative expenses of the plan. [DOL Reg § 2510.3-102; ERISA Tech Rel 92-01 (June 2, 1992) as modified by DOL News Rel 93-363 (Aug 27, 1993)] If the sole qualified benefit under the cafeteria plan is a dependent care assistance plan which does not fall within Section 3(1) of ERISA, then no trust is required in any event. [DOL Advisory Op 91-25A (July 2, 1991)]

Prohibited Transactions

Q 2:73 What is a prohibited transaction under ERISA?

ERISA prohibits certain transactions between the plan and a "party in interest" (defined in Question 2:74). The statute lists several broad classes of transactions that are prohibited unless permitted under a lengthy list of exceptions and exclusions (see Q 2:75). [ERISA §§ 406–408] (A parallel set of rules concerning transactions between tax-qualified retirement plans and "disqualified persons," contained in Code Section 4975, does not apply to welfare benefit plans.)

ERISA also prohibits self-dealing by plan fiduciaries (see Q 2:76).

Q 2:74   What is a party in interest?

The term "party in interest" encompasses the following seven categories, among others:

1. Any plan fiduciary (including any administrator, officer, trustee, or custodian), counsel, or employee of the employee welfare benefit plan;
2. Any person providing services to the plan;
3. An employer that has any employees covered by the plan;
4. Anyone having 50-percent-or-more control of an employer with employees covered by the plan;
5. A relative (spouse, ancestor, lineal descendant, or spouse of a lineal descendant) of anyone listed in (1) through (4);
6. Any organization that is 50-percent-or-more owned by anyone in (1) through (4); and
7. Any employee, officer, director, or 10-percent-or-more shareholder (or 10-percent-or-more partner or joint venturer) in (2), (3), (5), or (6).

[ERISA §§ 3(14)–3(15)]

Q 2:75   What transactions between plans and parties in interest does ERISA prohibit?

ERISA generally prohibits any transaction that directly or indirectly constitutes:

- A sale, exchange, or lease of any property between the plan and a party in interest;

- A loan of money or other extension of credit between the plan and a party in interest;

- The furnishing of goods, services, or facilities between the plan and a party in interest;

- The transfer or use of plan assets by or for the benefit of a party in interest; or

- The acquisition or holding of nonqualifying or excess qualifying employer securities or real property by the plan.

Extensive exceptions and exemptions apply to these provisions. [ERISA §§ 406–408]

Q 2:76 What acts by fiduciaries constitute prohibited self-dealing?

A fiduciary with respect to an ERISA plan cannot deal with the assets of the plan in his or her own interest or for his or her own account; receive any consideration for his or her own personal account from any party dealing with the plan in any transaction involving the plan; or act on behalf of a party whose interests are adverse to the plan, or of its participants or beneficiaries, in any transaction involving the plan. [ERISA § 406(b)]

Q 2:77 Can a prohibited transaction be a continuing violation?

Yes, a prohibited transaction such as a loan or lease is viewed as continuing in nature. Accordingly, it is subject to multiple penalties. For example, a lease between a plan and a party-in-interest which constitutes a prohibited transaction will be subject to a separate penalty for each year that it continues. [DOL Reg § 2560.502i-1(e)]

Q 2:78 Are exemptions from ERISA's prohibited transaction provisions available?

In addition to the exemptions and exclusions contained in the Act, ERISA authorizes the secretary of labor to exempt individual fiduciaries or transactions, or classes of fiduciaries or transactions, from the Act's prohibited transaction provisions. The DOL has granted numerous individual and class exemptions pursuant to this authority.

[ERISA § 408(a); Exemption Application Proc, 55 Fed Reg 32836 (Aug 10, 1990)]

Fiduciary Liability

Q 2:79 What liabilities does ERISA impose on fiduciaries?

ERISA imposes the following three types of liabilities on fiduciaries (including trustees):

1. Any fiduciary that breaches ERISA fiduciary duties is personally liable to the plan for any losses that result from a breach and must restore to the plan any profits made through use of plan assets. The fiduciary is also subject to other equitable and remedial relief including being removed (that is, prohibited from serving anymore as a plan fiduciary) and being required to pay interest and attorney's fees. [ERISA § 409(a)]

2. If a judicial proceeding is brought by the secretary of labor, fiduciaries can be subject to a civil fine and a penalty (see Qs 2:155, 2:156). [ERISA § 502(l)]

3. ERISA also imposes cofiduciary liability, that is, liability for the acts or omissions of other plan fiducuaries (see Q 2:82).

Q 2:80 May a fiduciary rely on information supplied by persons performing purely ministerial functions?

Generally, yes, the fiduciary may rely on information, data, analysis, and the like, furnished by persons who perform purely ministerial functions with respect to the plan, provided that the fiduciary has exercised prudence in selecting and in continuing to retain those persons. [DOL Reg § 2509.75-8, Q&A FR-11]

Q 2:81 If a fiduciary appoints trustees or other fiduciaries, does the appointing fiduciary retain any responsibility for the appointees' actions?

Provided that the power to make such appointments is expressly contained in the plan document (see Q 2:31), the appointing fiduciary generally will be responsible only for the selection and retention of such individuals. The appointing fiduciary should review the performance of trustees and other fiduciaries at reasonable intervals to ensure that their performance is in accordance with the plan documents and ERISA, and that it satisfies the needs of the plan. No particular method or procedure for doing so is specified under ERISA. [DOL Reg § 2509.75-8, Q&A FR-17]

However, the appointing fiduciary always remains subject to cofiduciary responsibility and to the attendant liabilities (see Q 2:82).

Planning Pointer. An appointment that was initially prudent and in the interests of the plan may cease to be so under later facts and circumstances. The appointing fiduciary is responsible for monitoring the appointee's acts and for removing and replacing an appointee as appropriate.

Q 2:82   How can a fiduciary be liable for the acts or omissions of another fiduciary?

A plan document may allocate or delegate fiduciary duties (including the duties of trusteeship). For example, the plan might designate a benefits committee as the named fiduciary for plan administration and an investment committee as the named fiduciary for the control and management of plan assets. However, even if the plan document carefully allocates or delegates fiduciary duties, a fiduciary nonetheless will be liable for another fiduciary's breach of fiduciary duty concerning the same plan (referred to as "cofiduciary responsibility") if the fiduciary:

- Knowingly participates in, or knowingly conceals, the act or omission of another fiduciary, knowing it to be a breach;
- Fails to comply with its own fiduciary responsibilities and thereby enables the other fiduciary to commit a breach; or
- Becomes aware of another fiduciary's breach and fails to make reasonable efforts under the circumstances to remedy it.

In other words, one fiduciary may become liable for the breach of another plan fiduciary if the first fiduciary's own performance is so inadequate that it creates an opportunity for the second fiduciary to commit a breach, or if the first fiduciary discovers the second fiduciary's breach and fails to take appropriate remedial action. [ERISA § 405(a)]

Q 2:83   May the plan exculpate a fiduciary from violations of fiduciary duty?

No, it may not. Although ERISA permits plans to include express authority to allocate or delegate fiduciary responsibility or to appoint an investment manager, any other provision in an agreement or instrument that purports to relieve a fiduciary from responsibility or liability for any responsibility, obligation, or duty under ERISA's fiduciary provisions is void as against public policy. [ERISA § 410(a)]

Q 2:84   May a plan insure its fiduciaries, or itself, against liability or losses resulting from fiduciary breaches?

Yes, a plan may purchase insurance for its fiduciaries or for itself to cover liability or losses caused by a fiduciary act or omission. However, the insurance must permit the insurer recourse against a fiduciary that has breached its fiduciary duty. [ERISA § 410(b)(1)]

Q 2:85   If fiduciary liability insurance is purchased by a fiduciary or plan sponsor rather than by the plan, must the policy allow recourse against the fiduciary?

No, if the fiduciary, the employer, or an employee organization purchases the policy, the insurance carrier need not be permitted recourse against the fiduciary. [ERISA §§ 410(b)(2), 410(b)(3)]

Q 2:86   May plan fiduciaries be indemnified out of plan assets?

They may not be indemnified for breaches of fiduciary duty. Indemnification would relieve the fiduciary from responsibility and liability to the plan, because it would effectively forfeit the plan's right to recover from the fiduciary plan losses caused by a fiduciary breach. [DOL Reg § 2509.75-4] However, indemnification of a fiduciary for expenses incurred in defending against a wrongful charge of fiduciary violations was held not to be barred by ERISA. [Packer Eng'g, Inc v Kratville, 965 F 2d 174 (7th Cir 1992)]

Q 2:87   May the plan sponsor indemnify plan fiduciaries?

Yes, an employer or employee organization generally may indemnify a plan fiduciary out of its own assets. [DOL Reg § 2509.75-4, Example (1)]

Nonfiduciary Liability

Q 2:88   Can a person who is not an ERISA fiduciary be liable for a breach of fiduciary duty?

The U.S. Supreme Court recently held that a non-fiduciary cannot be held liable under ERISA for monetary damages for a fiduciary's breach. In dictum, the majority opinion suggests that even non-monetary relief is not available. [Mertens v Hewitt Assoc, 113 S Ct 2063 (1993)] However, a U.S. district court has held that *Mertens* does not bar an action against a fiduciary for restitution or other equitable relief, as distinguished from monetary damages [Harris Trust & Savings Bank v Salomon Bros, Inc, 1993 U.S. Dist Lexis 11452 (ND Il 1993)]

Q 2:89   Can a person who is not an ERISA fiduciary be liable for civil penalities under ERISA?

Yes. In addition to being held liable for a breach of fiduciary responsibility, an ERISA nonfiduciary who knowingly participates in a breach of fiduciary responsibility may be subject to a civil penalty of 20 percent of the recovery amount in a judicial proceeding brought by the secretary of labor. [ERISA § 502(l)(1) Interim DOL Reg § 2570.80] Also, if the ERISA nonfiduciary is a party-in-interest to the welfare benefit plan and participates in a prohibited transaction involving the plan, a civil penalty of up to 5 percent of the amount involved (and an additional 100 percent if the violation is not corrected within 90 days after a final agency action order) may be imposed on the ERISA nonfiduciary. [ERISA § 502(i); DOL Reg § 2560.502i-1] (See Qs 2:155, 2:156.)

Bonding Requirement

Q 2:90   Who must be bonded?

Every fiduciary and every other person who handles funds or other property of the plan (as explained in Question 2:93) must be bonded. These individuals must be bonded to receive, handle, disburse, or otherwise exercise custody or control of plan funds or other plan property or to direct the performance of such functions. Certain exemptions may apply to banks, insurers, and other financial institutions. [ERISA §§ 412(a), 4l2(b)]

Q 2:91   Why is bonding required?

ERISA requires certain individuals who handle plan money to be bonded in order to provide protection against losses caused by their fraud or dishonesty, either directly or through collusion with others. Thus, bonding generally provides protection against losses from larceny, theft, embezzlement, forgery, misappropriation, wrongful conversion, willful misapplication, or other fraudulent or dishonest acts. The plan must be protected from loss, even though the person committing the act does not personally gain from the act. [ERISA § 412(a); Temp DOL Reg §§ 2580.412-6, 2580.412-9]

Q 2:92   Is bonding required for all plans?

No, if the only source from which benefits are paid is the general assets of an employer or employee organization, then the administrators, officers, and employees of such plans are exempt from the bonding requirement. [ERISA § 412(a)(1)]

Q 2:93   When are funds and property "handled"?

Individuals are considered to "handle" funds whenever their duties or activities involve a risk that the funds could be lost in the event of fraud or dishonesty. The duties that constitute handling relate to receipt, safekeeping, and disbursement of, access to, or decision-making power with respect to plan funds. Any person with the power to sign or endorse checks is considered to be handling plan funds. Certain acts are considered ministerial and thus do not fall within the bonding requirements. [Temp DOL Reg § 2580.412-6]

Q 2:94   What dollar amount is required for a bond?

The amount of the bond must be at least (1) $1,000 or (2) 10 percent of the amount of the funds handled, but in no case will the bond be less than $1,000 or more than $500,000, unless the secretary of labor prescribes a higher amount, subject to the 10-percent limitation. Further, the bond may not contain any deductible amount. [ERISA § 412(a); Temp DOL Reg § 2580.412-11]

Q 2:95   What form or type of bond is acceptable?

The bond must be in a form or of a type approved by the secretary of labor. Permissible forms and types include individual bonds and schedule or blanket forms of bonds that cover a group or class. [ERISA § 412(a); Temp DOL Reg § 2580.412-10]

Q 2:96   Which sureties can issue acceptable ERISA bonds?

Generally, a corporate surety holding a grant of authority from the secretary of the treasury must issue the ERISA bond. Bonds from certain companies authorized as reinsurers of federal bonds and certain arrangements with the underwriters at Lloyds, London, also qualify. [ERISA § 412(a); Temp DOL Reg § 2580.412-26]

Claims Procedures

Q 2:97   What is a claim?

A claim is a request made by or on behalf of a participant or beneficiary for a plan benefit. [DOL Reg § 2560.503-l(d)]

Q 2:98   When is a claim deemed to be filed?

A claim is considered filed when the participant or beneficiary follows a reasonable claims procedure established by the plan. [DOL Reg § 2560.503-1(d)]

If a plan has not established a reasonable claims procedure, the claim will be treated as filed when the claimant, or his or her authorized representative, makes a written or oral communication that is reasonably calculated to bring the claim to the attention of the organizational unit that customarily handles the employer's employee benefit matters, or to the attention of any officer of the employer. The claim is treated as brought to the attention of the appropriate organizational unit when it is first received by an individual in the unit. [DOL Reg § 2560.503-1(d)]

Q 2:99   What is a reasonable claims procedure?

A claims procedure is considered reasonable if it:

- Is described in the summary plan description (see Q 2:115);
- Neither contains any provision nor is administered in a fashion that unduly inhibits the filing or processing of plan claims;
- Complies with DOL regulation requirements for claim procedures; and
- Specifically provides for certain written notices to participants and beneficiaries.

[DOL Reg § 2560.503-l(b)]

Q 2:100   If a claim is denied, how soon must the participant be informed?

A participant or beneficiary whose claim for plan benefits is partially or wholly denied must be notified in writing within a reasonable period of time after the plan receives the claim. This period ordinarily cannot exceed 90 days. If an extension of time for processing is required, the claimant must receive written notice of the extension before the end of the initial 90-day period. The written notice must spell out the special circumstances necessitating the extension and the date by which the plan expects to render the final decision. The extension cannot exceed 90 days from the end of the initial 90-day period.

If the plan fails to act on the claim or fails to furnish the claimant with a notice of claim denial within a reasonable period, the claimant may treat the claim as denied and may appeal the denial under the plan's appeal procedure. [DOL Reg § 2560.503-1(e)]

Q 2:101   What procedural safeguards does ERISA require if a claim is denied?

ERISA employee welfare benefit plans must provide a two-step procedure for claim denials. If a participant's or beneficiary's claim is denied:

- The participant or beneficiary must be given adequate written notice setting forth the specific reasons for the denial, written in a manner calculated to be understood by the participant; and
- The participant or beneficiary must be afforded a reasonable opportunity for a full and fair review by a named fiduciary of the decision denying the claim.

[ERISA § 503]

Q 2:102   What information must the claim denial notice contain?

The written notice of claim denial issued by the plan administrator or insurer must give the following information in a manner calculated to be understood by the claimant:

- The specific reason(s) why the claim was denied;

- Specific reference to the pertinent plan provisions on which the denial was based;

- An explanation of what additional material or information is necessary, and why, for the claimant to perfect the claim; and

- An explanation of how to submit the denied claim for review.

[DOL Reg § 2560.503-1(f)]

Q 2:103 How long must a claimant have to appeal a denied claim?

A plan must allow the claimant at least 60 days after receipt of written notification of a claims denial to file a request for review of the denied claim. [DOL Reg § 2560.503-1(g)]

Q 2:104 What procedural rights does the claimant have on appeal?

The plan procedure for appealing and obtaining a review of a denied claim must allow the claimant or the claimant's duly authorized representative to make a written application to the plan requesting a review of the claim. The procedure must also enable the claimant to review pertinent documents and to submit issues and comments in writing. [DOL Reg § 2560.503-1(g)]

Q 2:105 Must the claimant be allowed to appear in person to appeal a claims denial?

No, ERISA imposes no such requirement. The plan may require that the appeals of denied claims be made solely upon written submissions. [DOL Reg § 2560.503-1(g)]

Q 2:106   How soon after the appeal is the claimant entitled to a decision?

A decision must generally be rendered within 60 days after the plan receives the request for review of the claim. If special circumstances require an extension of time for processing, written notice of the extension must be furnished to the claimant during the initial 60-day period. The extension cannot exceed an additional 60 days.

If the appropriate named fiduciary that reviews claims denials is a committee or board of trustees that holds meetings at least quarterly, a claim must be heard at the next meeting if it is received at least 30 days in advance of such meeting. If special circumstances require an extension of time for processing, the decision must be rendered by the third meeting after initial receipt of the claim.

If the plan fails to provide its decision on review to the claimant within these time periods, the claims appeal is treated as denied, and the claimant is free to bring a lawsuit for the benefits (see Q 2:111).

[DOL Reg § 2560.503-1(h)]

Q 2:107   What information must the decision on the appeal contain?

The named fiduciary's decision upon review must be written in a manner that is calculated to be understood by the claimant, state specific reasons for the decision, and give specific references to the pertinent plan provisions on which the decision is based. [DOL Reg § 2560.503-l(h)(3)]

Q 2:108   Do special claims procedures apply to health maintenance organizations (HMOs)?

Yes. If a federally qualified HMO provides a benefit claims procedure that meets the requirements of the federal Health Maintenance Organization Act of 1973 (HMO Act) (see Qs 5:7–5:28), it will satisfy the ERISA claims procedure requirements. [DOL Reg § 2560.503-1(j)] Thus, for example, if an employer offers a federally qualified HMO having a valid claims procedure under the HMO Act, it could require

HMO members with claims relating to medical care rendered by the HMO to follow the HMO's claims procedure.

Q 2:109   Do special claims procedure provisions apply to collectively bargained plans?

Yes, special rules apply to any plan established and maintained pursuant to a collective bargaining agreement (other than a plan covered by Section 302(c)(5) of the Labor Management Relations Act of 1947 concerning joint representation of the board of trustees). Such a plan is deemed to satisfy ERISA's initial claims procedure requirements if the collective bargaining agreement incorporates, by specific reference, provisions concerning (1) the filing of benefit claims and their initial disposition and (2) a grievance and arbitration procedure for denied claims. [DOL Reg § 2560.503-1(b)(2)]

Q 2:110   Are any covered plans exempt from ERISA's claims procedure requirements?

Yes, employee welfare benefit plans that provide only apprenticeship training benefits need not provide claims procedures at all. [DOL Reg § 2560.503-1(i)]

Q 2:111   Can a claimant bring a lawsuit for benefits without first following the plan's claims and appeals procedures?

Ordinarily, no. The courts generally have held that, when the plan provides reasonable claims and appeals procedures, a claimant must first exhaust his or her administrative remedies in order to bring a lawsuit for benefits. [Kross v Western Elec Co, Inc, 701 F 2d 1238 (7th Cir 1983)]

Q 2:112   What standard of review do the courts use in deciding whether or not the fiduciary's decision denying an appeal of a denied claim should be upheld?

If the plan document provides that the fiduciary has discretionary authority in determining eligibility, interpreting plan provisions, and ruling on appeals of denied claims, the courts generally will uphold the fiduciary's decision unless it is an abuse of discretion, or an arbitrary and capricious decision, or a violation of the law. Under this very limited form of judicial review, the fiduciary's decision will be given deference and upheld if it is based on substantial evidence, even if the court would have decided the claim differently. However, if the fiduciary has a conflict of interest, the court might give somewhat less deference to the fiduciary's exercise of his or her discretionary authority.

If, however, the plan document does not provide for such discretionary authority, the courts apply a *de novo* standard, and decide the merits of the claim without giving any special deference to the flduciary's interpretations and reasons for denying the claim appeal. Under this broad standard of judicial review, a court could interpret the plan or the goals underlying the plan differently than the individuals who are charged with responsibility for administering the plan and differently than the plan sponsor may have intended. [Firestone Tire & Rubber Co v Bruch, 488 US 809 (1989)]

Reporting and Disclosure

Q 2:113   What, in summary, are an employer's reporting and disclosure obligations under ERISA?

ERISA mandates that certain information about employee benefit plans be communicated to:

- Participants;
- The DOL;
- The IRS; and
- For certain retirement plans only, the Pension Benefit Guaranty Corporation (PBGC).

ERISA also contains requirements for retention of records relating to employee benefit plans and relating to the benefits of participants and beneficiaries. As used in ERISA, "employee benefit plan" means both pension plans (single- and multi-employer defined-benefit plans and defined-contribution plans) and welfare benefit plans (plans that provide medical, accident, disability, death, and other nonretirement benefits). Generally, the plan administrator is responsible for compliance with ERISA reporting and disclosure requirements.

Q 2:114   Are all ERISA welfare benefit plans subject to all the reporting and disclosure requirements of ERISA?

No. The DOL regulations provide exemptions for some (but not all) of the reporting and disclosure requirements within the following categories of welfare benefit plans:

1. Unfunded (see Q 2:130) or fully insured welfare benefit plans with fewer than 100 participants at the beginning of the plan year [DOL Reg § 2520.104-20];

2. Welfare benefit plans with fewer than 100 participants at the beginning of the plan year that are part of a group insurance arrangement providing benefits to the employees of two or more unaffiliated employers [DOL Reg § 2520.104-21];

3. Apprenticeship and training benefit programs [DOL Reg. § 2520.104-22];

4. Unfunded or fully insured welfare benefit plans providing benefits for a select group of management or highly compensated employees (commonly referred to as "top-hat" plans) [DOL Reg 2520.104-24];

5. Day care centers [DOL Reg § 2520.104-25]; and

6. Dues-financed welfare benefit plans maintained by employee organizations [DOL Reg § 2520.104-26].

Q 2:115   What is a summary plan description?

The summary plan description (SPD) is a written summary of the benefits under the plan plus a statement of participant rights under ERISA. The plan administrator of a welfare benefit plan is required to provide a summary plan description to active and retired plan participants.

Q 2:116   Must the SPD be a single booklet?

No, the SPD may consist of several documents. For example, some versions or inserts may apply only in certain geographic areas or to certain classes of employees. [DOL Reg § 2520.102-4]

Q 2:117   Does ERISA require that the SPD be written in a particular style?

Yes, it does. The format of a SPD must satisfy two general standards: It must be written in a manner calculated to be understood by the average plan participant, and it must be comprehensive enough to inform participants and beneficiaries of their rights and obligations under the plan. In preparing the SPD, the plan administrator must take into account the level of comprehension and education of typical plan participants and the complexity of the plan's terms. Technical jargon and long, complex sentences must be limited or eliminated entirely, and the use of clarifying examples, illustrations, cross-references, and a table of contents may be necessary.

The SPD cannot have the effect of misleading, misinforming, or failing to inform participants and beneficiaries. The advantages and disadvantages of the plan must be presented without either exaggerating the benefits or minimizing the limitations.

The descriptions of exceptions, limitations, reductions, and other restrictions of plan benefits cannot be minimized, rendered obscure, or otherwise made to appear unimportant. In addition, the exceptions, limitations, reductions, or restrictions of plan benefits cannot be summarized or described in a manner less prominent than the style, captions, printing type, and prominence used to describe or summarize plan benefits.

Foreign-Language Notice Requirement. If the English-language SPD would fail to adequately inform foreign-language participants of their rights and obligations under the plan, the SPD must provide assistance to plan participants in languages other than English under the following circumstances:

- If 25 percent of the plan's participants are literate only in the same non-English language, and the plan covers fewer than 100 participants at the beginning of the year, or
- If the lesser of 500 participants or 10 percent or more of all plan participants are literate only in the same non-English language, and the plan covers 100 or more participants at the beginning of the plan year.

The SPD must prominently display a notice in the non-English language offering assistance to participants and the procedures they must follow in order to obtain assistance. The assistance, which need not be written, must be given in the non-English language and be calculated to provide the participants with a reasonable opportunity to become informed about their rights and obligations under the plan. [DOL Reg §§ 2520.102-2, 2520.102-3(t)]

Q 2:118   Must any particular information be included in the summary plan description?

Yes, the DOL regulations contain a laundry list of technical information that must be included in the SPD. For example, the procedure for presenting claims and for appealing denied claims and a statement of ERISA rights must be included in it. In addition to such technical information, the SPD must set forth at least the following information regarding plan benefits:

- Requirements for eligibility to participate, including any age or service requirements.
- A summary of benefits, and, for welfare benefit plans, conditions for receiving them. A description of COBRA continuation rights should be included or else mentioned in group health plan SPDs with a statement that a copy of the continuation notice is available upon request. Additionally, group health plan SPDs will need to refer to family and medical leave payment provisions (see Chapter 15) and mention the procedure for reviewing qualified medical child support orders (QMCSOs). (See Qs 3:71–3:76).
- A clear statement of circumstances that could result in disqualification, ineligibility, or denial, loss, forfeiture, or suspen-

sion of benefits which might otherwise reasonably be expected to be covered by the plan based on the rest of the booklet description. Information on the plan's termination provisions must also be included. (Additional requirements regarding this issue are contained in ERISA Technical Release 84-1 (May 4, 1984).)

[DOL Reg § 2520.102-3] (Additional requirements apply to SPDs for employee pension plans.)

Q 2:119 Must an SPD be prepared for each federally qualified HMO offered by the employer?

No, the DOL regulations contain a limited exemption for federally qualified HMOs. If certain information is included in the SPD, the plan administrator may omit information on eligibility for that particular HMO, its covered benefits, the circumstances that may result in disqualification, ineligibility, or denial, loss, forfeiture, or suspension of benefits that the participant might otherwise reasonably expect from the HMO, the HMO's funding medium, and the HMO's claims procedure.

To qualify for this exemption, the SPD must inform participants that membership in one or more federally qualified HMOs is available and whether it is the plan's sole benefit or an alternative to other benefits. It also must state that the HMO will supply the participant, upon request, with written materials concerning the HMO's services, conditions for eligibility for particular benefits, circumstances under which services may be denied, and the procedures for obtaining services and for reviewing claims that are denied in whole or in part. Additionally, the SPD must state that these materials can be requested from the plan administrator. The plan administrator must transmit such requests for material promptly to the applicable HMOs. [DOL Reg § 2520.102-5] Note that no exemption from ERISA's SPD requirements exists for HMOs that are not federally qualified.

Q 2:120 When does the SPD have to be distributed?

The SPD must be furnished no later than 90 days after the individual becomes a plan participant or begins receiving benefits, or if later, 120 days after the plan is established. Thereafter, it must be distributed every ten years if there are no material modifications and every five years if there have been material modifications, that must, at that point, be incorporated into it. (See Q 2:122.) [ERISA § 104(b)(1)(B); DOL Reg §§ 2520.104a-3, 2520.104b-2]

Q 2:121   What methods can the employer use to distribute SPDs?

The plan administrator is required to use measures reasonably calculated to ensure actual receipt of the SPD by participants and beneficiaries, and the method or methods of delivery used must be likely to result in full distribution.

Workplace Distribution. In-hand distribution to the employee at his or her workplace is permitted. However, it is not acceptable merely to leave copies in locations frequented by employees, such as in the reception area or in the cafeteria.

Newsletter Articles. Printing the SPD or an update to it as an insert in a periodical (such as a union newspaper or internal company newsletter) is acceptable only if the periodical is comprehensive and up-to-date. The front page must display a prominent notice advising readers that the issue contains an insert, with important information about rights under the plan and ERISA, which should be read and retained for future reference. If some employees are not on the mailing list, other methods of distribution must be used in conjunction with the periodical, so that the methods taken together are reasonably calculated to ensure actual receipt.

Mailing. SPDs may be mailed, but those not sent by first-class mail must have return and forwarding postage guaranteed and address correction requested.

[DOL Reg § 2520.104b-1]

Q 2:122   Must SPDs be updated periodically?

Yes, they must be. Participants must be given an update summarizing material modifications to the plan no later than 210 days after the close of the plan year in which the modification or change is adopted, regardless of when the modification or change becomes effective. A revised SPD incorporating these changes must be issued no later than 210 days after the end of the plan year that is the fifth plan year the prior SPD was distributed. [ERISA § 104(b)(1); DOL Reg § 2520.104b-2] If no plan changes have been made since the prior SPD was distributed, ten years is substituted for five years.

The style and format requirements for SPDs, as well as the permissible methods of distribution and penalty for failure or refusal to provide a copy upon request, also apply to material modifications to SPDs.

Q 2:123   What COBRA continuation of group health plan coverage notices does ERISA require?

For group health plans, the plan administrator is responsible for the following three separate disclosures to employees regarding COBRA continuation of general health plan coverage:

1. When the plan first becomes subject to COBRA or, if later, when plan coverage begins, active employees and their spouses must be notified, within a specified time limit, of their right to elect continuation of group health plan coverage. [ERISA § 606(1); IRC § 4980B(f)(6)(A)]

2. When a COBRA qualifying event occurs, qualified beneficiaries must be notified, within a specified time limit, of their right to elect continuation of group health plan coverage. [ERISA § 606(4); IRC § 4980B(f)(6)(D)]

3. When the COBRA continuation of group health coverage ends, qualified beneficiaries must be notified of their right to elect to convert to individual coverage, if conversion rights are otherwise available under the group health plan. [Prop Treas Reg § 1.162-26, Q&A 43]

Model language for COBRA notices was provided in ERISA Technical Release 86-2 (June 26, 1986), but it should not be used without substantial updating for subsequent amendments to the law. (See Chapter 6 for a further discussion of COBRA.)

Q 2:124　What notice regarding qualified medical child support orders (QMCSOs) does ERISA require?

Effective on and after August 10, 1993, the plan administrator of a group health plan is responsible, upon receiving a medical child support court order, for immediately notifying the participant and each "alternate recipient" described in such court order of the plan's procedure for determining whether the court order is a qualified medical child support order (QMCSO) within the meaning of Section 609 of ERISA. Then, within a reasonable period after receiving the court order, the plan administrator must make a determination whether the court order is in fact a QMCSO and notify the plan participant and each alternate recipient of its conclusion. [ERISA § 609, as added by Section 4301 of OBRA '93] (QMCSOs are discussed in detail in Qs 3:71–3:76.)

Q 2:125　Are plan participants entitled to detailed notice of a partial or total claim denial?

Yes. For a detailed discussion of the claims process, see Questions 2:97 through 2:112.

Q 2:126　Are plan participants entitled to an annual statement of their plan benefits?

No, ERISA's annual benefit statement notice requirements apply only to pension plans. [ERISA §§ 105, 209] However, many employers voluntarily include welfare benefit plans in their annual benefit statements as a way of publicizing their comprehensive benefit programs.

Q 2:127　What is a summary annual report?

A summary annual report (SAR) is a brief summary of the Form 5500 series financial information filed with the IRS. This summary must be distributed annually to participants on or before the last day of the ninth month after the close of the plan year, or two months after the close of the period for which the extension of the due date for filing the annual report with the IRS was granted. Prescribed form language is provided for this purpose, and foreign-language notice requirements apply. [ERISA § 104(b); DOL Reg §§ 2520.104b-1,

2520.104b-10] SARs are subject to the same method of distribution requirements as are SPDs.

Certain plans are exempt from having to provide SARs. [DOL Reg §§ 2520.104-20–2520.104-26] (See Q 2:114.)

Q 2:128 What information must be provided on request from a participant or beneficiary?

The plan administrator of a welfare benefit plan must furnish or make available for inspection and copying, within 30 days of a request from a participant or beneficiary, a copy of any of the following:

- The last Form 5500 series annual report;
- The plan document, including any related collective bargaining agreement, trust agreement, contract, or other instrument under which the plan is established or operated;
- The most recent updated SPD; and
- Any plan termination report.

Several limited exemptions are available (see Q 2:114).

Q 2:129 What documents regarding welfare benefit plans must be filed with the IRS?

The plan administrator must file a Form 5500 series annual report for each ERISA Title I welfare benefit plan unless an exemption applies. [ERISA § 104] The Form 5500 series (which includes different, simpler versions for small plans) is designed to provide the IRS with detailed information on the qualification, financial condition, bonding, party-in-interest transactions, and other operations of the plan. The IRS furnishes the DOL (and, for certain pension plans, the PBGC) with a copy of the report. The annual report form must be filed with the IRS no later than the end of the seventh month following the end of the plan year, although the plan administrator may file for an additional two and a half-month extension. The plan administrator also must notify the IRS of a change in plan name, change in the name or address of the plan administrator, merger or consolidation of the plan with another plan, or termination of the plan. (Welfare benefit plans generally use the Form 5500 series annual report for such notifications.) [ERISA §§ 103, 104; 1992 Instructions for IRS Form 5500]

Fringe Benefit Plans. In addition, Code Section 6039D requires certain fringe benefit plans to file an annual report, and a new Schedule F has been added to the Form 5500 annual report for this purpose. Presently, the Section 6039D requirements only apply to cafeteria plans, educational assistance programs, and group legal service programs. IRS Notice 90-24 [1990-13 IRB 17] suspended the Section 6039D reporting requirements for Section 79, 105, 106, and 129 plans. Note, however, that if such plan is also a welfare benefit plan under Title I of ERISA, it is not relieved of the obligation to file the Form 5500 annual report and would be required to answer the questions applicable to ERISA Title I plans.

Q 2:130   What welfare benefit plans are exempt from the requirement of filing a Form 5500 with the IRS?

Several exemptions from the Form 5500 annual reporting requirements are available, as follows:

- *Small plans.* The Form 5500 filing is not required in the case of a welfare benefit plan that covered fewer than 100 participants as of the beginning of the plan year, and is fully insured, unfunded, or a combination of fully insured and unfunded.

  For this purpose, an unfunded welfare benefit plan is one that has its benefits paid as needed directly from the general assets of the employer. In order to be considered a fully insured welfare benefit plan, the benefits must be provided exclusively through insurance policies, the premiums of which must be paid directly by the employer from its general assets or partly from its general assets and partly from employee contributions (which the employer forwards within three months of receipt). [DOL Reg § 2520.104-20; 1993 Instructions for IRS Form 5500]

- *Top-hat plans.* An unfunded or insured welfare benefit plan for a select group of management or highly compensated employees is not required to file Form 5500. [DOL Reg § 2520.104-24; 1993 Instructions for IRS Form 5500]

- *State mandated plans.* No Form 5500 filing is required for plans maintained solely to comply with workers' compensation, unemployment compensation, or disability insurance laws, since those plans are exempt from ERISA. [ERISA § 4(b)(3); 1993 Instructions for IRS Form 5500]

Q 2:131 When is an accountant's report required to be filed with the IRS Form 5500 for a welfare benefit plan?

An independent qualified public accountant's opinion must be attached to the Form 5500 unless the plan is an employee welfare benefit plan that is unfunded, fully insured, or a combination of unfunded and fully insured. [DOL Reg § 2520.104-44; 1993 Instructions for IRS Form 5500; ERISA Tech Rel 92-01, 57 Fed Reg 23272 (June 2, 1992)] If the plan is funded by a voluntary employers' beneficiary association (VEBA) trust, the requirement of an independent qualified public accountant's opinion applies. [1993 Instructions for IRS Form 5500]

Q 2:132 What documents regarding welfare benefit plans must be filed with the DOL?

Required filings with the DOL include the following:

- *Summary plan description.* The SPD must be filed with the DOL within 120 days of the date the plan first becomes subject to ERISA. An updated SPD containing material modifications must be filed once each five years (once each ten years if there are no modifications; see Q 2:86). [ERISA § 104(b)(1)(B); DOL Reg § 2520.104b-2]

- *Material modifications.* All material modifications to the SPD that have been adopted during a plan year must be filed with the DOL within 210 days after the close of the plan year in which the modification is adopted, regardless of the effective date of the modification. [DOL Reg § 2520.104a-4]

- *Certain types of investments.* Common or collective trusts and pooled separate accounts, master trusts, and certain other investment entities can file certain financial information concerning their investments directly with the DOL. This must be done no later than the date on which the annual report is due. Further details on this filing requirement are contained in the 1993 Instructions for Form 5500 series reports. If the financial information is filed directly with the DOL, the plan is relieved from filing the same information as part of the Form 5500 annual report filing.

- *Top-hat plans.* An employer maintaining a top-hat welfare benefit plan primarily for the purpose of providing benefits for a select group of management or highly compensated employees (see Q 2:8) must provide plan documents to the secretary of labor upon request. [ERISA § 104(a)(3); DOL Reg. § 2520.104-24] In contrast, the ERISA exemption for top-hat pension plans requires affirmative action. [DOL Reg § 2520.104-23]

Q 2:133   What information regarding group health plans must be reported to the U.S. Department of Health and Human Services (DHHS)?

Effective for calendar years 1994 through 1998, sponsors and administrators of group health plans are required to report certain information to a newly created Medicare and Medicaid Coverage Data Bank to be maintained by the DHHS regarding all employees (including former employees) who elect coverage under a group health plan of, or contributed to by, the employer that covers at least one current or former employee. The purpose of this reporting requirement is to help identify the parties responsible for paying benefits covered by Medicare (under the Medicare secondary rules) and Medicaid (under the new exception to ERISA preemption of state laws). [ERISA § 101(f), added by Section 4301 of OBRA '93] (The data bank reporting requirements are discussed in detail in Qs 3:77–3:80.)

Q 2:134   What recordkeeping requirements does ERISA impose on employers?

ERISA requires employers to keep certain benefit records and copies of various plan documents and backup information (see Qs 2:135–2:137).

Q 2:135   What records relating to various plan documents must be kept and for how long?

ERISA has a blanket record retention requirement of six years from the date of filing for information relating to plan documents, SPDs, annual reports, SARs, individual benefit statements, and all other certifications and reports required to be filed under ERISA's reporting and disclosure rules (or which would be required to be filed but for an exemption). Employers are required to keep sufficiently detailed information and data necessary to verify, explain, clarify, or check such documents for accuracy and completeness, including vouchers, worksheets, receipts, and applicable resolutions. [ERISA § 107] Information required to be provided to the Medicare and Medicaid Coverage Data Bank (see Q 2:133 and Chapter 3) will also need to be retained.

Note that other laws may require record retention for longer periods.

Q 2:136   What records regarding benefit calculations must be kept?

Proposed DOL Regulation Section 2530.209 would impose strict requirements on the content, location, timing, format, and transfer of benefit records relating to calculations of pension plan benefits. In particular, the proposed pension regulation would require the employer to maintain sufficient records for each of its employees to determine the benefit due or that may become due to them. Since pension benefits might accrue over many years and are payable at retirement, these records could be required to be kept for the entire period of employment of each employee. No similar ERISA regulation has been issued about calculating benefits under welfare benefit plans; however, the minimum six-year record retention requirement discussed in Question 2:135 would still apply. [ERISA § 209; Prop DOL Reg § 2530.209]

ERISA Preemption of State Laws

Q 2:137   What is preemption of state law?

Preemption of state law is a legal principle under which federal law nullifies, in whole or in part, state laws on the same or a similar subject because federal law has "occupied the field." Preemption is not to be implied automatically; rather, it requires a clear and affirmative congressional command either explicitly stated in the statute itself or implicitly contained in its structure and purpose. [Jones v Rath Packing Co, 430 US 519, 525 (1977); Shaw v Delta Airlines, 463 US 85, 95 (1983); United Wire, Metal & Machine Health and Welfare Fund v Morristown Memorial Hosp; but see dissenting opinion in Morgan Guaranty Trust Co of NY v Tax Appeals Tribunal of the NY State Dept of Taxation, 80 NY 2d 44 (NY 1992)]

Q 2:138   Does ERISA supersede and preempt state laws affecting welfare benefit plans?

Generally, yes, it does. Section 514(a) of ERISA broadly preempts virtually all state laws that "relate" to employee welfare benefit plans subject to ERISA. For this purpose, state laws include state regulations, administrative interpretations, court decisions, and other state actions. "State" includes a state, any political subdivision thereof, or any agency or instrumentality of either, which purports to regulate, directly or indirectly, the terms and conditions of employee benefit plans covered by Title I of ERISA. [ERISA §§ 514(c)(1), 514(c)(2)] The Supreme Court has held that a state law "relates to" an ERISA plan if it has a connection with or reference to such a plan. [Shaw v Delta Airlines, 463 US 85, 95 (1983); United Wire, Metal & Mach Health and Welfare Fund v Morristown Memorial Hosp, 793 F Supp 524 (DC NJ 1992); but see dissenting opinion in Morgan Guaranty Trust Co of NY v Tax Appeals Tribunal of NY State Dept of Taxation, 80 NY 2d 44 (NY 1992)]

The several exceptions to ERISA's preemption provisions are discussed in the following questions. In addition, separate ERISA preemption provisions apply if the plan at issue is a multiple employer welfare arrangement (see Qs 2:149, 2:150).

ERISA does not preempt other federal laws. Thus, conduct that is permissible under ERISA might be prohibited under COBRA, the ADEA, or the Family and Medical Leave Act of 1993.

Q 2:139   What are the exceptions to ERISA's preemption of state laws purporting to regulate employee benefit plans?

There are several exceptions to ERISA's preemption provisions.

Saving Clause. ERISA contains a "saving clause" that keeps certain state laws free from preemption (see Q 2:140). Generally, whether attempted state regulation of the content of an employee benefit plan is preempted under the saving clause depends upon the type of plan at issue (that is, insured or self-insured).

Medicaid Laws. ERISA also does not preempt state laws that bar any employee welfare benefit plan provisions with the effect of limiting or excluding coverage or payment for health care because an individual is provided, or eligible for, Medicaid benefits or services. The preemption exception applies to the extent that the law is necessary for the state to be eligible to receive Medicaid reimbursement. [ERISA § 514(b)(8)]

Hawaii Prepaid Health Plan Act. ERISA does not preempt the Hawaii Prepaid Health Care Act as its substantive provisions existed on September 2, 1974. [ERISA § 514(b)(5)]

State Criminal Laws. ERISA does not preempt the general criminal laws of a state. [ERISA § 514(b)(4)] However, a criminal law that is limited in application to employee welfare benefit plans—for example, a state law providing that employee welfare benefit plan fiduciaries are criminally liable for breaches of fiduciary duty—is apparently preempted.

Q 2:140   What state laws are "saved" from preemption under ERISA's "saving clause"?

ERISA generally does not preempt state laws regulating insurance, banking, or securities—that is, they are "saved" from preemption. [ERISA § 415(2)(A)]

The most significant exemption for welfare benefit plans is the insurance law exemption, and the precise scope of this exemption has been a matter of broad debate and much litigation. The U.S. Supreme Court has held that a state insurance law falls within the scope of this exemption if the law regulates the "business of insurance." For this purpose, a state law is considered to regulate the business of insurance if the practice that it regulates satisfies a three-part test:

1. The practice has the effect of transferring or spreading a policyholder's risk;
2. The practice is an integral part of the policy relationship between the insurer and the insured; and
3. The practice is limited to entities within the insurance industry.

[Metropolitan Life Ins Co v Massachusetts, 471 US 724, 743 (1985), citing Union Labor Life Ins Co v Pireno, 458 US 119, 129 (1982)]

States continually attempt to regulate ERISA plans, and numerous such attempts have been held to be preempted by ERISA. The case law on ERISA preemption of state law is plentiful. For example, a state administrative rule that required a minimum jobsite ratio for pipefitters of three journeymen to one apprentice was preempted by ERISA because, in attempting to require employers to train their apprentices in accordance with the rule, it regulated the terms and conditions of an ERISA-covered apprenticeship plan. [Boise Cascade Corp v Peterson, 939 F 2d 637 (8th Cir 1991)] Similarly, ERISA preempts the New Jersey Family Leave Act, which requires employers to provide certain employees up to 12 weeks leave for the birth or adoption of a child or family member's serious illness and keep in force the employee's group health coverage at the same level as for active employees. The court noted that ERISA was designed specifically to avoid patchwork state regulation of multistate employers. ERISA also preempts New York's prevailing wage law concerning public construction projects to the extent that it requires employers to provide the prevailing level of benefits or their cash equivalent. [General Elec Co v New York State Dept of Labor, 891 F 2d 25 (2d Cir 1989)]

Planning Pointer. As a general rule, a state law (including a state law denominated as an "insurance law") which is phrased as "an employer shall do such and such" is very likely preempted by ERISA from applying to an ERISA-covered employee benefit plan. Such a law would not fall within the scope of ERISA's saving clause because the term "employer" is not limited to entities within the insurance industry.

Note, however, that even if a law is "saved" from preemption under ERISA's saving clause, ERISA's "deemer clause," discussed in Question 2:141, provides an exception to this exception.

Mandated Health Plan. Massachusetts has enacted a health care act that attempts to avoid ERISA preemption by providing that an employer does not have to establish an employee health benefit plan for its employees, but the employer will be required to pay a substantial tax to the state if it fails to do so. If it is ever implemented, the Massachusetts law probably will be challenged in the courts on the grounds that it is so punitive that it virtually forces employers to comply and, thus, is preempted by ERISA. It would not be saved from preemption as regulating the "business of insurance," since it is not limited to entities within the insurance industry and attempts instead to regulate employers directly. (See Q 3:5.)

Q 2:141   What is ERISA's "deemer clause"?

Section 514 of ERISA also provides that a state may not deem an employee benefit plan (other than one established primarily for the purpose of providing death benefits), nor any trust established under such a plan, to be an insurance company or other insurer, bank, trust company, or investment company or to be engaged in the business of insurance or banking for purposes of any law of any state purporting to regulate insurance companies, insurance contracts, banks, trust companies, or investment companies. [ERISA § 514(2)(B)] For example, a state could not treat a self-insured medical plan as an "insurance company" and attempt to regulate it as such. [FMC Corp v Holliday, 111 S Ct 403 (1990)] Accordingly, a self-insured plan is exempt from state insurance laws to the extent that they "relate to" the plan.

Claims Practices. ERISA also preempts state laws that regulate insurance companies providing claims and other administrative services to self-insured plans. Because entities other than insurance companies can process the claims and perform other administrative services, and there is no transferring or spreading of risk between the plan and the insurance company in such instances, the exception to ERISA preemption for laws regulating insurance has been held inapplicable. [Insurance Bd Under Social Ins Plan of Bethlehem Steel Corp v Muir, 819 F 2d 408 (3rd Cir 1987)]

Q 2:142   If an ERISA plan is fully insured, can state law regulate the content of the policy purchased to provide benefits under the plan?

In general, yes. State insurance law is not preempted as to fully insured welfare benefit plans because, although a state may not regulate the plan or the trust, it can regulate the content of the insurance policy. However, the applicable state law must regulate a practice which is the "business of insurance." Thus, for example, the Supreme Court has upheld the application of a state mandated benefit law to a policy under a fully insured medical plan. [Metropolitan Life Ins Co v Massachusetts, 471 US 724 (1985)] Similarly, the Court of Appeals for the Sixth Circuit held that a state law requiring a successor insurer under a medical plan to provide a substantially similar policy to the previous one was not preempted by ERISA. [International Resources Inc v New York Life Ins Co, 950 F 2d 294 (6th Cir 1991)] In contrast, the Court of Appeals for the Tenth Circuit refused to uphold the application of a state insurance law to an ERISA life insurance plan when the law, which invalidated a life insurance beneficiary designation of a spouse who divorced the insured before his or her death, also applied to retirement and compensation arrangements (and hence was not limited to the policyholder/insured relationship) and did not alter or spread policyholder risk. [Metropolitan Life Ins Co v Hanslip, 939 F 2d 904 (10th Cir. 1991)] Thus, it is important to be aware that not all state laws that are physically located within the state's insurance code will automatically be treated as "insurance" laws for ERISA preemption purposes. Each must be examined under the Supreme Court's three-prong test for the "business of insurance" (see Q 2:140).

Mandated Providers. There is also a variety of state laws that purport to mandate the types of remedial care providers that the plan must cover (for example, chiropractors, acupuncturists, and certified nurse midwives). One court has found that ERISA preempts these laws regardless of whether the plan is insured, because the law does not relate to the business of insurance. [Taylor v Blue Cross/Blue Shield of NY, 684 F Supp 1352 (ED La 1988)]

Claims Practices. The weight of court decisions supports the position that ERISA's provisions for administration of claims provide an exclusive remedy, and that state laws regulating claims practices of insurers are thus preempted when the insurance is provided pursuant to an ERISA employee welfare benefit plan. [Pilot Life Ins Co v Dedeaux, 481 US 41 (1987); In re Life Ins Co of North America, 857 F 2d 1190 (8th Cir 1988); Ramirez v Inter-Continental Hotels, 890 F 2d 760 (5th Cir 1989)]

Q 2:143 Does ERISA preempt state laws that attempt to require employer contributions to welfare benefit plans?

Yes, it does. [Stone & Webster Eng'g Corp v Ilsley, 690 F 2d 323 (2d Cir 1982), *affd on appeal without opinion, sub nom,* Arcudi v Stone & Webster Eng'g Corp, 463 US 1220 (1983)]

Q 2:144 Does ERISA preempt state laws that regulate insurance companies and third party administrators providing claims and other administrative services to self-insured plans?

Yes, it does. Since entities other than insurance companies can process the claims and perform other administrative services, and there is no transferring or spreading of insurance risk between the plan and the insurance company in such instances, the exception to ERISA preemption for laws regulating insurance has been held inapplicable. [Insurance Bd under Social Ins Plan of Bethlehem Steel Corp v Muir, 819 F 2d 408 (3rd Cir 1987)]

ERISA has also been held to preempt a state statute that attempted to regulate and tax third party administrators of ERISA plans. The appellate court found that the state law's reporting requirements imposed significant burdens on the ERISA plans, and held that the statute was not an insurance law saved from preemption because it did not involve the spreading of insurance risk. [NGS American, Inc v V Barnes, Civ No (5th Cir. 1993)]

Q 2:145   Does ERISA preempt state laws taxing employee welfare benefit plans?

Yes, ERISA does preempt these laws. [ERISA § 514(b)(5)(B)(i); National Carriers Conf Comm v. Heffernan, 454 F Supp 914 (D Conn. 1978)]

Q 2:146   Does ERISA preempt state laws taxing insurance policy premiums paid by employee welfare benefit plans?

No, it does not, because the tax is imposed on the insurance company, and not on the plan, even though the insurer generally passes on the tax cost to the plan. In addition, one federal appeals court has held that ERISA does not bar a California premium tax on a minimum premium plan insurer where the state calculates the tax using not only the premiums paid to the insurer, but also the benefits paid by the employer, as the base for the tax. [General Motors Corp v California State Bd of Equalization, 815 F 2d 1305 (9th Cir 1987), *cert denied,* 485 US 941 (1988)] California has not extended its tax position to tax benefits paid by an employer under self-insured plans that purchase stop-loss insurance coverage.

Q 2:147   May a state use its garnishment laws to attach an employee's interest in a welfare benefit plan?

Yes, it may. The U.S. Supreme Court has overturned a state law barring garnishment of ERISA plans. The Supreme Court noted that Congress has specifically barred alienation of pension benefits, but not of welfare benefits. The Court then went on to hold that ERISA does not preempt a general garnishment statute. [Mackey v Lanier Collection Agency & Serv Inc, 486 US 825 (1988)]

Q 2:148   Does ERISA preempt state labor laws affecting employee welfare benefit plans?

Yes, as long as the state law "relates" to an employee welfare benefit plan, ERISA apparently preempts it. The U.S. Supreme Court has affirmed an appeals court that held that ERISA preempted a state "prevailing wage" law (which mandated a certain level of contributions to employee welfare benefit plans for employers engaged in public works projects). [Local Union 598, Plumbers & Pipefitters Indus Journeymen & Apprentices Training Fund v JA Jones Constr Co, 846 F 2d 1213 (9th Cir 1988), *aff'd without opinion,* 109 S Ct 210 (1988)] In another context, a federal appellate court has held that ERISA preempts a state wage payment law as applied to severance pay benefits. [General Elec Co v NYS Dept of Labor, 891 F 2d 25 (2d Cir 1989)] ERISA has also been held to preempt the application of New York's age discrimination law to an ERISA severance plan [Barbagallo v General Motors Corp, 818 F Supp 573 (SD NY 1993)] and the application of an Indiana civil rights law to an ERISA plan in an AIDS case [Westhoven v Lincoln Foodservice Products, Inc, No 34A02-9206-CV-260 (Ind Ct App, July 26, 1993)].

Q 2:149   Can states regulate the benefits provided by multiple employer welfare arrangements (MEWAs)?

MEWAs are multiple employer arrangements that are not maintained or established pursuant to a collective bargaining agreement and that offer health benefit coverage. In many cases, the coverage is offered to small employers that might not be able to obtain group insurance from commercial carriers. [ERISA § 3(40)(A)]

States can regulate the benefits provided by a MEWA to varying degrees, depending on whether the MEWA is fully insured and on whether it is an "employee welfare benefit plan" covered under ERISA.

- If a MEWA is covered by ERISA (see Q 2:1) and is fully insured, state law regulating insurance applies only to the extent of standards regulating reserves and contributions and their enforcement. [ERISA § 514(b)(6)]
- If the MEWA is covered by ERISA (see Q 2:1) but is not fully insured, state law regulating insurance applies to the extent that the law is not inconsistent with ERISA. [ERISA § 514(b)(6)]
- If the MEWA is not subject to ERISA (that is, it is not sponsored by one or more employers or employee organizations), it is entirely subject to state law and regulation. This is the case, for example, if an insurance company sponsors the MEWA. [DOL Adv Op Ltrs 84-47A (Dec 5, 1984), 84-43A (Nov 6, 1984), 84-41A (Oct 26, 1984), 92-21A (Oct 19, 1992)]

- If the MEWA is not itself an employee welfare benefit plan covered under ERISA, each employer participating in the MEWA is considered to have its own ERISA plan. [ERISA § 514(a)(6); DOL Adv Ops 90-07A (Apr 6, 1990) and 90-10A (May 3, 1990)]

Q 2:150　If the MEWA is covered by ERISA and is not fully insured, can a state regulate the MEWA under its laws applicable to commercial insurance companies?

Yes, the DOL has held that there is nothing in ERISA that precludes the application of the same state insurance laws that apply to any insurer to an ERISA-covered MEWA that is not fully insured. In addition, a state insurance law will not be deemed to be inconsistent with ERISA because the law requires an ERISA-covered MEWA that is not fully insured to meet more stringent standards of conduct or because the law requires that it provide more or greater protections to plan participants and beneficiaries than those required by ERISA. Such protective measures may include a state's authorization to require and enforce registration, licensing, reporting, and similar requirements necessary to establish and monitor compliance with general state insurance laws or insurance laws specifically regulating MEWAs. [DOL Adv Op 90-18A (July 2, 1990)]

ERISA authorizes the secretary of labor to exempt from state insurance regulation ERISA-covered MEWAs that are not fully insured, either individually or by class. [ERISA § 514(b)(6)(B)] In view of DOL concerns over lack of adequate regulation of such MEWAs, it appears unlikely that the DOL will exercise its authority to grant exemptions.

Penalties and Enforcement

Q 2:151　What civil penalty applies to a failure to provide participants with information?

ERISA grants courts the discretion to impose a $100-per-day penalty on plan administrators who fail or refuse to comply with a request for certain information that ERISA requires the plan administrator to provide to participants and beneficiaries within 30 days after they request it. [ERISA § 502(c)] The plan administrator is personally liable if such a penalty is imposed, and the penalty is payable to the plan participant or beneficiary who requested the information. The Court of Appeals for the First Circuit recently upheld a lower court's assessment of $12,600 against an employer for its late response to a retirement plan participant's request for information concerning the plan. [Law v Ernst & Young, 956 F 2d 364 (1st Cir 1992)]

If a pension plan is making a qualified transfer of excess pension assets to a health benefits account, a $100-per-day penalty applies for each day the required notice to participants is late. [ERISA §§ 502(c)(1), 101(e)(1)]

Q 2:152 What ERISA penalty applies to failure to give the required notice of the right to COBRA continuation of group health plan coverage?

The $100-per-day penalty contained in ERISA Section 502(c) also applies to a failure or refusal to provide an initial COBRA notice and notice of COBRA rights when group health coverage is lost. Excise tax penalties may also apply. [IRC § 4980B] (See Chapter 6 for a discussion of the COBRA excise tax.)

Q 2:153 What is the civil penalty for failing to file annual reports?

ERISA Section 502 grants the DOL authority to impose up to a $1,000-per-day penalty on the plan administrator (see Q 2:11) for failure or refusal to file annual reports. Plans required to file under Code Section 6039D are also subject to a penalty of $25 per day, up to a maximum of $15,000, for late or incomplete filings. [IRC § 6652(e)]

The DOL has adopted enforcement procedures for assessing civil penalties (1) against parties in interest that engage in prohibited transactions with welfare benefit plans and (2) for failure to file annual reports. [ERISA § 502; DOL Reg §§ 2560.502c-2, 2560.502i-1, 2570.60–2570.71, and 2570.80–2570.87] The DOL also announced a special grace period beginning March 23, 1992, and ending December 31, 1992, during which filers of late or missing annual reports could qualify for reduced penalties for failure to file on a timely basis. If the special grace procedure was not complied with, the DOL has indicated that it may assess a penalty of $50 per day per plan for each late annual report until it is filed, and a penalty of $300 per day per plan (maximum $30,000) per plan for each failure to file until the annual report is filed.

Q 2:154 What is the civil penalty for failing to report information to the Medicare and Medicaid Coverage Data Bank?

The secretary of labor may assess a fine of up to $1,000 per violation on any employer, plan sponsor, insurer, third-party administrator, plan administrator, or any other person who maintains the information neccesary to enable the employer to comply with the Medicare and Medicaid Coverage Data Bank reporting requirements. For this purpose, failure to disclose the necessary information with respect to each covered individual under a group health plan is considered to be a separate violation. The secretary and others may also seek injunctive or equitable relief for violation of the Data Bank disclosure requirements. [ERISA § 502(c)(4), added by OBRA '93 § 4301]

Q 2:155 What are the penalties for a failure to comply with the fiduciary responsibility provisions of ERISA?

The fiduciary can be required to reimburse the plan for any losses caused by a fiduciary breach. The fiduciary may also be barred from serving as a fiduciary. Finally, if a judicial proceeding is brought by the secretary of labor for a breach of fiduciary responsibility, the secretary may assess a civil penalty of 20 percent of the recovery amount. [ERISA §§ 409, 502(e); Interim DOL Reg § 2570.80]

Q 2:156 What is the penalty for engaging in a prohibited transaction?

The secretary of labor may impose a penalty of up to 5 percent of the amount involved in the prohibited transaction relating to an ERISA welfare benefit plan. If the violation is not corrected within 90 days after a final agency action order, the secretary may assess an additional penalty of up to 100 percent of the amount involved. If the prohibited transaction is a continuing one (see Q 2:77), the penalties will be assessed for each year that the transaction continues. However, the penalties are suspended during timely hearings before an administrative law judge and appeals to the secretary of labor. [ERISA § 502(i); DOL Reg §§ 2560.502i-1, 2570.1–2570.12] (A similar penalty relating to tax-qualified retirement plans is contained in IRC § 4975.)

Q 2:157 How does ERISA protect participants and beneficiaries against interference with their rights?

ERISA makes it unlawful (1) to discharge, fine, suspend, expel, discipline, or discriminate against a participant or beneficiary for exercising any right to which he or she may become entitled under an ERISA plan or (2) to take such action against a participant or beneficiary for giving information or testifying in any inquiry or proceeding relating to ERISA. [ERISA § 510] ERISA also provides certain criminal penalties (see Q 2:158).

Note that an employee need not actually be participating in an employee benefit plan in order to fall within the scope of ERISA Section 510's protection. The Court of Appeals for the Sixth Circuit held that an individual who was discharged between her date of hire (when she was given orientation) and her starting date because of the employer's concern about high medical costs associated with her infant's illness was an employee and that her discharge therefore violated the provisions of ERISA Section 510. [Fleming v Ayers & Assoc, 948 F 2d 993 (6th Cir 1991)]

Q 2:158 How might ERISA violations result in criminal penalties?

It is illegal to use, to threaten to use, or to attempt to use fraud, force, or violence to restrain, coerce, or intimidate any participant or beneficiary for the purpose of interfering with or preventing the exercise of any ERISA right. Willful violators can be fined $10,000 or imprisoned for one year, or both. [ERISA § 511]

In addition, any person who is convicted of a willful violation of Part 1 of Title I of ERISA or any regulation or order issued under any such provision can be fined not more than $5,000 ($10,000 for violations of persons who are not individuals) or imprisoned for not more than one year. This applies to failure to comply with ERISA's reporting and disclosure duties, including but not limited to:

- Failure to prepare an SPD;
- Failure to provide each participant (and certain beneficiaries) with copies of the SPD and all material modifications;
- Failure to prepare and file an annual report with the IRS, including all required schedules thereto;
- Failure to file an SPD with the secretary of labor;
- Failure to make certain documents relating to the plan available for inspection by any plan participant or beneficiary;
- Failure to provide participants with an SAR;
- Failure to furnish a participant who makes a written request with a copy (for which a reasonable charge may be made) of the latest updated SPD, plan document, annual report, terminal report (if any), collective bargaining agreement, trust agreement, or other instruments under which the plan is established or operated.

[ERISA § 501]

Q 2:159   When does ERISA permit civil suits?

ERISA contains a comprehensive civil enforcement scheme. It allows civil suits by various parties to recover plan benefits, for breach of fiduciary duties, to enjoin acts or practices that violate ERISA or the terms of the plan, and to obtain other appropriate equitable relief.

Six main categories of civil action are expressly authorized under ERISA:

1. *Employee benefit and disclosure rights.* A participant or beneficiary may bring a civil action under ERISA in order to enforce ERISA's $100-per-day penalty provision for failure to provide certain plan materials upon request or to give required COBRA notices (see Qs 2:173, 2:174). [ERISA § 502(a)(1)(A)]

2. *Breach of fiduciary duty.* A participant, beneficiary, fiduciary, or the secretary of labor may bring a civil action for "appropriate relief" under Section 409 of ERISA. Under Section 409, any person who is a fiduciary under ERISA who breaches his or her duties under the plan is personally liable to make good to the plan any losses resulting from the breach and to restore any profits the fiduciary made through use of the plan's assets. Section 409 also permits a court to take "such other equitable or remedial relief as the court may deem appropriate." [ERISA §§ 502(a)(2), 409]

3. *Injunctive or equitable relief.* A participant, beneficiary, or fiduciary may bring a civil action under ERISA in order to enjoin any action or practice that violates Title I of ERISA or the terms of the plan, obtain "other appropriate equitable relief," redress such violations, or enforce Title I of ERISA or the terms of the plan. [ERISA § 502(a)(3)]

4. *Annual benefit statements.* A participant, beneficiary, or the secretary of labor may bring a civil action under ERISA to enforce the annual benefit statement provisions applicable to pension plans. [ERISA § 502(a)(4)]

5. *Enforcement by secretary of labor.* The secretary of labor may also bring a civil action under ERISA in order to enjoin any act or practice violating Title I of ERISA, obtain "other appropriate equitable relief," redress such violations; or enforce the provisions of Title I of ERISA. [ERISA § 502(a)(5)]

6. *Collection of monetary penalties.* The secretary of labor may bring a civil action under ERISA to collect the following penalties:

   a. The civil penalty of up to $1,000 per day applicable to a plan administrator's failure or refusal to file an annual report (that is, the Form 5500 series Annual Report required to be filed with IRS) or failure to provide material information in an annual report (which, because it is deficient, is treated as if it had not been filed) (see Q 2:153);

   b. The civil penalty of $1,000 per violation applicable to violations of the Medicare and Medicaid Coverage Data Bank reporting provisions of ERISA § 101(f);

    c. The civil penalty against parties in interest engaging in a prohibited transaction (see Q 2:156); or

    d. Civil penalties for violations by fiduciaries for prohibited transactions with ERISA plans (see Q 2:156). [ERISA § 502(a)(6); 502(c)]

Q 2:160   May an employee benefit plan be sued as a separate entity?

Yes, it may, However, any money judgment under Title I of ERISA against an employee benefit plan will only be enforceable against the plan as an entity and not against any other person unless his or her liability is established in his or her individual capacity under Title I of ERISA. [ERISA § 502(d)]

Q 2:161   Can an action under ERISA be brought in state court?

Generally not. ERISA provides that the U.S. district courts shall have exclusive jurisdiction of ERISA Title I actions brought by a participant, beneficiary, fiduciary, or the secretary of labor. Actions may be brought in a U.S. district court without regard to the amount in controversy or to the citizenship of the parties.

However, an exception is made for civil actions brought by a participant or beneficiary to recover benefits due him or her under the plan, to enforce his or her rights under the plan, or to clarify his or her rights to future benefits under the plan; actions can be brought either in a state court or a U.S. district court. [ERISA § 502(e)] However, an action to recover benefits brought in state court may be removed to federal court by the defendants (if done in a timely fashion). [Metropolitan Life Ins Co v Taylor, 481 US 58 (1987)]

Q 2:162   Can the exclusive jurisdiction of U.S. district courts under ERISA be defeated by filing, in a state court action, a complaint that asserts only state law causes of action?

Ordinarily, plaintiffs can play these types of games to stay in state court by taking advantage of what is known as the "well-pleaded complaint" rule. However, ERISA has been interpreted to provide an exception to the general rule.

The general rule is that a cause of action arises under federal law for purposes of having federal question jurisdiction only when the plaintiff's well-pleaded complaint raises federal law issues. Since preemption of a state law by a federal law is ordinarily a defense raised by the defendant, the issue of federal preemption thus would not appear on the face of a well-pleaded complaint and would not authorize removal of the case to a federal court.

However, an exception to the well-pleaded complaint rule occurs when Congress has so completely preempted a particular area that all state law causes of action are displaced and a complaint raising a claim in such area is necessarily federal in character. In Metropolitan Life Ins. Co. v. Taylor [481 US 58 (1987)], the U.S. Supreme Court held that a suit which purports to raise only state law claims but which falls within the scope of Section 502(a) of ERISA is necessarily federal in character by virtue of the clearly manifested intent of Congress. Accordingly, such a suit arises under the laws of the United States and is removable to federal court by the defendants.

Q 2:163 What additional protection does ERISA provide to individuals seeking redress under the statute?

In order to deter violations of ERISA, as well as to notify the relevant enforcement agencies of suits in which they might wish to intervene, a copy of the complaint in any civil or criminal action under ERISA (except an action brought by one or more participants solely to recover benefits due to them under the terms of the plan) must be filed by certified mail with both the secretary of labor and the secretary of the treasury. Both secretaries have the right, at their discretion, to intervene in any action (except that the secretary of the treasury may not intervene in an action under Part 4 of Title I relating to fiduciary duties). [ERISA § 502(h)]

Q 2:164 What other enforcement authority does ERISA provide to the secretary of labor?

ERISA grants the secretary of labor the express authority to make investigations, require production of books and records, and enter such places and question such individuals as the secretary deems necessary to determine if an ERISA violation exists. This assumes that the secretary has reasonable cause to believe a violation exists or the entry is pursuant to an agreement with the plan. The secretary is also expressly authorized to share information with other governmental agencies. [ERISA §§ 504, 506]

The secretary also has additional enforcement authority with respect to delinquent pension plan contributions. [ERISA § 502(b)] No parallel provisions are provided for contributions to welfare benefit plans.

Q 2:165 What is the effect of mandatory arbitration of claims on a participant's ability to bring an ERISA action?

When a participant signs an agreement containing an arbitration clause, the agreement appears to be enforceable under ERISA. The Court of Appeals for the Second Circuit held that Congress did not intend to preclude waiver of a judicial forum for claims for an ERISA violation and that arbitration is not inconsistent with ERISA's underlying purposes. The court noted that Congress's provision of exclusive federal jurisdiction of claims brought to enforce ERISA's substantive provisions concerns only which judicial forum is available, not whether an arbitral forum is available.

The court noted that no issue of possible inadequate union representation was present in the case under review, since no collective bargaining agreement existed. The employee signed the agreement containing the arbitration clause and thus could not complain that his rights were bargained away by a third party. Accordingly, statutory claims arising under ERISA may be the subject of compulsory arbitration. [Bird v Shearson Lehman/American Express, Inc, 926 F 2d 116 (2nd Cir 1991)] The dissent in that case protested that arbitration did not comport with the underlying purposes of ERISA because there is no general requirement that arbitrators of commercial disputes explain the reasons for their decisions or that they follow legal precedent. The dissent pointed to testimony before Congress that arbitrators in the securities industry frequently ignored legal precedent in favor of "rough justice."

An arbitration agreement contained in an individual employment agreement was also upheld under ERISA. [Fox v Merrill Lynch & Co, Inc, 453 F Supp 561 (SD NY 1978)] Arbitration provisions in contracts with service providers to ERISA plans have also been upheld. [Fabian Fin Serv v Kurt H Volk, Inc Profit-Sharing Plan, 768 F Supp 728 (CD Cal 1991)]

When the extent of an employer's obligation or the terms of a benefit plan are incorporated into a collective bargaining agreement, different concerns come into play, and conflicts may be required to be submitted to compulsory arbitration under the collective bargaining agreement. Much of the case law in this area involves disputes over the extent of the issues falling within the scope of the contractual grievance or arbitration procedures. If the claim is subject to binding arbitration, the effect on the claimant's ERISA claim appeal may be dispositive. A U.S. district court opinion held that a denial of medical and long-term disability coverage by the board of trustees of a Taft-Hartley welfare benefits fund is final and binding and must be given *res judicata* effect in the claimant's ERISA claim appeal action. This meant that the court could not undertake any review of the arbitrator's decision. [Kravik v Automotive Machinists Health and Welfare Fund, 13 EBC 2269 (ED Mont 1991)]

The Court of Appeals for the Ninth Circuit held that the doctrine of *res judicata* does not bar claims under ERISA Section 510 by employees who allege that they were laid off to prevent them from attaining the requisite service to qualify for pension benefits. The court held that an ERISA Section 510 claim concerns interference with attainment of rights under an ERISA benefit plan, not a collective bargaining agreement. The arbitrator therefore would have nothing to decide. In any event, participants are not required to exhaust grievance or arbitration remedies prior to bringing an action under Section 510 of ERISA. The court concluded that the participants were entitled to a *de novo* review of their ERISA Section 510 claims. [Amaro v Continental Can Co, 724 F 2d 747 (9th Cir 1984)]

Remedies for Breach of Fiduciary Duties

Q 2:166   What remedies are available against an ERISA fiduciary who breaches his or her fiduciary duties?

A plan fiduciary who breaches any of the responsibilities, obligations, or duties imposed upon fiduciaries by ERISA is personally liable to make good to the plan any losses resulting from the breach and to restore to the plan any profits of the fiduciary that have been made through use of assets of the plan by the fiduciary.

The fiduciary is also subject to such other equitable or remedial relief as the court hearing the action may deem appropriate, including removal of the fiduciary. [ERISA § 409(a)]

Q 2:167 May an ERISA plan sue, in its own name, a fiduciary of the plan for breach of fiduciary duties?

No. An action for breach of fiduciary duty may be brought by the secretary of labor, or by a participant, beneficiary, or other plan fiduciary. However, the plan itself is not included among those entitled to sue to enforce ERISA Section 409. [ERISA § 502(a)(2); Pressroom Unions-Printers League Income Sec Fund v Continental Assurance Co, 700 F 2d 889 (2d Cir 1983)]

Q 2:168 May a plan participant, beneficiary, or fiduciary sue a breaching fiduciary of the plan under ERISA Section 409 and recover damages in his or her individual capacity?

No. The participant, beneficiary, or fiduciary who brings an action for breach of fiduciary duty under ERISA Section 409 is suing on behalf of the plan itself. Thus, any recovery of monetary damages and other relief goes to the benefit of the plan only. [Simmons v Southern Bell Tel & Tel Co, 940 F 2d 614 (11th Cir 1991)]

Q 2:169 What kind of other equitable or remedial relief can a court require for a breach of fiduciary duty?

The statutory provision authorizing such other equitable or remedial relief "as the court may deem appropriate" gives the court very wide discretion in fashioning a remedy to address the particular fiduciary breach in the case before it. In addition to removal of the fiduciary, which is specifically authorized in ERISA Section 409, the court has available the traditional equitable remedies of injunction and specific performance.

The U.S. Court of Appeals for the Second Circuit upheld a lower court order permanently barring certain investment advisers from acting as fiduciaries or providing services to ERISA plans. The court noted that such a broad-based injunctive remedy may be appropriate when fiduciaries engage in egregious self-dealing. [Beck v Levering, 947 F 2d 639 (2d Cir 1991)]

Q 2:170 Is a fiduciary of an ERISA plan who commits a fiduciary breach subject to extra-contractual compensatory or punitive damages under ERISA?

No. In an action brought on behalf of the plan under ERISA Sections 409(a) and 502(a), the U.S. Supreme Court has held that ERISA does not provide for or permit extra-contractual compensatory or punitive damages. [Massachusetts Mut Life Ins Co v Russell, 473 US 134 (1985)]

Note. The U.S. Supreme Court decision in *Massachusetts Mutual* is limited to an action brought under ERISA Sections 409(a) and 502(a)(2). Thus, the issue of whether extra-contractual compensatory of punitive damages are allowable in actions brought under other provisions of ERISA is not yet finally settled, although most court decisions on this issue hold that extra-contractual or punitive damages are not available (see Q 2: 177).

Q 2:171 Can a plaintiff in an action for breach of fiduciary duty under ERISA Section 409(a) demand a jury trial?

It appears not. The remedies provided by ERISA Section 409(a) appear to be essentially equitable in nature, so that there is no constitutional entitlement to a trial by jury.

Q 2:172 What is the statute of limitations for an action for breach of fiduciary duty under ERISA?

An action against a fiduciary for breach of his or fiduciary duty must be commenced by the earlier of:

- Six years after (a) the date of the last action which constituted a part of the breach or violation or (b) in the case of an omission, the latest date on which the fiduciary could have cured the breach or violation; or

- Three years after the earliest date on which the plaintiff had actual knowledge of the breach or violation.

Exception. In the case of fraud or concealment, the action may be commenced within six years after the date of discovery of such breach or violation. [ERISA § 413]

In a decision by the U.S. Court of Appeals for the Seventh Circuit, the court held that the reference in the statute to actual knowledge was to be strictly construed, so that actual knowledge did not include constructive knowledge—that is, notice of facts which, in the exercise of reasonable diligence, would lead to actual knowledge.

The court of appeals also addressed the issue of whether the reference in the exception above to "fraud or concealment" referred to the nature of the factual allegations supporting the claim of breach of fiduciary duty (in this case, securities fraud), or to the steps taken by the fiduciary to cover up the breach. While recognizing that there was a split of opinion among the courts on the issue, the court of appeals concluded that the better view is that the phrase "in case of fraud or concealment" refers to steps taken by the defendant to hide the fact of the breach, rather than to the underlying nature of the plaintiff's claim. [Radiology Center, SC v Stifel, Nicolaus & Co, 919 F 2d 1216 (7th Cir 1990]

Remedies of Plan Participants and Beneficiaries

Q 2:173 Can a plan participant or beneficiary bring suit to recover plan benefits or to enforce his or her rights under the plan?

Yes, ERISA provides that a civil action may be brought by a participant or beneficiary (1) to recover benefits due him or her, (2) to enforce his or her rights under the plan, or (3) to clarify his or her rights to future benefits under the plan. [ERISA § 502(a)(1)(B)]

Q 2:174 Can a plan participant or beneficiary bring suit if the plan administrator fails to provide plan information as required under ERISA?

Yes, if the plan administrator fails or refuses to furnish the requested information within 30 days (unless such failure or refusal results from matters reasonably beyond the control of the plan administrator), the plan participant or beneficiary may bring suit and the court in its discretion may require the administrator to pay the plan participant or beneficiary up to $100 a day from the date of the failure or refusal.

A plan participant or beneficiary may also bring suit and in the court's discretion be awarded up to $100 a day for a plan administrator's failure to provide a required COBRA notice under ERISA Section 606. [ERISA §§ 502(a)(1)(A), 502(c)]

Q 2:175 Can a plan participant or beneficiary bring a civil action for any other reason under ERISA?

A participant or beneficiary can bring a suit (1) to enjoin any act or practice that violates ERISA or the terms of the plan or (2) to obtain other appropriate equitable relief to redress the violations or to enforce ERISA or the terms of the plan. [ERISA § 502(a)(3)]

Q 2:176 Can a plan participant or beneficiary bring an action for plan benefits without exhausting the plan's administrative remedies?

Generally not. The great weight of case law supports the view that, normally, the plan's administrative remedies must be exhausted before the plan participant or beneficiary can begin a legal action to recover benefits. For example, a recent decision by the U.S. Court of Appeals for the Sixth Circuit held that administrative appeal of a denied claim was a prerequisite to the commencement of a lawsuit, even though the wording of the plan document was written in permissive language (that is, a participant "may request a review"). [Baxter v CA Muer Corp, 941 F 2d 451 (6th Cir 1991)] However, if the issue involves COBRA rights, an emerging body of cases indicates that exhaustion of remedies is not required to enforce a statutory right. For a detailed discussion of the COBRA exhaustion issue, see C. Combe and I. Golub.

Q 2:177   May a plan participant or beneficiary suing for and receiving payment of plan benefits receive compensatory or punitive damages?

It appears not. The U.S. Court of Appeals for the Seventh Circuit held that neither compensatory nor punitive damages could be obtained in a suit by a participant or beneficiary either under Section 502(a)(1)(B) or Section 502(a)(3) of ERISA. The court relied heavily on the reasoning of the U.S. Supreme Court in *Massachusetts Mutual Life Ins. Co. v. Russell* [473 US 134 (1985)], to the effect that Congress did not intend to authorize remedies beyond those it enacted in ERISA [Harsch v Eisenberg, 956 F 2d 651 (7th Cir 1992); see also Reinking v Philadelphia Am Life Ins Co, 910 F 2d 1210 (4th Cir 1990) (extra-contractual damages for emotional distress not allowed under ERISA); Medina v Anthem Life Ins Co, 16 EBC 1533 (5th Cir 1993) (extra-contractual and punitive damages not allowable against an insurer that denied a health benefit claim)]

Q 2:178   Is a plan participant or beneficiary suing for plan benefits entitled to a jury trial?

While the issue is not settled, the weight of appellate authority indicates that the courts view such actions as essentially equitable in nature and, therefore, not subject to the constitutional requirement under the Seventh Amendment to the Constitution that actions at law are generally entitled to a jury trial if the plaintiff so elects. [See Pane v RCA Corp, 868 F 2d 631 (3d Cir 1989) and cases cited therein.]

Note. This is an issue which may have to be resolved ultimately by the U.S. Supreme Court.

Q 2:179   If a participant or beneficiary wins a suit for benefits, is he or she entitled to attorneys' fees and costs as well?

In the court's discretion, it may allow attorneys' fees and costs to either party in an ERISA action. [ERISA § 502(g)(1)] The U.S. Court of Appeals for the Sixth Circuit has indicated that the following factors are to be taken into account by the trial court in deciding whether an award of attorneys' fees should be made:

1. The degree of the opposing party's culpability or bad faith;
2. The ability of the opposing party to satisfy an award of attorneys' fees;
3. The deterrent effect of an award on other persons under similar circumstances;
4. Whether the party requesting attorneys' fees sought to confer a common benefit on all plan participants and beneficiaries or to resolve significant ERISA legal questions; and
5. The relative merits of the parties' positions.

While all the circuit courts of appeal appear to follow this five-factor analysis, one line of cases makes a presumption that a prevailing individual participant or beneficiary should ordinarily recover attorney's fees unless it would be unjust to do so. Another line of cases rejects such an assumption. [See Armistead v Vernitron Corp, 944 F 2d 1287 (6th Cir 1991) (no presumption in favor of prevailing plaintiff); Rodriguez v MEBA Pension Trust, 956 F 2d 468 (4th Cir 1992) (presumption in favor of prevailing plaintiff)]

Effect of the Proposed Clinton Health Plan

See Appendix A for a discussion of the proposed Clinton Health Plan.

Chapter 3

Medical Plans Generally

Medical plans are often the most important employee welfare benefit because employees rely upon and use them on a daily basis. These plans, regulated chiefly by the Internal Revenue Code (IRC; Code) and the Employee Retirement Income Security Act (ERISA), are also affected by a number of other federal and state laws. This chapter discusses the ground rules for medical benefits, including such basic concepts as funding types and cost sharing, coordination of benefits, and federal tax rules. This chapter also explains the new legal requirements concerning disability-based distinctions, adopted children, pediatric vaccines, family and medical leave, qualified medical child support orders (QMCSOs) and mandated reporting of detailed plan participant data to the new Medicare and Medicaid Coverage Data Bank. Employee assistance programs (EAPs) are also discussed in detail.

Basic Concepts

Q 3:1   What is medical care?

For federal income tax purposes, medical care is defined to include amounts paid for (1) the diagnosis, cure, mitigation, treatment, or prevention of disease, or for the purpose of affecting any structure or function of the body; (2) transportation, primarily for and essential to such medical care; and (3) insurance (including Medicare part B premiums) covering medical care. [IRC § 213(d)(1)]

A drug is considered to be a medical care expense only if it is a prescribed drug or insulin. [IRC §§ 213(b), 213(d)(3)]

Cosmetic Surgery. Cosmetic surgery or similar procedures are not considered to be medical care unless the surgery or procedure is necessary to ameliorate a deformity arising from, or directly related to, congenital abnormality, personal injury resulting from accident or trauma, or disfiguring disease. For this purpose, "cosmetic surgery" means any procedure that is directed at improving the patient's appearance and that does not meaningfully promote the proper function of the body or prevent or treat illness or disease. [IRC § 213(d)(9)]

Q 3:2   What types of medical care expenses are typically covered by employer-provided medical benefit plans?

There are a wide variety of employer-provided medical benefits. Benefits commonly covered by an employer-provided medical plan include some or all of the following:

- Hospital expenses
- Surgical expenses

- Physicians' services
- Nurses' services
- Prescription drugs
- Orthopedic appliances
- Dental care
- Vision care

Q 3:3 Will a plan generally cover all expenses that are considered medical care expenses for federal income tax purposes?

No, an employer-provided medical benefit plan generally will not cover all expenses that are considered to be medical care expenses for federal income tax purposes (although employers are free to choose to cover all such expenses). For example, expenses such as medical care transportation, other than by ambulance, are rarely covered. However, a medical reimbursement account or health care flexible spending arrangement (FSA) under a cafeteria plan, especially one funded with employee salary reduction amounts, in some cases will cover all or almost all expenses qualifying as medical care expenses for income tax purposes because it generally "wraps around" other employer-provided medical plan coverage. (See Qs 7:46–7:57 for a discussion of health care FSAs.)

Q 3:4 Does federal law require an employer to provide medical benefits?

Nothing in the IRC or any other federal law currently requires any employer to provide health care benefits (although numerous federal laws do regulate health coverage once it is offered). In addition, if an employer does offer a medical plan, the federal Health Maintenance Organization Act of 1973 (HMO Act) may require it to offer one or more federally qualified health maintenance organizations (HMOs) as an alternative choice. (HMOs are discussed in Chapter 4.)

Q 3:5   Does state law require an employer to provide medical benefits?

A number of states have laws mandating an employer to provide coverage, but ERISA generally preempts—and thus, invalidates—them (see Q 2:138). However, ERISA specifically leaves in effect the Hawaii Prepaid Health Care Act as its substantive provisions existed on the date ERISA became effective (see Q 2:139). Massachusetts has enacted a law that, if and when it becomes effective, would impose a stiff payroll tax on employers that do not provide benefits. Certain other states are considering adopting similar measures. Numerous state insurance laws require that insurance policies contain various minimum benefits, and such laws are not preempted by ERISA. (State insurance law is beyond the scope of this book. Workers' compensation laws represent a special situation under ERISA and are discussed at Questions 3:92 through 3:94.)

Massachusetts Surcharge. If and when the law becomes effective, all Massachusetts employers with six or more employees will be required to pay a 12-percent surcharge, called a "medical security contribution," on the first $14,000 (indexed) of an employee's wages, or about $1,680 per employee. This amount will be indexed to increases in health care cost inflation as set under the Massachusetts Act. The surcharge will apply to each employee working 30 or more hours a week, plus each employee working 20 or more hours a week who is a head of household or has worked at least five months.

The surcharge will not be imposed for any employee or spouse who has coverage through another employer. An employer that provides health insurance to its employees meeting specific benefit requirements, such as preventive and primary care services for children, may deduct the cost of the insurance from the surcharge, which would mean no surcharge at all for employers providing fairly comprehensive insurance to their employees. In addition, employers will be required to pay a second amount, called an "employment health insurance contribution," equal to 0.12 percent of the first $14,000 (indexed) of an employee's wages. This would amount to an additional $16.80 per employee.

A penalty of $35 per day or $5 per employee, whichever is higher, may be imposed on any employer that fails to make these health contributions. [Massachusetts Health Security Act, § 21, adding new

§ 14G to Chapter 151A of the Massachusetts General Laws (April 21, 1988)]

The effective date of the law has been postponed several times, and it is now scheduled to take effect in 1995. Whether this law ever takes effect and survives ERISA preemption standards remains to be seen (see Qs 2:137–150).

Q 3:6   When does an employer have a medical plan?

For purposes of Code Section 106, (concerning employer-provided accident and health insurance) and Code Section 105 (concerning the taxability of benefits received from employer-provided accident or health insurance), an employer-sponsored medical plan is an arrangement for the payment of amounts to employees in the event of personal injuries or illness. It is not necessary that such arrangements be in writing or that the employee's rights to benefits be enforceable, solely for purposes of determining whether such a plan exists for tax purposes. However (still for tax purposes only) if the employee's rights are not enforceable, an employer-provided plan nonetheless will be considered to exist if, on the date the employee became ill or injured:

- He or she was covered under a plan, or a program, policy, or custom having the effect of a plan, providing for the payment of amounts to the employee in the event of personal injuries or illness, and

- Notice or knowledge of such plan was reasonably available to the employee.

[Treas Reg § 1.105-5(a)]

COBRA. For purposes of the COBRA continuation of group health plan provisions, a separate definition of medical plan applies for COBRA purposes only and the IRS has issued a special proposal regulation concerning how to determine when a "group health plan" exists for COBRA purposes. See Chapter 6 for a discussion of COBRA.

ERISA. If a plan does exist, it may be required to comply with the plan document requirements of ERISA (see Qs 2:19–2:24).

Q 3:7   Is a medical benefit FSA under a cafeteria plan considered to be a medical plan?

Yes, it is. To qualify for favorable tax treatment accorded medical plans under Code Sections 105 and 106, medical FSAs must exhibit the risk-shifting and risk distribution characteristics of insurance. [Prop Treas Reg § 1.125-2, Q&A 7(a)] (See Chapter 7 for a detailed discussion of cafeteria plans.)

Q 3:8   Is a long-term care insurance plan considered to be a medical plan?

Long-term care insurance policies typically cover long-term nursing home care and other services not covered or not fully covered by Medicare or by the employer's regular medical plan. Typically, not all of the benefits included in such policies are clearly for Code Section 213 medical care. As a result, it is unclear whether a long-term care insurance plan is a Code Section 105 employer-provided medical plan, and the proper tax characterization of such arrangements has not been clarified by the Internal Revenue Service (IRS) or by Congress. Although the IRS has issued several private letter rulings allowing insurance companies to treat the reserves under a long-term care insurance policy as accident and health insurance reserves for insurance company corporate income tax purposes, those rulings have expressly declined to address the income tax treatment of the benefits payable to the policy beneficiaries. [Rev Rul 89-43, 1989-1 CB 213; Priv Ltr Ruls 91-06-040 (Nov 14, 1990), 91-06-041 (Nov 14, 1990)] (See Chapter 9 for a detailed discussion of long-term care insurance plans.)

Q 3:9   Is a Code Section 401(h) retiree medical account under a pension or annuity plan considered to be a medical plan?

No, it is not. The Code Section 401(h) provisions are a statutorily authorized method of setting aside funds in a pension or annuity plan before the plan participants retire in order to pay the cost of coverage under a medical plan in retirement. In effect, it is a "statutory holding tank" for funds that must be used for medical plan premiums or benefits and that cannot be used for pension benefits. Code Section 401(h) accounts are discussed in the chapter on funding and financing welfare benefits, at Qs 19:96 to 19:102.

Q 3:10 Is a minimum number of employees a prerequisite for a medical plan?

No, it is not. A medical plan may cover one or more employees. [Treas Reg § 1.105-5(a)]

Compare: For COBRA purposes, a "group health plan" must consist of at least two employees. See Q 6:4.

Q 3:11 Is a self-employed individual considered an employee?

No, an individual who is self-employed is not considered to be an employee for purposes of Code Sections 105 and 106. [IRC § 105(g); Treas Reg § 1.105-5(b)] Sole proprietors, partners, and more-than-2-percent S corporation shareholders are considered self-employed, while other shareholder-employees are not considered self-employed. [IRC § 1372] (See Qs 3:102 to 3:107 for a discussion of the tax treatment of the benefits of self-employed individuals.)

Compare: Under the special rules applicable to COBRA continuation of group health plan coverage, self-employed individuals are treated as employees for COBRA purposes only. See Qs 6:27 and 6:36.

Types of Plans

Q 3:12 How does an employer make medical benefits available to employees?

Most employer-provided plans take the form of medical care indemnity plans, also known as reimbursement plans. Under such a plan, the employee incurs a medical expense, and the employer's plan reimburses the expense either by paying the medical service provider (for example, hospital, surgeon) directly, or by paying the employee after the employee has paid the medical service provider.

In recent years, however, and primarily as a result of efforts to control rapidly escalating medical care costs, other types of medical care delivery systems have been incorporated into employer-provided plans, either as employee options or as mandated features. These include HMOs, preferred provider organizations (PPOs), and so-called "point-of-service" plans (which permit the employee to choose among several options each time he or she needs medical care).

Q 3:13   Must an employer ever offer a specific type of medical plan?

Yes, until October 24, 1995, the federal HMO Act requires an employer having an existing group health plan to include the option of membership in a federally qualified HMO in its benefit package if the HMO satisfies certain requirements. (See Chapter 5 for a detailed discussion of HMOs.) Employers without an existing group health plan are not regulated by the federal HMO Act.

Q 3:14   What is an HMO?

An HMO is a health care organization, composed of medical care providers and affiliated health care institutions, that agrees to provide a specified range of medical care for a set fee (commonly referred to as a capitation fee) to individuals residing in its geographic service area. The monthly fee covers the medical expenses incurred by the HMO member, regardless of the frequency or degree to which the HMO's medical services are used.

Example. An HMO agrees to provide specified medical care coverage for an employee and her family for a fee of $2,400 per year, regardless of whether their actual medical care expenses are more or less than that amount. If an HMO is offered as part of the employer's medical benefit plan, the employer will pay part or all of the HMO fee. Any amount that the employer does not pay is paid by the employee via payroll deduction.

Q 3:15   How are HMOs different from traditional medical plans?

The key distinguishing features of HMOs are that they:

- Provide care directly to members rather than reimbursing the cost of care obtained elsewhere; and
- Exercise control over access to the medical care providers and health care institutions.

These features are designed to provide the HMO with greater control over cost, quality of care, and determinations regarding the medical necessity of care. See Chapter 5 for a detailed discussion of HMOs.

Q 3:16   What is a PPO?

A PPO is a network of medical care providers who have agreed to provide various medical care services for specified fees. The network may be organized by the employer or by an outside entity such as an insurance company that either insures or administers the employer's plan. An employee who is covered by the PPO arrangement is generally required or encouraged to use a preferred provider. The expectation is that the cost to the plan will be less if the employee uses a preferred provider than if the employee were to use a medical care provider that is not a preferred provider.

Q 3:17   How is a PPO different from an HMO?

Generally, use of the PPO's preferred providers is strictly voluntary. Employer medical plans often allow the participant to select between the PPO and his or her own health care provider at any time, on a service by service basis. In contrast, membership in an HMO (generally for renewable one-year periods) restricts the employee to the use of the providers associated with that HMO for the duration of the membership period.

Q 3:18   What is a dental maintenance organization (DMO)?

A DMO is a type of health maintenance organization offering only dental care benefits. The federal HMO Act does not cover DMOs.

Funding Types and Cost Sharing

Q 3:19   How is an employer-provided medical benefit plan funded?

The employer has a wide choice of methods of funding the medical benefit plan, including no funding (self-insurance), full insurance, partial insurance (a minimum-premium plan or stop-loss insurance), or funding through a trust. (See Chapter 19 for additional discussion of these funding choices.)

Q 3:20 May the employer share the cost of the benefit plan with employees?

Yes, it may. The plan may be fully noncontributory, that is, the employees are not required to make a contribution from their pay in order to be covered. The plan may also be only partly noncontributory. For example, the plan may provide that the employee's own coverage is noncontributory, but that a contribution is required if the employee wishes to have dependent coverage. Finally, the plan may be fully contributory, requiring the employee to contribute for all of the coverage under the plan (employee-pay-all).

Q 3:21 Are there other ways in which employers can have employees bear part of the cost of medical care expenses?

Yes, there are. Two common methods of cost sharing are deductibles and coinsurance. When the plan provides for an annual deductible (for example, $250), the employee must pay for that amount of expenses with his or her own funds each year, and the plan pays only for the expenses over the deductible amount. In a coinsurance arrangement, the plan pays a specified percentage of the medical expenses (for example, 90 percent), while the employee pays the remainder (in this example, 10 percent).

> **Planning Pointer**. As a means of controlling plan costs, many employer-provided plans incorporate a combination of cost-sharing features. Thus, a single plan may require employee contributions and contain both deductible and coinsurance features.

However, simple cost sharing often does not provide sufficient incentive for the patient to be a more careful consumer of medical care services. In recent years, many employers have added "managed care" features to their health care plans in order to better control plan costs.

Q 3:22   What is managed care?

Managed care refers to controlling costs by managing, overseeing, or channeling health care services under an employee benefit plan to provide cost-effective care and avoid unnecessary services.

Q 3:23   What are some common forms of managed care?

Managed care features include the following:

- Utilization review, including preadmission certification, individual case management, and second surgical opinions, and
- Preferred providers

Q 3:24   What is utilization review?

Utilization review is a process used to determine the need, extent, and effectiveness of health care services. Typically, this determination is made (1) before the services are provided (for example, pre-admission certification or second surgical opinion programs), (2) during the course of services (for example, concurrent hospital review), or (3) after the services have been rendered (referred to as retrospective review). The earlier the review process is interjected, the more chance there is for affecting the course of treatment given and, as a result, the costs incurred for treatment.

Utilization review may be obtained as a part of a benefit package offered by an insurance carrier or may be "grafted onto" an existing program by retaining a third-party firm specializing in review and monitoring of health care services and service providers.

Q 3:25   What is pre-admission certification?

Under a plan providing for pre-admission certification, a participant normally is required to seek approval for nonemergency hospitalization in advance of admission to the hospital. Failure to do so may subject the participant to financial penalties in the form of lower benefit coverage or no coverage at all for the hospitalization in question. Plans that have a pre-admission certification requirement typically exempt emergency care from the pre-admission certification requirement, but require prompt post-admission notification of any emergency admission.

Q 3:26   What is concurrent review?

Concurrent review means monitoring a patient's care while he or she is in the hospital in order to better control the appropriateness and cost of medical care rendered and the duration of the hospital stay. The goal is to cut down on extra hospital days and excessive hospital tests and procedures without adversely affecting the quality of the patient's medical care.

Q 3:27   What is retrospective review?

Retrospective review is review of medical care services, typically hospitalization, after the fact. As such, the review is advisory in nature only; treatment alternatives are not proposed, and treatment is not modified or curtailed in the particular case. The chief benefit of retrospective review is in uncovering unnecessary services or unusual practice patterns—information that may be used as a basis for plan design modifications in the future or for decisions regarding the continued inclusion of a particular health care provider in a program.

Q 3:28   What is a second surgical opinion procedure?

Under a second surgical opinion procedure, a participant is required or encouraged to obtain a second opinion before obtaining certain specified nonemergency surgical procedures. To encourage the participant to do so, the plan typically covers the cost of a second surgical opinion in full and may also cover a third, "tie-breaker" opinion. Usually, the participant is not obligated to abide by the results of the second surgical opinion, but it is hoped that advice not to have surgery will encourage the patient to more fully consider alternate courses of treatment.

Failure to obtain a required second surgical opinion may result in a financial penalty such as reduced or no coverage for the surgical procedure.

Q 3:29 What is individual case management?

Individual case management involves special handling for cases that are expected to have unusually high costs, such as catastrophic illness, AIDS, cancer, and traumatic head injury cases. As soon as possible, case reviewers develop a proposed course of long-term treatment using cost-effective alternatives. Often, the medical plan covers treatments otherwise excluded if such treatment is recommended by the case management reviewers and agreed to by the patient and his or her physician. For example, the plan may not normally cover home health care or hospice care, but will provide it in an individual case management situation as an alternative to extended hospitalization.

Q 3:30 How are preferred providers incorporated into health care arrangements?

A panel of preferred providers (see Qs 3:16, 3:17) may be included in a health care arrangement in order to channel participants to preselected providers that will charge a pre-agreed fee. The plan's benefit structure may include a financial incentive to encourage participants to use the preferred providers, such as waiver of copayments and/or deductibles or a financial disincentive for failure to use the preferred provider.

Q 3:31 Does ERISA prevent employers from including managed care features in their medical plans?

No, an employer does not breach any ERISA fiduciary duties by incorporating managed care features into its plans. The decision to adopt or amend a plan is an employer function under ERISA, not a fiduciary function.

The Court of Appeals for the Third Circuit upheld a provision in an ERISA medical plan requiring that participants obtain pre-certification of hospitalizations or suffer a 30-percent reduction in the level of reimbursement of covered expenses under the plan. A participant who experienced shortness of breath associated with heart disease and who was hospitalized shortly thereafter was aware of his employer-provided medical plan's pre-certification provision but did not notify the hospital of it at the time he was admitted to the hospital, and he carried an outdated medical plan ID card that did not contain the required information. The plan's pre-certification procedure also permitted an individual admitted to the hospital on an emergency basis to notify the plan within 48 hours of the admission, but he failed to do that as well. When he subsequently submitted a claim for expenses, the plan applied the 30-percent penalty for failure to obtain the required certification of hospitalization.

The appellate court drew a distinction between ERISA's concern with the administration of benefit plans and with the design of such plans. It noted that ERISA does not impose a duty on employers to provide health care benefits to employees and held that ERISA's fiduciary responsibility provisions do not apply to the employer's design decisions and, hence, do not prohibit the inclusion of a penalty provision in the medical plan. Although the employee suffered significant economic deprivation, the employer did not violate ERISA by including a 30-percent penalty, even though the message conveyed by the pre-certification requirement could have been delivered by using a far lesser penalty. [Nazay v Miller, 949 F 2d 1323, 14 EBC (BNA) 1953 (3rd Cir 1991)]

Another method of encouraging employees to use a medical plan's managed care features is to incorporate "participating providers" and a nonassignment provision. Under such an arrangement, the employee is free to use either a participating or nonparticipating provider. The key mechanism for shifting utilization to the participating provider is the method of reimbursement. Typically, if the participant uses the participating provider, the plan pays the provider's fees directly to the provider and the participant only pays the copayment (if any). If the participant uses a nonparticipating provider, however, the plan's nonassignment clause would force the participant to pay the entire bill first and then submit a claim for reimbursement, subject to the plan's copayment requirement. Thus, for example, if the plan pays 70 percent for a particular medical service, the employee who uses a participating provider would pay only the 30 percent copayment, but the employee who uses a nonparticipating provider first would have to pay 100 percent of the bill and then submit a claim for the 70 percent covered by the plan, accompanied by a copy of a bill marked "paid." Sometimes, the plan also is designed to reimburse the preferred provider's charges at a higher percentage or in full.

These anti-assignment clauses have been challenged by nonparticipating providers. The Court of Appeals for the Ninth Circuit upheld such a plan design as not violating of ERISA. Noting that Congress expressly incorporated in ERISA a prohibition against assignment of pension benefits but did not do so for welfare benefits, the appellate court held that Congress intended to allow the free marketplace to work out "competitive, cost effective, medical expense reducing structures as might evolve." [Davidowitz v Delta Dental Plan of Calif, Inc, 946 F 2d 1476, 1481 (9th Cir 1991)] The Court of Appeals for the Eighth Circuit has also held that a general state law requiring free assignability of claims affects plan administration, including cost control measures, and thus "relates to" an ERISA plan and is preempted by ERISA. [Arkansas Blue Cross and Blue Shield v St Mary's Hosp, 947 F 2d 1341 (8th Cir 1991)]

> **Planning Pointer.** It is important to note, however, that how a decision to amend an ERISA plan is implemented is an area of fiduciary responsibility. Although case law under ERISA specifically dealing with managed care arrangements has been slow to develop, employers subject to ERISA should be mindful of the general ERISA duties regarding selection, monitoring, and retention of insurance carriers and other service providers to the plan and also should bear in mind the residual ERISA liability and cofiduciary liability. [Compare Corcoran v United HealthCare Inc 968 F 2d 1321 (5th Cir 1992), with Salley v EI DuPont de Nemours & Co, (5th Cir 966 F 2d 1011 1992). (See Chapter 2 for a detailed discussion of ERISA fiduciary responsibility and liability.)

Note. The employer's past course of conduct or the presence of a collective bargaining agreement may preclude the employer from unilaterally adopting or modifying a medical plan. The employer's ability to amend an ERISA-covered welfare benefit plan is discussed in detail in Qs 2:39–2:46.

Q 3:32   Aside from ERISA, is an employer or service provider subject to any other potential liability for implementing managed care?

This is a developing area of the law. Presumably, liability could exist for negligent selection of service providers. In addition, if the managed care program is administered improperly and, as a result, the patient is denied necessary and adequate medical care, it appears that the person or persons administering the managed care program could be liable if, for example, the managed care program's care guidelines are not soundly designed and/or carefully implemented.

The extreme need of employers to respond to rampant health care cost escalation has fostered (and, indeed, forced) the development of managed care arrangements as an alternative to cutting out costly medical programs altogether. The case law concerning employer liability for such arrangements is still developing. Careful planning and implementation should go a long way toward limiting exposure to potential litigation and liability in this area.

A U.S. district court case illustrates one type of potential liability associated with offering a managed care plan and the difficulty courts may have in analyzing these complex arrangements. An employer offered HMO coverage to its employees. A member of the HMO who had been receiving drug and alcohol rehabilitation on an outpatient basis was admitted as an inpatient for 15 days by his primary care physician at the HMO. At the end of this period, he was discharged despite his physician's and/or therapist's recommendation that he stay, and it was claimed that the HMO would neither approve treatment nor accept payment from the member's family for additional treatment. Two weeks later, the patient attempted to cross railroad tracks while intoxicated and was struck and killed by a train. The court held that ERISA does not preempt the medical malpractice claim because such a claim does not depend upon contractual entitlement to benefits. Rather, the medical malpractice claim was held to involve a separate issue of whether the HMO was liable, on an "ostensible agency" theory, for care that it arranged. [Kohn v Delaware Valley HMO, Inc, 14 EBC 2336 (ED Pa 1991), rehearing denied, 14 EBC 2597 (ED Pa 1992)]

Planning Pointer. The employer who offers an HMO, PPO, or managed care plan is also a potential "deep pocket" in such actions. The employer should try to obtain contractual protection against liability for care provided directly by, or arranged for by, an HMO, PPO, or managed care plan.

Coordination of Benefits

Q 3:33   What is a coordination of benefits (COB) provision?

A COB in a group health insurance plan specifies the plan benefits that are payable if health care expenses are covered by more than one plan.

Q 3:34   What is the purpose of a COB provision?

The principal purpose of a COB provision is to limit excess coverage, so that the employee will not receive reimbursements from more than one plan that in total exceed the actual amount of health care costs incurred. The COB provision also has a cost-control aspect, since it can significantly reduce the cost of the plan. In addition, the COB provision is designed to avoid claim delays, because it specifies which plans pay which benefits.

Q 3:35   Do all health plans have COB provisions?

No, but most plans do. If the plan provides benefits by means of an insurance contract, state insurance law may require the group health contract, and thus, indirectly, the plan, to contain a COB provision.

Q 3:36   What if only one plan has a COB provision?

Under the National Association of Insurance Commissioners (NAIC) Model COB Regulation, the plan without a COB provision is primary and the plan with the COB provision is secondary.

Q 3:37   Are COB provisions uniform?

No. COB provisions come in a variety of forms. However, as a practical matter, the COB provisions dealing with order of benefit determination (that is, which plan pays first and which plan pays second) are generally uniform regardless of whether the plans are insured or uninsured, and regardless of the state in which the insured plan is issued.

The NAIC, an association whose membership consists of the insurance commissioners from each state in the United States and the District of Columbia, has promulgated a model group COB regulation. The model regulation serves as a guide for the states when they choose to adopt COB rules. In June 1985, the NAIC promulgated a major modernization and updating of its model regulation. In subsequent years, it has made several changes in that model regulation.

Most, but not all, states have adopted COB rules or regulations. Those states that have no formal COB rules generally will not permit insurance policy forms to be used in the state if they have COB provisions that do not conform to the more significant provisions of the NAIC model regulation.

Plans that are not subject to state regulation tend to use the model's order of benefit determination provisions primarily to avoid situations in which both plans can end up in a secondary position, thereby depriving a claimant covered under two plans of primary coverage.

Q 3:38   Does ERISA preempt state COB laws for self-insured and/or insured medical plans?

Yes, ERISA preempts the application of state COB laws to self-insured medical plans. (See Questions 2:137–2:150 for further discussion of ERISA preemption principles.) However, when determining the federal common-law result under ERISA, courts may "borrow" from state COB principles or other federal laws to reach essentially the same result. [Reinforcing Iron Workers Local 426 Health and Welfare Fund v Michigan Bell Tel Co, 746 F Supp 668 (ED Mich 1990) (Although ERISA preempted the Michigan COB Act with respect to self-insured plans, ERISA contains no language regarding which plan would be liable on a primary basis for the dependent child's medical expenses. The court determined that the self-insured plan's rule that the father's plan must pay before the mother's plan was sexually discriminatory in violation of state law and Title VII of the federal Civil Rights Act of 1964. Instead, the court used the rule contained in the father's plan that the primary plan is that of the parent whose birthday occurs first in the year.)]

ERISA does not preempt state COB laws with respect to insured plans.

In a decision by the U.S. Court of Appeals for the Ninth Circuit, the court concluded that the federal courts should develop uniform federal common-law COB rules that apply nationwide for plans not subject to state COB laws because of ERISA preemption, rather than relying on particular state law rules. The court concluded, in accordance with the *Michigan Bell* decision above, that the earliest birthday rule was preferable to the father's plan primary rule because the earliest birthday rule is gender-neutral. The court also criticized the two plans for refusing to pay and thereby causing hardship to the beneficiaries, asserting that the plans should have found a way to pay the benefits and then work out the controversy between the plans. [PM Group Life Ins Co v Western Growers Assurance Trust, 953 F 2d 543, 14 EBC (BNA) 2233 (9th Cir 1992)]

Q 3:39 What are the general rules concerning coordination of insured plan benefits payable to someone who is covered both as an employee and as a dependent under separate plans?

Under the NAIC model regulation, if an individual has coverage under two plans, and one plan has no COB provision and the other plan does, the plan with no COB provision is primary and the plan with the COB provision is secondary. However, if both plans have COB provisions, the plan that covers the person as an employee is treated as the primary plan, and the plan that covers the person as a dependent is the secondary plan.

Example. A husband and wife work for different employers. Each has coverage as an employee, and the husband has elected dependent coverage. Both plans have COB provisions. For the husband's health care expenses, the husband's plan is the primary plan; for the wife's health care expenses, the wife's plan is primary and the husband's plan is secondary. The primary plan pays benefits in the normal manner, without regard to the secondary plan. The secondary plan generally pays the difference between a maximum amount (not more than the total expenses actually incurred) and the amount paid by the primary plan. The secondary plan never pays more than it would have paid if it had been the primary plan.

Note: The following questions explain the rules for "true" coordination of benefits. Many health plans, however, simply subtract the amount paid under other coverage from the benefits otherwise due, which is an "offset" provision. These plans sometimes incorrectly refer to the offset as a coordination of benefits provision.

Q 3:40 Which plan pays first when a retired individual is covered under a retiree medical plan and Medicare and is also covered as a dependent under a spouse's medical plan for active employees?

Formerly, this special situation resulted in all three plans asserting that they were the secondary payer, with no plan being willing to be the primary payer. In December 1990, the NAIC amended its model COB regulation to cover this situation by requiring that the plan covering the individual as a dependent of an active employee pays first, that Medicare pays second, and that the plan covering the individual as a retiree pays third. Not all states have adopted this change.

Q 3:41 What are the general rules for COB for dependent children when each parent has coverage?

The answer depends on whether or not the parents are separated or divorced.

Under the current NAIC model COB regulation, if the parents are not separated or divorced, the plan covering the parent whose birthday falls earlier in the year is the primary plan. If both parents have the same birthday, the plan that has been in effect longer is primary.

Prior to the current NAIC model COB regulation, when both parents had dependent coverage, the father's plan was the primary plan. To avoid situations in which both plans would end up in a secondary position during the period in which the states moved from the old rule to the new rule, the NAIC model COB regulation provided that in the event of conflict between the two rules, the old rule (that is, the father's plan as the primary plan) would prevail.

Under the NAIC model COB regulation, if the parents are separated or divorced, the plan of the parent with custody pays first. If the divorced parent with custody has remarried, the plan of the new spouse (that is, the step-parent's plan), pays second, and the plan of the parent without custody pays last.

> **Example.** A divorced parent, who has custody of a child but no plan coverage as an employee, has remarried and the new spouse has employee dependent coverage that includes the divorced parent's child. The new spouse's plan is primary for the child's health care expenses, and the noncustodial parent's plan is secondary.

If the parents are separated or divorced, and if the divorce decree or separation agreement provides for joint physical custody and has no provision designating either parent as the one having financial responsibility for the child's health care expenses, the most recent NAIC model regulation provides that the plan covering the parent whose birthday falls earlier in the year is the primary plan. Thus, in cases of joint custody, the rule is the same as the rule for parents who are not separated or divorced.

Q 3:42   How are insured plan benefits coordinated if an employee is laid off or retires?

The NAIC model regulation provides that if the employee is covered under two plans, under one as an active employee and under the other as a laid-off or retired employee, the active-employee coverage is primary. However, this rule applies only if both plans have it in their COB provisions or if they agree to its application.

Q 3:43   If none of the previous rules determine which plan pays first, how is the determination made?

The NAIC model COB regulation provides that if none of the previous rules determine which plan pays first, the plan covering the individual for the longer period of time is the one that pays first.

Q 3:44   How much does a secondary plan pay?

The NAIC model COB regulation provides that the secondary plan pays the difference between "total allowable expenses" and whatever the primary plan pays, as long as the secondary plan does not pay more than it would have paid had it been the primary plan. "Total allowable expenses" are generally expenses that are covered in whole or in part under either of the coordinating plans. The determination of what the secondary plan would have paid had it been the primary plan is made on an aggregate basis over the plan year rather than on a claim-by-claim basis.

As a result, a secondary plan might have to pay benefits for expenses that it does not cover if (1) those expenses were covered (but not in full) by the other plan, and (2) as a result of the operation of COB, it had savings (called a "credit balance") as a result of being the secondary plan during the current plan year. (This is different from an "offset" provision, under which the health plan with the offset provision would not pay for expenses that it does not cover.)

> **Example**. A secondary plan does not cover mental and nervous conditions. As a result of previous claims during the year, it has achieved COB savings of $5,000 compared to what it would have paid if it had been the primary plan. A claim of $2,000 is now submitted for treatment relating to mental and nervous disorders, $1,000 of which is payable by the primary plan. The secondary plan must pay the other $1,000 even though it does not cover expenses incurred in the treatment of mental and nervous conditions.

For a short time, the NAIC model COB regulation permitted plans to coordinate in ways that would allow them to preserve the deductibles and copayments inherent in their plans. For example, one permitted method would have allowed the secondary plan to pay the difference between what it would have paid on the claim had it been the primary plan and whatever the primary plan actually paid (essentially, an "offset"). However, those rules were removed from the NAIC model regulation.

Uninsured plans and insured plans in the few states that adopted the rule before it was repealed by the NAIC may still use this technique, although there is some doubt that it really results in cost-saving advantages to the plan. Plans that tend to favor this approach tend to be large employer plans that require little, if any, employee contribution for coverage. As employees covered by those plans realize that there is little advantage for their spouses to maintain their contributory employee health care coverage, they can be expected to have their spouses drop their own employee coverage and keep the dependent coverage. This migration away from duplicate coverage by a relatively small number of employees can erode any savings achieved by a more restrictive approach to what the secondary plan pays.

A recent amendment to the NAIC model regulation permits plans to take advantage of certain cost-containment penalties. Under this new rule, if the primary plan limits or excludes benefits when the plan participant fails to abide by the plan's cost-containment programs (such as pre-admission certification, PPO, or second surgical opinion), the amount of the penalty will not be considered an allowable expense. This feature is not available when a secondary plan's liability is generated by an HMO member seeking care outside the HMO, resulting in no liability to the primary HMO.

Example. A plan pays 90 percent of covered hospital expenses if pre-admission review is performed for voluntary admissions, but pays only 70 percent if such review is not performed. The secondary plan treats the 80 percent (the 10 percent copayment and the 70 percent paid under the pre-admission review penalty provision of the primary plan) as an allowable expense and pays only the 10 percent.

However, if the secondary plan has such a pre-admission review provision, and if the primary plan merely paid 90 percent of such expenses, the secondary plan would have to pay the extra 10 percent. This rule is available to protect the primary plan's cost containment features, not those of the secondary plan.

Q 3:45   **Can a state law prohibit an employee benefit plan from subtracting benefits payable under a state no-fault law or require the plan to be the primary payer with the no-fault insurance carrier as the secondary payer only?**

No, a state cannot regulate the terms of a self-insured medical plan, including whether it will pay primary or secondary to no-fault insurance coverage. [FMC Corp v Holliday, 498 US 52 (1990)]

Legal Parameters of Benefit Design

Q 3:46   **Do state insurance laws or state laws mandating the coverage of particular benefits or health care providers apply to group health plans?**

Sometimes, yes. However, ERISA's preemption provisions may bar the application of the state law to the particular group health plan. (ERISA preemption is discussed in detail in Qs 2:137–2:150.)

Q 3:47   **May a medical plan contain limits on certain types of covered benefits such as alcoholism or substance abuse or contain other disability-based limits?**

The freedom to limit coverage of particular benefits and/or conditions has been greatly constricted by the Americans With Disabilities Act of 1990 (ADA). Prior plan provisions are *not* "grandfathered," so all ADA-covered group health plans must comply with the ADA's requirements regardless of when the plan, or any particular benefit provision included in it, was adopted. Exactly how much flexibility employers have to limit coverage for cost or other reasons is currently unclear due to the strict (and perhaps impossible) standard of proof suggested by the Equal Employment Opportunity Commission (EEOC) Interim Final Rule under the ADA for demonstrating that a particular plan provision is not a subterfuge to evade the purposes of the ADA.

Some design practices, such as including universal limits that apply to all participants (both disabled and nondisabled) equally, or including uniformly applicable preexisting condition limits, are not considered to be disability-based distinctions and, as a result, are not affected by the ADA unless they are adopted for discriminatory reasons. Health-related insurance distinctions that are disability-based will violate the ADA unless they fall under the one of the ADA's exceptions. (The ADA requirements affecting medical plans are discussed in detail in Chapter 17.)

Q 3:48 Does federal law permit a medical plan to exclude acquired immune deficiency syndrome (AIDS) coverage?

Tax Penalties. There are no tax penalties for excluding medical treatment for AIDS.

ERISA. An employer was held not to have acted arbitrarily and capriciously or to have breached its ERISA duties in restricting the lifetime cap on health plan expenses for AIDS while not reducing it for other medical conditions. [McGann v H&H Music Co, 546 F 2d 401 (5th Cir 1991); see also Owens v Storehouse, 984 F 2d 394 (11th Cir 1993)] In addition, the exclusion of a condition entirely has been upheld under ERISA. [Johnson v District 2 Marine Eng'rs Beneficial Assoc—Assoc'd Maritime Officers Medical Plan, 857 F 2d 514 (9th Cir 1988)]

Employment Discrimination Laws. An employer covered by the Rehabilitation Act of 1973 or by the ADA may, under some circumstances, be barred from excluding AIDS coverage. (See Chapter 18 for further discussion of the federal Rehabilitation Act of 1973 and Chapter 17 for a discussion of the ADA). State laws, which are beyond the scope of this book, may also apply if they are not preempted by ERISA.

Q 3:49 Does federal law permit a medical plan to exclude adopted children and children placed for adoption?

No, it does not. Effective on and after August 10, 1993, ERISA Section 609(c) requires group health plans to cover adopted children and children who are placed for adoption (whether or not the adoption has become final). In addition, no preexisting condition limitations may apply to adopted and pre-adoptive children (even if preexisting condition limitations apply to other individuals under the plan), and they must be covered on the same terms and conditions as apply to natural children. For this purpose, a child is considered to be "placed for adoption" if a person has assumed and retains a legal obligation for total or partial support of the child in anticipation of adoption. [ERISA § 609(c), added by § 4301 of OBRA '93] A special transition rule provides that plan amendments need not be adopted until the first day of the 1994 plan year, provided that the group health plan is in operational compliance for the entire period from the effective date to the date the amendment is adopted. [§ 4301(d) of OBRA '93]

Group Health Plan. This requirement applies to all "group health plans" as that term is defined in Code Section 5000(b)(1), including any plan (including a self-insured plan) of, or contributed to by, an employer (including a self-employed person) or employee organization to directly or indirectly provide health care to the employees, former employees, the employer, others associated or formerly associated with the employer in a business relationship, or their families. [IRC § 5000(b), as amended by § 13561 of OBRA '93]

Q 3:50 Does federal law permit a medical plan to reduce or eliminate coverage for pediatric vaccines?

No, it does not. ERISA Section 609(d) and Code Section 4980B(f) require that group health plans may not reduce their coverage of the costs of pediatric vaccines below the level of coverage provided on May 1, 1993. The Consolidated Omnibus Budget Reconciliation Act (COBRA) excise tax penalty applies to violations. (See Chapter 6 for a detailed discussion of COBRA excise tax.) [ERISA § 609(d), added by § 4301 of OBRA '93; IRC § 4980B(f), as revised by § 13422(a) of OBRA '93]

Note. Although anticutback provisions are common in the rules governing retirement plans, the pediatric vaccine provision is the first time Congress has elected to permanently "vest" medical coverage at a particular level. If the plan had coverage for pediatric vaccines on May 1, 1993, that coverage cannot be cut back or diminished during the life of the medical plan.

Plan amendments need not be adopted until the first day of the 1994 plan year, provided that the group health plan is in operational compliance for the entire period from the effective date to the date the amendment is adopted. [§ 4301(d) of OBRA '93]

Q 3:51   What special rules apply to medical plans regarding New York hospital rates?

An employer's deduction for group health plan contributions will be disallowed if the plan fails to reimburse hospitals for inpatient services provided in New York (1) at the same rate that commercial insurers are required to reimburse hospitals for the same services for individuals not covered by a group health plan, or (2) at any other rate permitted under Code Section 162(n). "Group health plan," for this purpose, means a group health plan as defined in Code Section 5000(b)(1) (see Q 3:49). [IRC 162(n), added by § 13442(a) of OBRA '93] This requirement applies to inpatient hospital services provided to group health plan participants and beneficiaries between February 3, 1993 and May 11, 1995.

Q 3:52   May a medical plan impose limits on individuals who switch from HMO coverage to the medical plan?

No, if an individual switches to the medical plan during an open enrollment period, no exclusions, waiting periods, or health limits may be imposed on the individual. (See Chapter 5 for a detailed discussion of HMO coverage.)

Q 3:53   What conditions apply to individuals who take family or medical leave?

An individual who takes a family or medical leave that qualifies under the the Family and Medical Leave Act of 1993 (FMLA) is entitled to continue his or her group health plan coverage for the duration of the unpaid FMLA leave. The employer is required to continue its portion of premium contributions, and provision must be made for the employee to continue his or her contributions in order to maintain group health coverage in force. No exclusions or waiting periods may be imposed on individuals who return to active employment at the conclusion of an FMLA leave (even if they did not maintain group health coverage or their group health coverage terminated due to untimely premium payments during the leave). If the employee fails to return to employment at the conclusion of the FMLA leave, the employer may, in some circumstances, recover its portion of the premium payments. (These and other FMLA issues, as well as the interplay with COBRA, are discussed in detail in Chapter 15.)

Q 3:54 Does federal law require a medical plan to offer maternity benefits?

There is no federal requirement that a medical plan must offer maternity benefits. However, Title VII of the Civil Rights Act of 1964, as amended by the Pregnancy Discrimination Act of 1978, mandates that covered employers treat pregnancy in the same way as all other conditions. If employees have a choice of several health plans or options, each option must comply with this rule, regardless of who pays the premiums. Female employees cannot be forced to pay for more expensive dependent or family coverage in order to obtain maternity coverage. Equal treatment means that no separate deductibles may be allowed or maximum recoverable amounts imposed. Reimbursement must be provided for pregnancy-related conditions in the same way (for example, a fixed-dollar amount or a percentage of reasonable and customary charges) as for other conditions. Hospitalization and office visits (including prenatal and postnatal visits) must be covered on the same basis as for other conditions.

Preexisting condition limitations can be imposed, and benefits can stop, on the same terms as for any other medical conditions. Pregnancy-related conditions of nonspouse dependents are not required to be covered as long as the plan excludes the pregnancy-related conditions of nonspouse dependents of male and female employees equally. [42 USC § 2000e(k); EEOC Reg, Pt 1604, App, Q&As 21, 23-30] (See Chapter 18 for further discussion of Title VII.)

Q 3:55   Does federal law require a medical plan to cover abortions?

Yes, Title VII of the Civil Rights Act of 1964 does require that health insurance benefits be provided for abortions, but only when the pregnancy threatens the life of the mother if the fetus were carried to term. Medical complications arising from abortion, such as excessive hemorrhaging, must also be covered. [42 USC § 2000e(k); EEOC Reg, Pt 1604, App, Q&As 35-37] (See Chapter 18 for further discussion of Title VII.)

Q 3:56   Can an employer refuse to cover, or provide less medical coverage for, individuals who are eligible for Medicaid?

No. Effective on and after August 10, 1993, ERISA Section 609(b) requires that group health plans may not place any limits on group health plan eligibility or limit or exclude group health plan benefits because of a participant's or beneficiary's eligibility for or entitlement to, Medicaid. Group health plans also must pay plan benefits in accordance with any assignment made pursuant to state Medicaid laws by, or on behalf of, a plan participant or beneficiary. States are given a right to enforce compliance and ERISA's preemption provisions do not apply to such state actions. Plan amendments need not be adopted until the first day of the 1994 plan year, provided that the group health plan is in operational compliance for the entire period from the effective date to the date the amendment is adopted. [ERISA § 609(b), added by § 4301 of OBRA '93]

Q 3:57   Can an employer refuse to cover, or provide less medical coverage for, older employees or older spouses who are eligible for Medicare?

No, generally not. Individuals age 65 or older in "current employment status" (that is, the individual is an employee, the employer, or is associated with the employer in a business relationship) must be allowed to remain covered under the employer's group health plan under the same conditions as younger employees. A spouse age 65 or older of an individual in current employment status (regardless of such individual's age) must also be covered under the plan under the same conditions as spouses under age 65. This provision, formerly contained in the Age Discrimination in Employment Act of 1967 (ADEA), has been recodified as Section 1862(b)(1) of the Social Security Act [42 USC § 1395y] and as Code Section 5000(c).

No Affirmative Election Required. When this so-called *working-aged* provision was contained in the ADEA, a proposed regulation which was later withdrawn contained a requirement that the employee in the above situation had to make an affirmative choice to have the employer's group health plan be the primary payer; if not, the employer was permitted to pay secondary to Medicare. Despite the withdrawal of the proposed regulation containing that requirement, confusion still occasionally exists on this point. It is important to understand that group health plans are absolutely required to be primary to Medicare for this working-aged group (including any enrolled spouse age 65 or older of an employee of any age). The employee or spouse need not make any special written affirmation of the desire to have the employer's plan primary and Medicare secondary. The employee chooses to have the employer's plan as primary payer simply by staying in it, and chooses to have Medicare as primary payer by dropping out of the employer's plan; that is, Medicare becomes the primary payer when it is the employee's only available coverage.

Retirees. The working-aged provisions do not apply to former employees. An employer may provide that plan coverage of retired or terminated employees and their spouses and dependents, any of whom are eligible for Medicare, will be secondary to Medicare; and the use of wrap-around or Medicare supplemental coverage is not prohibited in these instances.

Small Plan Exclusion. Prior to August 10, 1993, a single-employer group health plan is exempt from the working-aged provisions of Code Section 5000 and the Social Security Act as long as it has less than 20 or more employees for each working day in each of 20 or more calendar weeks in the current calendar year or the preceding calendar year. In addition, if a multiemployer or multiple employer group health plan expressly elects the statutory exemption, then an employer participating in the plan and having less than 20 or more employees for each working day in each of 20 or more calendar weeks in the current or preceding calendar year, will also be exempt. [Social

Security Act § 1862(b)(1)(A), 42 USC § 1395y] On and after August 10, 1993, the prior calendar year has been eliminated from the above measuring period and only the current calendar year is used. Additionally, effective November 8, 1993, the number of employers with current employment status is determined using IRC controlled-group, affiliated-service group, and leased-employee rules. [42 USC § 1395y, as amended by § 13561 of OBRA '93]

Q 3:58   Can an employer refuse to cover, or provide less medical coverage for, an individual entitled to Medicare because the individual has kidney disease?

No, a group health plan may not differentiate in the benefits it provides to individuals entitled to Medicare because of end-stage renal kidney disease or the need for renal dialysis. [IRC § 5000(c), formerly contained in IRC § 162(i); Social Security Act § 1862(b)(1), 42 USC § 1395y(b)(1)(C)]

The group health plan (including, effective on and after August 10, 1993, retiree medical plans) must be the primary payer of benefits (and Medicare must be the secondary payer) for 18 months (formerly 12 months, for items and services furnished before February 1, 1991, for periods beginning before February 1, 1990). Accordingly, a covered group health plan that provides benefits for other conditions (for example, hospital care, physician care, or medically necessary care) cannot exclude benefits payable by Medicare for end-stage renal disease for this initial period. After the 18-month period, however, the coordinated provisions of Code Section 5000 and the Social Security Act permit the group health plan to become the secondary payer (unless another of the Social Security Act's Medicare secondary rules, such as the working-aged provisions discussed in Question 3:57, would come into play). [Social Security Act §§ 1862(b)(1)(C), 1862(b)(4), 42 USC § 1395y(b)(1)(C); Health Care Financing Administration (HCFA) Prop Reg § 411.62, 53 Fed Reg 22335 (June 15, 1988)] *Retiree* medical plans must be primary for end-stage renal disease for any individual who is entitled to medicare, regardless of age. This end-stage renal disease requirement, which had been scheduled to expire in 1995, has been extended until October 1, 1998. [42 USC 1395y(b), as amended by § 13561 of OBRA '93]

Note. The continued ability of group health plans to be secondary to Medicare has been placed in doubt by the EEOC's Interim Final Rule under the ADA. The EEOC apparently is taking the position that a limit on group health plan coverage for renal disease might constitute a prohibited disability-based distinction (see Chapter 17).

Definition of Group Health Plan. For purposes of the above Medicare rule relating to end-stage renal disease, a "group health plan" is any plan (including a self-insured plan) of, or contributed to by, an employer (including a self-employed person) to provide health care (directly or otherwise) to the employer's employees, former employees, others associated or formerly associated with the employer in a business relationship, or their families. [42 USC § 1395y(b)(1)(C) IRC § 5000(b)(1), as amended by § 13561 of OBRA '93]]

Q 3:59   Can an employer refuse to cover, or offer less coverage to, disabled employees or dependents who are eligible for Medicare?

No, if the employer's health plan is a large group health plan, it must fully cover such employees—or employers face a substantial excise tax (see Q 3:61). If an employee (or his or her covered dependent) is determined by the Social Security Administration to be disabled, the large group health plan must be the primary payer of benefits (that is, it pays first without any reduction for other coverage), and Medicare must be the secondary payer. [IRC § 5000(c); Social Security Act § 1862(b)(4)(A)(i)] The only permitted exception is the end-stage renal disease provisions discussed in Question 3:58.

Definition of Large Group Health Plan. A "large group health plan" is any plan (including a self-insured plan) of, or contributed to by, an employer (including a self-employed person) to provide health care, whether directly or otherwise, to the employees, former employees, the employer, and others associated or formerly associated with the employer in a business relationship, or their families, if the plan covers at least one employer that normally employed 100 or more employees on a typical business day during the previous calendar year. [IRC § 5000(b)(2), as amended by § 13561 of OBRA '93]]

If the plan is not a large group health plan, but the employer is subject to the ADA, refusing to cover disabled employees or dependents, or providing less coverage, may violate the ADA, unless it can be justified on the ground of increased insurance risk (see Q 17:10).

Q 3:60 Can a disabled employee who is not working be "active" covered for purposes of this Medicare coordination rule?

Although the HCFA had not issued final regulations defining an employee, it published proposed regulations under which a disabled individual who is not actively working will nonetheless be considered to be an active employee if he or she:

1. Is receiving payments from the employer that are subject to Federal Insurance Contributions Act (FICA) taxes (or would be but for such payments being exempt from FICA under the IRC); or

2. Is an employee under state or federal law or in accordance with case law; or

3. Is designated as an employee in the employer's records, that is, has not had his or her employment status terminated (for this purpose, payroll status is not controlling).

If none of these three criteria applied, the individual still could be an employee on the basis of all the facts relating to his or her situation. Factors that indicated employee status include:

- Payment by the employer of the same taxes paid on the individual's behalf as are paid for actively working employees;
- Accrual of vacation time or receipt of vacation pay;
- Participation in a benefit plan in which only employees may participate (individuals whose participation is mandated by COBRA may be disregarded);
- The right to return to duty if the individual's condition improves; or
- Accrual of sick leave.

[HCFA Prop Reg §§ 411.80-411.94; 55 Fed Reg 8491 (Mar 8, 1990)]

As of August 10, 1993, the HCFA proposed regulations have no application. The law now provides that the individual will be covered by the plan as primary if he or she has "current employment status," which is defined as status as an employee, the employer, or associated with the employer in a business relationship. [42 USC 1395y(b)(10) added by OBRA '93 13561(e)] It appears that the same standards applied under the working age primary provision (see Q 3:57), to determine employment status should be applicable to determine employment status for disability coverage primary to Medicare.

Q 3:61   What sanctions apply for violating these Medicare secondary rules?

Stiff penalties apply to violations of the Medicare secondary requirements. The federal government may bring an action against any entity, insurance policy, or plan to collect double damages for failure to pay as a primary payer. Individuals are also given a private right of action for double damages if the group health plan fails to pay benefits on a primary basis. Further, if a group health plan of any size violates one of these provisions, then the sponsoring employer or employee organization will be taxed by an amount equal to 25 percent of the employer's or employee organization's expenses incurred during the calendar year for each group health plan to which it contributes. [IRC § 5000(a); 42 USC § 1395y(a)(3)]

Q 3:62   Can an employer provide financial or other incentives not to enroll in the employer's group health plan to individuals who are entitled to Medicare benefits?

No. Where the employer's group health plan would be the primary payer and Medicare would be the secondary payer, it is unlawful for the employer or other entity to offer any financial or other incentive to an individual who is entitled to Medicare benefits not to enroll in the employer's group health plan, unless the incentive is also offered to all individuals who are eligible for coverage under the plan.

If the employer or other entity violates the above prohibition, it is subject to a civil money penalty of up to $5,000 for each violation. [Social Security Act § 1862(b)(3), 42 USC § 1395y(b)(3)]

Q 3:63 Must terminated and retired employees still be eligible for benefits?

Yes, under certain circumstances. Two federal laws, COBRA and the Retiree Benefits Bankruptcy Protection Act of 1988, require continuation of group health plan benefits and nonpension retiree benefits in bankruptcy respectively. (See Chapter 6 for further discussion of COBRA; see Chapter 18 for nonpension retiree benefits in bankruptcy.)

Q 3:64 Must a medical plan continue to cover military reservists called to active duty in the armed forces?

The answer to this question depends on the plan's provisions and how the reservist is carried on the employer's employment records. If coverage terminates, COBRA rights must be given (see Q 6:55).

Q 3:65 Must a medical plan cover care of veterans' nonservice-connected disabilities in a Veterans Administration (VA) facility?

Yes, it should—to the extent that it would otherwise cover the care—if it is a covered health plan contract. The Veterans' Health Care Amendments of 1986 invalidate provisions that exclude the coverage of care administered in a VA hospital or nursing home that is related to treatment of a veteran's nonservice-connected disability. The VA may recover the reasonable cost of any such care from any third-party payer, provided that the health plan contract would otherwise have covered the care or services if they had not been furnished by a department or agency of the United States. [38 USC § 629]

The reasonable cost is to be determined pursuant to VA regulations, reduced by any applicable plan deductible and copayment amounts that the third party can demonstrate would be payable under a comparable health plan contract to a nongovernmental facility. [38 USC § 629(c)(2)(b)]

Third-Party Payer. Third-party payers for these purposes generally include employers, employers' insurance carriers, and persons obligated to provide or pay expenses of health services under a health plan contract. [38 USC § 629(i)(3)]

Covered Health Plan Contract. Covered health plan contracts generally include insurance policies or contracts, medical or hospital service agreements, membership or subscription contracts, and similar arrangements for paying expenses for health services provided to individuals or for providing services to individuals. [38 USC § 629(i)(1)(A)]

Q 3:66 Must a medical plan cover inpatient care for military retirees and their dependents in military hospitals?

Yes, it should, on much the same terms and for much the same reasons that it should cover veterans' nonservice-connected disabilities (see Q 3:65). Title II of COBRA invalidates exclusions in health plan contracts for inpatient care received by military retirees and their dependents from military hospitals if the contract would otherwise cover such care. It authorizes the secretary of defense to recover the reasonable cost of any such services from third-party payers. Recovery is measured in the same way as for veterans' nonservice-connected disabilities, except that it will be based on Department of Defense regulations.

The definitions of "third-party payer" and "covered health plan contract" for military retirees are the same as for veterans' nonservice-connected disabilities. [10 USC § 1095; COBRA § 2001(b)]

Q 3:67 Are medical plans subject to ERISA?

Generally, an employer-sponsored medical plan is subject to ERISA and, as such, is subject to ERISA's COBRA continuation of health care requirements (which are parallel to, and coordinate with, the Code's COBRA provisions) pediatric vaccine coverage requirements, adopted and pre-adopted children coverage requirement, Qualified Medical Child Support Order (QMCSO) provisions and Medicare and Medicaid Coverage Data Bank provisions, as well as to ERISA's reporting and disclosure and fiduciary responsibility provisions. (See Chapter 2 for a detailed discussion of ERISA.)

Q 3:68   Is a medical plan subject to COBRA health care continuation requirements?

Yes, the medical plans maintained by most employers are subject to COBRA rules, with exceptions for small-employer, church, and government plans. (See Chapter 6 for a discussion of COBRA.)

Q 3:69   Are medical plans subject to tax nondiscrimination rules?

Yes. Code Section 105, which provides for the tax treatment of employer-provided accident and health benefits, does not impose any general nondiscrimination requirements; however, self-insured medical reimbursement plans must meet special nondiscrimination rules contained in Code Section 105(h) (see Qs 3:81–3:91).

Q 3:70   Do other federal laws affect employer-provided medical coverage?

Yes, they do. (Such federal laws are discussed generally in Chapters 15 through 18 and on a plan-by-plan basis in the other chapters of this book.)

Qualified Medical Child Support Orders

Q 3:71   Does a group health plan have to honor a qualified medical child support order (QMCSOs)?

Yes, it does. Effective on and after August 10, 1993, ERISA Section 609(a) requires a group health plan to honor QMCSO and pay benefits to any child who is an "alternate recipient" specified therein, or to the child's custodial parent or guardian who incurs covered expenses on the child's behalf. Plan amendments need not be adopted until the first day of the 1994 plan year, provided that the group health plan is in operational compliance for the entire period from the effective date to the date the amendment is adopted. [ERISA § 609(a), added by § 4301 of OBRA '93]

Q 3:72   When is a court order a QMCSO?

A "medical child support order" that meets certain statutory conditions is a QMCSO. A medical child support order is any court judgment, decree, or order (including approval of a settlement agreement) issued under a state's domestic relations or community-property law that (1) provides for child support or health benefit coverage for a child of a participant in a group health plan and (2) relates to benefits under such a plan. The medical child support order is "qualified" (that is, it is a QMCSO) if it: (1) recognizes an existing right, creates a right, or assigns the child the right to receive (as an "alternate recipient") benefits for which a participant or beneficiary is eligible under the group health plan; and (2) contains the additional information described in Question 3:73.

Court judgments, decrees, and orders issued under certain laws relating to medical child support also are QMCSOs.

[ERISA § 609(a)(2), added by § 4301 of OBRA '93]

Q 3:73   What information must be included in a QMCSO?

To be a QMCSO, the court order must specify:

- The name of the group health plan to which it applies;
- The name and last known address of the participant and each alternate recipient;
- A reasonable description of the type of coverage to be provided to each alternate recipient or the manner in which it is to be determined; and
- The period to which the order applies.

[ERISA § 609(a)(3), added by § 4301 of OBRA '93]

Disqualifying Provisions. A QMCSO cannot require a group health plan to provide any type or form of benefit or option not otherwise available under the plan, except to the extent necessary to meet medical child support laws described in new Section 1908 of the Social Security Act. [ERISA § 609(a)(4), added by § 4301 of OBRA '93]

Q 3:74   What are the plan administrator's responsibilities regarding a QMCSO?

ERISA requires a plan administrator to:

1. Adopt a written procedure for determining whether a court order meets the requirements of a QMCSO (the procedure must provide for the notification of each alternate recipient specified in the order to receive benefits and permit each such alternate recipient to designate a representative for receipt of notices);

2. Notify, immediately upon receipt of the court order, the participant and each alternate recipient listed in the order of the plan's procedure for determining whether the order is a QMCSO; and

3. Make the determination and notify the plan participant and each alternate recipient of its conclusion within a reasonable period after receiving the order.

[ERISA § 609(a)(5), added by § 4301 of OBRA '93]

A plan fiduciary will be discharged to the extent of payments made pursuant to their determinations, provided that it acts in accordance with ERISA's fiduciary standards in determining whether the court order is a valid QMCSO. [ERISA § 609(a)(6), added by § 4301 of OBRA '93]

Q 3:75   What rights do the alternate recipients named in a QMCSO have?

An alternate recipient must be treated as a group health plan beneficiary for all ERISA purposes except Title I reporting and disclosure.

For Title I reporting and disclosure purposes, the alternate recipient must be treated as a plan participant. [ERISA § 609(a)(7), added by § 4301 of OBRA '93]

Q 3:76   How is a QMCSO enforced?

ERISA's regular enforcement provisions (see Qs 2:15 to 2:179) apply; states are also given a right to enforce compliance and ERISA's preemption provisions do not apply to such state actions. [ERISA § 502(a), as amended by § 4301 of OBRA '93]

Medicare and Medicaid Coverage Data Bank Reporting Requirement

Q 3:77   What is the Medicare and Medicaid Coverage Data Bank?

The Medicare and Medicaid Coverage Data Bank, which is to be maintained by the DHHS, is designed to help identify the proper parties responsible for paying benefits covered by Medicare (under the Medicare secondary rules) and by Medicaid. The Data Bank will receive information regarding all employees (including former employees) who elect coverage under a group health plan of, or contributed to by, the employer that covers at least one current or former employee. ERISA Section 101(f) requires sponsors and administrators of group health plans to report such information to the Data Bank by January 31 of the next calendar year; however, the first required filing is due by February 28, 1995. The Data Bank reporting requirements currently only apply to information relating to calendar years 1994 through 1997, making the last report due by January 31, 1998. [ERISA § 101(f), revised by § 4301 of OBRA '93]

Q 3:78   What information must be reported?

The following information for each employee or former employee electing coverage under the group health plan must be reported to the Data Bank:

1. The name, address, and employer identification number (EIN) of the employer and of the group health plan;
2. The employee's name and Social Security number;
3. The type of coverage elected (single or family);
4. The name and Social Security number of the employee's covered spouse and covered dependents, if any; and
5. The period of coverage.

[Social Security Act § 1144, added by § 13561 of OBRA '93]

Disclosure of health status information, cost of coverage, or any coverage limitations or restrictions applying to any covered individual is prohibited. [ERISA § 609(f), added by § 4301 of OBRA '93]

Q 3:79 Who is responsible for reporting the required information?

Plan sponsors, plan administrators, insurers, third-party administrators, or others who maintain plan information must provide the required information either to the plan or directly to the Data Bank, as follows:

- *Multiemployer plans or a plan to which at least two employers contribute.* The information may be provided to the employer or directly to the Data Bank at the plan's option.
- *Employers with fewer than 50 employees on a "typical business day" during the calendar year.* The information must be provided directly to the Data Bank.
- *Everyone else.* The information may be provided to the employer or to the Data Bank, at the employer's option.

[ERISA § 609(f)(1), added by § 4301 of OBRA '93]

Q 3:80 What penalty applies to violation of the Medicare and Medicaid Coverage Data Bank reporting requirements?

The secretary of labor, the employer, or any other person referred to in ERISA Section 101(f)(1) may sue for an injunction or "other equitable relief." In addition, the secretary labor may assess a fine of up to $1,000 per violation on any employer, plan sponsor, insurer, third-party administrator, plan administrator, or any other person who maintains the information nceesary to enable the employer to comply with the reporting requirements. For this purpose, the failure to disclose the necessary information for each covered individual under a group health plan is considered to be a separate violation. For example, an employer failing to report the information for 8,000 plan members is potentially subject to a penalty of $8,000,000. [ERISA §§ 502(a)(7) and 502(c)(4), andded by § 4301 of OBRA '93]

The secretary of the DHHS may impose penalties on the unauthorized and willful disclosure of Data Bank information, including a penalty of $5,000 per violation. [ERISA § 502(a)(8), added by § 4301 of OBRA '93]

Code Section 105(h) Nondiscrimination Rules

Q 3:81   Do the nondiscrimination rules of Code Section 105(h) apply to all employer-provided medical plans?

No, the nondiscrimination standards of Code Section 105(h) apply only to self-insured plans. Employer-provided plans that are fully insured may contain discriminatory provisions without adversely affecting the favorable tax treatment of benefits actually received from the plan by employees.

Q 3:82   What is a self-insured plan?

A self-insured medical reimbursement plan is an employer plan that provides reimbursement to employees for expenses of medical care other than under a policy of accident and health insurance. [IRC § 105(h)]

A policy of accident and health insurance is either (1) a policy issued by a licensed insurer or (2) a reimbursement arrangement in the nature of a prepaid health care plan (for example, an HMO) that is regulated under federal or state law in a manner similar to the regulation of insurance companies. [Treas Reg § 1.105-11(b)(1)(i)]

Risk Shifting. Even a plan underwritten by an insurance company or a prepaid health care plan will be considered self-insured unless risk is shifted to the insurer or prepaid health care plan. Thus, a cost-plus policy or a policy providing only administrative or bookkeeping services will be considered self-insured. A plan will not be considered self-insured merely because one factor the insurer uses to determine the premium is the employer's prior claims experience. [Treas Reg § 1.l05-ll(b)(l)(ii)]

Captive Insurance Companies. A plan insured with a captive insurance company (that is, an insurance company that is fully or partially owned by the employer providing the plan) is considered insured only if, for the plan year, the premiums paid by unrelated companies are 50 percent or more of the total premiums received, and the policy of insurance is similar to policies sold to unrelated companies. [Treas Reg § 1.105-11(b)(1)(iii)]

Q 3:83   What rules are applicable to partially insured medical benefit plans?

For tax purposes, the portion of the plan that is self-insured is subject to the nondiscrimination rules contained in Code Section 105(h) and the part that is insured is not. [IRC § 105(h); Treas Reg § 1.l05-ll(b)(2)]

Compare: Under other statutes, such as ERISA, a partially insured plan might be treated as a single, self-insured plan (see Q 19:15).

Q 3:84   When is a self-insured plan nondiscriminatory under Code Section 105(h)?

In order for benefits received by highly compensated individuals to be fully excludable from gross income under Code Section 105, self-insured plans cannot discriminate in favor of highly compensated individuals and must satisfy both an eligibility test and a benefits test. [IRC § 105(h)]

Employees. In applying these nondiscrimination rules, all employees treated as employed by a single employer under the qualified pension controlled-group rules spelled out in Code Sections

414(b), 414(c), and 414(m) will be treated as employed by a single employer. [IRC § 105(h)(8)]

Q 3:85 Who is a highly compensated individual?

When applying the nondiscrimination tests of Code Section 105(h) to self-insured plans, highly compensated individuals are defined as:

- The five highest paid officers;
- Shareholders owning more than 10 percent of the value of the employer's stocks; and
- The highest paid 25 percent of employees, disregarding certain excludable employees who are not participating (those with less than three years of service at the start of the plan year, those under age 25 at the start of the plan year, part-time or seasonal employees, nonparticipants covered by a collective bargaining agreement, and nonresident aliens with no U.S.-source income).

[IRC §§ 105(h)(3) and (5)]

Q 3:86 When does a self-insured medical plan discriminate as to eligibility?

A self-insured medical plan discriminates in favor of highly compensated individuals with regard to eligibility to participate unless it benefits:

- 70 percent of all employees;
- 80 percent of all eligible employees, if at least 70 percent of all employees are eligible; or
- A nondiscriminatory classification of employees.

[IRC § 105(h)(3)(A)] When applying this discriminatory eligibility test, certain classes of employees may be excluded:

- Employees with less than three years of service before the plan year;

- Employees who have not attained age 25 before the plan year;
- Part-time (generally, less than 25 hours per week) and seasonal (generally, less than seven months per year) employees;
- Employees included in a unit of employees covered by a collective bargaining agreement, if accident and health benefits were the subject of good-faith bargaining; and
- Nonresident aliens with no U.S.-source income.

If certain standards contained in the regulation are met, part-time employees whose customary employment is less than 35 hours per week may be excluded. [IRC § 105(h); Treas. Reg. § 1.105-11(c)(2)(iii)]

Q 3:87 When does a self-insured medical plan discriminate as to benefits?

A self-insured medical plan will discriminate in favor of highly compensated individuals with regard to benefits unless all of the benefits provided to highly compensated individuals are provided on the same basis to all other individuals. This discrimination test is a "design" test rather than a "utilization" test: it measures benefit availability, not the amount of plan benefits actually received by participants. Significantly, the exclusions available for the discriminatory eligibility test (see Q 3:86) do not apply to this discriminatory benefits test. As a result, all participants within the controlled group must be counted when applying this discriminatory benefit test.

Proportionate to Compensation. If the plan covers highly compensated individuals, the plan will be treated as discriminatory as to benefits if the type and amount of benefits under the medical plan are proportionate to compensation. [Treas Reg § 1.10511(c)(3)(i)]

Related to Age or Service. The current regulations under Code Section 105 also treat as discriminatory a self-insured medical plan that has a maximum benefit limit (attributable to employer contributions) for any single benefit or combination of benefits, unless such maximum benefit limit is uniform for all participants and dependents of the participating employees and is not modified by reason of the participant's age or years of service. [Treas Reg § 1.105-11(c)(3)(i)]

Note: This appears to present a discrimination issue for self-insured retiree medical plans which condition entitlement to different levels of benefits coverage upon the number of years of service before retirement.

Discrimination in Operation. Self-insured medical plans are also prohibited from discriminating in operation. This will be a facts-and-circumstances inquiry, and the mere fact that highly compensated individuals use more benefits under the plan than other participants does not make the plan discriminatory in operation. [Treas Reg § 1.105-11(c)(3)(ii)] The duration of the benefit at issue is examined. If the benfit is added to the plan when a highly compensated individual needs it and then deleted, for example, discrimination in operation could occur.

Q 3:88 Do the Code Section 105(h) nondiscrimination rules apply to executive-only physical examination programs?

No, IRS regulations specifically exempt reimbursements paid under a plan for medical diagnostic procedures for an employee (but not for the employee's spouse or dependents), such as a self-insured executive-only physical examination plan. The allowable medical diagnostic procedures include routine medical examinations, blood tests, and X-rays. Further details are contained in IRS regulations. [Treas Reg § 1.105-11(g)]

Q 3:89 Does Code Section 105(h) allow a self-insured medical benefit plan to offset benefits from other sources?

Yes, it does. When applying the Code Section 105(h) nondiscrimination tests to a medical plan, that plan's benefits may be offset by benefits of the same type paid under a self-insured plan of the employer or another employer or under Medicare or another federal or state law or similar foreign law. [Treas Reg § 1.105-11(c)(1)]

Note: Other federal laws applicable to the medical plan may prohibit such offsets (see Qs 3:56–3:62).

Q 3:90   If an employer has multiple self-insured plans, are they tested separately under Code Section 105(h)?

Yes, they are, unless the employer chooses to designate two or more plans as a single plan for purposes of meeting the nondiscrimination rules. [Treas Reg § 1.105-11(c)(4)(i)]

Q 3:91   How are highly compensated individuals taxed if the plan is discriminatory under Code Section 105(h)?

Benefits paid to a highly compensated individual under a discriminatory plan are taxable to the extent they constitute an "excess reimbursement." [IRC § 105(h)(l)] The amount of the excess reimbursement depends upon whether the plan fails the eligibility test, the benefits test, or both.

Eligibility Test Failed. If the self-insured medical plan fails the eligibility test only, the taxable excess reimbursement to highly compensated individuals is calculated by taking the total reimbursements received by the highly compensated individual for the year and multiplying that total by a fraction, the numerator of which is the total plan year reimbursements to all highly compensated individuals and the denominator of which is the total plan year reimbursements to all plan participants.

Benefits Test Failed. If the self-insured medical plan fails the benefits test only, the taxable excess reimbursement is the portion of the reimbursement that is not available to all non-highly compensated individuals. For example, if the plan provides an annual maximum of $100,000 in reimbursements to highly compensated individuals and an annual maximum of only $50,000 to all other employees, a highly compensated individual who received $60,000 in benefits from the medical plan during that year would be taxed on $10,000 ($60,000 – $50,000), the portion that was not available to all non-highly compensated individuals.

Both Tests Failed. If the self-insured medical plan fails the eligibility and the benefits tests, the excess reimbursement is calculated in two steps. First, the benefits test is applied. The amount of excess reimbursement under that test, having already been taken into consideration, is then subtracted out of the numerator and denominator when the eligibility test is subsequently calculated. An example of how this works is contained in Treasury Regulations Section 1.105-11(e)(3).

Workers' Compensation

Q 3:92   Are employers required to provide employees with medical benefits under state workers' compensation laws?

Generally, yes. State workers' compensation laws require employers to provide benefits for job-related injuries and sickness. All such laws provide for reimbursement of medical expenses as one of the required benefits (disability income benefits and death benefits are also generally required benefits).

Q 3:93   Are medical benefit plans maintained in compliance with the requirements of state workers' compensation laws subject to ERISA?

A plan maintained *solely* for the purpose of complying with applicable state disability or workers' compensation laws is not subject to ERISA. [ERISA § 4(b)(3)]

However, rather than maintain a separately administered plan for worker's compensation benefits, some employers maintain a medical benefit plan for their employees that provides the medical benefits required by state workers' compensation laws and benefits for non-job-related injuries. The U.S. Supreme Court has held that such a multibenefit plan is subject to ERISA and that the application of a state worker's compensation law to the plan is preempted.

The first time the Supreme Court considered the issue, the state law in question concerned disability benefits (which presented the identical ERISA issues as would a state workers' compensation law).

In reviewing the applicability of the ERISA's workers' compensation plan exclusion to a multibenefit ERISA plan designed to satisfy a state's disability benefits law, the Court reasoned that, since the ERISA exclusion applies to plans, not portions of plans, a state cannot regulate the disability benefits portion of an employer's multibenefit ERISA plan. However, the Court reasoned, a state can require an employer to a maintain a separate plan solely to meet the state law requirements if, in the state's judgment, the disability benefits portion of the employer's multibenefit ERISA plan falls short of the state requirements. This latter holding stems from the Court's concern that employers will attempt to combine benefits not meeting the state requirements with other benefits in multibenefit ERISA plans, thereby avoiding falling into the Section 4(b)(3) exclusion from ERISA, in order to invoke ERISA preemption. If the state is not satisfied that the multibenefit ERISA plan satisfies the state requirements, it may compel the employer to maintain a separate plan that does comply. [Shaw v Delta Airlines, 463 US 85 (1983)]

In the *Shaw* decision, significantly, the Supreme Court drew a distinction between a "front-end" analysis (that is, whether the plan is an ERISA plan at all) and a "back-end" analysis (that is, once it is determined that plan is in fact an ERISA plan, ERISA Section 514 prevents states from regulating the plan directly under its disability and workers' compensation laws). The Court explained in *Shaw* that it was not holding that ERISA Section 514 preempts state disability laws, evidently out of a concern that the front-end analysis would be skipped over too lightly. However, it should be noted that, if a plan is an ERISA plan under the front-end analysis, then the result is precisely that; a state workers' compensation or disability benefits law cannot regulate the plan directly under the back-end analysis and is preempted. The Court's rather awkward explanation has caused some confusion to persist. There have been attempts to hook various benefit requirements onto state workers' compensation laws and make them stick under a somewhat bungled *Shaw* analysis.

Recently, the Supreme Court held such enlargements of state workers' compensation laws to be preempted by ERISA. [District of Columbia v The Greater Washington Bd of Trade, 113 SC 580 (1992)] In *Greater Washington,* the Court considered whether ERISA preempted a 1991 amendment to the workers' compensation law of the District of Columbia. Under the D.C. law provision, any employer providing health insurance coverage for an employee was required to provide health insurance coverage equivalent to the existing health insurance coverage during the period the employee received or was eligible to receive workers' compensation benefits (to a maximum of 52 weeks). The Court found that the D.C. law provision was preempted by ERISA because the benefits under the provision were tied to the level of benefits under the employer's ERISA plan, and the provision applied only to employers already providing benefits under ERISA plans.

The Supreme Court stated that the DC law specifically referred to welfare benefit plans regulated by ERISA and on that basis alone was preempted. Dismissing the District's argument that the law was part of its regulatory scheme for ERISA-exempt workers' compensation plans, and its attempt to use *Shaw* to bolster its position, the Court stated:

> It makes no difference that [the extension of health coverage provisions] are part of the District's regulation of, and therefore also "relate to," ERISA-exempt workers' compensation plans. The exemptions from ERISA coverage set out in § 4(b), 29 U.S.C. § 1003(b), do not limit the pre-emptive sweep of § 514 once it is determined that the law in question relates to an ERISA-covered plan. See *Alessi v. Reybestos-Manhattan, Inc.,* 451 U.S. 504, 525 [citation omitted] ("It is of no moment that New Jersey intrudes indirectly through a workers' compensation law, rather than directly, through a statute called 'pension regulation' "). [Greater Washington, at 584]. The Court attempted to clarify its *Shaw* analysis of when the ERISA Section 4(b)(3) front-end analysis is appropriate and when the ERISA Section 514 back-end analysis is appropriate. It pointed out that the statute in *Shaw* did not relate to ERISA plans, whereas the attempted extension of life and health insurance coverage at issue in *Greater Washington* did:

> We held that . . . [New York's Disability Benefits Law] was not preempted by § 514(a) because it related exclusively to exempt employee benefit plans "maintained solely for the purpose of complying with applicable. . .disability insurance laws" within the meaning of § 4(b)(3) . . . [citation omitted] The fact that employers could comply with the New York law by administering the required disability benefits through a multibenefit ERISA plan did not mean that the law related to such ERISA plans for preemption purposes. [citation omitted]

We simply held that as long as the employer's disability plan, "as an administrative unit, provide[d] only those benefits required by" the New York law, it could qualify as an exempt plan under ERISA § 4(b)(3). [citation omitted] . . .

As we have explained, the Disability Benefits Law upheld in *Shaw* — though mandating the creation of a "welfare plan" as defined in ERISA—*did not relate to a welfare plan subject to ERISA regulation.* [emphasis added] [The District of Columbia statute] does, and that is the end of the matter.

[Id, at 584]

The *Greater Washington* decision also overturned a contrary ruling by the Court of Appeals for the Second Circuit concerning a virtually identical Connecticut law. At issue in the Second Circuit case was a provision of the Connecticut workers' compensation statute that required employers who provide accident and health insurance or life insurance for employees to continue to do so for employees eligible to receive or receiving workers' compensation. The Connecticut law also provided that employers could do so by, among other alternatives, creating an injured employee's plan as an extension of any existing plan for working employees or by self-insurance. Seizing upon the language in *Shaw* concerning a state's ability to force the employer to choose between providing disability benefits in a separately administered plan and including the state-mandated benefits in its ERISA plan, the appellate court read it to mean that Connecticut could force the creation of a separate administrative unit *within* the ERISA plan to provide for this extension of health coverage. Accordingly, the appellate court held that the Connecticut statute was not preempted by Section 514 of ERISA because it fell within the ERISA Section 4(b)(3) exception. The Supreme Court rejected this type of argument in *Greater Washington,* essentially stating that once the front-end ERISA coverage hurdle is cleared by a multibenefit ERISA, the back-end Section 514 preemption analysis is limited to whether the state law is preempted from applying to the employer's ERISA medical plan as it is presently constituted:

[P]etitioners argue that § 514(a) should be construed to require a two-step analysis: if the state law "relate[s] to" an ERISA-covered plan, it may still survive pre-emption if employers could comply with the [state workers' compensation] law through separately administered plans exempt under § 4(b). . . . We cannot engraft a two-step analysis onto a one-step statute.

[RR Donnelley & Sons Co v Prevost, 915 F 2d 787 (2d Cir 1990), *cert denied,* 111 S Ct 1415, 113 L Ed 2d 468, (1991), overruled by District of Columbia v The Greater Washington Bd of Trade, 113 SC 580 (1992)]

Q 3:94   If an employer maintains a medical benefit plan subject to ERISA that provides coverage for job-related injuries or illnesses, are an employee's tort remedies against the employer under state law preempted?

Apparently not. In a U.S. district court decision, the court held that an employee's state court suit for personal injuries on the job, which were alleged to have been caused by the employer's negligence, was not preempted, even though the employer had an ERISA plan providing for medical and other benefits for such job-related injuries. The fact that the employee was covered under an ERISA plan and could claim benefits for medical expenses arising from the job-related injuries was not considered to make the lawsuit sufficiently "related to" the plan to justify preemption of the state law action. [Eurine v Wyatt Cafeterias, Inc, 14 EBC 1655 (ND Tex 1991); see also Nunez v Wyatt Cafeterias, Inc, 14 EBC 1388 (ND Tex 1991)]

> **Planning Pointer**. In three states (New Jersey, South Carolina, and Texas) an employer is permitted to opt out of workers' compensation insurance coverage. In those states, or in any other state where an employer may be permitted to establish an ERISA plan not subject to the minimum requirements of the state workers' compensation law, the employer should carefully consider the effect of not subjecting itself to the state workers' compensation law coverage. The workers' compensation laws, while taking away from employers certain common-law defenses, can also provide advantages to employers by limiting the extent of employee recoveries.

Deductibility of Employer Contributions

Q 3:95   May an employer deduct its contributions to or payments under a medical benefit plan?

Generally, yes, it may. [Treas Reg § 1.162-10(a)] However, employer contributions to a welfare benefit fund such as a voluntary employees' beneficiary association (VEBA) must also satisfy the additional requirements imposed by Code Sections 419 and 419A. (See Chapter 19 for a discussion of these funding requirements.)

Q 3:96   Are employers subject to any excise taxes based upon the way a medical plan is structured?

Yes, they are. If any group health plan does not comply with the Medicare disability provisions, the kidney disease provision, and the working-aged provisions discussed in Questions 3:56 through 3:60, the sponsoring employer or employee organization can be assessed an excise tax (equal to 25 percent of the employer's or employee organization's expenses incurred during the calendar year) for each group health plan of the employer or employee organization. Excise taxes may also be imposed for failing to provide COBRA continuation coverage correctly (see Q 3:61). (See Chapter 6 for a discussion of COBRA.)

Tax Treatment of Participants

Q 3:97   Are the employer's contributions to an employer-sponsored medical plan taxable to employees?

No, they are not. [IRC § 106; Treas Reg § 1.106-1)]

However, see Q 3:106 for a discussion of the special tax treatment applicable to more-than-2-percent shareholder employees of a Subchapter S Corporation.

Q 3:98   What if the employer's plan covers nonspousal cohabitants or "domestic partners"?

If the employer-provided health plan covers an individual other than the employee, his or her spouse, or his or her dependents, then the fair market value of coverage must be included in income by the employee and reported by the employer as wages. The IRS has ruled that a nonspousal cohabitant does not qualify as a spouse or dependent and that such individual's coverage is taxable to the employee. For this purpose, fair market value is determined based on how much an individual would have to pay for such coverage in an arm's-length transaction; for group medical coverage, this amount is the fair market value of the group coverage. [Priv Ltr Rul 90-34-048 (May 29, 1990), modified by Priv Ltr Rul 91-11-018 (Dec 14, 1990)]

In another private letter ruling, the IRS addressed whether coverage for a "principal domestic partner," defined by the medical plan in this instance as the unmarried equivalent of a husband or wife of the employee, was taxable to the employee. The IRS held that it was taxable unless applicable state law recognizes the arrangement as a common-law marriage. [Priv Ltr Rul 91-09-060 (Dec 6, 1990)]

Q 3:99   What is the tax treatment of employer-provided medical coverage for pre-adoptive children?

If the pre-adoptive child is a member of the employee's household and is placed with the employee by an authorized placement agency for legal adoption, the child qualifies as a dependent, and the child's coverage is nontaxable.

A privately placed pre-adoptive child is not a dependent under Code Section 152. Accordingly, the fair market value of group coverage for such a child is taxable to the employee and must be reported by the employer as wages. [Priv Ltr Rul 91-09-060 (Dec 6, 1990)]

Q 3:100   Are benefits actually received under an employer-provided medical plan taxable to employees?

Non-highly compensated employees are not taxed on benefits received under an employer-provided medical plan, regardless of whether the plan satisfies any applicable nondiscrimination requirements. However, if a self-insured medical plan discriminates in favor of highly compensated employees, then all or a part of the benefits received by such highly compensated employees will be included in their gross incomes. [IRS §§ 105(b), 105(h)] Also see Question 3:107 for the special rules applicable to more-than-2-percent shareholder-employees of Subchapter S corporations.

If an unmarried employee is permitted to cover a "domestic partner," benefits payable to that individual cannot be excluded from the employee's income under Code Section 105, unless applicable state law recognizes the arrangement as a common-law marriage. [Priv Ltr Rul 91-09-060 (Dec 6, 1990)] Reimbursements under an employer-provided medical plan received by an employee for medical expenses incurred by a privately placed pre-adoptive child cannot be excluded from the employee's income under Code Section 105. [Priv Ltr Rul 91-09-060 (Dec 6, 1990)]

Health Insurance Credit. Effective for taxable years beginning after December 31, 1990 and before January 1, 1944, taxpayers eligible for the earned income credit must reduce the amount of their medical care expenses taken into account for deduction purposes dollar-for-dollar by the amount of any allowable supplemental health insurance credit for the premium cost of coverage that includes one or more qualifying children (as defined for purposes of the earned income credit). [IRC §§ 32(b), 162(l)(3), 213(f)] Effective for taxable years beginning after December 31, 1993, the health insurance credit is repealed. [IRC § 32(b), as amended by § 13131 OBRA '93]

Q 3:101   If a self-insured medical plan is discriminatory, must the employer withhold taxes from the amount included in the gross income of highly compensated individuals?

No, employers generally are not required to withhold taxes on the amount of any medical care reimbursement made to or for the benefit of an employee under a self-insured medical reimbursement plan (as defined in Code Section 105(h)(6)(b)). [IRC § 3121(a)(2); IRC § 3401(20), added by OBRA '90 § 11703(f)]

Q 3:102   What is the income tax treatment of premiums paid for medical insurance coverage by a sole proprietor?

Under Code Section 162(l), a sole proprietor generally may deduct 25 percent of amounts paid for insurance providing medical coverage for the sole proprietor, his or her spouse, and dependents. The deduction cannot exceed the earned income of the sole proprietor from the trade or business for which the plan providing the medical care coverage is established. The deduction is allowable as a deduction in calculating adjusted gross income, but does not reduce net earnings from self-employment for purposes of the tax on self-employment income.

However, the deduction is not available if the sole proprietor is eligible for coverage under any subsidized health plan maintained by the employer of the individual or his or her spouse. [IRC § 162(l)]

Example. Joe, a sole proprietor, has a spouse with an employer-provided medical plan that includes optional family coverage. Whether or not the spouse elects family coverage, Joe cannot deduct 25 percent of any premiums he pays for medical insurance coverage, since he is eligible for coverage under his spouse's plan.

The 25-percent deduction, which originally was not available for insurance coverage provided, or amounts contributed, on or after June 30, 1992, has been retroactively restored by OBRA '93 and is now scheduled to expire on December 31, 1993, unless this deduction provision is further extended by Congress. [IRC § 162(l)(6); Tax Extension Act of 1991 § 110(a)(2); OBRA '93 13174]

Any medical benefits received under the medical insurance would qualify in full for exclusion from income under Code Section 104(a)(3).

Q 3:103   What is the income tax treatment of medical care coverage of a sole proprietor under a self-insured plan maintained by the sole proprietorship?

Since there are no amounts paid for insurance, the 25-percent deduction under Code Section 162(l) appears not to be available (the term "insurance" as used in Code Section 162(l) has not been clarified by regulations yet and apparently does not apply to self-funded medical expenses). Also, Treasury Regulations Section 1.105-5(b) provides that, benefits paid under a health plan to an individual who is self-employed in the business for which the plan is established, will not be treated as received through accident and health insurance for purposes of Code Sections 104(a)(3) and 105. Thus, the benefits received by the sole proprietor under the self-insured plan apparently will not be excludable in determining the sole proprietor's taxable income.

Q 3:104   What is the income tax treatment of premiums for medical insurance coverage paid by a partnership for coverage of its partners?

The IRS has ruled that when premium payments for medical insurance coverage are made without regard to partnership income, the premium payments are treated as guaranteed payments by the partnership under Code Section 707(c), deductible by the partnership on the partnership tax return, and includable in each partner's gross income. Provided that the conditions of Code Section 162(l) are met, the partner may deduct 25 percent of the premium (see Q 3:102) and may treat the remainder as a medical expense for purposes of Code Section 213.

Since the partners are not employees, the guaranteed payments are not subject to withholding at source by the partnership. [Treas Reg § 1.707-1(c)]

Alternatively, the partnership may choose to account for the payment of the medical insurance premiums as a reduction in distributions to the partners. In such event, the premiums are not deductible by the partnership, and distributable shares of partnership income and deductions and other items are not affected by payment of the premiums. Each partner may claim the 25-percent deduction to the extent permitted under Code Section 162(l). [Rev Rul 91-26, 1991-1 CB 184]

Q 3:105   What is the income tax treatment of medical care coverage provided to partners under a self-insured plan maintained by the partnership?

Since there are no amounts paid for insurance, the 25-percent deduction under Code Section 162(l) apparently is not available.

There is no clear and direct authority as to how a self-insured plan will be treated for income tax purposes. While Revenue Ruling 91-26 (see Q 3:104) deals only with an insured plan, it appears possible that the IRS would apply similar rules to a self-insured plan. Thus, if the medical benefits were payable without regard to partnership income, the payments presumably would be viewed by the IRS as guaranteed payments deductible at the partnership level and includable in the income of the partner receiving the benefits.

Alternatively, the partnership presumably could choose to account for the medical benefit payments to a partner as a reduction in distributions to the partner not deductible by the partnership and not affecting distributive shares of partnership income and deductions and other items. [See Rev Rul 91-26, 1991-1 CB 184]

Planning Pointer. The IRS position in Revenue Ruling 91-26, if applied to a self-insured plan, appears to provide harsh results in some situations. For example, assume a two-person 50-50 partnership with a self-insured medical plan, under which partner A has $100,000 in reimbursable medical expenses and partner B has $0 in reimbursable medical expenses. Under the revenue ruling, if applicable, it appears that A would have income of $100,000, or alternatively his or her distributions from the partnership would be reduced by $100,000. It appears that the partnership agreement should be able to provide that the partnership would treat the medical plan outlays as allocable ratably to the partners in accordance with their partnership shares. Thus, the $100,000 in plan medical expenses would be allocated $50,000 to A and $50,000 to B. It remains to be seen whether the IRS would agree with such an allocation.

Q 3:106   What is the income tax treatment of premiums for medical insurance coverage for shareholder-employees of Subchapter S corporations?

It depends on whether the shareholder-employee of the Subchapter S corporation is a more-than-2-percent shareholder or not. If the shareholder-employee is not a more-than-2-percent shareholder-employee, medical insurance premiums paid by the employee for services as an employee normally will be excludable from the shareholder-employee's income under Section 106 of the Code.

However, if the shareholder is a more-than-2-percent shareholder of the Subchapter S corporation, Code Section 1373 provides that, for purposes of applying the fringe benefit rules, the Subchapter S corporation will be treated as a partnership and a more-than-2-percent shareholder will be treated as a partner of the deemed partnership.

Applying this concept to premiums paid by a Subchapter S corporation for medical insurance premiums for its more-than-2-percent shareholder-employees, the IRS has ruled that the Subchapter S corporation can deduct the premiums paid as a business expense. However, the more-than-2-percent shareholder-employees must include the premiums paid for their coverage in gross income. Also, assuming the requirements of Code Section 162(l) are met, such shareholder-employees generally can deduct 25 percent of the premiums in calculating adjusted gross income and treat the remaining 75 percent as a medical expense for itemized medical expense deduction purposes.

It was also held that the Subchapter S corporation is required to file a Form W-2 for income tax purposes for each more-than-2-percent shareholder-employee having income from the premium payments. However, the income is not treated as wages for Social Security and Medicare tax FICA purposes, as long as the premium payments are made under a plan or system for employees and their dependents generally, or for a class or classes of employees and their dependents. If the premium payments are not made pursuant to such a plan or system, they then are subject to FICA tax. [Rev Rul 91-26, 1991-CB 184; IRS Ann 92-16, 1992-5 IRB 53]

Q 3:107   **What is the income tax treatment of medical benefits received by a shareholder-employee of a Subchapter S corporation under a self-insured medical plan?**

There is no direct authority on this question.

If the shareholder-employee is not a more-than-2-percent shareholder, medical benefits received by the shareholder-employee in the capacity of employee should be treated in the same way as benefits received by other employees; namely, the exemptions provided by Code Section 105(b) should apply.

If the shareholder-employee is a more-than-2-percent shareholder, and if the IRS applies the same rules as in Revenue Ruling 91-26 for insured plans, the medical benefit payments by the Subchapter S corporation would be deductible by it, but includable in the income of a more-than-2-percent shareholder-employee receiving such a benefit.

In addition, since there is no amount paid for insurance, the 25-percent deduction of Code Section 162(l) apparently would not be available to the more-than-2-percent shareholder-employee. [Rev Rul 91-26, 1991-CB 184]

Employee Assistance Programs

Q 3:108   What is an employee assistance program (EAP)?

An EAP is an employer-provided benefit which may encompass counseling, referrals, and possibly treatment for a stated list of concerns, such as:

- Anxiety;
- Stress;
- Depression;
- Drug abuse;
- Alcoholism;
- Work problems;
- Family or marital problems;
- Child care needs;
- Adolescent problems;
- Elder care needs (such as concerns relating to a sick or elderly parent, parent-in-law, or other family member);
- Financial worries; and
- Legal concerns.

EAPs run the gamut from being fairly limited in the scope of services covered to being broad-based programs designed to address numerous issues that affect workplace productivity. For example, a particular employer's EAP may focus solely on drug and alcohol abuse, while another employer's EAP may focus on everything from caring for a parent with Alzheimer's disease or a child with AIDS to marital counseling.

Q 3:109   Why do employers make EAPs available to their employees?

EAPs originally started as more or less informal programs to address lost workplace productivity due to excessive drinking and alcoholism. They have developed as a mechanism for an employer to help control the following situations that can result from substance abuse or other stressful personal and/or family circumstances:

- Absenteeism and tardiness;
- Impaired workplace productivity;
- Workplace accidents;
- Increased health costs associated with employee impairment; and
- Emotional and financial distress.

Q 3:110   What are the basic types of EAP?

It has been said that no two EAPs are alike. Despite the variability among individual employers' programs, they can be roughly classified into a few groups.

First, EAPS may be internal or external. An internal EAP is an in-house program of the employer that may be affiliated with the personnel department or the medical department. An external EAP, is a third-party organization that contracts with the employer to provide EAP services through its own network of professionals, counselors, and referral services in return for a monthly fee.

Second, EAPs may be roughly divided according to how comprehensive their services are. Full-service EAPs combine diagnosis, counseling, and referral for treatment or services. Often, a series of visits to a counselor or referral provider, such as two to seven visits, will be covered. Less comprehensive EAPs operate more like central clearinghouses for information and referral regarding services such as day care, elder care, community-based counseling programs, part-time nursing services, and companion services. Some EAPs consist of a telephone hotline to a trained counselor who makes an assessment and provides a referral to sources of professional help or community services, as indicated. To the extent the hotline is accompanied by a panoply of services, the hotline-type EAP will fall into the full-service or assessment and referral groups.

If the EAP does not cover the cost of the referral services or covers only a certain number of visits, some of the referral services may qualify as covered medical expenses under the employer's medical plan.

Q 3:111   Is EAP participation voluntary?

EAP participation may be voluntary, through self-referral, or it may be suggested by the manager of an employee whose performance appears to be impaired. Some employer programs also make referral to an EAP mandatory upon identification of an employee as a substance abuser. The continued legality of mandatory referrals may be in question, however, following the enactment of the ADA (see Chapter 17).

Q 3:112   Are EAP services always confidential?

EAP programs generally are designed to provide a confidential source of help for employees.

Disclosure to Employer. Some EAP programs involve disclosure to the employer, such as to the employer's medical department or personnel department. This may raise numerous employment law issues that are beyond the scope of this book. In general, however, particularly if an external EAP is involved, employee confidentiality generally is a priority, and employers sometimes even pay the monthly fee specified by the external EAP without knowing which employees have requested services during the month.

The EAP is itself subject to regulation and may be required by law to disclose certain information, such as child abuse. In addition, psychotherapists may be required to notify an intended victim and/or the police of anticipated harm. The EAP's duty of disclosure is also beyond the scope of this book (but is addressed in the *Employee Assistance Law Answer Book* (Panel Pub, a div. of Aspen Pubs, Inc., 1990)).

Q 3:113 Is an EAP an ERISA plan?

Although EAPs do not resemble conventional employee benefit programs, they may nonetheless fall within the scope of ERISA's definition of an employee welfare benefit plan. Under Section 3(1) of ERISA, an employee welfare plan includes plans that are established or maintained to provide, among other things, benefits in the event of sickness, accident, or disability. Although an EAP may cover various unconventional services, it may also cover benefits in the event of sickness or disability and thus constitute an ERISA plan.

The DOL has issued several advisory opinion letters on this issue, taking the position that benefits for the treatment of drug and alcohol abuse, stress, anxiety, depression, and similar health and medical problems constitute "medical" benefits or benefits "in the event of sickness, accident, or disability" within the meaning of Section 3(1) of ERISA.

A narrower question is presented by an EAP that provides only an initial evaluation and referral. If the initial assessment is performed by a trained health professional or counselor, it is possible that an ERISA plan will exist. The Court of Appeals for the Sixth Circuit recently found an EAP to be an ERISA plan. [In re General Motors Corp, No 92-2017 (6th Cir Sept 1, 1993)]

However, if the EAP coordinator has no special training and simply makes referrals from a published list of community resources, it appears that the EAP will not be considered an ERISA plan. Recently, the DOL found such a "bare-bones" program not to constitute an ERISA plan, because:

- The EAP provided only telephone referrals and not medical benefits or benefits in the event of sickness within the meaning of Section 3(1) of ERISA;

- The EAP toll-free number and hotline provided no more than generally available public information when making telephone referrals to employees. (Referrals were made to agencies selected from an annual publication of the Florida Department of Health and Rehabilitative Services.)

- The EAP coordinators had no special training in counseling or a related discipline;

- The EAP did not employ any counselors, either on an in-house or contractual basis; and

- Other than the initial referral, the EAP did not provide any other benefits free of charge.

[DOL Adv Op No 91-26 (July 19, 1991); see also DOL Adv Op Nos. 92-12A (April 20, 1992), 83-35A (June 27, 1993)]

Q 3:114 What are the consequences of an EAP being an ERISA plan?

If the EAP meets the definition of an ERISA welfare benefit plan, then all of the ERISA duties and responsibilities apply, including the reporting and disclosure requirements of Title I of ERISA.

This means that the employer would be required, among other things, to take the following actions:

1. Prepare and distribute an SPD, updated as necessary via a summary of material modifications,

2. File the SPD and summary of material modifications with the DOL, and

3. File an annual report (Form 5500) with the IRS.

The DOL has not yet addressed how an employer is to provide full and fair review of an appeal of a denied claim under a confidential EAP program.

Q 3:115   Is an EAP subject to COBRA?

Yes, if the EAP falls within the definition of an ERISA welfare benefit plan and it also provides "medical care" as defined in Code Section 213, then COBRA continuation rights must be offered. [ERISA § 607(1)] (COBRA is discussed in detail in Chapter 6.)

Effect of the Proposed Clinton Health Plan

See Appendix A for a discussion of the proposed Clinton Health Plan.

Chapter 4

Retiree Medical Benefits

Retiree benefits have been the focus of much attention as health care costs continue to escalate. Employers have become painfully aware of the true cost of coverage as a result of Statement of Financial Accounting Standards No. 106, Employers' Accounting for Postretirement Benefits Other Than Pensions (FAS 106), which requires employers to project the future unfunded liability associated with such benefits and accrue the expense of providing them over the course of active employment. As a result, the cost-containment and managed care tools and techniques discussed in Chapter 3 have been applied in the redesign of retiree medical plans in an effort to make them less costly. Some employers have attempted (some successfully and some not) to simply terminate their retiree medical plans as being too expensive to maintain any longer. This chapter discusses the reasons for the intense focus on retiree medical costs, employer responses, and legal issues that arise upon plan redesign, cutback, or termination.

Basic Concepts

Q 4:1   Why are retiree medical benefits the focus of such interest and concern?

Retiree medical benefits have traditionally taken a back seat to medical benefits for active employees because the active employee plans cover more individuals, cost more, and are more directly tied to day-to-day employee morale and productivity. However, as medical costs continue to soar, medical technology improves, and individuals live longer, generous retiree medical benefit plans have become increasingly costly as well. Recent accounting developments have highlighted the magnitude of the financial impact of the future promise under many of these plans, and, as a result, employer attention is turning toward redesigning such plans to make them more cost-efficient or toward other, substitute means of delivering dollar-efficient benefits.

Q 4:2   What significant changes are occurring with regard to retiree medical benefits?

Retiree medical benefits are no longer sacrosanct. Employers are incorporating the same cost-saving features and managed care mechanisms that have proven successful in past years under active employee medical plans. They are also shifting more of the responsibility for prudent purchase of medical services onto retirees by requiring them to contribute (or to contribute more) to the cost of retiree medical coverage directly or through increased deductibles, copayments, and lower plan limits. Alternatively, or in conjunction with plan redesign, employers are investigating the feasibility of prefunding part or all of the future liability for retiree medical benefits on a tax-favored basis.

In addition, a few employers are now taking a previously unheard of step: They are terminating retiree medical benefits altogether, usually for reasons of cost. Biting the bullet in this regard represents an often painful balance of employee relations factors with corporate goals and budgetary factors.

Q 4:3 What legal issues are implicated in addressing current retiree medical plan concerns?

While no law requires an employer to offer a medical plan to its employees, numerous laws regulate the manner in which such a plan, once offered, must be designed and administered. One chief concern when looking at plan modifications that could be characterized as cutbacks is whether such modifications would violate any federal law directly or indirectly governing the content of employee benefit plans, as well as state and local laws to the extent they are not preempted by the Employee Retirement Income Security Act (ERISA). One new federal law requirement to bear in mind is the requirement effective on and after August 10, 1993, that "group health plans" covering retirees must be *primary* to Medicare for end-stage renal disease for 18 months, regardless of whether the individual is also entitled to Medicare for any other reason (including age). [IRC § 5000; Social Security Act § 1862(b)(1), 42 USC § 1395y(b)(1), as amended by OBRA '93, § 13561] See Q 3:60 for a discussion of the Medicare secondary requirements. A second concern is whether the employer has voluntarily assumed (either affirmatively in writing or through a course of conduct) a greater obligation to provide benefits than is required by such laws, in a manner that cannot later be reversed or that can be reversed only with great difficulty should the employer subsequently want or need to do so.

Obligation to Provide Retiree Medical Benefits

Q 4:4 Is an employer legally obligated to provide retiree medical benefits?

There is no law that requires private employers to provide retiree medical benefits for its former employees. Employers are free, as a matter of corporate management discretion, to decide whether or not to adopt retiree medical benefit plans. In addition, the decision to adopt a plan is not an ERISA fiduciary function. [Belade v ITT Corp, 909 F 2d 736 (2d Cir 1990); Moore v Metropolitan Life Ins Co, 856 F 2d 488 (2d Cir 1988)]

Q 4:5   Once an employer decides to offer a retiree medical plan, does it have a duty to employees and potential plan participants to adopt the best plan it can afford?

No, it does not. The employer is under no duty to act solely in the interests of employees and potential plan participants and beneficiaries when determining what the content of the plan will be. [*Belade*, 909 F 2d 736 (2d Cir 1990); *Moore*, 856 F 2d 488 (2d Cir 1988)]

Q 4:6   Are retiree medical benefits a form of deferred compensation that vests upon retirement?

No, they are not. Retiree medical benefits are not a form of deferred compensation that is "earned" incrementally over the course of an employee's service for the employer or that "vests" because the employee's service has been completed.

Note, however, that if the retiree medical plan covered pediatric vaccines on May 1, 1993, that level of coverage for that particular benefit has "vested" by operation of law rather than due to having been earned (see Q 3:50). Many retiree medical plans are simply a continuation of the medical plan for active employees, often with the retiree paying a greater share of the cost, so the pediatric vaccine benefit (however infrequently it might be used by the retiree population) is an item about which to be aware.

Q 4:7   Once an employer voluntarily offers retiree medical benefits, does ERISA require that retirees become vested in them?

Generally, no. ERISA does not contain any vesting provisions for welfare benefit plans. The U.S. Court of Appeals for the Sixth Circuit, in the benchmark case on the issue, held that there is no basis for finding mandatory vesting in ERISA of retiree welfare benefits. The appellate court noted that the legislature, rather than the courts, should determine whether mandatory vesting of retiree welfare benefits is appropriate. Absent such legislative action, the parties are free to set out by agreement or by private design, as set forth in the plan documents, whether retiree medical benefits vest or whether they can be terminated. [In re White Farm Equipment Co, 788 F 2d 1186 (6th Cir 1986); see also Wise v El Paso Natural Gas Co, 16 EBC 1791 (5th Cir 1993)]

Note, however, that pediatric vaccine coverage has "vested" by operation of law (see Q 3:50).

Q 4:8 Once an employer voluntarily offers retiree medical benefits, does the Consolidated Omnibus Budget Reconciliation Act (COBRA) require that retirees become vested in them?

No, it does not. As discussed in Chapter 6, COBRA rights also apply to retiree benefits. COBRA continuation coverage, if elected, delays the termination date of retiree medical benefits but does not prohibit the employer from changing the benefit levels from time to time or from terminating the plan.

COBRA requires that a "qualified beneficiary" must be given the right to elect COBRA continuation coverage that is (1) identical to that provided to similarly situated beneficiaries who have not undergone a qualifying event and (2) identical to the coverage the qualified beneficiaries themselves received immediately before the qualifying event, except for certain permitted differences (see Q 6:86). The statute and the regulations define the required level of coverage at the time it is elected. Nothing in COBRA, however, prevents the employer from subsequently amending or modifying such coverage as to all participants or from terminating the plan. [IRC § 4980B(f)(2); ERISA § 602(1); Public Health Service Act (PHSA) § 2102; Prop Treas Reg § 1.162-26, Q&As 22, 23]

Q 4:9 Are retiree medical benefits a mandatory subject of collective bargaining?

It depends upon whether the individuals are currently employees or are currently retired. An employer is required to bargain in good faith with a union representing its employees about the benefits active employees will receive when they retire. However, retirees are not considered to be "employees" under the National Labor Relations Act of 1935, as amended. Thus, an employer is not required to bargain over welfare benefits for already retired employees. Rather, benefits for current retirees are a permitted subject of bargaining, and the employer may agree to bargain about them but is not required to do so. [Allied Chem & Alkali Workers of Am Local Union No 1 v Pittsburgh Plate Glass Co Chem Div, 404 US 157 (1971)]

Q 4:10   If an employer offers retiree medical benefits pursuant to a collective bargaining agreement, do those employees who attain retirement age during the period of the collective bargaining agreement become vested in the retiree medical benefits?

Possibly yes. Although retiree medical benefits legally are not a form of deferred compensation, there is another layer of potential employer liability in the collective bargaining context resulting not from the retiree medical plan provisions, but from the separate collective bargaining agreement. The theory underlying some of the case law construing collective bargaining agreements is that active employees who agree to forego current wages in exchange for future benefits at retirement have, upon attaining retirement, an expectation of receiving those benefits throughout retirement. In this instance, the exchange is not characterized as the employer's receipt of the employee's current employment service in return for future deferred compensation, but rather may be characterized as the employee's sacrifice of current compensation in return for promised future benefits upon retirement.

In the collective bargaining context, the Court of Appeals for the Sixth Circuit applied an "inference" that retiree medical benefits are "status benefits." In other words, once retiree status is attained, there is an inference that the parties likely intended the benefits to continue beyond the term of the collective bargaining agreement and for as long as retiree status is maintained:

> Thus, when the parties contract for benefits which accrue upon achievement of retiree status, there is an inference that the parties likely intended those benefits to continue as long as the beneficiary remains a retiree. This is not to say that retiree insurance benefits are necessarily interminable by their nature. Nor does any federal labor law policy identified to this court presumptively favor the finding of interminable

rights to retiree insurance benefits when the collective bargaining agreement is silent. Rather, as a part of the context from which the collective bargaining agreement arose, the nature of such benefits simply provides another inference of intent. Standing alone, this factor would be insufficient to find an intent to create interminable benefits. In the present case, however, this contextual factor buttresses the already sufficient evidence of such intent in the language of this agreement itself. [International Union, United Auto, Aerospace and Agric Implement Workers of Am v Yard-Man, Inc, 716 F 2d 1476, 1482 (6th Cir 1983), *cert denied*, 465 US 1007 (1984)]

Numerous courts have used this "status" benefit theory to find that retiree medical benefits have vested where the provisions of the collective bargaining agreement (particularly ambiguous provisions) or other extrinsic evidence supports an inference of an intention to provide lifetime vesting. However, where the contract language clearly limited the duration of retiree medical benefits to the term of the agreement, it was held that retiree medical benefits did not continue beyond the expiration of the collective bargaining agreement. [Arndt v Wheelabrator Corp, 763 F Supp 396 (ND Ind 1991); District 17, UMW v Allied Corp, 765 F 2d 412 (4th Cir 1985), *cert den* 105 S Ct 3227]

Other cases have rejected or simply ignored the "status" benefit theory on the basis that it is illogical to infer an intent to vest retiree benefits every time an employee is eligible to receive them on his or her retirement date, because ERISA explicitly exempts welfare benefits from its vesting requirements. [Anderson v Alpha Portland Indus Inc, 836 F 2d 1512 (8th Cir 1988); see also Senn v United Dominion Indus Inc, 951 F 2d 806 (7th Cir 1992)] The case law in this area is quite extensive and continues to evolve.

Planning Pointer. Because the inference of an intent to provide lifetime benefits might be applied by a court to the employer's conduct, employers desiring to avoid a commitment to lifetime retiree medical benefits at a particular level should attempt to carefully craft both plan and collective bargaining agreement provisions to clearly limit the duration of retiree medical benefits to the term of the collective bargaining agreement. Note that the employer's particular collective bargaining situation may not afford enough latitude to achieve this result.

Cost Containment Through Plan Redesign

Q 4:11 What contributes to the rapid escalation in the cost of retiree medical benefits?

Double-digit medical inflation, new medical technologies, and the government's attempts to shift more of the cost of the Medicare program onto the private sector all fuel the spiraling cost of medical care.

In addition, inappropriate plan design can magnify the effect of these other forces. For example, a plan that provides retiree medical benefits to every employee who retires will be paying for the cost of medical benefits over the period from retirement to death for both long-service employees and short-service employees. When short-service employees obtain a benefit extending for such a long period relative to their period of employment with the sponsoring employer, the benefit derived from coverage is disproportional to the employment services received by the employer.

Many retiree medical plans also have been neglected while employers implement managed care and other cost-containment provisions in their medical plans for active employees. Only in the past few years have employers focused on using these same techniques to control retiree medical costs.

Q 4:12 What options are available to an employer seeking to control retiree medical costs?

An employer has wide flexibility to achieve some control of retiree medical costs, subject to a potential legal limit on its ability to change its plan (the legal limits on plan cutbacks are discussed in Questions 4:15 through 4:20). This can be accomplished in a number of ways, including:

- Redefining the target group to incorporate pension-type goals, so that retiree medical benefit dollars are focused on the company's longer-service employees; and

- Reducing benefit costs through plan design.

Q 4:13   How can an employer incorporate pension-type goals into retiree medical plans?

To incorporate pension-type goals, employers may consider reformulating employer contributions for retirees to reflect age, length of service, or a combination of both. Under this type of design, employer contributions toward the premiums for retiree medical coverage would be more (and employee contributions would be less) for older, longer-service employees. However, since benefits would then differ according to age or length of service, using this approach for a self-insured plan raises a possible discrimination issue under Code Section 105(h) and the regulations thereunder (see Q 4:18).

The employer contribution might also be structured to differentiate between retirees who are eligible for Medicare and those who are not.

Q 4:14   How can an employer reduce retiree medical benefit costs through plan design?

An employer can help reduce retiree medical benefit costs through plan design by shifting more of the risk (of utilization and medical cost increases) to retirees and to other plans. A number of mechanisms used singly or in combination create a shift of some of the risk, such as adding or increasing retiree contributions, deductibles, and copayments, adding or lowering annual and/or lifetime plan maximums. or revising coordination of benefits provisions. Alternatively, the employer could offer a "defined-benefit" or "defined-dollar" plan. The retiree would be responsible for everything beyond those defined limits, creating a total shift of risk to retirees and other plans beyond the amount expressly assumed by the employer.

In addition to risk shifting, the plan design could focus the purchase of medical care and services on more cost-efficient options by providing financial incentives for using them (and, often, financial penalties for not following the managed care procedures). The particular plan redesigns may vary considerably from employer to employer, depending upon how aggressively the employer seeks to control plan costs. The basis of managed care is directing or monitoring the access to care to assure that the care provided or reimbursed under the plan is medically necessary and cost-efficient, while providing incentives to health care providers to cut out unnecessary or duplicative services and to reduce or contain the price charged for necessary care and services.

Plan Cutbacks—Legal Issues

Q 4:15   Once an employer has adopted a retiree medical plan, must a particular level of benefits be maintained?

In general, the employer has broad design flexibility to reduce the future level of retiree medical benefits.

However, the employer must clearly and unambiguously reserve the right to alter or diminish benefits under the plan. [Dague v Gencorp Inc No 5:91CV2617 (ND Ohio, August 27, 1993)] If the employer engages in a course of conduct that a court may find to have effectively guaranteed a particular level of benefits, the employer may find itself required to maintain that particular level of benefits even though it had not originally intended to do so. [Schalk v Teledyne Inc, 13 EBC 1167 (WD Mich, Nov 30, 1990); Chervin v Sulzer Bingham Pumps Inc, 13 EBC 1089 (D Ore 1990); but see Erdman v Bethlehem Steel Corp Employee Welfare Plans, 607 F Supp 196 (WD NY 1985)]

Notwithstanding this clear right, an employer cannot alter or diminish benefits under the plan in such a way as to violate federal law or, to the extent not preempted by ERISA, state insurance law. However, ERISA probably would preempt the application to ERISA welfare benefit plans of general state labor laws prohibiting employment discrimination in the terms, conditions, and privileges of employment.

In addition, an employer cannot change plan coverage terms retroactively if employees thereby would be deprived of benefits for which they had already incurred expenses based upon the coverage terms clearly communicated to them. The Court of Appeals for the Third Circuit has held that an employer that intended to exclude coverage for motorcycle accidents under its medical plan but failed to do so cannot retroactively amend the plan to deprive employees of benefits. [Confer v Custom Eng' Co, 14 EBC 2065 (3rd Cir 1991)]

So long as the employer has expressly reserved the right to cut back benefits, however, nothing in ERISA prohibits an employer from doing so prospectively—including cutting back coverage for future expenses incurred for conditions that were first manifested or for which the employee first sought treatment prior to the date of the plan amendment. [McGann v H & H Music Co, 14 EBC 1729 (5th Cir 1991); see also, Owens v Storehouse Inc, 14 EBC 1550 (ND Ga 1991)]

Q 4:16 Is an employer subject to a collective bargaining agreement free to amend, modify, or terminate a retiree medical plan prior to expiration of the collective bargaining agreement?

Not necessarily. The terms of the collective bargaining agreement and the plan will need to be examined to see if the employer has the express authority to unilaterally change the plan prior to the expiration of the collective bargaining agreement without subjecting itself to an unfair labor practice charge. Some collective bargaining agreements simply incorporate by reference employer-provided plans that clearly reserve the employer's right to amend or modify the plan at any time. [Benedict v United Intermountain Telephone Co, 17 EBC (BNA) 1044 (ED Tenn 1933) (collective bargaining agreement did not prohibit charging retirees a premium); United Steelworkers v Newman-Crosby Steel, Inc, 16 EBC (BNA) 2760 (DRI, 1993) (collective bargaining agreement cannot be modified by changes to the plan and summary plan description, both of which were amended to add the authority to make cutbacks)] Ambiguity in a collective bargaining agreement may create an opportunity for a court to consider extrinsic evidence concerning whether lifetime health benefits were promised. [Bidlack v Wheelabrator Corp, No 89C 360 (7th Cir, May 19, 1993)]

Q 4:17 Is an employer subject to a collective bargaining agreement free to terminate retiree medical coverage upon expiration of the collective bargaining agreement?

The answer is not clear-cut and will depend upon the terms of the collective bargaining agreement, the plan, and applicable case law. There is a substantial body of case law, and different courts have come to opposite conclusions based upon their scrutiny of the underlying documents. In addition, some courts have applied an inference that retiree medical benefits are a "status" benefit that vest upon attainment of retirement. Thus, the employer's ability to terminate retiree medical coverage upon the expiration of a collective bargaining agreement may come down to a facts-and-circumstances determination in each particular case.

Q 4:18   Can an employer have a retiree medical plan with benefits based upon age and length of service?

This has been the subject of considerable discussion in recent years as employers attempt to redesign retiree medical plans to incorporate pension-type goals such as rewarding longer-service employees.

The current regulations under Code Section 105 treat self-insured medical plans as discriminatory if the plan has a maximum benefit limit (attributable to employer contributions), unless the portion of the maximum benefit attributable to employer contributions is uniform for all participants and dependents and is modified by reason of the participant's age or years of service. [Treas Reg § 1.105-11(c)(3)(i)]. This means that if a self-insured retiree medical plan provides differing levels of benefits based upon years of service, a Code Section 105(h) nondiscrimination issue exists. In addition, requiring greater contributions of younger participants in a self-insured retiree medical plan would also raise a nondiscrimination issue under Code Section 105(h) because younger participants would receive fewer benefits per premium dollar.

Q 4:19   If an employer includes retiree medical benefits in an "early-out" program, can it cut back or terminate those benefits at a later date?

It depends upon how those benefits are included in the early-out or early retirement incentive program. In a federal district court case, the court upheld an employer's addition of deductible and copayment features to its medical plan for active and retired employees based upon the employer's unambiguous reservation of the right to amend the plan stated in the summary plan description. It concluded that benefits generally did not vest at any particular level upon retirement. However, prior to the addition of those changes, a group of employees had accepted the employer's offer of a special early retirement program in connection with a plant closing, workforce downsizing, and other employer-initiated actions. They signed written acceptance agreements that released the employer from liability for certain claims and stated that they had reviewed the benefits applicable to them and accepted them. The court concluded that, as to the employees who accepted the separate early retirement program, the employer may have entered into a bilateral contract to provide vested retiree medical benefits at a particular level in return for defined consideration (the release). [Sprague v General Motors Corp, 13 EBC 2678 (ED Mich 1991)]

Q 4:20   If an employer reduces severance pay by the value of retiree medical benefits as permitted under the Age Discrimination in Employment Act (ADEA), can the employer subsequently amend, modify, or terminate the retiree medical plan?

The answer depends upon the level of retiree medical benefits that will be available after the amendment or modification. The Older Workers Benefits Protection Act (OWBPA) amendments to the ADEA require that the value of retiree health benefits that can be used to reduce severance pay and that is payable as a result of a contingent event unrelated to age must meet minimum, specified standards. If the employer does utilize such a reduction, that minimum statutory level of retiree medical benefits must continue to be made available, or the employer will be subject to an action for specific performance by any "aggrieved individual" for failing to fulfill its obligation to provide retiree medical benefits. [ADEA § 4(l)2)(F); 29 USC § 623(l)(2)(F)]

> **Planning Pointer.** An employer contemplating reducing the level of retiree medical benefits in order to reduce its FAS 106 liability (see Chapter 20) should consider whether coordinating severance pay and retiree medical benefits in this fashion effectively ties its hands regarding wholesale redesign of its retiree medical program.

Funding Options

Q 4:21 What options are available to an employer that wishes to reduce FAS 106 liability by prefunding its liability for retiree medical benefits on a tax-advantaged basis?

Employers have several options for prefunding retiree medical benefits, including:

- The welfare benefit fund rules of Code Sections 419 and 419A;
- A Code Section 401(h) account under a pension or annuity plan;
- A profit-sharing retirement plan; and
- Transfer of pension plan surplus.

In addition, the employer could finance its liability for retiree medical benefits using corporate-owned life insurance (COLI). Each of these methods could be used alone or in conjunction with plan redesign techniques.

Q 4:22 How much of the employer's liability for retiree medical benefits can be funded under the welfare benefit fund rules of Code Sections 419 and 419A?

Code Sections 419 and 419A welfare benefit fund rules allow tax-deductible funding of a reserve for postretirement medical insurance benefits if certain conditions are satisfied. The reserve must be funded over the working lives of the employees and be actuarially determined on a level basis, using assumptions that are reasonable in the aggregate. The IRS has not issued formal guidance on how this funding limit applies to existing retirees, who have no remaining working lives.

The amount that the employer contributes cannot include any amount to cover anticipated inflation, and separate accounting is required for key employees. However, the income on the reserve for postretirement medical benefits accumulates on an after-tax basis unless certain exceptions apply.

A more detailed discussion of this funding method is contained in Chapter 19.

Q 4:23   How much of the employer's liability for retiree medical benefits can be funded using a Code Section 401(h) account under a pension or annuity plan?

The employer can establish and maintain a separate account, called a Section 401(h) account, under a pension or annuity plan, to pay for sickness, accident, hospitalization, and medical expenses of retired employees, their spouses, and dependents. Various requirements must be met in order for the employer to do so.

One of the key requirements is that the retiree medical benefits must be subordinate to the retirement benefits under the plan and cannot exceed 25 percent of the total contributions (for pension, retiree medical, and life insurance) made to the pension or annuity plan since the date the Code Section 401(h) account was established under the pension plan. Within these limits, however, the total cost of retiree medical benefits (including anticipated inflation), can be prefunded, and earnings will accumulate in the Section 401(h) account tax-free. Since the flexibility to prefund in this manner depends upon the contributions made to the pension plan, this method will be less useful for employers with well-funded pension plans.

Code Section 401(h) accounts are discussed more fully in Chapter 19.

Q 4:24   Can an employer fund its liability for retiree medical benefits under a profit-sharing retirement plan?

Although a Code Section 401(h) account cannot be maintained under a profit-sharing plan (because it is not a pension or annuity plan), an employer can always increase contributions under a profit-sharing plan to cover part or all of the cost of retiree medical benefits. No special segregated account is necessary. By utilizing a defined contribution plan to do so, the employer can use a retirement-type vehicle to obtain tax-free accumulation of earnings. On the other hand, when the benefits are paid out of the plan, they are taxable retirement benefits. The employer has no power to force the individual to use such funds for retiree medical benefits (although it can encourage the individual to do so).

Q 4:25   Can an employer transfer any portion of a pension plan surplus in order to fund retiree medical benefits?

Yes, Code Section 420 provides a special mechanism for a "qualified transfer" of a part of the surplus under a defined benefit pension plan (other than a multiemployer plan) to a Code Section 401(h) account once each year, provided certain requirements are met.

Two of the applicable requirements may limit the attractiveness of this option. First, in order to have a qualified transfer, the pension plan must provide that the accrued benefits of any plan participant or beneficiary become nonforfeitable as if the plan had terminated immediately before the qualified transfer. This full vesting of accrued benefits may have a substantial cost impact on the employer. Second, the "applicable employer cost" of the retiree medical benefits that are furnished must be at least as high, during the year of the qualified transfer and the four years after it, as during the two taxable years before the year of the qualified transfer.

Accordingly, an employer contemplating a wholesale redesign and reduction of retiree medical benefits may not wish to be locked into a particular level of benefits in this fashion. Section 420 "qualified transfers" are discussed in more detail in Chapter 19.

Q 4:26   Does financing with COLI help reduce FAS 106 liability?

Corporate-owned life insurance (COLI) can be purchased to cover the employer's liability for benefits under a retiree medical plan. The policies are wholly owned by the employer and subject to the claims of the employer's creditors. The employees have no right or interest in the insurance policies on their lives.

This technique is designed to assure adequate cash flow and possible tax advantages. However, it does not constitute a funding method for the welfare benefit plan, does not meet the requirements for creation of a "plan asset" under FAS 106, and is not intended to create a plan asset for ERISA purposes. Thus, although it is a method for financing retiree medical liability, it does not reduce the amount of that liability for FAS 106 purposes.

The structure and use of COLI is discussed in more detail in Chapter 19.

Q 4:27 Can retirement plan benefit payments be deferred and used as a pre-tax cafeteria plan contribution for retiree medical coverage?

One of the more innovative ideas for financing the cost of retiree medical benefits is the suggested use of pension plan payouts as a pre-tax cafeteria plan contribution toward retiree medical plan coverage. This technique, dubbed the "qualified cafeteria plan hybrid" has been discussed for many years and has been described in detail in "New Cafeteria Plan Ideas—Qualified Cafeteria Plan Hybrid: Appetizing Addition to Retiree Funding Menu?" [Case & Colemen, 5 *Benefits Law Journal*, No 4, Winter 1992-93, p 533 et seq, and follow-up letters in the same journal].

There are several technical issues that must be reviewed when considering the implementation of a qualified cafeteria plan hybrid. Perhaps the key issue regarding such a technique is whether qualified retirement plan payments constitute "cash" within the meaning of Code Section 125, and may be annually assigned, prior to receipt by the retiree, as a pre-tax contribution toward retiree medical coverage under a cafeteria plan (see Q 7:43–7:45). If this technique is considered valid by the IRS, then an employee would avoid taxation of retiree benefits altogether by essentially converting the retirement plan benefit into a Section 106 employer contribution for accident or health insurance and then receiving retiree medical benefit expense reimbursements tax-free under Code Section 105. The IRS has not yet ruled on the validity of this technique, so employers considering implementing such a program should obtain the guidance of experienced legal counsel.

Chapter 5

Health Maintenance Organizations

Many employers offer the option of membership in one or more health maintenance organizations (HMOs) as part of their medical benefit packages. Often, "federally qualified" HMOs are included because of the mandatory requirements of the federal Health Maintenance Organization Act of 1973 (HMO Act). This chapter explores the special rules that apply to an employer when it offers federally qualified HMOs to its employees.

Basic Concepts

Q 5:1   What is an HMO?

An HMO is an independent health care organization that serves a specific geographic area, called the "service area." The HMO consists of a contractually related group of physicians, referral specialists, hospitals, and other medical professionals that provides care directly to its members. Unless otherwise authorized by the HMO, members must receive covered care from the HMO's affiliated medical personnel and health care institutions within the HMO's service area. In return for a set monthly fee, HMO members are entitled to use the HMO's full range of medical professionals and services. Individual services may require copayments, such as a $10 for every office visit. Specific medical benefits offered by a particular HMO may vary, but, in general, HMOs stress preventive care such as physical examinations, immunizations, and well-baby care. HMOs also provide coverage for emergencies outside the service area. Many HMOs have reciprocal agreements allowing one another's members to use their facilities.

HMOs that satisfy federal requirements regarding their structure and operation can apply for a designation of "federally qualified." Federally qualified HMOs are regulated by the U.S. Department of Health and Human Services (DHHS).

Q 5:2   What are the main types of HMOs?

There are three main types, or models, of HMOs: group, staff, and independent practice association (IPA). Both group and staff-model HMOs usually have one or a series of health centers or clinics at which a broad array of primary care physicians and some specialists practice regularly. In the staff model, the physicians are salaried; in the group model, some or all of them own the practice. From the consumer's point of view, however, the group and staff model HMOs are virtually indistinguishable; both are essentially a form of one-stop shopping.

IPAs, on the other hand, usually lack central health care offices and generally consist of coordinated groups of physicians who practice out of their own offices. Member physicians will generally take a certain percentage of patients who receive services through the HMO, as well as regular fee-for-service patients. A member in an IPA, therefore, may receive general care at one physician's office, pediatric care at a second physician's office, gynecological care at a third location, and so forth. The functional components of IPA model HMOs are often, therefore, geographically removed from one another, unlike centrally organized group or staff model HMOs. Various hybrid HMO arrangements also have developed. [HHS Reg § 417.103]

Q 5:3   When must an employer offer an HMO as part of its medical benefit package?

Until the mandatory provisions of the HMO Act expire in 1995 or until changed by enactment of President Clinton's health plan, a covered employer having at least 25 employees who reside in a federally qualified HMO's service area must offer the option of membership in a federally qualified HMO (see Q 5:7) in addition to its existing medical plan if the HMO mandates the employer (see Q 5:12–5:17) and meets certain requirements. Employees who reside in the HMO's service area thus get a "dual-choice" of medical programs: a choice between coverage under the existing medical plan and coverage under the HMO. [42 USC § 300e-9(a)] However, the employer need not offer every HMO that mandates it (see Q 5:19).

An employer is subject to the HMO Act if it

1. Was covered under the minimum wage provisions of the Fair Labor Standards Act during any quarter in the prior calendar year,
2. Had 25 or more full or part-time employees during any quarter in the prior calendar year; and
3. Offers a health benefit plan to eligible employees.

State and local governments are also covered by this law. [42 USC § 300e-9 (a)(1); HHS Reg § 417.150]

Certain states provide certification for HMOs. In addition, Connecticut, Michigan, New York, Rhode Island, Washington, and West Virginia have mandatory dual-choice statutes patterned after the federal law. To the extent that the Employee Retirement Income

Security Act (ERISA) does not preempt these statutes, the employer must comply with them as well.

Q 5:4   Is an HMO subject to Internal Revenue Code (Code) nondiscrimination rules?

No, ordinarily it is not. An HMO generally involves the shifting of risk, and is in effect an insured plan, so Code Section 105(h) rules that govern self-insured plans do not affect the HMO offering. However, the HMO and the employer are subject to the coverage rules of the HMO Act (see Qs 5:27–5:35). [Treas Reg § 1.105-11(b)(1)]

Q 5:5   Is an employer's offering of an HMO subject to ERISA?

Yes, it is. The application of ERISA to an HMO offering involves some unique considerations (see Qs 5:49–5:57).

Q 5:6   Is an employer's offering of an HMO subject to the Consolidated Omnibus Budget Reconciliation Act (COBRA) health care continuation requirements?

Yes, it is. See Chapter 6 for a discussion of COBRA.

Federal Qualification—Benefits

Q 5:7   What is a "federally qualified" HMO?

A federally qualified HMO is one that meets the standards specified in the HMO Act. These standards relate to both organization and operation. A federally qualified HMO must offer a minimum required package of health care benefits, have a quality assurance program, and provide a grievance procedure. Certification of federally qualified status must be obtained from the DHHS. The HMO's service area is then the "federally qualified service area." Only a federally qualified HMO can "mandate" an employer, a process that is discussed in Questions 5:12 through 5:17.

Q 5:8 What benefits must a federally qualified HMO offer?

A federally qualified HMO is required by law to offer a minimum required level of benefits, called "basic health services." Except where specifically limited by law, the basic health services generally must be provided to members without limitation as to time and cost. They include:

- Inpatient and outpatient hospital services
- Physicians' services, including consultant and referral services
- Emergency services, including reimbursement for medically necessary inpatient or outpatient emergency services both inside and outside the service area from non-HMO providers and
- A limited amount of short-term outpatient mental health care, including both evaluation and crisis intervention services

[42 USC § 300e-9(d); HHS Reg §§ 417.101, 417.106(b)(1)]

Q 5:9 May a federally qualified HMO offer additional health services?

Yes, a federally qualified HMO may also offer additional health care services, called "supplemental health services." The regulations contain a laundry list of permitted supplemental health services. If the HMO chooses, it can incorporate one or more supplemental services into its basic package, which it offers uniformly to all employers. Alternatively, it may choose to offer one or more supplemental health services as elective coverage riders. [HHS Reg §§ 410.101(d), 417.102]

Q 5:10 May an employer require a federally qualified HMO to offer particular health services?

An employer generally may not insist that a federally qualified HMO offer (or not offer) particular health services. The basic health services that the HMO must offer are nonnegotiable. However, supplemental health services are negotiable, unless the HMO has chosen to incorporate them into its basic health services package.

[HHS Reg § 417.102(b)] Additionally, supplemental health services that are required under state law are not negotiable.

Even if a particular service is optional with the HMO, the HMO must also be appropriately licensed under state law in order to be able to offer the service.

> **Planning Pointer.** Most HMOs offer a series of coverage riders that will allow employers to choose the extra coverage necessary to align coverage available under the HMO option more closely with that available under the employer's existing medical program.

Q 5:11 If federal law changes require employers to include a specific benefit in their medical plans, can they make the federally qualified HMO follow suit?

Changes in federal law applicable to employers generally omit any reference to benefits offered pursuant to an HMO option. An employer could be placed in violation of the law if the HMO refused to also offer the required benefit. As a practical matter, however, the HMO would be requested by all of its member employers to comply and probably would do so in order to keep the business or remain competitive. In the past, the DHHS has indicated that it will not assist in enforcing a mandate against an employer if an HMO fails to offer services that the employer is legally obligated to provide or make available to its employees. (See also Q 5:49). HMO coverage will also be subject to FMLA requirements (see Chapter 15).

Federal Qualification—The Mandate

Q 5:12 What must a federally qualified HMO do to "mandate" or "activate" an employer?

Before October 24, 1995, when the federal HMO Act's mandatory dual-choice provisions are scheduled to expire, or until superseded by enactment of President Clinton's health care program, a federally qualified HMO can "mandate" an employer. [HMO Act of 1973, as amended by the HMO Amendments of 1988] If the federally qualified HMO provides an employer with certain required information about its operations and finances within a specified time period, the employer must respond to the HMO and, possibly, offer coverage under the HMO to its employees as an alternative to its existing medical program. The federally qualified HMO must request inclusion in the employer's benefit plan and must submit the required information (see Q 5:13) to the employer or to the employer's designee at least 180 days, but no more than 365 days, before the expiration or renewal date of a health benefit contract, employer-employee contract, or collective bargaining agreement. State law may allow a longer period for approaching a state or local government. [HHS Reg §§ 417.152(a), 417.151(b)]

Q 5:13   What information must the mandate include?

The required information consists of the following eleven items:

1. Evidence of federally qualified status.
2. A description of the HMO's federally qualified service area and the dates on which basic and supplemental services are provided within the service area.
3. Type of HMO (group, staff, IPA, or hybrid model (see Q 5:18).
4. If the HMO is an IPA, a list of member physicians by name, specialty, and whether they are accepting new patients from the HMO membership. This list must be current within 90 days of the HMO's request for inclusion in the employer's benefit program.

   If the HMO is a type other than an IPA, a list of the HMO's ambulatory care facilities and each facility's address, days and hours of operation, whether it is accepting new patients from the HMO membership, and a list of the names and specialties of the facility's providers of basic and supplemental health services. This information must also be current within 90 days of the date the HMO requests inclusion in the employer's benefit package.
5. The hospitals affiliated with the HMO.
6. The type of legal entity plus the identity of the members of the HMO's policymaking body and the principal managing officer of the HMO.

7. Capacity of the HMO to enroll new members and the likelihood of any future limitations on enrollment.

8. The HMO's most recent audited annual financial statements.

9. The proposed contract between the HMO and the employer, public entity, or designee.

10. Sample copies of the HMO's marketing brochures and literature.

11. Rates, including copayments, for basic health services and for those supplemental health services that are uniformly included in the HMO's basic package. The rates may be expressed as either the rates currently being charged or the estimated rates for these services. If current rates are provided, the date on which they became effective must also be included.

[HHS Reg § 417.152(c)]

Q 5:14   Does a federally qualified HMO's mandate have to contain any particular language?

No, the letter from the HMO does not have to include any particular language informing the employer that it is being officially mandated by the HMO. It simply must request inclusion in the employer's benefit package and include the required information concerning the HMO (see Q 5:13).

Q 5:15   How long does an employer have to respond to a mandate by a federally qualified HMO?

The employer has 60 days after receipt of the HMO's request and mandate package to respond in writing to the HMO. [HHS Reg § 417.152(d)]

Q 5:16   How does an employer respond to a mandate by a federally qualified HMO?

Assuming receipt of a valid mandate or activation package, the employer must respond with information on its employees and program of medical coverage. The employer must state whether it has at least 25 employees in the HMO's federally qualified service area. If so, the employer must also provide the HMO with the following information:

- The expiration or renewal dates of its health contracts;
- The amount of the employer's (and, where applicable, the employees') current contribution for health benefits, including the dates on which those contribution levels became effective
- The expiration date of any collective bargaining agreements covering those employees and
- If the employer is a public entity, a description of health benefits, including limitations and exclusions, required for employees of the public entity by state law or regulation

[HHS Reg § 417.152(d)]

Q 5:17   What if the HMO's mandate is defective?

If the federally qualified HMO's request for inclusion in the employer's benefit package does not contain all of the required information (see Q 5:13), the employer has 60 days to inform the HMO in writing that the request is defective and give the basis for that conclusion. The employer does not have to take any further action regarding the HMO until the HMO corrects the defect. [HHS Reg § 417.152(e)]

Employer Obligations

Q 5:18   How many federally qualified HMOs must the employer offer?

An employer that has been validly mandated prior to October 24, 1995 must offer the option of membership in at least one group or staff model federally qualified HMO and in at least one IPA model federally qualified HMO in each service area in which at least 25 of its employees reside. This assumes, of course, that one of each type is available in the service area. In other words, offering two federally qualified HMOs, one of each type, is sufficient to meet the employer's obligation. [HHS Reg § 417.154(a)]

For purposes of satisfying the employer's obligation under the federal HMO Act, a hybrid HMO (1) that has individual physicians and other health professionals under contract with the HMO or (2) that is a combination of one or more associations, medical groups, staff, and individual physicians and other health professionals under contract with the HMO is lumped into the same category as IPAs.

The 25-employee rule also applies when an employer is mandated by a second federally qualified HMO of the same type as the first, with a service area that overlaps the service area of the federally qualified HMO currently being offered by the employer. In this event, the employer also must offer the option of membership in the second HMO, at least in the nonoverlapping area, if it has at least 25 employees who reside in the nonoverlapping area covered by the second federally qualified HMO. [HHS Reg § 417.154(b)]

Q 5:19   Must the employer offer the first federally qualified HMO that approaches it?

No, the employer is not obligated to offer its employees the option of membership in the first federally qualified HMO or HMOs that make a timely and valid request. It may offer any other federally qualified HMO of the same type covering the same service area, as long as the HMO is willing to be offered and the employer offers the minimum number of federally qualified HMOs required by law. [HHS Reg § 417.154(c)]

Q 5:20   To which employees must an employer offer a federally qualified HMO?

Once it is validly mandated, the employer must offer the option of membership in a federally qualified HMO to its employees and their eligible dependents who reside in the HMO's federally qualified service area at the same time that a health benefit plan is offered to them. [HHS Reg § 417.153]

Planning Pointer. Taken literally, this rule could present an employee relations problem if only some of the employees in an employment location, and not others, receive a benefit. HMOs are sometimes willing to accept members who live close to, but not in, the service area, as long as those individuals understand that they must use services from that HMO's medical professionals.

Q 5:21 Is it sufficient to offer the federally qualified HMO to all of the employer's employment locations situated within the HMO's federally qualified service area?

Generally, no, it is not. The dual-choice mandate (see Q 5:3) is based on how many employees reside in the federally qualified service area, not on how many are employed at a facility or job site physically located within the federally qualified service area. [HHS Reg § 417.153(b)]

Thus, employees who live within a federally qualified HMO's service area, but who work at a job site or facility outside the service area, are entitled to be offered the option of membership in the federally qualified HMO.

Planning Pointer. This means that a special annual enrollment period (see Q 5:30) will have to be provided to such employees, even if the HMO option is not available to any other employees at the employment location. There is no obligation to offer the federally qualified HMO to employees who work in the service area, but do not reside in it. [HHS Reg § 4l7.153(b)]

Q 5:22 When must the employer make the option of membership in a federally qualified HMO available to its employees?

If the employer has received a valid mandate and there is no collective bargaining agreement, the employer must include the option of membership in a federally qualified HMO in any health benefit plan offered to eligible employees when the health contract is renewed or negotiated. If the term of the contract is not fixed or exceeds one year, the contract is treated as renewable on its earliest anniversary date. For self-insured plans, the budget year is treated as the term of the contract. The employer and the HMO are free to agree on a different effective date for the HMO offering. [HHS Reg § 417.156]

Example. A retailer with a January 1 medical plan anniversary date may not wish to hold an HMO enrollment period in the middle of its busy November and December holiday season. It could, if the federally qualified HMO agreed, schedule the open enrollment during the slower February inventory period.

Q 5:23   How does an employer satisfy its obligation to offer a federally qualified HMO when there is a collective bargaining agreement?

If an employer has employees who are represented by a bargaining representative when the HMO requests inclusion in the employer's health benefit program, the employer must refer the offer of membership in the federally qualified HMO to the bargaining representative. The HMO's request for inclusion must be raised in the collective bargaining process at the following times, unless otherwise mutually agreed upon:

- When a new agreement is being negotiated;
- At the times provided in the agreement for discussion of changes, if the agreement is for a fixed term of more than one year and provides that its terms concerning health benefits may be renegotiated during the term of the agreement; or
- In accordance with a specific process to review HMO offers.

If the bargaining representative accepts the offer, the employer must make the option of membership in the HMO available to each represented employee. However, if the bargaining representative rejects the offer, the employer has no further obligation with respect to that federally qualified HMO. [HHS Reg §§ 417.153(c), 417.156(a)]

Q 5:24   Must an employer give a federally qualified HMO access to its employees and to its premises?

If it has been validly mandated, the employer can be required to give a federally qualified HMO access to its employees and, depending on the circumstances, to its premises. At a minimum, the federally qualified HMO must be given "fair and reasonable access" to employees who reside in the HMO's federally qualified service area.

This access must be given not less than 30 days prior to and during the group enrollment period (see Qs 5:31, 5:33) in order that the HMO may present and explain its program. This access includes the opportunity to distribute the following kinds of information:

- Educational literature
- Brochures
- Announcements of meetings and
- Other relevant printed materials

The employer cannot provide access to eligible employees that is "less restrictive or less favorable than the access it provides other offerors of alternatives included in the health benefits plan, whether or not these offerors elect to avail themselves of that access." [HHS Reg § 417.155(a)]

Q 5:25 Can the employer review and approve the federally qualified HMO's offering materials in advance?

Yes, an employer is allowed to review in advance the offering materials that the federally qualified HMO will use with its employees. The HMO must provide the employer the opportunity to review and revise its materials prior to distribution. However, an employer may correct only "factual errors and misleading statements," unless the HMO agrees to more extensive changes or more extensive changes are required by law. Furthermore, the employer must complete its review promptly so that it will not interfere with or delay the group enrollment period. [HHS Reg § 417.155(b)]

Q 5:26 Must an employer sign the federally qualified HMO's group service contract?

No, the employer does not have to sign the specimen contract provided by the HMO.

Planning Pointer. As a practical matter, it may be prudent to have some sort of written agreement with the HMO covering such items as when the employer must forward monthly premium payments, how enrollments are to be handled, when and for how long the annual enrollment period will be held, any restrictions on the HMO's use of the employer's logo, the HMO's provision of information that the employer may need to satisfy its ERISA reporting and disclosure requirements, and possibly, a hold-harmless agreement.

Q 5:27 Can the HMO limit the offering to some, but not all, employees and dependents?

As long as the employees reside in the service area, a federally qualified HMO may not pick and choose which employees it will allow to join. For example, it cannot limit coverage to employees under age 65. The employer's definition of eligible employee is controlling. [HHS Reg § 417.150] However, the employer and the HMO may negotiate the definition of eligible dependents for HMO coverage purposes.

> **Planning Pointer.** HMOs will generally have either coverage that is broad enough, or elective dependent coverage riders that are sufficient, to let the employer make the offer of membership in the federally qualified HMO available to all its employees and their eligible dependents.

Q 5:28 Must an employer offer a federally qualified HMO to its retired employees?

No, an employer that offers employees the option of membership in one or more federally qualified HMOs does not have to make HMO coverage available to retired employees. If the HMO agrees, an employer may voluntarily extend the option to retired employees.

Q 5:29 Can the HMO force the employer to include the HMO as an option in the employer's benefit program?

No, a federally qualified HMO cannot do so directly. A recent district court case held that no private right of enforcement exists under the federal HMO Act. Accordingly, even though an employer was refusing to comply with the federal HMO Act, the federally qualified HMO in question could not obtain a preliminary injunction to force the employer to include it as an option in the employer's benefit package. The court held that the sole enforcement mechanism provided in the statute is for the Secretary of the DHHS to punish the wrongdoing employer with repeated fines until compliance is achieved. [Health Care Plan Inc v Aetna Life Ins Co, 14 EBC 1823 (WD NY 1991)] (For a discussion of penalties under the HMO Act, see Question 5:47.)

HMO Enrollment

Q 5:30   When must employees be allowed to enroll in a federally qualified HMO?

Employees must be permitted to select from among the different alternatives in the employer's health benefit program (including HMO options) as follows:

- All eligible employees must be permitted to choose during the annual group open enrollment period (see Qs 5:31 and 5:32)
- New employees must be permitted to choose when they first become eligible for health benefits
- Individuals who move into the service area of a federally qualified HMO for which they were not previously eligible must be permitted to choose when they move since they have become eligible for membership because of their change in residence and
- Individuals covered by another alternative which ceases operation must be permitted to choose at the time the other alternative ceases

[HHS Reg § 417.155(e)(2)]

Q 5:31   What is a group open enrollment period?

A group open enrollment period is an annual period of at least 10 working days when the option of membership in one or more federally qualified HMOs (or of switching from the HMO to one of the employer's other health plan offerings) must be made available to employees. [HHS Reg §§ 417.150, 417.155(c)]

Q 5:32 May an employer impose a health test or preexisting-condition limitation on employees during the group on open enrollment period?

No, generally employers must permit any eligible employee or dependent to enroll in a federally qualified HMO offered by the employer—or to transfer out of HMO coverage to a non-HMO alternative—during the group open enrollment period or upon the occurrence of any of the other circumstances described in Question 4:30, without imposing waiting periods, exclusions, or limitations based upon health status as a condition either of enrollment in an HMO or of transfer from HMO to non-HMO coverage. [HHS Reg § 417.155(c)] However, employers may continue to impose conditions for the non-HMO alternative on individuals who are not switching out of an HMO.

Q 5:33 May an HMO condition enrollment or reenrollment during group or open enrollment upon health status, health care needs, or age?

No, a federally qualified HMO may not discriminate against members or individuals by imposing conditions on enrollment or on reenrollment during the group open enrollment period based upon the health status, health care needs, or age of the member or individual. [HHS Reg § 417.107(d)]

Q 5:34 Must a federally qualified HMO accept mid-year enrollments of individuals who declined HMO coverage during group open enrollment?

No, it does not have to do so. A federally qualified HMO is required to accept unlimited health risks only during the annual group open enrollment period. At other times, it is free to accept or reject enrollment (other than from new hires and transfers into the service area) and to impose a health test. However, the federally qualified HMO must nonetheless admit an individual who failed a health test if he or she applies during any subsequent open enrollment period (see Qs 5:31–5:34).

Q 5:35   Are employees who select an HMO excluded from additional benefits offered by the employer?

No, they are not. Employees may not be penalized in any fashion because they elect coverage with a federally qualified HMO. An employer must continue to make freestanding dental, optical, or prescription drug benefits available to any employee who would be eligible for them upon electing the non-HMO option, unless the benefits are included in the prepaid package of basic services that the HMO provides to its members. A benefit is freestanding if it is:

1. Not integrated or incorporated into the employer's basic health benefit package or major medical plan; and
2. Either (1) insured by a different carrier from that which provides the employer's basic health benefit package or major medical plan or (2) has a premium separate from that which covers the employer's basic health benefit package or major medical plan.

The examples that follow illustrate the application of these rules, along with the application of the rules discussed in Questions 5:31 through 5:35.

Example 1. An employer offers a medical plan, a separate dental plan, and a federally qualified HMO. The HMO does not cover dental expenses. The dental plan allows anyone who previously declined dental plan coverage to join at any time upon submission of satisfactory evidence of good health. Employee A is enrolled in the medical and dental plans and wants to switch to HMO coverage during the next annual group open enrollment period, but wants to continue his dental coverage. Employee A must be allowed to continue his dental coverage if he enrolls in the HMO.

Example 2. The facts are the same as in Example 1, except that Employee B is enrolled in the medical plan but not the dental plan. Employee B wants to elect dental coverage during the open enrollment period. Employee B does not have to be automatically waived into the dental plan, because the automatic waiver of health conditions applies only to joining an HMO or switching from an HMO to alternative health plan coverage during a group open enrollment period. However, Employee B must be allowed the opportunity to enroll in the dental plan and must meet any conditions, such as providing satisfactory evidence of good health, otherwise applicable to late enrollment imposed by the dental plan on all late enrollees.

Example 3. Company A has a medical plan that incorporates dental coverage. There is no freestanding dental plan. Company A also offers two federally qualified HMOs whose service areas include the town in which Employee C resides. Employee C is currently covered by Company A's medical plan but wants to switch to one of the HMOs during the next annual group enrollment period. If Employee C joins the HMO, Company A does not have to "break out" dental benefits and continue that portion only of the medical plan coverage for Employee C, regardless of whether the HMO offers any dental coverage. In this case, Employee C may be required to choose between the whole medical plan and the HMO coverage.

Of course, an employee cannot be deprived of other benefits, such as disability or group term life insurance, merely because he or she chooses coverage under a federally qualified HMO. [HHS Reg § 417.155(d)]

Q 5:36   Must an employee elect or decline HMO coverage in writing?

Generally, employees must make an affirmative written selection from among the different alternatives (including HMO options) included in the employer's health benefit plans the first time the option of coverage by a particular federally qualified HMO becomes available. Thus, an affirmative written selection is required

- During the group open enrollment period in which the alternative of membership in any particular federally qualified HMO is first offered to an eligible group of employees
- When a new hire is first offered a selection among health benefit alternatives and

- When an employee moves his or her residence into the service area of an HMO offered by the employer for which the employee was not previously eligible

For subsequent group enrollment periods, the employer need not obtain an affirmative written election, except from employees who are switching from one alternative to another. [HHS Reg § 417.156(e)(1)]

Q 5:37   When does HMO coverage become effective?

If an employee elects coverage under a federally qualified HMO offered by the employer, coverage becomes effective on the day the employee's current coverage would expire or would be automatically renewed. The employer and the HMO may mutually agree to a different effective date. [HHS Reg § 417.155(g)]

Contributions

Q 5:38   When are payments for HMO coverage made?

The employer pays a monthly premium, theoretically in advance, on behalf of each HMO member. This amount is billed directly to the employer. A federally qualified HMO is permitted to charge a late payment penalty on accounts receivable that are in arrears. [HHS Reg §§ 417.104(a), 4l7.104(d)]

Additionally, HMOs may impose copayments on individual services, but the law limits the amount that may be charged, so that copayments will not create a barrier to obtaining necessary medical care. For basic health services, a federally qualified HMO cannot impose copayment charges exceeding 50 percent of the HMO's total cost of providing the particular service to its members, or 20 percent of the total cost of providing the entire package of basic health services.

Copayment charges in any year for a member cannot exceed 200 percent of the total annual premium cost that would have been charged for coverage containing no copayments. The member is responsible for demonstrating that he or she has met this limit. [HHS Reg § 417.104(a)(4)]

Additionally, the HMO Act allows federally qualified HMOs to permit members to obtain up to 10 percent of basic services from nonaffiliated providers. An HMO may charge an additional, reasonable deductible for services obtained in this manner. [42 USC § 300e(b)(1)]

Q 5:39 Must employers contribute toward the monthly cost of HMO coverage?

Yes, the HMO Act requires the employer to contribute toward the monthly cost of coverage under a federally qualified HMO if the employer contributes toward any of its other medical plan options. [42 USC § 300e-9(c)]

Q 5:40 How much must the employer contribute toward the monthly cost of HMO coverage?

Generally effective on October 24,1988 (the date of enactment of the HMO Amendments of 1988), employers that have been validly mandated by a federally qualified HMO must contribute an amount toward the HMO's monthly premium that does not "financially discriminate" against an employee who enrolls in the HMO. This rule applies regardless of whether the HMO's mandate was received before or after October 24, 1988. However, collective bargaining agreements in effect on October 24, 1988, are not superseded. [42 USC § 300e-9(c)] Until 1995, when the mandatory dual-choice provisions of the HMO Act are scheduled to expire, the HMO Act does not regulate the amount of the employer's contribution toward a voluntarily offered federally qualified HMO. However, beginning in 1995, voluntarily offered HMOs will become subject to the same financially nondiscriminatory standard that applies to HMOs that have validly mandated the employer. [134 Cong Rec H9613 (Oct 5, 1988)]

Prior to amendments to the HMO Act made in 1988, an employer had to include the option of membership in a federally qualified HMO in its health benefit plan on "terms no less favorable," respecting the employer's monetary contribution or its designee's cost for health benefits calculated in dollars and cents, than the terms on which the other alternatives in the health benefit plan are included. If more than one non-HMO health benefit alternative was offered, the employer's HMO contribution had to be: "equal, in terms of dollars and cents, to the largest amount of the contribution that would be paid for that individual employee to any other alternative which is included in the health benefits plan." [HHS Reg §§ 417.157(a), 4l7.157(b)]

Q 5:41 Is there a limit on how much an employer must contribute toward the cost of the federally qualified HMO?

Yes, there is. As a general principle, an employer need not pay more for health benefits just because it offers its employees the option of membership in a federally qualified HMO than it would otherwise have to pay for them under a collective bargaining agreement or other contract (for example, health insurance contract) in effect at the time the employer includes the HMO in its health benefit plan. The contribution made on behalf of any individual employee need not be more than what the HMO actually charges as its monthly premium. [42 USC § 300e-9(c); HHS Reg § 417.157]

Q 5:42 How does an employer ensure that its contribution to a federally qualified HMO is not financially discriminatory?

Under the 1988 amendments to the federal HMO Act, an employer's contribution to a federally qualified HMO will not be considered financially discriminatory if the employer's method of determining its contributions on behalf of all employees is (1) reasonable and (2) designed to ensure employees a fair choice among health benefit plans. [42 USC § 300e-9]

The Health Care Financing Administration recently issued a proposed regulation reflecting this standard. Employer contributions for HMO coverage will not be considered financially discriminatory if:

1. The contributions for the HMO and the non-HMO alternative are equal;

2. They are based on demographics (age, sex, family status, and other factors that are reasonable predictors of use, experience, costs, or risk);

3. The employer pays the same percentage of premiums for each health alternative that the employer offers;

4. The employer's policy is that all employees must contribute to their health care plan and the employer requires that employees make a reasonable contribution toward HMO coverage (a contribution equal to 50 percent or less of the required employee contribution to the principal non-HMO alternative plan is reasonable); or

5. The employer's HMO contribution is a negotiated amount that is mutually acceptable to the employer and the HMO (however, the employer cannot insist on any contribution arrangement that would cause the HMO to violate any rules, such as the community rating requirement,) to which it is subject).

[HHS Prop Reg § 417.157, 56 Fed Reg 30723 (July 5, 1991)]

Q 5:43 What if the HMO's monthly premium exceeds an employer's required monthly contribution?

Any amount by which the HMO's monthly premium charge exceeds the required monthly employer contribution may be charged to employees as the required employee contribution toward HMO coverage.

Q 5:44 Must the employer provide payroll deductions for the employees' share of HMO premiums?

Yes, the employer must provide payroll deductions as a means of paying employee contributions toward a federally qualified HMO if it does so for the non-HMO alternatives in the employer's health benefit program. [42 USC § 300e-9(c); HHS Reg § 417.158]

Q 5:45   If the employer permits employees to pay for medical coverage by salary reduction, must it also allow employees who select the HMO option to pay for it by salary reduction?

Generally, yes. If an employer offers its employees membership in an HMO that has validly mandated the employer, the employer's contribution toward the federally qualified HMO must be financially nondiscriminatory (see Q 5:39). When an employer permits employees to pay for medical coverage by salary reduction, after-tax employee contributions are converted into pre-tax employer contributions, thereby increasing the amount of employer contributions toward the coverage. This "premium conversion," which is governed by the Code Section 125 cafeteria plan rules (see Q 7:43–7:45), makes the coverage option for which it is available more financially attractive for employees by lowering its out-of-pocket premium cost. Accordingly, failure to offer it in connection with the HMO option could be viewed as financially discriminatory.

Note that, prior to October 24, 1995, the financial nondiscrimination requirement only applies to federally qualified HMOs that have validly mandated the employer. After that date, which is subject to a special transition rule for collectively bargained plans (see Q 5:40), the financial nondiscrimination requirement will apply to all federally qualified HMOs offered by the employer whether or not offered voluntarily and regardless of the date on which the option of membership in the HMO was first offered to employees.

Termination of Coverage

Q 5:46   What health benefits must an employer offer an employee who loses HMO benefits because of a transfer?

An employer may, of course, transfer an employee. And, because of the transfer, the employee may move out of the qualified service area of a federally qualified HMO in which he or she is currently enrolled. In this case, the employer must let the employee select from among its health benefit program alternatives without waiting for the next annual group enrollment period; it must give the employee the opportunity to join (1) any federally qualified HMOs the employer offers in the employee's new area of residence or (2) the employer's traditional plan. [HHS Reg § 417.155(e)(2)]

Q 5:47   What happens if the employee moves out of the HMO's service area but continues to work at the same employer location?

If an employee voluntarily moves out of the federally qualified HMO's federally qualified service area, the employer must still give the employee the opportunity to select among the different alternatives within the employer's health benefit program at that time, regardless of when the next group enrollment period is scheduled to be held. [HHS Reg § 417.155(e)(2)]

HMO Act Penalties

Q 5:48   What penalties can be imposed on an employer that violates the HMO Act?

Presently, an employer that violates those federal HMO Act requirements discussed in this chapter that involve offering the plan, contributing to the plan, and providing payroll deductions is subject to a penalty of up to $10,000 for each 30-day period of noncompliance per violation. However, the penalty may not be assessed until the employer has been given notice and an opportunity to present its views on the charge.

The Secretary of the DHHS is to consider the gravity of the noncompliance and the demonstrated good faith of the employer when determining the amount of the penalty or an agreed-upon compromise course of action, in attempting to achieve rapid compliance.

This $10,000 penalty does not apply to the federal government, state and local governments, the District of Columbia, or certain churches. However, state and local governments that receive funding under certain portions of the Public Health Services Act may have their funds terminated if they fail to comply with the federal HMO Act. [42 USC §§ 300e-9(d), 300e-9(f)]

ERISA Considerations

Q 5:49   Is an HMO a separate ERISA plan?

The Department of Labor (DOL) does not consider a federally qualified HMO that is offered as an alternative to the employer's medical plan to be a separate ERISA plan obligated to comply with ERISA on its own. Rather, a federally qualified HMO is considered a benefit under an employer's health benefit plan, regardless of whether the offering is compulsory under state or federal law. The DOL's view is that:

> Section 1310(a) of the HMO Act . . . assume[s] a preexisting plan established by an employer for the purpose of providing health benefits and require[s] that the QHMO [federally qualified HMO] membership option be included in that plan. Since this preexisting health benefits plan must be established by an employer, the provisions of ERISA will apply to the plan to the extent the plan offers benefits listed under Section 3(1) of Title I, whether those benefits are offered through a QHMO or otherwise. . . . Accordingly, the Department is of the opinion that the provisions of Title I of ERISA are applicable, in relevant part, to a plan that offers a QHMO option pursuant to the HMO Act and HHS [Health and Human Services] regulations thereunder, regardless of whether the employer enters into a contract with the QHMO as to the specific terms and conditions of coverage, and without regard to the terms of any such contract.

[Preamble to Final Reg, 29 CFR Pts 2520, and 2560, 46 Fed Reg 5882, Jan 21, 1981] A district court recently found an HMO offered by an employer to its employees to be an ERISA plan. [Dutch v Travelers Health Network of Louisiana, Inc, 16 EBC (BNA) 2310 (ED La 1993)] Additionally, several of the malpractice cases discussed in Q 5:58 appear to assume that the HMO is an ERISA plan.

Of course, if the federally qualified HMO is voluntarily offered by the employer as the only health plan option, the HMO would be considered to be the ERISA plan rather than merely an option under a preexisting ERISA plan.

In either event, the federally qualified HMO will need to satisfy the various ERISA section 609 requirements. (See Q 2:18.)

Q 5:50   Is an employer required to file a separate Form 5500 Annual Report for each HMO it offers with the Internal Revenue Service (IRS)?

No. If the federally qualified HMO is offered as an alternative to the employer's medical plan, the DOL has taken the position that an HMO is a benefit under the employer's medical package rather than a separate ERISA Title I plan. In such case, the employer must only include a separate Schedule A for each HMO. [DOL Reg §§ 2520.104-44(b)(1)(ii), 2520.104-44(e)] Of course, if the HMO is the only medical plan made available to employees in that particular geographic area, then the HMO would constitute an ERISA Title I plan and a separate Form 5500 Annual Report would be required.

Note that the special less-than-100-participant exemption from the Form 5500 filing requirement contained in DOL Regulation Section 2520.104-20 applies to the entire medical package, not to each HMO option individually. Accordingly, it is useful only for employers with very small medical plans.

Q 5:51   Is an employer required to produce an ERISA summary plan description (SPD) for each federally qualified HMO that it offers?

No, the employer does not have to produce an SPD for each federally qualified HMO that it makes available to its employees provided that it includes certain information in its medical plan SPDs regarding the availability of HMOs. The exact information that must be included to qualify for this exclusion is discussed in Question 2:119. Note that no similar exclusion from ERISA's SPD requirements is available for HMOs that are state-certified only.

Q 5:52   Can a plan sponsor be liable for a breach of fiduciary duty because it makes membership in a federally qualified HMO available?

DOL regulations and advisory opinion letters have not addressed this particular issue.

In 1978, when acceptance of HMOs by employers was critical to HMOs' financial survival, the DOL's administrator of pension and welfare benefit programs stated in a DOL news release that he did not believe a plan sponsor could be held liable for a breach of ERISA fiduciary duty merely because it made membership in a federally qualified HMO available as a benefit under the plan. He noted that HMOs can receive federal qualification only if the Department of Health, Education and Welfare (now the Department of Health and Human Services) is satisfied that the HMO will be operated in accordance with the federal HMO Act's provisions concerning fiscal soundness, nature of services, and other matters. [DOL News Rel USDL 78-188 (Mar 10, 1978), CCH Pension Plan Guide Transfer Binder 1975-1979, § 22,880]

However, others now may take the view that, at least where an employer has a choice of HMOs, the selection of an HMO should be based on reasonable investigation and comparison. Arguably, the ERISA fiduciary duties that apply to the selection of insurance carriers and service providers to the plan apply with equal force to the selection of HMOs, since HMOs can be characterized as both insurers and service providers. A thornier question is presented when only one federally qualified HMO is available in a particular geographic area, and that HMO validly mandates the employer but is perceived as unacceptable for some reason. The interplay between ERISA duties of prudence and the HMO Act's mandate have yet to be addressed in the case law, and neither of these two federal laws preempts the other.

Q 5:53   Does the employer have a duty to inquire into the accuracy of a federally qualified HMO's descriptive materials or into the HMO's operations?

In a 1978 news release, DOL stated that "[g]enerally, an employer would be justified under ERISA in offering a qualified HMO without making independent investigation into these matters and in assuming that the descriptive material furnished by a [federally] qualified HMO is adequate." [DOL News Rel USDL 78-188 (Mar 10, 1978), CCH Pension Plan Guide Transfer Binder 1975-1979, ¶ 22,880]

However, ERISA's fiduciary responsibility provisions suggest that a greater degree of employer involvement may be required. With regard to the HMO's descriptive materials, the HMO regulations specifically grant the employer the right to review and revise HMO materials prior to their distribution to employees (see Q 5:25). Although the HMO regulations permit an employer to correct only factual errors and misleading statements unless the HMO specifically allows further changes or further changes are required by law, this review, at the very least, should be performed. With regard to the HMO's operations, some hold the view that a degree of inquiry is necessary to fulfill the employer's ERISA duties of prudence in the selection of health care insurers and service providers.

Q 5:54   Does an employer have ERISA fiduciary responsibility for a federally qualified HMO's internal business and financial affairs?

The DOL has never issued a regulation or formal advisory opinion letter on this matter. The 1978 DOL news release on HMOs addressed this issue, stating that making membership in a federally qualified HMO available to employees "would not ordinarily result in the management of the HMO's assets being subject to the fiduciary responsibility provisions of ERISA." [DOL News Rel USDL 78-188 (Mar 10, 1978), CCH Pension Plan Guide Transfer Binder 1975-1979, § 22,880] However, some may take the position that the employer nonetheless must investigate the federally qualified HMO's internal business and financial affairs to some extent (to precisely what extent remains a subject of debate) in order to meet its ERISA burden of prudent selection of a service provider.

Q 5:55   Are employee contributions toward HMO coverage considered to be ERISA plan assets which must be held in trust?

Yes, employee contributions toward HMO coverage are considered to be plan assets. However, the DOL currently has suspended enforcement of the trust requirement with respect to HMOs (see Questions 2:68–2:72).

Q 5:56   Do these special ERISA rules apply to HMOs that are only state certified?

No, they do not. The limited exemptions from ERISA SPD and claims procedure requirements do not apply to HMOs that are only state-certified. The DOL's rationale was that it was unable to verify whether the various state laws regulating nonqualified HMOs would necessarily provide sufficient protection to participants to warrant relief from the requirements of ERISA. However, the limited exemptions for small plans and unfunded plans discussed in Chapter 2 might apply. Also, the DOL's press release concerning ERISA fiduciary liability (see Q 5:50) addressed only federally qualified HMOs. [Preamble to Final Reg, 29 CFR Pts 2520, 2560, 46 Fed Reg 5882, Jan 21, 1981]

Q 5:57 Does ERISA preempt state mandatory HMO laws?

Yes, arguably it does. Since an HMO is generally regarded as akin to an insurance plan, ERISA will not preempt state HMO laws if they regulate practices that constitute the business of insurance. However, for a state insurance law to be saved from ERISA preemption, the practice must satisfy a three-part test:

1. It must have the effect of transferring or spreading risk;
2. It must be an integral part of the policy relationship between the insurer and the insured; and
3. It must be limited to entities in the insurance industry.

[Metropolitan Life Ins Co v Massachusetts, 471 US 724 (1985)]

However, a state law that attempts to require employers to offer state-certified HMOs arguably would fail this three-part test because it regulates the employer-employee relationship.

Liability for Managed Care

Q 5:58 Could an employer be liable for health care decisions made by the HMO or for health care provided or arranged for by the HMO?

This is a developing area of the law. Physicians have traditionally been treated as independent contractors, thereby insulating other entities from liability under a master-servant theory. However, HMOs select a panel of primary and referral health care providers, engage in utilization and quality review, and may exercise oversight to such a degree as to alter the traditional legal relationship. Even if the HMO does not exercise the requisite control, it nonetheless functions as an intermediary in the sense that it puts members (including the employer's employees) into contact with a preselected group of health care providers. Courts have wrestled with the implications of managed care arrangements such as HMOs, and in egregious cases have started to use various legal theories to hold an HMO liable for actions taken (or not taken) by health care providers within its system.

A recent U.S. district court case held that ERISA does not preempt the medical malpractice claim concerning care given (or not given) to a member because it does not depend upon contractual entitlement to benefits. In that case, a member of the HMO who had been receiving drug and alcohol rehabilitation on an outpatient basis was admitted as an inpatient for 15 days by his primary care physician at the HMO. He was then discharged despite his physician's and/or therapist's recommendation that he not be discharged at that time. It is claimed that the HMO would neither approve treatment nor accept payment from the member's family for additional treatment. Two weeks after he was discharged, the member was struck and killed by a train as he attempted to cross railroad tracks while intoxicated. The court held that the medical malpractice claim involves a separate issue of whether the HMO is liable, on an "ostensible agency" theory, for care arranged for by it. [Kohn v Delaware Valley HMO Inc, 14 EBC 2336 (ED Pa 1991), denied on rehearing, 14 EBC 2597 (ED Pa 1992]

HMOs also could be held liable for the actions of health care providers under a negligent selection theory. In another recent case, an HMO's credentialing process for its referral specialists consisted of determining only if the physician was licensed to practice medicine, that he or she had admitting privileges to hospitals and could dispense narcotics. The HMO did not conduct a personal interview, check references, or inquire as to the physician's standing in the medical community. This process failed to uncover that, as of the date hired, one of the referral specialists was the object of a number of medical malpractice suits, four of which had been concluded in favor of the plaintiff patients. The court indicated that, since HMO members were limited in their choice of referral specialists, the inclusion of an unqualified or incompetent physician would pose an foreseeable risk of harm to the HMO's members. The HMO thus owed a duty to its members to investigate the competence of prospective HMO providers. The court nonetheless ruled in the HMO's favor in this case due to a special state law that shielded the HMO from liability. [Harrell v Total Health Care Inc, no WD 39809, slip op (Mo Ct App W Dist, Apr 25, 1989), *aff'd,* 781 SW 2d 58 (Mo 1989)]

These and other health law case developments (discussed in Chapter 3) point inevitably to the next concern: whether an employer that offers such a program, which provides care directly to employees rather than reimbursing care obtained independently by employees, could be liable for the HMO's actions, and thus liable for alleged medical malpractice. Even though the employer may be offering the HMO under compulsion of law, the employer may nonetheless be viewed as being responsible for putting the employee into contact with the health care providers in the HMO's system.

Note. Under ERISA, the line of liability may already be in place, since the plan administrator's ERISA fiduciary duties extend to the selection and monitoring of service providers. How much care must go into the selection of managed care organizations such as HMOs has been a subject of considerable discussion among practitioners, who differ on whether an employer must engage in an in-depth investigation of the operations of an HMO before offering it to employees. This is due in part to the legal requirement, under the federal HMO Act, that a validly mandated employer must include the HMO in its employee benefits package whether it wants to or not and in part to the fact that the HMO already bears the imprimatur of the federal and state qualification/licensing process (whatever the thoroughness of that process may be).

Planning Pointer. Since employers typically permit employees to switch in or out of an HMO option once a year, the employee generally will be required to remain a member of the HMO for at least a year. During that time, the member will be limited to the HMO's facilities and authorized providers and referral providers except to the extent the HMO's benefit package permits the member to obtain care from nonaffiliated health care providers. To the extent that the HMO member does not want to bear the cost of obtaining care "outside the system," the member must stay within the system. Regardless of whether the employer conducts an in-depth quality and/or financial review prior to offering the

HMO, it should take steps to avoid possible liability for the actions that HMOs, or their referral providers, take during the period the employer offers such HMOs as an option in its benefit package. The employer should try to obtain, in advance of any offering of the HMO to its employees, contractual protection against liability for the care that the HMO provides or arranges as well as its decisions not to provide or arrange for care or services in any given situation.

Chapter 6

COBRA Requirements for Continuation of Coverage under Group Health Plans

The Consolidated Omnibus Budget Reconciliation Act of 1985 (COBRA) imposes a duty on employers to provide continuation of group health coverage to employees, spouses, and dependents under certain circumstances. This chapter explains the purpose of COBRA continuation as well as the rights and obligations of employers and employees under the Act.

Overview

Q 6:1 What is the purpose of the COBRA continuation of coverage rules?

The COBRA continuation of coverage rules are intended to provide access to affordable health insurance when an employee loses a job, is laid off, or retires, or when a person receiving health coverage under a spouse's plan divorces or is widowed. Because there is a real risk that the employee or spouse will be left without access to affordable health insurance in these situations, Congress acted in 1985 to reduce this risk. A portion of the COBRA statute requires employers to provide continuation coverage at group rates to employees, their spouses, and their dependents. The employer must permit "qualified beneficiaries" to elect to continue their health insurance under the plan for 18, 29, or 36 months, depending on the "qualifying event" that entitles the person to coverage. The employees may be required to pay premiums for the continuation coverage, but the employer generally is not permitted to charge more than 100 percent of the employer's own cost for the coverage plus a 2 percent administrative service charge. Employers must be careful to observe the COBRA continuation of coverage provisions: There are strict and far-reaching sanctions for violations.

Q 6:2 Where can the COBRA continuation of coverage requirements be found?

Virtually identical COBRA continuation coverage provisions are included in:

- Code Section 4980B of the Internal Revenue Code, 26 USC 4980B (formally, these provisions were in Code Section 162(k), 26 USC Section 162(k)

- Sections 601 through 608 of the Employee Retirement Income Security Act of 1974 (ERISA), 29 USC Sections 1161 through 1168

- Section 2201 through 2209 of the Public Health Service Act (PHSA), 42 USC Sections 300bb-1 through 300bb-8

The proposed Treasury regulations issued on June 15,1987, refer to Former Code Section 162(k) and are presently codified as Proposed Treasury Regulations Section 1.162-26.

Q 6:3   When must an employer provide the option of continuing group health plan coverage?

The COBRA continuation of coverage rules mandate that individuals have the option of continuing coverage whenever all three of the following elements are present:

1. The employer is not exempt under COBRA and maintains or contributes to a group health plan (including a self-insured plan) to provide health care (directly or indirectly) to the employer's employees, former employees or the families of such employees or former employees (see Q 6:4–6:24);
2. The individual is a qualified beneficiary (see Q 6:24–6:32, 6:58); and
3. A qualifying event occurs that causes the qualified beneficiary to lose coverage under the group health plan (see Q 6:42–6:59).

[IRC §§ 4980B(f),4980B(g)(2), 5000(b)(1); ERISA § 601(a); PHSA § 2101(a); Prop Treas Reg § 1.162-26, Q&A 18(e)]

Covered Plans

Q 6:4   What is a "group health plan" for COBRA continuation of coverage purposes?

For COBRA continuation of coverage purposes, a group health plan is any plan (including a self-insured plan) maintained or contributed to by an employer or employee organization (see Q 6:5) that provides "medical care" as defined in Code Section 213(d) (see Q 6:6) to at least two or more employees, former employees, the employer, other associated or formerly associated with the employer in a business relationship, or their families. In addition, one or more individual insurance policies in any arrangement that involves the provision of medical care to two or more employees is also a group health plan for this purpose. [IRC § 4980B(g)(2); IRC § 5000(b)(1) as amended by OBRA '93 Section 13561; Prop Treas Reg § 1.162-26, Q&A 7(a)] (Note: For COBRA's definition of "plan," see Qs 6:14 through 6:22.)

Q 6:5 What is a plan that is "maintained or contributed to by an employer" for COBRA purposes?

The proposed COBRA regulations use a "but for" test. They state that a plan is maintained by an employer if the employee would not have been able to receive coverage at the same cost if the employee were not employed by the employer. Therefore, even if the employee pays the entire cost of plan coverage, the employer will be obligated to follow COBRA's continuation coverage rules as long as the employee receives a favorable rate because he or she is employed by the employer. [Prop Treas Reg § 1.162-26, Q&A 7(a)]

However, proposed regulations do not treat a union-only plan as maintained by an employer if the plan is maintained by the union, the employer does not contribute, and the employer is not involved in administering the plan (for example, by providing dues checkoff). [Prop Reg § 1.162-26, Q& A 7(a)]

Note that, although ERISA includes union-only plans to which the employer does not contribute as ERISA-covered welfare benefit plans (see Q 2:1), ERISA uses the separate COBRA definition of "group health plan" for purposes of its continuation of group health plan requirements contained in ERISA Sections 601 through 608.

Q 6:6 What is "medical care"?

A COBRA group health plan provides "medical care" within the meaning of Code Section 213(d). Code Section 213(d) defines medical care to include "the diagnosis, cure, mitigation, treatment, or prevention of disease" and "any other undertaking for the purpose of affecting any structure or function of the body"; transportation "primarily for and essential to" medical care is also included in the Code definition. [IRC §§ 4980B(g)(2), 5000(b)(1); Prop Treas Reg § 1.162-26, Q&A 7(a)]

However, the proposed COBRA regulations exclude programs that further general good health but do not relieve or alleviate health or medical problems and are generally accessible to, and used by, employees, whatever their state of health. For example, a fitness program or swimming pool used generally by employees would not qualify as a program of health care. [Prop Reg § 1.162-26, Q& A 7(c)]

First-aid treatment available only to current employees, at an on-site facility, during the employees' working hours is not considered medical care if the employees are not charged for the treatment and the care is limited to illness and injury occurring during working hours. [Prop Treas Reg § 1.162-26, Q&A 7(e)]

Employer-maintained drug and alcohol treatment programs are considered to be medical care. [Prop Treas Reg § 1.162-26, Q&A 7(c)]

For taxable years after 1990, "medical care" under Code Section 213 does not include cosmetic surgery or similar procedures, unless the surgery or procedure is necessary to ameliorate a deformity arising from, or directly related to, congenital abnormality, personal injury resulting from an accident or trauma, or disfiguring disease. The term "cosmetic surgery" means any procedure that is directed at improving the patient's appearance and does not meaningfully promote the proper function of the body or prevent or treat illness or disease. [IRC § 213(d)(9), added by OBRA '90 § 11342(a)]

> **Planning Pointer.** Most employer group health plans do not provide coverage for cosmetic procedures. However, for those plans that do provide such coverage, the 1990 law changes would excuse them from offering continuation benefits for cosmetic surgery or similar procedures excluded from coverage under Code Section 213.

Q 6:7 Is a medical plan of a government entity considered to be a group health plan for COBRA purposes?

The definition of group health plan used for COBRA purposes under the Code specifically excludes a plan of the federal government or other governmental entity. [IRC § 5000(d)] However, parallel provisions of the PHSA apply COBRA continuation requirements generally to state and local government employers that receive funding under that Act. [PHSA § 2201 et seq]

Q 6:8   Are self-insured plans subject to COBRA?

Yes, group health plans are not exempt from COBRA solely by reason of being self-insured. [IRC §§ 4080B(g)(2), 5000(b)(1)]

Q 6:9   Is a plan maintained by a voluntary employees' beneficiary association (VEBA) subject to COBRA?

Yes, group health plans maintained by VEBAs organized in whole or in part to maintain such a plan are subject to COBRA. [ERISA §§ 607(1), 607(3)(1)]

Q 6:10   Are cafeteria plan flexible spending arrangements (FSAs) subject to COBRA?

Yes, medical FSAs under cafeteria plans are subject to COBRA. [Prop Treas Reg §§ 1.125-2, Q&A 7(b)(3), and 1.162-26, Q&A 7(a)] Exactly how this is to be accomplished is not clear, since the theories underlying the COBRA continuation of coverage regulations and the cafeteria plan regulations do not mesh well. The IRS has not yet provided specific guidance on this issue.

Q 6:11   Are employee assistance programs (EAPs) subject to COBRA?

Yes, an EAP apparently is subject to COBRA if it provides medical care such as coverage of psychiatric or mental health visits and not merely information and referrals to professional counselors. The IRS has not issued specific guidance on EAPs and COBRA continuation of group health plan requirements. (See Question 6:6 for the definition of medical care used for COBRA purposes and Questions 3:108 through 3:115 for a further discussion of EAPs.)

Q 6:12   Are long-term care plans subject to COBRA?

Yes, a long-term care plan (which typically covers nursing home care and other services not covered, or not very generously covered, by Medicare) apparently will be subject to COBRA if it covers Section

213 medical care. The IRS has not issued specific guidance on COBRA and long-term care plans (see Chapter 9).

Q 6:13   Are plans maintained solely for corporate directors, agents, independent contractors, and the self-employed subject to COBRA?

For plan years beginning on or after January 1, 1990, a plan maintained solely for corporate directors, agents, independent contractors, and self-employed individuals is subject to the COBRA continuation of coverage rules. The definition of "covered employee," contained in Code Section 4980B, was changed to include any individual who is, or was, provided coverage under a group health plan by virtue of the performance of services by the individual for one or more persons maintaining the plan, including a self-employed individual under Code Section 401(c)(1). [IRC § 4980B(f)(7)]

Definition of "Plan" for COBRA Purposes

Q 6:14   Is a medical plan ever considered to be two or more separate group health plans, not a single plan, for COBRA purposes?

Yes, the proposed COBRA regulations contain a scheme for "dis-aggregating," or breaking down, plans in order to break arrangements into their constituent group health plans. The smaller units are then treated as separate plans for COBRA compliance purposes, even if the aggregate has traditionally been referred to as a single plan, or is reported on Form 5500 as a single plan.

> **Example.** A multiple employer welfare arrangement (MEWA) with four participating employers provides both a high-option and a low-option benefit schedule. Under the proposed COBRA regulations, the MEWA contains eight plans: a low-option and a high-option plan for each of the four employers.

[Prop Treas Reg § 1.162-26, Q&A 10]

Q 6:15   What is the significance of the number of plans?

The number of group health plans maintained by an employer is significant for several determinations, including:

- Cost of COBRA continuation coverage; and
- Beneficiaries' right to elect separate coverage.

All references to a "group health plan" in the proposed COBRA regulations mean a separate group health plan as determined under the disaggregation rules. [Prop Treas Reg § 1.162-26, Q&A 10]

Q 6:16   How is the number of COBRA plans calculated?

The disaggregation rules are applied in the following order, and in the way that creates the smallest number of plans:

1. "Different benefit package or option rule" (see Q 6:17);
2. "Choice of benefit combination rule" (see Q 6:20);
3. MEWA status (see Q 6:25);
4. If there is a MEWA, which participating employers are considered a single employer (see Q 6:30);
5. "Identical insurance contract rule" (see Q 6:20);
6. Determination of segregated assets under self-funded plans (see Q 6:21); and
7. Determination of collectively bargained and noncollectively bargained plans (see Q 6:22).

[Prop Treas Reg § 1.162-26, Q&A 10]

Q 6:17   Are different benefit packages treated as separate plans?

Yes, each benefit package or option (for example, a choice of deductibles or different catastrophic limits) offered under an arrangement must be treated as a separate group health plan.

Example 1. An employer offers two types of coverage. They are identical except that one has a $250 deductible, and the other a

$500 deductible. Each type of coverage is considered a different benefit package, and thus a separate group health plan.

Example 2. The coverages are identical except that the catastrophic limit is $1,000 for one coverage and $2,000 for the other; they, too, are treated as different benefit packages and separate group health plans.

[Prop Treas Reg § 1.162-26, Q&A 10(c)]

Q 6:18   Are there any benefit packages or options that do not create separate group health plans?

Yes, there are. Different classifications of coverage (for example, self-only or self-and-family coverage) are not treated as separate options and therefore do not require another level of disaggregation; nor will a deductible defined as a uniform percentage of compensation, say, 1 percent, create multiple group health plans. [Prop Treas Reg § 1.162-26, Q&A 10(c)]

Q 6:19   Are benefit combinations treated as separate group health plans?

Yes, they are. Availability of the benefit combinations determines what constitutes a separate benefit plan. For instance, an arrangement that would be considered a single plan except that employees can elect either medical coverage alone or medical plus dental coverage consists of two plans: a medical plan and a medical plus dental plan. If the employee can choose medical and/or dental coverage independently of each other, there are two separate plans for COBRA purposes, but they are a medical-only plan and a dental-only plan. [Prop Treas Reg § 1.162-26, Q&A 10(c), Example 4]

Q 6:20   Does coverage under separate insurance contracts with identical terms create separate group health plans?

Yes, it does. Under an insured arrangement, if two or more groups of employees are covered under separate contracts between an insurer or insurers and one or more participating employers, each separate contract is treated as a separate group health plan even if all contract terms are identical. [Prop Treas Reg § 1.162-26, Q&A 10(d)]

Q 6:21 When is a self-funded arrangement treated as two or more group health plans?

Each segregated portion of a self-funded arrangement is treated as a separate group health plan. A portion of the arrangement is segregated if benefits under any portion are payable only from the assets available under that portion, and assets available to pay benefits under one portion cannot be applied to any other portion. This rule is applied whether or not a trust is used, and whether or not stop-loss insurance or insurance for only a portion of the benefits is provided.

Example 1. An employer maintains an arrangement under which employees may obtain medical and dental coverage together on an all-or-nothing basis. The arrangement is funded through a trust. The trust's assets are segregated into two parts: one to pay only medical benefits, the other to pay only dental benefits. The segregated-assets rule requires the arrangement to be treated as two separate plans.

Example 2. The funding arrangements are the same as in Example 1, but employees can independently elect medical coverage, dental coverage, or both. As explained in Question 6:138, the arrangement is already treated as two separate plans (a medical-only and a dental-only plan), so the segregated-assets rule does not cause any further division.

Example 3. An employer maintains an arrangement that is a single plan in all respects except that the employee can choose between medical-only coverage and medical-plus-dental coverage. The arrangement is funded through a trust whose assets are segregated into two parts. One part is available to pay only medical benefits; the other to pay only dental benefits. Because the COBRA disaggregation rules are applied in a specified order to create the smallest number of plans, the arrangement must first be broken down into two separate plans (medical and medical plus dental). Then the segregated-assets rule requires the second plan to be broken down further into a medical plan and a dental plan, because the assets under each portion are unavailable to pay benefits under the other portion. In other words, there are three plans in the arrangement: two separate medical plans and a dental plan.

[Prop Treas Reg § 1.2-26, Q&A 10(f)]

Q 6:22 What is a collectively bargained plan?

The proposed COBRA regulations give a nontraditional definition of this term. The plan must be maintained under a collective bargaining agreement between or among one or more unions and one or more employers. If both union and nonunion employees or former employees and their families are covered, the employer is considered to have two separate plans: one that is collectively bargained and one that is not. [Prop Treas Reg § 1.162-26, Q&A 12]

Covered Employers

Q 6:23 Are all employers subject to COBRA?

Although most employers are obligated to follow COBRA's rules if they provide group health plans, certain employers are exempt:

- Federal, state, and local governments (although the PHSA imposes similar Cobra requirements for state and local governments receiving funds under that Act); and

- Churches, conventions and associations of churches, and certain church-controlled organizations.

There is also an exemption for small employers (see Qs 6:26–6:32). [IRC § 4980B(d); ERISA § 601(a); § 2101(b)(2)]

Q 6:24 Does COBRA cover multiple employer welfare arrangements (MEWAs)?

Yes, it does. A plan that is maintained by several employers and that meets the ERISA Section 3(40) definition of a MEWA is generally considered to be a separate group health plan with respect to each employer maintaining the arrangement. [Prop Treas Reg § 1.162-26, Q&A 10(d)]

Q 6:25   Are any employers too small to be subject to COBRA?

Yes, some are. Exempt employers are those that, in the year preceding the year for which exemption is sought, had fewer than 20 employees on a "typical business day" (see Q 6:26). [IRC § 4980B(d)(1); ERISA § 601(b); PHSA § 2201(b)(1)]

Q 6:26   How is the typical-business-day standard satisfied?

The typical-business-day standard is satisfied if, and only if, the employer had fewer than 20 employees (as defined in Question 6:18) on at least 50 percent of its working days during the preceding calendar year. [Prop Treas Reg § 1.162-26, Q&A 9(b)] For this purpose, the entire 12-month period must be considered.

Q 6:27   Which individuals are counted as "employees" in deciding whether an employer is too small for its group health plans to be subject to COBRA?

Both part-time and full-time employees are counted. Additionally, at least one court has held that temporary employees should also be counted. [Martinez, 13 EBC (BNA) 1348 (D Colo 1991)] Persons defined as self-employed under Code Section 401(c)(1), such as partners and sole proprietors who provide services to the business, are also counted. Agents and independent contractors (and their employees, agents, and independent contractors) and corporate directors are also counted if they are eligible to participate in an employer-maintained group health plan. [Prop Treas Reg § 1.162-26, Q&A 9(c)] Nonresident aliens with no U.S. source income apparently also must be counted for the purposes of the small-employer exemption.

It is important to note that once it is determined that the plan is subject to COBRA, the statute uses a separate definition of "covered employees" for purposes of determining who is entitled to COBRA rights under such a plan (see Q 6:36).

Q 6:28   Are entities under common control aggregated to determine eligibility for the small-employer exemption?

Yes, they are. For purposes of the minimum-size requirement, the employer and all other entities under common control with it are considered to be a single employer. The controlled-group rules of Code Section 414 apply for this purpose. [IRC § 414(t)] However, if the group health plan is part of a MEWA as defined in Section 3(40) of ERISA, then the slightly different controlled-group rules of Section 3(40) of ERISA are used to determine whether two or more employers are treated as a single employer for purposes of COBRA's minimum-size requirement. [Prop Treas Reg § 1.162-26, Q&A 9(d); see IRC § 414(t) for the common-control rules]

Q 6:29   Does the small-employer plan exemption apply to any of a MEWA's sponsoring employers?

The small-employer plan exemption is available to any MEWA sponsors that normally employed fewer than 20 employees during the preceding calendar year. Only the larger employers participating in the MEWA are required to comply with COBRA.

The rules of ERISA Section 3(40)(B), concerning trades or businesses under common control, are used to determine whether two or more employers are treated as a single employer in the MEWA.

Example 1. Employers A, B, and C maintain a MEWA. C had 13 employees during the preceding calendar year. C is exempt from COBRA.

Example 2. Assume the same facts as in Example 1. A, which does not qualify for the small-employer exemptions, violates COBRA. Only A will be subject to sanctions under COBRA; B and C will not be affected.

Example 3. Assume the same facts as in Example 1, except that C acquires two wholly owned subsidiaries, D and E. D and E had more than 20 employees each during the preceding calendar year. Under the small-employer rule, C, D, and E constitute a single employer that participates in the MEWA and that, because of its size, is immediately subject to COBRA's requirements (see Q 6:24). If E violates COBRA, C and D, the other employers in its group of

trades or businesses, will be subject to COBRA sanctions. However, E's violation will not affect A and B, because each of them
is treated as a separate employer maintaining a separate group
health plan.

[Prop Treas Reg § 1.162-26, Q&A 10(b), Examples 2, 3]

Q 6:30   How does the small-employer exemption apply to multiemployer plans?

A multiemployer plan, which is a plan maintained by at least two
unrelated employers (that is, not in the same controlled group)
pursuant to one or more collective bargaining agreements, is treated
as a single group health plan for COBRA purposes. [ERISA 3(37(A);
Prop Treas Reg § 1.162-26, Q&As 9(d), 12(a)] Accordingly, for the
small-employer exemption to apply, every participating employer
(determined under the controlled-group rules) must have fewer than
20 employees on a typical working day.

Q 6:31   What happens if an employer in an exempt small-employer plan increases its workforce?

The answer depends upon the type of plan which is being affected
by the workforce increse.

Single-employer plan: A "workforce increase" is caused by an
increase in the number of employees of a single employer, through
hiring or through the addition of another employer to the *same*
controlled group. The plan will eventually become subject to COBRA,
but not immediately. The plan becomes subject to COBRA on the
following January 1: the first day of the calendar year immediately
following the calendar year in which the employer's workforce
exceeded 20 employees on an average day. This rule applies even if
the plan year is not a calendar year. [Prop. Treas. Reg. § 1.162-26,
Q&A 9(d)] In contrast, if an *unrelated* employer were to be added to
a single-employer plan, no workforce increase occurs; instead, a
MEWA would be created.

MEWA: If the workforce of an exempt employer participating in a
MEWA increases (either due to hiring more employees or due to
adding another employer to the *same* controlled group) and, as a

consequence, that employer loses the small-employer exemption, the effect on the small-employer exemption is the same as for a single-employer plan. That participating employer's small-employer exemption ceases effective as of the first day of the calendar year next following the calendar year in which the 20-employee threshold is met. No other employers participating in the MEWA are affected. [Prop Treas Reg § 1.162-26, Q&As 9(d), 10(d)]

Multiemployer Plan. If any employer participating in the multiemployer plan exceeds the 20-employee threshold mid-year due to a workforce increase (hiring more employees or adding another employer within the same controlled group), then all participating employers lose the exemption effective as of January 1 of the next calendar year. However, the proposed COBRA regulations provide a special "safety valve" for multiemployer plans. The multiemployer plan can maintain its exemption from COBRA continuation of coverage rules if all employers crossing the 20-employee threshold cease to maintain the plan before February 1 following the January 1 on which the plan would become subject to COBRA. In other words, multiemployer plans have a month after the close of the plan year to review the workforce records of each sponsoring employer, "weed out" the larger employers, and thereby maintain the plan's exempt status. But if the employers over the 20-employee threshold do not drop out of the plan before the February 1 deadline, the entire multiemployer plan becomes subject to the COBRA continuation of coverage requirements, retroactive to January 1 of that year. [Prop Treas Reg § 1.162-26, Q&A 9(d)] In contrast, if a new, *unrelated* employer with 20 or more employees were to join the multiemployer plan, the entire plan (and all participating employers) become subject to COBRA immediately and the "safety valve" rule does not apply. [Prop Treas Reg § 1.162-26, Q&A 9(d)]

Q 6:32   What happens if an employer covered by COBRA decreases its workforce below 20 employees?

In the year of the decrease, the COBRA requirements continue to apply to qualifying events occurring in that year. If the employer continues to satisfy the small-employer exemption requirements during the next calendar year, the employer is not subject to COBRA with respect to qualifying events occurring in that year. However, the employer must continue to meet its COBRA responsibilities to individuals who became qualified beneficiaries (1) in the year the employer's workforce dropped below 20 and (2) in prior calendar years. [IRC § 4980B(d)(1), as amended by OBRA § 11702(f)]

MEWAs. If a workforce decrease experienced by an employer participating in a MEWA causes it to qualify for the small-employer exemption during the next calendar year, the other employers participating in the MEWA are unaffected. [Prop. Treas. Reg. § 1.162-26, Q&A 10(d)]

Multiemployer Plans. If a multiemployer plan is subject to COBRA, the decrease in the size of a participating employer below the 20-employee threshold does not cause either that employer or the multiemployer plan to become exempt from COBRA; *all* participating employers (determined under the controlled-group rules) must individually satisfy the small-employer exemption in order for the multiemployer plan (and all participating employers) to be exempt from the COBRA continuation of coverage rules. [Prop Treas Reg § 1 162-26, Q&A 9(d)]

Q 6:33   What special COBRA requirements apply if the employer goes bankrupt?

If an employer files for protection under Title 11 of the United States Code, a broad group of retirees, their spouses or surviving spouses, and their dependents become qualified beneficiaries. The group is unusually broad because the statute picks up individuals whose coverage is lost or diminished because of a bankruptcy proceeding within one year before or after the qualifying event, and because lifetime COBRA continuation coverage is extended to retirees and those who were surviving spouses at the time they became qualified beneficiaries. (See Qs 6:35 and 6:48.)

Q 6:34   When a merger or acquisition occurs, which employer must provide COBRA continuation coverage?

In a typical stock-based transaction, the acquiror is legally required to assume all liabilities of the target, including the responsibility for providing COBRA continuation coverage to qualified beneficiaries who went through a qualifying event before the date of the merger or acquisition. The proposed COBRA regulations adopt this approach.

In contrast, although the parties to a sale of assets normally negotiate the allocation of liabilities to be assumed by the acquiror or retained by the seller, the proposed COBRA regulations specifically preclude the conventional treatment of asset sales. The "successor employer" (the buyer or acquiring employer) is primarily responsible for providing COBRA continuation coverage. Significantly, this means that the buyer or acquiring employer is also required to cure COBRA violations in existence on the date of the merger or acquisition. [Prop Treas Reg § 1.162-26, Q&A 5]

> **Planning Pointer.** COBRA's divergence from standard corporate practice makes the due diligence review before consummation of an acquisition even more important.

Qualified Beneficiaries

Q 6:35   Who is a "qualified beneficiary"?

Four classes of individuals are defined as qualified beneficiaries, based on their status on the day before the qualifying event (see Question 6:42):

1. A person who is a covered employee under a group health plan;
2. A covered employee's covered spouse;
3. A covered employee's covered dependent child; and
4. In bankruptcy situations, certain retirees and their spouses (including widows and widowers) and dependents.

[IRC § 4980B(g); ERISA § 607; PA § 2208; Prop Treas Reg § 1.162-26, Q&A 15(a)]

Q 6:36   Who is a "covered employee"?

A "covered employee" is any individual who has, or had, coverage under a group health plan subject to COBRA, by reason of the performance of service by the individual for one or more persons maintaining the plan. This broad definition also includes individuals such as independent contractors and partners (see Q 6:37). Mere eligibility for coverage, without actual coverage, does not make a person a covered employee. Note that retirees and former employees receiving group health coverage because of their previous employment are considered covered employees. [IRC § 4980B(f)(7); ERISA § 607(2); PH S Act § 2208(2); Prop Treas Reg § 1.162-26, Q&A 16(a)]

Q 6:37   Can a self-employed individual be a covered employee?

Yes, for plan years beginning on or after January 1, 1990, a self-employed individual who actually participates in a group health plan subject to COBRA is a covered employee. This rule applies to individuals such as partners and sole proprietors, who are self-employed under the definition of Code Section 401(c)(1); it also applies to agents, independent contractors, and corporate directors. [IRC § 4980B(f)(7); ERISA § 607(2); P § 2208(2); Prop Treas Reg § 1.162-26, Q&A 16(b), which has not been revised to reflect the 1990 amendment to COBRA's definition of "covered employee"]

Q 6:38   Are there special rules for nonresident aliens?

Yes, there are. A person whose status as a covered employee is attributable to a period of time in which he or she was a nonresident alien without U.S.-source income cannot become a qualified beneficiary. Such a person's spouse and dependents cannot become qualified beneficiaries by reason of their relationship to the alien employee. [Prop Treas Reg § 1.162-26, Q&A 15(d)]

Note. Nonresident aliens without U.S.-source income are, however, apparently counted for purposes of applying COBRA's small-employer exemption, as discussed in Question 6:27, because the statute does not contain a similar exclusion for that purpose.

Q 6:39   What if the employee is entitled to Medicare?

If the employee is entitled to Medicare (rather than merely eligible for Medicare) on the day before a qualifying event, he or she cannot become a qualified beneficiary. An exception occurs if the bankruptcy rule applies see Q 6:24). [Prop Treas Reg § 1.162-26, Q&A 15]

Note. The continued validity of this rule with regard to individuals who become entitled to Medicare due to disability or due to end-stage renal disease has been placed in question due to the Equal Employment Opportunity Commissions's (EEOC) interim guidance issued under the Americans With Disabilities Act of 1990 (ADA), which generally provides that disability-based distinctions in group health plans may violate the ADA. [EEOC Interim Guidance on Application of ADA to Health Insurance, reprinted at 109 Daily Labor Rep E-1 (June 9, 1993)]

For a situation in which an employee who is a qualified beneficiary subsequently becomes entitled to Medicare, see Questions 6:92 and 6:93.

Q 6:40   If a qualified beneficiary subsequently acquires a new family member, does that new family member also become a qualified beneficiary?

No, only one measuring date is used to determine who is a qualified beneficiary: the day before the qualifying event. On that date, the class of qualified beneficiaries entitled to elect COBRA coverage is closed. If new spouses, newborn children, or adopted children join a qualified beneficiary's family after that day, they do not become qualified beneficiaries, even if they are subsequently enrolled in the plan. [Prop Treas Reg § 1.162-26, Q&As 15, 17(a)]

Q 6:41   Can a retiree be a qualified beneficiary?

Generally not. Although the definition of a covered employee to whom a qualifying event can occur specifically includes anyone whose group health plan coverage results from status as a former employee, a retired employee cannot lose coverge as a result of terminating employment or reducing hours of employment. Retirees can, however, lose coverage and become "qualified beneficiaries" as a result of a bankruptcy filing (see Qs 6:42, 6:48). [Prop Treas Reg § 1.162-26, Q&A 16]

Qualifying Events

Q 6:42   What is a qualifying event?

A qualifying event is any one of the following (but only if it results in a loss of group health plan coverage):

1. Termination of a covered employee for any reason other than gross misconduct;
2. Reduction in the number of hours a covered employee is employed;
3. Medicare entitlement for a covered employee; or
4. Commencement of a bankruptcy proceeding concerning an employer from whose employment the covered employee retired.

In addition, a qualifying event occurs with respect to the covered employee's spouse and dependents when coverage is lost because:

1. The covered employee dies;
2. A retiree or former employee whose group health plan coverage resulted wholly or partially from covered employment dies;
3. A spouse obtains a divorce or separation from the covered employee; or
4. A child of the covered employee ceases to fit the group health plan's definition of a dependent child.

[IRC § 4980B(f)(3); ERISA § 603; PA § 2203]

Q 6:43   Why are the qualifying-event provisions included in COBRA?

COBRA is intended to provide a "bridge" in coverage for a limited period of time, so the individual can get other group or individual health care coverage. For this reason, events that do not result in loss of group health plan coverage are not within the scope of COBRA. For example, if a plan covers spouses who are legally separated from employees covered by the plan, legal separation would not mean a loss of coverage; therefore, the employer sponsoring such a plan would not be required to offer continuation coverage to the estranged spouse of the employee.

Although it might seem that the purpose of COBRA is to protect the worker, in fact, there are only two situations in which an active covered employee can have the status of a qualified beneficiary under COBRA: termination, for reasons other than gross misconduct, and reduction of hours of employment. [Prop Treas Reg § 1.162-26, Q&A 15]

Q 6:44 Must group health plan coverage actually cease in order to be considered "lost" for COBRA purposes?

Group health plan coverage need not cease entirely in order for a COBRA qualifying event to occur. For COBRA purposes, a loss of coverage is considered to occur when the covered individual ceases to be covered under the same terms and conditions as were in effect immediately before the qualifying event. Thus, a "loss" would occur if benefits decrease or are cut back due to a qualifying event. For example, suppose that an employee goes from full-time to half-time employment and, as a result, the employee's health plan coverage is reduced by half. In that instance, a "loss" of coverage would occur due to a reduction in hours, so COBRA rights are triggered. [Prop Treas Reg § 1.162-26, Q&A 18(c)]

Q 6:45 Can a reduction in coverage be a qualifying event?

Yes, it can, as long as the covered employee, spouse, or dependent child is no longer covered under the terms and conditions in effect immediately before the qualifying event, *and the loss of coverage results from the occurrence of one of the specified events,* such as termination of employment. If an employer merely amends its group health plan to cut back coverage generally, but the cutback is not related to one of the specified COBRA events, a qualifying event does not occur. [Prop Treas Reg § 1.162-26, Q&A 16]

Q 6:46 What if the loss of coverage is not simultaneous with the event?

General Rule. Unless the plan provides otherwise, a qualifying event that results in a loss of group health plan coverage is deemed to occur when the event occurs, not when coverage is lost. For instance, if a terminated employee is entitled to a six-month extension of coverage (for whatever reason), the loss does not occur until the end of the six-month extension period. However, the date of an employee's termination will be treated as the date of the qualifying event, unless the plan provides otherwise. [Prop Treas Reg § 1.162-26, Q&A 18(c); Gaskell et al v The Harvard Cooperative Society, 93-1024 and 93-1102 (1st Cir, August 25, 1993).]

Special Plan Provision Rule. A group health plan may provide that the qualifying event occurs on the date coverage is actually lost, provided that the plan also provides that the notice period, described in Q 6:64, also begins on the date coverage is actually lost. [IRC § 4980B(f)(8); ERISA § 607(5)]

Q 6:47 What if an employer reduces coverage in anticipation of a qualifying event?

In nonbankruptcy situations, an elimination or reduction of coverage is disregarded in determining whether the qualifying event causes a loss of coverage. In other words, the "loss" of coverage is measured from the level of coverage in force before the employer's anticipatory cutback. [Prop Treas Reg § 1.162-26, Q&A 16]

The proposed COBRA regulations do not give any specific time period during which the cutback must occur in order to be treated as an anticipatory cutoff of benefits (see Q 6:86).

Planning Pointer. All the facts and circumstances must be assessed in deciding whether benefits were indeed cut back in anticipation of a qualified event. Presumably, the amount of time involved will be relevant. Note, however, that the proposed regulations are clear that the loss of coverage need not occur immediately after the qualifying event, as long as it occurs during the maximum period for continuation of COBRA coverage (see also Q 6:50).

Q 6:48   When is coverage "lost" in an employer bankruptcy?

In an employer bankruptcy, a "substantial elimination" of coverage of a qualified beneficiary, who is a retiree or a spouse or surviving spouse of a retiree or a dependent child of a retiree, that occurs within one year before or after the date the bankruptcy proceeding was begun is treated as a loss of coverage. In other words, COBRA's bankruptcy provisions pick up any substantial loss of coverage over a two-year period. [IRC § 4980B(f)(3); ERISA § 603(6)]

Substantial Elimination of Coverage. The proposed COBRA regulations do not cover the bankruptcy provisions of COBRA, so there is as yet no IRS guidance concerning what will qualify as a "substantial elimination" of coverage.

Q 6:49   Is the Federal Deposit Insurance Corporation (FDIC) or a bank that takes over the assets and employees of a failed bank obligated to continue COBRA coverage for the failed bank's employees?

In a decision by the U.S. Court of Appeals for the Tenth Circuit, the court considered the situation where a state bank failed and went into receivership and the FDIC was appointed receiver and liquidating agent. At the same time, the bank ceased operations and terminated its health plan. Another bank then purchased some of the failed bank's assets and assumed depositor liability. The purchasing bank also hired some of the failed bank's employees and operated a branch at the failed bank's location. The purchase agreement explicitly provided that the purchasing bank had no obligation under the failed bank's employee benefit plans. The court concluded that the failed bank ceased doing business when it went into receivership, and that neither the FDIC nor the purchasing bank was a successor employer required to provide COBRA continuation coverage to the employees of the failed bank. [Leiding v FDIC, No 90-5078 (10th Cir Aug 12, 1991)]

However, in December 1991, federal banking legislation was enacted which provides that the FDIC, in its capacity as a successor of a failed depository institution (whether acting directly or through a bridge bank) has the same obligation to provide COBRA continuation coverage as the failed institution would have had if it had not failed. The same requirement applies to any successor to the failed depository institution.

An entity is considered a successor to the failed depository institution during any period if:

1. The entity holds substantially all of the assets or liabilities of the failed insititution, and
2. The entity is any of the following:

   —The FDIC;

   —A bridge bank, or

   —An entity that acquired the assets or liabilities of the failed institution from the FDIC or a bridge bank.

The legislation applies to plan years beginning on or after the date of enactment (December 19, 1991), regardless of whether the qualifying event occurred before, on, or after the date of enactment. [Pub L 102-242, § 451, 102d Cong 2d Sess, 105 Stat 2382]

Note. The federal banking legislation did not contain conforming amendments to the COBRA provisions of ERISA and the Code. Presumably, at some point, conforming amendments will be enacted.

Q 6:50 Can a voluntary termination, such as quitting or abandoning a job, constitute a qualifying event?

Yes, it can, if it occurs while the plan is subject to COBRA and it results in a loss of group health plan coverage. Unless the employee was guilty of gross misconduct, it is irrelevant whether employment was terminated, or hours were reduced, voluntarily or involuntarily. [Prop Treas Reg § 1.2-26, Q&A 19]

Q 6:51 Is involuntary termination, for example, firing, a qualifying event?

Yes, it is (if it occurs while the plan is subject to COBRA and it results in a loss of group health plan coverage) unless the employee is guilty of gross misconduct. [IRC § 4980B(f)(3)(B)]

Q 6:52   What behavior qualifies as "gross misconduct" that would make a terminated employee ineligible for COBRA coverage?

Neither the statute nor the proposed COBRA regulations define the term "gross misconduct." Therefore, employers must make their own determinations about what constitutes gross misconduct. [Rev Proc 87-28, 1987-1 CB 770] A California case looked to the definition of gross misconduct contained in that state's unemployment insurance law (even though it was not required to) because of the similarity in purpose between the two laws. The court in that case found that a single incident of the employee's discussion of confidential information was not gross misconduct for purposes of determining the employee's entitlement to COBRA continuation of group health plan coverage. [Paris v F Korbel & Bros Inc, 751 F Supp 834 2489 (ND Cal 1990)] However, this case probably would have reached the opposite conclusion had the single piece of confidential information been of vital importance to the employer's business, such as disclosure of a heavily guarded secret formula or recipe for the company's main product or of the code for the company's main vault, for instance. Other cases have upheld the employer's determination of gross misconduct where the behavior at issue involved mishandling of employer funds or stealing employer property. [Burke v American Stores Employee Benefit Plan, 1993 US Dist LEXIS 2614 NC Ill (Mar. 2, 1993) (stealing company property); Karby v Standard Products Co, 1992 WL 333931 (DSC 1992) (conversion of company property to private use and failure to disclose receipt of an interest-free loan from the employer's supplier); Avina v Texas Pig Stands, Inc, 1991 US Dist LEXIS 132957 (WD Tex 1991) (cash handling and invoice irregularities, failure to improve store performance)] In one case, a court found that embezzlement of company funds by the company's president constituted misconduct, but that he was nonetheless entitled to COBRA because his termination of employment was *voluntary* rather than due to such misconduct. In that case, the president been permitted to resign from the company. [Conery v Bath Associates, 803 F Supp 1388 (ND Ind 1992)]

Planning Pointer. Because the penalties for violating COBRA are so stringent (see Qs 6:128–6:141), employers are likely to restrict their claims of gross misconduct to the most egregious types of employee behavior.

Q 6:53　Is a strike or walkout a qualifying event?

If a strike or walkout that occurs while the plan is subject to COBRA results in a loss of group health plan coverage, it is a qualifying event. [Prop Treas Reg § 1.2-26, Q&A 19; 898 F 2d 887 (2d Cir 1990)]

Q 6:54　Is a layoff a qualifying event?

Yes, it is, if it occurs while the plan is subject to COBRA and it results in a loss of group health plan coverage. [Prop Treas Reg § 1.2-26, Q&A 19]

Q 6:55　Is a call to active duty in the armed forces a qualifying event?

Assuming that the employee is either terminated from employment or is placed on leave of absence or otherwise can be said to suffer a reduction in hours, a COBRA qualifying event will occur if, as a result, he or she loses group health plan coverage. [IRS News Rel 90-142 (Nov 21, 1990); IRS Notice 90-58, 1990-2 CB 345]

Q 6:56　When does termination of employment occur for individuals other than common-law employees?

Termination occurs, for COBRA purposes, with the termination of the relationship (for example, a corporate directorship) that gave rise to the individual's treatment as an employee for COBRA purposes (see Q 6:18). [Prop Treas Reg § 1.2-26, Q&A 18(b)]

Q 6:57　Can a qualifying event ever occur with regard to an employee's spouse or dependent even if the employee remains covered?

Yes, it can. For example, a new retiree's spouse receiving coverage without cost might lose coverage six months after the employee's retirement because the spouse elects not to pay a premium required to retain coverage; therefore, the employee's retirement is a qualifying event, and the retiree's spouse is a qualified beneficiary. The same rule would apply if coverage were lost because of a divorce. [Prop Treas Reg § 1.162-26, Q&A 18(e), Examples 2, 3]

Q 6:58 Can placing a disabled employee on inactive-employee status be a qualifying event?

Yes, it can be. However, even if there is a reduction in hours because of placement on inactive status, there will be a qualifying event only if there is also a "loss" of group health plan coverage within the maximum applicable COBRA continuation period. [Prop Treas Reg § 1.162-26, Q&A 18(b)]

Q 6:59 Can an event that occurs before a plan is subject to COBRA serve as a qualifying event?

No, it cannot. COBRA does not obligate group health plans to offer continuation coverage to individuals whose coverage is lost because of events that take place before the plan becomes subject to COBRA requirements. This is true even if the individual is entitled to an extension of plan coverage that lasts until a date after the plan becomes subject to COBRA. [Prop Treas Reg § 1.162-26, Q&A 18(d)] However, the proposed COBRA regulations do require that COBRA continuation coverage be extended to anyone who experiences, once the group health plan becomes subject to COBRA, what would otherwise be a "second qualifying event" if COBRA had been in effect at the time of the first event (see Q . 6:101). [Prop Treas Reg § 1.162-16, Q&A 42]

Notice to Participants

Q 6:60 Must the plan notify employees and spouses of the existence of COBRA continuation rights before a qualifying event occurs?

Yes, it must. The group health plan must notify all covered employees and spouses of their COBRA rights when the plan first comes under COBRA. When employees and spouses first become eligible to participate in a plan, the plan must give them written notice of their COBRA rights. [IRC § 4980B(f)(6); ERISA §§ 606(1), 606(3); PHS Act §§ 2206(1), 2208(c); ERISA Tech Rel 86-2]

Q 6:61   Must plan administrators use any particular language for the required notices?

No particular language is required. The Department of Labor (DOL) has published model notice language for these purposes, but the language must be updated in light of intervening amendments to COBRA. Although the DOL considers use of the model notice good-faith compliance with a reasonable interpretation of COBRA in the absence of regulations, using the model notice is not the only way to achieve good-faith compliance. Nonconforming notices will be assessed on a case-by-case basis, considering all relevant circumstances. [ERISA Tech Rel 86-2]

The Department of Health and Human Services (DHHS) has published similar model language for use by state and local plans, which language also must be updated in light of intervening amendments to COBRA. [52 Fed Reg 604 (January 7, 1987)]

Q 6:62   Is there a prescribed method for distributing initial notices?

Yes, there is. Sending the notice by first class mail to the last known address of covered employees and their spouses is deemed a good-faith effort at compliance under DOL rules. [ERISA Tech Rel 86-2]

Q 6:63   Must the employee and spouse be sent separate notices?

A single notice is sufficient if the spouse's last known address is the same as the covered employee's; but if the employer or plan administrator is aware that the spouses have different addresses, separate notices must be mailed. [ERISA Tech Rel 86-2]

Q 6:64   Who must notify the plan administrator when a qualifying event occurs?

The answer depends on the nature of the qualifying event.

When Employer Is Required to Give Notice. The employer must give notice within 30 days of the occurrence of a qualifying event concerning (1) the employee's or ex-employee's death, (2) termination of employment or reduction in hours, (3) the employee's becoming eligible for Medicare, or (4) the commencement of a bankruptcy proceeding. The 30-day notice period can be counted from the date of loss of coverage (if the loss occurs later than the event) rather than from the date of the earlier event, if the plan expressly so authorizes and also expressly provides that the COBRA continuation period will start on the date coverage is lost rather than on the date of the event.

Special Rule for Multiemployer Plans. In the case of a multiemployer plan, the plan document may provide for a notice period that is longer than 30 days, regardless of when the qualifying event occurs. [IRC § 4980B(f)(6)(B); ERISA § 606(a)(2)] For employment termination or reduction in hours only, multiemployer plans may also provide that the plan administrator will make the determination that a qualifying event has occurred rather than requiring notice from the employer. [IRC § 4980B(f)(6); ERISA § 606(b)]

When Employee Is Required to Give Notice. In order to secure continuation coverage, the covered employee or qualified beneficiary must first provide notice of divorce, legal separation, or a dependent child's loss of dependent status under the plan's definition of dependency to the plan administrator. The notice must be given within 60 days of the later of (1) the date of the qualifying event or (2) the date that coverage would be lost because of the qualifying event. [IRC § 4980B(f)(6))C); ERISA § 606(a)(3); PHSA § 2206(3); Prop Treas Reg § 1.2-26, Q&A 33]

Q 6:65   Must each affected qualified beneficiary give notice of a qualifying event (for example, a divorce or separation from a covered employee) that will cause more than one qualified beneficiary to lose coverage?

No, separate notices are not necessary. A timely notice of a qualifying event sent by a covered employee or by any affected qualified beneficiary will preserve the COBRA election rights of all qualified beneficiaries involved. [Prop Treas Reg § 1.2-26, Q&A 33]

Q 6:66 What must the plan administrator do after being notified of a qualifying event?

On receiving timely notice of a qualifying event, a plan administrator has 14 days to notify everyone who is a qualified beneficiary with respect to that event that a qualifying event has occurred. Notice to a qualified beneficiary who is married to a covered employee counts as notice to all other qualified beneficiaries in the same household. [IRC § 4980B(f)(6); ERISA § 606; PHS Act § 2206]

Q 6:67 What happens if a qualified beneficiary turns down COBRA continuation coverage?

Each person gets only "one bite at the apple" to elect coverage as, and receive the rights of, a qualified beneficiary. Turning down COBRA continuation coverage terminates a person's status as a qualified beneficiary at the end of the election period (defined in Q 6:74). In fact, if a covered employee later adds such an individual to the employee's coverage (for example, if one spouse adds the other during an annual open enrollment period) and a qualifying event subsequently affects the covered employee, the individual who had originally rejected COBRA coverage will not be able to regain the status of a qualified beneficiary. [Prop Treas Reg § 1.162-26, Q&A 17(b)]

Q 6:68 What happens if the plan administrator is not notified of a qualifying event?

If the covered employee or qualified beneficiary fails to notify the plan administrator of a divorce, separation, or child's loss of dependency status, the group health plan is not required to offer the qualified beneficiary the option of COBRA continuation coverage. [Prop Treas Reg § 1.162-26, Q&A 33]

Q 6:69 Is the plan administrator relieved of the duty to notify qualified beneficiaries of their COBRA rights if it hires others to perform that duty?

No. According to the DOL, the plan administrator's duty to notify qualified beneficiaries of their COBRA rights is a statutory duty that cannot be delegated to others (that is, although the plan administrator can delegate the COBRA function, it continues to retain the legal responsibility for it). Accordingly, the DOL has held that a plan administrator that enters into an arrangement or agreements with a service provider or other parties to provide COBRA notices must take steps to ensure that the qualified beneficiaries are in fact properly notified. [DOL Adv Op 90-A (May 31, 1990)]

Q 6:70 What happens if the plan administrator fails to notify qualified beneficiaries of their COBRA rights?

A plan administrator who fails to provide a required COBRA notice to a qualified beneficiary can incur substantial excise tax liability and ERISA penalties, which are discussed fully in Qs 6:127 through 6:141.

In addition, failure to give notice or failure to provide adequate notice in a timely manner may subject the plan administrator to liability for COBRA benefits for which it might not have been liable if timely adequate notice had been given.

In U.S. district court case, under the terms of a medical plan a dependent would lose coverage at age 19 unless the dependent was a full-time student. The dependent in the case had a serious accident shortly after his 19th birthday. The employee provided the plan administrator with information which, upon due inquiry, would have revealed that the dependent was not a full-time student. However, the plan administrator erroneously determined that plan coverage continued and failed to give a COBRA notice. Some time later, it was determined that coverage in fact had been lost at age 19, and the employee was asked to refund benefits paid erroneously. The court held that the plan administrator had failed to fulfill its fiduciary duties in determining whether coverage was in force and in failing to give a COBRA notice. The court assumed that if notice had been given, the dependent would have elected COBRA coverage in view of the serious injuries suffered by the dependent, and thus COBRA continuation coverage was held to be in effect. [Swint v Protective Life Ins Co, 779 F Supp 532 (SD Ala 1991)]

Q 6:71   Is special treatment of COBRA notices required where the person entitled to elect COBRA coverage is mentally incapacitated?

Two court decisions indicate that a plan administrator may have to take extraordinary steps in providing notice where the person entitled to elect COBRA continuation coverage is not mentally able to make an informed decision. In a decision by the U.S. Court of Appeals for the Eleventh Circuit, the facts involved an employee who was in a persistent vegetative state as a result of strokes. After being kept on the payroll for a time, the employee became entitled to either 12 months continuation with no cost or 18 months of COBRA coverage. A proper COBRA notice was given, and the employee's spouse asked for further information, including a summary plan description which was not provided. No COBRA election was made and the 12-month continuation coverage took effect. Shortly before the expiration of the 12-month period, the spouse was appointed legal guardian of the employee and attempted to elect COBRA coverage. The Court of Appeals held that a COBRA notice to an incompetent beneficiary is not effective unless it is accompanied by plan documents that allow the person acting on behalf of the incompetent beneficiary to make an informed and intelligent decision. Since the spouse had not been provided with a summary plan description, the COBRA notice was held to be ineffective, and the spouse-guardian's election of COBRA continuation coverage was allowed. [Meadows v Cagle's Inc, 954 F 2d 686 (11th Cir 1992)]

In a U.S. district court case, an employee was given a timely COBRA notice and elected coverage and paid the first COBRA premium. The employee then became mentally incompetent and failed to pay the next premium due, resulting in cancellation of the COBRA coverage. Some months later, a guardian for the incompetent was appointed, who attempted to reinstate the coverage by paying the delinquent premiums. The court ruled that the employer was required to reinstate the COBRA coverage. The court held that where a COBRA beneficiary misses a premium payment due to mental incapacity, the deadline for payment is tolled for a reasonable period of time until the beneficiary or legally appointed guardian is able to cure the deficiency. [Sirkin v Phillips Colleges Inc, 14 EBC 2193 (DN J 1991; see also Branch v G Bernd Co, 14 EBC 2817 (11th Cir 1992) (MD Ga 1991)]

Planning Pointer. If the plan administrator is aware that a COBRA beneficiary is mentally incompetent, it may be prudent to provide the COBRA election notice and premium payment notices to the legal representative (if any) or spouse or other person handling the incompetent's affairs, as well as to the incompetent.

Q 6:72 Can an employer or plan administrator be held liable for a COBRA continuation notice sent in error?

It appears that in some situations there could be liability.

In a U.S. district court case, the court considered a situation where an employee of the employer erroneously advised the plan administrator to send out a COBRA notice and election form, even though the former employee receiving the notice was not entitled to COBRA continuation coverage. The former employee completed the election of coverage form and returned it to the plan administrator. The court held that the administrative error in sending out the COBRA notice and election form could not be construed as a binding offer of coverage, since the statute and the terms of the plan did not provide for such coverage. [Smith v Genelco, Inc, 777 F Supp 750 (ED Mo 1991)]

However, in a decision by the U.S. Court of Appeals for the Eleventh Circuit, an employer was held to be estopped from retroactively denying COBRA benefits after first approving coverage, even though the former employee was not entitled to COBRA continuation for himself and his dependents under the then-current version of the COBRA statute because he was covered under his wife's health benefit plan. The court applied a federal common-law theory of equitable estoppel, which consists of the following five elements:

1. The party to be estopped misrepresented material facts;
2. The party to be estopped was aware of the true facts;
3. The party to be estopped intended that the misrepresentation be acted on or had reason to believe the party asserting the estoppel would rely upon it;
4. The party asserting the estoppel did not know, nor should it have known, the true facts; and

5. The party asserting the estoppel reasonably and detrimentally relied on the misrepresentation.

The appellate court concluded that all five elements of equitable estoppel had been met in the case and held that COBRA coverage applied. [National Companies Health Benefit Plan v St Joseph's Hospital, 929 F 2d 1558 (11th Cir 1991)]

COBRA Election and Enrollment

Q 6:73   Who is entitled to make a COBRA election?

Any qualified beneficiary who would otherwise lose coverage under a group health plan must be given an opportunity to elect to continue his or her group health plan coverage. (See Questions 6:77 through 6:88 for a discussion of the type of coverage that must be provided.)

Q 6:74   What is the minimum permitted election period?

Every qualified beneficiary must be given an election period of at least 60 days to decide whether to elect COBRA continuation coverage. [IRC § 4980B(f)(5)(A)(i)]

Q 6:75   When does the COBRA election period begin?

The COBRA election period begins on the later of:

1. The date the qualified beneficiary would lose coverage because of a qualifying event, or

2. The date the qualified beneficiary is notified of the right to elect continuation coverage.

[IRC § 4980B(f)(5)(A)] (See Questions 6:44 through 6:48 for a discussion of when and under what conditions "loss" of coverage occurs.)

Q 6:76   What if the plan administrator does not send the notice on time?

The plan administrator's failure to send a timely notification that a qualifying event has occurred will extend the election period. Therefore, the qualified beneficiary is not penalized for the delay. [IRC § 4980B(f)(5); ERISA § 605; PHS Act § 2205; Prop Treas Reg § 1.162-26, Q&A 32]

Q 6:77   Is the COBRA continuation election considered made when it is sent or when it is received?

An election of COBRA continuation coverage is treated as made on the date that notice of election is sent to the employer or plan administrator. [Prop Treas Reg § 162-26, Q&A 35]

Q 6:78   Are qualified beneficiaries who waive COBRA continuation coverage allowed to change their minds?

Yes, a change is permitted under certain circumstances. A waiver can be revoked at any time before the end of the election period; a waiver or revocation of waiver is treated as made on the date it is sent to the employer or plan administrator. [Prop Treas Reg § 1.162-26, Q&A 35]

Q 6:79   Must group health plan coverage be provided during the interim period when the qualified beneficiary is deciding whether to elect COBRA coverage?

After a qualified beneficiary elects COBRA continuation coverage, coverage generally must be provided retroactively to the date when it would have been lost. Indemnity or reimbursement arrangements have two alternatives: (1) coverage can be extended during the election period; or (2) if the plan permits retroactive reinstatement, the qualified beneficiary can be dropped from the plan and reinstated when an affirmative election is made. [Prop Treas Reg § 1.2-26, Q&A 34]

It is important to note that coverage must be retroactively restored when the qualified beneficiary *elects* COBRA continuation coverage, even if he or she does not immediately pay for it. Employers cannot withold COBRA continuation coverage until all outstanding premiums are paid, since qualified beneficiaries have an additional 45-day period after election to forward the initial premium payment (which may include all outstanding premiums due). This will also impact the coverage representations that the employer, plan administrator, or third-party administrator makes in response to questions from providers during the election period and before the initial COBRA premium has been paid (see Qs 6:120, 6:121). [Communications Workers of America, District One, AFL-CIO v NYNEX Corp, 898 F 2d 887 {2d Cir. 1990)] (For a detailed discussion of the obligations of the group health plan during the COBRA election period and prior to payment of the initial premium, see C.M. Combe, I Golub, *COBRA Handbook* (Panel Publishers, 1993)).

In the case of a waiver followed by a revocation of the waiver, the group health plan is not required to provide retroactive coverage for the period from the loss of coverage until the date the waiver is revoked. [Prop Treas Reg § 1.62-26, Q&A 35]

Q 6:80 What happens to claims incurred by the qualified beneficiary before making a decision about COBRA continuation coverage?

The group health plan is under no obligation to pay additional claims for covered plan expenses incurred during the election period until COBRA continuation coverage is actually elected and, if applicable, until premium payments have been made. [Prop Treas Reg § 1.2-26, Q&A 34(b)]

Q 6:81 How do direct service plans, such as health maintenance organizations (HMOs), handle payment for services rendered during the election period but before an election is made?

Direct service plans and walk-in clinics have two options during the election period for dealing with a qualified beneficiary who has not made an election and paid the initial premium. The first option is to require the qualified beneficiary to choose between (1) electing and paying for the coverage, or (2) paying the reasonable and customary charge for the plan's services on a fee-for-service basis. Qualified beneficiaries who take the fee-for-service option must be reimbursed for their payments within 30 days of making the election and paying the required initial premium.

The other option is for the plan to treat the qualified beneficiary's use of the facility as a constructive election of COBRA continuation coverage, requiring him or her to pay any applicable charge for coverage; however, the qualified beneficiary must be notified of the meaning of the constructive election before using the facility. [Prop Treas Reg § 1.62-26, Q&A 34(c)]

Q 6:82 Can an employer speed up the decision by withholding money or benefits?

No, it cannot. Employers are specifically forbidden to withhold benefits otherwise available to the qualified beneficiary, including payment for claims relating to covered expenses incurred before the qualifying event, to force a quicker decision about COBRA rights. A waiver of COBRA rights obtained by threats to withhold any benefit is invalid. [Prop Treas Reg § 1.162-26, Q&A 36]

Q 6:83 Must each qualified beneficiary be allowed to make an independent election?

Yes, each must be allowed to make an independent election concerning COBRA continuation coverage. This would include, if applicable, the right to receive COBRA continuation of core coverage only and to switch to another group health plan during an open enrollment period. [Prop Treas Reg § 1.622-26, Q&A 37]

Q 6:84 Can the employee elect COBRA coverage on behalf of family members?

An employee's affirmative election to receive COBRA coverage on his or her own behalf and on that of his or her covered spouse and dependents is binding on the spouse and dependents. Proposed regulations state that the employee's affirmative election is effective to bind other family members even if the covered employee has a choice between core-only coverage and core plus noncore coverage (see Qs 6:90-6:94), and selects core-only coverage. [IRC § 4980B(f)(5)(B); Prop Treas Reg § 1.2-26, Q&A 37]

Q 6:85   Can a covered employee decline coverage on behalf of his or her spouse and dependents?

No, although a covered employee can make an affirmative election of coverage that is binding on the spouse and dependents, the covered employee cannot decline coverage on their behalf. If the covered employee turns down COBRA coverage, the spouse must be given an opportunity to elect it. Similarly, only the covered employee's affirmative election of coverage is binding on dependents; if the spouse also rejects COBRA continuation coverage, each dependent child must also be given an opportunity to elect it. [IRC § 4980B(f)(5); ERISA § 605; PHS Act § 2205; Prop Treas Reg § 1.62-26, Q&A 37]

Type and Extent of Required Coverage

Q 6:86   What type of coverage must be offered to qualified beneficiaries?

When coverage is lost because of a qualifying event, COBRA gives qualified beneficiaries the right to elect group health plan coverage that is identical to:

1. The coverage provided to similarly situated beneficiaries who have not undergone a qualifying event, and
2. The coverage the qualified beneficiaries themselves received immediately before the qualifying event.

If the continuation coverage offered differs from the beneficiaries' prior coverage (except for the permitted differences discussed in Questions 6:90 through 6:94), the group health plan will not be in compliance with COBRA requirements unless other complying coverage is offered. As discussed in Question 6:38, coverage limitations introduced in anticipation of a qualifying event are disregarded in assessing the adequacy of continuation coverage. [IRC § 4980B(f)(2); ERISA § 602(1); PHSA § 2102; Prop Treas Reg § 1.162-26, Q&A 22]

Q 6:87 Must qualified beneficiaries demonstrate insurability in order to quality for continuation coverage?

No, they need not do so. Continuation coverage cannot be conditioned on evidence of insurability, and employers are not allowed to discriminate against qualified beneficiaries who lack this evidence. [IRC § 4980B(f)(2); ERISA § 602(4); PHSA § 2102; Prop Treas Reg § 1.622-26, Q&A 22]

Q 6:88 What is the effect on continuation coverage if the employer changes the coverage available to employees who have not undergone a qualifying event?

Such changes do not affect the employer's obligation to offer continuation coverage, unless the employer completely ceases to offer any group health plan at all.

When COBRA continuation coverage is changed or terminated, the employer must allow COBRA continuees to switch to any of the group health plans the employer still maintains. When a qualified beneficiary does elect to switch plans, all credits toward satisfaction of deductibles, copayments, catastrophic limits, and other such limits must be carried over to the new plan. [IRC § 4980B(f)(2)(B)(ii); ERISA § 602(4); PHSA § 2202; Prop Treas Reg § 1.162-26, Q&A 23]

Q 6:89 Must a plan permit qualified beneficiaries to participate in an open enrollment period?

Yes, it must. An open enrollment period is the time in which an employee covered by a group health plan can select a different group health plan or add or eliminate coverage of family members. Any open enrollment period available to active employees must be made available to qualified beneficiaries; for instance, qualified beneficiaries must be permitted to add newly eligible dependents not previously enrolled if the plan otherwise permits it. Each qualified beneficiary in a family must be given the same opportunity to change plans that is given to an active employee. [Prop Treas Reg § 1.162-26, Q&A 30]

Q 6:90   Must a qualified beneficiary who elects continuation coverage take (and pay for) all the coverage he or she had just before the qualifying event?

No, electing identical coverage is not necessary. COBRA contains a series of rules about "core coverage." If, immediately prior to the qualifying event, the qualified beneficiary was covered by a plan that included both core and noncore coverages, the qualified beneficiary must be given a choice of continuing only the core coverage or all of the prior coverage. [Prop Treas Reg § 1.162-26, Q&A 24] The two exceptions to this rule are discussed in Question 6:83.

Q 6:91   What is core coverage under COBRA?

Generally, most health benefits are treated as mandatory core coverage. Vision care and dental benefits are noncore coverage. However, vision or dental benefits that are required under applicable local law are core coverage; so are vision care that, under local law, must be provided by a physician (rather than paramedical personnel such as opticians) and dental care or oral surgery occasioned by accidental injuries. [Prop Treas Reg § 1.162-26, Q&A 25]

Q 6:92   What does COBRA require from plans offering both core and noncore coverage?

If the premium for core coverage is at least 95 percent of the premium for all coverage that the qualified beneficiary received immediately before the qualifying event, the plan need not give the beneficiary the option of electing only core coverage as continuation coverage. If the employer offers a plan with both core and noncore coverages and also maintains at least one other plan limited to core coverage for similarly situated active employees, qualified beneficiaries under the "mixed" plan need not be offered core-only coverage under this plan. But the employer must give them the option of continuation coverage under any other plan the employer maintains for similarly situated active employees. [Prop Treas Reg § 1.162-26, Q&A 24]

Q 6:93   Must employers let qualified beneficiaries elect continuation of noncore coverage only?

If the noncore coverage was offered as a free-standing plan before the qualifying event, qualified beneficiaries must be permitted to make an independent election of noncore coverage as their sole continuation coverage. However, qualified beneficiaries who were covered under single plans joining core and noncore coverage need not be offered the opportunity to continue only the noncore portion. [Prop Treas Reg § 1.162-26, Q&A 27]

Q 6:94   Can a qualified beneficiary elect continuation coverage in the form of core coverage plus only one of two noncore benefits provided before the qualifying event?

It depends on how the noncore coverages were made available before the qualifying event. If the employer offered the medical, dental, and vision coverage in a single package, the qualified beneficiary need be given a choice only between continuing core-only coverage and continuing core plus *all* noncore coverage. Thus, the qualified beneficiary does not have to be given the choice of core plus dental coverage, or core plus vision coverage.

However, if there were separate free-standing plans, independent of the core plan, that provided the vision and dental coverage, the employer is deemed to offer three separate group health plans. Qualified beneficiaries must be given the choice of continuation coverage under any one, two, or all three of the plans. For example, they can elect continuation of the dental coverage only. [Prop Treas Reg § 1.162-26, Q&A 27]

Q 6:95   When COBRA continuation coverage is elected, how are deductibles handled?

The commencement date of continuation coverage seldom falls on the first day of the period used to compute deductibles. COBRA recognizes this fact and requires that the qualified beneficiary be given credit for expenses incurred toward the group health plan's deductibles during the time before the continuation period began. Credit must be given as if the qualifying event had never occurred. [Prop Treas Reg § 1.162-26, Q&A 28]

If the group health plan's deductible is not a fixed amount but is based on the covered employee's compensation, the plan is entitled to treat the employee's compensation as frozen at the level used to compute the deductible immediately before COBRA continuation coverage began. [Prop Treas Reg § 1.162-26, Q&A 28]

Q 6:96   If family members select different continuation options, how is the remaining deductible amount computed?

The answer depends on the plan's terms before the qualifying event. If deductibles were computed separately for each covered individual, the remaining deductible amount is simply carried forward for each individual.

However, if the plan computed the deductible on a family basis, including a family deductible satisfied by completing a specified number of individual deductibles, each "new family unit" must be given credit for the preexisting family unit's remaining deductible amount.

Example 1. The group health plan imposes a single, annual $500 family deductible. Before their COBRA continuation coverage commenced, the Smith family satisfied $400 of this amount. Mrs. Smith and daughters Rachel and Evelyn elect a single plan providing core plus noncore coverage; Mr. Smith and son Edward elect core-only coverage. There are now two "family units," and each unit must be credited with $400 toward the $500 annual deductible requirement for family coverage.

Example 2. The facts are the same as in Example 1, except that the group health plan requires families to satisfy a maximum of three $200 individual deductibles a year, for a total family deductible of $600. Before COBRA continuation coverage commenced, Mr. Smith and Edward had each satisfied an individual deductible, giving the family $400 credit toward the $600 family deductible. If the family makes the COBRA continuation elections given in Example 1, each new family unit must be credited with $400 toward the family deductible, regardless of which family member incurred the deductible expenses.

Example 3. The facts are the same as in Example 2, except that Mr. Smith and Edward instead elect a continuation option offered as an alternative to COBRA coverage; Mrs. Smith, Rachel, and Evelyn elect COBRA continuation coverage. Each new family unit must be credited with $400 toward the family deductible, no matter what type of continuation coverage is elected.

[Prop Treas Reg § 1.162-26, Q&A 28]

Q 6:97 How are annual plan limits handled for COBRA coverage?

Plan limits, including copayment limits, annual catastrophic limits on out-of-pocket expenses, limits on specific benefits (such as maximum days of hospitalization), and annual or lifetime limits on the total dollar amount of expenses reimbursable under the plan, must be treated in the same way as deductibles (see Qs 6:95, 6:96). [Prop Treas Reg § 1.162-26, Q&A 29]

Duration of Coverage

Q 6:98 What is the maximum required COBRA continuation period?

If the qualifying event is termination of the covered employee's employment or reduction in the covered employee's hours, the maximum required coverage period ends 18 months after such event, unless the "second qualifying event" rule or the Social Security disability rules (see Q 6:91) apply. The maximum required coverage period is 36 months for all other qualifying events, except for the employer's filing for Title 11 bankruptcy protection. [Prop Treas Reg § 1.162-26, Q&A 39]

COBRA continuation coverage for retirees of bankrupt companies (and for their spouses if the spouses were qualified beneficiaries at the time of the bankruptcy) extends for life. If the qualifying event is the employer's bankruptcy, continuation coverage for surviving spouses and dependent children of retirees extends for 36 months after the retiree's death. [IRC § 4980B(f)(2); ERISA § 603; PHSA § 2202(2)]

Q 6:99 From what date is the maximum COBRA continuation period counted?

The general rule is that the COBRA coverage period begins on the date of the qualifying event, regardless of whether the loss of coverage occurs then or later. Accordingly, any "tail" or extension of full health coverage (for example, for three months after termination of employment) would count toward the COBRA continuation period as long as the coverage is identical to that offered to the employee immediately prior to the qualifying event (see Qs 6:86-6:97).

However, the COBRA continuation period can be counted beginning with the date coverage is actually "lost" provided that:

- The plan document expressly provides for counting the COBRA continuation period from the date of loss, and

- The plan document also expressly provides that the employer's period for notifying the plan administrator of certain qualifying events (the employee's death, termination, reduction of hours, or becoming eligible for Medicare, or the employer's commencement of a bankruptcy proceeding involving certain retirees) will begin with the date of the loss of coverage. (See Question 6:55 for a discussion of how long the employer has for notifying the plan administrator of these events.)

[IRC § 4980B(f)(8)] (See Questions 6:45 and 6:47 for a discussion of when and under what conditions coverage is considered to be "lost" for COBRA purposes.)

Q 6:100 Can a plan terminate the coverage of a qualified beneficiary for cause during the COBRA continuation period?

Yes, a group health plan can terminate the coverage of a qualified beneficiary for cause, on the same basis that it can terminate for cause the coverage of a similarly situated active employee who has not undergone a qualifying event. However, for COBRA purposes, termination for cause does not include termination for failure to make timely payments to the plan. (Premiums for COBRA coverage are discussed in Questions 6:107 through 6:126.) [Prop Treas Reg § 1.162-26, Q&A 38]

Q 6:101 Are there circumstances under which the maximum COBRA continuation period must be extended?

Yes, there are three circumstances under which the maximum COBRA continuation period may be extended. First, the "second qualifying event" rule states that if a qualifying event gives rise to an 18-month continuation period and a second qualifying event occurs during that 18-month period, the COBRA continuation period is extended to 36 months for qualifying beneficiaries who became qualified beneficiaries because of the first qualifying event and were still covered under the plan when the second qualifying event occurred.

> **Example.** Mr. Jones terminates employment and elects COBRA continuation coverage for himself, his spouse, and his two children. Two months later, he dies. The original 18-month continuation period is automatically extended to 36 months for his survivors who are still enrolled on the date of the second qualifying event.

[IRC § 4980B(f)(2); ERISA § 603; PHSAct § 2202(2); Prop Treas Reg § 1.162-26, Q&A 40]

Second, if an employee who has experienced the qualifying event of termination of employment or reduction in hours becomes entitled to Medicare within the 18-month COBRA period, his or her spouse and/or children who are qualified beneficiaries may extend their COBRA continuation coverage for up to an additional 18 months (a total of 36 months altogether). A technical amendment to the statute may be necessary to achieve this result, which is described in the legislative history. The statute appears to inadvertently grant a longer extension. [IRC § 4980B(f)(2)(B); ERISA § 602(2)(A); PHSA § 2202(2)(A)]

Third, the Social Security disability rule provides that any qualified beneficiary who is determined to have been disabled at the time of a qualifying event that was either a termination of employment or a reduction in hours is entitled to a total of up to 29 months of COBRA continuation coverage rather than 18 months. To qualify, such individual must notify the plan administrator of the determination of disability under the Social Security Act within 60 days after the determination and before the end of the first 18 months of COBRA continuation. The qualified beneficiary also must notify the plan administrator within 30 days of a final determination that the qualified beneficiary is no longer disabled, and the special extension of continuation coverage will terminate as of the month that begins more than 30 days after the date of such final determination. [IRC §§ 4980B(f)(2)(B)(i)(IV), 4980B(f)(6)(C); ERISA §§ 602(2), (3); PHSA §§ 2202(2)(A), 2202(3)].

Q 6:102　Is early termination of the COBRA continuation period ever permitted?

Yes, COBRA continuation coverage terminates on the *earliest* of the following five dates:

1. The date on which the employer ceases to provide any group health plan to any employee (including successor plans).
2. The date on which plan coverage ceases because any premium required under the plan with respect to the qualified beneficiary has not been paid (see Q 6:125).
3. The date on which a qualified beneficiary first becomes, after the date he or she elects COBRA continuation, covered under any other group health plan, as an employee or otherwise. There have been numerous court cases concerning whether preexisting health care coverage also "becomes effective" after the date of the COBRA election, thus permitting termination of COBRA coverage [see, for example, *National Companies. Health Plan v. St. Joseph's Hospital,* 929 F 2d 1558 (11th Cir. 1991)].

   However, continuation coverage must be continued if the other coverage contains any exclusion or limitation with respect to any preexisting condition of such beneficiary. Additionally, IRS Notice 90-58 states that military health plans are not "group health plans" for purposes of this cutoff rule. [IRS Notice 90-58, 1990-2 CB 345]

4. The date on which a qualified beneficiary first becomes, after the date he or she elects COBRA continuation, entitled to Medicare benefits (that is, he or she has actually applied for Medicare). The date on which he or she reaches 65 is irrelevant; entitlement to benefits, not mere eligibility, is required. However, Medicare entitlement does not terminate the COBRA continuation period for individuals who become qualified beneficiaries because their employer filed for Title 11 protection.

Although the DHHS has taken the position that employers may not cut off the COBRA coverage of employees who become entitled to Medicare due to end-stage renal disease, this position was recently rejected by the Court of Appeals for the Fifth Circuit. The Fifth Circuit held that the Social Security law's end-stage renal provisions mandated the order of payment (by requiring that employer-provided group health plans be the primary payer, and Medicare the secondary payer, for the first 18 months of an individual's Medicare entitlement solely because of end-stage renal disease and that it does not apply to a health plan's decision to terminate coverage. [Blue Cross & Blue Shield of Texas, Inc v Shalala (5th Cir 1993)]

However, the continued validity of the Fifth Circuit's interpretation may now be in question as a result of the ADA Act of 1990. The EEOC has issued interim guidance under the ADA which generally takes the position that all disability-based distinctions in group health plans, including limitations expressly applying to end-stage renal disease, may violate the ADA. [EEOC Interim Guidance on Application of ADA to Health Insurance, reprinted at 109 DLR E-1 (June 9, 1993)]

5. In the case of extension of the 18-month period because of Social Security disability, the date on which a qualified beneficiary loses Social Security disability status (see Q 6:101).

6. The date on which coverage of a qualified beneficiary is terminated for cause if otherwise provided in the plan for non-COBRA participants (see Q 6:90).

[Prop Treas Reg § 1.2-26, Q&A 38; IRC § 4980B(f)(2)(B); ERISA § 602(2); PHSA § 2202(2)] Note that the cases express contradictory views regarding whether preexisting coverage with another employer cuts off the continuation coverage period [Oakley v City of Longmont, 890 F 2d 1128 (10th Cir 1989) (employee's preexisting coverage under spouse's group health plan does not cut off COBRA continuation coverage); Brock v Primedica Inc, 904 F 2d 295 (5th Cir 1990) (where employee had coverage under spouse's plan, there is no COBRA continuation)]

Q 6:103   Can COBRA coverage for existing qualified beneficiaries be cut off if the employer's workforce drops below 20 employees?

No, any individual who has a qualifying event in the calendar year during which an employer covered by COBRA becomes small enough to qualify for the small-employer exemption (plus any COBRA continuees from prior calendar years) cannot have his or her COBRA continuation coverage rights cut off. However, if the employer continues to satisfy the small-employer exemption in the following calendar year, no further individuals become qualified beneficiaries entitled to COBRA continuation rights (see Q 6:23). [IRC § 4980B(d)(1), as amended by OBRA 89 § 11702(f)]

Q 6:104   After the COBRA continuation period ends, must the qualified beneficiary be given a chance to enroll in an individual conversion health plan?

If the plan does not contain a conversion privilege, continuees have no right to convert. However, continuees must be allowed to exercise any conversion privilege existing under the plan when their continuation coverage ends at the expiration of the maximum continuation period. [Prop Treas Reg § 1.162-26, Q&A 43]

Q 6:105   How long must the qualified beneficiary be given to elect the conversion plan?

The qualified beneficiary must be given the option to exercise the conversion privilege during the 180-day period that ends on the date that the COBRA continuation period expires. [IRC § 4980B(f)(2)(E); ERISA § 602(5); PHSA § 2202; Prop Treas Reg § 1.162-26, Q&A 43]

Q 6:106   What are the employer's obligations to qualified beneficiaries who elect region-specific plans and then move outside the plans' service areas?

If a qualified beneficiary relocates to an area not served by the region-specific plan (for example, an HMO) in which he or she is participating, and if the employer has employees in the new area, the qualified beneficiary must be given the same right to elect alternative coverage that would be offered to an active employee who transferred to the new location while continuing to work for the employer. [Prop Treas Reg § 1.162-26, Q&A 30]

Premiums

Q 6:107   Who pays for COBRA continuation coverage?

The employer may, if it wishes, pay all or part of the cost of COBRA continuation coverage. However, the employer is not required to pay for the coverage; a group health plan can charge a qualified beneficiary up to the full amount of the "applicable premium" (see Q 6:109).

Q 6:108   When can a state pay COBRA premiums on behalf of a qualified beneficiary?

A state Medicaid program may pay the COBRA premiums for individuals whose income does not exceed the federal poverty level and whose resources do not exceed twice the maximum amount that an individual may have and obtain supplemental security income (SSI) benefits in that state, if the state determines that the savings in expenditures under Medicaid resulting from such enrollment is likely to exceed the amount of COBRA premiums. This rule applies only if the COBRA continuation coverage is under a group health plan provided by an employer with 75 or more employees. [Social Security Act §§ 1902(a)(10)(F), 1902(u); 42 USC § 1396a, added by OBRA '90 § 4713]

Further, if the state determines that enrollment in a group health plan would be more cost-effective than Medicaid coverage, it can compel enrollment in group health plans provided that it pays any applicable COBRA premiums and all deductibles, co-insurance, and other cost sharing for services otherwise covered by Medicaid. [Social Security Act § 1906, 42 USC § 1396b, added by OBRA '90 § 4713]

Q 6:109 How is the applicable premium that the qualified beneficiary can be required to pay calculated?

The applicable premium generally equals 100 percent of the cost of the coverage provided to similarly situated beneficiaries who have not experienced a qualifying event, plus an additional 2 percent for administrative expenses. For this calculation, it is irrelevant whether the employer, the employee, or both pay the premiums for the group health coverage of active employees who have not suffered a qualifying event. [IRC §§ 4980B(f)(2)(C) and 4980B(f)(4)(A); ERISA §§ 602(3), 601(1); PHSA §§ 2202(3), 2204; Prop Treas Reg § 1.162-26, Q&A 44]

In the case of extension of coverage due to Social Security disability (see Q 6:92), the employer may charge an applicable premium for the 19th month through the 29th month of up to 150 percent of the cost of coverage provided to similarly situated employees who have not experienced a qualifying event. [IRC § 4980(f)(2)(C)]

Q 6:110 Which individuals are similarly situated for purposes of determining the applicable premium?

The legislative history of COBRA defines "similarly situated" individuals as those defined in the plan who have not suffered a qualifying event. Their medical conditions need not be similar to those of the qualified beneficiaries. Group health plans are not permitted to use a definition of similarly situated that violates the Equal Pay Act of 1963, Title VII of the Civil Rights Act of 1964, or other similar laws prohibiting discrimination in employment. See Chapter 13 for a discussion of these laws. Nor may categories be created that would inappropriately increase the cost of COBRA continuation coverage to non-highly-compensated employees.

Q 6:111   How is the cost of an insured plan calculated for applicable premium purposes?

Promised regulations on cost determinations under COBRA have not been issued, so it is unclear whether an employer that has traditionally taken administrative expenses into account when setting the premiums for active employee plans can continue to do so, given the 2-percent administrative surcharge permitted under COBRA.

Q 6:112   How is the cost of a self-insured plan calculated?

The statute provides two alternative methods for calculating the cost of a self-insured plan. Under the first, a self-insured plan's cost of providing continuation coverage for any period is equal to a reasonable estimate of the cost of providing coverage for the same period for similarly situated beneficiaries. The reasonable estimate must be actuarially determined, taking into account any factors prescribed by regulations. Apparently, health care cost inflation can be taken into account.

The second alternative permits the employer to define the cost as the applicable premium for similarly situated beneficiaries for the previous determination period, adjusted for cost-of-living changes by using the gross national product (GNP) implicit price deflator for the 12-month period ending on the last day of the sixth month of that prior determination period. However, this method cannot be used for a self-insured plan if there is any significant difference in either the coverage under the plan or the employees covered under the plan since the prior determination period. [IRC § 4980B(f); ERISA § 604(2); PHSA § 2204(2)]

Presumably, when the COBRA cost regulations are issued, they will include guidelines for identifying a "significant difference."

Q 6:113   What is the time period used to calculate COBRA premiums?

COBRA premiums are calculated in advance for a fixed period of time, called the "determination period." For any applicable premium, the determination period is 12 consecutive months. [IRC § 4980B(f); ERISA § 604(2); PHSA § 2204(3)]

Q 6:114 What is the premium determination period for an employer with several group health plans?

The 12-month period chosen as the determination period need not coincide with the plan year or other significant date for any of the employer's group health plans. Therefore, several plans with different plan years or policy anniversary dates can use a single, uniform determination period. [Prop Treas Reg § 1.162-26, Q&A 45]

Q 6:115 Does each qualified beneficiary have a separate determination period?

No, a group health plan may choose a single, uniform determination period for calculating the premium for all COBRA beneficiaries, provided that the plan uses this period consistently from year to year. Each qualified beneficiary is not entitled to have a personal determination date based on the date his or her COBRA continuation coverage begins. [Prop Treas Reg § 1.162-26, Q&A 45]

Q 6:116 Can a plan increase the premium charged to a COBRA continuee who adds new dependents?

Yes, a premium increase is permitted if the increased family size causes a change in the coverage classification under the terms of the plan. The plan can charge the applicable premium for the new coverage classification.

Example. George Stone, a single man, terminates employment and elects COBRA continuation coverage; his premium for individual enrollment is $45 a month. A few months later, he marries and enrolls his wife during the plan's election of coverage period for newly eligible dependents. For the relevant determination period, the plan's premium is $70 per month for an individual plus one dependent. The plan can charge Mr. Stone the higher premium immediately.

[Prop Treas Reg § 1.162-26, Q&A 30(d)]

Q 6:117   Can a COBRA continuee who chooses a different plan during an open enrollment period be charged the premium for the new coverage?

Yes, the plan can charge the qualified beneficiary the applicable premium for the newly selected coverage option, even if the qualified beneficiary must pay more than under the prior COBRA continuation coverage.

Example 1. When a qualifying event occurs, Brad Johnson and his family are enrolled in a low-option medical plan. Brad elects COBRA continuation coverage on behalf of the entire family; the monthly premium is $125. A few months later, the sponsoring employer conducts an annual enrollment period. Brad switches his and his family's coverage to the high-option medical plan; the plan's premium is $175 a month. The plan can charge Brad the higher premium immediately.

Example 2. Assume the same facts as in Example 1, except that Brad and one child choose the high-option medical coverage during the open enrollment period, but his wife and their other child keep the low-option medical coverage. The Johnson family now consists of two family units. The plan can charge $125 for the family unit with low-option medical coverage, and $175 for the family unit with the high-option coverage. Note that the plan must credit each family unit with expenses accrued toward annual deductibles, benefit copayments, and plan limits (see Qs 6:86–6:88).

[Prop Treas Reg § 1.162-26, Q&A 30(d)]

Q 6:118   Must COBRA continuees absorb increases in the premium charged by a group health plan to similarly situated individuals who have not undergone a qualifying event?

The statute and regulations mandate predetermined, fixed COBRA rates for each 12-month determination period. Once an employer sets a determination date for a group health plan, that becomes the only date on which rates for COBRA continuation coverage can change. [Prop Treas Reg § 1.162-26, Q&A 45]

It is not clear from the regulations whether an exception to this rule is made when a plan amendment increasing or decreasing coverage leads to a premium increase or decrease for active-employee coverage. It is also unclear whether an employer that adds significant new health benefits to a group health plan in the middle of a determination period and consequently raises the rates for active employees may also raise rates for qualified beneficiaries.

Planning Pointer. In practice, a conservative approach would be to "batch" all benefit increases and make them effective on the annual determination date, so that their cost can be factored into the COBRA continuees' premium for the ensuing 12-month period.

Q 6:119 When determining COBRA cost, must an employer take into account experience refunds and policy dividends received from an insurance company?

The proposed COBRA regulations do not deal with the proper handling of experience refunds and policy dividends paid by an insurance company as a result of favorable (that is, lower than expected) claims experience for the policy year. Until regulations are issued, employers presumably will be held to a good-faith standard provided that their interpretation of the statute is reasonable and not applied in a discriminatory manner.

Q 6:120 When is the first payment for COBRA continuation coverage due?

The group health plan may not require payment of any premium due for the period beginning with the date coverage would otherwise be lost until 45 days after the individual makes his or her COBRA election. [IRC § 4980B(f)(2); ERISA § 602(3); PHSA § 2202(3)]

As discussed in Question 6:74, there is a 60-day election period, so the group health plan may have to wait up to 105 days (60 plus 45) before it gets the premium for such period. If the loss of coverage is not simultaneous with the qualifying event, this waiting period could be even longer. Additionally, since the election period must last 60 days after the later of the date coverage is lost or the plan administrator sends notification to the beneficiary that the qualifying event has occurred, a late notice automatically extends the permitted period for paying the batch of premiums. In such a case, the first payment will be for three or four months of coverage. [IRC § 4980B(f); ERISA § 602(3); PHSA § 2202(3); Prop Treas Reg § 1.162-26, Q&A 48]

Q 6:121   Can the employer take any steps to speed up the payment of the initial premium?

No, the employer is not allowed to withhold money or other benefits owed to a qualified beneficiary until the beneficiary pays for COBRA continuation coverage. However, the plan can delay payment of claims incurred during the election period and the initial 45-day grace period until the qualified beneficiary makes a timely election to get COBRA continuation coverage and also pays the initial premium during the 45-day grace period. Special rules are provided for HMOs and other direct service providers. [Prop Treas Reg § 1.162-26, Q&A 34]

Q 6:122   How must the first payment be credited?

The COBRA continuee's first payment must be applied toward continuation coverage retroactive to the date that coverage would have been lost because of a qualifying event. However, if the qualified beneficiary first waived coverage, then revoked the waiver and made a timely election of COBRA continuation coverage, the first premium payment is not used to pay for the period covered by the waiver. [Prop Treas Reg § 1.2:26, Q&A 47]

Q 6:123   After the initial payment, can the qualified beneficiaries be required to pay premiums quarterly or semiannually?

No, they must be given the option of paying premiums for COBRA continuation coverage in monthly installments. Other payment options can also be made available. [IRC § 4980B(f); ERISA § 604(2)(C); PHSA § 2202(3)]

Q 6:124   When are premium payments deemed made?

The proposed COBRA regulations do not state whether a payment is made when the qualified beneficiary sends it or when the plan receives it. One possible approach applies the rule used to determine when an election of COBRA coverage is made (see Q 6:68) and treats a payment as made when it is mailed. Under this approach, the employer would wait a few days for overdue payments that could have been mailed on time, rather than cutting off coverage on the last day of the grace period.

Q 6:125   What is the grace period, if any, for making premium payments?

A special grace period is required for the first payment (see Q 6:111). For other payments, the qualified beneficiary must be allowed a grace period for forwarding premium payments. The grace period must be either 30 days after the due date, or any longer period permitted by the terms of the plan or the contract between the employer and an insurer, HMO, or other entity covering similarly situated beneficiaries. For example, an employer that contracts with its health insurer for a 90-day grace period to forward overdue premiums must provide at least a 90-day grace period to qualified beneficiaries. [IRC § 4980B(f); ERISA § 604(2)(C); PHSA § 2202(2); Prop Treas Reg § 1.162-26, Q&A 48]

Q 6:126   Can the employer cancel coverage during the grace period and then reinstate it if the qualified beneficiary pays the overdue premium?

This approach is generally not permitted. COBRA continuation coverage may be terminated for failure to make timely premium payments, but payments are considered timely if they are made within the grace period discussed in Questions 6:120 and 6:125. [Prop Treas Reg § 1.2-26, Q&A 48]

COBRA Enforcement and Sanctions

Q 6:127   Which agencies have the power to enforce COBRA?

COBRA divides enforcement authority among three agencies: the IRS, the DHHS, and the DOL. According to the Conference Report issued for COBRA, the secretary of labor issues the regulations dealing with disclosure and reporting; the secretary of the treasury (that is, the IRS) makes rules for required coverage, deductions, and income inclusions; and the secretary of health and human services issues the regulations for continuation coverage provided by state and local governments. The DHHS regulations must conform to those issued by the other two agencies. [HR Rep No 453, 99th Cong, 1st Sess 562-563 (1985), quoted in ERISA Tech Rel 86-2]

The IRS has not yet issued final regulations. However, detailed guidance can be found in the Notice of Proposed Rulemaking published on June 15, 1987. The IRS has also signaled its intent to provide model plan language and issue revenue rulings on questions that are not addressed in the regulations.

The DOL has issued ERISA Technical Release 86-2, which contains model language (not yet updated for later COBRA amendments) for providing notices to employees. The DHHS has issued a similar notice. (See Q 6:61.)

Q 6:128   How are COBRA violations penalized?

COBRA violations are penalized by an excise tax that may be assessed against an employer or a multiemployer plan. The tax may also be assessed against persons responsible for administering or providing benefits under a plan (other than in their capacity as employees) if the culprit was responsible for administering or providing benefits under the plan, and the culprit's act or failure to act was partially or wholly responsible for the COBRA violation.

The excise tax replaced a rule that penalized the employer for COBRA violations by limiting the deductibility of contributions to group health plans violating COBRA, and by including certain group health plan costs in the gross income of highly compensated employees. Under the draconian "one mistake" rule for plan years prior to 1989, a single COBRA violation for one day affecting only a single employee, was enough to cause the loss of the employer's deduction for all contributions and expenses of all its group health plans. The loss of the employer's tax deduction was applied on a controlled-group basis. [Former IRC §§ 106, 162(k); IRC § 4980B; Prop Treas Reg § 1.162-26, Q&As 3, 4]

Q 6:129   How much is the excise tax imposed for COBRA violations?

The excise tax is $100 per day per qualified beneficiary for the duration of the noncompliance period (see Qs 6:130, 6:131), with a maximum of $200 per day per family, regardless of the number of qualified beneficiaries affected by the violation. [IRC §§ 4980B(b)(1), 4980B(c)(3)]

Note. Effective as of August 10, 1993, the COBRA excise tax may also be assessed if group health plan coverage for pediatric vaccines is reduced below the level in effect on May 1, 1993. This separate provision is discussed in Chapter 3, which covers medical care in general.

Q 6:130   When does the noncompliance period used to calculate the excise tax begin?

The noncompliance period begins on the date the COBRA violation first occurs. However, for failure to provide coverage, the noncompliance period does not begin until 45 days after the written request is made.

An "inadvertent failure" rule exempts from excise taxation any part of the period for which it is established (to the satisfaction of the secretary of the treasury) that no potentially liable person knew, or should have known by exercising reasonable diligence, that the violation existed. However this rule does not apply in situations in which the special audit rule (see Q 6:125) applies. [IRC §§ 4980B(b)(2)(A), 4980B(b)(3), 4980 B(c)(1)

Q 6:131 When does the noncompliance period end?

The period of noncompliance ends on the earlier of (1) the date on which the violation is corrected or (2) six months after the last day of the maximum applicable COBRA continuation period (excluding a failure to make timely premium payments). [IRC § 4980B(b)(2)(B)]

Q 6:132 When is a COBRA violation considered "corrected"?

A COBRA violation is considered corrected if (1) it is retroactively removed to the extent possible and (2) the financial position of the qualified beneficiary, or beneficiary's estate, is as good as it would have been if the violation had not occurred. For this purpose, it is assumed that the beneficiary would have elected the coverage that was most favorable in light of the expenses he or she had incurred since the beginning of the violation. [IRC § 4980B(g)(4); Conf Rep to accompany HR 4333, HR Rep No 1104, 100th Cong, 2d Sess, Vol II, at 24 (1988)]

Q 6:133 Is there a grace period before the excise tax applies?

Yes, there is. No excise tax applies to COBRA violations corrected during the first 30 days after any potentially liable person knows (or should have known by the exercise of reasonable diligence) of the violation. The violation must have a reasonable cause. The grace period is unavailable for cases of willful neglect and violations that were not corrected before the special audit rule (see Q 6:134) is applied. [IRC §§ 4980B(c)(1), 4980B(b)(3)]

Q 6:134 Does an audit of the employer affect the excise tax?

Yes, it does. The special audit rule imposes a minimum excise tax on COBRA violations that are not corrected before the date when a notice of examination of income tax liability is sent to the employer, if the violations occurred or continue to occur during the period under examination. [IRC § 4980B(b)(3)]

Q 6:135   What is the excise tax under the special audit rule?

Under the special audit rule, the minimum excise tax per affected qualified beneficiary is either $2,500 or the otherwise applicable excise tax, whichever is less. But if an employer's (or multiemployer plan's) violations for any year are more than de minimis, the minimum excise tax imposed is the smaller of the otherwise applicable excise tax or $15,000. [IRC § 4980B(b)(3)] The IRC does not define de minimis.

Q 6:136   Is there a maximum excise tax that can be imposed with respect to a single-employer plan?

There is no limit on the excise tax that can be assessed for a willful violation. However, if the violation was not willful, and the employer had reasonable cause for its actions, the maximum excise tax with respect to a single-employer plan for any taxable year is generally the lesser of:

- $500,000 or

- 10 percent of the aggregate amount paid or incurred by the employer (or predecessor employer) during the preceding taxable year for group health plans.

[IRC §§ 4980B(c)(4)(A), 4980B(e)(1)(A)(i)]

Q 6:137   Is there a maximum excise tax that can be imposed for a violation committed by a multiemployer plan?

There is no limit on the excise tax that can be assessed upon a willful violation. Otherwise, the maximum tax in any taxable year on the trust forming a part of the plan is the lesser of $500,000 or 10 percent of the amount paid or incurred during the taxable year to provide medical care (directly or through insurance, reimbursement, or otherwise). [IRC § 4980B(e)(l)(A)(ii)] In addition, if an employer participating in a multiemployer plan is assessed the excise tax, the single-employer plan maximum (see Q 6:136) applies to that employer. [IRC § 4980B(c)(4)(B)]

Q 6:138 Is there a maximum excise tax that can be imposed on persons other than employers or multiemployer plans?

For COBRA violations that are not willful and are due to reasonable cause, the maximum aggregate amount of tax that may be imposed on persons other than employers or multiemployer plans for COBRA violations concerning all plans during the taxable year is $2 million. There is no maximum excise tax for willful violations. [IRC § 4980B(c)(4)(C)]

Q 6.139 Who—other than employers or multiemployer plans—can be liable for excise tax?

Individuals responsible for administering benefits or making benefits available under the plan can be held liable if their actions or failures to act wholly or partially caused a COBRA violation. [IRC § 4980B(e)(1)(B)]

Benefit providers or administrators that are bound by a legally enforceable agreement to make COBRA coverage available are fully liable for a failure to make COBRA coverage available, but they are not liable for other violations unless they took responsibility for performing the act to which the failure relates. [IRC § 4980B (e)(2)(A)]

Benefit providers are liable for failure to comply with a written request for COBRA coverage sent by the qualified beneficiary if the qualifying event is a divorce, legal separation, or child's loss of dependency status or by the employer or plan administrator for all other qualifying events. [IRC § 4980B(e)(2)(B)] But liability will not be imposed if the employer's act or failure to act made it impossible for the person to make COBRA coverage available. [Conf Rep to accompany HR 4333, HR Rep No 1104, 100th Cong, 2d Sess, Vol II, at 26 (1988)] A person providing coverage under the plan will not be liable for failure to comply with a written request to make COBRA coverage available sooner than 45 days after the date the notice is provided to such person. [IRC § 4980B(b)(2)] The legislative history indicates that this provision will not override a written agreement between an employer and a third party that obligates the third party to provide continuation coverage. [Conf Rep to accompany HR 4333, HR Rep No 1104, 100th Cong, 2d Sess, Vol II, at 27 (1988)]

Q 6:140   May the IRS waive the excise tax penalty for a COBRA violation?

Yes, it may. Part or all of the excise tax may be waived if failure to comply was due to reasonable cause and not to willful neglect, with the result that the payment of such tax would be excessive in proportion to the failure involved. The legislative history of COBRA states that excessiveness is judged by the seriousness of the failure to comply with COBRA, not by the taxpayer's ability to pay. [IRC § 4980B(c)(5); Conf Rep to accompany HR 4333, HR Rep No 1104, 100th Cong, 2d Sess, Vol II, at 27 (1988)]

Q 6:141   What is the ERISA penalty for failure to notify employees and qualified beneficiaries of their COBRA rights?

The ERISA Section 502(c) penalty of up to $100 per day applies to the plan administrator's failure to provide:

- Written notice to each covered employee and his or her spouse of COBRA continuation rights at the time their group health care coverage commences (see Q 6:60); and
- Notice to the qualified beneficiary that a qualifying event has occurred (see Qs 6:66, 6:58 to 6:72).

[ERISA §§ 502(c), 606(1), 606(4)]

Plan Year

Q 6:142   What is a group health plan's plan year?

The plan year designated in the plan document is determinative: not the plan year shown on the Form 5500 annual report to IRS. [Prop Treas Reg § 1.62-26, Q&A 13]

Q 6:143   What is the plan year of a plan without a plan document?

Many group health plans still operate without a plan document, even though ERISA may require one (see Q 2.19–2.22). IRS provided somewhat convoluted guidelines for such plans, based on the plans' measuring years for plan limits and deductibles. Self-funded plans without measuring years were to use either the calendar year or the employer's tax year, whichever was later, as their plan year. [Prop Treas Reg § 1.126-26, Q&A 13]

Chapter 7

Cafeteria Plans

The benefit needs of employees differ and, therefore, cafeteria plans, which permit a choice from a menu of welfare benefit options, have become quite popular. Cafeteria plans, however, entail unique and complex structural concerns. This chapter reviews the basic concepts and tax requirements of cafeteria plans.

Basic Concepts

Q 7:1   What is a cafeteria plan?

A cafeteria plan is an employer-provided plan that offers participants the opportunity to choose between cash, and one or more "qualified benefits." Cash includes actual cash and/or taxable benefits. Qualified benefits generally are nontaxable benefits such as medical or dental coverage. At a minimum, to meet Internal Revenue Code (the Code) requirements, the cafeteria plan must offer at least one currently fully taxable benefit (or cash) and one qualified benefit. [IRC § 125(d)(1); Prop Treas Reg § 1.125-2, Q&A 3]

Q 7:2   What is the importance of using a cafeteria plan?

Without a Cafeteria Plan. Generally, an employee who is offered a choice among taxable and nontaxable benefits is treated, for tax purposes, as having received the taxable benefits. This is true even if he or she does not elect such benefits or makes the election prior to the year in which he or she would have received them. The employee would be required to include the taxable benefits in gross income at the time he or she could have received them. [Prop Treas Reg § 1.125-1, Q&A 9; Treas Reg § 1.451-2]

With a Cafeteria Plan. However, if the choice is made available under a cafeteria plan that satisfies the nondiscrimination requirements of Code Section 125, the result will be entirely different. The participant will not be required to include the cash (or currently taxable benefits) in gross income merely because he or she has the opportunity to choose among cash and the qualified benefits under the cafeteria plan, before the cash actually becomes currently available to him or her. Thus, Code Section 125 protects participants from being treated as having "constructively received" the cash or currently taxable benefits. It is an exception to the general income tax rules governing constructive receipt of income. [Prop Treas Reg §§ 1.125-l, Q&A 9, and 1.125-2, Q&A 2]

Written Plan

Q 7:3 Must a cafeteria plan be in writing?

Yes, Code Section 125 requires that a cafeteria plan be a separate written benefit plan. [IRC § 125(d)(1); Prop Treas Reg. § 1.125-1, Q&A 2]

Q 7:4 What must the plan document of a cafeteria plan contain?

The plan document must:

1. State the eligibility requirements for participation in the plan.
2. Set forth the procedures that a participant must follow to make a valid benefit election under the plan, including:
   — The period during which participants are permitted to make elections,
   — To what extent the participant's election will be irrevocable, and
   — How long the participant's election will remain effective.
3. Specifically describe each of the benefits available under the plan.
4. State the periods during which benefits will be provided.
5. Describe how the employer will contribute to the plan (such as pursuant to a salary reduction agreement between the employer and the employee or by nonelective employer contributions to the plan or both).
6. Describe the maximum amount of elective (or salary reduction) contributions available to any employee under the plan by stating either:
   — The maximum dollar amount or percentage of compensation that employees may make as elective contributions, or
   — A method for determining such an amount or such a percentage.
7. State the plan year of the cafeteria plan.

If the cafeteria plan includes the choice of receiving benefits contained in other separate written plans, such as a group term life insurance plan or a dependent care assistance plan, the benefits under these other plans need not be fully described in the cafeteria plan document as well. Instead, an employer is permitted to incorporate them by reference to the other plan or plans. But if the cafeteria plan offers different maximum levels of coverage, for example, these differences must be described in the cafeteria plan document. [Prop Treas Reg §§ 1.125-1, Q&A 3, and 1.125-2, Q&A 3]

Eligible Employees

Q 7:5 Who can participate in a cafeteria plan?

All participants in a Code Section 125 cafeteria plan must be employees. [IRC § 125(d)(1)(A); Prop Treas Reg § 1.125-1, Q&A 4] Note, however, that full-time, non-employee life insurance salespeople are considered employees. [IRC § 7702(a)(20)]

Q 7:6 May a cafeteria plan cover spouses and other beneficiaries of the participant?

Yes, it may. Although spouses and beneficiaries cannot be active participants and cannot be given the opportunity to select among cafeteria plan benefits or to purchase specific alternatives offered under the plan, a qualified cafeteria plan may provide benefits to spouses and to other beneficiaries of participants. In other words, spouses and other beneficiaries can benefit from the employee's selection of an option for them, such as family medical insurance coverage. If the participant dies, the spouse will not be treated as an active participant merely because he or she then may have to choose among various death benefit settlement options or distribution options. [Prop Treas Reg § 1.125-1, Q&A 4] Note, however, that if spouses or dependents elect COBRA continuation of group health plan coverage, or such coverage is elected on their behalf, such individuals generally should be accorded the rights of a participant. The Internal Revenue Service (IRS) has not yet issued guidance on exactly how this is to be accomplished in the context of a cafeteria plan. See Chapter 6 for a discussion of COBRA.

Q 7:7 May a Code Section 125 cafeteria plan cover former employees?

Yes, it may. Former employees are considered to be employees for this purpose. However, a Code Section 125 cafeteria plan cannot be established predominantly for the benefit of the employer's former employees. Thus, an employer could not, for instance, maintain a retiree-only cafeteria plan. [Prop Treas Reg § 1.125-1, Q&A 4]

Q 7:8 May a cafeteria plan cover partners, sole proprietors, or S corporation shareholders?

No, generally it may not. All participants in a cafeteria plan must be employees. Partners and sole proprietors, who are self-employed, may not be treated as employees for cafeteria plan purposes. [IRC §§ 126(d)(1)(A) and 401(c); Prop Treas Reg § 1.125-1, Q&A 4] Additionally, an employee who is a more-than-2-percent shareholder in an S corporation on any day during the taxable year cannot participate in a cafeteria plan maintained by the S corporation. [IRC § 1372]

> **Planning Pointer.** This rule can be quite significant for benefit design in the dependent care area. If an employer maintains a dependent care program as an independent benefit, a partner, a sole proprietor, or a more-than-2-percent S corporation shareholder is eligible; however, if the program is offered under a cafeteria plan, that person must be excluded.

Permitted Benefit Choices

Q 7.9 What kind of choice must a cafeteria plan offer a participant?

It must offer a choice between cash and a "qualified benefit" (as defined at Qs 7:31–7:36). A currently fully taxable benefit generally is considered the same as cash for this purpose (see Q

7:35). [IRC § 125(c)(1)(B); Prop Treas Reg §§ 1.125-1, Q&A 5, 1.125-2, Q&As 3, 4]

Q 7:10 Is a choice between cash and a qualified benefit available through pre-tax salary reductions enough to meet this test?

Yes, it is, because salary reduction contributions are treated as employer contributions (See Qs 7:14–7:16).

Q 7:11 How must a plan be structured to ensure that qualified benefits do not lose their favorable tax treatment?

The employer must adopt certain procedures for benefit elections in order to ensure that participants are not deemed to have constructively received—and are not therefore taxed on—taxable benefits (including cash) that they have not elected to receive. To do this, the employer plan must ensure that the choice of benefits is made before the taxable benefits become "currently available." [Prop Treas Reg §§ 1.125-1, Q&As 9, 15, 1.125-2, Q&A 2]

A benefit will not be treated as currently available on the date that the participant makes a benefit election under the cafeteria plan, provided that:

1. The election form specifies the future period for which the benefit will be provided; and
2. The participant makes his or her election before the beginning of the specified period.

[Prop Treas Reg § 1.125-1, Q&A 15] No particular form of election is mandated.

Q 7:12 When is a benefit considered currently available, and therefore taxable?

A benefit is treated as currently available to a participant if the participant is free to receive it either:

1. At his or her discretion; or

2. By making an election or giving notice of intent to receive it.

However, the mere ability to elect or to give notice of intent to receive a benefit in advance of actual receipt of the benefit does not in itself make the benefit currently available, and therefore taxable, if the benefit does not become available until some specified time in the future, and there is a substantial risk of forfeiture of the benefit. [Prop Treas Reg § 1.125-1, Q&A 14]

Q 7:13   Is a benefit currently available if receipt is limited or restricted?

If there is a substantial limitation or restriction on the participant's receipt of the benefit, it will not be treated as being currently available, provided that (1) the participant may under no circumstances receive the benefit before a particular time in the future and (2) there is a substantial risk that the participant will not receive the benefit if he or she does not fulfill specified conditions during the period before the particular time in the future. [Prop Treas Reg § 1.125-1, Q&A 14]

Salary Reduction

Q 7:14   What is a salary reduction contribution?

A salary reduction contribution, or elective contribution, is one made pursuant to a salary reduction agreement between an employer and a participant. Under a salary reduction agreement made before the salary becomes currently available (see Qs 7:11–7:13), required participant contributions are made on a pre-tax basis; that is, they are not included in the employee's taxable income. [Prop Treas Reg § 1.125-1, Q&A 6]

Q 7:15   How does the IRS view salary reduction (elective) contributions, and why is this significant?

Generally, an employee contribution made on a pre-tax basis is, for tax purposes, considered to be an employer contribution that is made by the employer on the participant's behalf. This means that salary reduction (elective) contributions are generally treated as employer contributions for applicable nondiscrimination tests. [Prop Treas Reg § 1.125-1, Q&A 6]

Q 7:16 Are salary reduction (elective) contributions required to be held in trust?

Although the IRS views salary reduction contributions as *employer* contributions for tax purposes because they are not considered to be constructively received by cafeteria plan participants, the Department of Labor (DOL) views them as *employee* contributions. Accordingly, the DOL's final regulation on the trust requirement for employee contributions to ERISA welfare benefit plans, which contains no specific mention of cafeteria plans, would apparently require elective contributions for cafeteria plan benefit options, including medical reimbursement accounts, to be deposited in trust. The DOL has confirmed this interpretation, but suspended enforcement while it considers whether to grant a class exemption or individual exemptions from the trust requirement in these circumstances. [DOL Reg § 2510.3-102, ERISA Tech Rel Nos 88-1 (Aug 12, 1988), 92-01, 52 Fed Reg 23272 (June 2, 1992)]

Period of Coverage

Q 7:17 What period must a cafeteria plan election cover?

Except for the initial plan year, or a short plan year in which the cafeteria plan year is being changed, the period of coverage of a qualified cafeteria plan generally must be 12 months. Coverage cannot be elected on a month-by-month or expense-by-expense basis. [Prop Treas Reg §§ 1.125-1, Q&As 17, 18, 1.125-2, Q&A 7(b)(3)]

Q 7:18 Why is the period of coverage important?

An election to participate in a cafeteria plan must be made before the period of coverage to avoid constructive receipt of income. [Prop Treas Reg § 1.125-1, Q&A 15]

Elections

Q 7:19   Must an individual make an affirmative election to participate in a cafeteria plan?

Yes, individuals generally must make an affirmative election (usually in writing) to participate in a cafeteria plan. [Prop Treas Reg § 1.125-1, Q&A 8]

Under a negative option approach, an individual is deemed to have selected a cafeteria plan benefit (usually a salary reduction benefit) unless he or she returns the form and affirmatively rejects participation. Individuals who fail to return the form or fail to respond are treated as electing a cafeteria plan benefit. When this approach is used for the initial period of coverage under the cafeteria plan, it does not appear to conform to the intent of the proposed cafeteria plan regulations. Although opinions differ, the more conservative view is that this particular type of initial negative option does not always reflect a "choice" between cash and qualified benefits; the negative option provides no proof that the participant ever received the form, or that the participant did not simply forget to fill it out. It may also violate state laws requiring specific written authorization from the employee prior to making deductions for benefit plan contributions from his or her paycheck.

Newer methods of benefit administration, such as enrollment by means of automatic voice response telephone programs or computer linkup, also can be used to permit individuals to elect or reject cafeteria plan enrollment. These arrangements generally include a computer-generated written confirmation of the individual's election in order to establish written proof of the election. These computer-generated elections with written confirmations are generally thought to satisfy the affirmative election requirement under the cafeteria plan regulations.

Q 7:20   May a cafeteria plan use a one-time election that renews automatically unless the participant revokes it?

An initial affirmative election followed by a negative option which automatically renews and extends the initial written election for succeeding periods of coverage is referred to as an "evergreen election." In other words, once made, the affirmative election to participate in the cafeteria plan stays in force indefinitely unless it is affirmatively revoked. The proposed regulations do not expressly prohibit this evergreen approach.

Q 7:21   What happens if an employee changes his or her mind once the election becomes effective?

If the plan permits revocation of an election once the coverage period has begun, cash or fully taxable benefits are generally considered currently available, and thus taxable, even if the employee does not receive them. It does not matter whether participants ever actually exercise the right or whether the revocation is prospective only. Subject to the exceptions discussed in the following questions, participant elections must be irrevocable during the period of coverage. [Prop Treas Reg §§ 1.125-1, Q&A 15, 1.125-2, Q&A 6(a)]

Q 7:22   Are there any exceptions to the prohibitions against revocation of an election to participate in a cafeteria plan?

Yes, exceptions are provided for:

- Changes in family status (see Q 7:23)
- Separation from service (see Q 7:24)
- Cessation of required contributions (see Q 7:25)
- Changes in health plan costs and coverage (see Qs 7:26–7:28)
- Elective contributions under cash or deferred (i.e., Code Section 401(k)) arrangements (see Q 7:29).

[Prop Treas Reg § 1.125-2, Q&A 6]

Q 7:23   May a revocation be permitted because of a change in family status?

Yes, it may be. A participant may be (but is not required to be) permitted to revoke his or her election under the cafeteria plan for the remainder of the period of coverage (and, if the plan permits, to make a new election for the remainder of the period of coverage) on account of changes in family status, including:

- Marriage;
- Divorce;
- Death of a spouse or child;
- Birth of a child of, or adoption of a child by, the employee;
- Termination of a spouse's employment;
- Commencement of employment by the employee's spouse;
- A switch from part-time to full-time employment, or vice versa, by either the employee or the employee's spouse;
- The taking of an unpaid leave of absence by either the employee or the employee's spouse; and
- A significant change in the employee's or the spouse's health coverage that is attributable to the spouse's employment.

Both the revocation and the new election must be on account of, and consistent with, the change in family status. A benefit election change is considered to be consistent with a family status change only if the election change is necessary or appropriate as a result of the family status change. [Prop Treas Reg §§ 1.125-1, Q&A 8, 1.125-2, Q&A 6(c)]

Q 7:24   May a revocation of a participant's election be permitted if the employee separates from service?

Yes, a participant who separates from service may be (but is not required to be) permitted to revoke his or her election and terminate the receipt of benefits for the remainder of the period of coverage. However, the plan must bar separated employees who revoke coverage from making new benefit elections if they return to service during the same period of coverage. [Prop Treas Reg § 1.125-2, Q&A 6(d)]

Q 7:25   May a plan permit a revocation because of the employee's cessation of contributions?

Yes, it may. The cafeteria plan may provide that a benefit will cease to be provided to an employee who fails to make the required premium payments for that benefit. However, the plan also must prohibit the employee from making a new benefit election for the remainder of the period of coverage. [Prop Treas Reg § 1.125-2, Q&A 6(d)]

Q 7:26   May a plan permit revocations because of health plan cost changes?

If the cost to employees of a health plan provided by an independent, third-party provider (for example, an independent insurance company or a health maintenance organization (HMO)) under a cafeteria plan significantly increases, the cafeteria plan may (but is not required to) permit participants to revoke their elections for the remainder of the period of coverage and receive prospective coverage under another plan that provides similar coverage. The plan is also permitted to automatically adjust participant contributions to reflect premium *increases* or *decreases* charged by an independent third-party provider. [Prop. Treas. Reg. § 1.125-2, Q&A 6(b)(1)]

Q 7:27   May a plan permit revocations because of changes in health plan coverage?

Yes, it may. A plan may permit a participant in a health plan option provided by an independent third party (for example, an independent insurance company or an HMO) to revoke his or her election if coverage is significantly curtailed or ceases and to receive prospective coverage under a plan that offers similar coverage. [Prop Treas Reg § 1.125-2, Q&A 6(b)(2)]

Q 7:28   May a plan permit revocation because of changes in the spouse's health care plan?

Yes, it can, if there is a significant change in the health care coverage of the employee or the spouse attributable to the spouse's employment. [Prop Treas Reg § 1.125-2, Q&A 6(c)] For example, if an employee elected coverage only for himself because his spouse had coverage through her employer, and the spouse then left employment during the year and lost her coverage, the employee could be permitted to revoke his election and make a new election covering his spouse as well as himself.

Recently, the IRS was asked whether a "change in family status" would occur in the following two situations:

1. A spouse, covered under her employer's medical plan, is no longer entitled to receive benefits because the medical expenses have exceeded the plan's maximum reimbursement limit.

2. A spouse, covered under her employer's medical plan, becomes eligible for Medicare at age 65 and her plan becomes a secondary payer.

The IRS concluded that neither situation constituted a "change in family status," because neither was attributable to the spouse's employment or former employment. [IRS Information Ltr, Mar 4, 1992]

Q 7:29 Do the irrevocable-election rules apply to a cash or deferred (Code Section 401(k)) option?

No, they do not. Instead, the plan must follow the rules of Code Sections 401(k) and 401(m) that apply to 401(k) plans. [Prop Treas Reg § 1.125-2, Q&A 6(f)]

Q 7:30 Does the plan have any recourse if an employee simply stops making required contributions?

Yes, it does. A plan may provide that a benefit will cease if an employee fails to make a required premium payment, as long as it prohibits the employee from making a new election for the remainder of the coverage period. [Prop Treas Reg § 1.125-2, Q&A 6(e)]

Benefits

Q 7:31 Which benefits are qualified benefits?

The following specific benefits are qualified benefits under a cafeteria plan:

- Group term life insurance coverage for benefits of up to $50,000 that is excludable from gross income under Code Section 79 (see Q 11:56);

- Group term life insurance coverage that is includable in gross income solely because the death benefit is more than $50,000 (see Qs 11:56 and 11:57);

- Coverage under an accident or health insurance plan that is excludable from income under Code Section 106 (see Chapter 3);

- Coverage under a qualified group legal services plan that qualifies under Code Section 120 (since the income exclusion for these services expired on June 30, 1992 and apparently will not be reinstated by Congress, group legal services are no longer a qualified benefit under a cafeteria plan) (see Qs 8:63–8:77);

- Coverage under a dependent care assistance plan that qualifies under Code Section 129 (see Qs 8:1–8:21);

- Participation in a qualified cash or deferred arrangement that is part of a profit-sharing or stock bonus plan under Code Section 401(k); and

- Any other benefit permitted under the regulations.

[IRC § 125(f); Temp Treas Reg § 1.125-2T; Prop Treas Reg §§ 1.125-1, Q&As 5, 7, 1.125-2, Q&As 4, 5]

Cafeteria plans maintained by certain educational organizations may also include postretirement life insurance provided that all contributions for such insurance are made before retirement and such life insurance does not have a cash surrender value at any time. [IRC § 125(d)(2)(C)]

Q 7:32   Are there any tax-favored benefits that are not qualified benefits?

Yes, there are several. The statute specifically excludes scholarships and fellowships under Code Section 117, educational assistance programs under Code Section 127, and fringe benefits under Code Section 132. Also, meals and lodging excluded under Code Section 119 are ineligible because they are furnished for the convenience of the employer and are not elective in place of other employer-provided compensation or benefits. [IRC § 125(f); Temp Treas Reg § 1.125-2T; Prop Treas Reg § 1.125-2, Q&A 4(d)]

Q 7:33   Is group term life insurance on the lives of the participant's spouse and children a qualified benefit?

Generally, it is not considered to be a qualified benefit because group term life insurance on the lives of the participant's spouse and children is not excludable from income under Code Section 79. If it is treated as a *de minimis* benefit under Code Section 132, it is not permitted to be included in the cafeteria plan as a qualified benefit. [IRC § 125(f)]

However, IRS Notice 89-110 provided that, for plan years ending on or before December 31, 1991, dependent life insurance could be included in a cafeteria plan provided that it was treated as cash under Proposed Treasury Regulations Section 1.125-2, Q&A 4(b). For plan years ending after December 31, 1991, dependent life insurance cannot be included in a cafeteria plan if it would be eligible for the Code Section 132 *de minimis* benefit exclusion if it were offered outside the cafeteria plan. [IRS Notice 89-110, 1989-2 CB 447] (See Q 12:10.)

Q 7:34   What happens if a qualified benefit fails a nondiscrimination test of some other IRC section?

The definition of the term "qualified benefit" formerly did not hinge on satisfaction of any separate nondiscrimination test applicable only to that benefit. However, when former Code Section 89 was repealed, the statutory authority formerly contained in Code Section 125 to disregard the benefit's discriminatory status under other applicable IRC sections also was repealed. Accordingly, it is unclear whether the failure of any cafeteria plan benefit to satisfy other applicable IRC sections, such as Code Section 105(h) for self-insured medical plans or Code Section 79 for group term life insurance plans, disqualifies the entire cafeteria plan. [Former IRC § 125(e); IRC § 125(f)]

Q 7:35 When can a benefit be treated as cash?

In general, a benefit is treated as cash if it (1) does not defer compensation and (2) either (a) is purchased with after-tax dollars or (b) the employee is treated as receiving, *for all federal income tax purposes* (including reporting and withholding), cash compensation equal to the full value of the benefit at that time and purchasing benefit with after-tax dollars. [Prop Treas Reg § 1.125-2, Q&A 4(b)]

Q 7:36 Can a cafeteria plan ever offer deferred compensation as a qualified benefit?

Yes, but only if the plan offers an option to make elective contributions under a cash or deferred arrangement that qualifies as a Code Section 401(k) plan. [IRC § 125(d)(2); Prop Treas Reg §§ 1.125-1, Q&A 7, 1.125-2, Q&A 4(c)]

However, with the exception of the Code Section 401(k) plan option and a special exception for certain postretirement group life insurance plans maintained by educational institutions, use of a cafeteria plan to defer compensation is strictly forbidden. [IRC § 125(d)(2)(A); Prop Treas Reg § 1.125-1, Q&A 7, 1.125-2, Q&As 4(c), 5(a)]

Q 7:37 What does the prohibition against deferred compensation mean?

It means that a cafeteria plan cannot offer participants the opportunity to simply defer or delay compensation they have earned, and thus delay the resulting tax liability.

It also means that a qualified cafeteria plan cannot be used to defer compensation by indirect means. Any available benefits that are not used during the period of coverage are forfeited at the end of the period of coverage. [Prop Treas Reg §§ 1.125-1, Q&A 7, 1.125-2, Q&A 5(a)] This is referred to as the "use it or lose it" rule.

Q 7:38 What plan provisions can violate this ban on indirect deferred compensation?

Permitting employees to carry over unused benefits from one period of coverage to the next violates the prohibition against having deferred compensation in a cafeteria plan. It does not matter whether the benefits or contributions carried over are converted, automatically or electively, into another taxable or nontaxable benefit or used to purchase additional benefits of the same type.

Permitting participants to use contributions for one plan year to purchase benefits to be provided in a subsequent year also violates the prohibition against indirect deferred compensation. [Prop Treas Reg §§ 1.125-1, Q&A 7, 1.125-2, Q&A 5(a)]

Including life, health, disability, or long-term care insurance coverage having a savings or investment feature, such as whole life insurance, would operate to permit the deferral of compensation in violation of this limitation. [Prop Treas Reg § 1.125-2, Q&A 5(a)]

Q 7:39 How does the "use it or lose it" rule affect the way vacation pay options must be structured?

A cafeteria plan may permit participants to receive either additional or fewer paid vacation days on an elective basis. However, non-elective vacation days must be treated as used before elective vacation days. Unused elective vacation days cannot be carried over to another plan year. Unused elective vacation days may be cashed out provided that the participant receives the cash by the earlier of (1) the last day of the cafeteria plan's year or (2) the last day of the employee's taxable year to which pretax contributions used to purchase the unused days relate. If the unused elective vacation days are not cashed out, they must be forfeited. [Prop Treas Reg § 1.125-2, Q&A 5(c)]

Q 7:40 Does the prohibition against deferred compensation affect insurance-type benefits?

Yes, it does. A cafeteria plan may not permit participants to purchase insurance (life, health, disability, or long-term care) that has a savings or investment feature, such as whole life insurance. However, a cafeteria plan may pay a reasonable premium rebate or policy dividend if the rebate or dividend is paid before the close of the 12-month period immediately following the plan year to which the rebate or dividend relates. [Prop Treas Reg § 1.125-2, Q&As 5(a), 5(b)]

Q 7:41 May a plan use forfeited salary reduction amounts to pay plan benefits or to provide lower-priced benefits?

It is consistent with the theory of risk shifting and risk distribution to allow the participants as a group to benefit from the group experience. However, any related benefit formula or credit against premium amounts cannot be based upon individual benefit use or guarantee individual participants a specified level of benefit.

Cafeteria plans may, in accordance with the standards above, reduce premiums required of participants for flexible spending arrangements based on "experience gain," that is, the amount by which premiums paid from all sources plus any income exceed all claims paid plus reasonable administrative costs. As an alternative, the cafeteria plan may pay participants policy dividends or premium refunds (see Q 7:57). Both of these courses of action are voluntary and are not required to be included in the cafeteria plan. [Prop Treas Reg § 1.125-2, Q&A 7(b)(7)]

One unresolved issue is whether employers can simply keep the amounts forfeited under the "use it or lose it" rule. The DOL has taken the position that employee contributions to cafeteria plans, including salary reduction contributions made on a pre-tax basis, are plan assets for ERISA purposes. Under this view, ERISA's fiduciary responsibility provisions would prohibit use of any forfeited employee contributions for the benefit of the sponsoring employer (see Chapter 2). [ERISA Tech Rel 92-01, 57 Fed Reg 23272 (June 2, 1992)]

Q 7:42   Can the employer make up forfeited benefits outside the qualified cafeteria plan?

No, the employer cannot take actions outside the cafeteria plan that it is prohibited from taking within the plan. Thus, for example, the employer may not make cafeteria plan participants whole by providing them with a bonus outside the plan equal to the amount of unused reimbursement account benefits forfeited at the end of the plan year. [Prop Treas Reg § 1.125-1, Q&A 17]

Premium Conversion Plans

Q 7:43   What is a premium conversion plan?

In a premium conversion plan, the employee is offered a choice of cash or pre-tax payment of employee contributions, typically for medical coverage. It can either stand alone as a cafeteria plan under Code Section 125 or be one of several choices under a cafeteria plan. The "conversion" refers to the deemed conversion of employee contributions into *employer* contributions by having the employee pay them on a pre-tax basis via a salary reduction agreement as described in Question 7:44.

Q 7:44   Is a premium conversion plan a qualified benefit?

Yes, it is. The proposed IRS regulations state that an employee's payment of premiums for employer-provided medical coverage on a pre-tax basis through salary reduction constitutes employer-provided coverage under Code Section 106. [Prop Treas Reg §§ 1.125-1, Q&A 6, 1.125-2, Q&A 4(a)] The plan document must provide that the employer will make employer contributions pursuant to salary reduction agreements under which participants elect to reduce their compensation or to forgo increases in compensation and to have such amounts contributed, as employer contributions, by the employer on their behalf. Such amounts contributed are treated as employer contributions to the extent that the agreement relates to salary that has not actually or constructively been received and that does not subsequently become available to the participant. In other words, the contributions are "converted" from after-tax employee contributions to pre-tax employer contributions. [Prop Treas Reg § 1.125-1, Q&A 6] Presumably, salary reduction agreements can also be used for disability income benefits or Code Section 79 group term life insurance.

As a result of being treated as pre-tax employer contributions, contributions toward the cost of health insurance made on a salary reduction basis do not count toward the Code Section 32 health insurance tax credit that otherwise may be available to taxpayers who qualify for the earned income tax credit. [IRC § 32(b)(2), as amended by OBRA 190 § 11111(a)] The health insurance tax credit is repealed for taxable years after 1993. [OBRA '93 § 13131]

> **Planning Pointer.** Disability income benefits under an employee-pay-all disability plan are excludable from income under Code Section 104 if the coverage is paid for with after-tax contributions. If an employee pays for such coverage on a salary reduction basis, however, the coverage is employer-paid, and hence the disability income benefits under the plan become taxable to the disabled participant to the extent that they are attributable to employer contributions not included in gross income. Accordingly, the employer may wish to consider whether the premium conversion option for disability income coverage should be offered to employees and, if offered, whether the tax effect of selecting (or not selecting) the salary reduction option should be spelled out in employee communications. A similar concern arises with group term life insurance coverage in excess of $50,000. Because it may be taxable under Code Section 79, employers may wish to consider whether the life insurance would be more advantageous to employees if offered on an after-tax, employee-pay-all basis.

Q 7:45   If a premium conversion option is made available for medical coverage, must it also be provided for federally qualified HMOs?

If the employer allows employees to elect to pay for medical coverage on a pre-tax basis, the employer would appear to be obligated to allow employees to pay for federally qualified HMO coverage on a pre-tax basis as well. Under the federal Health Maintenance Organization Act, the employer must contribute toward the HMO's monthly premium an amount that does not financially discriminate against an employee who enrolls in the federally qualified

HMO. Since pre-tax premiums are treated as employer contributions, an employer that did not allow this option for HMO enrollment could be considered to be making HMOs available on a basis that discriminates financially (see Q 5:41).

Flexible Spending Arrangements

Q 7:46   What is a flexible spending arrangement (FSA)?

An FSA is an account credited with a certain level of contributions (either employer-paid contributions or employee-paid contributions, or both) to reimburse specified expenses up to a specified maximum reimbursement level. The account generally is an unfunded book account of the employer. [Prop Treas Reg § 1.125-2, Q&A 7(C)]

Under the typical FSA, the employee designates an amount of salary reduction contribution for the plan year and directs the employer to credit that amount to the FSA. If the amount designated by the employee also represents the amount of dollars that can be drawn out of the FSA as benefits, the FSA is said to take a "contribution equals benefits approach" because a one-to-one relationship exists between the amount of salary reduction contributions and the maximum available benefits under the FSA. However, a one-to-one relationship is not required, and some employers use employer monies to provide a higher level of available reimbursement from the FSA than the salary reduction contributions credited to the FSA. The maximum amount of reimbursement however, cannot be substantially in excess of the total employee-provided and employer-provided "premium." The maximum amount of reimbursement available under the FSA will satisfy this rule if it is less than 500 percent of the premium. [Prop Treas Reg § 1.125-2, Q&A 7(C)]

Q 7:47   What types of expenses may be reimbursed under a health FSA?

Reimbursements under a health FSA must be specifically for medical expenses as defined in Code Section 213. For taxable years after 1990, health FSAs may no longer reimburse cosmetic surgery or similar procedures, unless the surgery or procedure is necessary to ameliorate a deformity arising from, or directly related to, congenital abnormality, personal injury resulting from an accident or trauma, or disfiguring disease. [IRC § 213(d)(3), added by OBRA 1990 § 11342]

A health FSA cannot reimburse premium payments for other health insurance coverage, such as for other coverage purchased by the employee or coverage maintained by an employer of the employee's spouse. Apparently, a health FSA cannot be used to make pre-tax premium payments for the medical plan that it "wraps around." However, employee premiums for current coverage under the health plan may be paid on a salary reduction basis through the "ordinary operation of the cafeteria plan" (it is not clear exactly what that means). Thus, a premium conversion option for the medical plan that the FSA wraps around still can be offered as a separate, free-standing option under the cafeteria plan or can be split off as a second cafeteria plan. [Prop Treas Reg §§ 1.125-1, Q&A 17, 1.125-2, Q&A 7(b)(4)]

Q 7:48   Is a health FSA required to qualify as a Code Section 105 accident or health plan?

Yes, a health FSA must be a bona fide accident or health plan under Code Sections 105 and 106. [Prop Treas Reg § 1.125-2, Q&A 7(a)]

Q 7:49   Must a health FSA be the primary payer and Medicare a secondary payor?

Yes, it appears that a health FSA, as a Code Section 105 medical plan, is subject to the requirements of Code Section 5000. Accordingly, the Code Section 5000 provisions requiring the medical plan to be the primary payer and Medicare to be the secondary payer will apply under certain circumstances to the health FSA. (See Questions 3:57–3:62 for a discussion of Medicare secondary rules.)

Note that characterization as a "group health plan" also means that the health FSA would be required to meet the additional requirements for group health plans contained in new Section 609 of ERISA dealing with coverage of pediatric vaccines, coverage of adopted children, and qualified medical child support orders. (See Qs 3:49, 3:50, and 3:71–3:76).

Q 7:50   What insurance-type characteristics must a health FSA exhibit?

Under a health FSA:

1. Coverage need not be provided through a commercial insurance contract, but the health FSA must exhibit the risk-shifting and risk-distribution characteristics of insurance;

2. The reimbursement arrangement cannot have the effect of eliminating all, or substantially all, risk of loss to the employer maintaining the plan;

3. Reimbursements must be paid specifically to reimburse the participant for medical expenses incurred previously during the period of coverage;

4. Reimbursements can not be paid to the participant in the form of cash or any other taxable or nontaxable benefit (including health coverage for an additional period), without regard to whether or not the employee actually incurs medical expenses during the period of coverage; and

5. The maximum amount of coverage must be available at all times during the period of coverage (reduced by prior reimbursements for the same period of coverage).

[Prop Treas Reg § 1.125-2, Q&A 7]

If the risk of loss of the employer maintaining the plan or other insurer is negated, either under the arrangement itself or by some other means that is outside the plan, the arrangement does not shift and redistribute risk. [Prop Treas Reg §§ 1.125-1, Q&A 17, 1.125-2, Q&A 7(a)] Thus, for example, if an employee quits his or her job after submitting huge covered claims to a health FSA but after paying only a few salary reduction contributions to the FSA, thus leaving the FSA in a deficit position, the employer cannot require that the employee refund the excess of the FSA benefits paid over the salary reduction contributions actually made.

A health FSA must also meet the general requirements for an FSA discussed in Questions 7:54 through 7:57.

Although Proposed Treasury Regulations Section 1.125-2 refers to the earlier Proposed Treasury Regulations Section 1.125-1 to indicate that the risk-sharing and risk-distribution requirement has always been present for health options under cafeteria plans, what is genuinely new is the interpretation, discussed at Question 7:51 that coverage under a health FSA must be uniform at all times during the period of coverage.

Q 7:51　Why must health FSA coverage be uniform throughout the period of coverage?

Coverage under a health FSA must be uniform throughout the period of coverage in order to shift risk to the employer. The maximum amount of reimbursement under the health FSA must be available at all times during the period of coverage and cannot hinge on how much the participant has contributed to the health FSA to date in the coverage period.

In other words, the employer cannot refuse to pay a claim for covered benefits, to the extent it does not exceed the annual maximum reimbursable amount elected, solely because it is greater than the amount of the participant's salary reduction contributions received thus far in the period of coverage. Rather, the book account for the particular participant must be credited immediately with the full amount of reimbursement elected for the period of coverage and the participant must be given the right to draw it all out in covered benefits at any time during the period of coverage. For this purpose, employers must make benefit payments on at least a monthly basis but are permitted to hold claims until the total amount submitted is at least a specified, reasonable minimum amount, such as $50.

The employer is permitted to reduce the maximum amount of reimbursement available under the FSA at any time during the period of coverage by the amount of prior reimbursements attributable to the same period of coverage. [Prop Treas Reg § 1.125-2, Q&A 7(b)(2)]

Q 7:52　Is there a limit on the amount of expenses that can be reimbursed by a health FSA?

Yes, there is. The maximum amount of reimbursement to a participant for a period of coverage must be less than 500 percent of the total "premium" (employer-paid and employee-paid contribution to the FSA of the participant). [Prop Treas Reg § 1.125-2, Q&A 7(c)]

Q 7:53 How does a plan ensure that participants cannot manipulate the amount of coverage under a health FSA?

A benefit under a cafeteria plan cannot be operated in a manner that allows participants to purchase coverage under an accident or health plan only for periods for which they expect to incur expenses. Thus, for example, if participants are allowed to elect coverage on a month-by-month or expense-by-expense basis, reimbursements will not be considered to flow from a qualified benefit. However, reimbursements based upon a 12-month period (or the initial plan year or changed plan year, if shorter) will not be considered to operate to enable participants to purchase coverage only for periods during which medical care will be incurred. Zero balance accounts (ZEBRAs), under which the participant contributes only the exact dollar amount of expenses to be reimbursed, are forbidden. [IRS News Release IR-84-22 (Feb 10, 1984); Prop Treas Reg §§ 1.125-1, Q&A 17, 1.125-2, Q&As 7(a), 7(b)(3)]

Q 7:54 When must an expense reimbursable by a health FSA be incurred?

Expenses reimbursed under a health FSA must be incurred during the participant's period of coverage under the FSA. For this purpose, an expense is incurred when the medical care service is received; other dates, such as the date on which the employee is formally billed or charged, the date the participant pays for the expense, or the date proof of expenses is submitted, are not controlling. An FSA cannot make advance reimbursements of future or projected expenses.

An expense is not treated as incurred during a period of FSA coverage if it is incurred before the later of:

- The date on which the FSA is first in existence, or

- The date on which the participant first becomes enrolled under the FSA.

A cafeteria plan may permit covered medical care expenses to be reimbursed after the close of the period of coverage in which they were incurred. [Prop Treas Reg §§ 1.125-1, Q&A 17, 1.125-2, Q&A 7(b)(6)]

Q 7:55   What type of substantiation must a plan require for claims for reimbursement from a health FSA?

A health FSA claim can be reimbursed only if the participant provides:

1. A written statement from an independent third party that a medical expense in a specified amount has been incurred and the amount of that expense; and

2. A written statement from the participant that the expense has not been reimbursed by, or is not reimbursable under, any other health plan coverage.

[Prop Treas Reg § 1.125-2, Q&A 7(b)(5)]

Q 7:56   What design restrictions are applicable to dependent care FSAs under cafeteria plans?

Dependent care FSAs also must comply with the incurred expense, timing, and anti-manipulation principles that apply to health FSAs, as well as the claim substantiation standards. [Prop Treas Reg § 1.125-1, Q&A 18] However, dependent care FSAs are *not* required to provide uniform coverage throughout the coverage period, as is required for health FSAs (see Q 7:51). [Prop Treas Reg § 1.125-2, Q&A 7(b)(8)]

Q 7:57   Can unused contributions under a health FSA be used to reimburse excess expenses under a dependent care FSA or vice versa?

No, they cannot. A health FSA cannot reimburse dependent care expenses; nor can a dependent care FSA reimburse health expenses. If any contributions remain unused in an FSA at the close of the period of coverage, they must be forfeited under the "use it or lose it" rule discussed in Question 7:37. However, the proposed treasury regulations do permit an FSA that has an experience gain for a period of coverage to use the excess of premiums paid (both employer- and employee-paid) plus income, if any, over total claims reimbursement and reasonable administrative expenses to be returned to the premium payers as dividends or premium refunds. In no case may this be done based directly or indirectly on individual claims experience. [Prop Treas Reg § 1.125-2, Q&A 7(b)(4)]

Code Section 125 Nondiscrimination Rules

Q 7:58 Must cafeteria plans satisfy any nondiscrimination rules?

Yes, they must. To qualify as a Code Section 125 cafeteria plan, the plan must pass an eligibility test, a contributions and benefits test, and a concentration test.

Q 7:59 What is the nondiscriminatory eligibility test imposed by Code Section 125?

A Code Section 125 cafeteria plan cannot discriminate in favor of highly compensated individuals as to eligibility to participate in the plan. [IRC § 125(b)(1)(A)]

Highly Compensated Individuals. Under Code Section 125, highly compensated individuals are defined as:

- Officers,
- More-than-5-percent shareholders,
- Highly compensated employees, or
- A spouse or dependent of any of the above individuals.

This definition is different than that contained in Code Section 414(s), and this definition of highly compensated individuals is a facts and circumstances determination. [IRC § 125(e)(1); Prop Treas Reg § 1.125-1, Q&A 13]

Q 7:60   Are there any exceptions or safe harbors for the eligibility test?

Yes, there is one. A plan's eligibility requirements are not deemed to favor highly compensated individuals if the plan satisfies the following four statutory safe-harbor criteria:

1. It meets the nondiscriminatory classification test contained in Code Section 410(b)(2)(A)(i). This statute deals with minimum coverage requirements for qualified retirement plans.

2. It does not require more than three years of service as a precondition for participation.

3. The plan imposes a uniform minimum service requirement for all employees.

4. Employees who satisfy this uniform participation requirement commence plan participation no later than the first day of the first plan year beginning after the condition is satisfied.

[IRC § 125(g)(3)]

Q 7:61   What is the nondiscriminatory contributions and benefits test imposed by Code Section 125?

A Code Section 125 cafeteria plan cannot discriminate in favor of highly compensated participants with regard to contributions and benefits. [IRC § 125(b)(1)(B)] For this purpose, the cafeteria plan will not be considered discriminatory with regard to contributions and benefits if qualified benefits and total benefits (or the employer contributions allocable to each) do not discriminate in favor of highly compensated participants. [IRC § 125(c)]

Q 7:62   Are there any exceptions or safe harbors for the nondiscriminatory contributions and benefits test?

Yes, there is one statutory safe harbor. But this one applies only to health benefits. Health benefits will be treated as nondiscriminatory if:

- Contributions on behalf of each participant equal either:

— 100 percent of the cost of the coverage of the majority of similarly situated highly compensated participants, or

— at least 75 percent of the cost of the coverage of the similarly situated participant having the highest cost health benefit under the plan; and

- Contributions or benefits that exceed those described above bear a uniform relationship to compensation.

[IRC § 125(g)(2)]

Q 7:63 What is the nondiscriminatory 25-percent-concentration test imposed by Code Section 125?

If a Code Section 125 cafeteria plan provides more than 25 percent of its nontaxable benefits (excluding group term life insurance in excess of $50,000) to key employees, the key employees are not eligible for cafeteria plan tax treatment. [IRC § 125(b)(2)]

Key Employees. For this purpose, a key employee is any individual who, at any time during the plan year or any of the prior four years, is one of the following:

- An officer with annual compensation greater than 50 percent of the Code Section 415(b) limit (for 1993, 50 percent of this limit is $57,820.50);
- One of the ten largest owners having compensation greater than the Code Section 415(c) limit (for 1993, $30,000);
- A more-than-5-percent owner; or
- A more-than-1-percent owner having compensation in excess of $150,000.

[IRC § 416(i)(1)]

Q 7:64 Are collectively bargained plans subject to these nondiscrimination rules?

No, they are not. [IRC § 125(g)(1)]

Tax Treatment of Cafeteria Plan Benefits

Q 7:65   Can a benefit ever become taxable because it is offered through a cafeteria plan?

Yes, it can. For example, a disability income insurance benefit will be taxable, even if it is funded entirely or partially with employee salary reduction contributions, because the coverage is treated as funded with employer contributions. [IRC § 105(d) and Prop Treas Reg § 1.125-1, Q&A 5]

Q 7:66   What are the tax consequences of a plan that is discriminatory under Code Section 125?

A highly compensated participant in a discriminatory cafeteria plan is taxed on the combination of the taxable benefits with the greatest aggregate value that the employee could have selected under the cafeteria plan, regardless of whether he or she actually did select that particular benefit combination. These amounts are first allocated to the taxable benefits actually selected and then on a pro rata basis to the nontaxable benefits actually selected. A numerical example of how this works is provided in the regulations. [Prop Treas Reg § 1.125-1, Q&As 10, 11]

The amounts are treated as received by the highly compensated participant in his or her taxable year "within which ends the plan year with respect to which an election was or could have been made." [Prop Treas Reg § 1.125-1, Q&A 12]

There are no adverse tax consequences on participants who are not highly compensated. [Prop Treas Reg § 1.125-1, Q&A 10]

Q 7:67   Are cafeteria plan benefits subject to Social Security tax?

The answer depends on the rule for the specific benefit. A qualified benefit that is already subject to Social Security Federal Insurance Contribution Act (FICA) taxes does not become nontaxable when offered under a qualified cafeteria plan. Thus, for example, the cost of group term life insurance coverage amounts over $50,000, which is includable in an employee's income and is subject to FICA tax, will not escape such taxes merely because it is offered as a benefit under a cafeteria plan. The IRS has issued a notice clarifying this interpretation. [IRS Notice 88-82, 1988-2 CB 398]

Effective for group term life insurance coverage provided after 1990, an employer is not required to withhold and pay over the employee's share of the FICA tax with respect to coverage for periods during which an employment relationship no longer exists between the employee and the employer. However, the employer is required to include on the W-2 statement provided to the former employee the portion of the compensation applicable to the imputed value of the group term life insurance and the amount of FICA tax due on such value. The former employee is required to pay his or her portion of the FICA tax directly to the IRS. (See Q 11:73 as to how the tax is to be taken into account on the former employee's Form 1040.) [IRC § 3102(d), as added by OBRA 1990 § 5124(a)]

Q 7:68   Is the amount of salary reduction used to "purchase" qualified benefits subject to FICA tax or federal unemployment tax?

No, it is not. This can produce both employee and employer savings if the salary reduction applies to compensation below the FICA wage base ($55,500 for the 6.20 percent Old Age, Survivors, and Disability Insurance (OASDI) tax for 1993; $135,000 for the 1.45 percent Hospital Insurance (HI) tax for 1993). Starting in 1994, the HI tax applies to all wages, regardless of amount [OBRA '93 § 13207]

Planning Pointer. Employers and employees should be aware that the FICA savings may reduce the ultimate Social Security benefit slightly.

Q 7:69   Does receipt of dependent care assistance benefits under a cafeteria plan reduce the child care tax credit otherwise available to the employee?

Yes, it can. For a discussion of the interplay between Code Section 129 dependent care assistance plan benefits (which can be offered as a qualified benefit under a cafeteria plan) and the dependent care tax credit, see Question 8:18.

Reporting and Disclosure Requirements

Q 7:70   Must the plan administrator file a Form 5500 with the IRS for the cafeteria plan?

Yes. Opinions differ, however, on how this is to be done. First, Code Section 6039D requires that certain information be filed with the IRS annually, and new Schedule F to the Form 5500 Annual Report is designed to fulfill this requirement. Second, Title I of ERISA requires that a Form 5500 Annual Report must be filed for a medical plan or other ERISA welfare benefit plan (unless exempted by regulation), and many of the questions on the Form 5500 are designed to satisfy this ERISA Title I requirement. Some employers file a single Form 5500 for the entire cafeteria plan package and answer all relevant questions. Others file for each "ERISA Benefit" option (for example, the medical FSA) separately. If a separate Form 5500 is being filed for a premium conversion option, opinions differ as to whether the ERISA Title I questions must be answered in addition to the Code Section 6039D questions.

In 1991, it was reported that some DOL field officers were taking the position that the Form 5500 filing for a salary reduction cafeteria plan had to include an audit of the salary reduction amounts by an independent public accounting firm. The DOL subsequently issued a technical release providing interim relief from the audit requirement while it continues to consider "the extent to which reporting and disclosure relief may be appropriate for contributory plans with respect to which relief from the trust requirement is made available." This information extends until the adoption of final regulations providing relief from the trust and reporting requirements of Title I of ERISA. [ERISA Tech Rel No 92-01, 57 FR 23272, June 2, 1992, as modified by DOL News Release 93-363 (Aug 27, 1993)]

Effect of Other Laws

Q 7:71   Is a cafeteria plan subject to the ERISA?

Yes, it is. Cafeteria plans containing ERISA-governed benefits, such as a health flexible spending account (see Q 7:46), are subject to

ERISA. Some disagreement among practitioners exists concerning whether a free-standing premium conversion plan is an ERISA welfare benefit plan. See Questions 7:43 through 7:45 for further discussion of premium conversion plans (that is, plans that permit employee contributions to be made on a pre-tax salary reduction basis) and Chapter 2 for a discussion of ERISA.

Q 7:72 Is a cafeteria plan subject to the Consolidated Omnibus Budget Reconciliation Act (COBRA)?

Yes, a cafeteria plan is affected by the COBRA continuation of coverage requirements to the extent it includes group health benefits, such as a health FSA or reimbursement account (see Q 7:46–7:57). Employees electing health benefits made available under the cafeteria plan have a right to COBRA protection to the same extent as beneficiaries of other group health plans.

Note, however, that if the spouse or dependent elects COBRA continuation of group health plan coverage, or such coverage is elected on their behalf, such individuals generally should be accorded the rights of a participant. The IRS has not yet issued guidance on exactly how this is to be accomplished in the context of a cafeteria plan. (See Chapter 6 for a discussion of COBRA.)

Q 7:73 What amount of FSA group health plan coverage must be offered to COBRA-eligible individuals?

It appears that the amount of FSA coverage that must be made available for a COBRA election initially is the amount of FSA coverage in effect on the date of the qualifying event. For example, if an employee elects FSA coverage for a calendar year of $1,200 (at a salary reduction of $100 a month), is reimbursed for medical expenses of $200, and then is divorced on March 30, the divorced spouse can elect COBRA coverage of $1,000 for the remainder of the year, contributing (on an after-tax basis) $102 a month for nine months. As of the start of the next year, the divorced spouse can elect any amount of FSA coverage that an employee could elect. If there are dependents who also lose FSA coverage because of the divorce, each such dependent must also be offered the option of electing COBRA FSA coverage of

$1,000 (initially) at a monthly after-tax contribution of $102 a month for nine months. [CCH Pension Plan Guide, ¶ 26, 337]

Planning Pointer. While there would appear to be little advantage to contributing on an after-tax basis for FSA group health plan coverage, it does present a potential to "beat the system." In the example above, the divorced spouse could, for example, arrange for needed major surgery in January of the next year, elect the maximum amount of FSA coverage permitted under the plan for that year, pay one or two months' contributions, get reimbursed for all of the hospital and surgical bills, and then discontinue contributions. There appears to be little the employer can do to avoid such potential abuse of the FSA plan.

Q 7:74 How does the Americans with Disabilities Act (ADA) of 1990 affect health care FSAs?

Because health care FSAs are self-insured medical plans, they are prohibited from including in the FSA any disability-based distinction which would be treated as a "subterfuge to evade the purposes of the [ADA]." Exactly what this means is discussed in detail in Question 17:11.

Q 7:75 How does the Family and Medical Leave Act (FMLA) of 1993 affect cafeteria plans?

To the extent that any benefit offered under the cafeteria plan constitutes a "group health plan" for FMLA purposes, employees may continue their coverage during the period of leave provided they continue to pay the premiums (see Q 15:13).

Chapter 8

Dependent Care Assistance, Educational Assistance, and Group Legal Services

Three other forms of fringe benefits that employers frequently provide to their employees are dependent care assistance, educational assistance, and group legal services. Each has its own set of tax consequences, and each is affected by similar, but subtly different, additional tax rules, which this chapter reviews. (Note that the favorable tax rules for educational assistance will expire after December 31, 1994 (unless extended by Congress) and that the favorable tax rules for group legal services expired on June 30, 1992 and apparently will not be further extended by Congress.

Dependent Care Assistance

Q 8:1 What is a dependent care assistance program?

A dependent care assistance program is an employer-provided program of care for employees' dependents. Benefits may take the form of employer-maintained dependent care centers, cash reimbursement of dependent care expenses incurred by the employee, or both.

Q 8:2 Does the Employee Retirement Income Security Act (ERISA) apply to dependent care assistance programs?

No, generally such programs are not subject to ERISA. However, if the employer provides or sponsors a day care center, ERISA does apply. [ERISA § 3(1); DOL Adv Op 88-10A (Aug 12, 1988)] See Chapter 2 for a discussion of ERISA.

Q 8:3 Are employees taxed on benefits received from an employer-provided dependent care assistance program?

If the dependent care assistance program satisfies the requirements of Internal Revenue Code (Code) Section 129, the employee can exclude the reimbursements or the value of the services from income, up to the specified limits. [IRC § 129]

Q 8:4 May partners, S corporation shareholders, and sole proprietors receive tax-favored dependent care assistance benefits under an employer-provided program?

Yes, they may. The term "employee" as used in Code Section 129 includes a self-employed individual. A sole proprietor is treated as his or her own employer, and a partnership is treated as the employer of each of its partners. [IRC §§ 129(e)(3), 129(e)(4)]

Q 8:5   Can an employee who receives dependent care assistance benefits under an employer-provided program also claim the Code Section 21 tax credit for dependent care?

Not necessarily. Benefit payments received under a Code Section 129 employer-provided dependent care assistance program reduce the amount of expenses that may be taken into consideration under the federal income tax credit for dependent care assistance under Code Section 21 on a dollar-for-dollar basis. [IRC § 21(c)]

Q 8:6   Does the dependent care assistance program have to be in writing?

Yes, even though ERISA may not always apply to these programs (see Q 8:2), a separate provision contained in Code Section 129 requires that the employer-provided dependent care assistance program be set out in a separate written plan. [IRC § 129(d)(1)]

Q 8:7   What is the exclusive benefit requirement for employer-provided dependent care assistance programs?

Code Section 129 requires that an employer-provided dependent care assistance program be for the exclusive benefit of employees. [IRC § 129(d)(1)]

Q 8:8   What disclosure of program benefits is required to be made to eligible employees?

Code Section 129 imposes two disclosure requirements. First, the sponsoring employer must provide reasonable notification of the availability and terms of its program to eligible employees. [IRC § 129(d)(6)]

Second, the plan must furnish each employee who has received benefits in the preceding calendar year with a written statement by

January 31 showing the amounts paid or expenses incurred by the employer in providing dependent care assistance to the employee. [IRC § 129(d)(7)]

Q 8:9   What is the maximum amount of tax-favored benefits that may be provided by a dependent care assistance program?

Code Section 129 contains an overall dollar limit on the permissible amount of employer-provided dependent care assistance benefits plus an earned-income limitation that may further reduce (or completely eliminate) the dollar amount allowable. The maximum aggregate dollar amount of excludable employer-provided dependent care assistance benefits under Code Section 129 is the lesser of:

- $5,000 if the participant is single or is married and files a joint tax return; or

- $2,500 if the participant is married and files a separate tax return; or

- The earned income of the participant, if single; or

- If the participant is married, the "earned income" of the spouse who earned the lesser amount during the calendar year.

[IRC §§ 129(a)(2) and 129(b)]

Earned Income. A spouse who is incapacitated or who is a fulltime student for at least five months during the calendar year is treated as having earned income of not less than $200 per month if there is one qualifying dependent and not less than $400 per month if there are two or more qualifying dependents. [IRC §§ 21(d), 129(b)(2), 129(e)(2)]

On-Site Care. Dependent care assistance received from the employer's on-site facility is to be valued based on the use of the on-site facility by the employee's dependent(s) and the value of the services provided by the facility with respect to such dependent(s). [IRC § 129(e)(8)]

Q 8:10 If the employee's spouse does not work and is neither disabled nor a full-time student, can the employee receive any reimbursements under the employer's dependent care assistance program?

No, under these circumstances, the earned-income limitation discussed in Question 8:9 would reduce the amount of benefits available under the employer's plan to zero. [IRC §§ 21(d), 129(b)]

Q 8:11 Under the employer's plan, who can be a qualifying dependent?

To be excludable under Code Section 129, the dependent care expenses must be incurred in caring for a "qualifying individual." This includes any individual falling into one of the following three categories:

1. A dependent of the employee who is under the age of 13 and for whom the employee can claim a dependent tax deduction (personal exemption);
2. A dependent of the employee who is physically or mentally incapable of caring for himself or herself; or
3. The spouse of the employee, if the spouse is physically or mentally incapable of caring for himself or herself.

[IRC § 21(b)(1); Family Support Act of 1988, Pub L No 485, 100th Cong, 2d Sess (1988), § 703]

Q 8:12 What types of dependent care expenses can the employer's program cover?

The expenses must be for household services and care of qualifying dependents. The expenses must be incurred to enable the employee to be gainfully employed. Examples of expenses that may be paid for or reimbursed under a Code Section 129 plan include:

- At-home child care;

- Household services related to the care of elderly or disabled adults living with the employee who are "qualifying individuals" (see Q 8:11);
- Care at licensed nursery schools and kindergartens; and
- Dependent care centers meeting state or local government requirements and providing day care for more than six individuals (but not overnight or sleep-away camps).

The services cannot be provided by an individual for whom the employee or the employee's spouse can claim a personal tax exemption or by the employee's child under age 19 (determined as of the close of the taxable year). [IRC §§ 21(b)(2), 21(e)(6), 129(e)]

If the qualifying individual is not a dependent under the age of 13, dependent care expenses which are incurred outside the home can be taken into account only if the qualifying individual regularly spends at least eight hours a day in the employee's household. [IRC § 21(b)(2)(B)]

Q 8:13   Are employer-provided dependent care assistance programs subject to nondiscrimination rules?

Yes, they are. In order for the benefits to be excludable from federal income tax when received by employees, the plan may not discriminate in favor of highly compensated employees (as defined in Code Section 414(q)) or their dependents. To be nondiscriminatory, the plan must pass an eligibility test, a benefits test, a 25-percent-concentration test, and a 55-percent-concentration test. [IRC §§ 129(d)(2), 129(d)(3), 129(d)(4), and 129(d)(8)]

Q 8:14   What are the nondiscrimination tests?

Code Section 129 imposes the following four nondiscrimination requirements on employer-provided dependent care assistance plans:

1. *Eligibility test.* The program must benefit employees who qualify under a classification set up by the employer and found by the Internal Revenue Service (IRS) not to discriminate in favor of highly compensated employees (as defined in Code Section 414(q)) or their dependents.

2. *Benefits test.* The contributions or benefits under the program cannot discriminate in favor of highly compensated employees (as defined in Code Section 414(q)) or their dependents.

3. *25-percent-concentration test.* Not more than 25 percent of the amounts the employer pays or incurs for dependent care assistance during the year may be provided for more-than-5-percent owners of the stock or of the capital or profits interest in the employer at any time during the year (or their spouses or dependents).

4. *55-percent-concentration test.* The average benefits provided to non-highly compensated employees under all such plans of the employer must be at least 55 percent of the average benefits provided to highly compensated employees. In the case of any benefits provided through a salary reduction agreement, employees whose compensation is less than $25,000 may be disregarded when applying this test.

[IRC §§ 129(d)(2), 129(d)(3), 129(d)(4), 129(d)(8)]

Q 8:15   What are the tax consequences if the employer's dependent care assistance program fails the Code Section 129(d) requirements?

If the employer's dependent care assistance program fails any of the nondiscrimination requirements or other requirements (such as the separate written plan requirement) imposed by Code Section 129, only highly compensated employees will be taxed on the benefits received from the program. Non-highly compensated employees will not be affected and their plan benefits will continue to be excludable from federal income taxes up to the applicable limit under Code Section 129.

Q 8:16 Is the employer required to pay Social Security Federal Insurance Contribution Act (FICA) or Federal Unemployment Tax Act (FUTA) taxes on, or withhold taxes from, dependent care assistance program payments?

No, as long as it is reasonable for the employer to believe that payments from its Code Section 129 dependent care assistance program are excludable from the employee's gross income, such program payments are not subject to:

- FICA tax;
- FUTA tax; or
- Federal income tax withholding requirements.

[IRC §§ 3121(a)(18), 3306(b)(13), 3401(a)(18)]

Q 8:17 Can a dependent care assistance program be made a part of a cafeteria plan?

Yes, it can. A dependent care assistance program is a "qualified benefit" under the Code Section 125 cafeteria plan rules. Dependent care assistance programs can be included as a flexible spending arrangement (FSA) option and paid for by employee salary reduction or by employer contributions, or both. However, partners, sole proprietors, and more-than-2-percent shareholders in an S corporation would not be eligible to participate in the dependent care assistance plan, because cafeteria plans may only have employees as participants. See Chapter 7 for a discussion of the cafeteria plan rules, including the additional Code Section 125 nondiscrimination rules that would apply to such an arrangement. [IRC § 125(f); Prop Treas Reg §§ 1.125-1, Q&A 18, 1.125-2, Q&A 7(b)(8)]

Q 8:18 What is the dependent care tax credit?

Code Section 21 contains a tax credit for certain dependent care assistance expenses incurred by the taxpayer to enable him or her to be gainfully employed. Note, however, that benefit payments received under a Code Section 129 employer-provided dependent care assistance program will reduce the amount of expenses that may be taken into consideration under the federal income tax credit for dependent care assistance under Code Section 21 on a dollar-for-dollar basis. [IRC § 21(c)] The income level of the employee and his or her spouse will determine whether the employer-provided program benefit exclusion or the tax credit is more favorable.

The credit cannot exceed the individual's income tax liability, and married couples generally must file joint returns in order to claim the credit. [IRC §§ 21(a), 21(e)(2)]

Q 8:19 Does the employer have any obligation to help the employee determine which tax benefit—the exclusion or the credit—is more advantageous?

No, applicable tax rules do not presently require such disclosure. The requirement that an employer with a dependent care assistance program disclose to the employees that both the exclusion and the credit are available to them, and outline the circumstances under which one may be more advantageous than the other, was contained in the proposed Treasury regulations under former Code Section 89, which has been repealed.

Q 8:20 Is there any information that the employee must provide the IRS?

Yes, there is. An employee claiming a dependent care credit or exclusion must provide the name, address, and taxpayer identification number of each dependent care provider. Failure to provide this information will result in loss of the credit or exclusion unless the employee can show to the IRS's satisfaction that the taxpayer exercised due diligence in attempting to provide the information. If the dependent care provider is a tax-exempt organization, the requirement of a tax identification number does not apply, but the name and address of the tax-exempt organization must be provided on the tax return. [IRC §§ 21(e)(9), 129(e)(9), 6109(a)(3)]

Q 8:21   Is an employer required to report any dependent care assistance program information to the IRS?

Yes, in addition to any potential requirement of filing due to being an ERISA plan, Code Section 6039D separately requires that an annual return for the plan must be filed with the IRS. [IRC § 6039D] The IRS has specified that the Form 5500 Annual Report is to be used for this purpose.

Educational Assistance Programs

Q 8:22   What is an educational assistance program?

An educational assistance program is an employer-provided plan to assist employees in furthering their educations.

Q 8:23   Does ERISA apply to educational assistance programs?

ERISA does not apply if the plan is unfunded, that is, if payments are made solely from the general assets of the employer or employee organization. [DOL Reg § 2510.3-1(k); DOL Adv Op 89-10A (July 6, 1989)] See Chapter 2 for a discussion of ERISA.

Q 8:24   Are employees taxed on educational assistance benefits?

Under Code Section 127, if a plan meets certain requirements, employer payments up to a specified limit are excludable from an employee's federal gross income. [Treas Reg § 1.127-1] This favorable tax treatment originally expired on June 30, 1992, but it has been retroactively restored in full by the Omnibus Budget Reconciliation Act of 1993. However, as this book goes to press, this favorable tax treatment is scheduled to expire yet again, for taxable years beginning after December 31, 1994, unless Congress acts to extend the application of Code Section 127. [IRC § 127(d), OBRA '93, § 13101]

Without the Code Section 127 exclusion, benefits are taxable. However, if the education expense incurred by the employee is job-related, the expense may be either excludable from the employee's gross income or deductible by the employee (see Q 8:54–8:62).

Q 8:25 May partners, S corporation shareholders, and sole proprietors receive tax-favored educational assistance program benefits under an employer-provided plan?

Yes, they may, since they are treated as employees for purposes of Code Section 127, which governs employer-provided educational assistance programs. A sole proprietor is treated as his or her own employer, and a partnership is treated as the employer of each of its partners. [IRC §§ 127(c)(2), 127(c)(3)]

Q 8:26 Does the educational assistance program have to be in writing?

Yes, although ERISA does not apply to an unfunded educational assistance program (see Q 8:23), a separate provision contained in Code Section 127 requires that the employer-provided educational assistance program be set out in a separate written plan in order for the program's benefits to be excludable from income when they are received by employees. [IRC § 127(b)(1)]

Q 8:27 What is the exclusive benefit requirement for employer-provided educational assistance programs?

Code Section 127 requires that an employer-provided educational assistance program be for the exclusive benefit of employees. [IRC § 127(b)(1)]

Q 8:28 What disclosure of program benefits is required to be made to eligible employees?

The sponsoring employer must provide reasonable notification of the availability and terms of its educational assistance program to eligible employees. [IRC § 127(b)(6)]

Q 8:29   What is the maximum amount of tax-favored benefits that may be provided by an educational assistance program?

The maximum amount excludable from income in a taxable year is $5,250. [IRC § 127(a)(2)] Note the scheduled expiration of the exclusion after December 31, 1994 unless further extended by Congress (see Q 8:24).

Q 8:30   May an educational assistance program provide benefits to spouses or dependents who are not employees of the employer?

Spouses and dependents cannot be eligible under a plan that qualifies as an educational assistance program for tax purposes. [IRC § 127; Treas Reg § 1.127-2(d)]

Q 8:31   What types of educational assistance can the employer's program cover?

Qualifying educational assistance includes tuition, fees and similar payments, and the cost of books, supplies, and equipment. It does not include the cost of tools or supplies that may be retained after completion of a course, meals, lodging, or transportation; or any payment for any course or other education involving sports, games, or hobbies. [IRC § 127(c)(1); Treas Reg § 1.127-2(c)] Note that expenses that do not qualify under a Code Section 127 program may possibly qualify as a working condition fringe benefit under Code Section 132 or as a qualified scholarship reimbursement under Code Section 117.

Q 8:32   Can the employer's program cover graduate courses?

Yes it can, starting in 1991. Payments for any graduate-level courses of a type normally taken by an individual pursuing a program that leads to a law, business, medical, or similar advanced academic or professional degree are covered by the Code Section 127 exclusion beginning in 1991. The term graduate-level course means a course taken by an employee who has received a bachelor's degree (or its equivalent) or who is receiving credit toward a more advanced degree. [IRC § 127(c)(1), as amended by OBRA '90 § 11403]

Q 8:33 Are employer-provided educational assistance programs subject to nondiscrimination rules?

Yes, they are. In order for the benefits to be excludable from federal income tax when received by employees, the plan may not discriminate in favor of highly compensated employees (as defined in Code Section 414(q)) or their dependents. To be nondiscriminatory, the plan must pass an eligibility test and a 5-percent concentration test.

Q 8:34 What are the nondiscrimination tests?

Code Section 127 imposes the following two nondiscrimination requirements on employer-provided educational assistance programs:

1. *Eligibility test.* The program must benefit employees who qualify under a classification set up by the employer and found by the IRS not to discriminate in favor of highly compensated employees (as defined in Code Section 414(q)) or their dependents.

2. *5-Percent concentration test.* No more than 5 percent of the amounts paid or incurred by the employer for educational assistance during the year may be provided to more-than-5-percent owners of the stock or of the capital or profits interest of the employer (or to their spouses or dependents).

[IRC §§ 127(b)(2), 127(b)(3)]

Q 8:35 What are the tax consequences if the employer's educational assistance program fails the Code Section 127 nondiscrimination tests?

If the employer's educational assistance program fails either of the nondiscrimination tests imposed by Code Section 127, it appears that all employees, not just the highly compensated, will be taxed on the benefits received from the program. [IRC §§ 127(a), 127(b)] However, if the expenses are job-related, they may be deductible by the employee. [Treas Reg § 1.162-5]

Q 8:36   Is the employer required to pay FICA or FUTA taxes on, or withhold taxes from, educational assistance program payments?

No, as long as it is reasonable for the employer to believe that payments from its Code Section 127 educational assistance program are excludable from the employee's gross income, such program payments are not subject to

- FICA tax or FUTA tax; or
- Federal income tax withholding requirements.

[IRC §§ 3121(a)(18), 3306(b)(13), 3401(a)(18)]

Q 8:37   Can educational assistance be offered in a cafeteria or salary reduction plan?

No, it cannot be. The plan must not give eligible employees a choice between educational assistance and other remuneration includable in gross income. [IRC §§ 125(f) and 127(b)(4); Treas Reg § 1.127-2(c)(2)]

Q 8:38   Is an employer required to report any educational assistance program to the IRS?

An annual return for the plan must be filed with the IRS. [IRC § 6039D] The IRS has specified that the Form 5500 Annual Report is to be used for this purpose, but the instructions to this form currently exempt Code Section 127 plans providing only job-related training that is deductible under Code Section 162.

Qualified Scholarships and Tuition Reductions

Q 8:39 Is an educational assistance program the only way in which an employee can receive tax-free treatment of amounts received for educational expenses?

No. As pointed out in Question 8:24, if the educational expenses are job related, employer reimbursement of such expenses can qualify as a working condition fringe benefit under Code Section 132(d), excludable from income.

In addition, in limited circumstances, employers may be able to exclude reimbursed educational expenses on the ground that the amounts received are either qualified scholarships or qualified tuition reductions under Code Section 117. Provided the payments meet the qualification requirements of Code Section 117, they are excludable from gross income.

Q 8:40 What is the qualified scholarship exclusion from income?

Under Code Section 117(a), gross income does not include any amount received as a qualified scholarship by an individual who is a candidate for a degree at an educational institution described in Code Section 170(b)(1)(A)(ii), except to the extent the amount represents payment for services rendered. [IRC § 117(c)]

The term "qualified scholarship" means any amount received by an individual as a scholarship or fellowship grant to the extent the individual establishes that, in accordance with the conditions of the grant, such amount was used for qualified tuition and related purposes. [IRC § 117(b)(1), Prop Treas Reg § 1.117-6(c)(1)]

Q 8:41 What are qualified tuition and related expenses?

The term "qualified tuition and related expenses" means the following:

- Tuition and fees required for enrollment or attendance at the educational institution; and

- Fees, books, supplies, and equipment required for courses of instruction at the educational institution.

[IRC § 117(b)(2)]

Incidental expenses are not treated as related expenses. Incidental expenses include expenses for room and board, travel, research, clerical help, equipment, and other expenses that are not required. [Prop Treas Reg § 1.117-6(c)(2)]

The terms of the scholarship or fellowship grant need not expressly require that the amounts received be used for tuition and related expenses. However, to the extent the terms of the grant (1) specify that the grant cannot be used for tuition and related expenses or (2) designate a portion of the grant for other purposes, such amounts will not qualify for exclusion from income. [Prop Treas Reg § 1.117-6(c)(1)]

Q 8:42   What is a scholarship or fellowship grant?

A scholarship or fellowship grant is a cash amount paid or allowed to, or for the benefit of, an individual to aid in the pursuit of study or research. It also may be in the form of a reduction in the amount owed by the recipient to an educational organization for tuition, room and board, or any other fee. The grant may be funded by a governmental agency, college or university, charitable organization, business, or any other source. [Prop Treas Reg § 1.117-6(c)(3)]

Q 8:43   What is an educational organization as described in Code Section 170(b)(1)(A)(ii)?

An "educational organization," as described in Code Section 170(b)(1)(A)(ii), if it has as its primary function the presentation of formal instruction, normally maintains a regular faculty and curriculum, and normally has a regularly enrolled body of pupils or students in attendance at the place where its educational activities are regularly carried on. [Prop Treas Reg § 1.117-6(c)(5)]

Q 8:44   Who is a candidate for a degree?

A candidate for a degree is any one of the following:

- A primary or secondary school student;
- An undergraduate or graduate student at a college or university who is pursuing studies or conducting research to meet the requirements for an academic or professional degree; or
- A full-time or part-time student at an educational institution described in Code Section 170(b)(1)(A)(ii) that
  - Provides an educational program that is acceptable for full credit toward a bachelor's or higher degree or offers a program of training to prepare the student for gainful employment in a recognized occupation, and
  - Is authorized under federal or state law to provide such a program and is accredited by a nationally recognized accreditation agency.

[Prop Treas Reg § 1.117-11(c)(4)]

Q 8:45   Is a qualified scholarship excludable from gross income if it is provided in return for services?

No. The portion of any amount received as a qualified scholarship that represents payment for teaching, research, or other services required as a condition for receiving the grant is not excluded from income. [IRC § 117(c)]

A requirement of the grant that the recipient pursue studies, research, or other activities primarily for the benefit of the grantor is treated as a requirement to perform services. A grant conditional upon past, present, or future teaching, research, or other services also constitutes payment for services. [Prop Treas Reg § 1.117-6(d)(ii)]

Q 8:46   If only a portion of a scholarship or fellowship grant is a payment for services, how is the exclusion determined?

An allocation must be made, based on what is reasonable compensation for the services performed as a condition of the grant. [Prop Treas Reg § 1.117-6(d)(3)]

Q 8:47   How are these rules on payment for services applied?

Example 1. If a qualified scholarship is provided under a requirement that the individual work for the grantor after graduation, the entire amount of the scholarship is includable in the recipient's income as wages. [Prop Treas Reg § 1.117-6(d)(5), Examples (1) and (2)]

Example 2. If an individual receives a $6,000 scholarship from a university that requires the individual to work as a researcher for the university, and a researcher without a scholarship is paid $2,000 for such services, $4,000 is excludible from gross income and $2,000 must be included in income as wages. [Prop Treas Reg § 1.117-6(d)(5), Example (5)]

Example 3. Tuition assistance payments made by a university on behalf of a faculty member to other schools, attended by the faculty member's children, with which the university had no reciprocal agreement, were held not to qualify as scholarships and were held to be taxable as compensation. [Knapp v Commissioner, 867 F 2d 749 (2d Cir 1989)]

Q 8:48   What is a qualified tuition reduction exclusion from income?

Gross income does not include any qualified tuition reduction [IRC § 117(d)(1)], except to the extent that it represents payment for services rendered. [IRC § 117(c)]

Q 8:49   What is a qualified tuition reduction?

The term "qualified tuition reduction" means the amount of any reduction in tuition provided to an employee of an educational organization described in Code Section 170(b)(1)(A)(ii) for the education, normally below the graduate level at such organization or another such organization, of the following:

- The employee; or
- Any person treated as an employee, or whose use is treated as an employee use, under the fringe benefit rules in Code Section

132(f) (this includes the spouse and dependent children of the employee of the educational institution).

[IRC § 117(d)(2)]

Q 8:50   Does this mean that no qualified tuition reduction can be provided for graduate-level education?

No. There is a limited exception in the case of the education of an individual who is a graduate student at the educational institution and who is engaged in teaching or research activities for the educational institution. For such individuals, the general requirement that the education must be below the graduate level does not apply. [IRC § 117(d)(5)]

Q 8:51   Are there nondiscrimination rules that apply to qualified tuition reduction programs?

Yes. A qualified tuition reduction provided to a highly compensated employee is excludable from the individual's gross income only if such reduction is available on substantially the same terms to each member of a group of employees that is defined under a reasonable classification set up by the employer that does not discriminate in favor of highly compensated employees. Highly compensated employees are defined in Code Section 414(q), the definition used for qualified pension plan purposes. [IRC § 117(d)(3)]

Q 8:52   If a qualified tuition reduction program is discriminatory, are the benefits taxable to all participants, or only to those in the highly compensated employee category?

If the qualified tuition reduction program is discriminatory in favor of highly compensated employees, the highly compensated employees lose the entire benefit of the exclusion from gross income. However, employees who are not highly compensated and who received a qualified tuition reduction obtain the benefit of the income exclusion. [Priv Ltr Rul 90-41-085 (July 19, 1990)]

Q 8:53   Is a qualified scholarship program or a qualified tuition reduction plan subject to ERISA?

No, as long as the program is unfunded, it is not subject to ERISA. The definition of a "welfare plan" is not considered to include a scholarship program. ("Scholarship program" includes tuition and education expense refund programs, under which payments are made solely from the general assets of the employer.) [DOL Reg § 2510.3-1(k)]

Job-Related Educational Benefits

Q 8:54   How are employer-provided educational benefits treated for federal income tax purposes if the benefits do not qualify for exclusion under Code Sections 127 or 117?

If the educational benefits are job-related, they may be excluded from the employee's gross income as a working condition fringe benefit. If the amounts paid by the employer are for education relating to the employee's trade or business of being an employee of the employer, so that, if the employee paid for the education, the amount paid could be deducted as a business expense by the employee under Code Section 162, the costs of the education may be excluded as a working condition fringe. [Treas Reg § 1.132-1(f)(1)]

If the educational expenses are not job-related, and are not eligible for exclusion under Code Sections 127 or 117, they are fully taxable to the employee.

Q 8:55   What employer-provided educational benefits are considered deductible as employee business expenses under Code Section 162, and thus excludable from gross income?

Educational expenses are deductible as ordinary and necessary business expenses by an employee if the education:

- Maintains or improves skills required by the employee in his or her employment; or

- Meets the express requirements of the employer, or the requirements of applicable law or regulation, imposed as a condition
  of the retention by the employee of an established employment
  relationship, status, or rate of compensation.

[Treas Reg § 1.162-5(a)]

Q 8:56　What kinds of educational expenses are considered expenses incurred to maintain or improve skills required in the employee's job?

Educational expenses incurred to maintain the employee's skills
include refresher courses or courses dealing with current developments as well as academic or vocational courses (whether or not
leading to an academic degree), as long as the expenses are not
required to meet minimal educational requirements of the employee's
job and do not qualify the employee for a new trade or business.
[Treas Reg § 1.162-5(c)(1)]

Q 8:57　When is an employer-provided educational benefit considered to be incurred in order to meet the express requirements of the employer, and therefore excludable from gross income?

The requirement must be imposed for a bona fide business
purpose of the employer, and only the minimum education necessary
to the employee's retention of his or her employment relationship,
status or rate of compensation is considered to be required. Education
in excess of that required may qualify as expenses incurred to
maintain or improve the employee's skills (see Q 8:56). [Treas Reg
§ 1.162-5(c)(2)]

Q 8:58　What employer-provided educational benefits do not qualify as deductible employee business expenses, and therefore are not excludable from gross income?

Employer-provided educational benefits do not qualify as deductible employee business expenses when the education:

- Is required by the employee in order to qualify for the minimum educational requirements of his or her position; or
- Is part of a program of study pursued by the employee that will lead to qualifying the employee for a new trade or business.

Once the employee has met the minimum educational requirements for his or her position, the employee will be treated as continuing to meet those requirements even if they are changed. Thus, educational expenses to meet such changed requirements by an employee who formerly met the old requirements may qualify as expenses to maintain or improve the employee's skills. [Treas Reg § 1.162-5(b)(2)(i)]

Q 8:59   What expenses qualify as educational expenses?

Educational expenses include tuition, books, and other incidental expenses, such as laboratory fees. Local travel between the employee's place of business and the educational institution is deductible, but local travel between the employee's home and the educational institution is considered a nondeductible commuting expense by the IRS unless the education is on a strictly temporary basis. [IRS Pub 17, "Your Federal Income Tax for Individuals" (1992 ed), 226] Travel expenses, including those for meals and lodging, incurred while away from home overnight to obtain work-related education are generally deductible as employee business expenses. [Treas Reg § 1.162-5(e)]

Q 8:60   Can the employer exclude the cost of the educational benefit from the employee's gross income if the employer reimburses or advances the cost to the employee in cash rather than paying the cost directly to the educational institution?

Yes it can, provided the reimbursement or advance payment arrangement satisfies IRS requirements for an "accountable plan," which are, in general, that the employer must:

1. Determine that the expenses would be deductible by the employee;

2. Obtain substantiation of the expenses; and

3. Require repayment of excess reimbursements within a reasonable period of time.

[Treas Reg § 1.62-2(c)]

Q 8:61   Are employer-provided educational benefits not qualifying under Code Sections 127 or 117 subject to income tax withholding?

If the educational expenses are deductible employee business expenses, and if the employer pays the cost directly or reimburses the employee for the cost under an "accountable plan," no income tax withholding is required. [IRC § 3401(a)(19); Treas Reg 31.3401(a)-4] If the cost of the educational benefits does not qualify as a deductible employee business expense and therefore does not qualify as a working condition fringe under Code Section 132, income tax withholding is required. [Temp Treas Reg § 31.3401(a)-1T]

Q 8:62   Are employer-provided educational benefits not qualifying under Code Sections 127 or 117 subject to FICA and FUTA tax?

If the educational expenses are deductible employee business expenses, and if the employer pays the cost directly or reimburses the employee for the cost under an "accountable plan," no FICA or FUTA tax applies. However, if the cost is not a deductible employee business expense and therefore is not a working condition fringe benefit for Code Section 132 purposes, FICA and FUTA taxes apply. [IRC §§ 3121(a)(20), 3306(b)(16); Treas Reg §§ 31.3121(a)-3(a), 31.3306(b)-2(a)]

Group Legal Services Plans

Q 8:63   What is a group legal services plan?

A group legal services plan is an employer-funded program to provide personal legal services to employees, their spouses, and their dependents.

Q 8:64 Does ERISA apply to group legal services plans?

Yes, it does. [ERISA § 3(1); DOL Reg § 2510.3-1(a)(2)] See Chapter 2 for a discussion of ERISA.

Q 8:65 Are employees taxed on benefits received from employer-provided group legal services plans?

No unless Congress acts to extend Code Section 120. Under Code Section 120, if the plan met specific requirements, certain contributions and benefits were excludable from the employee's gross income. The exclusion applied to insurance coverage (whether through an insurer or self-insured) with a value of up to $70 each taxable year. The value of coverage in excess of that amount was not excluded from gross income. [IRC §§ 120(a), 120(d)] This favorable tax treatment is not available for taxable years beginning after June 30, 1992 or for amounts paid after that date in a taxable year beginning in 1992, unless Congress acts to further extend Code Section 120. [IRC § 120(e); Tax Extension Act of 1991, § 104(a)(2)] While Congress in OBRA '93 extended certain tax provisions, it did not extend the favorable tax treatment of group legal services plans.

Q 8:66 Could partners, shareholders, and sole proprietors receive tax-favored group legal services benefits under an employer-provided plan?

Yes, they could. The term "employee" as used in Code Section 120 included a self-employed individual. A sole proprietor was treated as his or her own employer, and a partnership was treated as the employer of each of its partners, who in turn, were treated as employees. [IRC §§ 120(d)(1), 120(d)(2)]

Q 8:67 Was the Code Section 120 exclusion available regardless of how the group legal services plan was funded?

No, it was not. The employer could not self-fund the plan, that is, pay reimbursements of legal expenses out of the employer's general assets. The employer had to make payments to:

- Insurers, or other organizations or persons that provide personal legal services, or indemnification against the cost of personal legal services, in exchange for a prepayment or payment of a premium;

- A group legal services trust that was tax-exempt under Code Section 501(c)(20) or to another tax-exempt entity permitted to receive such payments; or

- Providers of legal services under the plan as prepayments.

[IRC § 120(c)(5); Prop Treas Reg § 1.120-2(g); IRS Gen Couns Mem 39485 (Sept. 30, 1985)]

Q 8:68   Did the group legal services plan have to be in writing?

In addition to the ERISA written plan document requirement, a separate provision contained in Code Section 120 required that the employer-provided group legal services plan be set out in a separate written plan in order for the plan's benefits to be excludable from income when they were received by employees. [IRC § 120(b)]

Q 8:69   What was the exclusive benefit requirement for employer-provided group legal services plans?

Code Section 120 required that an employer-provided group legal services plan be for the exclusive benefit of employees or their spouses or dependents. [IRC § 120(b)]

Q 8:70   Was the employer required to obtain a determination letter from the IRS in order for the plan to qualify under Code Section 120?

Yes, the employer had to apply for and obtain a determination letter from the IRS that its group legal services plan was a plan qualified under Code Section 120. [IRC § 120(c)(4); Treas Reg § 1.120-3]

Q 8:71 What was the maximum amount of tax-favored benefits that may be provided by a group legal services plan?

The maximum amount of excludable benefits for legal services that could be provided by an employer-provided Code Section 120 plan in any taxable year was limited to benefits provided through employer contributions equal to an insurance value of $70. [IRC § 120(a)]

Q 8:72 What was the tax effect if the $70 annual limit on the excludable amount was exceeded?

The employee was taxed on the excess. However, if a tax-exempt trust was a part of the plan, it did not lose its tax-exempt status. [IRC § 120(a)(2), Conf Rpt to accompany HR 4333, H Rpt 1104, 100th Cong, 2d Sess (1988), at 80]

Q 8:73 What types of legal service expenses could the employer's plan cover?

Personal legal expenses which were specified in the plan qualified. These included obtaining alimony or a split of community property; protecting or asserting rights to property of a decedent in the capacity of heir or legatee of the decedent; and claims for damages for personal injury (other than compensatory damages). [Prop Treas Reg § 1.120-2(c)] The plan also could provide a limited initial consultation about whether the recipient needed personal legal services. [Prop Treas Reg § 1.120-2(c)(4)]

Personal legal expenses generally did not include legal expenses connected with or pertaining to (1) a trade or business; (2) the management, conservation, or preservation of property held for the production of income by the employee or a spouse or dependent; or (3) the production or collection of income by the employee or a spouse or dependent. [Prop Treas Reg § 1.120-2(c)(1)]

Q 8:74   Were employer-provided group legal services plans subject to nondiscrimination rules?

Yes, they were. In order for benefits to be excludable from federal income tax when received by employees, the plan could not discriminate as to contributions or benefits in favor of highly compensated employees (as defined in Code Section 414(q)) and certain other individuals. To be nondiscriminatory, the plan also had to pass an eligibility test and a 25 percent concentration test. [IRC § 120(c)(1)]

Q 8:75   What were the nondiscrimination tests?

Code Section 120 imposed the following three nondiscrimination requirements on employer-provided group legal services plans:

1. *Eligibility test.* The plan had to benefit employees who qualify under a classification set up by the employer and found by the IRS not to discriminate in favor of highly compensated employees (as defined in Code Section 414(q)). Employees covered by a collective bargaining agreement could be excluded if group legal services benefits were the subject of good-faith bargaining.

2. *Contributions and benefits test.* Contributions or benefits under the plan could not discriminate in favor of employees who were officers, shareholders, self-employed, or highly compensated, or their spouses or dependents. Contributions or benefits that varied by years of service were not discriminatory if the formula did not favor the highly compensated group. However, if benefits increased as compensation increased, the benefits are discriminatory in favor of the highly compensated. [IRC § 120(c)(1); Prop Treas Reg § 1.120-2(e)(3)]

3. *25 percent concentration test.* Not more than 25 percent of the amounts contributed under the plan during the year could be provided for shareholders or owners who directly or indirectly held more than 5 percent of the stock or of the capital or profits interest in the employer (or for their spouses or dependents).

[IRC §§ 120(c)(2) and 120(c)(3)]

Proposed Treasury Regulations would have added a further test: the plan could not discriminate in favor of highly compensated employees in actual operation. A persistent pattern of greater utilization by highly compensated employees could disqualify the plan. [Prop Treas Reg §§ 1.120-2(e)(2), 1.120-2(e)(3)(ii)]

Q 8:76　Was the employer required to pay FICA or FUTA taxes on group legal services plan payments?

No, as long as it was reasonable for the employer to believe that payments from its Section 120 educational assistance program were excludable from the employee's gross income, such program payments were not subject to

- FICA tax;
- FUTA tax; or
- Federal income tax withholding requirements.

[IRC §§ 3121(a)(17), 3306(b)(12); IRS Pub 15, Cir E, Employer's Tax Guide (1992)]

Q 8:77　Was an employer required to report any group legal services plan information to the IRS?

Yes. In addition to the Form 5500 Annual Report required to be filed due to Title I of ERISA, Code Section 6039D separately required that an annual return be filed with the IRS. The IRS specified that the Form 5500 Annual Report was to be used for this purpose also. This requirement apparently applies for periods after the expiration of Code Section 120 on July 1, 1992.

Chapter 9

Group Long-Term Care Insurance

Group long-term care insurance is a rapidly developing benefit designed to provide financial assistance to, or on behalf of, individuals (usually older individuals) whose ability to care for themselves has become significantly diminished or impaired. This chapter discusses what group long-term care insurance is, how it is treated for tax and other purposes, and whether it can be included in cafeteria plans.

Basic Concepts

Q 9:1 Why is group long-term care insurance becoming increasingly popular?

A number of factors have converged to facilitate the development of group long-term care insurance, including the following:

- There is a greater percentage of older individuals than before. Older individuals presently constitute approximately 10 percent of the population of the United States, and this percentage is expected to increase to over 25 percent in the next 60 years or so.
- Individuals are living longer, leading to a projected increase in the number of older people in the future.
- Improvements in medical technology help to extend life but may not always restore health. As a result, individuals in an impaired condition may live substantially longer.
- Neither governmental medical programs nor private employer medical plans offer extensive coverage for skilled nursing care, hospice care, and home care; and custodial care is almost always excluded.

Q 9:2   What is long-term care?

"Long-term care" is a term without a precise definition as yet. It generally refers to financial protection against potentially devastating costs associated with long-term care for functionally disabled individuals who are unable to care for themselves because of a chronic or long-term nonremediable physical or mental condition. Long-term care covers both medical and nonmedical support services provided in a setting other than an acute care unit of a hospital.

Q 9:3   When is an individual considered functionally disabled?

An individual is considered functionally disabled when he or she cannot perform some or all of the "activities of daily living" (ADLs). While there is no officially agreed-upon definition, ADLs are generally viewed as including:

- Bathing
- Dressing
- Eating
- Maintaining continence
- Transferring (moving from a bed or chair)

- Walking
- Using the toilet

Coverage under group long-term care insurance policies is typically triggered by the inability to perform a specific number (such as two or three, for example) of ADLs. Some policies also consider the individual's ability to take medication.

Covered Benefits

Q 9:4   What types of care and services are typically covered by group long-term care insurance?

Group long-term care insurance policies typically cover the following services, usually for employees and spouses, retirees and spouses, and in some cases also the employee's parents and parents-in-law:

- Nursing home care
- Home health care
- Adult day care
- Respite care (temporary care provided to allow the caregiver some time away from the patient)

Group long-term care insurance policies frequently incorporate managed care features to control costs, such as individual case management. Long-term care encompasses more than just medical care; it also includes a broad range on nonrehabilitative personal and social services, such as transportation, meal preparation, housekeeping services, and help with the ADLs, such as eating, dressing, and bathing. Such additional nonmedical services are custodial in nature and generally are not covered, or are covered only for a strictly limited duration, under traditional medical insurance.

The National Association of Insurance Commissioners (NAIC) has adopted a model law and regulation to serve as a guide for state legislation. Alzheimer's disease is specifically required to be covered.

Note that long-term care benefits might also be provided as an accelerated death benefit feature of a life insurance policy. Accelerated death benefits are discussed in Chapter 12.

Q 9:5   Is group long-term care insurance considered accident and health insurance?

Not entirely. Group long-term care insurance is a hybrid product— one that combines various features of (1) life insurance (through buildup of individual reserves sometimes characterized as similar to group universal life insurance); (2) medical insurance; and (3) other coverage not falling under either of those two general categories, such as custodial care, certain adult day care services and respite care.

Legislative proposals have been introduced in Congress to clarify in a way favorable to the insureds the federal income tax treatment of long-term care insurance coverage and benefits. The legislative proposals would grant long-term care insurance meeting certain specified statutory requirements the same favorable tax treatment accorded to accident and health insurance. However, as this book goes to press, no bill has been passed.

Tax Treatment of Employers

Q 9:6   Can employers deduct the cost of group long-term care insurance?

There is no clear guidance on this issue.

It appears that an employer may be able to deduct the full premium cost under Code Section 162 as reasonable compensation, even though long-term care insurance clearly covers items falling outside of the Section 213 definition of medical care. However, if the group long-term care insurance is viewed as deferred compensation or as including any features that the Internal Revenue Service (IRS) would consider to be deferred compensation, the employer's ability to deduct such premium payments may be limited. The IRS has not issued any guidance on whether long-term care insurance would constitute an arrangement for the deferral of compensation. [IRC §§ 162 and 404; Treas Reg § 1.162-10]

Employer-paid long-term care insurance is very rare, and virtually all plans are entirely employee-paid.

Tax Treatment of Coverage Provided to Employees

Q 9:7 How are employees taxed on the monthly value of employer-paid group long-term care insurance?

There is presently no clear guidance on this issue.

Code Section 106 shields employees from taxation on the value of monthly value of coverage under employer-paid accident and health insurance plans. As defined in the regulations, accident and health insurance is an arrangement for the payment of amounts to employees in the event of personal injuries or sickness. The terms "personal injuries" and "sickness" arguably are broad enough to cover benefits under a group long-term care insurance plan. [IRC § 106; Treas Reg § 1.105-5(a)] However, because the IRS has not yet ruled on whether employer-paid long-term care insurance would qualify as "accident and health insurance" under Code Section 106, the tax treatment of the value of long-term care insurance coverage paid for by an employer is unclear and the appropriate tax treatment to employees thus remains an open issue.

Tax Treatment of Benefits Received by Employees

Q 9:8 How are employees taxed on benefits received from employer-paid group long-term care insurance?

There is no clear guidance on this issue.

As noted above, the IRS has not ruled on whether employer-paid group long-term care insurance enjoys the same favorable tax treatment as accident and health insurance under Code Sections 104 and 105. The exclusion from income under Code Section 105 applies to benefit payments received from employer-paid accident and health insurance plans only if one of the following conditions is satisfied:

- The amount must be paid, directly or indirectly, to reimburse an individual for expenses incurred for medical care within the meaning of Code Section 213 for the taxpayer, his or her spouse, and his or her dependents as defined under Code Section 152; or

- The amount must constitute payment for the permanent loss or loss of the use of a member or function of the body, or the permanent disfigurement of the taxpayer, his or her spouse, or a dependent within the meaning of Code Section 152 and it be computed without regard to the period the employee is absent from work.

These limitations create several problems when applied to benefit payments from employer-paid group long-term care insurance. First, payments made to or on behalf of parents and in-laws would not qualify for this exclusion. Second, not all of the benefits under the plan are likely to qualify as medical care within the meaning of Code Section 213. Third, although the benefits could be characterized, alternatively, as payments in respect of the loss of one or more body members or bodily functions, the IRS might not agree with this characterization.

Accordingly, it appears that not all of the benefits received from employer-paid group long-term care insurance will be excludable under Code Section 105. As this book goes to press, the IRS has not ruled on whether all or a portion of the benefits received would be excludable from the employee's income or whether the entire benefit would be taxable.

Q 9:9 How are employees taxed on benefits received from employee-pay-all group long-term care insurance?

There is no clear guidance on this issue.

If employees pay the entire premium for group long-term care insurance coverage on an after-tax basis, the tax treatment of benefits received from such a plan would be governed by Code Section 104 rather than Code Section 105. Code Section 104 excludes from gross income any benefit payments received from "accident or health insurance for personal injuries or sickness," to the extent such insurance is not paid for by the employer or attributable to employer contributions that were not includable in the employee's gross income.

For this purpose, "personal injury" is defined as an externally caused sudden hurt or damage to the body brought about by an identifiable event, and the term "sickness" is defined to include all other mental illnesses, bodily infirmities and disorders, and diseases. These terms appear to be deliberately broad, and the benefits provided by a group long-term care insurance plan would appear to fall within the scope of such definitions. Significantly, the Code Section 104 exclusion is not contingent upon either (1) the payments being made for Code Section 213 "medical care" or (2) loss of a body member or bodily function. As this book goes to press, the IRS has not ruled on whether all or a portion of the benefits received would be excludable from the employee's income or whether the entire benefit would be taxable.

Characterization under Other Laws

Q 9:10   Is group long-term care insurance subject to ERISA?

Yes, it can be. Despite some confusion about how it is to be characterized, group long-term care insurance apparently does cover, at least in part, "medical, surgical, or hospital care or benefits, or benefits in the event of sickness, accident, disability" within the meaning of Section 3(1) of ERISA. Although long-term care insurance plans typically are offered to employees on an employee-pay-all basis, such a plan will still be considered as maintained by an employer (and hence subject to ERISA) if the employer promotes or endorses the program. [29 CFR § 2510.3-1(j)]

Accordingly, ERISA's requirements regarding plan documents, summary plan descriptions, Form 5500 Annual Report filings, summary annual reports, and fiduciary responsibilities would apply. Additionally, to the extent that group long-term care insurance plans also satisfy the definition of "group health plan" contained in new

Section 609 of ERISA (added by the Omnibus Budget Recondiliation Act of 1993), it also would be subject to the Medicare and Medicaid Coverage Data Bank reporting requirements (see Chapter 3).

Q 9:11 Do the COBRA continuation of coverage requirements apply to group long-term care insurance?

Apparently, yes. Although Congress may never have intended such a result, group long-term care insurance plans may fall within COBRA's definition of a covered "group health plan." A covered group health plan for COBRA continuation of coverage purposes is a plan which provides "medical care" within the meaning of Code Section 213 and which is "maintained or contributed to by the employer." (These requirements are discussed in Chapter 6.)

Q 9:12 Does the Family and Medical Leave Act of 1993 (FMLA) apply to group long-term care insurance?

Apparently, yes. Although Congress may never have intended this result, group long-term care insurance plans may fall within the FMLA's provisions concerning group health plans. As such, the coverage could be continued during the period of FMLA leave provided the employee paid the premiums (see Q 15:23).

Inclusion in Cafeteria Plans

Q 9:13 Can long-term care insurance be included under the employer's cafeteria plan?

The answer is currently unclear.

The Code Section 125(d)(2) provision that a cafeteria plan cannot include any plan that provides for "deferred compensation" appears to raise a possible barrier to including long-term care insurance in a cafeteria plan. IRS regulations provide that a cafeteria plan operates to permit the deferral of compensation if the plan permits participants to use contributions for one plan year to purchase a benefit that will be provided in a subsequent plan year, such as "long-term care insurance coverage with a savings or investment feature such as whole life insurance." [Prop Treas Reg § 1.125-2, Q&A 5(a)] Long-term care insurance typically does provide coverage in future plan years and does build up substantial reserves similar to whole life insurance. Thus, long-term care insurance may be considered a form of "deferred compensation," even if paid for with employee after-tax contributions.

Even if the group long-term care insurance were not viewed as deferred compensation, including it in a cafeteria plan on an employer-paid or salary reduction (pre-tax) basis would raise additional issues. First, the employer's contribution must be for one of the "qualified benefits" permitted under Code Section 125. Group long-term care insurance arguably may qualify as employer-provided accident and health insurance under Code Section 106 (see Q 9:7). Even if Code Section 106 were satisfied, it only operates to shield employees from taxation of the monthly value of such coverage. Whether the employer could deduct its premium payments for such coverage is unresolved (see Q 9:6). Further, excludability of the benefits received would then be governed by Code Section 105, which may not fully shield such employer-paid benefits from inclusion in gross income (see Q 9:8) and in any case, would not exclude benefits received by or on behalf of in-laws or parents. The employer could, however, offer long-term care insurance on an after-tax basis separately from the cafeteria plan.

The current uncertainty over the tax treatment of long-term care insurance has generally prevented employers from providing it as an employer-subsidized benefit or on a salary-reduction basis under cafeteria plans. If Congress or the IRS should provide partial or fully favorable tax treatment, long-term care insurance presumably would become a widely available feature under cafeteria plans.

Chapter 10

Disability Income Plans

Disability income plans are employer plans, some mandated by state law, that provide partial income replacement for employees who become disabled. Because employer-provided disability income benefits are generally taxable to employees, the Internal Revenue Code (Code) nondiscrimination requirements of Code Section 105(h) generally do not apply to disability income benefits. However, disability income plans have their own traps and pitfalls, which are reviewed in this chapter.

Basic Concepts

Q 10:1   What is a disability income plan?

A disability income plan is a plan that provides income-replacement benefits to employees who are unable to work because of illness or accident. This type of plan does what its name implies; it "replaces" a portion of the income or compensation lost while the employee is disabled. Thus, the level of benefits generally is dependent upon the employee's predisability income level, not on the nature and extent of his or her particular disability. Typically, the plan benefits consist of a stream of income payments, usually paid on a monthly or weekly basis, although some plans also contain a cash lump-sum feature.

Q 10:2   Does federal law require employers to provide employees with disability income benefits?

No, there is no federal law that requires employers to provide employees with disability income benefits. However, numerous state law requirements exist.

Q 10:3   Are employers required to provide employees with disability income benefits under state law?

Yes, employers must, at a minimum, provide disability income protection for job-related disabilities. All states have workers' compensation laws that require coverage of job-related disabilities. Depending on the laws of the state involved, coverage may be provided through employer contributions to a state insurance fund, self-insurance, or insurance with an insurance carrier. (See Chapter 19 for a discussion of funding issues and Chapter 2 for a discussion of ERISA preemption of state workers compensation laws.)

In addition, California, Hawaii, New Jersey, New York, Rhode Island, and Puerto Rico have temporary disability laws requiring coverage for disabilities that are not job related. Here too, the employer can generally choose from among several options: participating in a state fund, self-insuring, or insuring with a private insurance carrier. (Rhode Island, for example, requires participation in the state fund.) The disability income benefits are limited in amount (generally, one half to two thirds of the employee's weekly wage, subject to statutory minimums and maximums) and temporary in nature (52 weeks or less). The benefits are generally funded through employee and employer contributions (except California and Rhode Island, where the employer is required to provide only an employee-pay-all plan).

Many employers provide disability benefits over and above those mandated by state laws.

Q 10:4   What types of disability income plans do employers typically provide?

As might be expected, employers voluntarily offer a wide variety of income-replacement-type disability plans. Types of plans include:

1. *Wage continuation or sick pay.* The employer continues payment of all or part of the employee's salary for a specified period of disability.

2. *Short-term disability income benefits.* (These are also sometimes referred to as temporary disability benefits or "TDI.") The employee receives a portion of his or her regular wages under a formal plan of short-term disability benefits (for example, for 13 weeks, 26 weeks, or the like) under an insured, trusteed, or self-insured arrangement. (See Chapter 19 for further discussion of funding.)

3. *Long-term disability income benefits.* This coverage, which usually starts after short-term disability income benefits cease, generally provides a partial income-replacement benefit to employees who are not likely to return to work because of the total and/or permanent nature of their disabilities. This type of plan will frequently provide for offsets for other disability or retirement-type benefits, such as disability or retirement benefits under Social Security or under a retirement plan.

Q 10:5   Does the Employee Retirement Income Security Act (ERISA) apply to disability income-type plans?

The answer depends on the type of plan at issue. ERISA's definition of a covered "employee welfare benefit plan" includes plans providing benefits in the event of sickness or disability. However, an unfunded short-term disability plan is treated as a payroll practice and not as a welfare benefit plan subject to ERISA (see Q 2:14).

In addition, ERISA does not cover any plan maintained solely for the purpose of complying with applicable workers' compensation laws or unemployment compensation or disability insurance laws. The U.S. Supreme Court has interpreted this ERISA exemption to require that plans maintained to comply with state disability laws also must be administered separately in order to qualify for the exemption. Thus, if an employer's plan provides broader benefits than those required to satisfy the state temporary disability law, ERISA governs the entire plan, and the state temporary disability law cannot regulate it (even if the portion intended to comply with the state disability requirement is deficient). The state law can, however, require the employer to maintain a separate plan to satisfy the state temporary disability law if the employer's ERISA plan does not do so. [ERISA §§ 3(1), 4(b)(3); Shaw v Delta Airlines, 103 S Ct 2890 (1983)] (See Chapter 2 for a discussion of ERISA.)

Q 10:6   Do employers also typically provide any dismemberment benefits?

Yes, some employers also provide dismemberment benefits. This type of plan generally offers a flat payment for loss of a leg, arm, eye, or the like. Such benefits generally are combined with accidental death benefit insurance. (See Chapter 12 for a discussion of accidental death and dismemberment benefits.)

Q 10:7   Does the Family and Medical Leave Act (FMLA) apply to disability income and dismemberment benefits?

Yes, it does. See Chapter 15 for a detailed discussion of the FMLA, including particularly the FMLA's provisions regarding sick pay.

Q 10:8   Does the Consolidated Omnibus Budget Reconciliation Act (COBRA) apply to disability income or dismemberment plans?

No, it does not. COBRA applies only to certain group health plans. (See Chapter 6 for a discussion of COBRA.)

Q 10:9   Do any tax nondiscrimination rules apply to disability plans?

Generally, the Internal Revenue Code does not impose any nondiscrimination rules on disability plans. However, if a disability plan is funded using a Code Section 501(c)(9) voluntary employees' beneficiary association (VEBA) trust, then the plan (other than certain collectively bargained plans) must meet the following nondiscrimination rules imposed by Code Section 505(b):

1. Each class of benefits must be provided under a classification of employees that is found by the Internal Revenue Service (IRS) not to discriminate in favor of highly compensated employees; and

2. The benefits within each class of benefits must not discriminate in favor of highly compensated employees.

If a disability income benefit funded under a VEBA trust is tied to compensation, only the first $200,000 indexed by the IRS (for 1993, the indexed amount is $235,840) can be taken into account for years before 1994. For 1994 and later, the compensation limit is set at $150,000, indexed to the cost of living starting in 1995. In the case of a plan maintained pursuant to one or more collective bargaining agreements in effect on August 10, 1993, the new compensation limit takes effect on the later of January 1, 1994 or the date the last collective bargaining agreement terminates (without regard to any extension, amendment, or modification after August 10, 1993). [IRC §§ 505(a), 505(b)(2), 505(b)(7), OBRA '93, § 13212(c), (d)] (See Chapter 19 for further discussion of VEBAs.)

In addition, a variety of other federal laws affect these types of employer-provided plans and prohibit discrimination on the basis of pregnancy or other disabilities. (See Chapters 17 and 18 for further discussion of these other federal laws.) Specific standards under the Federal Age Discrimination in Employment Act of 1967 (ADEA) are discussed in the following questions.

Note. In enacting changes to the VEBA nondiscrimination rules in the Deficit Reduction Act of 1984 (DEFRA), Congress in the legislative history indicated that integration of VEBA disability benefits with Social Security benefits was to be allowed subject to rules comparable to the integration rules in the pension area, and that special limits were to apply to the disability income benefits where both the disability pension benefits and the VEBA disability income benefits were integrated with Social Security. However, no Treasury regulations have been issued to implement the congressional intent, and, in view of substantial changes made since 1984 in the pension integration rules, it appears that changes in the Social Security integration procedures of VEBAs are not necessary until Treasury regulations are forthcoming.

Q 10:10   Are disability income plans subject to the Age Discrimination in Employment Act of 1967 (ADEA)?

Yes, they are. Disability income benefits are part of the terms, conditions, and privileges of employment governed by the ADEA. [ADEA § 4(a); 29 USC § 623(a)(1988)] See Chapter 16.

Q 10:11   Can an employer limit eligibility for disability income coverage based on age?

No, eligibility for disability income coverage cannot be denied based on age, at least for individuals within the age group protected by ADEA (age 40 and older) and within the group protected by applicable state law (sometimes age 18 and older). For example, an employer subject to the ADEA could not extend disability income coverage to its employees under age 60 and deny coverage to anyone who becomes disabled after age 60. However, under the "benefit package" approach in the Equal Employment Opportunity Commission (EEOC) regulations, a benefit may be eliminated based on age if another benefit of at least equal value is provided instead (see Qs 16:2–16:27).

Q 10:12   Can an employer limit the amount or duration of disability income benefits based on age?

Yes, it can, provided that the employer follows the guidelines contained in the ADEA regulations expressly restored by the Older Workers Benefit Protection Act of 1990 (OWBPA). Those regulations require that any reduction in the amount or duration of disability income benefits must be justified on the basis of cost equivalency— that is, the cost of the reduced benefits for older employees must be no less than the cost of benefits provided to younger employees. Two approaches for achieving cost equivalency are provided under the EEOC regulations: the "benefit-by-benefit" approach and the "benefit package" approach. (The specific rules regarding cost-justified reduction in benefits are discussed in greater detail in Questions 16:8 through 16:27.)

Q 10:13   Can an employer increase an employee's share of the cost of disability income benefits based on age?

No, the employee's share of the cost of disability income benefits cannot increase with age. Essentially, such a practice is viewed as a mandatory reduction in take-home pay in violation of the ADEA. It is permissible, however, for the employer to require that employees bear the same proportion of the cost of the plan. Older employees may be required to make larger absolute dollar contributions than younger employees if the cost of the coverage increases by age, as long as the proportion of the total cost paid by the employee remains constant. For example, the employer might decide to bear 50 percent of the cost of disability income coverage and charge employees 50 percent of the cost. As long as older employees were not charged more than 50 percent of the cost, such an arrangement would not violate the ADEA. (See Qs 16:15, 16:16.)

Q 10:14   How much time does an employer have to bring a disability income plan into compliance with the ADEA as amended in 1990 by the OWBPA?

New Plans. A disability income plan established on or after October 16, 1990 must comply from its inception.

Existing Plans. A disability income plan that existed on October 16, 1990 and that remains unmodified was required to be brought into compliance no later than April 15, 1991. However, if any modifications were made to the plan before April 15, 1991, the plan was required to be in compliance as of the date the plan was modified. Special effective date rules apply to state and local governmental disability income plans.

Benefits in Pay Status. Disability income benefits that commenced before October 16, 1990 and that continue after such date pursuant to an arrangement in effect on that date are not subject to the OWBPA amendments to the ADEA, provided that no substantial modification to the arrangement is made with the intent of evading the purposes of the OWBPA.

(For further details, see Q 16:6.)

Tax Treatment of Employers

Q 10:15 Are employer contributions to, or payments under, a disability income plan deductible for federal income tax purposes?

Yes, generally they are, provided that they are an ordinary and necessary business expense. [IRC § 162(a); Treas Reg § 1.162-10] However, if the disability income benefits are provided through a welfare benefit fund such as a Code Section 501(c)(9) VEBA trust, the employer contributions must also satisfy the requirements of Code Sections 419 and 419A in order to be deductible by the employer. (See Chapter 19 for further discussion of Code Sections 419 and 419A.)

Tax Treatment of Employees

Q 10:16 Are employees taxed on the cost of employer-provided disability coverage?

No, covered employees are not taxed on the cost of the disability coverage received from the employer. This is true for both income-replacement-type disability plans and dismemberment plans. [IRC §§ 61(a)(1), 104(a)(3), 105(a), 106] (Taxation of the benefits actually received from the plan is discussed in Questions 10:17 through 10:26.

Q 10:17   Are benefits paid under a dismemberment-type plan taxable to the employee?

No, Code Section 105 contains a blanket exclusion from federal gross income for benefit payments received by employees under an employer-provided dismemberment-type plan. Benefit payments derived from employer contributions will not be taxable to the employee or other recipient if they:

1. Constitute payment for the permanent loss, or loss of use of, a member or function of the body; and
2. Are computed with reference to the nature of the injury without regard to the period the employee is absent from work.

[IRC §§ 104(a)(3), 105(c)]

The portion of dismemberment-type benefit payments attributable to employee contributions is excluded from federal gross income under Code Section 104.

Q 10:18   Are benefits paid under a disability income plan taxable to the employee?

Yes, they are—to the extent that the disability income benefits are attributable to employer contributions or payments. However, to the extent that the disability income benefits are attributable to the employee's own contributions, they are not taxed. [IRC §§ 104(a)(3), 105(a)] If the employee contributions are made by means of salary reduction under a cafeteria plan, the contributions are deemed to be employer contributions, and the disability income benefits attributable to such contributions are therefore taxable. (See Q 7:43.)

Income replacement-type benefits received under workers' compensation laws as compensation for personal injuries or sickness are fully tax-free, even though they are attributable to employer contributions. [IRC § 104(a)(1)] However, benefits received pursuant to state temporary disability laws (see Q 10:3) for non-job-related disabilities are not exempt insofar as they are attributable to employer contributions. [Treas Reg § 1.104-1(b)]

Q 10:19   How does an employer calculate the amount that is taxable to an employee receiving disability income payments under a plan involving both employer and employee contributions?

In order to properly report taxable income paid to its employees, the employer must calculate the portion of the amounts received under the disability income plan that is attributable to employer contributions (including contributions made by means of salary reduction under a cafeteria plan). The actual method of allocating employer contributions varies, depending on whether the plan is insured or uninsured and, if insured, whether individual or group policies are used to fund the disability income benefits. (See Qs 10:20–10:26.)

Q 10:20   What if the employer contributes a different amount for each class of employees under the disability income plan?

If the ratio of employer to employee contributions differs by class of employees (for example, salaried and hourly), the employer must determine the ratio of employer to employee contributions for the employee class to which the recipient belongs. [Treas Reg § 1.105-1(c)(2)]

In a recent private letter ruling, the IRS held that where an employer amended a long-term disability plan that had been fully employer-paid to provide that employees earning over a certain salary level would pay the full cost of their coverage with after-tax contributions, the group of employees paying the cost of their coverage constituted a separate class of employees. In addition, they were considered to be covered under a new plan, so that long-term disability benefits received by such separate class of employees were tax-free under Code Section 104(a)(3). [Priv Ltr Rul 91-11-027 (Dec 19, 1990)]

Q 10:21   What if the plan contains other types of benefits besides disability income benefits?

If the disability income benefits are part of a larger plan providing multiple benefits and the contributions of the employer and employees for the disability income coverage are not separately identified, the employer must determine the employer-provided portion of each disability income benefit payment based upon the respective employer and employee contributions to the overall plan. [Treas Reg § 105-1(c)(3)]

Q 10:22 How is the taxable amount determined if a group insurance policy is used to fund the disability income plan?

If the disability income benefits are funded using a group insurance policy, the determination of what portion of each disability income payment is deemed attributable to employer contributions, and thus taxable to the employee, is quite complex. The reason is that the premium cost attributable to an individual employee under a group insurance policy is not readily determinable. Once the employee class is determined, if required (see Q 10:20), the employer calculates the income amount of the payment by multiplying the total payment by a fraction whose numerator is the net employer-paid premiums for the appropriate "experience period" and whose denominator is the total net premiums for the appropriate experience period.

Net premiums are premiums paid, less policy dividends and experience-rating credits. [Treas Reg § 1.105-1(d)(2)]

Experience Period. If the net premiums for three or more prior policy years are known at the beginning of the calendar year, the three prior years are the appropriate experience period. If the three prior policy years' net premiums are not known at the beginning of the calendar year, two years' net premiums may be used. If two years' net premiums are not known, one year's net premiums may be used. If not even one prior policy year's net premiums are known, the computation may be made by using either:

1. A reasonable estimate of the net premiums for the first policy year; or

2. The net premiums for the current policy year, if they are ascertained during the calendar year.

Example. An employer adopts a new contributory disability income plan on January 1, 1993, and funds the plan with an experience-rated group insurance policy. The policy year is the same as the calendar year. For 1993, the employer will not know the net premiums for the year, because the policy dividend for the year will not be determined until some time in 1994. Thus, the employer must make a reasonable estimate of the net premiums for that year to determine the disability income amounts attributable to employer contributions for 1993. As of January 1, 1994, the net premiums for the year 1993 *still* will not be known; therefore, the employer may continue to use a reasonable estimate of the net premiums for the year 1993 to determine the taxable benefits for 1994. Alternatively, the employer may wait until the insurer declares the 1993 policy year dividend and use the actual net premiums for 1993 to determine the portion of 1994 disability income payments attributable to employer contributions.

[Treas Reg § l.105-1(d)(2)]

Q 10:23 How is the taxable amount determined if the disability income plan is self-insured?

If the disability income plan is self-insured, the determination of what portion of each disability income payment is deemed attributable to employer contributions, and thus taxable to the employee, is similar to that for plans funded with group insurance (see Q 10:22). A ratio of employer contributions to all contributions is applied to the payment, using the appropriate employee class (see Q 10:20) and experience period. [Treas Reg § 1.105-1(e)]

Experience Period. If the plan has been in effect for at least three years before the calendar year, the employer contributions and total contributions for those three years are used for the allocation. If the plan has existed for only two prior years or one prior year, those periods are used. If the uninsured plan has not been in effect for one full year at the beginning of the calendar year, the determination of the taxable amount may be made on the basis of the portion of the year preceding the determination, or the determination may be made periodically (such as monthly or quarterly) and used for the succeeding period. [Treas Reg § 1.105-1(e)]

Example. An employer adopts a new contributory plan in 1993, and the employee receives disability income benefits early in 1993 and then leaves employment on April 15, 1993. The employer may determine the taxable portion of the benefits based on contributions during the period January 1 to April 15, 1993, on contributions for the month of March 1993, or on contributions for the first quarter of 1993.

Q 10:24 How is the taxable amount determined if individual insurance policies are used to fund a disability income plan?

If individual insurance policies are used to fund a disability income plan, the portion of each disability income payment deemed attributable to employer contributions, and thus taxable to the employee, is determined by multiplying the total payment by a fraction whose numerator is the employer-paid premiums under the individual policy for the current policy year and whose denominator is the total premiums (employer- and employee-paid) under the individual policy for the current policy year. The calculation may be expressed by the following formula:

$$\text{Taxable amount} = \text{payment} \times \frac{\text{employer--paid premiums}}{\text{all premiums}}$$

[Treas Reg § 1.105-1(d)(1)]

Q 10:25 How is the taxable amount of disability income payments determined if each employee in a cafeteria plan is given the option of contributing to the disability income coverage on a salary reduction basis or on an after-tax basis?

There is no official guidance on this point. The rules contained in the Treasury regulations applicable to group insurance and self-insured plans (see Qs 10:22, 10:23) do not seem to fit. It appears that the disability plan could be viewed as containing two classes of employees: those who contribute the full cost of their coverage (the after-tax class) and those who contribute nothing (the pre-tax class). Those who contributed the full cost of their coverage (that is, contributed on an after-tax basis) would receive the disability benefits tax-free under Code Section 104(a)(3). Those who contributed on a pre-tax basis would receive their disability benefits on a fully taxable basis under Code Section 105(a).

Note. This interpretation appears to be supportable under Treasury Regulation Section 1.105-1(c)(2), which provides that a separate determination of the portion of the amounts attributable to employer contributions is to be made for each class of employees where the plan provides that some classes of employees contribute but others do not, or that the employer will make different contributions for different classes of employees, or that different classes of employees will make different contributions, and where in any such case the employer contributions and employee contributions for the class of employees can be ascertained. An example is given of a plan under which contributions are required from first-year employees, but not from other employees. As long as the employee and employer contributions for the first-year employees can be ascertained separately, the calculation of taxable income for such class can be done separately from the non-first-year employees.

Q 10:26 How is the taxable amount of disability income payments determined if the plan is amended to change the respective contributions by the employer and employees?

In a private letter ruling, the IRS considered an employer's long-term disability plan, which had in the past been paid for completely by the employer. The plan was amended to provide that employees earning below a specified salary amount would continue to receive the coverage at no cost, while employees earning at or over that amount would pay the full cost of their coverage with after-tax dollars. The ruling reached the following conclusions:

1. The group of employees paying the full cost of their coverage would be treated as a separate class of employees from the group of employees receiving the coverage at no cost;

2. The coverage under the amended plan for the group of employees paying the full cost of their coverage would be treated as a new plan; and

3. The coverage under the amended plan for the group of employees paying the full cost of their coverage would be considered attributable solely to employee contributions, so that disability benefits received by that group will be received free of income tax under Code Section 104(a)(3).

[Priv Ltr Rul 91-11-027 (Dec 19, 1990)]

Thus, where a plan is amended in a manner similar to that in the ruling, the three-year look-back procedure (see Qs 10:22, 10:23) to determine the allocation between employer and employee contributions may be unnecessary and inappropriate.

Q 10:27   Are taxable disability income benefits subject to mandatory wage withholding?

Whether mandatory withholding (that is, wage payroll withholding required by the IRC) applies depends upon who is paying the benefits.

Employer Payments. Withholding is mandatory if the employer—or an agent of the employer—makes the payments. [IRC §§ 3401, 3402; Treas Reg § 31.3401(a)-1(b)(8)] This means that if, for example, the employer maintains a self-insured plan and retains an insurance company or other claims administrator to handle claims payments, the payments will be subject to mandatory wage withholding. The IRS has indicated that withholding is not mandatory if the employer is handling the disability income payments but is acting on behalf of a third-party payer, that is, a trust that has assumed the insurance risk. [Priv Ltr Rul 85-32-035]

Third-Party Payer. Withholding is not required if the payments are made by an insurer under an insured plan, or by a trust that has assumed the insurance risk for payment of the benefits. [IRC § 3402(o); Treas Reg § 31.3402(o)-3]

Q 10:28   Can the employee make a third-party payer withhold?

Yes, an employee who wants to have federal income tax withheld from his or her disability income payments may generally do so by making a request of the payer on IRS Form W-4S or a form of the payer identical to the IRS form, unless the plan is exempted (see Q 10:29) or is governed by a contrary provision in a collective bargaining agreement (see Q 10:32). This is called "voluntary" withholding, because the IRC does not require it absent a request from the employee. This rule applies to temporary disability or sick pay. [IRC §§ 3402(o)(1)(C), 3402(o)(2)(C), 3402(o)(3), 3402(o)(4)]

The amount requested to be withheld must generally be a whole-dollar amount, and at least $20 on a weekly basis. If a payment covers only part of a week, the amount to be withheld is prorated.

Example. The amount to be withheld is $20 per week. A final payment upon the employee's return to work consists of 40 percent of a workweek (that is, two nonworking days in a five-day work-week). The amount to be withheld from the final payment is $8.

The third-party payer may permit the employee to elect withholding on a percentage basis (for example, 20 percent) rather than on a whole-dollar-amount basis. The percentage elected must be at least 10 percent.

If the withholding amount elected would reduce the net payment to the employee to below $10, no income tax withholding applies. [IRC § 3402(o)(3); Treas Reg §§ 31.3402(o)-3(a), 31.3402(o)-3(b), 31.3402(o)-3(c)]

Q 10:29   Are all recipients of long-term disability income benefits entitled to demand that a third-party payer withhold?

No, they are not. The voluntary withholding provision applies to "sick pay" or "temporary" benefits. [IRC §§ 3402(o)(1)(C), 3402(o)(2)(C)] The regulations interpret this exception as exempting the plan from all voluntary withholding if *all* amounts paid under the plan are paid to individuals who are totally and permanently disabled. The totally and permanently disabled standard means that the employee must be unable to engage in any substantial gainful activity because of a medically determinable physical or mental impairment that either (1) can be expected to result in death or (2) has lasted or can be expected to last for a continuous period of at least 12 months. [Treas Reg § 31.3402(o)-3(h)(1)(i)]

Planning Pointer. Many total and permanent disability plans have definitions of disability that are somewhat more liberal than the tax law definition. Therefore, this exemption from the application of the voluntary withholding requirements has quite limited application.

Q 10:30 When does a valid request for voluntary withholding by a third-party payer take effect?

The third-party payer must honor the request for all disability income payments made more than seven days after it receives the request. The payer may choose to honor the request sooner. [Treas Reg § 31.3402(o)-3(d)]

Q 10:31 May an employee change or withdraw a voluntary withholding request?

Yes, the employee may change or terminate the request for voluntary withholding at any time. The third-party payer must honor a written request to change or terminate voluntary withholding by the eighth day after receipt. [Treas Reg §§ 31.3402(o)-3(d), 31.3402(o)-3(e)]

Q 10:32 Can a collective bargaining agreement override the voluntary withholding rules?

Yes, it can. If third-party payer disability income is paid pursuant to a collective bargaining agreement, and the agreement provides for withholding in specified amounts, the agreement will determine the amount to be withheld, and individual elections will not be valid. For this exception to apply, the payer must be furnished with payees' Social Security numbers and sufficient information for it to determine the amount to be withheld. The payer, however, does not withhold from employees who have filed withholding exemption statements with the employer to the effect that they had no income tax liability in the prior year and expect to incur no income tax liability in the current year. [IRC § 3402(o)(5); Treas Reg § 31.3402(o)-3(i)]

Q 10:33   Are taxable disability income payments subject to Social Security withholding?

Disability income payments attributable to employer contributions or payments (including salary reduction contributions made under a cafeteria plan) are subject to Federal Insurance Contributions Act (FICA), or Social Security, withholding only for benefits paid in the month of disability or in the first six months following the month of disability. [IRC § 3121(a)(4)]

Q 10:34   Who is responsible for Social Security withholding?

The employer is responsible for Social Security withholding. However, if benefits are paid by a third-party payer, the third-party payer is treated as the "employer" and is liable for the employer's share of the FICA tax and for withholding the employee's share of the FICA tax. The third-party payer can avoid liability for the employer's share of the tax—and shift liability to the employer— provided that it:

1. Withholds the employee's portion of the FICA tax;
2. Deposits the withheld tax by the required due date; and
3. Lets the employer know, on or before the due date of the employer deposit, the amount of taxable payments made on which it has withheld and deposited FICA tax.

Upon receiving such a notification from the third-party payer, the employer is then obliged to pay the employer's share of the FICA tax. [IRC § 3121(a)(4); Treas Reg § 31.3121(a)(2)-2]

Q 10:35   How are disability income payments required to be reported?

The third-party payer must, by January 15 of the year following the payments, provide the employer with a written statement containing the following information:

1. The payee's name and, if there is voluntary withholding (see Qs 10:27–10:34), the payee's Social Security number;
2. The total amount of sick pay paid to the payee; and

3. The total amount, if any, withheld.

[Treas Reg § 31.6051-3]

An employer receiving a third-party payer statement must furnish the information to the IRS and to the payee. The report must include a breakdown of the total payment into the portion, if any, attributable to employee contributions (and therefore nontaxable) and the taxable portion (see Qs 10:18–10:24). The employer may use the same Form W-2 that it uses for regular wages, or it may provide a separate Form W-2 for the disability income payments. [Treas Reg § 31.6051-3]

Alternatively, the third-party payer and the employer may enter into an agency agreement whereby the third-party payer files the Form W-2 in lieu of the employer. [Treas Reg § 31.6051-3]

Note. Apparently, the complexity of the reporting and withholding requirements for sick pay payments when a third-party payer is treated as the employer has caused a good deal of confusion among employers and third-party payers, and some erroneous reporting and depositing of withheld taxes.

Recently, the IRS issued a detailed notice giving explicit instructions concerning the completion and filing of IRS Form 941 (the employer's quarterly return of withheld taxes), the annual Form W-2 (the wage and tax statement), and Form W-3 (transmittal of income and tax statements), including illustrations of how the forms are to be completed. The notice covers the situation where the third-party payer transfers the FICA liability to the employer, as well as the situation where the third-party payer does not transfer the FICA tax liability to the employer. [IRS Notice 91-26, 1991-34 IRB 14]

Tax Treatment of Self-Employed Persons and Subchapter S Corporation Shareholder-Employees

Q 10:36   What is the income tax treatment of insurance premiums paid by a sole proprietor for disability income insurance coverage?

It has been held that premiums paid for disability income insurance coverage by a sole proprietor are a personal expense and, thus, not deductible. [IRC § 262; Rev Rul 58-90, 1958-1 CB 8; Marvin v Blaess, 28 TC 710 (1957)]

Q 10:37 What is the income tax treatment of disability income benefits received by a sole proprietor under an insured plan maintained by the sole proprietorship?

The benefits received from an insured disability income benefit plan are excludable from gross income under Code Section 104(a)(3). [Rev Rul 58-90, 1958-1 CB 88]

Q 10:38 What is the income tax treatment of disability income benefits received by a sole proprietor under a self-insured plan maintained by the sole proprietorship?

Treasury Regulation Section 105-5(b) provides that benefits paid under an accident or health plan to an individual who is self-employed in the business with respect to which the plan is established will not be treated as received through accident and health insurance for purposes of Code Sections 104(a)(3) and 105. Thus the exclusion under Section 104(a)(3) is not applicable, and the benefits are not excludable or deductible from the sole proprietor's gross income.

Q 10:39 What is the income tax treatment of insurance premiums paid by a partnership for disability income insurance coverage of its partners?

Based on the position the IRS has taken concerning medical insurance premiums (see Q 3:104), it appears that if the premium payments are made without regard to partnership income, the premium payments will be treated as guaranteed payments by the partnership under Code Section 707(c), deductible by the partnership on the partnership tax return and includable in each partner's income.

Since the partners are not employees, the guaranteed payments are not subject to withholding at source by the partnership. [Treas Reg § 1.707-1(c)]

Alternatively, the partnership may choose to account for the payment of the disability insurance premiums as a reduction in distributions to the partners. In such event, the premiums are not deductible by the partnership, and distributable shares of partnership income and deductions and other items are not affected by payment of the premiums. [Rev Rul 91-26, 1991-1 CB 184]

Q 10:40 What is the income tax treatment of disability income benefits received by a partner from an insured disability income plan maintained by the partnership?

The disability income benefits are excludable from gross income under Code Section 104(a)(3).

Q 10:41 What is the income tax treatment of disability income benefits received by a partner under a self-insured disability income plan maintained by the partnership?

There is no clear and direct authority as to how a partnership's self-insured disability income benefit plan will be treated for income tax purposes. Based on the IRS position in Revenue Ruling 91-26 (see 10:39), it appears possible that the IRS would apply similar rules to a self-insured plan. Thus, if the disability income payments were payable without regard to partnership income, the payments presumably would be viewed as guaranteed payments deductible at the partnership level and includable in the income of the partner receiving the disability income benefits.

Alternatively, the partnership presumably could choose to account for the disability income payments to a partner as a reduction in distributions to the partner that (1) is not deductible by the partnership and (2) does not affect distributive shares of partnership income and deductions and other items. [Rev Rul 91-26, 1991-1 CB 184]

Note. It appears that the partnership agreement should be able to provide for allocating the disability payments ratably among all the partners in accordance with their partnership shares (see Planning Pointer in Q 3:105).

Since the benefits are provided through a self-insured plan and not through accident and health insurance, the Code Section 104(a)(3) exemption from income of insured disability income payments is not available to the partner receiving the benefits. [Treas Reg § 1.105-5(b)]

Q 10:42   What is the income tax treatment of insurance premiums paid by a Subchapter S corporation for insured disability income coverage maintained for shareholder-employees of the Subchapter S corporation and the benefits received by the shareholder-employees?

If the shareholder-employee of the Subchapter S corporation is not a more-than-2-percent shareholder, the premiums paid by the employer for services as an employee normally will be excludable from the shareholder-employee's income under Code Section 106, and the disability income insurance benefits will be taxable, to the extent they are attributable to employer contributions.

However, if the shareholder-employee is a more-than-2-percent shareholder of the Subchapter S corporation, the Subchapter S corporation is deemed a partnership and the shareholder-employee is treated as a partner in the partnership. [IRC § 1373]

Based on Revenue Ruling 91-26 (1991-1 CB 184), it appears that the premiums will be deductible by the Subchapter S corporation as a business expense and that the more-than-2-percent shareholder employees must include the premiums paid for their coverage in gross income.

Q 10:43   What is the income tax treatment of disability income benefits received by shareholder-employees of a Subchapter S corporation under an insured disability income plan maintained by the Subchapter S corporation?

Based on Revenue Ruling 91-26 (1991-1 CB 184), it appears that any benefits received under insured disability income coverage maintained by a Subchapter S corporation will be exempt from the income of the more-than-2-percent shareholders under Code Section 104(a)(3).

Q 10:44   What is the income tax treatment of disability income benefits received by a shareholder-employee of a Subchapter S corporation from self-insured disability income coverage maintained by the Subchapter S corporation?

There is no direct authority on the question. If the shareholder employee is not a more-than-2-percent shareholder, disability income benefits should be subject to tax under Code Section 105(a). If the shareholder-employee is a more-than-2-percent shareholder, and if the IRS applies the rules of Revenue Ruling 91-26 (1991-1 CB 184), the disability income payments would be deductible by the Subchapter S corporation, and includable in the gross income of the shareholder-employee receiving the benefits. Since the plan does not provide accident and health insurance, the exclusion from income under Code Section 104(a)(3) is not available. [Rev Rul 91-26, 1991-1 CB 184; Treas Reg § 1.105-5(b)]

Chapter 11

Group Term Life Insurance Plans

One of the major employee welfare benefits is group term life insurance. Group term life insurance coverage, although it may be taxable to the employee to some extent, is entitled to special treatment under Code Section 79 if the plan conforms to the requirements of that section. This chapter discusses the ground rules.

Basic Concepts

Q 11:1   What is term life insurance for Section 79 purposes?

Term life insurance, broadly defined, is life insurance that provides death benefit coverage only for a specified period (the term), with no cash value, loan value, or other permanent benefit under the policy.

Permanent life insurance (e.g., whole life insurance or universal life insurance), on the other hand, combines life insurance protection with a savings element and generally has a cash and loan value.

A right to convert or to continue life insurance after group term life insurance coverage terminates is not a permanent benefit, nor is any other feature that provides no economic benefit other than current insurance protection to the employee (for example, a double indemnity rider) or term life insurance under which the premium remains level for a period of five years or less. [Treas Reg § 1.79-0]

If an employer provides that employees who retire have vested rights to group term life insurance coverage in retirement and/or the employer funds the retiree coverage through a voluntary employees' beneficiary association (VEBA) or retired lives reserve, the coverage will not be considered to be paid-up or permanent insurance, as long as the insurance company does not provide a permanent guarantee of coverage to the retired employee. [IRC § 83(e)(5)]

Q 11:2   What is a group term life insurance plan?

A group term life insurance plan is an insurance arrangement whereby an employer provides term life insurance coverage to a class of employees (the group).

Q 11:3   Are employer-provided group term life insurance plans eligible for favorable tax treatment?

Yes, they are. An employer generally may deduct its contribution to a group term life insurance plan. In addition, if a plan meets the definition of group term life insurance contained in Section 79 of the Internal Revenue Code (the Code) and the regulations issued under that Code section (see Q 11:4), the covered employees generally receive favorable federal income tax treatment, which includes an exclusion from gross income for the cost of up to $50,000 of employer-provided coverage and taxation of amounts over $50,000, according to a table (referred to as "Table I") promulgated by the Internal Revenue Service (IRS) that is used to determine the amount of imputed income (see Qs 11:56, 11:57).

If the plan discriminates in favor of any key employee (see Q 11:41), all key employees lose the favorable tax treatment granted under Code Section 79. Key employees under a discriminatory group term life insurance plan are denied the benefit of the $50,000 exclusion and are taxed on all coverage on the basis of cost determined under Table I in the Treasury regulations (see Q 11:57) or actual cost, whichever is higher. [IRC § 79(d)(1)] In addition, certain "grandfathered" employees (see Q 11:48) who retire after 1986 under a discriminatory plan lose the benefit of a complete exemption from tax on their group term life insurance coverage. (The applicable discrimination rules are discussed in Questions 11:40 through 11:48, and the tax consequences of a discriminatory plan are discussed in Questions 11:61 through 11:63.)

Q 11:4 How does an employer-provided group term life insurance plan qualify for favorable tax treatment under Code Section 79?

To qualify for favorable tax treatment under Code Section 79, the employer-provided group term life insurance coverage for employees must meet the following four conditions:

1. The coverage must provide a general death benefit that is fully excludable from income in the hands of the beneficiary under Code Section 101(a) (see Qs 11:12, 11:13);

2. The coverage must be provided to a group of employees (see Qs 11:14–11:24);

3. The coverage must be provided under a policy that is "carried directly or indirectly by the employer" (see Qs 11:25–11:37); and

4. The amount of coverage provided to each employee must be computed under a formula that precludes individual selection (see Qs 11:38, 11:39).

Q 11:5   Does Code Section 79 apply only to term life insurance policies?

Generally, Code Section 79 does not apply to a policy containing a permanent value, that is, a cash value, paid-up value, or other value extending beyond one year. However, under limited circumstances, a policy containing a permanent benefit may qualify under Section 79 if an allocation that meets IRS requirements is made between the term and permanent elements and the value of the permanent benefit is taken into account in determining the employee's taxable income (see Qs 11:31, 11:32).

Q. 11:6   Can an employer provide group term life insurance coverage for its employees under Section 79 by purchasing a group policy from its wholly owned life insurance subsidiary?

Yes, the IRS has ruled that where a parent corporation carries insurance on its employees' lives under a group term life insurance policy purchased from a wholly owned life insurance subsidiary, the coverage qualifies as group term life insurance for Section 79 purposes, and the premiums are deductible by the parent to the extent they constitute reasonable compensation for services rendered. [Rev Rul 92-93, 1992-2 CB 45]

Note. The same result should apply in other affiliated corporation situations, such as where a parent life insurance company insures the employees of a wholly owned subsidiary or where a brother-sister corporate relationship exists between the insurer and the employer whose employees are insured. The revenue ruling also indicates that the same favorable treatment is available where a life insurance company insures its own employees.

Caveat. An employer considering its Section 79 group term life insurance plan with a life insurance affiliate should consider carefully the possible application of the prohibited transaction rules of the

Employee Retirement Income Security Act of 1974 (ERISA). (See Chapter 3.) For example, the Department of Labor (DOL) takes the position that insuring or reinsuring an ERISA plan with a foreign insurance affiliate generally constitutes a prohibited transaction in the absence of an individual prohibited transaction exemption.

Q 11:7   Can spouses and dependents be insured under a Code Section 79 group term life insurance plan?

No, Code Section 79 prohibits inclusion of spouses and dependents under an employer-provided group term life insurance plan. Such plans can only cover employees. [Treas Reg § 1.79-3(f)(2)] (The definition of "employee" for this purpose is discussed in Qs 11:14–11:19. See Qs 12:1–12:10 for a discussion of dependent life insurance and Q 7:33 for a discussion of dependent life insurance in cafeteria plans.)

Q 11:8   Can group term life insurance provided under a tax-qualified retirement plan qualify for Code Section 79 treatment?

No, it cannot. The Code Section 79 exemption for the first $50,000 of coverage is unavailable. The cost of group term life insurance provided under a tax-qualified retirement plan may be determined in one of two ways:

1. By using an IRS table (the so-called PS-58 table, contained in Revenue Rulings 55-747 and 66-110) that has rates substantially in excess of the rates used under Code Section 79; or

2. By using the insurance company's published rates for individual one-year term policies offered to all standard risks. [IRC §§ 79(b)(3), 72(m)(3); Rev Rul 55-747, 1955-2 CB 228, as amplified by Rev Rul 66-110, 1966-1 CB 12]

Q 11:9   Can state law affect the coverage eligible for special treatment under Code Section 79?

Yes, it can. Code Section 79 does not apply to amounts of group term life insurance in excess of the limits imposed under applicable state law. [Treas Reg § 1.79-1(e)]

When Code Section 79 first became law in 1964, a number of states had laws that substantially limited the amount of group term life insurance that an employer could provide to its employees under policies within those states' jurisdictions. However, at present, only one state, Texas, has limits on the amount of group term life insurance under a policy delivered in Texas, and Texas now permits amounts of group term life insurance not in excess of the greater of $100,000 or four times the employee's annual compensation. Thus, an executive earning $500,000 in annual compensation could have $2 million in group term life insurance under Texas law. [Tex Ins Code, Art 3.50(1)(d)]

Q 11:10   Is an employer-provided group term life insurance plan subject to ERISA?

Yes, it is. (See Chapter 2 for a discussion of ERISA.)

Q 11:11   Does the Age Discrimination in Employment Act of 1967 (ADEA) apply to employer-provided group term life insurance?

Yes, it does. The ADEA prohibits discrimination because of age in all compensation, terms, conditions, and privileges of employment, including all employee benefits. [29 USC § 630(l)] (For further details, see Chapter 16 and Qs 11:49–11:53.)

General Death Benefit Requirement

Q 11:12   What type of benefit must a plan offer to qualify as group term life insurance under Code Section 79?

The first of the four requirements that must be satisfied in order for insurance to be characterized as "group term life insurance" under Code Section 79 is that the group term life insurance plan must offer a "general death benefit." This is a benefit that is payable upon death without any special conditions. A life insurance benefit under a travel accident policy or an accidental death double indemnity rider does not qualify as group term life insurance under Code Section 79, because the death benefit is not a general death benefit. However, travel accident insurance and accidental death benefits receive favorable tax treatment under other IRC provisions. (See Chapter 12 for a discussion of these and other death benefits.)

Q 11:13   What is a survivor monthly income benefit, and can it qualify as a general death benefit?

The typical survivor income group term life insurance benefit is payable in the form of a monthly income benefit to a qualified survivor or survivors (for example, spouse or children). It is payable when the employee dies only if there is a qualified survivor living at the time of the employee's death. Factors such as a qualified survivor's death, a spouse's remarriage, or a child's attainment of a specified age (for example, 21), may vary the term (that is, the duration), or the amount of the survivor income benefit, or both.

The Treasury regulations under Code Section 79 expressly recognize that a survivor income group life insurance benefit qualifies as life insurance. [Treas Reg § 1.79-3(b); Priv Ltr Rul 85-09-046; Estate of J Smead, 78 TC 43 (1982); Estate of John Connelly, Sr v United States, 551 F 2d 545 (3d Cir 1977)] One federal district court decided that an uninsured survivor income benefit plan was not life insurance for tax purposes, suggesting that treatment as life insurance depends upon the existence of a definite death benefit that is payable in any event upon the employee's death. [Davis v United States, 323 F Supp 858 (WD W Va 1971)] The *Davis* case has not been followed generally or in the authorities cited above, and it does not appear to be a correct interpretation of the law on this point.

"Group of Employees" Requirement

Q 11:14   What types of employees may a Code Section 79 group term life insurance plan cover?

The second of the four requirements that must be satisfied in order for insurance to be characterized as "group term life insurance" under Code Section 79 is that coverage be provided to a group of employees. The "group of employees" required by Code Section 79 consists of either (1) all employees of the employer or (2) fewer than all the employees if membership in the group is determined solely on the basis of age, marital status, or factors related to employment, such as membership in a union, duties performed, compensation received, and length of service.

For Code Section 79 purposes, a requirement of participation in the employer's pension, profit-sharing, or accident and health plan is considered to be a "factor related to employment," even if employee contributions to the plan are required. Ownership of stock is not a factor relating to employment; however, a requirement of participation in the employer's stock bonus plan may be a factor related to employment. [Treas Reg § 1.79-0]

Q 11:15 Who can be an "employee" under a Code Section 79 group term life insurance plan?

The Code Section 79 definition of "employee" includes:

- Common-law employees;
- Full-time life insurance salespersons; and
- Persons who formerly performed services as employees, such as retired employees.

[Treas Reg § 1.79-0]

Q 11:16 Are corporate directors and independent contractors employees under Code Section 79?

No, these two classes of individuals are not "employees" under Code Section 79. Accordingly, coverage provided to independent contractors is not eligible for the $50,000 exclusion granted under Code Section 79. Similarly, coverage provided to corporate directors in their capacity as such also is not eligible because corporate directors are independent contractors rather than employees. [Enright, 56 TC 1261 (1971)]

Q 11:17   Does stock ownership affect characterization as an employee?

No, it does not. Employees who are also shareholders (other than certain S corporation shareholders) may generally be part of a group of employees for Code Section 79 purposes.

Q 11:18   Can an S corporation shareholder or a partner be treated as an eligible employee?

No, generally such an individual cannot be. A partner is never eligible as an employee under Code Section 79. A more-than-2-percent direct or indirect shareholder in an S corporation is treated as a partner in a partnership and therefore is not eligible for tax-favored treatment under Code Section 79 either. [IRC § 1372; Treas Reg § 1.79-0]

Q 11:19   Does coverage for dependents qualify for favorable tax treatment under Code Section 79?

No, Code Section 79 governs only group term life insurance on the life of the employee. [Treas Reg § 1.79-3(f)(2)] (See Chapter 12 for a discussion of dependent life insurance.)

Q 11:20   Must an employer-provided group term life insurance plan cover a minimum number of employees to qualify under Code Section 79?

Yes, it must. Generally, a plan cannot qualify for favorable tax treatment under Code Section 79 unless, at some time during the calendar year, coverage is provided to at least ten full-time employees who are members of the group of employees. All life insurance provided under policies carried directly or indirectly by the employer is taken into account in determining whether the test is met. [Treas Reg § 1.79-1(c)(1)]

Q 11:21   What happens if a plan fails the minimum size requirement?

Generally, the plan will not qualify as group term life insurance under Code Section 79. However, there are two exceptions, one for single-employer plans and one for multiemployer union-type plans.

Q 11:22   If a single-employer plan fails the minimum size requirement, how can it still qualify under Code Section 79?

A single-employer life insurance plan covering fewer than 10 full-time employees may qualify as group term life insurance under Code Section 79 provided that the following requirements are met:

1. The coverage is provided to all full-time employees or, if evidence of insurability affects eligibility, to all full-time employees who provide evidence of insurability satisfactory to the insurer;

2. The amount of insurance provided is computed either as a uniform percentage of compensation or on the basis of coverage brackets established by the insurer; and

3. The required evidence of insurability that affects an employee's eligibility for, or amount of, insurance is limited to a medical questionnaire completed by the employee that does not require a physical examination.

When computing the amount of insurance provided, the amount treated as provided may be reduced in the case of employees who do not provide evidence of insurability satisfactory to the insurer. [Treas Reg § 1.79-1(c)(2)]

Coverage Brackets. If the amount of insurance coverage under a plan with fewer than 10 employees is available in different amounts rather than in a single, uniform amount or single, uniform percentage of compensation, then the insurance must meet the following limitations in order to qualify under Code Section 79:

1. Generally, no coverage bracket may exceed 2½ times the next lower bracket, and the lowest bracket must be at least 10 percent of the highest bracket; and

2. The insurer may establish a separate schedule of coverage brackets for employees who are over age 65, but

   —No bracket in the over-65 schedule may exceed 2 1/2 times the next lower bracket, and

   —The lowest bracket in the over-65 schedule must be at least 10 percent of the highest bracket in the under-65 schedule.

[Treas Reg § 1.79-1(c)(2)]

The IRS will look at substance, not just form, in considering whether this test is met.

Example. A plan covering fewer than 10 full-time employees met the coverage bracket requirements of the regulations on its face. But it was not qualified as a Code Section 79 plan because, although it contained three coverage brackets, no employee in fact had ever been covered under the middle bracket. Treating the plan as if it had only two coverage brackets, the IRS concluded that the plan failed because the top bracket was more than 2½ times the next bracket (the lowest bracket). [Rev Rul 80-229, 1980-2 CB 133]

Insurability. The IRS also ruled that a plan covering fewer than 10 full-time employees failed to qualify as a Code Section 79 plan because, although the insurer determined eligibility for coverage on the basis of a medical questionnaire only, the premium rate was three times the standard premium rate unless the insured employee agreed to furnish additional medical information or to undergo a medical examination. [Rev Rul 75-528, 1975-2 CB 35]

Q 11:23   If a multiemployer plan fails the minimum size requirement, how can it still qualify for Code Section 79 treatment?

Another exception to the general rule that a plan subject to Code Section 79 must cover ten or more full-time employees applies if the following requirements are met:

1. The insurance is provided under a common plan to the employees of two or more unrelated employers;

2. The insurance is restricted to, but mandatory for, all employees of the employer who belong to or are represented by an organization (such as a union) that carries on substantial activities in addition to obtaining insurance; and

3. Evidence of insurability does not affect an employee's eligibility for insurance or the amount of insurance.

[Treas Reg § 1.79-1(c)(3)]

Q 11:24 Can any employees be excluded when applying either of the two exceptions to the minimum size rules?

Yes, employees need not be taken into account when applying the minimum size rules (for example, the rule that "all" employees must be covered) if:

1. They are ineligible for insurance under the terms of the policy because they have not been employed for a waiting period, not to exceed six months, specified in the policy;

2. They are part-time employees, that is, employees whose customary employment is for not more than 20 hours in any week, or five months in any calendar year; or

3. They have reached the age of 65.

[Treas Reg § 1.79-1(c)(4)]

Note. Since the ADEA generally applies to employers with 20 or more employees, an employer with less than 10 employees may exclude employees age 65 or older without violating the ADEA. However, in some situations state age discrimination laws may be applicable.

Policy Carried Directly or Indirectly by the Employer

Q 11:25 What is a "policy" under Code Section 79?

The third of the four requirements that must be satisfied in order for insurance to be characterized as "group term life insurance" under Code Section 79 is that the policy be "carried directly or indirectly by the employer." For this purpose, a "policy" normally is a single group life insurance contract under which a life insurance company provides group term life insurance coverage to employees of the employer.

Q 11:26 Must two or more policies issued by one insurer be treated as one policy for Code Section 79 qualification purposes?

Yes, the general rule is that two or more insurance policies or obligations of the same insurer (or its affiliate, such as a subsidiary) must be aggregated and treated as a single insurance policy for

Code Section 79 purposes if they are sold in conjunction. Obligations that are offered or made available to a group of employees are considered sold in conjunction if they are offered or made available because of the employment relationship. [Treas Reg § 1.79-0]

In determining whether the obligations are sold in conjunction, neither the actuarial sufficiency of the premium charged for each obligation nor the facts that the obligations (1) are in separate documents, (2) receive separate state insurance department approval, or (3) are independent of one another are taken into account. A group of individual contracts under which life insurance is provided to a group of employees may be a single policy. Also, two benefits provided to a group of employees—one term life insurance and the other a permanent benefit—may be considered a single policy, even if one of the benefits is provided only to employees who decline the other benefit. [Treas Reg § 1.79-0]

Q 11:27 Can an employer ever elect to treat two or more term policies issued by the same insurer (or its affiliate) as separate policies?

Yes, an employer may elect to treat two or more policies of the same insurer (or its affiliate) that provide no permanent benefits as separate policies if the premiums are properly allocated among such policies. [Treas Reg § 1.79-0]

> **Planning Pointer.** In order to treat the policies as separate, the employer, aided by the insurer, must be able to demonstrate that the basic and supplemental policies are truly separate and free-standing and that the premiums are calculated independently and are not interdependent. [Priv Ltr Ruls 86-38-050, 88-16-031]

Q 11:28 Why would an employer want to treat two or more group term obligations as separate policies?

Such an election may be desirable if an employer that provides basic group term life insurance coverage to employees also offers employee-pay-all coverage under a separate supplemental group term life insurance policy with the same insurer.

Electing to treat the supplemental policy as a separate policy may enable the employer to treat the supplemental policy as a policy that it does not carry directly or indirectly (see Q 11:33), thus saving employees from possible imputed income on such coverage. However, if the employer provides basic insurance that is noncontributory, the employer may prefer not to elect to treat the basic and supplemental policies as separate policies, since employee contributions offset the imputed income attributable to amounts of coverage in excess of $50,000. [IRC § 79(a)(2)]

Q 11:29   If employees are covered by both a term policy and a permanent policy issued by the same insurer (or its affiliate), can the employer ever treat them as two separate policies?

Yes, the Code Section 79 regulations recognize that many insurers selling group term life insurance plans also mass market permanent life insurance programs on an employee-pay-all basis, and that an employer should not automatically be treated as having a single policy for tax purposes merely because it happened to purchase two policies from the same insurance carrier. Accordingly, the employer may elect to treat the obligation providing the permanent benefits as a policy separate from the term policy if:

1. The insurer sells the permanent obligation directly to the employee, who pays the full cost thereof;

2. The employer's participation with respect to sales of the permanent obligation to employees is limited to selection of the insurer and the type of coverage, to sales assistance activities such as providing employee lists to the insurer or permitting the insurer to use the employer's premises for solicitation, and to the collection of premiums through payroll deduction;

3. The insurer sells the obligation on the same terms and in substantial amounts to individuals who do not purchase (and whose employers do not purchase) any other obligation from the insurer; and

4. No employer-provided benefit is conditioned on purchase of the obligation.

[Treas Reg § 1.79-0]

Q 11:30 Why would an employer want to treat a term life insurance policy and a permanent life insurance policy issued by the same insurer (or its affiliate) as two separate policies?

Such an election is desirable for two reasons:

1. The employer would avoid possible disqualification of the group term life insurance policy under Code Section 79, since qualifying group term life insurance generally is not permitted to contain a permanent feature unless restrictive requirements contained in the regulations are met; and

2. Even if the restrictive requirements for permanent benefits are met, the Code Section 79 tax treatment for the employees under the combined plan would be onerous.

Q 11:31 When can Code Section 79 apply to a single insurance policy with both a term and a permanent feature?

Code Section 79 may apply to a policy containing a permanent value (that is, a cash value—paid-up value, or other value extending beyond one year), provided that the policy meets the following requirements:

1. The policy or the employer must designate in writing the part of the death benefit provided to each employee that is group term life insurance; and

2. The part of the death benefit that is provided to an employee and designated as the group term life insurance benefit for any policy year is not less than the difference between the total death benefit provided under the policy and the employee's deemed death benefit at the end of the policy year.

[Treas Reg § 1.79-1(b)]

This rule is intended, in part, to discourage insurance carriers from packaging permanent life insurance with term life insurance, in an attempt to obtain the favorable Code Section 79 group term life insurance treatment for the entire package. The rule requires the package to be broken down into term and permanent components, and results in unfavorable tax treatment for the permanent life insurance portion of the package. (The tax treatment is described in Question 11:69.)

The amount of the deemed death benefit (DDB) at the end of any policy year may be expressed by the following equation:

$$DDB = \frac{R}{Y}$$

R = the greater of

— the net level premium reserve at the end of the policy year for all benefits provided to the employee by the policy or

— the cash value of the policy at the end of the policy year.

Y = the net single premium for insurance (the premium for one dollar of paid-up, whole life insurance) at the employee's age at the end of the policy year.

The net level premium reserve (R) and the net single premium (Y) are based on the 1958 Insurance Commissioners' Standard Ordinary mortality table plus 4 percent interest. [Treas Reg §§ 1.79-1(d)(3), 1.79-1(d)(4)]

Q 11:32 Should an employer seek Code Section 79 treatment for a single policy combining permanent benefits?

No, generally it should not. Because of the conservative mortality table and interest rate that the regulations use to value the permanent benefit, the cost of the coverage imputed as income to the employee may equal or exceed the actual premium paid. If the coverage is not subject to Code Section 79, the employee is taxed only on the actual premium paid by the employer. [Treas Reg § 1.61-2(d)(2)(ii)(a)]

Q 11:33 When is the employer considered to be "directly or indirectly carrying" a policy for purposes of Code Section 79?

A policy is considered to be "carried directly or indirectly by the employer" if:

1. The employer pays any part of the cost of the life insurance directly or indirectly; or

2. The employer or two or more employers arrange for their employees to pay the cost of the life insurance and charge at least one employee less than the Table I cost of his or her insurance and at least one other employee more than the Table I cost of his or her insurance.

[Treas Reg § 1.79-0]

Q 11:34 How is an employee-pay-all plan treated under these rules?

Under the second part of the "carried directly or indirectly" test, an employee-pay-all group term policy may be treated as employer-provided (and, hence, result in imputed income for some employees) if the premium rates charged to the employees "straddle" the Table I rates under Code Section 79. A straddle occurs whenever some of the rates charged to participating employees are above the Table I rates and other rates charged to participating employees are below the Table I rates. This straddling rule in the regulations has its origin in the legislative history of Code Section 79, which indicates that Congress was concerned that younger employees might be required to subsidize older employees by having to contribute more than the actual cost of coverage for young employees, while older employees would be permitted to contribute less than the actual cost of their coverage. [HR Rpt No 749, 88th Cong, 1st Sess, at 40 (1963); S Rpt No 830, 88th Cong, 2d Sess, at 46 (1964)]

Q 11:35   Why can it be undesirable for an employee-pay-all plan to be treated as an employer-provided group term life insurance?

If the straddling rule would cause an employee-pay-all group term life insurance plan to be treated as employer-provided, then such coverage would be taxable under the rules of Code Section 79. This would result in some employees being taxed on amounts of coverage in excess of $50,000 even though they paid for it with after-tax dollars. Since the Table I cost is reduced by employee contributions, as a practical matter only employees with large amounts of employee-pay-all insurance purchased at less than Table I rates might be required to include a portion of the value of such coverage in gross income.

Additionally, because of the Code Section 79 nondiscrimination rules, the employee-pay-all group term life insurance plan that straddles Table I could raise nondiscrimination and tax issues affecting not only the employee-pay-all coverage but also employer-paid coverage having a common key employee participant. [Temp Treas Reg § 1.79-4T, Q&A 10] (The Code Section 79 nondiscrimination rules are discussed in Questions 11:40 through 11:48.) However, there are several ways that an employee-pay-all plan can overcome this obstacle (see Q 11:36).

Q 11:36   How can an employee-pay-all plan avoid the impact of the straddling rule that applies under Code Section 79?

There are several ways. One way to avoid the impact of the straddling rule is to have an entity independent of the employer sponsor the plan. Additionally, the impact can arguably be avoided via the rate structure. If employee-pay-all rates at all ages are at or below the Code Section 79 Table I rates, no imputed income should result. [Priv Ltr Rul 86-38-050]

Non-employer Plan. Several IRS private rulings have held that employee-pay-all group term life insurance plans provided through a trust, such as one maintained by a VEBA, are not considered to be carried directly or indirectly by the employer and, therefore, are not subject to Code Section 79. [Priv Ltr Ruls 84-30-138, 82-23-052, 81-29-070]

Note: If an employee-pay-all group term life insurance plan maintained by a VEBA does not fall under Code Section 79, then the Code Section 505(b) compensation limit applies to the benefits under the plan (see Q 19:68).

Another private ruling held that an employee-pay-all group term life insurance arrangement sponsored by an insurance brokerage and employee benefit consulting firm, under which the sponsor selected a bank trustee to hold the policy and recommended an insurer to the trustee, was not a policy carried directly or indirectly by the employer of the group of employees involved. [Priv Ltr Rul 84-31-040]

Presumably, in all of the rulings cited above, the straddling rule would have applied—and resulted in imputed income to some employees—if the group policy had been considered carried by the employer.

Q 11:37 **Does an employee-pay-all group term life insurance policy that has nonsmoker premium rates at or below Table I rates and smoker premium rates above Table I rates trigger the straddling rule?**

No, it apparently does not. An IRS ruling considered an employee-pay-all group term life insurance policy that had separate premium rates for nonsmokers and smokers. The nonsmoker rates were all below Table I rates, and the smoker rates were all above Table I rates. The premium rates for each group of employees were sufficient to make both the nonsmokers' and smokers' coverages self-supporting and independent of each other and independent of the employer's basic life plan. The IRS ruled that the employer could elect to treat the nonsmoker and smoker coverages as two separate policies for purposes of Section 79. Since neither policy straddled the Table I rates, neither policy would be considered to be carried directly or indirectly by the employer and thereby subject to Section 79. [Priv Ltr Rul 91-49-003 (Sept 10, 1991)]

Benefit Formula Precluding Individual Selection

Q 11:38   How can a benefit formula "preclude individual selection" so as to satisfy Code Section 79?

The fourth and last of the requirements that must be satisfied, in order for insurance to be characterized as "group term life insurance" and qualify for favorable tax treatment under Code Section 79, is that the amount of insurance provided to each employee must be computed under a formula that "precludes individual selection" of the amount of coverage. The formula must be based on factors such as age, years of service, compensation, or position. The factors used to determine eligibility for a large amount of coverage cannot be based on position and apply to only one person, such as the corporate president, or the plan will involve individual selection and not qualify for Code Section 79 treatment. [Treas Reg § 1.79-1(a)(4); Towne, 78 TC 791 (1982); see also Whitcomb, 81 TC 505 (1983)]

In a recent private letter ruling, IRS held that a plan provision allowing employees the option of reducing their coverage to avoid computed income would not be considered to be individual selection and would not disqualify the plan as a Code Section 79 plan. [Priv Ltr Rul 93-19-026, Feb 11, 1993]

Q 11:39   Can a benefit formula meet this test if coverage varies according to how much an employee elects to contribute?

The amount of insurance provided may be determined under a limited number of alternative schedules based on the amount each employee elects to contribute, without being considered individual selection. However, the amount of insurance provided under each such schedule must be computed under a formula that precludes individual selection. [Treas Reg § 1.79-1(a)(4)] There is no official guidance on the maximum number of alternative schedules tied to the amount of employee contributions that can be provided and still be considered to be a "limited" number.

Nondiscrimination Rules

Q 11:40 What are the basic nondiscrimination rules under Code Section 79?

Code Section 79 imposes two nondiscrimination requirements on employer-provided group term life insurance plans:

1. *Eligibility to Participate.* The group term life insurance plan may not discriminate in favor of "key employees" (see Q 11:41) with regard to eligibility to participate; and
2. *Benefits Test.* The group term life insurance plan may not discriminate in favor of participants who are "key employees" with respect to the type and amount of benefits available under the plan.

[IRC § 79(d)(1)]

Q 11:41 Who is a "key employee," in whose favor a plan cannot discriminate?

A "key employee" is any employee who meets any of the following four tests at any time during the plan year or has met them at any time during any of the preceding four plan years:

1. The employee is an officer of the employer whose annual compensation from the employer exceeds 50 percent of the defined-benefit plan dollar limit under Code Section 415(b)(1)(A). (For 1993, the annual compensation figure works out to $57,821.) The number of employees treated as officers is limited to 50 or, if fewer, the greater of either three officers or 10 percent of the employees.
2. The employee has annual compensation from the employer in excess of the defined-contribution plan dollar limit contained in Code Section 415(c)(1)(A) ($30,000 in 1993) and is one of the 10 employees owning (or treated as owning) the largest interest in the employer.
3. The employee is a more-than-5-percent direct or indirect owner of the employer.

4. The employee is a more-than-1-percent direct or indirect owner of the employer and receives annual compensation from the employer in excess of $150,000.

[IRC §§ 79(d)(6), 416(i)(1); Treas Reg § 1.416-1, Q&A T-12]

If a retiree had key-employee status at the time of retirement or separation from service on or before October 27, 1990, the retiree remains a key employee throughout retirement. Effective on and after October 28, 1990, all former employees (not just retirees) who had key-employee status at the time of retirement or separation from service continue to be classified as key employees. [IRC § 79(d)(6), as amended by OBRA 1990 § 11703(e)(1)]

Determination of Officer Status. The determination of an individual's status as an officer is made on the basis of the facts, not just the employee's title. Thus an employee who has the title but not the authority of an officer (for example, someone designated as assistant secretary for document-signing purposes) is not an officer. Conversely, an employee who does not have the title but has the authority of an officer is an officer for key-employee purposes. [Treas Reg § 1.416-1, Q&As T-13, T-14]

Q 11:42 When is eligibility to participate discriminatory under Code Section 79?

A group term life insurance plan discriminates with regard to eligibility to participate *unless* any one of the following tests is satisfied:

1. The plan benefits 70 percent or more of all employees of the employer;

2. At least 85 percent of all employees who are participants are not key employees;

3. The plan benefits employees who qualify under a classification established by the employer that the IRS has found not to discriminate in favor of key employees; or

4. The plan is part of a cafeteria plan that meets the cafeteria plan requirements of Code Section 125. (See Chapter 7 for a discussion of cafeteria plans.)

When applying this eligibility test, employees with less than three years of service, part-time or seasonal employees, employees covered under a collective bargaining agreement where the plan benefits were the subject of good-faith bargaining, and nonresident aliens with no U.S.-source earned income from the employer may be excluded. [IRC § 79(d)(3)]

> **Planning Pointer.** The 85-percent eligibility test is quite a liberal one. For example, assume that an employer with 500 employees has 15 key employees. If the employer provides group term life insurance only to the 100 highest-paid employees, and excludes the 400 lowest-paid employees, the employer's plan would satisfy the 85-percent eligibility test. [Temp Treas Reg § 1.79-4T, Q&A 9]

Q 11:43   When are benefits discriminatory under Code Section 79?

If the plan covers a key employee, benefits are available on a discriminatory basis *unless* the plan provides:

1. A fixed amount of insurance that is the same for all covered employees;
2. Coverage as a uniform percentage of total compensation or of basic or regular rate of compensation; or
3. Benefits that are nondiscriminatory based on all the facts and circumstances.

[IRC §§ 79(d)(4) and (d)(5); Temp Treas Reg § 1.79-4T, Q&A 9]

Q 11:44   Are group term life insurance policies tested separately in determining whether the employer's plan is discriminatory?

The answer depends on whether the policies cover a common key employee.

Mandatory Aggregation of Active Coverage. All policies that provide group term life insurance coverage to a common key employee or common key employees and that are carried directly or indirectly by the employer are a single plan for nondiscrimination testing. [Temp Treas Reg § 1.79-4T, Q&A 5]

> **Example.** A key employee has $50,000 of group term life insurance under one policy and an additional $250,000 of coverage under a separate group policy. The two policies are treated as a single plan for nondiscrimination testing purposes.

Mandatory Aggregation of Active and Retiree Coverage. A policy that provides group term life insurance to a key employee and a separate policy that will provide coverage to the same key employee after retirement or separation from service must be treated as a single plan. [Temp Treas Reg § 1.79-4T, Q&A 5]

Permissive Aggregation of Plans. An employer may choose to treat two or more policies that do not provide coverage to a common key employee as a single plan in order to satisfy the nondiscrimination rules; for example, the employer has one policy covering non-key employees only, and a second policy covering key employees. [Temp Treas Reg § 1.79-4T, Q&A 5]

Q 11:45   Can a plan that provides separate layers of coverage pass these nondiscrimination tests?

Yes, it can. If a plan provides layers of coverage based on percentages of compensation, each layer of coverage is tested separately. Thus, if an employer with 500 employees and 15 key employees provides coverage of 100 percent of compensation for all 500 employees and an additional 100 percent of compensation for the 100 highest-paid employees, the plan would not discriminate as to the amount of benefits, because the additional layer of coverage would satisfy the 85-percent eligibility test, and the amount of coverage would be the same (as a percentage of compensation) for all the members of the 100-employee subgroup.

The determination of the subgroups of employees to be tested can make allowances for reasonable differences in insurance (as a multiple of compensation) because of rounding, the use of compensation brackets, or other similar factors. [IRC § 79(d)(5); Temp Treas Reg § 1.79-4T, Q&A 9]

Q 11:46 How is additional group term life insurance that employees purchase under a Code Section 79 plan treated for nondiscrimination testing purposes?

As long as the option to purchase additional coverage at the employee's own expense (including on a pretax basis under a cafeteria plan) is available on a nondiscriminatory basis, the fact that key employees exercise the option to a greater extent than other employees does not make the plan discriminatory.

However, if additional insurance coverage that is available to any key employee is not available on a nondiscriminatory basis to non-key employees, the plan will be discriminatory, even though the employees are paying the full cost of the coverage. [Temp Treas Reg § 1.79-4T, Q&A 10]

Q 11:47 How are the Code Section 79 nondiscrimination rules applied to a plan covering both active and retired employees?

A plan that covers both active and former employees will fail the nondiscrimination tests unless both groups satisfy the tests. (See Question 11:48 for certain grandfathered employees who are excluded from these tests.)

However, both the eligibility test and the benefits test are applied separately to active and former employees. If only former employees who have retired are eligible for coverage, the retirees are tested separately.

Example. A plan provides group term life insurance equal to two times compensation for all active employees and one times final compensation (based on average annual compensation for the final five years) for all former employees. It is nondiscriminatory. However, if the coverage for former employees were limited to key employees only, the plan would be considered discriminatory. [Temp Treas Reg § 1.79-4T, Q&As 7, 8]

In applying the coverage tests to former employees, the employer may make reasonable mortality assumptions regarding former employees who are not covered by the plan, but must be considered in testing. Also, any former employee who terminated employment before the earliest date of termination of any former employee covered by the plan may be excluded from the testing group. [IRC § 79(d)(8); Temp Treas Reg § 1.79-4T, Q&As 7, 8]

Q 11:48 What is the effect of the Deficit Reduction Act of 1984 (DEFRA) "grandfather" rules under Code Section 79?

The grandfathered group under Code Section 79 consists of two categories. It includes:

1. Employees and retired employees who
   a. Attained age 55 on or before January 1, 1984,
   b. Were employed by the employer or a predecessor employer at any time in 1983, and
   c. Are covered under a group term life insurance plan of the employer "in existence" on January 1, 1984, or a "comparable successor" to the plan in existence on January 1, 1984; and
2. Employees who retired on or before January 1, 1984, and who, when they retired, were covered under the plan "in existence" on January 1, 1984, or a predecessor plan.

Plan in Existence on January 1, 1984. A plan in existence on January 1, 1984, is a plan that had executed the group policy or policies providing the benefits under the plan on or before that date and had not terminated them before that date. [Temp Treas Reg § 1.79-4T, Q&A 2]

Comparable Successor Plan. A comparable successor plan is a plan maintained by the employer or a predecessor that does not increase the benefits for a particular employee. Thus, increases in coverage for nongrandfathered employees will not cause the grandfathered employees to lose their favored status. [TRA '86 § 1827(b)(3)] If caused by an increase in compensation, an increase in the amount of life insurance coverage based on a percentage of compensation will not be considered an increase in benefits causing loss of grandfathered status. [Temp Treas Reg § 1.79-4T, Q&A 3] [This temporary regulation does not reflect the statutory changes made by the Tax Reform Act of 1986 (TRA '86) and is overly broad in defining what is not a comparable successor plan.]

Effect on Discrimination Testing. If the conditions for grandfather status continue to be met, the entire amount of group term life insurance coverage on the grandfathered employees may be disregarded when performing the Code Section 79 nondiscrimination tests. [Tax Reform Act of 1984 (TRA '84) § 223(d)(2), as amended by TRA '86 § 1827(b)(2); Priv Ltr Rul 91-49-010 (Aug 30, 1991)]

Effect of Plan Discrimination. If, after disregarding the coverage of the grandfathered group, the plan fails the nondiscrimination rules for other reasons (for example, the coverage of nongrandfathered employees is discriminatory), grandfathered employees who retire on or after January 1, 1987 lose the benefit of the grandfathered status (see Q 11:60).

Retirement Before 1987. The IRS, in a recent private letter ruling, has taken the position that in order for an employee to be considered retired before 1987, the employee had to have both actually retired and attained "retirement age" (generally, the earliest age at which the employee could retire with an actuarially unreduced pension benefit) before 1987. [Priv Ltr Rul 90-43-041 (July 31, 1990)] It is arguable, however, that actual retirement before 1987 is all the statute requires.

Other Plan Design Limitations

Q 11:49   Can an employer subject to the ADEA limit eligibility for group term life insurance benefits based upon age?

No, eligibility for group term life insurance coverage cannot be denied based upon age, at least for individuals within the age group protected by the ADEA (age 40 and older) and that protected by the applicable state law (sometimes age 18 and older). For example, an employer subject to the ADEA could not extend group term life insurance coverage to its employees under age 60 and deny coverage to anyone over age 60.

Q 11:50   Can an employer subject to the ADEA limit the amount of group term life insurance benefits based upon age?

Yes, provided that the employer follows the guidelines contained in the ADEA regulations expressly restored by the Older Workers Benefit Protection Act of 1990 (OWBPA). Those regulations require that any reduction in the amount of group term life insurance benefits must be justified on the basis of cost equivalency, that is, the cost of the reduced benefits for older employees must be no less than the cost of benefits provided to younger employees. Two approaches for achieving cost equivalency are provided under the Equal Employment Opportunity Commission (EEOC) regulations: the "benefit-by-benefit" approach and the "benefit package" approach. The specific rules regarding cost-justified reduction in benefits are discussed in greater detail in Questions 16:8 through 16:21.

Q 11:51 Can an employer subject to the ADEA increase the employees' share of the cost of group-term life insurance based upon age?

No, the employee's share of the cost of group term life insurance benefits cannot increase with age. Essentially, such a practice is viewed as a mandatory reduction in take-home pay in violation of the ADEA. It is permissible, however, for the employer to require that employees bear the same proportion of the cost of the plan. Older employees may be required to make larger absolute-dollar contributions than younger employees if the cost of group term life insurance coverage increases by age, as long as the proportion of the total cost paid by the employee remains constant. For example, the employer might decide to bear 50 percent of the cost of group term life insurance coverage and charge the employees 50 percent of the cost. As long as older employees were not charged more than 50 percent of the cost applicable to their age bracket, such an arrangement would not violate the ADEA (see Qs 16:15, 16:16).

Q 11:52 Can an employer subject to the ADEA limit eligibility, based upon age, for extension of group term life insurance during disability?

Some group term life insurance plans contain a provision that extends coverage to an employee who becomes disabled for the duration of the disability without premium cost (referred to as a "disability waiver" benefit). Typically, such a provision would apply only in the case of disabilities occurring before a specified age, such as age 60. Such a provision has been found by the EEOC not to be discriminatory as long as the cost of the group term life insurance without the disability waiver is at least equal to the cost of the group term life insurance with the disability waiver at the next lower age bracket, for example, ages 55-59. [EEOC Notice N-915.023 (Mar 21, 1988)]

Q 11:53   Can employer-provided group term life insurance be reduced or eliminated at retirement?

Yes, it can. The ADEA currently does not apply to retired employees. Once an older employee has retired or otherwise terminated employment, the employer can reduce or eliminate group term life insurance benefits without violating the ADEA. [ADEA §§ 2, 4, 11(f) 29 USC 621, 623, 630(f); EEOC Reg § 1625.10(f)(1)(i)] (See Q 16:3.)

Tax Treatment of Employer Contributions

Q 11:54   Are an employer's contributions for group term life insurance coverage for employees tax-deductible?

Yes, an employer's contributions for group term life insurance for employees are generally tax-deductible as ordinary and necessary business expenses. However, no deduction is allowed if the employer is a direct or indirect beneficiary of the policy. In addition, an employer's deductions for contributions to a welfare benefit fund, such as a VEBA or a retired lives reserve held by an insurer, are subject to the special limitations applicable to welfare benefit funds. (See Qs 19:39–19:42 and Qs 19:45–19:47.) [IRC §§ 162(a), 264(a)(1), 419, 419A]

Q 11:55   Does an employer's deduction hinge on compliance with Code Section 79?

No, it does not. Code Section 79 deals exclusively with whether the value of employer-provided coverage is taxable to employees and, if so, to what extent.

Income Tax Treatment of Coverage Provided to Employees

Q 11:56   How, generally, are employees taxed for group term life insurance coverage under Code Section 79 when the plan is not discriminatory?

If a Code Section 79 group term life insurance plan is not discriminatory, an employee who has coverage of $50,000 or less has no imputed income subject to federal income tax. If the coverage exceeds $50,000, the employee has imputed gross income equal to the "cost" of his or her group term life insurance in excess of $50,000 of coverage, less any employee contributions for the coverage (including any contributions toward the first $50,000 of coverage). [IRC §§ 79(a), 79(d); Treas Reg § 1.79-3] (Taxation of employees if the plan is discriminatory is discussed in Question 11:61.)

Q 11:57 How should the employer calculate the annual amount that is included in the employee's gross income under Code Section 79?

The computation is made on the basis of each period of coverage, which consists of each calendar month or portion of a calendar month during which coverage is provided.

Except in the case of a key employee under a discriminatory plan (see Q 11:61), the total amount of coverage for the period then is reduced by $50,000. The remaining amount of coverage under the plan for the particular employee is valued using the Table I cost contained in the regulations, *based on the employee's age on the last day of the taxable year.* Table I provides the following costs:

Five-Year Age Bracket	Cost per $1,000 of Protection for One-Month Period
Under 30	$ .08
30 to 34	.09
35 to 39	.11
40 to 44	.17
45 to 49	.29
50 to 54	.48
55 to 59	.75
60 to 64	1.17
65 to 69	2.10
70 and above	3.76

If the amount of coverage varies during the month (for example, if the coverage is tied to salary and the employee receives a raise during the month), the amount of coverage is considered the average of the amounts payable at the beginning and at the end of the month.

If the plan does not provide for a lump-sum form of payment either automatically or as an option—for example, if it provides a survivor income life insurance benefit only—the amount of coverage is equal to the present value of the stream of payments. If the beneficiary's age affects the present value of the benefit—for example, if a survivor income benefit is payable to a spouse for life—the beneficiary's age is the age at the nearest birthday as of June 30 of the calendar year. [Treas Reg § 1.79-3; Temp Treas Reg § 1.79-3T]

The monthly costs are aggregated for the taxable year, and this amount is then reduced by employee contributions (including any contributions toward the first $50,000 of coverage). Employee salary reduction contributions under a cafeteria plan are not considered employee contributions for this purpose (see Q 11:19).

Q 11:58 How are employee contributions toward coverage taken into account when calculating imputed income under Code Section 79?

After the cost of the group term life insurance is determined for the entire taxable year (see Question 11:56 for non-key employees and Question 11:62 for key employees), that amount is reduced by employee contributions, if any, toward the group term life insurance for the entire year, including employee contributions for coverage under $50,000 (but excluding employee salary reduction contributions under a cafeteria plan).

Employee contributions that represent a payment for a different taxable year (other than amounts applicable to regular pay periods extending into the next taxable year) cannot be used to offset the current cost. Thus, a prepayment of postretirement insurance cost would not reduce the taxable cost currently.

Employee contributions toward group term life insurance coverage that is already excludible from imputed income (for example, coverage while disabled or coverage when a charity is the beneficiary) cannot be used to offset imputed income on coverage that is not excludable.

If employee contributions are made on an unallocated basis for multiple insured benefits, one of which is group term life insurance, the individual employee's contributions for the portion that is the group term life insurance coverage must be determined by ascertaining (1) how much of the amounts all employees covered for the multiple insured benefits have contributed is allocable to the purchase of group term life insurance and (2) the pro rata portion of this allocable amount attributable to the individual employee, based on the ratio of the amount of group term life insurance on the employee to the total amount on all the employees. [IRC § 79(a); Treas Reg § 1.79-3(e)]

Q 11:59   Are disabled employees subject to tax under Code Section 79?

No, an employee who has terminated employment with the employer and is disabled has no imputed income under Code Section 79, regardless of whether or not the group term life insurance plan is discriminatory. For this purpose, employment is considered terminated when the individual no longer renders services to the employer as an employee. An individual is considered disabled when he or she is unable to engage in any substantial gainful activity because of any medically determinable physical or mental impairment that can be expected to result in death or to be of long-continued and indefinite duration. [IRC §§ 79(b)(1), 72(m)(7); Treas Reg § 1.79-2(b)]

Each year, the individual must provide proof of qualifying disability with the individual's income tax return. [Treas Reg § 1.79-2(b)(4)(ii)]

Planning Pointer. The disability test is a strict one, and an employee may qualify for disability benefits under the employer's disability plan and yet not be considered disabled for Code Section 79 purposes.

Q 11:60   Does an employee who has retired have imputed income under Code Section 79?

Generally, he or she does if coverage exceeds $50,000 or if the retiree is a key employee (see Q 11:41) under a discriminatory plan.

Grandfathered Employees. Until 1984, there was a complete exclusion from income for coverage provided after an employee had retired and attained "retirement age" (generally the earliest age at which the employee could retire with an actuarially unreduced pension). Accordingly, individuals who took early retirement would be subject to income tax on the amount of their retiree group term life insurance coverage in excess of $50,000 until they attained retirement age. Upon the retiree's attainment of retirement age, the coverage ceased to be taxable.

Retired individuals who are in the grandfathered group are still eligible for this prior law exclusion. [TRA '84 § 223(d)(2), as amended by TRA '86 § 1827(b); Treas Reg § 1.79-2(b)(3)] (The grandfather rules are discussed in Question 11:48.) However, any grandfathered employee who retires after 1986 and retires under a plan that is discriminatory loses the benefit of the retiree exemption. For non-key employees, this means that income on coverage in excess of $50,000 in retirement would be taxable at Table I rates. For key employees, the entire amount of retiree group term life insurance coverage would be taxable at the higher of Table I rates or actual cost. (For what constitutes "retirement" prior to 1987, see Question 11:48.)

Q 11:61 What are the tax consequences if the employer's group term life insurance plan fails the Code Section 79 nondiscrimination tests?

If the group term life insurance plan discriminates in favor of any key employee (see Q 11:41), all key employees are affected. Each key employee under a discriminatory plan loses the $50,000 exemption and is taxed on the full amount of coverage for the entire year, less his or her own contributions, at the greater of Code Section 79 Table I cost or actual cost. [IRC § 79(d)(1)]

Employees who are not key employees are not affected and continue to qualify for favorable taxation under Code Section 79. [IRC §§ 79(a), 79(d)(1)]

Any grandfathered individuals who did not retire before January 1, 1987, will lose grandfather protection. Those who are non-key employees and who otherwise would have qualified for the prior law exclusion will then be taxed on the value of their coverage for the year in excess of $50,000. Those who are key employees will lose the benefit of the total exclusion under prior law, lose the benefit of the current $50,000 exclusion, and will be taxed on all coverage for the year, less employee contributions, using the higher of Table I rates or actual cost.

Q 11:62   How is "actual cost" determined under a discriminatory group term life insurance plan?

Actual cost generally is determined by apportioning among covered employees the net premium (the group premium less policy dividends, premium refunds, or experience-rating credits) attributable to the group term life insurance plan during the taxable year. An employer that has multiple coverages with the same insurer must reasonably allocate the total premiums paid to the insurer between the group term life insurance coverage and the other types of coverage.

The portion of the net premium for group term life insurance apportioned to a particular key employee is generally determined by the following steps:

Step 1. Select a premium table for the entire group (rates in this table are referred to as "tabular premium" rates). For this purpose, the 1960 Basic Group Table published by the Society of Actuaries ordinarily must be used; however, if the group policy contains a reasonable premium rate table (based on recognized mortality assumptions) on an attained-age basis with age brackets not exceeding five years, that table may be used instead to determine the tabular premiums.

Step 2. Determine the ratio of the net amount of premiums for the entire group to the total amount of tabular premiums for the entire group.

Step 3. Multiply the tabular premium for the key employee at his or her age by the ratio determined in step 2.

Example. Mr. Jones, a key employee, has group term life insurance of $100,000 under a discriminatory plan. The tabular premium at Mr. Jones' age is $1 per month per $1,000 of coverage. The tabular annual premium on an attained-age basis for the group is $100,000, and the actual net annual premium for the group is $150,000. Since the ratio of the actual premium to the tabular premium for the group is 1.5 to 1.0, Mr. Jones' actual premium cost would be $1.50 per month per $1,000 of coverage, or $150 per month ($1,800 for the year).

Exception. If the insurer calculates the mortality charge for coverage for a key employee separately (for example, the charge is based on a medical examination), and the mortality charge plus a proportionate share of the loading charge for the coverage for the group is higher than the amount determined under the allocation method above, the actual cost for that key employee is the higher amount. Any cost for key employees calculated under this method is excluded in applying the general allocation method to other key employees. [Temp Treas Reg § 1.79-4T, Q&A 6]

Q 11:63 What if the plan is discriminatory under Code Section 79 for only a part of a taxable year?

If a plan is discriminatory for any part of the key employee's taxable year, it is treated as discriminatory for the entire taxable year. [Temp Treas Reg § 1.79-4T, Q&A 11]

Q 11:64 Are there any planning strategies an employee can use to avoid imputation of income under Code Section 79?

Yes, the employee may, provided certain conditions are met, designate a charity (that is, any organization described in Code Section 170(c)) as the beneficiary of the policy. The employee may also designate the employer as the beneficiary. These strategies may be used by all employees, including key employees under a discriminatory plan.

Q 11:65 When will designating a charity as beneficiary avoid imputed income under Code Section 79?

The charity must be designated as the sole beneficiary for the entire period during the taxable year for which the employee receives the amount of the coverage subject to the designation (although the designation may be revocable). The charity may be designated as beneficiary for a specific amount or for a fractional amount of the total coverage.

> **Example.** An employee has $50,000 of coverage for the first six months of a taxable year. On July 1, her coverage increases to $60,000 because of a salary increase. She designates a charity as beneficiary for $10,000 for the second six months, and thereby avoids any imputed income in that year. The following taxable year, she would have to maintain the designation of the charity as the sole beneficiary of $10,000 during the entire taxable year to avoid imputed income. If she revoked the charitable beneficiary designation during that taxable year, no charitable beneficiary designation exclusion would apply for any part of that taxable year.

[IRC § 79(b)(2)(B); Treas Reg § 1.79-2(c)]

Q 11:66   When will designation of the employer as beneficiary avoid imputed income under Code Section 79?

The requirements are basically the same as those for charitable beneficiary designations. [IRC § 79(b)(2)(A)] However, if the employer is the nominal beneficiary under the policy but there is an arrangement whereby the employer is required to pay over all or a portion of the death proceeds to the employee's estate or beneficiary, the employer is not considered the beneficiary with respect to such amount, and the employee does not avoid imputed income. [Treas Reg § 1.79-2(c)(2)]

> **Planning Pointer.** Some state group insurance laws prohibit an employer from being designated as a beneficiary of an employee's group life insurance. Also, designating the employer as beneficiary can jeopardize the tax deductability of the employer's premium payments. [IRC § 264(a)(1)]

Q 11:67   Can an assignment other than to a charity or to the employer avoid imputed income for an employee under Code Section 79?

No, it cannot, although such assignment may provide estate tax advantages (see Q 11:86). Because the employer provides the group life insurance by reason of the employment of the insured individual, the employee who makes an assignment continues to have imputed income under Code Section 79. When determining the amount of imputed income, any employee contributions made by the assignee are treated as paid by the employee (see Q 11:92). [Rev Rul 73-174, 1973-1 CB 43]

Q 11:68   Can an employee deduct his or her contributions for group term life insurance coverage?

No, premiums that an individual pays for life insurance coverage are considered a nondeductible personal expense. However, employee contributions reduce the taxable cost of group term life insurance (see Q 11:58). [IRC § 262]

Planning Pointer. A group term life insurance plan qualifying under Code Section 79 can be made part of a cafeteria plan, so that employee contributions can be made on a salary reduction basis. (See Chapter 7 for a discussion of cafeteria plans.)

Q 11:69   If a policy contains both term and permanent benefits and is subject to Code Section 79, how is the employee's coverage taxed?

The employee is taxed on the portion of the policy designated as group term life insurance in accordance with the general rules of Code Section 79. The employee is also taxed on the cost of the permanent coverage, reduced by any amount the employee has paid for the permanent coverage (see Question 11:1 for a definition of "permanent coverage").

The cost of the permanent coverage for an employee is no less than the amount that is expressed by the following equation:

Cost of permanent coverage for an employee = $X(DDB2 - DDB1)$

X =   the net single premium for insurance (the premium for $1 of paid-up whole life insurance) at the employee's age at the beginning of the policy year (X is calculated using the 1958 Insurance Commissioners' Standard Ordinary mortality table plus 4 percent interest).

DDB2 = the employee's deemed death benefit at the end of the policy year.

DDB1 = the employee's deemed death benefit at the end of the preceding policy year.

(The definition of the "deemed death benefit" is discussed in Question 11:31).

Q 11:70   What is the tax treatment under Code Section 79 of policy dividends under a policy combining a permanent feature?

If the employee pays nothing for the permanent coverage, all policy dividends the employee actually or constructively receives are fully taxable. If the employee has contributed to the cost of the permanent coverage, a portion of the dividends is includible in the employee's income. The includible amount is expressed by the following equation:

$$\text{Includible amount} = (D + C) - (PI + DI + AP)$$

D = the total amount of dividends the employee actually or constructively received under the policy in the employee's current taxable year and all preceding taxable years.

C = the total cost of the permanent coverage for the employee's current taxable year and all preceding taxable years.

PI = the total amount of premium for the permanent coverage included in the employee's income for the employee's current taxable year and all preceding taxable years.

DI = the total amount of dividends included in the employee's income in all the employee's preceding taxable years.

AP = the total amount the employee has paid for permanent coverage in the employee's current taxable year and all preceding taxable years.

[Treas Reg § 1.79-1(d)(5)]

Q 11:71 If the policy year and the employee's taxable year are different, how is the cost of the permanent coverage allocated between taxable years?

The cost of permanent coverage for a policy year is allocated first to the employee's taxable year in which the policy year begins and may be expressed by the following equation:

$$\text{Cost of permanent coverage for taxable year in which policy year begins} = F \times C$$

F = the fraction representing that portion of the premium for the policy year that is paid on or before the last day of the employee's taxable year.

C = the cost of permanent benefits for the policy year.

Any part of the cost of the permanent benefit that is not allocated to the employee's taxable year in which the policy year begins is allocated to the employee's following taxable year. [Treas Reg § 1.79-1(d)(6)]

Q 11:72 Is imputed income under Code Section 79 subject to federal income tax withholding?

No, it is not. However, the employer must report each year's imputed income amount on a Form W-2 filed with the IRS and provide the employee with a copy of the W-2. [Treas Reg §§ 1.6052-1, 1.6052-2]

Q 11:73 Is imputed income under Code Section 79 subject to Social Security tax?

Yes, it is subject to the Federal Insurance Contributions Act (FICA, or Social Security) tax. Withholding of the employee's share of the FICA tax is required. The IRS allows employers to treat any period not exceeding one year as a payroll period for this purpose. Thus, an employer can elect to withhold on the imputed income under Code Section 79 only once a year. [IRC § 3121(a)(2)(C); IRS Notice 88-82, 1988-2 CB 398]

Cafeteria Plans. The FICA tax and the resultant withholding requirement apply even if the group term life insurance is provided under a cafeteria plan. [IRC § 3121(a)(5)(G); IRS Notice 88-82, 1988-2 CB 398] A benefit that is otherwise subject to FICA taxes does not become nontaxable merely because it is included under a cafeteria plan. Thus, for example, the cost of group term life insurance coverage amounts over $50,000, which is includible in an employee's income and is subject to FICA tax, will not escape such taxes as a result of being offered as a benefit under a cafeteria plan.

Retirees. The FICA tax and withholding requirements for group term life insurance do not apply to individuals who separated from service before 1989 and do not return to work for the same employer or a successor employer thereafter. For persons who retire during or after 1989 and who have imputed income under Section 79, such imputed income is subject to FICA tax. Effective for group term life insurance coverage provided after 1990, an employer is not required to withhold and pay over the retiree's share of the FICA tax with respect to coverage for periods during which an employment relationship no longer exists between the retiree and the employer. However, the employer is required to include on the W-2 statement provided to the former employee the portion of the compensation applicable to the imputed value of the group term life insurance and the amount of FICA tax due on such value. The former employee is required to pay his or her portion of the FICA tax directly to the IRS. The Form 1040 return instructions for 1992 provide that the amount of the FICA tax due is to be added to line 53 on page 2 of Form 1040, and the words "Uncollected Tax" added on the dotted line next to line 53. [IRC § 3102(d)]

Q 11:74   Is imputed income under Code Section 79 subject to federal unemployment tax (FUTA)?

No, it is not subject to FUTA. [IRC § 3306(b)(2)(C)]

Q 11:75   If employer-provided group term insurance coverage does not qualify under Code Section 79, what are the tax consequences for employees?

If the policy does not qualify under Code Section 79, and the proceeds are payable to a beneficiary designated by the employee, the premiums paid by the employer are included in the employee's gross income.

However, special rules may apply if the insurance is provided pursuant to a tax-sheltered annuity governed by Code Section 403(b), or if the insurance is provided under a pension or profit-sharing plan. [Treas Reg § 1.61-2(d)(2)(ii)(a)]

Income Tax Treatment of Death Benefits

Q 11:76 Are death benefits paid under a Code Section 79 group term life insurance plan subject to federal income tax?

No, death benefit proceeds are not taxable to the beneficiary. The general rule is that all life insurance death benefits (or proceeds) are fully exempt from federal income tax. [IRC § 101(a)] However, if the insurance carrier also pays the beneficiary interest on the proceeds, the interest is fully taxable. [IRC § 101(c)]

Q 11:77 If a death benefit is paid out in installments, or as an annuity, how are the payments taxed?

The amount of the death benefit is prorated over the expected payout period, so that a portion of each payment representing life insurance proceeds is received tax-free, and the remaining portion (deemed to represent investment earnings accruing on the death proceeds until all payments are made) is taxable.

If the group term life insurance policy does not provide for a lump-sum benefit as one option under the policy (for example, it is a survivor-income-benefit-only policy), the death proceeds equal the present value of the anticipated future payments at the date of death. [IRC § 101(d)(2); Treas Reg § 1.101-4(b)]

The interest rate used to calculate the taxable portion of the payments is the one the insurer uses to calculate the amount of the payments. However, the IRS prescribes the mortality tables used to calculate the present value of death benefits payable in the form of an annuity, the anticipated payout period, and so forth. The mortality tables under Code Section 72 regulations, which apply to annuities, are used for this purpose. [IRC § 101(d)(2)(B)(i); Treas Reg § 1.101-7]

Q 11:78   Are death benefits from a group term life insurance plan payable in the form of a life annuity subject to the Code Section 72 provisions governing annuities?

No, they are not. Life insurance proceeds payable in the form of an annuity are governed by Code Section 101(d) and the regulations thereunder; annuities are governed by Code Section 72 and the regulations thereunder. The income tax treatment is similar, but not identical, and the treatment under Code Section 101(d) is generally more favorable to the recipient.

For example, Code Section 101(d) permits the payee of a life annuity payout to continue to exclude a portion of each payment from income even after the payee has outlived his or her life expectancy and thus recovered the death benefit tax-free. [Treas Reg § 1.101-4(c)] In contrast, Code Section 72 makes the annuity payments fully taxable once the annuitant has recovered the investment in the contract. [IRC § 72(b)(2)]

Tax Treatment of Premium Rebates

Q 11:79   Does an employer have income when it receives a premium rebate under a group term life insurance policy?

A premium rebate, generally referred to as an experience refund or policy dividend, may be paid by the insurer if the financial experience under the group policy has been favorable.

Assuming the employer has taken a federal income tax deduction for the premium payments it has made (as is normally the case), the employer must include a premium rebate in its federal gross income, unless the prior deduction did not reduce the employer's federal income tax. If the employer did not take a tax deduction for its premium payments or if the deduction did not result in a tax benefit, the premium rebate is not taxable. [IRC § 111].

Q 11:80   In what year is an employer required to take a taxable premium rebate into its federal gross income?

If the employer is on a cash-basis method of accounting, a taxable premium rebate is taken into income in the taxable year in which the premium rebate is actually or constructively received. [Treas Reg § 1.451-1(a)]

If the employer is on an accrual-basis method of accounting, a taxable premium rebate is taken into income in the taxable year when (1) all the events have occurred that fix the right to receive the premium rebate and (2) the amount of the premium rebate is fixed with reasonable certainty. [Treas Reg § 1.451-1(a)]

A group policy dividend was held not to be subject to accrual for federal income tax purposes until the board of directors of the insurer had declared a dividend out of surplus and the amount of the dividend had been fixed by a calculation of the insurer's actuaries. [O Liquidating Corp, 19 TCM 154 (1960), *revd* on other grounds, 292 F 2d 225 (3rd Cir 1961)]

Note. If the group insurance policy were deemed to be a "welfare benefit fund" under Section 419(e)(3)(C) of the Code and IRS regulations thereunder, then the deductibility of the premiums would be subject to the account limit rules under Code Sections 419 and 419A. The employer can avoid having to treat such a group policy as a welfare benefit fund by satisfying requirements for the Code Section 419(e)(4)(B) exemption for a "qualified nonguaranteed contract," including the requirement that the employer treat any premium rebate payable with respect to the policy year as received or accrued in the taxable year in which such policy year ends.

Most group insurance policies generally are not treated as welfare benefit funds under existing IRS regulations, so compliance with the requirements for qualified nonguaranteed contract status does not appear to be necessary to avoid welfare benefit fund treatment (see Qs 19:21–19:25).

Q 11:81   What is the federal income tax treatment of premium rebates paid to employees under a contributory or employee-pay-all group term life insurance plan?

If the employee premiums were paid with after-tax contributions, a premium rebate received by an employee is nontaxable to the extent that it does not exceed the employee's cumulative after-tax contributions. To the extent that the premium rebate exceeds the employee's cumulative after-tax contributions, or if the contributions by the employee were made on a pre-tax basis under a cafeteria plan, the employee is subject to tax on the rebate. [IRC § 72(e), Treas Reg § 1.72-1(d)]

> **Planning Pointer.** Generally, premium rebates paid to employees under employee-pay-all plans are not taxable when employee contributions have been made on an after-tax basis, especially for employees who have contributed under the plan for a number of years. The employer may wish to apportion a premium rebate among covered employees by taking into account length of participation or cumulative employee contributions, so as to eliminate any reportable taxable income. Such an apportionment may also be desirable in the interests of fairness to the contributing employees.

Q 11:82   Is a taxable premium rebate paid to employees subject to wage withholding for federal income tax, FICA, and FUTA purposes?

Yes, it is. The IRS has held that a taxable premium rebate to employees constitutes wages for the purpose of federal income tax withholding, and for the FICA and FUTA purposes. [Priv Ltr Rul 92-03-033 (Oct 22, 1991)]

Q 11:83   What is the federal income tax treatment if the employer or insurer, instead of paying employees a premium rebate, waives employee contributions under the group life insurance policy for a limited period?

In order to avoid the administrative complexities of apportioning a premium rebate among the covered employees and paying a cash amount to each employee, it is a common practice to waive future employee contributions for a limited period sufficient to use up the amount of the group policy surplus. While there is no direct authority on the federal income tax treatment of such a waiver program, it appears that the employee would be viewed as constructively receiving cash in the amount of the waived premiums and then would be deemed to have contributed the cash to the group life insurance policy as premiums. As long as the waived premiums do not exceed the employee's cumulative after-tax contributions to the group policy, the employee should have no income for federal income tax purposes.

Q 11:84   What are the federal income tax consequences if the surplus under a group life insurance policy, instead of being paid as a premium rebate, is used to establish or increase the amount of a premium stabilization reserve?

A premium stabilization reserve is a reserve held by the insurance company for the purpose of leveling the costs of the group policy over a number of policy years. As long as the reserve is reasonable in amount, the insurance company obtains a tax deduction for increases in the amount of such a reserve. [IRC § 807(c)(6)] It is common for such a reserve to be established under an employee-pay-all group life insurance policy to avoid having to change the employee contribution rates frequently.

Establishment and maintenance of a premium stabilization reserve by the insurer appears to have no adverse tax consequences for either the employer or the employees covered by the group life insurance policy. [Rev Rul 69-382, 1969-2 CB 28] However, if the premium stabilization reserve is held by a VEBA, see Question 19:36.

Federal Estate and Gift Taxation

Q 11:85   Are group term life insurance death benefits includable in the deceased employee's federal gross estate?

Generally, yes, they are. Life insurance proceeds are includable in the insured employee's gross estate if they are payable to the insured employee's estate. They are also included in the gross estate if they are payable to a beneficiary but the insured possesses "incidents of ownership" in the insurance at the time of death. [IRC § 2042] Generally, the employee will have incidents of ownership because the employee will have the right to designate the beneficiary or beneficiaries. In addition, the employee often has the right to assign the coverage. ("Incidents of ownership" are discussed further in Question 11:88.)

Q 11:86   Is there anything the employee can do to try to remove the death benefit from his or her federal gross estate?

Yes, the employee can assign his or her group term life insurance coverage. Although assignment will not avoid imputed income to the employee on the coverage provided on the employee's life, it may result in the proceeds payable upon the employee's death being excluded from his or her federal gross estate (see Q 11:85). Thus, assignment could be a successful estate planning technique.

Q 11:87   What kind of assignment of group life insurance coverage is necessary to remove it from the employee's gross estate?

The employee must make an absolute assignment of all incidents of ownership under the policy (see Q 11:88) and the group policy and state law must permit such an assignment. [Rev Rul 69-54, 1969-1 CB 221, as modified by Rev Rul 72-307, 1972-1 CB 307]

Group policies now generally permit assignment by gift, and most states have statutes specifically recognizing the validity of such gifts. Even if a state does not have specific laws on the subject, assignments should be valid under general principles of contract and insurance law.

Planning Pointer. The employee should make the assignment while he or she is healthy, to increase the chances of estate planning success (see Q 11:89).

Q 11:88   What are the "incidents of ownership" the employee must surrender to make a successful assignment?

The meaning of the term "incidents of ownership" is not limited to ownership in the pure legal sense. Incidents of ownership include the right of the insured or the insured's estate to the economic benefits of the policy. They also include the power to change the beneficiary, to surrender or cancel the policy, to assign the policy, and to revoke an assignment. [Treas Reg § 20.2042-1(c)(2)] Additionally, they include any reversionary interest having a value of more than 5 percent of the value of the policy immediately before the insured's death.

The power to select a mode of payment of the death proceeds may, by itself, constitute an incident of ownership. [Estate of James H Lumpkin, Jr v Commissioner, 474 F 2d 1092 (5th Cir 1973); but see to the contrary Estate of John Connelly, Sr v United States, 551 F 2d 545 (3d Cir 1977), *nonacq*, Rev Rul 81-128, 1981-1 CB 469] However, the privilege to convert to an individual policy of life insurance upon termination of employment has been held not to constitute an incident of ownership. [Estate of J Smead, 78 TC 43 (1982), *acq in result*, 1984-2 CB 2] The fact that an employee may in effect cancel the group term life insurance coverage by terminating employment has also been held to be too limited a right to constitute an incident of ownership. [Landorf v United States, 408 F 2d 461 (Ct Cl 1969); Rev Rul 72-307, 1971-1 CB 221]

Q 11:89   Can an assignment fail because the employee dies too soon after it is made?

Yes, it can. The assignment must be made more than three years before the employee's death; otherwise the proceeds will be includible in the employee's gross estate. [IRC § 2035]

Q 11:90   Must a term policy be reassigned each year?

No, generally a group term life insurance policy is considered a continuing policy as long as premiums are paid to keep it in force. Therefore, once the initial assignment has been in effect for more than three years, the death proceeds will be excluded from the federal gross estate, and a renewal of the assignment each year is not required. [Rev Rul 82-13, 1982-1 CB 132]

However, some caution should be exercised about changes in carrier and modifications of the policy. The IRS has allowed a broadly worded assignment that purportedly applied to future group term life insurance with the same or a different insurance carrier to carry over when one insurance carrier replaced another, but the group term life insurance plan itself was unchanged. [Rev Rul 80-289, 1980-2 CB 270] The legal result should be the same if the group term life insurance plan is modified somewhat, as long as it can be considered a successor to the original plan.

However, the IRS has imposed a new three-year period in a case in which the original assignment did not purport to carry over to a new insurance carrier or successor plan and the new insurance carrier required a new assignment to be executed. [American National Bank v United States, 832 F 2d 1032 (7th Cir 1987)]

Q 11:91 Will the estate tax be affected if the assignee pays the employee's share of the premiums under a contributory group term life insurance plan?

It may be. One federal appeals court permitted a portion of the proceeds to be excluded from the insured's gross estate when the assignee of an individual life insurance policy had paid the premium and the insured died within three years of the assignment. The exclusion was based on the ratio that the premiums paid by the assignee bore to the total premiums paid. [Estate of Morris Silverman, 61 TC 338 (1973), aff'd, 521 F 2d 574 (2d Cir 1975)] Thus, in a case involving contributory or employee-pay-all group term life coverage, there may be an advantage to having the assignee pay the employee's contributions for the first three years following the assignment. (This will not affect the employee's income tax liability; see Question 11:67.)

Q 11:92 Should employees generally assign their group life insurance to remove it from their federal gross estates?

There is no hard and fast rule. A decision must be based on the individual facts and circumstances of each case. Most estates are entitled to a federal "unified credit" equivalent to a $600,000 tax exemption, unless the amount is used up by lifetime gifts. [IRC §§ 2010 and 2001] In addition, property passing to a spouse at death is generally eligible for an unlimited marital deduction. [IRC § 2056] Thus, many employees with modest estates need not be concerned about the federal estate tax. However, employees with larger estates may find that an assignment of group term life insurance serves a bona fide estate planning purpose and may result in significant savings in federal estate taxes.

Q 11:93   Will an assignment result in federal gift tax liability?

The answer again depends on the employee's facts and circumstances. If an employee's assignment of group term life insurance is a gift, federal gift tax rules will apply. However, an assignment of group term life insurance rarely gives rise to a gift tax liability at the time of assignment. The value of the gift at the time of assignment is generally quite small. Thus the gift (unless it is a gift of a future interest) is generally eligible for an annual exclusion of $10,000, which can be increased to $20,000 if the gift is not to the employee's spouse and the employee's spouse consents to the gift. If the assignment is to the employee's spouse, a 100-percent marital deduction is generally available. Finally, if the gift is not excluded from gift tax as a result of the annual exclusion or the marital deduction, the gift tax can usually be avoided by claiming the unified tax credit, subject to a phase-out rule for certain wealthy individuals. [IRC §§ 2503(b), 2505, 2513, 2523, 2001]

Q 11:94   How is an assignment valued for federal gift tax purposes?

The IRS has ruled that an assignment of group term life insurance made on the day preceding the date the monthly premium became due has no value for gift tax purposes. If the assignment was made during the month (under a monthly premium policy), presumably the value of the gift would be only a fraction of the monthly premium. For example, if an assignment was made on the fifteenth day of a 30-day month, one half of the monthly premium would be the value of the gift. [Rev Rul 84-147, 1984-2 CB 201]

An employee who is not a key employee under a plan that is discriminatory under Code Section 79 (see Qs 11:40–11:47) may use the Table I rates in the Code Section 79 regulations (see Q 11:57) to determine this premium cost. The employee may also use the actual cost of the coverage. [Rev Rul 84-147,1984-2 CB 201]

The standards for a key employee under a discriminatory plan are somewhat less clear. The IRS has held that actual cost has to be used. [Rev Rul 84-147, 1984-2 CB 201] However, the ruling was issued before Code Section 79 was amended to provide that key employees under a discriminatory plan would be taxed on the higher of actual cost or Table I "cost." Presumably, a key employee in a discriminatory plan must use the higher of the two cost figures for gift tax valuation purposes.

Retired Lives Reserve. The presence of a retired lives reserve apparently has no effect on the gift tax value of an assignment, although there is no specific authority on this point. The typical retired lives reserve fund is unallocated; that is, no specific portion of the reserve is allocable to any individual employee. In addition, the insurance company generally does not guarantee that the reserve will be adequate to continue coverage in retirement for any specified period. However, if a specific amount is set aside for the employee-assignee, as may be the case if key employees are covered by the retired lives reserve, the amount set aside may have to be taken into account for gift tax purposes.

Chapter 12

Death Benefits Other Than Employee Group Term Life Insurance

In addition to group term life insurance for employees, employers may choose to offer various death benefit plans. This chapter examines the application of the Internal Revenue Code (the Code), the Employee Retirement Income Security Act of 1974 (ERISA), and other regulatory concerns for some of the more common types of employer-provided death benefits: dependent group life insurance, accidental death benefits, business travel accident plans, group universal life (GUL) insurance, uninsured death benefits, split-dollar life insurance, bonus life insurance and death benefits under qualified retirement plans. In addition, this chapter discusses developments in new employee benefit products such as accelerated death benefits and living benefits. Corporate-owned life insurance (COLI) is discussed in Chapter 19.

Dependent Group Term Life Insurance

Q 12:1   What is a dependent group term life insurance plan?

A dependent group term life insurance plan is a plan covering a group of employees that provides the participating employees with group term life insurance coverage on the lives of the employees' dependents (that is, spouses and children). In the event of the death of an employee's dependent covered for insurance, the death proceeds generally are payable to the employee.

Q 12:2   Who pays for the cost of a dependent group term life insurance plan?

Depending on the terms of the plan, the cost of the dependent group term life insurance coverage may be paid for entirely by the employer, or shared by the employer and the participating employees, or the participating employees may pay the full cost of the coverage. In a majority of cases, dependent group term life insurance plans provide that the participating employees pay the full cost of the dependent coverage.

Q 12:3   Is a dependent group term life insurance plan subject to ERISA?

If the employer pays all or part of the cost of the dependent group term life insurance plan, ERISA applies. [ERISA § 3(1)] If the plan is an employee-pay-all plan, ERISA possibly may apply, depending on the extent of the employer's sponsorship or involvement in the plan. Department of Labor (DOL) regulations exempt a group insurance program from treatment as an ERISA employee welfare benefit plan only if it satisfies the following four requirements:

1. No contributions are made by the employer;

2. Participation in the program is completely voluntary;

3. The employer's sole functions with respect to the program are, without endorsing the program, to (a) permit the insurer to publicize the program to employees and (b) collect premiums through payroll deduction and to remit them to the insurer; and

4. The employer receives no consideration in the form of cash or otherwise in connection with the program, other than reasonable compensation (excluding any profit) for administrative services actually rendered in connection with payroll deductions.

[DOL Reg. § 2510.3-1(j)]

Q 12:4 Are dependent group term life insurance plans subject to the Age Discrimination in Employment Act (ADEA)?

Yes, they are. The ADEA prohibits discrimination because of age in all compensation, terms, conditions, and privileges of employment, including all employee benefits. [29 USC § 630(l), as amended by § 102 of the Older Workers Benefits Protection Act (OWBPA)] (For an explanation of the ADEA, see Chapter 16.)

Q 12:5 Can the employer deduct its premium payments for dependent group term life insurance?

Yes, if the employer pays premiums for dependent group term life insurance, then its premium payments can be deducted, provided that they are an ordinary and necessary business expense. [IRC § 162(a); Treas Reg § 1.162-10] However, if the dependent group term life insurance benefits are provided through a welfare benefit fund such as a Code Section 501(c)(9) voluntary employees' beneficiary association (VEBA) trust, any employer contributions must also satisfy the requirements of Code Sections 419 and 419A in order to be deductible by the employer (see Qs 19:20–19:52 for further discussion of Code Sections 419 and 419A).

Q 12:6   Are the employee's own contributions toward dependent group term life insurance coverage deductible?

No, premiums that an employee pays for life insurance coverage for his or her dependents are considered a nondeductible personal expense. [IRC § 262]

Q 12:7   Is the cost or value of dependent group term life insurance coverage provided to an employee by his or her employer included in the employee's gross income for federal income tax purposes?

Before 1989, Treasury regulations for many years had provided that, when the employer paid part or all of the cost of the coverage but the coverage did not exceed $2,000 on the life of the spouse or child, the coverage was considered incidental and not includible in the employee's gross income. If the employer paid all or a part of the cost of the coverage, and the dependent coverage on a spouse or child exceeded $2,000, the cost of the entire coverage (determined using Table I in the Code Section 79 regulations) less the employee's contributions toward the coverage was includible in the employee's gross income. However, since the employer paid no part of the cost of employee-pay-all coverage, employee-pay-all coverage appeared to be tax-free under this rule, even if the rates charged "straddled" Table I (see Q 11:34) [Treas Reg § 1.61-2(d)(2)(ii)(b); TD 6888, 1966-2 CB 23]

In 1989, the Treasury Department amended the regulations to provide that the cost (determined under Table I) of group term life insurance on the life of a spouse or dependent provided in connection with the employee's performance of service is fully taxable. The $2,000 incidental amount of coverage rule was eliminated. At the same time, the Treasury Department issued regulations under Code Section 132 (dealing with the tax treatment of fringe benefits) stating that dependent group term life insurance could not qualify as an excludable *de minimis* fringe benefit. [Treas Reg §§ 1.612(d)(2)(ii)(b), 1.132-6(e)(2)]

Following widespread objections to this change in the Internal Revenue Service (IRS) position, the IRS then issued Notice 89-110 (1989-2 CB 447) stating that, until further notice:

1. If the employer-provided dependent group term life insurance has a face amount of $2,000 or less, it will be deemed to be an excludable *de minimis* fringe benefit under Code Section 132; and

2. In determining whether dependent group life insurance with a face amount higher than $2,000 is a *de minimis* fringe benefit, only the excess, if any, of the cost of such insurance (determined under Table I) over the amount paid by the employee for such insurance will be taken into account.

Therefore, unless and until the IRS takes further action,

- Dependent group life insurance coverage with a face amount of $2,000 or less is tax-free to the employee, and

- In the case of dependent group life insurance coverage with a face amount higher than $2,000, the employee may possibly be receiving a tax-free *de minimis* fringe benefit, depending on the amount of the coverage and the level of his or her contribution toward the coverage.

Under this rule, it appears that employee-pay-all group term dependent life insurance coverage ordinarily should not give rise to any imputed taxable income to employees, even if the rates charged straddle Table I, and the straddle rule in the Code Section 79 regulation were found to be applicable.

Q 12:8 Is dependent group term life insurance subject to Code Section 79 income tax treatment?

No, Code Section 79 applies only to group term life insurance coverage on the employee's own life. It does not apply to group term life insurance on the lives of the employee's dependents. [Treas Reg § 1.79-3(f)(2)]

Because Section 79 does not apply, employee-pay-all dependent life insurance maintained by a VEBA will be subject to the $150,000 compensation limit contained in Code Section 505(b)(7) (see Q 19:68).

Q 12:9 How are the death benefit proceeds under a dependent group term life insurance plan taxed?

Dependent group term life insurance death benefit proceeds are treated as life insurance proceeds for federal income and estate tax purposes. Therefore, the death benefit proceeds are exempt from federal gross income when received by the employee/beneficiary. Since the deceased spouse or child generally has no incidents of ownership in the policy, the proceeds are not includible in the deceased spouse's or child's estate for federal estate tax purposes. [IRC §§ 101(a), 2042; Treas Reg § 1.101-1(a)(1)]

Q 12:10 Can dependent group term life insurance be made part of a cafeteria plan?

Originally, Treasury regulations permitted the inclusion of dependent group term life insurance in a cafeteria plan, and also permitted employee contributions for the coverage to be made on a salary reduction, that is, pre-tax, basis. [Temp Treas Reg § 1.125-2T] However, regulations proposed subsequently took the position that, because dependent group term life insurance is a fringe benefit under Code Section 132, it is not treated as a qualified benefit or cash under Code Section 125 and, therefore, cannot be a part of a Section 125 cafeteria plan even if the dependent coverage is purchased with after-tax employee contributions. [Prop Treas Reg § 1.125-2, Q&A 4(d); IRC § 125(f)]

Because the application of this new IRS position would have disqualified some existing cafeteria plans that were offering dependent group term life insurance as a cafeteria plan option, the IRS announced that, for plan years ending before 1992, dependent group term life insurance could be included in a cafeteria plan provided it was treated as cash, regardless of whether it is eligible for exclusion as a *de minimis* fringe benefit under Code Section 132. The IRS notice went on to say that, if the dependent group term life insurance was included in the cafeteria plan, the amount includible in the employee's gross income was the greater of the Table I cost or the amount of the employee's contributions for the coverage: a questionable conclusion. For plan years ending after 1991, the IRS notice states that dependent group term life insurance cannot be included in a cafeteria plan if the benefit would be eligible for exclusion as a *de minimis* fringe benefit under Code Section 132. [IRS Notice 89-110, 1989-2 CB 447]

In view of the position taken by the IRS in its proposed regulation and notice, there appears to be no tax advantage to including dependent group term life insurance in a cafeteria plan.

Accidental Death Benefits

Q 12:11 What is an accidental death benefit plan?

An employer-provided accidental death benefit plan provides coverage for death resulting from accidental means. It does not provide benefits for death resulting from illness or natural causes. If the accidental death benefit is combined with a dismemberment insurance feature, it is referred to as an accidental death and dismemberment (AD&D) plan. Dismemberment benefits generally cover permanent loss of a body member or function or loss of use of a body member or function (for example, loss of a limb or loss of eyesight) and usually are paid as a lump sum.

Q 12:12 How does an employer typically provide AD&D coverage?

In many cases, an employer that provides group term life insurance to employees will provide AD&D insurance under the same or an additional group policy.

Q 12:13 Is an AD&D plan subject to ERISA?

Generally yes, it is. The ERISA definition of a covered "employee welfare benefit plan" includes plans maintained for the purpose of providing benefits in the event of disability, accident, or death. If the AD&D insurance is an adjunct to a group term life insurance plan, the two coverages will ordinarily be treated as part of a single plan for ERISA purposes.

Q 12:14   Is an accidental death and dismemberment plan subject to the ADEA?

Yes, it is. The ADEA prohibits discrimination because of age in all compensation, terms, conditions, and privileges of employment, specifically including all employee benefits. [29 USC § 630(l), as amended by § 102 of the OWBPA] (For an explanation of the ADEA, see Chapter 16.)

Q 12:15   Can the employer deduct its premium payments for AD&D insurance?

Yes, the premiums attributable to both the accidental death benefit coverage and the dismemberment coverage can be deducted, provided that they are an ordinary and necessary business expense. [IRC § 162(a); Treas Reg § 1.162-10] However, if the AD&D benefits are provided through a welfare benefit fund such as a Code Section 501(c)(9) VEBA trust, the employer contributions must also satisfy the requirements of Code Sections 419 and 419A in order to be deductible by the employer. (See Questions 19:52 through 19:69 for further discussion of Code Sections 419 and 419A.)

Q 12:16   Is employer-provided AD&D coverage taxable income to employees?

No, it is not. An employee's gross income does not include employer-provided coverage under an accident or health plan. [IRC § 106]

The dismemberment portion of the coverage is clearly exempt from federal gross income under Code Section 106. For a time, IRS private rulings had been taking the position that employer premiums for the accidental death benefit insurance portion of the AD&D coverage did not qualify for this exemption and instead constituted taxable death benefit coverage. However, more recent private rulings have abandoned that interpretation and appear to concede that the employer premiums for accidental death coverage are exempt under Code Section 106: a position that is a sounder interpretation of the statute. [Priv Ltr Ruls 88-01-015, 87-46-024] It is also consistent with that taken by the IRS and the Treasury Department in the proposed regulations issued under former Code Section 89. [Former Prop Treas Reg § 1.89(a)-1, Q&A 1(f)(1)(ii)]

Accidental death benefit insurance coverage is not considered group term life insurance for Code Section 79 purposes and therefore does not give rise to imputed income under Code Section 79.

Q 12.17 How are the death benefit proceeds under an employer-provided accidental death benefit plan taxed?

Accidental death benefit proceeds are treated as life insurance proceeds for federal income and estate tax purposes. Therefore, the death benefit proceeds are (1) exempt from income tax and (2) includible in the employee's federal gross estate if they are payable to the employee's estate or if the employee had any incidents of ownership in the policy. [IRC §§ 101(a), 2042; Treas Reg § 1.101-1(a)(1); Commissioner v Estate of Noel, 380 US 678 (1965)] (See Questions 11:85 through 11:94 for a discussion of the federal estate and gift taxation of group term life insurance, which also applies generally to group accidental death insurance.)

Q 12:18 What is the income tax treatment of the dismemberment benefits that are received by an employee under employer-provided AD&D coverage?

Dismemberment benefits received by an employee under an employer-provided AD&D plan will be excluded from the gross income of the employee pursuant to Code Section 105(c) to the extent the payments are for the permanent loss or loss of use of a body member or function or for the permanent disfigurement of the employee, and the benefits are computed with reference to the nature of the injury without regard to the period the employee is absent from work. [IRC § 105(c)]

Business Travel Accident Insurance

Q 12:19 What is business travel accident insurance?

Employers frequently purchase group travel accident insurance policies that cover employees in the event of accidental death or injury while traveling on the employer's business. The amounts of coverage are generally related to compensation (for example, two times salary).

Q 12:20 Is a business travel accident insurance plan subject to ERISA?

Yes; because such a plan provides disability and death benefits in the event of an accident while traveling on company business, it is an ERISA plan. [ERISA § 3(1)] See Chapter 2 for a discussion of ERISA.

Q 12:21 Is a business travel accident plan subject to the ADEA?

Yes, it is. The ADEA covers all compensation, terms, conditions, and privileges of employment, including all employee benefit plans. [29 USC § 630(l), as amended by § 102 of the OWBPA] (For an explanation of the ADEA, see Chapter 13.)

Q 12:22 Can the employer deduct its premium payments for business travel accident insurance?

Yes, generally the premiums can be deducted, provided that the business travel accident insurance is an ordinary and necessary business expense. [IRC § 162(a); Treas Reg § 1.162-10]

Q 12:23 Is employer-provided business travel accident insurance coverage taxable to employees?

No, it is not. Gross income of an employee does not include employer-provided coverage under an accident or health plan. [IRC § 106]

Q 12:24 How are the proceeds of business travel accident insurance taxed?

The tax treatment of policy proceeds under a business travel accident plan depends on whether the triggering event was the employee's accidental injury or death.

Accidental Injury. If the proceeds are paid due to the employee having sustained a covered accidental injury, the proceeds relating to such accidental injury are excludable from federal gross income under Code Section 105(c).

Death of the Employee. The death benefit proceeds under an employer-provided business travel accident insurance plan are treated as life insurance proceeds for federal income and estate tax purposes, so the death benefit proceeds are (1) exempt from income tax, and (2) includible in the employee's federal gross estate if they are payable to the employee's estate or if the employee had any incidents of ownership in the policy. [IRC §§ 101(a) and 2042; Treas Reg § 1.101-1(a)(1)]

Group Universal Life Insurance

Q 12:25 What is group universal life (GUL) insurance?

GUL insurance is an outgrowth of individual universal life insurance. The typical universal life insurance policy is a species of permanent life insurance that provides a savings element in addition to pure insurance protection. The pure insurance portion is also referred to as the "term insurance" element, but should not be confused with group term life insurance.

Under the traditional forms of permanent life insurance (for example, whole life insurance), the factors the insurance company uses in determining a policy's benefits and cash values, such as amounts at risk, expenses, term insurance protection costs, and interest rates, are not disclosed. The distinguishing characteristic of a GUL policy is that, unlike other forms of permanent life insurance, it "unbundles" the components of a permanent life insurance policy and accounts for them separately. Unbundling the various elements enables employees to see how much of the policy is pure insurance protection and how much money (cash value) is accumulating in the savings element and at what interest rate. Accordingly, employees can evaluate the merits of the policy both for the level of insurance protection available and for the potential savings that can be achieved.

Interest rates under GUL policies typically reflect—and are adjusted from time to time based upon—current market rates. The amount of pure insurance protection under the policy at any time can be either a level amount over the life of the policy or can be an amount that declines over the life of the policy. In this latter type, the savings element (the cash value) will accumulate faster because the cost of the pure insurance protection portion also declines over the life of the policy.

Q 12:26   What is variable GUL insurance?

Under a type of insurance known as variable GUL, the employee can select from a number of investment options for the savings element of the policy, such as equity funds and money market funds, or let some or all of the savings element accumulate at specified interest rates.

Q 12:27   How is GUL insurance typically provided to employees?

To date, GUL insurance has been marketed almost entirely as an elective employee-pay-all benefit which may supplement the employer's basic group term life insurance coverage. Employee premiums for GUL generally are paid through payroll deduction, although employees may also be able to pay additional amounts directly in cash to the insurer.

Typically, available coverage is based on the employee's compensation, and the employee has a choice regarding the coverage amount, for example, one, two, or three times compensation.

Q 12:28   Is GUL insurance subject to Code Section 79 group term life insurance treatment?

No, generally it is not. GUL is considered a single, integrated permanent insurance policy and not a policy of group term life insurance. [IRC § 7702]

A policy having permanent elements can be subject to Code Section 79 if (1) the policy or the employer separately states in writing the part of the death benefit provided to each employee that is "group term life insurance" and (2) the designated group term portion of the benefit is at least a certain amount (calculated under a formula contained in the regulations). Because designating an insurance policy with permanent coverage as "group term life insurance" can produce adverse tax consequences for employees (see Qs 11:27, 11:28), it is unlikely that employers would deliberately structure the GUL arrangement or write its employee communications so as to bring it within Code Section 79.

Even if GUL coverage could be deemed to have met the above conditions (either through deliberate or inadvertent action), Code Section 79 does not apply to employee-pay-all coverage unless it is arranged for by the employer and the term rates paid by the employees "straddle" the Table I rates. This result can be avoided by offering the GUL coverage with rates that do not straddle Table I or by having the coverage sponsored by someone other than the employer, such as an independent insurer, a Code Section 501(c)(9) VEBA trust, an independent consultant, or an independent insurance broker, so that the employer has no part in arranging for the coverage other than providing payroll deductions (see Qs 11:34–11:36.) [Treas Reg §§ 1.79-0, 1.79-1(a), 1.79-1(b)]

Q 12:29   Is a GUL plan an employee benefit plan subject to ERISA?

Despite the fact that GUL is an employee-pay-all plan, it may be subject to ERISA, depending on the amount of employer involvement. DOL regulations exempt a group insurance program from treatment as an ERISA employee welfare benefit plan only if it satisfies the following four requirements:

1. No contributions are made by the employer;

2. Participation in the program is completely voluntary;

3. The employer's sole functions with respect to the program are, without endorsing the program, to (a) permit the insurer to publicize the program to employees and (b) collect premiums through payroll deduction and to remit them to the insurer; and

4. The employer receives no consideration in the form of cash or otherwise in connection with the program, other than reasonable compensation (excluding any profit) for administrative services actually rendered in connection with payroll deductions.

[DOL Reg § 2510.3-1(j)]

The first, second, and fourth requirements in the DOL regulation ordinarily can be easily satisfied. However, the third requirement presents a facts and circumstances issue, and in many cases it may be difficult to be sure of the result. A number of DOL opinion letters take the view that the employer's involvement in developing and implementing the group program must be quite limited in order not to constitute employer sponsorship. [DOL Ops. 83-3A (Jan 17, 1983), 82-9A (Feb 1, 1982), 81-56A (June 29, 1981)]

The DOL requirement precluding employer involvement is much stricter than a similar test, under Code Section 79, for determining whether a group permanent insurance policy covering employees of an employer can be treated as a separate policy from a group term insurance policy of the insurer (or affiliate) also covering employees of the employer. [Treas Reg § 1.79-0] The tax regulation does not contain an employer "sponsorship" concept and appears to permit substantial employer involvement in assisting sales of the coverage to employees (see Q 11:29).

Q 12:30   Is a GUL plan subject to the ADEA?

Generally, yes. The ADEA prohibits discrimination because of age in all compensation, terms, conditions, and privileges of employment, specifically including all employee benefits. [29 USC § 630(l), as amended by § 102 of the OWBPA] (For an explanation of the ADEA, see Chapter 16.)

Q 12:31   Are employer contributions to GUL coverage tax-deductible?

At this time, GUL coverage is generally an employee-pay-all proposition (see Q 12:25). However, employer premium payments are presumably tax-deductible on the same terms and subject to the same limitations as premium payments for other employee life insurance (see Q 11:54).

Q 12:32   How are GUL death benefit proceeds treated for federal income tax purposes?

Death benefit proceeds under GUL coverage receive the same favorable income tax treatment as other forms of life insurance proceeds, providing that the GUL policy meets the general tax definition of a life insurance policy contained in Code Section 7702. (The insurance carrier generally monitors compliance with the requirements of Code Section 7702.) Accordingly, the total death benefit under the GUL policy, including the savings element of the policy, is received by the beneficiary free of income tax. [IRC § 101(a)]

If the GUL death benefit proceeds are paid in the form of installment payments or as a life annuity rather than in a single lump sum, the proceeds are treated as received ratably over the payout period. The portion of each payment constituting the ratable portion of the death benefit proceeds is received tax-free, and the balance of each payment representing investment earnings on the death benefit proceeds is taxable. [IRC § 101(d)]

Q 12:33   How are GUL payments to an employee during his or her lifetime treated for federal income tax purposes?

A payment to an employee during his or her lifetime can occur due to a total surrender of the GUL policy, a partial withdrawal, or a policy loan. Each of these types of payments is taxed similarly to other forms of permanent life insurance.

Total Surrender. The recovery of an employee's tax basis under the GUL policy, usually equal to his or her contributions, is tax-free. The gain under the GUL policy—that is, the amount by which the cash value of the employee's coverage exceeds the employee's tax basis in the policy—is subject to income tax. In addition, if the GUL policy is a "modified endowment contract" and the surrender is made prior to age 59½, a penalty tax may apply to the gain. (See further discussion in Question 12:34.) [IRC § 72(e)]

If the employee elects no later than 60 days after surrender to receive the surrender proceeds either in installments or as a life annuity, the employee's tax basis is recovered pro rata over the projected payout period, and the balance of each payment is taxable. [IRC § 72(h)] If the employee outlives the projected payout period under a life annuity payout, and thus recovers his or her entire tax basis in the policy, the remaining payments are fully taxable. However, if the employee dies before his or her tax basis is recovered, a deduction for the unrecovered basis is allowed on the employee's final tax return or to the beneficiary (if there is a death benefit payable upon the death of the annuitant). [IRC § 72(b)]

Partial Withdrawal. Unless the employee's GUL coverage is a modified endowment contract (see Question 12:34), a partial withdrawal is tax-free to the extent that it does not exceed the employee's tax basis in the GUL policy. The portion (if any) of the withdrawal that exceeds the employee's tax basis in the GUL policy is taxable. [IRC § 72(e)(5)]

Policy Loan. Unless the employee's GUL coverage is a modified endowment contract (see Q 12:34), receipt of a policy loan has no income tax consequences to the employee. The amount of the loan is not taxable, and it does not affect the employee's tax basis in the policy. [IRC § 72(e)(4)] Interest that the employee pays on the GUL policy loan generally is treated as a nondeductible personal interest expense, unless the proceeds of the policy loan are invested so that the policy loan interest qualifies as "investment interest." [IRC §§ 163(d), 163(h)(1), 163(h)(2)]

Q 12:34   What is a modified endowment contract, and how does this characterization affect employee taxation on lifetime payouts under a GUL policy?

A modified endowment contract is a contract that meets the general tax law definition of a life insurance contract in Code Section 7702 but that fails a "seven-pay test" (see Q 12:35–12:38). Generally, the modified endowment contract rules do not apply to life insurance contracts entered into on or before June 20, 1988 (see Q 12:39). [IRC § 7702A] If GUL coverage of an employee constitutes a modified endowment contract, then lifetime distributions, withdrawals, and policy loans will receive less favorable tax treatment than under other types of policies.

Distributions (for example, withdrawals) under a policy that is a modified endowment contract are taxed on a taxable income-out-first (before nontaxable principal) basis rather than on the tax-free recovery rules applicable to other life insurance policies (see Q 12:33.) If the employee takes out a policy loan, such a loan will be treated as a policy distribution and taxed on an income-out-first basis. Similarly, if the employee obtains a loan from a party other than the insurance carrier using the modified endowment contract as security for such loan, the loan is treated as triggering a policy distribution taxable on an income-out-first basis. (In contrast, loans relating to other life insurance policies have no tax effect; see Question 12:33.) [IRC § 72(e)(10)]

Furthermore, a 10-percent penalty tax is imposed on the taxable amount of a distribution from a modified endowment policy to an employee who is under age 59½, unless one of the following exceptions applies:

- The employee is disabled, as defined in Code Section 72(m)(7); or

- The distribution is part of a series of substantially equal periodic payments made (not less frequently than annually) for the life or life expectancy of the employee or the joint lives or joint life expectancies of the employee and his or her beneficiary.

[IRC § 72(v)]

Q 12:35 What is the "seven-pay test" that the employee must satisfy to avoid the modified endowment contract treatment for his or her GUL coverage?

The seven-pay test of Code Section 7702A requires that the amount of premiums paid under the contract at any time during the first seven contract years cannot exceed the total of all the net level premiums that would have been paid on or before that time, if the contract provided for paid-up future benefits after the payment of seven net level annual premiums. The IRC provides computational rules for determining the amount of the seven net level premiums. [IRC § 7702A(c)]

If the employee's GUL coverage fails to satisfy the seven-pay test, then it is treated as a modified endowment contract and the unfavorable tax consequences discussed in Question 12:34 follow. [IRC § 7702A(b)]

Q 12:36 If GUL coverage satisfies the seven-pay test for the first seven years, is it assured of escaping modified endowment contract treatment thereafter?

No, it is not, because such assurance generally exists only if there is no material change in the coverage. If there is a material change under the contract (apparently including a coverage increase based on increased compensation), the coverage is treated as a new contract subject to a new seven-pay test, with certain adjustments to reflect the cash surrender value of the contract at the time.

Generally, a material change includes any increase in future benefits under the contract except:

- An increase attributable to the payment of premiums necessary to fund the lowest level of the death benefit and certain ancillary benefits payable in the first seven contract years;
- An increase attributable to the crediting of interest or other earnings (including policyholder dividends); or
- To the extent provided in Treasury regulations, any cost-of-living increase based on an established broad-based index (such as the consumer price index (CPI)) that is funded ratably over the remaining period during which premiums are required to be paid under the contract.

[IRC § 7702A(c)(3); Conf Rept on the Technical and Miscellaneous Revenue Act (TAMRA) of 1988, Pub L No 100-647, 100th Cong, 2d Sess, Vol II, 104-105 (1988)]

Planning Pointer. GUL coverage that is dependent on changes in compensation may always be subject to seven-pay testing (creating a succession of overlapping seven-pay tests). Thus the insurer and employee may have to continuously monitor and limit the amount of premium payments if they want to avoid modified endowment contract status.

Q 12:37 If an employee's GUL coverage fails the seven-pay test at any time, can the failure be cured?

Yes, it can be. To do so, the portion of the premiums paid during the contract year that caused the failure must be returned to the employee with interest no later than 60 days after the end of the contract year. The interest on the returned premiums is taxable. If the premiums are not returned with interest within the specified period, the coverage beginning on the date of failure is considered to be a modified endowment contract. [IRC §§ 7702A(e)(1)(B), 7702A(e)(1)(C)]

Q 12:38 If the failure of the seven-pay test is not cured, will prior distributions (including loans) also become subject to modified endowment contract treatment?

Yes, they will, to some extent. Distributions made at any time during the contract year of the failure are affected. In addition, the Code specifies that regulations are to be promulgated that will provide that prior distributions made in anticipation of the failure to meet the seven-pay test wil be affected. The Code also states that any prior distribution made within two years of the failure is to be treated as made in anticipation of the failure. [IRC § 7702A(d)]

Q 12:39 Does the date on which GUL coverage begins affect the application of the modified endowment contract rules?

Yes, it does. The rules generally apply to contracts entered into after June 20, 1988. The date on which an individual employee's coverage commences is presumably the operative date. [IRC § 7702A(a)(1)]

However, if the death benefit under an old GUL contract increases by more than $150,000 over the death benefit in effect on October 20, 1988, the coverage will become subject to the seven-pay test if a material change (see Q 12:36) occurs thereafter. [TAMRA § 5012(e)(2)]

> **Planning Pointer.** If the amount of GUL coverage under a pre-June 21, 1988 contract, is tied to compensation, the $150,000 death benefit increase limit could in time be exceeded, and the coverage thereafter be subject to the seven-pay test.

The safe haven is also unavailable if (1) the death benefit is increased after June 20, 1988, and (2) the employee did not have a unilateral right under the contract before June 21, 1988 to obtain the increase without producing evidence of insurability. Additionally, the safe haven for preexisting coverage is not available for any group term life insurance coverage issued before June 21, 1988 that is converted after June 20, 1988 to GUL coverage. [TAMRA § 5012(e)(3)]

Uninsured Death Benefits

Q 12:40   Are uninsured death benefits subject to ERISA?

Generally, yes. ERISA's definition of a covered "employee welfare benefit plan" includes plans providing benefits in the event of death, regardless of whether or not the plan is insured. [ERISA § 3(1)] (See Question 2:12 for a discussion of when a "plan" exists for ERISA purposes.)

Q 12:41   Is an uninsured death benefit plan subject to the ADEA?

Yes, it is. The ADEA covers all compensation, terms, conditions, and privileges of employment, including all employee benefits. [29 USC § 630(l), as amended by § 102 of OWBPA] (For an explanation of the ADEA, see Chapter 16.)

Q 12:42   May an employer deduct an uninsured death benefit it pays on behalf of an employee?

Yes, the amount will generally be deductible when paid, assuming the payment represents reasonable compensation for the employee's past services. [IRC § 162] However, if the benefit is self-funded using a VEBA, the additional requirements of Code Sections 419 and 419A also must be satisfied (see Qs 19:52–19:69).

Q 12:43   Are employer-provided uninsured death benefits taxable income to the recipient?

An employer-provided death benefit that is insured is entirely excluded from the recipient's taxable income under Code Section 101(a). However, if the employer-provided death benefit is uninsured, only the first $5,000 of the death benefit payment(s) is excludable from income. The $5,000 exclusion applies whether the payment is made to the estate of the employee or to a beneficiary, and whether the benefit is paid directly or to a trust. Uninsured death benefit amounts in excess of $5,000 are fully taxable, regardless of whether the employer's payment is voluntary or is made pursuant to a contractual obligation. [IRC §§ 101(b), 102(c)(1); Treas Reg § 1.101-2(a)(1)]

Exceptions. Even though they are not insured with a commercial life insurance carrier, certain state employee life insurance plans may be recognized as life insurance under state law; therefore, the death benefit payments qualify for the Code Section 101(a) life insurance exemption instead of being limited to the $5,000 exclusion for uninsured death benefit payments. [IRC § 7702; Ross v Odom, 401 F 2d 464 (5th Cir 1968)] In addition, a church self-funded death benefit plan is treated as life insurance even though the plan is not a life insurance contract under state law, provided it otherwise meets the requirements of life insurance contract status under Code Section 7702, so that the death benefit payments qualify for the Code Section 101(a) life insurance exemption also. [IRC § 7702(j)]

Q 12:44   What death benefits qualify for the $5,000 exclusion from federal gross income?

The Code Section 101(b) exclusion for uninsured death benefits applies to amounts payable by the employer because of an employee's death. It does not apply to amounts that would have been payable to the employee during his or her life as compensation for services, such as uncollected salary or bonuses.

In addition, this exclusion generally does not apply to amounts that the employee had a nonforfeitable right to receive while living (although it does apply to a lump-sum distribution under a tax-qualified pension, profit-sharing, or stock bonus plan, or under a tax-sheltered annuity purchased by a school or a publicly supported charity). If, for example, payments made under a deferred-compensation contract in respect of a deceased employee would have been paid to the employee if he or she had continued to live, the payments following death are fully taxable.

Furthermore, the exclusion does not apply to payments to a survivor under a joint and survivor annuity with a starting date before the employee's death, and it does not apply to interest payments on the uninsured death benefit amount held by the employer under an agreement to pay interest thereon. [IRC § 101(b); Treas Reg § 1.101-2(a)(2)]

Q 12:45 Is the special $5,000 income tax exclusion available on a per-employer, per-employee, or per-payee basis?

The $5,000 exclusion for uninsured death benefits provided by an employer applies on a per-employee basis. An individual's estate and beneficiaries are jointly entitled to one $5,000 death benefit exclusion with respect to that individual. [IRC § 101(b)(2)(A)]

If there is more than one payee for the uninsured death benefit, the $5,000 exclusion is apportioned among the payees according to the ratio of the amount received by the particular payee to the total death benefits. [Treas Reg § 1.101-2(a)(3)]

Q 12:46 Is a death benefit funded through a VEBA treated as an uninsured death benefit or as life insurance proceeds?

Apparently, an uninsured death benefit provided through a VEBA would qualify for exemption of the death benefit proceeds only up to $5,000. Complete exemption from income taxation as a life insurance death benefit hinges upon a contractual arrangement that meets the IRC definition of life insurance under Code Section 7702. That definition requires that the contract be a life insurance contract under state law. [IRC §§ 101(a), 7702(a)] As a general rule, state laws do not appear to recognize a death benefit provided by a VEBA as a life insurance contract.

Split-Dollar Life Insurance

Q 12:47   What is a split-dollar plan?

A split-dollar plan is a life insurance plan under which both the employer and the employee have interests in permanent life insurance policy coverage on the employee's life. At the employee's death, the employer receives a specified portion of the death proceeds, and the employee's estate or beneficiary receives the balance of the proceeds.

Under the prototype split-dollar plan developed many years ago, the employer paid only the portion of the annual policy premium that equaled the increase in the policy's cash value for that year, and the employee paid the remainder of the premium. At the employee's death, the employer received the cash surrender value of the policy (thus recouping most or all of its cost for the policy), and the employee's estate or beneficiary received the remainder of the death proceeds. Many variations of this prototype exist, generally involving the employer's payment of a larger portion, or even all, of the annual premium.

Ownership of the policy generally takes one of two forms. Under the endorsement method, the employer is the owner of record of the policy, and an endorsement is added to the policy to identify the employee's beneficial interest in the policy. Under the alternative arrangement, the collateral assignment method, the employee is the owner of record of the policy, but a collateral assignment of the policy is made to the employer to evidence the employer's beneficial interest in the life insurance. For federal tax purposes, the IRS takes the position that the tax results are the same whether the endorsement method or the collateral assignment method is used. [Rev Rul 64-328, 1964-2 CB 11]

Q 12:48 Is split-dollar life insurance subject to ERISA?

Generally, yes. ERISA's definition of a covered "employee welfare benefit plan" includes plans providing benefits in the event of death. [ERISA § 3(1)] (See Question 2:12 for a discussion of when a "plan" exists for ERISA purposes.)

Q 12:49 Can the employer deduct its premium payments under a split-dollar plan?

No, it cannot, because an employer cannot deduct premiums on a life insurance policy covering the life of an officer or employee if the employer is a beneficiary, directly or indirectly, under the policy. [IRC § 264(a)(1)]

Q 12:50 Does the employer's payment of part or all of the annual premium for split-dollar insurance coverage result in taxable income to the employee?

Yes, it does. The employee is taxed on the value of the death benefit coverage provided by the employer, based on the cost of one year of term insurance. The amount of death benefit protection payable to the employee's estate or beneficiary is valued according to the IRS's PS-58 table, which is based on the attained age of the employee. However, if the life insurance company's published one-year term rates for standard risks under newly issued policies are lower than the PS-58 rates, the insurer's rates may be used. After the value of the death benefit coverage for the employee is calculated, the employee-paid portion of the annual premium is subtracted to arrive at the amount taxable to the employee. [Rev Rul 64-328, 1964-2 CB 11; Rev Rul 66-110, 1966-1 CB 12]

Additionally, the total value of any benefits other than term insurance protection that the employee receives under the split-dollar plan, less any amounts contributed by the employee for them, is includible in the employee's gross income. Thus, cash policy dividends and any policy dividends applied to provide the employee with additional term insurance or paid-up insurance coverage on a nonforfeitable basis will be included in the employee's gross income (unless their value is offset by employee contributions). [Rev Rul 66-110, 1966-1 CB 12]

Planning Pointer. Because the PS-58 rates are based on obsolete mortality tables and low interest rates, the insurer's rates are generally substantially lower.

Q 12:51 What is the income tax treatment of death benefit proceeds under a split-dollar plan?

The death benefits paid under a split-dollar life insurance plan are proceeds of life insurance; so, the amounts received by both the employer and the employee's estate or beneficiary generally are fully exempt from income tax. [IRC § 101(a)] However, if the employer is subject to the corporate alternative minimum tax, a portion of the death proceeds may be subject to the corporate alternative minimum tax. Earnings on the cash value owned by the employer may also have to be taken into account for corporate alternative minimum tax purposes. [IRC § 56(g); Prop Treas Reg § 1.56(g)-l(c)(5)]

Q 12:52 What is the federal estate tax treatment of death proceeds under a split-dollar insurance plan?

The death benefit proceeds under a split-dollar insurance plan are treated as life insurance proceeds for federal estate tax purposes. Accordingly, the portion of the death benefit proceeds payable to the employee's estate are includible in the employee's federal gross estate. And, any portion of the proceeds payable to a named beneficiary are also includible in the employee's federal gross estate if the employee possessed any incidents of ownership in the policy at the time of death. Also, if the employee transferred ownership of his or her interest in the policy within three years of death, such interest will be included in his or her federal gross estate. [IRC §§ 2042, 2035]

Q 12:53 What is a split-dollar plan "rollout," and what are its tax consequences to the employee and employer?

A "rollout" is the termination of a split-dollar arrangement with regard to a particular employee through the placement by the employer of complete ownership and control of the life insurance policy in the hands of the employee. In return for giving up its interest in the policy, the employer may, depending on the contractual understanding of the parties, withdraw from the policy the cash surrender value amount or some lesser amount, such as an amount equal to its contributions, or even turn over the policy to the employee without receiving anything in return.

If the split-dollar plan is, for example, a prototype plan (see Question 12:47), under which the employer contributes an amount equal to the increase in cash value each year, and the employer gives the employee full ownership at some future time (for example, at the employee's retirement) in return for payment to the employer of an amount equal to the cash value at the time of rollout, then there should be no income tax consequences to the employee as a result of the rollout.

However, if the employer receives less on a rollout than the amount of the cash value attributable to its contributions, the employee might have imputed taxable income for federal income tax purposes. Unfortunately, there is no official guidance on this issue and there are only two IRS private rulings on the subject. One private ruling involved a plan under which the employer and employee each would pay a specified portion of the annual premium and each would own a specified portion of the cash value of the policy. At a later time, the employer then would assign the policy outright to the employee without receiving anything in return. The IRS ruled in this case that, at the time of the policy rollout, the employee would have income equal to the cash value of the policy minus the amount the employee contributed toward the cash value. [Priv Ltr Rul 79-16-029, relying on Rev Rul 64-328, 1964-2 CB 11;, IRC § 83 (compensatory transfers of property to employees)] The ruling appears correct in holding that the transfer of the employer's interest to the employee would be a taxable event. However, it appears that the increase in cash value attributable to the employee's own contributions should be taxable not at rollout, but only if and when the policy is surrendered. [IRC § 72(e)]

A second private ruling concerned a proposed split-dollar plan using the endorsement method (see Q 12:47), under which the employee would contribute the PS 58 cost (that is, the value of the term insurance protection), and the employer would pay the balance of the premiums. After seven years, the employer would borrow its contributions to the policy (thus recouping its premium payments) and would then transfer complete ownership to the employee. The IRS ruled that the employee would have income equal to the cash value of the policy (net of the loan) minus the amount of the employee's own contributions. [Priv Ltr Rul 83-10-027]

When a taxable rollout to the employee occurs, the employer should be able to deduct any amount treated as taxable compensation to the employee because, at that point in time, the employer is no longer a direct or indirect beneficiary of the policy. At the same time, however, the employer apparently would have to recognize any gain (attributable principally to investment earnings accumulated prior to rollout) on the cash value considered transferred to the employee. [IRC § 83(h); Priv Ltr Ruls 79-16-029, 83-10-027]

Q 12:54 What is a "reverse" split-dollar plan, and what are its tax consequences to the employee?

A reverse split-dollar plan is a relatively new type of split-dollar plan. As its name implies, it is the reverse of the prototype split-dollar plan (see Q 12:47). Under a reverse split-dollar plan, the employer pays a portion of the premium equal to the "value" of the term insurance protection element of the policy and is the beneficiary for that portion of the death proceeds. The employee pays the remainder of the premium, designates the beneficiary of the balance of the death proceeds, and owns the cash value of the policy.

The value of the term insurance protection is determined using the high PS-58 rates instead of the insurer's standard one-year term rates, which generally are substantially lower. Under some reverse split-dollar arrangements, the employer pays the PS-58 cost of the term protection for a number of years in advance, thereby reducing or eliminating the employee's contributions and resulting in a faster buildup in the policy cash values.

There are no IRS rulings or other legal authority on the tax treatment of reverse split-dollar plans. Proponents of reverse split-dollar plans contend that the employee should have no income tax consequences, because the employer is paying full value (PS-58 costs) in return for the term insurance protection it is receiving. However, it is doubtful that the IRS or the courts will agree with that analysis.

Because the actual term costs under the policy generally are substantially lower than the PS-58 term costs, the employer's payments result in cash value increases well in excess of those attributable to the employee's own premium payments. Thus, the IRS might hold that the employee has received taxable compensation equal to that excess (and the earnings on that excess) at the point or points in time that the employee's interest in the cash values derived from the employer's contributions becomes nonforfeitable or freely transferable. [IRC § 83]

Bonus Life Insurance

Q 12:55   What is a "bonus" life insurance plan?

A "bonus" life insurance plan is an arrangement under which an employer pays all or a portion of the premium cost for life insurance coverage for one or more employees either to the employer directly or on his or her behalf to the insurance carrier. The employer treats its payments as cash bonuses to the covered employees. Typically, the life insurance involved is a form of permanent life insurance, such as whole life insurance or universal life insurance and individual policies rather than a group policy ordinarily provide the life insurance coverage. The insurance policy is wholly owned by the employee.

Q 12:56   What is the income tax treatment of a bonus life insurance plan?

Under a bonus life insurance plan, the employer generally treats the bonus payments it makes as compensation payments that are fully tax deductible by the employer. The employer also treats the payments as wages to the covered employees, subject to income tax withholding and Federal Insurance Contributions Act (FICA) and Federal Unemployment Tax Act (FUTA) taxation. In some cases, the employer may "gross up" the payments to the covered employees to reimburse the employee for some or all of the income tax liabilities the employee has with respect to the bonus payments.

Planning Pointer. It is generally assumed that the bonus life insurance plan is not a group term life insurance plan for purposes of Code Section 79. However, in order to avoid possible application of, and adverse tax treatment under, Code Section 79 (see Q 11:32), it may be advisable for the employer to give the eligible employees the choice of taking the bonus payment in cash instead of receiving the life insurance coverage.

Q 12:57   Is a bonus life insurance plan subject to ERISA?

It appears to be an open issue. Since the employer treats its payments as current compensation and employee cash wages, it can be argued that no ERISA plan is created. The position that no ERISA plan exists appears to be strengthened considerably if the employees are given the choice of taking the employer payments in cash in lieu of applying them to the cost of the life insurance coverage.

Death Benefits under Qualified Retirement Plans

Q 12:58   Can a tax-qualified retirement plan provide death benefit coverage for plan participants?

Yes, it can. Under a tax-qualified retirement plan, the employer can provide the employees with death benefit protection, through insurance or otherwise, provided the death benefit coverage is "incidental" to the retirement benefits. [Treas Reg § 1.401-1(b)(1)]

Q 12:59   How does the incidental test apply in the case of life insurance coverage provided under a qualified pension plan?

The IRS has developed several tests for determining whether a preretirement death benefit under a pension plan is incidental. They are as follows:

1. A life insurance or uninsured death benefit will be considered incidental if the cost of the death benefit for a participant provided by employer contributions and earnings does not

exceed 25 percent of the total cost of all benefits for the participant. [Rev Rul 70-611, 1970-2 CB 89] This test applies to a term life insurance contract.

2. If the pension plan is funded in part through the purchase of ordinary insurance contracts (for example, whole life insurance), up to, but not including, 50 percent of the employer contributions for a particular participant may be applied to an ordinary insurance contract on the participant's life. [Rev Rul 74-307, 1974-2 CB 126] This test is deemed to be consistent with the first test (the 25-percent test) because the ordinary insurance contract provides death benefits and retirement benefits.

3. A life insurance death benefit in a qualified pension plan will be considered incidental if the death benefit before retirement does not exceed the greater of 100 times the monthly retirement benefit, or the cash value of the policy. [Rev Rul 68-31, 1968-1 CB 151]

Q 12:60   How does the incidental test apply in the case of life insurance coverage provided under a qualified profit-sharing plan?

In the case of life insurance courage provided under a qualified profit-sharing plan, the incidental test applies as follows:

1. Not more than 25 percent of the employer's current contributions and forfeitures allocated to the employee's account may be applied to life and/or accident or health insurance coverage.

2. If ordinary life insurance (for example, whole life insurance) is purchased, the percentage is increased up to, but not including, 50 percent. If accident or health insurance is also purchased, the premium for the accident or health insurance plus one-half the premium for the ordinary life insurance cannot exceed 25 percent of the employer's contributions plus forfeitures.

3. If the profit-sharing plan permits funds accumulated for a specified period to be distributed, funds accumulated for the required period may be applied to life insurance or health insurance coverage without regard to the incidental test.

Generally, funds must be accumulated under a profit-sharing plan for at least two years before distribution. [Rev Rul 61-164, 1961-2 CB 58]

Q 12:61 How does the incidental test apply to life insurance purchased with voluntary employee contributions?

The incidental test has no application to life insurance purchased with voluntary employee contributions (that is, after-tax employee contributions). Thus, the full amount of such contributions may be applied to the purchase of life insurance if the plan so permits. [Rev Rul 69-408, 1969-2 CB 58]

Q 12:62 What rules apply in determining whether the life insurance is purchased with employer contributions or not?

If the qualified retirement plan specifies that the life insurance premiums will be paid with employee contributions, the plan provision will apply. However, if the plan is silent, the life insurance premiums will be considered to be paid first from employer contributions and plan earnings. Whether the life insurance coverage is purchased in whole or in part with employer contributions is important in determining the income tax treatment of the life insurance coverage (see Q 12:63) [Rev Rul 68-390, 1968-2 CB 175]

Q 12:63 Is an employee taxed on life insurance coverage provided under a qualified retirement plan?

Yes, unless the coverage is provided with the employee's own after-tax contributions. If the life insurance coverage is provided through employer contributions and/or plan earnings, the value of the life insurance coverage (that is, the value of the term protection) is taxable income to the employee each year. [IRC § 72(m)(3); Treas Reg § 1.72-16(b)(2)]

Q 12:64   How should an employer determine the value of the life insurance protection taxable to an employee under a qualified retirement plan?

The value of the life insurance protection is determined in the same way as for life insurance protection under a split-dollar plan (see Q 12:50).

The employer generally is required to use the PS-58 table promulgated by the IRS to value the life insurance protection. However, if the life insurance company providing the coverage has published one-year term rates for standard risks under newly issued policies that are lower than the PS-58 rates, the insurer's one-year term rates may be used instead. [Rev Rul. 64-328, 1964-2 CB 11, 66-110, 1966-1 CB 12]

Q 12:65   How are life insurance death benefits paid to an employee's estate or beneficiary under a qualified retirement plan treated for federal income tax purposes?

If the life insurance policy provided only term life insurance coverage, the entire death benefit is exempt as life insurance proceeds under Code Section 101(a). However, if the life insurance policy had a cash reserve value (for example, coverage was provided under a whole life insurance policy), only the pure death benefit protection portion of the policy (that is, the difference between the total death benefit and the cash value) is exempt as life insurance proceeds under Code Section 101(a).

The cash value portion is treated as a pension benefit and is taxable in accordance with the rules of Code Section 72. In addition to actual contributions made by the employee, the employee's tax basis, which is recovered tax-free by the estate or beneficiary, also includes the value of the term coverage that was taxed to the employee while living. In general, if the death benefit constitutes a lump sum distribution, the cash value portion of the death benefit will be eligible for the $5,000 employer death benefit exclusion under Code Section 101(b). [Treas Reg §§ 1.72-16(c), 1.72-8(a), 1.402(a)-1(a)(5), (6)]

Q 12:66 Can tax-qualified retirement plans provide preretirement death benefits to employees other than through the purchase of life insurance?

Yes, as long as the incidental death benefit test is satisfied.

Generally, qualified pension plans, but not qualified profit-sharing plans, are required to offer to participating employees a qualified preretirement survivor annuity death benefit payable to the surviving spouse of a deceased employee. The amount of the qualified preretirement survivor annuity is based on the amount of the employee's vested pension benefit and must fall within a specified minimum and maximum amount. [IRC §§ 401(a)(11), 417]

The employer does not have to absorb the cost of the preretirement survivor annuity and may charge the cost of the benefit through a reduction in the amount of vested pension benefits. However, under many plans the employer subsidizes the cost of the qualified preretirement survivor annuity in whole or in part. [Treas Reg § 1.401(a)-20, Q&A-21]

Unless the qualified preretirement survivor annuity is fully subsidized by the employer, the employee must be given the opportunity to waive the benefit with the consent of his or her spouse. [Treas Reg § 1.401(a)-20, Q&As 37, 38]

Q 12:67 Can tax-qualified retirement plans provide postretirement death benefits?

Yes, they can. Generally, qualified retirement plans are required to pay retirement benefits to a married employee in the form of a qualified joint and survivor annuity for the employee and the employee's spouse, unless the employee, with the consent of his or her spouse, elects to take the retirement benefits in another form of payment provided under the plan. No election need be provided if the benefit is fully subsidized by the employer. [IRC §§ 401(a)(11), 417; Treas Reg § 1.401(a)-20, Q&As 37, 38]

A qualified retirement plan may also include death benefit features in other forms of retirement benefit features and options it offers. For example, it may offer a life annuity with 10 years' payments guaranteed, or a joint and survivor annuity for the employee and someone other than a spouse. However, any distributions must satisfy the minimum distribution requirements of Code Section 401(a)(9) and very detailed regulations thereunder, including the requirement that any death benefits must be incidental to the retirement benefits. [IRC § 401(a)(9)(G); Prop Treas Reg § 1.401(a)(9)-2]

Accelerated Death Benefits

Q 12:68 What is an "accelerated" death benefit?

An "accelerated" death benefit is an elective benefit under a life insurance policy whereby the insured can, on request, obtain a portion of the face amount of the policy prior to death if one or more specific health conditions exist. This is a relatively new type of life insurance policy benefit which is being made available by many life insurance companies. It is provided in recognition of the fact that there are people who have enormous pre-death medical and health-related expenses, and that a prepayment of life insurance death benefits can provide a source of financing to meet those extraordinary needs.

Q 12:69 What kinds of medical or health-related conditions may qualify an insured to elect accelerated death benefits under a life insurance policy?

There is a substantial variety among the accelerated death benefit products being offered currently by life insurance companies. Typically, the insured can request and obtain an accelerated death benefit upon the occurrence of one of the following events (some policies cover more than one event):

- A terminal illness (that is, a medical condition from which the insured is expected to die within a fairly short specified time period, such as 6 months or 12 months);
- A dread disease or catastrophic illness (for example, AIDS, heart attack, stroke, cancer, renal failure); or
- Extended or permanent confinement in a nursing home or similar facility.

Generally, the life insurance companies offering such a product limit the amount that can be taken out to a percentage of the face amount (such as 50 percent).

Q 12:70   Is an accelerated death benefit payable in a lump sum?

Not necessarily. It may be payable in a lump sum or in install-ments. A terminal illness or dread disease benefit is more likely to be paid in a lump sum, while a benefit for a nursing home confinement is more likely to be paid in installments (for example, 2 percent of the face amount a month for 25 months).

Q 12:71   How is the face amount of the policy reduced?

This can vary also by the type of accelerated death benefit payment and the carrier involved. One method is to reduce the face amount directly by the amount paid. Other methods include treating the payment as a loan secured by a lien on the policy for the amount advanced. If it is handled as a loan, interest may be charged on the loan from the date of payment of the accelerated death benefit to the date of death.

Q 12:72   If the policy has a cash value (for example, group universal life insurance), how does a payment of an accelerated death benefit affect the cash value?

This depends on how the product is structured by the insurance company involved. The most commonly used method appears to be to reduce the face amount and the cash value by the same percentage. For example, if an employee with a group universal life policy face amount of $100,000 and a cash value of $30,000 received a lump sum accelerated death benefit of $50,000, under this method the employee would be left with a policy having a face amount of $50,000 and a cash value of $15,000. However, some insurance companies follow other methods, which may reduce the cash value to a greater or lesser degree, or not at all.

Q 12:73   What is the federal income tax treatment of an accelerated death benefit received by an employee under a group life insurance policy?

There is no specific authority at this time on the federal income tax treatment of accelerated death benefit payments received by an insured employee under a group life insurance policy.

However, proposed regulations issued under Code Section 7702 (the tax definition of life insurance) suggest what the answer will be. The proposed regulations provide that, for purposes of Code Section 7702, the amount payable as a *qualified* accelerated death benefit is treated as a death benefit. [Prop Treas Reg § 1.7702(e)]

A qualified accelerated death benefit is one that meets the following three requirements;

1. The accelerated benefit is payable only if the insured becomes terminally ill;

2. The amount of the accelerated benefit is equal to or more than the present value of the reduction in the death benefit otherwise payable upon the death of the insured; and

3. The ratio of the cash surrender value of the contract immediately after the payment of the accelerated benefit *to* the cash surrender value immediately before the payment, is equal to or greater than the ratio of the death benefit immediately after the payment of the accelerated benefit *to* the death benefit immediately before the payment.

[Prop Treas Reg § 1.7702(e)]

In determining the present value of the reduction in the death benefit (see the second requirement above), the insurer must use as the discount interest rate the greater of (a) the applicable federal interest rate as determined under Code Section 846(c)(2), or (b) the interest rate for policy loans under the contract, and must assume that the insured dies 12 months after the date of payment of the accelerated benefit. [Prop Treas Reg § 1.7702(d)(2)]

A group life insurance policy (whether term or universal life) should be able to be amended easily to provide an accelerated death benefit for terminal illness that satisfies the definition of a qualified accelerated death benefit in the proposed regulations.

While the proposed regulations do not address the income tax treatment of the qualified accelerated death benefit payment in the hands of the insured, the fact that it is treated as a death benefit for purposes of Code Section 7702 suggests that it will also be treated as a death benefit for purposes of the exemption death benefit proceeds of life insurance under Code Section 101(a). A terminal illness payment that does not meet the definition of a qualified accelerated death benefit presumably would not receive death benefit treatment under Code Section 101(a).

Q 12:74   What is the federal income tax treatment of an accelerated death benefit received by an insured employee under a group life insurance policy for medical reasons other than terminal illness?

Here also, there is no specific authority at this time, but the proposed regulations under Code Section 7702 suggest what the tax treatment may be. The proposed regulations provide that an additional benefit will not be treated as part of the cash value of the life insurance contract for purposes of Code Section 7702, if it meets the following three requirements:

1. The benefit is payable solely upon the occurrence of a morbidity (that is, health) risk;

2. The charges for the benefit are separately stated and currently imposed by the terms of the contract, and

3. The charges for the benefit are not included in premiums taking into account in determining the investment in the contract for purposes of calculating gain under Code Section 72, and are not included in premiums paid under Code Section 7702.

[Prop Treas Reg § 7702-2(f)(1)] An example is given of a policy with a death benefit of $10,000, a cash value of $40,000, and a morbidity benefit satisfying the above three requirements which pays $70,000 in complete satisfaction of the contract upon the occurrence of a specified morbidity risk. Of the $70,000 payment, $40,000 constitutes a cash value payment, and $30,000 is the morbidity payment. [IRS Prop Reg § 1.7702-2(f)(2), Ex 1]

Although the proposed regulations do not address the income tax treatment of the morbidity payment received by the insured, it suggests that the benefit ($30,000 in the example) will be treated as an accident and health insurance benefit exempt under Code Section 105(c) (to the extent attributable to employer contributions) and under Code Section 104(a)(3) (to the extent attributable to employee contributions).

If a morbidity benefit does not satisfy the three requirements in the proposed regulations, it may adversely affect the status of the contract as a life insurance contract under Code Section 7702, as well as result in income tax liability for some or all of the payment on the part of the insured employee.

Planning Pointer. If the employer wishes to add a terminal illness benefit, a morbidity benefit, or both to a group life insurance policy for its employees, it seems prudent to have the policy conform to the requirements in the proposed regulations, in order to obtain likely favorable tax treatment of the benefits.

[Prop Treas Reg. § 1.7702-2, as amended by IRS Notice 93-27 (July 2, 1993)]

Note. The above changes to Code Section 7702 will become effective no earlier than publication of final regulations on the subject.

Q 12:75 Are employers likely to favor an accelerated death benefit option as a part of their group life insurance programs for employees?

Offering an accelerated death benefit option of the terminal-illness-type under a group term life insurance plan or under a GUL plan can be done without major employer cost. Also, providing such an option may relieve employee pressures on the employer to increase catastrophic coverage limits under the employer's medical plan.

By providing an accelerated death benefit option tied to permanent nursing home status, the employer may be able to avoid the need to increase medical plan coverage or to institute a program of long-term care coverage.

Living Benefits

Q 12:76   What is a "living benefit"?

A "living benefit" is similar to an accelerated death benefit, except it is paid by a third party rather than by the insurance company that issued the life insurance policy. A living benefit allows the insured to receive the proceeds payable upon death while still living, at an actuarially discounted value based upon the expected remaining lifetime of the individual. Living benefits are also known as "viatical settlements."

Q 12:77   How is a living benefit different from an accelerated death benefit?

The terms "accelerated death benefit" and "living benefits" are often used interchangeably. However, an accelerated death benefit is paid by the insurance company that issued the policy (the second party), and ownership of the policy is not transferred. In contrast, a living benefit is the receipt of proceeds of a life insurance policy through sale of the policy to a third-party company—the living benefits company—or to an investor, with the living benefits company acting as broker.

Q 12:78   How is the living benefit paid?

A living benefit company will pay cash, typically 50 percent to 80 percent of the face amount of an individual life insurance policies of a terminally ill individual, and sometimes, of an individual who has attained a specified age, such as 83 or older. The living benefit company in return typically takes an irrevocable absolute assignment of the policy.

Q 12:79   Why would an insured individual want a living benefit?

A living benefit is attractive to an individual with a catastrophic illness, including AIDS, or with limited financial resources. If the individual has a catastrophic illness, the cost of medical treatment can be an incredible burden during what is already a difficult time, and a terminally ill patient requiring expensive and extensive care can become destitute, particularly an individual who has little or no long-term disability insurance. A living benefit allows the individual to access the cash value of the life insurance policy while still living, usually to help pay medical bills.

Q 12:80　Why is a need for living benefits and similar products developing?

Employer-covered group health plans continue to become more "cost-effective" (a term that covers everything from cutting back on expensive care to restricting access to certain types of treatments through gatekeepers and case management), and lower lifetime health benefit limits sometimes are included in the employer's health benefit plan. This can result in less medical coverage being available to terminally ill patients. (See for example, Owens v Storehouse, 16 EBC 1737 (11th Cir 1993), and McGann v H & H Music Co, 546 F 2d 401 (5th Cir 1991), in which an employer's decision to drastically lower the lifetime benefit limit for AIDS but not for other illnesses and conditions was upheld.) Additionally, employer-provided medical plans rarely cover experimental care, which might have the effect of excluding certain courses of treatments for diseases such as AIDS.

Q 12:81　Are living benefits a "ghoulish" practice?

It initially may appear unsavory for a third party to purchase a life insurance policy at a discount and then receive the full proceeds when the individual dies, while the original beneficiaries (usually close family members) receive no life insurance proceeds. However, living benefits, if fairly valued, can be viewed as a positive new product that fills a critical need within the insurance industry. The patient obtains access to much-needed funds to pay for hospital and doctor bills and for basic living expenses. Additionally, to the extent that treatments given to terminally ill patients are experimental, living benefits provide funds for experimental research and allow such patients to cross-subsidize one another. To avoid the appearance of doing beneficiaries out of the insurance proceeds, living benefit companies often require an irrevocable assignment from all of the designated beneficiaries as well and will not purchase the policy unless all of them so agree. At least one state also requires that the insured individual be certified as mentally competent prior to making the assignment.

Recently, several states reportedly have questioned whether "brokered" living benefits (that is, those in which the living benefits company acts as an intermediary that arranges for the sale of the policies to independent investors) may violate state securities laws. Living benefits companies that purchase policies with their own capital do not appear to run afoul of these laws. [Kerr, Now, AIDS Patients' Lives Are Drawing Speculators, NY Times, Aug 29, 1992, p 1, col 1]

Q 12:82 How does a living benefit differ from traditional life insurance?

The life insurance industry offers various types of life insurance policies that are priced according to life expectancy and mortality rates. If the insured individual dies earlier than anticipated, the insurance company pays more than it planned (because there was less time for investment earnings to grow). If the insured individual dies later than anticipated, the insurance company makes money. Accordingly, traditional life insurance is a financial wager that a group of individuals will live long enough, and pay enough premiums before they die, so that the insurance company will profit. One well-known insurance company executive has distilled this concept underlying traditional life insurance into a single sentence: "You die, we pay; you live, you pay."

Living benefits, on the other hand, involve risk up front. The living benefits company pays out the percentage of face value to the ill individual and does not collect any premiums. It thus can never make any more money than the difference between the face value of the policy and the percentage of face value that it has already paid out to the insured. The living benefits company then bears the risk that its profit margin will be eroded (via loss of the time value of money) by various developments, among them:

- The individual recovers; or
- The individual lives longer than expected; or

- A life-extending treatment may be developed; or
- A medical breakthrough may occur; or
- The future financial viability of the insurance company could be endangered by events not foreseeable at the time of the living benefit payment.

In addition, if a waiver of premiums due to disability is not available, the living benefits company must pay the premiums to keep the policy in force, which will further reduce its ultimate profit. Accordingly, living benefits payable by a living benefits company could be characterized as: "You die or live, we pay either way."

Q 12:83 When the living benefit company takes an irrevocable assignment of an individual's life insurance policy, does the company have an insurable interest in the individual's life?

Generally, yes. Insurable interest generally is measured at the time the insurance is originally purchased from the insurance company. In other words, the person who purchases the policy from the insurance company must, at that time, have an insurable interest in the life of the insured (and an individual always has an insurable interest in his or her own life). Exceptions to this general rule do exist in a few states, however.

Q 12:84 Is a living benefits option available only from independent, non-insurance companies?

Yes, the living benefit company provides the service directly to the individual insureds. Occasionally, it will do so at the request of an insurance carrier that has been asked to provide an accelerated death benefit but that has no formal mechanism in place for doing so.

Q 12:85 Are living benefit payments taxable to the insured?

If an insured accepts a cash payment of a percentage of the face value of a life insurance policy on his or her life and irrevocably assigns the policy, the payment is taxable to the insured to the extent that it exceeds the insured's tax basis in the policy.

The living benefit payment thus can change what would have been nontaxable life insurance death proceeds into taxable income. However, it permits the insured access, during his or her lifetime, to funds that would otherwise be payable only upon his or her death, in order to pay medical bills and other expenses.

Chapter 13

Fringe Benefits

Many exclusions or partial exclusions from gross income are provided for as fringe benefits under Code Section 132, a catchall section covering all manner of employer-provided benefits: no-additional-cost services, qualified employee discounts, working condition fringe benefits, *de minimis* fringe benefits and qualified transportation benefits. These "perks" include airplanes, computers, cars, taxi fares and occasional meals, on-premises athletic facilities, employer-provided eating facilities, occasional typing of personal letters by a secretary, occasional personal use of a copying machine, occasional theater and sports tickets, coffee and doughnuts, soft drinks, transit passes, parking, use of company telephones for personal phone calls, shopping discounts, and so forth. This chapter gives an overview of the five major types of fringe benefit expenses governed by Code Section 132 and then provides a more detailed explanation of several specific types of fringe benefits.

Introduction

Q 13:1   What are fringe benefits under Code Section 132?

Many federal laws regulating employee benefits refer to employer-provided pension and welfare benefit plans generically as fringe benefits. For tax purposes, Code Section 132 provides a catchall for several categories of benefits that are not excludable from gross income under other IRC sections. Fringe benefits that are covered under Code Section 132 are excluded from the gross income of the employee. [IRC § 132(a)]

Q 13:2   What fringe benefits are governed by Code Section 132?

Code Section 132 governs any fringe benefit that qualifies as any of the following:

- No-additional-cost service (see Qs 13:3-13:14)
- Qualified employee discount (see Qs 13:15-13:26)
- Working condition fringe benefit (see Qs 13:27-13:31)
- *De minimis* fringe benefit (see Qs 13:66-13:69) or
- Qualified transportation fringe benefit (see Qs 13:91-13:99)

[IRC § 132(a)]

Special rules also apply to on-premises gyms and other athletic facilities (see Qs 13:85-13:90) and on-premises eating facilities (see Qs 13:70-13:75). [Treas Reg § 1.132-1(a)]

No-Additional-Cost Services

Q 13:3   What is a no-additional-cost service?

A no-additional-cost service is any service provided by an employer to an employee for the employee's personal use if:

1. The service is offered for sale to non-employee customers by the employer in the ordinary course of its line of business;
2. The employee performs substantial services in that same line of business; and
3. No substantial additional cost is incurred by the employer in providing the service to the employee.

The value of a no-additional-cost service is excluded from an employee's gross income under Code Section 132. [IRC §§ 132(a), 132(b); Treas Reg §§ 1.132-1(a)(1), 1.132-2(a)(1)]

Q 13:4   What types of services may qualify as no-additional-cost services under Code Section 132?

No-additional-cost services are excess capacity services, such as hotel accommodations provided by an employer that is a hotelier; transportation by aircraft, train, bus, subway, or cruise line if the employer is in one of those lines of business; and telephone services provided by a telephone company. [Treas Reg § 1.132-2(a)(2)]

Q 13:5   What types of services do not qualify as no-additional-cost services?

The Code Section 132 exclusion for no-additional-cost services does not include non-excess capacity services, such as the facilitation by a stock brokerage firm of stock purchases. (Non-excess capacity services may, however, be eligible for a qualified employee discount of up to 20 percent of the value of the service provided, see Question 13:23.) [Treas Reg § 1.132-2(a)(2)]

Q 13:6   Do services provided only to employees qualify as no-additional-cost services?

No, they do not. A key requirement for services to qualify as no-additional-cost services is that the employer must provide them to the general public as well. Services primarily provided to employees and not to the employer's customers do not qualify. [IRC § 132(b)(1); Treas Reg §§ 1.132-2(a)(1)(i), 1.132-4(a)(ii)]

Q 13:7   Must a no-additional-cost service be provided to employees for free?

No, the service does not have to be provided entirely free to qualify as a no-additional-cost service under Code Section 132. All that is required is that the employer cannot incur substantial additional cost in providing the service to the employee—for example, forgoing revenue because the service is provided to an employee rather than to a non-employee customer. Any amounts paid by the employee for the service are disregarded.

The Code Section 132 exclusion for a no-additional-cost service applies regardless of whether the service is provided at no charge or at a reduced price. The benefit may also be provided through a partial or total rebate of the price the employee pays for the service. [IRC § 132(b); Treas Reg §§ 1.132-2(a)(1)(ii), 1.132-2(a)(3)]

Q 13:8   For purposes of the no-additional-cost rule, how is the employer's cost of providing the service to employees determined?

For the Code Section 132 exclusion for no-additional-cost services to apply, the employer cannot incur substantial additional cost (including revenue that is forgone because the service is provided to an employee rather than to a non-employee customer) in providing the service to the employee.

When calculating the cost incurred by the employer, any amount paid for the service by the employee is disregarded, and the employer must include the cost of labor incurred in providing services to employees. Labor costs must be included even if the employer does not incur non-labor costs in providing the service to the employee.

This is true even if the individuals providing the services otherwise would have been idle and regardless of whether the services were provided outside normal business hours. If, however, the services being provided to the employee were "merely incidental" to the primary service being provided by the employer, then the employer generally will not be treated as having incurred substantial additional cost.

Internal Revenue Service (IRS) regulations contain two examples of items that would be considered merely incidental:

1. The in-flight services of a flight attendant and cost of in-flight meals provided to airline employees flying on a space-available basis would be incidental to the primary service that is being provided (that is, air transportation); and

2. Maid service provided to hotel employees renting hotel rooms on a space-available basis would be incidental to the primary service being provided (that is, hotel accommodations).

[Treas Reg § 1.132-2(a)(5)]

Note that if airline employees are permitted to take personal flights and receive reserved seats rather than flying on a space-available basis, the employer forgoes potential revenue and the employees receiving such free flights are not eligible for the no-additional-cost exclusion. [Treas Reg § 1.132-2(c)]

Q 13:9 Can an employee's family members also receive no-additional-cost services?

Yes, they can. Under the Code Section 132 exclusion from an employee's gross income for a no-additional-cost service, the term "employee" is defined broadly to include several categories of individuals, as follows:

1. Current employees in the employer's line of business;

2. Former employees who have separated from service in such line of business or who have retired from such line of business by reason of disability;

3. A widow or widower of an employee who either died while employed in the employer's line of business or separated from service in the employer's line of business due to retirement or disability; and

4. The spouse and dependent children of any of the above (a dependent child includes a son, stepson, daughter, or step-daughter who is also a dependent of the employee or whose parents are both deceased and who has not attained age 25).

5. In addition, use of air transportation by the parents of the employee will be treated as use by the employee.

[Treas Reg § 1.132-1(b); IRC § 132(g)]

All employees who are treated as employed by a single employer under the controlled group rules of Code Sections 414(b), 414(c), 414(m), or 414(o) are treated as employed by a single employer. Also, any partner who performs services for a partnership is treated as employed by the partnership. [Treas Reg §§ 1.132-1(b)(1), 1.132-1(c)]

Q 13:10   What is the line of business limitation?

A no-additional-cost service or qualified employee discount treatment is only available if the service or property is offered for sale to non-employee customers in a line of business in which the employee/recipient also performs substantial services. [Treas Reg § 1.132-4(a)(1)]

The employee can only exclude from gross income those no-additional-cost services or qualified employee discounts in the line(s) of business in which he or she performs substantial services. [Treas Reg § 1.132-4(a)(1)] If an employee performs services directly benefitting more than one line of business, he or she is treated as performing substantial services for all such lines of business (and, so, could qualify to receive no-additional-cost services or qualified employee discounts from all of them).

Q 13:11   How are lines of business determined?

The Code Section 410(b) line of business rules do not apply under Code Section 132. Instead, an employer's line of business is determined by reference to the *Enterprise Standard Industrial Classification Manual* (ESIC Manual) prepared by the Statistical Policy Division of the U.S. Office of Management and Budget. An employer will be treated as having more than one line of business if it offers paying customers property or services in more than one ESIC Manual two-digit code classification. [Treas Reg § 1.132-4(a)(2)]

Mandatory aggregation of lines of business: Two or more lines of business must be treated as a single line of business under the following circumstances:

1. If it is uncommon in the employer's industry for any of the separate lines of business to be operated without the others;

2. If it is common for a substantial number of employees (excluding those who work at the employer's headquarters or main office) to perform substantial services for more than one of the employer's lines of business, so that determining which employees perform substantial services for particular lines of business would be difficult; or

3. If the employer's retail operations located on the same premises are in separate lines of business but would be considered to be in one line of business if the merchandise were offered for sale at a department store.

Special rules apply for affiliates of commercial airlines and for certain air transportation organizations. Special grandfather rules are provided for certain retail department stores, for affiliated groups operating airlines, and for telephone service provided to predivestiture retirees. [Treas Reg §§ 1.132-4(a)(3), 1.132-4(b)–(g)]

Q 13:12 Can an employee receive a no-additional-cost service from an unrelated employer?

Yes, an employee of one employer can receive tax-free no-additional-cost services from a second, unrelated employer. In order to do so, all of the following three requirements must be satisfied:

1. The two unrelated employers must have a written reciprocal agreement permitting each employer's employees performing

substantial services in the same line of business to receive no-additional-cost services from the other employer;

2. The service received by the employee from the unrelated employer is the same type of service generally provided to non-employee customers in the line of business in which the employee works and in the line of business from which the employee receives the service (so that it would be a no-additional-cost service to the employee if provided directly by the employee's own employer); and

3. Neither employer incurs substantial additional cost either in providing such service to the other employer's employees or under the agreement.

However, if one of the employers receives a substantial payment from the other regarding the reciprocal agreement, the paying employer will be considered to have incurred substantial additional cost. Services performed under the reciprocal agreement would then be disqualified from treatment as no-additional-cost services. [Treas Reg § 1.132-2(b)]

Q 13:13 What nondiscrimination requirements apply to no-additional-cost services under Code Section 132?

In order for the value of a no-additional-cost service to be excluded from a highly compensated employee's gross income, the benefit must be available on substantially the same terms to all employees of the employer, or to a group of employees under a reasonable classification set up by the employer that does not discriminate in favor of highly compensated employees. [Treas Reg § 1.132-8(a)(1)] For this purpose, the definition of "highly compensated employee" contained in Code Sections 414(q), (s), and (t) is used. [IRC § 132(i)(6); Treas Reg § 1.132-8(f)]

The nondiscrimination test is applied by aggregating the employees of all related employers except that employees in different lines of business generally are not aggregated. [Treas Reg § 1.132-8(b)(1)]

Q 13:14   What happens if a no-additional-cost benefit is discriminatory?

If any portion of the no-additional-cost benefit is discriminatory, the highly compensated employees cannot exclude from gross income either (1) any portion of the value of the benefit or (2) the value of any related fringe benefit program. [Treas Reg § 1.132-8(a)(2)]

Employee Discounts

Q 13:15   What is an employee discount?

An employee discount is the price at which an employer offers property or services for sale to customers minus the price at which the property or service is offered to the employee. [Treas Reg § 1.132-3(b)(1)]

Q 13:16   What is a "qualified employee discount"?

A qualified employee discount is a discount that meets certain guidelines. If those guidelines are met, then Code Section 132 provides that the value of a qualified employee discount is excluded from the employee's gross income. [Treas Reg § 1.132-3(a)(1)]

Q 13:17   How large can a qualified employee discount be under Code Section 132?

The portion of an employee discount that qualifies for the Code Section 132 exclusion from gross income is as follows:

1. *Property.* For property sold to an employee at a discount, the maximum excludable portion of the discount is the price at which the property is being offered to non-employee customers in the ordinary course of the employer's line of business multiplied by the gross profit percentage (see 13:21).
2. *Services.* For services sold to an employee at a discount, the maximum excludable portion of the discount is 20 percent of

the price at which the services are being offered to non-employee customers.

[IRC § 132(c)(1); Treas Reg § 1.132-3(a)(1)]

The portion, if any, of the discount exceeding the above limits is required to be included in the gross income of the employee. [Treas Reg § 1.132-3(e)]

Q 13:18   What form may a qualified employee discount take?

The qualified employee discount may consist of price reductions, cash rebates from the employer, or cash rebates from a third party. The exclusion will apply regardless of whether the property or service is provided at a reduced charge or at no charge at all. [Treas Reg § 1.132-3(a)(4)] Of course, any portion of the discount exceeding the allowable limit must be included in the gross income of the employee. [Treas Reg § 1.132-3(e)]

Q 13:19   If the employer offers the property or service to its non-employee customers at a discounted price, how is the amount of the Code Section 132 qualified employee discount affected?

The price charged to non-employee customers is the starting point from which a qualified employee discount is calculated. If the employer offers the property or service to its non-employee customers at a discounted price and sales at discounted prices equal at least 35 percent of the employer's gross sales for its prior tax year, then the price at which the employer is considered to offer the property or service for sale to its non-employee customers will be the discounted price. [Treas Reg § 1.132-3(b)(2)]

This discounted price for non-employee customers is calculated by taking the price at which the property or service is being offered to non-employee customers at the time of the employee's purchase and reducing it by the percentage discount at which the greatest percentage of the employer's discount gross sales was made for the prior tax year. The qualified employee discount is then calculated using this lower price for non-employee customers. [Treas Reg § 1.132-3(b)(2)(iv)]

Q 13:20 What property qualifies for a tax-free employee discount?

Any property offered for sale to customers in the ordinary course of the employer's line of business in which the employee performs substantial services is "qualified property," except for real property and personal property (whether tangible or intangible) of a kind commonly held for investment. [Treas Reg § 1.132-3(a)(2)] Thus, employee discounts on the purchase of securities, commodities, or currency, or of either residential or commercial real estate, are not qualified employee discounts and are therefore not excludable from gross income under Code Section 132. [IRC § 132(c)(4); Treas Reg § 1.132-3(a)(2)(ii)]

Q 13:21 When determining the qualified employee discount on property, how is the employer's gross profit percentage calculated?

The qualified employee discount on property sold to an employee at a discount generally is equal to the employer's gross profit percentage for the prior tax year. The gross profit percentage is calculated by taking the employer's aggregate sales price of such property sold by the employer to non-employee customers for the prior tax year (determined using generally accepted accounting principles) and subtracting from it the employer's aggregate cost of the property for the prior tax year, then dividing the resulting amount by the aggregate sales price of property sold to non-employee customers for the prior tax year. [IRC § 132(c)(2); Treas Reg § 1.132-3(c)]

If substantial changes in the employer's business make it inappropriate for the prior year's gross profit margin to be used for the current year, the employer must redetermine the gross profit percentage to be used for the remainder of the current year by reference to an appropriate industry average. [Treas Reg § 1.132-3(c)(iv)]

Aggregation of employers. The gross profit percentage required to be aggregated under Code Sections 414(b), 414(c), 414(m), or 414(o) for employers who do not have the same tax year must be calculated on a 12-month period that is selected and used on a consistent basis. [Treas Reg § 1.132-3(c)(1)(ii)]

Employees performing services for more than one line of service. If an employee performs substantial services in more than one line of the employer's business, the applicable gross profit percentage for determining the amount of employee discount that is excludable from the employee's gross income is the one for the line of business in which the property is sold. [Treas Reg § 1.132-3(c)(2)]

Department stores. Special rules apply to the leased sections of department stores. [Treas Reg § 1.132-3(d)]

Q 13:22   What if the goods are damaged, distressed, or returned?

No amount will be taxable to the employee under Code Section 132 for damaged, distressed, or returned goods made available by the employer, as long as the employee pays a price equal to or exceeding the fair market value of the goods in such shape. [Treas Reg § 1.132-3(b)(3)]

Q 13:23   How is a qualified discount on services calculated?

Code Section 132 provides that an employee's excludable discount for services may be up to 20 percent of the price at which the employer offers such services to non-employee customers in the ordinary course of business. The portion of a discount in excess of that limit is treated as taxable employee wages. [IRC § 132(c)(3); Treas Reg § 1.132-3(e)]

Q 13:24   Can an employee's family members also receive a tax-free employee discount on services?

Yes, they may. For purposes of the qualified employee discount, the term "employee" is broadly defined to include the following:

1. Current employees in the employer's line of business;

2. Former employees who have separated from service in such line of business or who have retired from such line of business by reason of disability;

3. Any widow or widower of an employee who either died while employed in the employer's line of business or separated from service in the employer's line of business due to retirement or disability; and

4. The spouse and dependent children of any of the above (a dependent child includes a son, stepson, daughter, or step-daughter who is also a dependent of the employee or whose parents are both deceased and who has not attained age 25).

[Treas Reg § 1.132-1(b)]

Q 13:25   Can qualified employee discounts be provided by a second, unrelated employer?

Yes, they can. Although there is no counterpart to the rule described in Question 13:12 (regarding no-additional-cost services) for employee discounts, qualified employee discounts may nonetheless be provided either directly by the employer or indirectly by a third party. As an example, employees of an appliance manufacturer could receive a qualified employee discount on that manufacturer's appliances sold at a retail store, if the retail store also sells the appliances to its non-employee customers. [Treas Reg § 1.132-3(a)(5)]

Q 13:26   What nondiscrimination rules apply to qualified employee discounts?

In order for the value of an employee discount to be excluded from a highly compensated employee's gross income, the benefit must be available on substantially the same terms to all employees of the employer, or to a group of employees under a reasonable classification set up by the employer that does not discriminate in favor of highly compensated employees. [Treas Reg § 1.132-8] For this purpose, the definition of highly compensated employees contained in Code Sections 414(q), (s), and (t) is used. [IRC §§ 132(i)(1), 132(i)(6)]

The nondiscrimination test is applied by aggregating the employees of all related employers except that employees in different lines of business are not aggregated. [Treas Reg § 1.132-8(b)]

Working Condition Fringe Benefits

Q 13:27   What is a working condition fringe benefit?

A working condition fringe benefit is any property or service provided by an employer to an employee that would be allowable as a deduction under Code Sections 162 or 167 if the employee paid for the property or service. Code Section 132 provides that the fair market value of the property or service is excluded from the employee's gross income if the employee could have deducted it as a business expense (disregarding the Code Section 67(a) minimum required amount for miscellaneous itemized deductions). [IRC § 132(d); Treas Reg § 1.132-5(a)]

If other IRC sections require substantiation (see 13:28) in order for a deduction under Section 162 or 167 to be allowable, those substantiation requirements would have to be met in order for the expense to be excludable under Code Section 132. [Treas Reg § 1.132-5(a)(1)(ii)]

If a deduction is allowable to the employee under an IRC section other than Code Sections 162 or 167, the property or service does not qualify as a working condition fringe benefit under Code Section 132. [Treas Reg § 1.132(a)(1)(iii)]

Q 13:28   What minimum requirements must be met in order for employer-provided property or services to be working condition fringe benefits?

Three basic requirements apply, as follows:

1. If the employee had purchased the property or service, he or she would have been entitled to a business expense deduction. [IRC § 132(d)]

2. The employee's use of the property or service must be related to the employer's trade or business. [IRC §§ 162, 167; Treas Reg § 1.132-5(a)(2)]

3. The employee's use of such property must be substantiated by adequate records or sufficient evidence corroborating the employee's own statement. [Treas Reg § 1.132-5(c)]

Additionally, other requirements may have to be met in order for the particular item to be a working condition fringe benefit.

Q 13:29 What property or services constitute working condition fringe benefits?

Among the employer-provided items whose fair market value may be excluded from gross income as a working condition fringe benefit under Code Section 132 (if the detailed requirements applicable to each are satisfied) are the following:

- Cars (business or demonstration use)
- Chauffeur services
- Transportation for security concerns (such as terrorist activity, death threats, and threat of kidnapping or serious bodily harm)
- Airplanes and air transportation
- Bodyguards
- Use of consumer goods for product testing and evaluation
- Travel expenses, including for meals and lodging
- Word processors and computers
- Entertainment

Note that the applicable regulations contain detailed requirements related to the exclusion for many of the above items. [Treas Reg § 1.132-5] Employer-provided aircraft is discussed in further detail in Questions 13:32 through 13:45, and the special requirements applicable to employer-provided cars are discussed in Questions 13:46 through 13:65. Prior to 1993, employer-provided parking generally was treated as a working condition fringe benefit. However, starting in 1993, employer-provided parking is now a qualified transportation fringe benefit subject to dollar limits and is no longer a working condition fringe beneift. [IRC § 132(f)(7)] (See Qs 13:91–13:99.)

Q 13:30 What employer-provided products and services are not working condition fringe benefits?

A physical examination program provided by the employer is not excludable as a working condition fringe benefit. This is true even if the value of the program might be deductible to the employee under Code Section 213. [Treas Reg § 1.132-5(a)(1)(iv)] It might, however, be excludable under Code Sections 106 and 105 as an accident and health plan (see Chapter 3).

At one time, the IRS took the position that outplacement assistance was not excludable as a working condition fringe benefit. In a reversal of position, the IRS ruled that if the employer derives a substantial business benefit from the provision of outplacement services that is distinct from the benefit of paying additional compensation, such as promoting a positive corporate image, maintaining employee morale, and avoiding wrongful termination suits, the provision of outplacement services generally may be treated as a working condition fringe benefit. However, if the employee can elect to receive cash or other taxable benefits in lieu of the outplacement services, the outplacement services will not qualify as a working condition fringe benefit and will be taxable as compensation. [Rev Rul 92-69, 1992-36 IRB 5]

Q 13:31 What nondiscrimination rules apply to working condition fringe benefits?

Except for product testing programs, Code Section 132 does not impose any nondiscrimination rules on the availability of the exclusion for working condition fringe benefits. Therefore, an employer can make working condition fringe benefits available to selected employees if it wishes. [Treas Reg § 1.132-5(q)]

Aircraft

Q 13:32 Is an employee's use of a private aircraft owned or leased by the employer a working condition fringe benefit?

Use of an employer-provided noncommercial aircraft (for example, a private airplane or helicopter) is a tax-free working condition fringe benefit where the flight is taken purely for business purposes. The amount excludable from income as a working condition fringe benefit is the amount that the employee could deduct as a business expense if the employee had paid for the flight on the aircraft. Thus, a flight that is purely business is totally excludable from income. [Treas Reg § 1.132-5(k)]

Q 13:33 If an aircraft trip is made by an employee for both business and personal reasons, what is the tax treatment of the trip?

If the trip is primarily for the employer's business, the employee must include in income the excess of all the flights that comprise the trip over the value of the flights that would have been taken had there been no personal flights but only business flights. Thus, if an employee flies on a company plane from New York to San Francisco primarily on business but takes some extra time to sightsee in San Francisco, the trip is fully exempt as a working condition fringe.

However, if the employee flies on the company plane to Seattle for sight-seeing, the employee must include in income the excess of the value of the three trips (New York to San Francisco, San Francisco to Seattle, and Seattle to New York) over the two trips that would have been taken purely as a business trip (New York to San Francisco and San Francisco to New York). [Treas Reg § 1.61-21(g)(4)(ii)]

Q 13:34 What if the trip on a company aircraft is primarily a personal trip, and the business purpose is secondary?

If the employee combines in one trip both personal and business flights on an employer-provided aircraft and the trip is primarily personal, the employee includes in income the value of the personal flights that would have been taken had there been no business flights but only personal flights.

For example, if the employee flies from New York to Seattle for personal reasons, but stops en route in San Francisco for some incidental business, the employer would be taxed on the value of direct flights from New York to Seattle and Seattle to New York. [Treas Reg § 1.61-21(g)(4)(iii)]

Q 13:35   What if members of the employee's family fly on the company aircraft along with the employee?

If the trip is primarily a business trip and the employee's spouse is along for business reasons, the trip for both the employee and the spouse is exempt as a working condition fringe benefit. However, if the spouse is not along for business reasons, or if the employee brings along children for personal reasons, the value of their flights is generally includable in the employee's gross income. [Treas Reg § 1.132-5(k)]

Q. 13:36   What rules apply for valuing taxable trips in an employer-provided aircraft?

The value of a taxable flight on an employer-provided aircraft may be based on the fair market value of the flight. [Treas Reg §§ 1.61-21(b)(6), 1.61-21(b)(7)] Alternatively, the value of a flight can be determined under the special rules of the base aircraft valuation formula, also known as the Standard Industry Fare Level Formula (SIFL). The SIFL cents-per-mile rate applicable for the period during which the flight was taken is multiplied by the aircraft multiple (based on the takeoff weight of the aircraft), and then the applicable terminal charge is added. The SIFL rates and terminal charges are calculated by the Department of Transportation and revised semiannually. [Treas Reg § 1.61-21(g)(5)]

Q 13:37   Are the SIFL valuation rules the same for all employees?

No. The aircraft multiple, which is based on the takeoff weight of the aircraft, is different for a control employee (see 13:38-13:40) and a noncontrol employee. For example, if the company airplane is 25,001 pounds or more, the aircraft multiple is 31.3 percent for a noncontrol employee. However, for a control employee, the aircraft multiple is 400 percent, producing a much higher value for the personal flights of a control employee than for an employee who is not a control employee. [Treas Reg § 1.61-21(g)(7)]

Q 13:38 Who is a control employee?

In the case of a nongovernment employer, a control employee includes an employee earning $50,000 or more who is one of the following:

1. A board- or shareholder-appointed, -confirmed, or -elected officer of the employer (limited to the lesser of 10 employees or 1 percent of all employees); or
2. Among the top 1 percent most highly paid employees, not in excess of 50 employees.

A control employee also includes an employee who owns a 5-percent or greater equity, capital, or profits interest in the employer, or who is a director of the employer. [Treas Reg § 1.61-21(g)(8)]

Q 13:39 Who is a control employee in the case of a government employer?

A control employee of a government employer includes an elected official, or an employee whose compensation equals or exceeds the compensation paid to a federal government employee holding an Executive Level V position. [Treas Reg § 1.61-21(g)(9)]

Q 13:40 Does a control employee include a former employee?

Yes, in some cases. An employee who was a control employee of the employer at any time after reaching age 55, or within three years of separation from the service of the employer, is a control employee with respect to flights taken after separation from the service of the employer. However, these employees are not counted in applying the limitations in Question 13:38 (e.g., the 50-employee limit). [Treas Reg § 1.61-21(g)(11)]

Q 13:41 Do the higher valuation rules for control employees also apply to the personal trips on company aircraft by family members of the control employee?

Yes, they do. Since the value of their personal trips is taxable to the control employee, the same valuation rules apply in determining the value of their trips. However, the value of a flight by a child who is less than two years old is deemed to be zero. [Treas Reg § 1.61-21(g)(1)]

Q 13:42 What if some passengers on a company-provided aircraft are traveling primarily for business purposes and other passengers are traveling primarily for personal reasons?

Under a special seating capacity rule, if 50 percent or more of the regular passenger seating capacity of the aircraft is occupied by individuals traveling primarily on the employer's business, the value of any flight by an employee who is not traveling primarily on business is valued at zero (i.e., is tax-free). For this purpose, an employee is deemed to include a retired or disabled employee, the spouse of a deceased employee, and the spouse or dependent child of an employee, as well as a partner of a partnership. It does not include an independent contractor or director of the employer.

For example, a control employee goes on a business trip on a seven-seat company plane and takes only his spouse and child with him as nonbusiness guests. The control employee will be taxed on the value of the trip for the spouse and the child. However, if three other primarily business travelers are added as passengers, the spouse and child can travel tax-free. [Treas Reg § 1.61-21(g)(12)]

Q 13:43 How does the 50-percent seating capacity rule apply where the trip involves multiple flights?

The 50-percent seating capacity rule must be met both at the time the individual whose flight is being valued boards the aircraft and at the time the individual deplanes.

Example. A control employee is flying on a seven-seat plane from New York to San Francisco on business and takes along his spouse and child as nonbusiness guests. Three other company employees are also aboard on company business. The plane stops in Chicago and two of the company employees get off there. The control employee will be taxed on the value of the flight from New York to San Francisco for the spouse and child, since the 50-percent rule was not met both at the beginning and at the end of the flight from New York to San Francisco. [Treas Reg § 1.61-21(g)(12)(ii)]

Q 13:44 Can the employer use either the fair market value rule or the special SIFL rule in valuing the employer-provided aircraft usage?

Yes. However, if the employer uses the special rule it must use it for all purposes. If the employer uses the special SIFL rule for one employee, it must use it for all employees in the same calendar year.

The employee can use the special SIFL rule only if the employer has used it for withholding and reporting purposes. However, the employee is free to use the fair market value rule even if the employer uses the special SIFL rule. [Treas Reg § 1.61-21(c)(2)] If the employee chooses to use the fair market value rule, the employee must use it for all flights within the same calendar year. [Treas Reg § 1.61-21(g)(14)(ii)]

Q 13:45 Is the amount of taxable employer-provided aircraft travel subject to wage withholding?

Yes, it is. [IRC §§ 3121(a), 3201(b), 3401(a)]

Cars and Other Vehicles

Q 13:46   Is the use of an employer-provided vehicle excludable as a working condition fringe benefit?

Yes, it can be. An employee can exclude the amount that he or she could deduct as a business expense under Code Section 162 or Code Section 167 if he or she had paid for the availability of the vehicle himself or herself. [Treas Reg § 1.132-5(b)(1)(i)] The amount that would not be deductible is a taxable fringe benefit that must be included in the employee's gross income.

> **Example.** Employee A has an employer-provided vehicle available to him for one year. Assume that, were the vehicle to be used only for personal use, the value of its availability would be $2,000. Assume that the employee drives the vehicle 6,000 miles for his employer's business and an additional 2,000 miles for non-employer business. To calculate the value of the working condition fringe benefit, the $2,000 is multiplied by a fraction, the numerator of which is the business-use mileage (6,000) and the denominator of which is the total use mileage (8,000). The result, $1,500, is the value of the working condition fringe benefit. Accordingly, only $500 of the value of the availability of the car does not qualify as a working condition fringe benefit and would be included in the employee's gross income.

If other employees also use the vehicle, their use is included in determining the value of the working condition fringe benefit. [Treas Reg §§ 1.132-5(b)(1)(i), 1.132-5(b)(1)(v)]

Q 13:47   What kind of employer-provided vehicles qualify?

When determining whether part or all of the use of an employer-provided vehicle may be excluded from the employee's gross income as a working condition fringe benefit under Code Section 132, qualifying vehicles include any motorized vehicle manufactured primarily for use on public streets, roads, and highways. [Treas Reg §§ 1.132-5(b)(1), 1.61-21(e)(2)]

Q 13:48   What if the employer-provided vehicle is very expensive?

If the employee uses an employer-provided vehicle in part for personal purposes, the working condition fringe benefit exclusion does not apply to the personal miles driven by the employee. This is because if the employee had paid for the availability of the vehicle, he or she would not be able to deduct any part of the payment attributable to personal miles under Code Section 162 or 167. It does not matter if the employee would have chosen a less expensive vehicle. Nor does the result change even if the decision to provide an expensive rather than an inexpensive car is made by the employer for bona fide noncompensatory business reasons. [Treas Reg § 1.132-5(b)(1)(iii)]

Q 13:49   What if the employee uses more than one employer-provided vehicle?

The working condition fringe benefit exclusion is determined separately for each employer-provided vehicle. [Treas Reg § 1.132-5(b)(2)]

Q 13:50   Is the employee required to substantiate his or her business use of an employer-provided car?

Yes, the value of the use of a company car provided to an employee for use in the employer's business will be treated as a fully taxable fringe benefit, and not a working condition fringe benefit, unless the employee can substantiate the amount of his or her business use. [Treas Reg § 1.132-5(c)(1); Temp Treas Reg § 1.274-5T(a)]

Q 13:51   In particular, what must be substantiated?

The business use of an employer-provided car must be substantiated. To do so, the following elements must be documented:

- Amount of each separate expenditure for the car (for example, cost of purchase, maintenance, repairs)
- Amount of each business use (that is, mileage)
- Amount of total use during the taxable period

- Date of expenditure relating to the car or date of business use and
- Business purpose for the expense or use

[Temp Treas Reg §§ 1.274-5T(b)(6), 1.280F-6T(b)(1)(i)]

Q 13:52 What kinds of records will be considered adequate?

A deduction for expenses related to the business use of a car must be substantiated by adequate records. The following items may, singly or in combination, be adequate records: account books, diaries, or logs; trip sheets; statements of expense (for example, expense reports); and receipts, paid bills, or similar documentary evidence. [Temp Treas Reg § 1.274-5T(c)(2)]

Each required element of business use (see Q 13:51) must be substantiated.

Certain vehicles that are likely to be used only a *de minimis* amount for personal purposes are exempt from the substantiation requirements. A list of these vehicles is included in the Treasury regulations and includes, among other things, such vehicles as forklifts, cement mixers, dump trucks, cranes and derricks, certain moving vans, refrigerated trucks, and delivery trucks with seating for the driver only. [Temp Treas Reg § 1.274-5T(k)(2)]

Q 13:53 When must the records used for substantiation be prepared?

Records generally must be made at or near the time of the expenditure or use—at a time when the taxpayer has full present knowledge of each element of the expenditure or use (such as the amount, time and place, business purpose, and business relationship). Expense account statements prepared from account books, diaries, logs, or similar records made at or near the time of the expenditure or use will also be treated as made at or near the time of the expenditure or use if they are submitted to the employer by the employee in the regular course of good business practice. [Temp Treas Reg § 1.274-5T(c)(2)(ii)(A)]

Q 13:54   Is a written record always required?

Generally yes, but the record of the business use of a car also may be substantiated in a "computer memory device with the aid of a logging program." [Temp Treas Reg § 1.274-5T(c)(2)(ii)(C)]

If the employee fails to keep adequate written records relating to each element of the business expense relating to, or use of, the car, then he or she may be forced to attempt to substantiate the business expense or use in the following ways:

1. By his or her own oral or written statement, containing information in detail as to the element in question, and

2. By other corroborative evidence.

[Temp Treas Reg § 1.274-5T(c)(3)]

Q 13:55   What if some of the documentation needed to substantiate the business use of a car is confidential?

If any information concerning the elements of the expense or use (such as place, business purpose, or business relationship) is confidential in nature, it need not be recorded in the account book, diary, log, statement of expense, trip sheet, or similar record, provided that:

1. It is recorded at or near the time of the expense or use, and

2. It is available elsewhere for the IRS district director to substantiate such element of the expense or use.

[Temp Treas Reg § 1.274-5T(c)(2)(ii)(D)]

Q 13:56   Is there a safe harbor for substantiating an employee's use of an employer-provided vehicle for business only?

Yes, there is. The working condition fringe exclusion under Code Section 132 for the value of the use of the vehicle applies only if applicable substantiation requirements are met. A safe harbor substantiation rule is provided, under which the employer must maintain a written policy statement expressly limiting the use of the vehicle to business use only. [Treas Reg § 1.132-5(e)]

Q 13:57   What must be contained in the employer's written policy statement concerning business use only?

The employer must prohibit all nonbusiness use of the vehicle. Under the safe harbor substantiation rule for business use only of an employer-provided vehicle, an employer's written policy statement must satisfy the following five conditions:

1. The vehicle must be owned or leased by the employer and must be provided to one or more employees for use in connection with the employer's trade or business;

2. When not being used in the employer's trade or business, the vehicle must be kept on the employer's business premises except when it is temporarily located elsewhere (for example, for maintenance or repairs);

3. No employee using the vehicle lives at the employer's business premises;

4. Under the employer's written policy, no employee may use the vehicle for personal purposes except for *de minimis* personal use (such as stopping for lunch between two business deliveries); and

5. The employer reasonably believes that employees do not use the vehicle for personal use (except for *de minimis* use).

To avoid lengthy documentation of business use, employees also in fact must not use the vehicle for any personal use except for *de minimis* personal use. Evidence must exist that would enable the Commissioner to determine whether all of these conditions are met. [Treas Reg § 1.132-5(e), Temp Treas Reg 1.274-6T(a)(2)]

Q 13:58   What if the employer makes a vehicle available to the employee for both business use and commuting?

If the employer provides a vehicle to the employee for both business use and commuting use, the amount of the working condition fringe benefit excludable under Code Section 132 is the value of the availability of the vehicle to the employee for uses other than commuting purposes, provided that:

1. Applicable substantiation requirements are met (a safe harbor substantiation rule is provided under which detailed use records will not be required if the employer maintains a written policy statement on commuting use of the vehicle that contains certain specified information [Treas Reg § 1.132-5(f)]); and

2. A special rule for valuing commuter use is used and such value is either included in the employee's income or reimbursed by the employee.

[Treas Reg § 1.132-5(f)]

Q 13:59 What information must be contained in the employer's written policy statement on business and commuting use?

Under this second safe harbor substantiation rule, the employer's written policy statement must prohibit all personal use of the vehicle other than commuting. The policy statement will be considered to do so if it satisfies the following five conditions:

1. The vehicle must be owned or leased by the employer, provided to one or more employees for use in connection with the employer's trade or business, and be so used;

2. For *bona fide* noncompensatory business reasons, the employer requires the employee to commute to and/or from work in the vehicle;

3. The employer has established a written policy under which neither the employee nor any individual whose use would be taxable to the employee, may use the vehicle for personal purposes, other than for commuting or *de minimis* personal use (such as a stop for a personal errand);

4. The employer reasonably believes that, except for *de minimis* personal use, neither the employee nor any individual whose use would be taxable to the employee uses the vehicle for personal purposes except commuting; and

5. The employee required to use the vehicle is not a control employee required to use an automobile.

[Temp Treas Reg § 1.274-6T(a)(3)(i)]

To avoid lengthy documentation of business and commutation use, the employee must either reimburse the employer for the value of the commuter use or include a commuting value of $1.50 per one-way commute (e.g., from home to work or from work to home) in gross income. [Temp Treas Reg §§ 1.61-2T(f)(3), 1.274-6T(a)(3)(ii)]

Also, evidence must exist that would enable the Commissioner to determine whether the use of the vehicle meets these five conditions. [Temp Treas Reg § 1.274-6T(a)(3)]

Q 13:60   How is the taxable personal use of an employer-provided vehicle calculated?

The taxable value of the personal use or unsubstantiated business use of, or expense relating to, an employer-provided car must be included in the employee's gross income. Several valuation methods are available, including the following:

1. Fair market value method (see 13:62);
2. Annual lease value method (see 13:63);
3. Cents-per-mile method (see 13:64); and
4. Commuting value method (see 13:65).

The employee may use a special valuation rule (that is, any method other than the fair market value method) only if the employer does also, or if the employer does not meet the first condition of Question 13:61 and one of the other three conditions of Question 13:61 is satisfied. [Treas Reg § 1.61-21(c)(2)(ii)] Once the employer selects one of the special valuation rules, Treasury regulations impose conditions on when and if the employer can switch methods.

Use by more than one employee. When applying a special valuation rule for any vehicle used by more than one employee at the same time (for example, an employer-sponsored commuting pool), the employer must use the same rule to value the use of the vehicle by each employee who shares the use of it, and the employer must allocate the value of the vehicle's use based on the relevant facts and circumstances among the employees sharing its use. [Treas Reg § 1.61-21(c)(2)(ii)(B)]

Q 13:61 Do any special conditions apply when electing special vehicle valuation rules?

Yes. Starting in 1993, a previous requirement that the employer notify the employee of the employer's use of a special valuation rule has been eliminated. [57 Fed Reg 62192 (Dec 30, 1992)] Instead, the IRS regulations now provide that neither the employer nor the employee may use a special valuation rule unless one of four conditions is satisfied. The four conditions are:

1. The employer treats the value of the benefit as wages for reporting purposes within the prescribed time;
2. The employee includes the value of the benefit in income within the prescribed time;
3. The employee is not a control employee (see Q 13:38); or
4. The employer demonstrates a good faith effort to treat the benefit correctly for reporting purposes.

If no one of these four conditions is met, both the employer and employee must use the general valuation rules based on facts and circumstances.

Generally, the employee may use a special valuation rule only if the employer has used the rule. However, the employee may use a special valuation rule not used by the employer if the employer does *not* treat the value of the benefit as wages for reporting purposes (see Condition 1 above) and Condition 2, 3, or 4 is met. The employee may always use the general valuation rules based on facts and circumstances. [Treas Reg § 1.61-21(c)]

Q 13:62 How is the fair market value of an employer-provided vehicle determined?

Under the fair market value method, the value of the employer-provided vehicle equals the amount that an individual would be required to pay in an arm's-length transaction in order to lease the same or comparable vehicle, on the same or comparable conditions, and in the geographic area in which the vehicle is available for use.

In computing the fair market value of the car, the fair market value of specialized equipment not susceptible to personal use or any telephone added to the car is disregarded if necessitated by, and attributable to, the employer's business needs. However, the value of the specialized equipment is included if the employee uses it in a trade or business other than that of the employer. [Treas Reg § 1.61-21(b)(4)]

Q 13:63 How does the annual lease value method work?

The annual lease value of an automobile is calculated by determining its fair market value as of the first date it is made available to any employee for personal use and then selecting a dollar range from the Annual Lease Value Table contained in Treasury Regulation Section 1.61-21(d)(2)(iii). If the car is available to the employee for only part of a calendar year, the fair market value is either a prorated annual lease value or a daily lease value.

If the employer and employee jointly own the car, the annual lease value is reduced according to a formula contained in the regulations. If the employee contributes toward the price but does not receive any ownership interest in the car, his or her contribution is disregarded. In general, an employee's ownership interest will not be recognized unless it is reflected in the title of the car; even then, it will not be recognized if the title does not reflect the benefits and burdens of ownership. [Treas Reg § 1.61-21(d)(2)(ii)]

Revaluation of the car. The value used under this rule must be recalculated every four years. [Treas Reg § 1.62-21(d)(2)(iv)]

Fleet-average valuation rule. If the employer has a fleet of 20 or more automobiles and certain requirements are satisfied, the employer may use a fleet-average value for purposes of calculating the annual lease values of the automobiles in the fleet. [Treas Reg § 1.61-21(d)(5)(v)]

Q 13:64   How does the cents-per-mile valuation rule work?

The cents-per-mile valuation method may be used to value an employee's personal use of an employer-provided vehicle where:

1. The employer reasonably expects the vehicle will be regularly used in the employer's trade or business throughout the calendar year (or a shorter period of ownership); or

2. The vehicle is primarily used by employees during the calendar year and is actually driven at least 10,000 miles in that calendar year.

However, in order to use the cents-per-mile valuation rule, the value of the car cannot exceed $12,800 (as adjusted by Code Section 280F(d)(7) for 1989 and later years). Under the cents-per-mile rule, the value of the benefit provided in the calendar year is the standard mileage rate provided in the applicable Revenue Ruling or Revenue Procedure, multiplied by the number of personal miles that the employee has driven (i.e., for personal purposes). The standard mileage rate is to be applied to personal miles independently of business miles. For this purpose, personal miles means all miles for which the employee used the automobile except those driven in the employee's trade or business of being an employee of the employer.

Regular use in an employer's trade or business. Whether the car or vehicle is regularly used in the employer's trade or business will be determined based on the facts and circumstances. The car will be treated as being used in such a manner if:

1. At least 50 percent of the car's total annual mileage is for the employer's business, or

2. The car is generally used each workday to transport at least three of the employer's employees to and from work in an employer-sponsored commuting vehicle pool.

[Treas Reg § 1.61-21(e)(1)(iv)]

However, if the vehicle is used only infrequently for business use, such as for occasional trips to the airport or between the employer's multiple business premises, such use will not constitute use of the vehicle in the employer's trade or business. [Treas Reg § 1.61-21(e)(1)(iv)(B)]

Joint ownership. If the employee has contributed toward the purchase price of the car or toward the cost of leasing the car in return for a percentage ownership interest in the vehicle or lease, the value of the vehicle will be reduced according to a formula contained in the Treasury Regulations. However, if the employee's ownership interest is not reflected in the title of the vehicle, it will not be recognized. An ownership interest reflected in the title of the vehicle will not be recognized if, under the facts and circumstances, the title does not reflect the benefits and burdens of ownership. [Treas Reg § 1.61-21(e)(1)(iii)(B)]

Excluded and included items. When valuing the use of a vehicle using the cents-per-mile method, the fair market value of maintaining and insuring the vehicle is included. However, if the employer does not provide fuel, the cents-per-mile rate can be lowered by up to 5.5 cents or the amount specified in an applicable Revenue Ruling or Revenue Procedure. Outside the United States, Canada, or Mexico, fuel provided by the employer may also reduce the cents-per-mile rate. [Treas Reg §§ 1.61-21(e)(1), 1.61-21(e)(3)]

Q 13:65 How does the commutation value rule work?

Under the commutation valuation rule, the employee may include in his or her gross income $1.50 per one-way commute (e.g., from home to work or from work to home) if the following six conditions are met:

1. The vehicle is owned or leased by the employer;
2. The vehicle is provided to one or more employees for use in connection with the employer's trade or business and is used in the employer's trade or business;
3. The employer requires the employee to commute to and/or from work in the vehicle for *bona fide* noncompensatory business reasons;
4. The employer has established a written policy forbidding use of the vehicle for personal purposes other than commuting or *de minimis* personal use (such as stopping for a personal errand

on the way between a business delivery and the employee's home);

5. The employee does not use the vehicle for any personal purpose other than commuting and *de minimis* personal use; and

6. The employee who is required to use the vehicle for commuting is not a control employee as defined in Treasury Regulation Sections 1.61-21(f)(5) and (6). (However, this limitation only applies if the vehicle is an automobile.)

[Treas Reg § 1.61-21(f)(1)]

For this purpose, personal use by an employee is anything not in the employee's trade or business of being an employee of the employer. [Treas Reg § 1.61-21(f)(1)]

De Minimis Fringe Benefits

Q 13:66   What is a *de minimis* fringe benefit?

A *de minimis* fringe benefit is any property or service provided by an employer to its employees, the value of which is so small as to make accounting for it unreasonable or administratively impracticable (after taking into account the frequency with which similar fringe benefits are provided by the employer to its employees). [Treas Reg § 1.132-6(a)] The value of a *de minimis* fringe benefit may be excluded from the employee's gross income under Code Section 132.

Q 13:67   What kinds of property or services constitute *de minimis* fringe benefits?

Examples of *de minimis* fringe benefits include the following:

- Occasional typing of personal letters by a company secretary
- Occasional personal use of an employer's copying machine (as long as 85 percent of the use of the machine is for business purposes)
- Occasional cocktail parties, group meals, or picnics for employees and their guests

- Traditional birthday or holiday gifts with a low fair market value
- Occasional theater or sporting event tickets
- Coffee, doughnuts, and soft drinks
- Use of company telephones for local calls
- Flowers, fruit, books, or similar property provided to employees under special circumstances (such as on account of illness, outstanding performance, or family crisis)

[Treas Reg § 1.132-6(e)]

The following items are also excludable as *de minimis* fringe benefits if they meet detailed guidelines:

- Dependent group term life insurance
- Meals, meal money, and local transportation fare
- Eating facilities

[Treas Reg § 1.132-6; IRS Notice 89-110, IRB 1989-2 CB 447 postponing the effective date of Treas Reg § 1.132-6(e)(2) as applied to dependent group term life insurance until further notice.]

Note that if the employer gives the employee cash for the above items, the cash is not excludable from the employee's gross income as a *de minimis* fringe benefit (except for occasional meal money and local transportation fare), even if the value of the in-kind benefit (the item itself) would be. This is because it would not be unreasonable or administratively impracticable to account for the cash. [Treas Reg § 1.132-6(c)]

Prior to 1993, an employer-provided public transit pass provided at a discount not exceeding $21 per month (in 1992) was exempt as a *de minimis* fringe benefit. However, starting in 1993, a transit pass (public or private) is a qualified transit fringe benefit and is no longer a *de minimis* fringe benefit. [IRC § 132(f)(7)] (See Qs 13:91–13:99.)

Q 13:68　What products and services do not qualify as *de minimis* fringe benefits?

The following benefits cannot be excluded from gross income under Code Section 132 as *de minimis* fringe benefits:

- Season tickets to sporting or theatrical events
- The commuting use of an employer-provided automobile or other vehicle more than one day a month
- Membership in a private country club or athletic facility, regardless of the frequency with which the employee uses the facility
- Use of employer-owned or leased facilities (such as an apartment, hunting lodge, boat) for a weekend.

Even if the value of these items may not be excluded as *de minimis* fringe benefits, the value of these items may possibly be excluded under other statutory provisions, such as the exclusion for working condition fringe benefits. [Treas Reg § 1.132-6(e)(2)]

Q 13:69 Do any nondiscrimination requirements apply to *de minimis* fringe benefits?

Except for employer-provided eating facilities, *de minimis* fringe benefits are not subject to any nondiscrimination rules under Code Section 132. IRS regulations provide detailed requirements for employer-provided eating facilities. [Treas Reg § 1.132-6(f)]

Employer-Operated Eating Facilities

Q 13:70 What kinds of facilities qualify as employer-operated eating facilities for employees?

An employer-operated facility for employees is any facility that:

1. Is owned or leased by the employer;
2. Is operated by the employer;
3. Is located on or near the employer's business premises; and
4. Furnishes meals that are provided before, during, or immediately after the employee's workday.

For this purpose, meals include food, beverages, and related services provided at the facility. [Treas Reg § 1.132-7(a)(2)]

Q 13:71   Do *de minimis* fringe benefits include the value of meals provided to employees at an employer-operated eating facility for employees?

Yes, the value of meals provided to employees in employer-sub-sidized cafeterias, dining rooms, and other eating facilities is treated as an excludable *de minimis* fringe benefit under Code Section 132, provided that:

1. On an annual basis, the revenue from the facility equals or exceeds the direct operating costs of the facility [Treas Reg § 1.132-7(a)(1)(i)]; and

2. In addition, for the exclusion to be available to highly compen-sated employees, access to the facility must also be available under a reasonable classification set up by the employer that does not discriminate in favor of highly compensated employees [Treas Reg § 1.132-7(a)(1)(ii)].

Q 13:72   When calculating revenue from employer-operated eating facilities, what items need not be counted?

If the employer can reasonably determine the amount of meals furnished for the convenience of the employer under Code Section 119, then both the costs and the revenues associated with them may be disregarded under Code Section 132. Code Section 119 provides an exclusion from the employee's gross income for the value of meals provided by the employer if the meals are furnished on the employer's premises, for the convenience of the employer (a facts and cir-cumstances determination), and on working days. [Treas Reg § 1.119-1(a)(1)] (See the discussion of meals and lodging furnished for the convenience of the employer in Questions 13:100 through 13:117.)

Q 13:73   What items constitute the direct operating costs of an employer-operated eating facility?

For purposes of the Code Section 132 exclusion for *de minimis* fringes, the direct operating costs of an employer-operated eating facility include the following costs:

- Food and beverages
- Labor for personnel whose services relating to the facility are performed primarily on the premises
- Payment to another with whom the employer has contracted to run the facility, to the extent that the amount would be direct operating costs if the employer operated the facility directly

[Treas Reg §§ 1.132-7(b)(1), 1.132-7(b)(3)]

Revenues and direct operating costs may be determined separately for each dining room or cafeteria or on an aggregate basis. [Treas Reg § 1.132-7(b)(2)]

Q 13:74 What nondiscrimination rules apply to the exclusion of an employer-provided eating facility under Code Section 132 as a *de minimis* fringe benefit?

Highly compensated employees (as defined in Code Section 414(q)) cannot exclude from gross income any portion of the value of meals provided at an employer-operated eating facility, unless the benefit is made available on substantially the same terms to:

1. All employees of the employer; or
2. A nondiscriminatory classification of employees (a facts and circumstances determination).

[Treas Reg §§ 1.132-7(a)(1)(ii), 1.132-8(d)]

This discrimination test is applied by aggregating the employees of related employers under Code Section 414(b), 414(c), 414(m), or 414(o), to the extent that such employees regularly work at or near the facility. Employees in separate lines of business are not to be aggregated, and the nondiscrimination test is applied separately to each facility. [Treas Reg § 1.132-8(b)]

Even if a highly compensated employee must include the value of the meals provided to him or her at a discriminatory facility, he or she may nonetheless exclude from gross income the value of meals at nondiscriminatory facilities. [Treas Reg § 1.132-8(a)(2)(ii)(B)]

Deemed nondiscrimination. Even if access to an employer-operated eating facility is available to a classification of employees that discriminates in favor of highly compensated employees, the classification will nonetheless not be treated as discriminatory as long as the facility is not used by executive group employees more than a *de minimis* amount. Executive group employees, for this purpose, are defined as in Code Section 414(q), but substituting "top 1 percent" for "top 10 percent" in the definition of top-paid group contained therein. [Treas Reg § 1.132-8(d)(5)]

Q 13:75   How are employees taxed on nonexcluded meals furnished at employer-provided eating facilities?

If the Code Section 132 *de minimis* fringe benefit exclusion is not available for the value of employer-provided meals, the recipient must include the following in gross income:

1. The fair market value of the meals, minus
2. The sum of:
   a. The amount (if any) paid for the meals and
   b. The amount specifically excluded under any other IRC section.

[Treas Reg § 1.132-7(c)]

Code section 119. For a description of the total exclusion under Code Section 119, see Question 13:72.

Valuation. The fair market value of meals to be allocated to an individual is determined in accordance with the rules contained in Treasury Regulation Section 1.61-21(j). Two methods are provided, as follows:

1. *Direct meal subsidy.* The sum of the individual meal subsidies for each meal consumed by the employee during the calendar year, less the amount paid by the employee; or
2. *Indirect meal subsidy.* Allocation of the aggregate meal value (deemed to be 150 percent of the total operating costs of the particular facility), less the facility's gross receipts, among employees in any manner reasonable under the circumstances.

[Treas Reg § 1.162-21(j)(2)]

Occasional Meal Money and Local Transportation Fare

Q 13:76 Are occasional meal money and local transportation fare excludable from gross income under Code Section 132 as *de minimis* fringe benefits?

Yes, they can be. To qualify, the meals, meal money, and local transportation fare provided must be reasonable and also must satisfy the following three requirements:

1. They must be provided on an occasional basis, not a regular or routine basis;
2. They must be provided because overtime work necessitates an extension of the employee's normal work schedule (even if the overtime work was reasonably foreseeable); and
3. Meals or meal money must be provided to enable the employee to work overtime.

[Treas Reg § 1.132-6(d)(2)]

Meal money and local transportation fare calculated based on the number of hours worked do not qualify as *de minimis* fringe benefits. [Treas Reg § 1.132-6(d)(2)]

Meals and meal money that do not qualify as *de minimis* fringe benefits might be excludable under Code Section 119 (see Q 13:72).

Special rules apply to taxi fare (see Q 13:78) and commuting under unsafe conditions (see Qs 13:79-13:85; see also Qs 13:91-13:99 regarding qualified transportation fringe benefits.)

Transportation in Unusual Circumstances and Unsafe Conditions

Q 13:77 What special rules apply to employer-provided transportation such as taxi fare?

Ordinarily, employer-provided transportation (such as taxi fare) for commuting to and from work is not excludable as a *de minimis* fringe benefit under Code Section 132 because commuting is a nondeductible personal expense under Code Section 262. However, if (1) the employer provides transportation to and/or from work because of unusual circumstances, and (2) it is unsafe, based on the facts and circumstances, for the employee to use other available means of transportation, the employee may include in gross income $1.50 per trip per one-way commute for employer-provided transportation. [Treas Reg § 1.132-6(d)(2)(C)(iii)] This special value cannot be used by control employees as defined in Treasury Regulation Sections 1.61-21(f)(5) and 1.61-21(f)(6).

Q 13:78 When do unusual circumstances exist?

For purposes of the Code Section 132 exclusion, the determination of whether unusual circumstances exist regarding the employee in question is based on the facts and circumstances. For example, being called to work at 2:00 A.M. when the employee's regular work schedule is 9:00 A.M. to 5:00 P.M. would be an unusual circumstance. Another example is a temporary change in the employee's work schedule, such as working late for a two-week period. [Treas Reg § 1.132-6(d)(2)(iii)(B)]

Q 13:79 When do unsafe conditions exist?

For the Code Section 132 exclusion, factors that indicate whether an employee's use of alternate transportation is unsafe include the history of crime in the geographic area surrounding the employee's workplace or residence, and the time of day during which the employee must commute. [Treas Reg § 1.132-6(d)(2)(iii)(C)]

Employer-Provided Transportation Due to Unsafe Conditions

Q 13:80 What additional exclusion is available for employer-provided transportation due to unsafe conditions?

Treasury Regulation Section 1.61-21(k) provides a special partial exclusion from gross income for employer-provided transportation meeting the following four conditions:

1. The transportation is provided solely because of unsafe conditions to an employee who would otherwise walk or use public transportation at the time of day he or she must commute;

2. The employer has established a written policy (such as in the employer's personnel manual) stating that the transportation is not provided for any other personal purposes and the employer's practice in fact conforms with the policy;

3. The transportation is not used for any personal purposes except commuting due to unsafe conditions; and

4. The recipient employee is a "qualified employee" (see 13:81.)

[Treas Reg § 1.61-21(k)(1)]

If the preceding conditions are met, the includable value of each one-way trip to or from work is $1.50, regardless of the actual fair market value of the trip.

Q 13:81 Who is a "qualified employee" for purposes of receiving transportation solely due to unsafe conditions?

"Qualified employees," for this purpose, are nonexempt hourly employees in an employment classification eligible to receive overtime pay at least one and one-half times the regular rate. [Treas Reg § 1.61-21(k)(6)(i)(A)] Employees receiving compensation in excess of the Code Section 414(q)(1)(C) limit are excluded. [Treas Reg § 1.61-21(k)(6)(i)(B)]

Recordkeeping requirement. The employer must be in compliance with the record-keeping requirements of the Fair Labor Standards Act of 1938, as amended, concerning wages, hours, and other conditions of employment, or else its employees will be disqualified from treatment as "qualified employees" for purposes of this special transportation exclusion and no part of such employer-provided transportation will be excludable. [Treas Reg §§ 1.61-21(k)(6)(iii), 1.61-21(k)(6)(v)]

Q 13:82 For purposes of the Code Section 61 exclusion, when are unsafe conditions considered to exist?

Unsafe conditions will be considered to exist if a reasonable person would, under the facts and circumstances, consider it unsafe for the employee to walk to or from home, or to use public transportation at that particular time of day. Factors that indicate unsafe conditions include a history of crime in the geographic area surrounding either the employee's workplace or residence at the time of day the employee must commute. [Treas Reg § 1.61-21(k)(5)]

Q 13:83 What type of employer-provided transportation counts toward the special exclusion for unsafe conditions?

The employer-provided transportation must consist of a motorized, wheeled vehicle purchased by the employer (or purchased by the employee and reimbursed by the employer) from an unrelated third party for the purpose of transporting the employee to or from work. The vehicle must have been manufactured primarily for use on public streets, roads, and highways (for example, a bus or automobile). [Treas Reg §§ 1.61-21(f)(4),1.61-21(k)(4)]

Q 13:84 How are qualifying trips valued?

If the requirements of Treasury Regulation Section 1.61-21(k) regarding employer-provided transportation for unsafe conditions are met, the amount includable in each employee's gross income is $1.50 per one-way commute (i.e., from home to work or from work to home). [Treas Reg § 1.61-21(k)(3)]

On-Premises Athletic Facilities

Q 13:85 What is an on-premises athletic facility?

On-premises athletic facilities include gyms, pools, golf courses, and any other athletic facilities. [Treas Reg § 1.132-1(e)(1)]

Q 13:86 Can the value of on-premises athletic facilities be excluded from the employee's gross income?

Yes, it can. Gross income does not include the value of any on-premises athletic facilities that the employer provides to its employees. [Treas Reg § 1.132-1(e)(1)]

Q 13:87 What conditions must be satisfied in order for the value of on-premises athletic facilities to be excluded under Code Section 132?

In order for the value to be excludable from the employee's gross income, the facility must meet the following three conditions:

1. It must be located on the employer's premises;
2. It must be operated by the employer; and
3. Substantially all of its use during the calendar year must be by the employer's employees and their spouses and dependent children.

The Code Section 132 exclusion does not apply if the athletic facility is made available to the general public through membership sales, rental, or similar arrangements. [Treas Reg § 1.132-1(e)(1)]

Q 13:88 When is the athletic facility considered to be on the premises of the employer?

The athletic facility must be located on the premises of the employer, but need not be located on the employer's business premises. Whether the premises are owned or leased by the employer does not matter; a leasing employer need not even be a named lessee on the lease as long as the employer pays reasonable rent. However, athletic facilities that are facilities for residential use (such as a resort with accompanying athletic facilities) do not qualify. [Treas Reg § 1.132-1(e)(2)]

Health club, country club, and other memberships do not qualify for the on-premises athletic facility exclusion unless the employer owns or leases and operates the facility and substantially all of the facility's use is by the employer's employees and their spouses and dependent children. [Treas Reg § 1.132-1(e)(3)]

Q 13:89   When is the employer considered to be operating an on-premises athletic facility?

The employer will be treated as operating an on-premises athletic facility if it does so through its own employees or it contracts with another to operate the facility. [Treas Reg § 1.132-1(e)(4)]

If the facility is operated by more than one employer, it is treated as being operated by each employer. [Treas Reg § 1.132-1(e)(4)]

Q 13:90   May an employee's family members also use the employer's on-premises athletic facilities on a tax-free basis?

Yes, they can. An "employee" for purposes of the exclusion for on-premises athletic facilities, is defined broadly to include the following:

1. Current employees of the employer;

2. Former employees who separated from the employer's service due to retirement or disability;

3. Any widow and widower of an employee who either died while employed by the employer or separated from service due to retirement or disability; and

4. Any spouse or dependent child of the above, including any son, stepson, daughter, or stepdaughter who is a dependent of the employee or whose parents are both deceased and who has not attained age 25 (if Code Section 152(e), dealing with a child of divorced parents, applies, the child will be treated as a dependent of both parents).

[Treas Reg § 1.132-1(b)]

Qualified Transportation Fringe Benefits

Q 13:91   What is a qualified transportation fringe benefit?

A qualified transportation fringe benefit includes any of the following provided by an employer to an employee:

- Transportation in a commuter highway vehicle if such transportation is in connection with travel between the employee's residence and place of employment
- A transportation pass
- Qualified parking

[IRC § 132(f)(1), as added by the Energy Policy Act of 1992, Pub L No 102-486, 102d Cong, 2d Sess (Oct 24, 1992), effective for benefits after 1992]

Q 13:92   What is a "commuter highway vehicle"?

A "commuter highway vehicle" is defined as any vehicle that has a seating capacity of at least six adults (excluding the driver) and for which at least 80 percent of the mileage use is reasonably expected to be:

1. For purposes of transporting employees in connection with travel between their residences and their place of employment; and

2. On trips during which the number of employees transported for such purposes is at least half of the adult capacity of the vehicle (not including the driver).

[IRC § 132(f)(5)(B)]

Q 13:93   What is a "transit pass"?

A "transit pass" is any pass, token, fare card, voucher, or similar item entitling a person to free or reduced price transportation if such transportation:

1. Is on mass transit facilities (public or private); or

2. Provided by any person in the business of transporting persons for compensation or hire in a highway vehicle which has a seating capacity of at least six adults (excluding the driver).

[IRC § 132(f)(5)(A)]

Q. 13:94　What is "qualified parking"?

"Qualified parking" is parking provided to an employee on or near the business premises of the employer or on or near a location from which the employee commutes to work by means of:

- Mass transit facilities

- A highway vehicle for hire, which has a seating capacity of at least six adults (excluding the driver)

- A commuter highway vehicle or

- A carpool

Qualified parking does not include any parking on or near property used by the employee for residential purposes. [IRC § 132(f)(5)(C)]

Example. Employee A drives from his home to a commuter railway station, parks his car, and takes the train to work. If the employer pays for the cost of parking at the railway station, it is a qualified transportation fringe benefit.

Q 13:95　Are all qualified transportation fringe benefits exempt from income tax?

No, not in all cases. There are dollar limits on the amounts that can be excluded from the employee's income. If the amount of the qualified transportation fringe benefit exceeds the applicable dollar limit, the excess is income to the employee. [IRC § 132(f)(2)]

Q 13:96   What are the dollar limits on qualified transportation fringe benefits?

In the case of transportation in a commuter highway vehicle, and also in the case of a transit pass, there is a dollar limit of $60 a month. If the employee receives both the benefits, there is a combined limit of $60 a month.

> **Example.** Employee B is provided by her employer with transportation in a commuter highway vehicle at a cost of $40 a month and with a transit pass costing $35 a month. B has gross income each month of $15 ($40 + $35 – $60).

In the case of qualified parking, the dollar limit on the exclusion from income is $155 per month. [IRC § 132(f)(2)]

Q 13:97   Are the dollar limits on qualified transportation fringe benefits indexed for inflation?

Yes. Starting in 1994, the dollar limits will be adjusted annually to reflect cost-of-living changes. If an increase is not a multiple of $5, the increase will be rounded to the next lowest multiple of $5. [IRC § 132 (f)(6)]

Q 13:98   Can the employer reimburse an employee in cash for the cost of a qualified transportation fringe benefit?

Yes, the employer generally does not have to pay the cost of a qualified transportation fringe benefit in advance or directly to the provider of the service, but can reimburse the employee in cash.

However, in the case of a transit pass, cash reimbursement is permitted only if a voucher or similar item which may be exchanged only for a transit pass is not readily available for direct distribution by the employer to the employee. [IRC § 132(f)(4)]

Q 13:99   Is a qualified transportation fringe benefit received by an employee subject to income tax withholding or to Social Security (FICA) and the Federal Unemployment Tax Act (FUTA)?

To the extent that the qualified transportation fringe benefit is excludable from gross income under Code section 132(f), it is not subject to income tax withholding, or to FICA or FUTA. However, to the extent the benefit is taxable (that is, to the extent the dollar limits are exceeded), income tax withholding and FICA and FUTA apply. [IRC §§ 3401(a)(19), 3121(a)(20), 3306(b)(16)]

Meals and Lodging Furnished for the Convenience of the Employer

Q 13:100   Is the value of meals furnished by an employer to an employee and/or his or her family included in the employee's gross income?

The value of meals furnished by an employer to an employee, his or her spouse, or any dependent of the employee can be excluded from the employee's gross income if two requirements are met, as follows:

1. The meals are furnished on the business premises of the employer, and
2. The meals are furnished for the convenience of the employer.

[IRC § 119(a)]

Q 13:101   Is the value of lodging furnished by an employer to an employee and/or his or her family included in the employee's gross income?

The value of lodging furnished by an employer to an employee, his or her spouse, or any dependent of the employee can be excluded from the employee's gross income if three requirements are met, as follows:

1. The lodging is furnished on the business premises of the employer;
2. The lodging is furnished for the convenience of the employer; and
3. The employee is required to accept the lodging as a condition of employment.

[IRC § 119(a); Treas Reg § 1.119-1(b)]

Q 13:102   Does the meals exclusion apply if the employee receives a cash meal allowance?

No. In order for the exclusion to apply, the meals must be furnished in kind, not (1) in the form of cash or (2) under an option to take the meals either in kind or in cash. [Treas Reg § 1.119-1(e)] The U.S. Supreme Court held that a state trooper who received cash meal allowances from his employer was not entitled to the exclusion because the meals were not provided by the employer in kind. [Kowalski v United States, 434 US 77 (1977)]

Q 13:103   Does the meals exclusion apply to an employee if the employer provides groceries rather than finished meals?

The authorities are split on this issue. The U.S. Court of Appeals for the Ninth Circuit held that meals do not include groceries. [Tougher v Commissioner, 441 F 2d 1148 (9th Cir 1971)] However, the U.S. Court of Appeals for the Third Circuit found that groceries were meals that could qualify for exclusion if the other statutory requirements were met. [Jacob v United States, 493 F 2d 1294 (3d Cir 1974)]

Q 13:104   What is considered to be the business premises of the employer?

The term "business premises of the employer" generally means the place of employment of the employee. [Treas Reg § 1.119-1(c)(1)] The U.S. Tax Court has stated that the term "on the business premises" with respect to lodging means either (1) living quarters that constitute an integral part of the business property or (2) premises on which the employer carries on some of its business activities. The tax court held that a residence a mile away from the employer's mill was not on the business premises. [Gordon S Dole, 43 TC 697, 707 (1965), *affd per curiam*, 351 F 2d 308 (1st Cir. 1965)]

If an employee is furnished lodging by his or her employer in a camp located in a foreign country, the camp will be treated as the business premises of the employer, provided that the following three conditions apply:

1. The place at which the employee renders services is in a remote area where satisfactory housing is not available on the open market;

2. The camp is located (as near as practicable) in the vicinity of the employee's workplace; and

3. The camp lodging is furnished in a common area (or enclave) which is not available to the public and which normally accommodates 10 or more employees.

[IRC § 119(c); Treas Reg §§ 1.119-1(c)(2), 1.119-1(d)]

Q 13:105 Is actual physical presence on the business premises of the employer required for the meals and lodging exclusions to be allowed?

Generally yes. In a decision by the U.S. Court of Appeals for the Sixth Circuit, it was held that meals and lodging provided to an employee in an employer-owned residence only "two short blocks" from the place of employment were not provided on the business premises of the employer. [Commissioner v Anderson, 371 F 2d 59 (6th Cir 1966), *cert denied*, 387 US 906 (1967)] However, in a later decision by the U.S. Tax Court, *Anderson* was held to be not applicable to a situation where lodging was furnished directly across the street from the workplace, and the IRS has acquiesced in the tax court decision. [Jack B Lindeman, 60 TC 609 (1973), *acq* 1973-2 CB 2]

Q 13:106 When are meals deemed furnished for the convenience of the employer?

The question of whether meals are furnished for the convenience of the employer is one of fact to be determined by analysis of all the facts and circumstances in each case. [Treas Reg § 1.119-1(a)(1)]

In determining whether meals are furnished for the convenience of the employer, the fact that a charge is made for such meals and the fact that the employee may accept or decline such meals are factors that are not to be taken into account. [IRC § 119(b)(2)]

IRS regulations interpreting the convenience of the employer requirement set out separate guidelines for (1) meals furnished without a charge and (2) meals furnished with a charge. [Treas Reg §§ 1.119-1(a)(2), 1.119-1(a)(3)]

Q 13:107 When are meals provided without a charge considered furnished for the convenience of the employer?

Under IRS regulations, meals furnished without a charge will be regarded as furnished for the convenience of the employer if the meals are furnished for a substantial noncompensatory business reason of the employer. If a substantial noncompensatory business reason exists, the meals will be considered furnished for the convenience of the employer even if the meals are furnished also for a compensatory reason. The determination of whether a substantial noncompensatory business reason exists will be based on all the surrounding facts and circumstances. A mere declaration by the employer that such a business reason exists is not enough. [Treas Reg § 1.119-1(a)(2)(i)]

Q 13:108 What are some substantial noncompensatory business reasons of the employer for providing meals without charge to the employee?

IRS regulations give a number of illustrations of substantial noncompensatory business reasons, as follows:

1. The meals are furnished to the employee during working hours to have the employee available for emergency calls during the meal period. It must be shown that emergencies have actually occurred, or can reasonably be expected to occur, which have resulted or can expect to result in the employee being called to work during the meal period. [Treas Reg § 1.119-1(a)(2)(ii)(a)]

   An example is given of a hospital that maintains a cafeteria on its premises for the hospital staff during their working hours. Each employee is at times called upon to work during the meal period. The employer does not require the employees to remain on the premises during meal periods, but they rarely leave. The meals are considered provided for the convenience of the employer, and the value of the meals is excluded from the employee's federal gross income. [Treas Reg § 1.119-1(f), Example (9)]

2. The meals are furnished to the employee during working hours because the employer's business requires that the employee must be restricted to a short meal period, such as 30 or 45 minutes, and the employee could not be expected to eat elsewhere in such a short meal period. Meals can qualify under this rule if the employer's peak work load occurs during the normal lunch hours. [Treas Reg § 1.119-1(a)(2)(ii)(b)]

   An example is given of a teller working in a bank in which the peak work load occurs during normal lunch hours, who is given only 30 minutes for lunch. [Treas Reg § 1.119-1(f), Example (3)]

3. The meals are furnished to the employee during working hours because the employee could not otherwise secure proper meals within a reasonable meal period, as, for example, because there are insufficient eating facilities in the vicinity of the employer's premises. [Treas Reg § 1.119-1(a)(2)(ii)(c)]

4. While a meal furnished before or after working hours generally will not qualify for exclusion from income, an exception is made for restaurant and food service employees. In the case of restaurant and food service employees, a meal furnished during, immediately before, or immediately after the working hours of the employee will be regarded as furnished for a substantial noncompensatory business reason of the employer. [Treas Reg §§ 1.119-1(a)(2)(i), 1.119-1(a)(2)(ii)(d)] However, a

meal given to a restaurant worker or food service employee on the employee's day off would not qualify for exclusion from income. [Treas Reg § 1.119-1(f), Example (2)]

5. If substantially all the meals for employees who are furnished meals satisfy the convenience of the employer test, meals furnished to other employees will be considered to satisfy this test also. [Treas Reg § 1.119-1(a)(2)(ii)(e)]

6. If the employer would have furnished a meal during working hours for a substantial noncompensatory reason, but the employee's duties prevented him or her from eating during working hours, a meal served immediately after working hours would qualify for exclusion from the employee's gross income. [Treas Reg § 1.119-1(a)(2)(ii)(f)]

Q 13:109 When will meals be considered to be furnished for a compensatory business reason?

Meals will be regarded as furnished for a compensatory business reason when the meals are provided for one of the following reasons:

1. To promote the morale or good will of the employee, or

2. To attract prospective employees.

[Treas Reg § 1.119-1(a)(2)(iii)]

Q 13:110 When are meals furnished with a charge considered to be provided for the convenience of the employer?

If the employer provides meals for which a charge is made by the employer, and the employee is given a choice of accepting the meals and paying for them or of not paying for them and providing his or her meals in another manner, the meals will not be considered as provided for the convenience of the employer.

However, if an employee is charged an unvarying amount irrespective of whether he or she accepts the meals, the amount of the flat charge itself is not includable in the employee's compensation and the value of the meal is excludable if the meal is provided for the convenience of the employer (using the same rules applied to meals provided without a charge).

If the meals furnished for a flat charge do not meet the convenience of the employer test, the employee is required to include the value of the meals in income regardless of whether the value exceeds or is less than the amount charged for the meals. However, the value of the meals may be deemed to be equal to the amount charged for them, in the absence of evidence to the contrary. [Treas Reg § 1.119-1(a)(3)]

> **Planning Pointer.** It appears that if the value of the meals exceeds the amount charged for them, in some cases the employer-operated eating facilities rules under the fringe benefit rules of Code Section 132 may make the excess amount a nontaxable *de minimis* fringe benefit (see Qs 13:70-13:75).

Q 13:111 When is an employee considered to accept lodging as a condition of employment?

The requirement that the employee must accept the lodging as a condition of employment means that the employee is required to accept the lodging in order to perform the duties of his or her employment properly. For example, lodging is considered accepted as a condition of employment if the lodging is furnished because the employee is required to be available for duty at all times, or because the employee could not perform the services required unless furnished with lodging. [Treas Reg § 1.119-1(b)]

If the three requirements for the lodging exclusion are met (see Q 13:101), the exclusion applies irrespective of whether a charge is made, and irrespective of whether the lodging is furnished as compensation under an employment contract or statute fixing the terms of employment. [IRC § 119(b)(1); Treas Reg § 1.119-1(b)]

Q 13:112 What is the tax treatment if the employee is charged a flat amount for the lodging?

If the employer furnishes the employee lodging for which the employee is charged an unchanging amount irrespective of whether the employee accepts the lodging, the amount charged is not, as such, includable in gross income. In addition, if the three-part test for the lodging exclusion is satisfied (see Q 13:101), the value of the lodging is also excludable from the employee's federal gross income.

If the test for exclusion is not met, the value of the lodging is includable in the employee's federal gross income, regardless of whether it exceeds or is less than the amount charged. In the absence of evidence to the contrary, the value of the lodging can be deemed to be equal to the amount charged. [Treas Reg § 1.119-1(b)]

However, see the special statutory exception in the case of employees of educational institutions who are provided with "qualified campus lodging" (see Qs 13:113–13:116).

Q 13:113 What special treatment applies to lodging provided to employees of educational institutions?

If the lodging provided to an employee of an educational institution does not qualify for exclusion under the three-part test of Code Section 119 (see Q 13:101), it may qualify for exclusion in whole or in part as "qualified campus lodging." [IRC § 119(d)]

Q 13:114 What institutions are considered educational institutions for this purpose?

An educational institution for this purpose is defined as one which normally maintains a regular faculty and curriculum and normally has a regularly enrolled body of pupils or students in attendance at the place where its educational activities are regularly carried on. [IRC §§ 119(d)(4), 170(b)(1)(A)(ii)]

Q 13:115 What lodging is considered to be "qualified campus lodging"?

"Qualified campus lodging" is lodging which does not meet the general three-part test for exclusion and which is:

1. Located on or in the proximity of a campus of the educational institution, and

2. Furnished to the employee, his or her spouse, and any of his or her dependents by or on behalf of the educational institution for use as a residence.

[IRC § 119(d)(3)]

Q 13:116 Is the exclusion for qualified campus housing unlimited?

No. The exclusion does not apply to the extent that the employee pays an inadequate rent. The amount in excess of:

1. The lesser of:

   a. Five percent of the appraised value of the qualified campus housing, or

   b. The average of the rentals paid by persons other than employees or students during the calendar year for comparable lodging provided by the educational institution, over

2. The rent paid by the employee for the qualified housing during the calendar year

is includible in the employee's income.

[IRC § 119(d)(2)]

For example, assuming that the 5-percent-of-appraised-value limitation applies, this means that if the rent paid by the employee for qualified campus lodging equals or exceeds 5 percent of appraised value, no amount is includible in the employee's gross income, even if the fair rental value is greater than the rental payments made. However, if the rent payments in such a case are less than 5 percent of the appraised value of the qualified campus housing, the difference is includable in the employee's gross income.

Q 13:117   Is the value of meals and lodging furnished to employees subject to income tax withholding and to Social Security (FICA) and federal unemployment (FUTA) taxes?

To the extent that the amounts are excluded from gross income under Code Section 119, they are not subject to income tax withholding or to FICA and FUTA taxes. On the other hand, the value of meals and lodging that is not excludable under Code Section 119 is subject to income tax withholding and to FICA and FUTA taxation. [IRC §§ 3401(a), 3121(a)(19), 3306(b)(14); Treas Reg § 31.3401(a)-1(b)(9)]

Employee Gifts and Achievement Awards

Q 13:118   If an employer makes a gift to an employee in cash or in property, how is the gift treated by the employee for federal income tax purposes?

While a gift generally is not subject to federal income tax, the IRC contains a specific exception to the general rule. The Code provides that, in general, any amount transferred by, or for the benefit of, an employer to, or for the benefit of, an employee is not to be excluded from gross income, even though it constitutes a gift for tax purposes. [IRC § 102(c)(1)]

There are two specific limited exceptions to the rule that employee gifts are includable in gross income. They are (1) employee achievement awards and (2) *de minimis* fringe benefits.

[IRC § 102(c)(2)]

Q 13:119   What is an employee achievement award?

The term "employee achievement award" means an item of tangible personal property which is:

1. Transferred by the employer to an employee for length-of-service achievement or safety achievement;
2. Awarded as part of a meaningful presentation; and

3. Awarded under conditions and circumstances that do not create a significant likelihood of the payment of disguised compensation.

[IRC § 274(j)(3)(A)]

Q 13:120   What is not considered tangible personal property for purposes of the employee achievement award rules?

Tangible personal property obviously does not include cash. It also does not include a certificate, other than a nonnegotiable certificate conferring only the right to receive tangible personal property. Also excluded are vacations, meals, lodging, tickets to theatrical and sporting events, and stocks, bonds, and other securities. [Prop Treas Reg § 1.274-8(c)(2)]

Q 13:121   What is a meaningful presentation?

Whether an employee achievement award is presented in a meaningful presentation is determined by a facts and circumstances test. The presentation need not be elaborate, but it must be a ceremonious observance emphasizing the recipient's achievements in the area of safety or length of service. [Prop Treas Reg § 1.274-8(c)(3)]

Q 13:122   When will an award be considered payment of disguised compensation?

An award will be considered disguised compensation, disqualifying the award as an employee achievement award, if the conditions and circumstances surrounding the award create a significant likelihood that it is payment of compensation. Examples include the following:

- Making the awards at the time of annual salary adjustments
- Making the awards as a substitute for a prior program of cash bonuses
- Providing the awards in a manner that discriminates in favor of the highly compensated, or

- Where the fully deductible cost to the employer is grossly disproportionate to the fair market value of the item

[Prop Treas Reg § 1.274-8(c)(4)]

Q 13:123   What qualifies as a length-of-service award?

An award does not qualify as a length-of-service award if it is presented for less than five years employment with the employer or if the award recipient has already received a length-of-service award during the same year or in any of the four prior calendar years (other than an award that qualified as a *de minimis* fringe benefit under Code Section 132(e)(1)).

An award presented upon the occasion of a recipient's retirement is a length-of-service award. However, in some circumstances, a traditional retirement award can be treated as a *de minimis* fringe benefit under Code Section 132(e)(1). [IRC § 274(j)(4)(B); Prop Treas Reg § 1.274-8(d)(2)]

Q 13:124   What qualifies as a safety achievement award?

An award will not be treated as an award for safety achievement if awards for safety achievement (other than awards qualifying as *de minimis* fringe benefits) during the same year have previously been awarded to more than 10 percent of the eligible employees, or if the award is to a noneligible employee—that is, a manager, administrator, clerical employee, or other professional employee. An eligible employee must have worked full time for the employer for at least one year before the safety achievement award is presented. [IRC § 274(j)(4)(C); Prop Treas Reg § 1.274-8(d)(3)]

Q 13:125   May the employer deduct the cost of an employee achievement award?

Yes, to a limited extent. The deduction limit varies depending upon whether the employee achievement award is or is not a qualified plan award (see Q 13:126), as follows:

1. If the award is not a qualified plan award, the deductible cost of the award, when added to the cost of all other employee achievement awards that are not qualified plan awards and that are made in the same taxable year to the employee, may not exceed $400;

2. If the award is a qualified plan award, the deductible cost of the award, when added to the cost of all other employee achievement awards (both qualified plan awards and those not qualified) made to the employee in the same taxable year, must not exceed $1,600.

[IRC § 274(j)(2); Prop Treas Reg § 1.274-8(b)]

Q 13:126   What is a qualified plan award?

A qualified plan award is an employee achievement award that is presented pursuant to an established written plan or program that does not discriminate in terms of eligibility or benefits in favor of highly compensated employees. The following conditions apply:

1. The definition of highly compensated employees in Section 414(q) of the Code is used for this purpose.

2. Whether an award plan is established is determined from all the facts and circumstances of the case, including the frequency and timing of changes to the plan.

3. Whether the award plan is discriminatory is determined from all the facts and circumstances of the case, and a plan may be found discriminatory in operation even though the written terms of the plan are nondiscriminatory.

Even if a nondiscriminatory written plan exists, no award presented by the employer in a taxable year will be considered a qualified plan award if the average cost of all employee achievement awards during the taxable year under any qualified plan exceeds $400. The average cost is determined by dividing (1) the sum of the costs of all employee achievement awards (without regard to the deductibility of the costs) by (2) the total number of employee achievement awards presented.

In determining the average cost, employee achievement awards of nominal value ($50 or less) are not taken into account.

[IRC § 274(j)(3)(B); Prop Treas Reg § 1.274-8(c)(5)]

Q 13:127 Is an employee required to include the value of an employee achievement award in gross income?

An employee is not required to include in gross income the value of an employee achievement award he or she receives if the cost to the employer does not exceed the amount allowable as a deduction to the employer for the cost of the employee achievement award (see Qs 13:125, 13:126).

If the cost to the employer of the employee achievement award is allowable as a deduction only in part, the employee must include in gross income the greater of:

1. An amount equal to the portion of the employer's cost that is not allowable as a deduction (but not in excess of the value of the award); or
2. The amount by which the value of the award exceeds the amount allowable as a deduction to the employer.

[IRC § 74(c)(2); Prop Treas Reg §§ 1.74-2(a), 1.74-2(b)]

If a tax-exempt employer is involved, the amount deductible is determined as if the employer were taxable. [IRC § 74(c)(3); Prop Treas Reg § 1.74-2(d)(2)]

Example. The employer gives an employee achievement award costing $425 and having a fair market value of $475. Assuming the deductible limit of $400 applies, the employee would have gross income of $75, since the fair market value exceeds the cost to the employer. [Prop Treas Reg § 1.74-2(c), Example (3)]

Q 13:128 How do the employee achievement award rules apply to partnerships and sole proprietorships?

In applying the deduction limitations of Code Section 274(j)(2) to employee achievement awards made by a partnership, the limitations apply to the partnership as well as to each member of the partnership. [IRC § 274(j)(4)(A); Prop Treas Reg § 274-8(d)(1)]

In applying the deduction rules of Code Section 274(j) and the exclusion from gross income rules of Code Section 74(c), any award made by a sole proprietorship to the sole proprietor will not be treated as an employee achievement award. [Prop Treas Reg §§ 1.274-8(c)(1), 1.74-2(d)(1)]

Planning Pointer. Since the proposed regulations bar only sole proprietorships from qualifying for the exclusion, it appears that a partner in a partnership could receive an employee achievement award qualifying for full or partial exclusion from gross income under Code Section 74(c).

Q 13:129 Is an employee achievement award that exceeds the excludable amount under Code Section 74(c) always taxable?

While employee achievement awards in excess of the excludable limits of Code Section 74(c) generally are subject to income tax (see Q 13:127), in very limited circumstances the excess may be eligible for exclusion on the basis that it is a *de minimis* fringe benefit under Code Section 132(e)(1). [Prop. Treas Reg § 1.74-2(e)] (See Qs 13:66 through 13:69 for a discussion of *de minimis* fringe benefits.)

Q 13:130 Is an employee achievement award received by an employee subject to income tax withholding and to Social Security (FICA) and federal unemployment tax (FUTA)?

To the extent that the employee achievement award is excludable from gross income under Code Section 74(c), it is not subject to income tax withholding, nor to FICA and FUTA. However, to the extent the award is includable in gross income, income tax withholding and FICA and FUTA are applicable. [IRC §§ 3401(a)(19), 3121(a)(20), 3306(b)(16)]

Chapter 14

Vacation and Severance Pay Plans

Vacation and severance pay benefit packages can raise troublesome issues relating to the Employee Retirement Income Security Act of 1974 (ERISA). In addition, "golden parachute" plans, a type of severance pay plan, can be subject to onerous income tax rules. This chapter reviews these areas.

Vacation Pay Plans

Q 14:1   What is a vacation pay plan?

A vacation pay plan is an employer plan that provides compensation payments to employees for specified periods of vacation, including payments for vacation time that has been earned but not actually taken. Such a plan also generally includes compensation for specified holidays, whether or not those days are actually taken off. Vacation pay plans, like other employee benefit plans, can take a wide variety of forms; the benefits may be vested or unvested, the plan may be funded or unfunded, and the plan may be a single-employer plan or a multiemployer plan.

Q 14:2   Are funded vacation pay plans subject to ERISA?

Yes, they are. The ERISA definition of an employee welfare benefit plan lists vacation benefits as one of the types of benefits such a plan provides (see Q 2:5). [ERISA § 3(1)] In addition, the U.S. Supreme Court has held that a funded vacation pay plan is an ERISA welfare benefit plan. [Mackey v Lanier Collection & Agency Serv Inc, 108 S Ct 2182 (1988)] ERISA's definition of an employee welfare benefit plan also incorporates, by reference, the benefits listed in Section 302(c) of the Labor Management Relations Act of 1947, which includes funded vacation benefits. [ERISA § 3(1); DOL Adv Op No 79-89A (Dec 26, 1979)]

Q 14:3   Are unfunded vacation pay plans subject to ERISA?

No. Most vacation pay plans are unfunded and are paid out of the employer's general assets. Department of Labor (DOL) regulations take the position that payments for vacation and holidays made from an employer's general assets do not constitute an employee welfare benefit plan, but merely a "payroll practice," and thus are not subject to ERISA. [DOL Reg § 2510.3-1(b)(3)(i)] The U.S. Supreme Court has upheld this regulation as a correct interpretation of the law. [Massachusetts v Morash, 109 S Ct 1668 (1989)] A California court has held that an unfunded vacation pay plan is not an ERISA plan. [Millard v Restaurant Enterprises Group, Inc, 16 EBC (BNA) 1951 (Cal Ct App 4th, 1993)]

Q 14:4   Are vacation pay plans subject to state laws?

The answer depends on whether the vacation pay plan is an ERISA plan. If the vacation pay plan is subject to ERISA, that is, funded (see Qs 14:2, 14:3), and the state law or regulation "relates to" the plan, ERISA generally preempts the state law or regulation, and the vacation pay plan is not subject to the state law or regulation. However, the U.S. Supreme Court has held that ERISA does not preempt state laws relating to garnishment of vacation benefits provided through a welfare benefit plan, because there is no parallel provision to ERISA Section 206 (which prohibits assignment or alienation of pension benefits) for ERISA welfare benefit plans. [Mackey v. Lanier Collection Agency & Service, Inc., 108 S Ct 2182 (1988)] (See Chapter 2 for a discussion of ERISA preemption.)

Q 14:5   Is vacation pay taxable income to employees?

Yes, it is. Vacation pay is taxable and is subject to income tax wage withholding. [IRC § 61; Treas. Reg. § 31.3401(a)-(1)(b)(3)] Vacation pay is also subject to Social Security (FICA), and Federal Unemployment (FUTA) taxes. [IRC §§ 3121(a), 3306(b)]

Q 14:6   May the employer deduct vacation pay expense?

Yes, it may. Vacation pay is generally deductible as reasonable compensation for prior services rendered. [IRC § 162; Treas Reg § 1.162-10] However, special rules apply to accrual-basis employers.

Q 14:7   When may an accrual-basis employer deduct vacation pay?

An accrual-basis taxpayer can generally deduct for a taxable year only (1) vacation pay paid in that taxable year plus (2) vacation pay (a) earned and vested in that taxable year and (b) paid within 2½ months after the close of the taxable year. [IRC §§ 461(h), 404(a)(5); Prop Treas Reg § 1.461-4(d)(6), Ex 1; Temp Treas Reg § 1.404(b)-1T, Q&A 2]

Severance Pay Plans

Q 14:8   What is a severance pay plan?

A severance pay plan is a plan that provides payments to employees upon termination of employment. Generally, the payments are proportionate to length of employment.

The plan may be a permanent program or a limited program (for example, an "open-window" program that offers a group of employees cash payments, increased pension benefits, or both as inducements to voluntarily retire or to separate from employment within a certain time period).

The plan may cover voluntary separations, involuntary separations, or both, and may place conditions on payment of benefits (for example, no benefits are provided if the employee goes to work for a competitor). In addition, the plan may deny benefits if the employee is terminated for cause, that is, it may include a "bad-boy" provision.

Q 14:9   Are funded severance pay plans considered employee benefit plans subject to ERISA?

Yes, funded severance pay plans are clearly subject to ERISA's definition of employee welfare benefit plans to which include plans providing benefits in the event of unemployment (see Q 2:5). [ERISA § 3(1)]

Q 14:10   Are unfunded severance pay plans subject to ERISA?

Yes, they are. For a time, some employers took the position that an unfunded severance pay plan, particularly one that was maintained on an informal basis, was a payroll practice or fringe benefit, and therefore not an ERISA plan (see Q 2:5). However, in recent years, a number of federal appellate courts have decided that unfunded severance pay plans do constitute ERISA plans, even if they are not established with all the formalities of other welfare plans. [Gilbert v Burlington Indust, Inc, 765 F 2d 320 (2d Cir 1985); Holland v Burlington Indust, Inc, 772 F 2d 1140 (4th Cir 1985); Blau v Del Monte Corp, 748 F 2d 1348 (9th Cir. 1985) cert denied 474 N.S. 865 1985)] The issue has been resolved by the U.S. Supreme Court, which has stated that an unfunded severance pay plan is an ERISA plan. [Firestone Tire and Rubber Co v Bruch, 109 S Ct 948 (1989)]

However, a voluntary separation plan under which the employee received a one-time lump-sum payment was held not to be an ERISA plan because there were no continuing payments and thus no need for continuing administration. [Wells v General Motors Corp, 881 F 2d 1661 (5th Cir 1989), *cert denied* 110 S Ct 1959 (1990)]

Planning Pointer. It appears prudent for an employer to treat an unfunded severance pay program as an ERISA plan and to comply with all ERISA requirements, such as a formal written plan document, summary plan description, and the like.

Additional case law concerning when a "plan" exists for ERISA purposes is discussed in Chapter 2.

Q 14:11   Do ad hoc severance payments or internal policies providing severance benefits constitute severance pay plans that are subject to ERISA?

Yes, either of these could constitute an ERISA plan, depending on the facts and circumstances. [Blau v Del Monte Corp., 748 F 2d 1348 *(9th Cir 1985), cert denied* 474 US 865 (1985); Petrella v NL Indust, Inc, 529 F Supp 1357 (DNJ 1982)]

Q 14:12   What if the severance policy has never been communicated to employees?

Keeping a severance policy secret will not keep it from possibly being an ERISA plan. No formal, written plan is required for a plan to be subject to ERISA. ERISA covers a welfare benefit plan if it is established or maintained by an employer or an employee organization, or both, that are engaged in any activities or in any industry that affects commerce. [ERISA § 4(a)] If ERISA covers the plan, then ERISA requires that it be established pursuant to a written instrument, but that is the responsibility of the plan administrator and plan fiduciaries rather than a prerequisite to coverage under ERISA. [Blau v Del Monte Corp, 748 F 2d 1348 (9th Cir 1985), *cert denied* 474 US 865 (1985)]

Q 14:13   Are individual contractual arrangements with executives for severance benefits a severance pay plan subject to ERISA?

Yes, such contractual arrangements could possibly constitute an ERISA plan. At least one court has held that a series of individual executive employment contracts providing "golden parachute" payments upon a change in control constitutes an ERISA severance pay plan. [Purser v Enron Corp, 10 EBC 1561

(WD Pa 1988)] See Questions 14:27 to 14:21 for a discussion of golden parachute provisions.

Q 14:14   Do individual employment arrangements with executives constitute a plan subject to ERISA?

It appears that an individual employment contract, or selected portions thereof, might be considered an ERISA plan. This is a developing area of the law. Previously, courts generally have taken the position that individual employment agreements are not ERISA plans. [See Lackey v Whitehall Corp, 704 F Supp 201 (D Kan 1988); McQueen v Salida Coca-Cola Bottling Co, 652 F Supp 1471 (D Colo 1987)] However, at least one court has held that a series of individual executive employment contracts providing "golden parachute" payments upon a change in control constitutes an ERISA severance pay plan. [Purser v Enron Corp, 10 EBC 1561 (WD Pa 1988)] More recently, in DOL Advisory Opinion 91-02A (July 2, 1991), the DOL considered a severance arrangement entered into by an employer as consideration for an individual's acceptance of employment as general counsel and the accompanying move across country. Even though the severance arrangement covered only one individual, the DOL found it to be a severance pay plan governed by ERISA.

Q 14:15   Under ERISA, is a severance pay plan considered a welfare benefit plan or a pension plan?

Generally, the DOL views a severance pay plan as a welfare benefit plan, not a pension plan, provided the severance pay plan meets the following requirements:

1. Payments are not contingent, directly or indirectly, upon the employee's retirement;

2. The total amount of the payments does not exceed the equivalent of twice the employee's annual compensation in the year preceding the termination; and

3. Payments are completed by these deadlines:

(a) In the case of an open-window plan (see Q 10:8), within 24 months after the later of termination or normal retirement age, and

(b) In all other cases, within 24 months after termination.

[DOL Reg § 2510.3-2(b)]

Planning Pointer In view of the more onerous ERISA requirements that attach to a pension plan (compared to a welfare benefit plan), strict compliance with the conditions in the DOL regulation is advisable.

Q 14.16 May an employer-provided severance pay plan provide that the amount of severance pay will be determined on a case-by-case basis?

Evidently, yes it may. The U.S. Court of Appeals for the Third Circuit held that, as long as the plan explicitly states such a limitation, nothing in ERISA prevents an employer from providing its employees with benefits on a case-by-case basis. Accordingly, while the employer was barred from correcting, one day before the employee was terminated, a printer's error accidently listing more generous severance pay benefits than it had intended to offer, the employee's reduced benefit was nontheless upheld on the basis of the express statement in the plan that the employer reserved the right to determine benefits on a case-by-case basis. [Hamilton v Air Jamaica, Ltd, 945 F 2d 74 (3rd Cir 1991)]

Q 14:17 How does the Age Discrimination in Employment Act (ADEA) regulate the content of severance pay plans?

The Older Workers Benefits Protection Act of 1990 (OWBPA) amended the federal Age Discrimination in Employment Act of 1967 (ADEA) to add substantive regulation of severance programs as follows:

1. Reduction of severance pay by certain other benefits is prohibited, with limited exceptions, and

2. A waiver of ADEA claims that is required to be executed as a condition of receipt of severance benefits must be "knowing and voluntary"

The statute contains certain minimum conditions that a waiver of ADEA claims must meet in order for it to be treated as knowing and voluntary. (See Qs 14:18 to 14:21.)

Q 14:18 Can an employer subject to the ADEA reduce or deny severance pay if an employee is eligible for, or receives, retirement benefits?

The ADEA, as amended by the OWBPA, prohibits an employer from reducing or eliminating severance pay solely because the employee is eligible for retirement benefits or will receive retirement benefits. However, the statute contains a limited exception: If severance pay is payable as a result of a contingent event that is not related to the employee's age (for example, a plant closing or layoff), the severance pay can be reduced by "pension sweeteners" (that is, additional pension benefits that are payable solely as a result of the contingent event) if the individual is eligible for an immediate and unreduced pension. [ADEA § 4(1)(2)(A)(ii), 29 USCA § 623(1)(2)(A)(ii) (Supp 1992)]

For purposes of this exception, severance pay includes Code Section 501(c)(17) supplemental unemployment benefits, which may extend to 52 weeks. Their primary purpose and effect is to continue benefits until the individual becomes eligible for an immediate and unreduced pension, whereupon they cease. [ADEA § 4(1)(2)(C), 29 USCA § 623(1)(2)(C) (Supp 1992)]

Q 14.19 Can an employer subject to the ADEA reduce or deny severance pay if an employee is eligible for, or receives, retiree health benefits?

The ADEA, as amended by the OWBPA, prohibits an employer from reducing or eliminating severance pay solely because the employee is eligible for retiree health benefits or will receive retiree health benefits. However, the statute contains a limited exception: If severance pay is payable as a result of a contingent event that is not related to the employee's age (for example, a plant closing or layoff), the severance pay can be reduced by the value of retiree health benefits under certain limited circumstances. These include:

1. The employee must be eligible for an immediate pension;
2. If the employee receives actuarially reduced pension benefits, the value of retiree health benefits that may be subtracted from severance pay must be reduced by the same percentage as the percentage reduction in pension benefits; and
3. The retiree health benefits must have a certain minimum value in order to be subtracted from severance pay.

[ADEA § 4(1)(2), 29 USCA § 623(1)(2) (Supp 1992)]

Minimum Required Retiree Health Benefits. For retiree health benefits to be a permitted reduction of severance pay payable as a result of a contingent event unrelated to the employee's age, one of the following conditions must apply:

1. Retiree health benefits for retirees under age 65 must be at least "comparable" to Medicare benefits under Title XVIII of the Social Security Act; or
2. Retiree health benefits for retirees age 65 and above must be "comparable" to 25 percent of Medicare benefits under Title XVIII of the Social Security Act.

The ADEA directs that if the employer's obligation to provide retiree health benefits is of limited duration, the value of each individual's benefit is to be calculated at a rate of $3,000 per year for benefit years before age 65 and $750 per year for benefit years beginning at age 65 and above. However, if the employer's obligation to provide retiree health benefits is of unlimited duration, the value for each individual is to be calculated at a rate of $48,000 for individuals below age 65 and $24,000 for individuals aged 65 and above. The age of the individual used for this purpose is his or her age on the date of the contingent event. The above dollar amounts are to be indexed based upon the dollar value of the medical component of the DOL's urban consumer price index. If the retiree health benefits are contributory, the above limits will be reduced by the percentage that the individual is required to pay. [ADEA § 4(1)(2), 29 USCA § 623(1)(2) (Supp 1992)]

Future Liability of Employer. If the employer has reduced severance pay that is payable due to a contingent event unrelated to age by the permitted value of retiree health benefits, the employer will be subject to an action for specific performance by any "aggrieved individual" if it subsequently fails to fulfill its obligation to provide retiree health benefits. [ADEA § 4(1)(2), 29 USCA § 623(1)(2) (Supp 1992)]

Q 14:20   Can an employer subject to the ADEA reduce severance pay by the value of pension benefits and retiree health benefits?

Yes, in the case of a contingent event unrelated to age, such as a plant closing or layoff, an employer may reduce the amount of severance pay by the value of certain "pension sweeteners," or certain retiree health benefits, or both (see Qs 14.18 and 14:19). [ADEA § 4(1)(2), 29 USCA § 623(1)(2) (Supp 1992)]

Q 14:21   Can an employer subject to the ADEA require an individual to sign a waiver as a condition of receiving severance benefits?

Yes, under very limited circumstances: A waiver made on or after October 16, 1990, must be "knowing and voluntary." The ADEA as amended by OWBPA sets forth certain minimum requirements for a waiver to be treated as knowing and voluntary:

1. The waiver must be part of a written agreement between the individual and the employer that is written in a manner calculated to be understood by the individual, or by the average individual eligible to participate;

2. The waiver must specifically refer to rights to claims that may arise under the ADEA;

3. The individual does not waive rights or claims that may arise after the date the waiver is executed;

4. The individual waives rights or claims only in exchange for cash or other consideration in addition to anything of value to which the individual is already entitled;

5. The individual is advised in writing to consult with an attorney prior to executing the agreement;

6. The individual is given a period of at least 21 days (45 days in the case of an exit incentive or other employment termination program offered to a group or class of employees) to consider the agreement;

7. The agreement provides that, for a period of at least seven days after the date it is executed, the individual may revoke it and the agreement will not become effective or enforceable until the seven-day period has expired; and

8. If the waiver is requested in connection with an exit incentive or other employment termination program offered to a group or class of employees, the employer must satisfy additional statutory disclosure requirements (see Q 16:38).

[ADEA § 7(f)(1), 29 USCA § 626(f)(1) (Supp 1992)]

Q 14:22   Must an employer provide severance pay if the former employee becomes employed by a successor employer?

It depends on the terms of the plan. If the severance plan clearly provides that no severance benefits are payable if the former employee goes to work for a successor employer, the plan provisions generally will be given effect. However, if the plan is silent or ambiguous as to whether severance benefits are payable when an employee goes to work for a successor employer, severance benefits may have to to be paid. [Barnett v Petro-Tex Chem Corp, 893 F 2d 800 (5th Cir 1990); Flick v Borg-Warner Corp, 892 F 2d 285 (3rd Cir 1989)]

In one case, the U.S. Court of Appeals for the First Circuit examined a written severance pay plan that provided benefits in the event of termination due to "lack of work." The employer in question had orally advised several employees that they would not receive severance pay if they continued in employment with an acquiring employer. The transferred employees, who did not miss a day of work, sued for severance pay under the former employer's plan and won. The appellate court refused to recognize as valid an attempted oral modification to the former employer's severance pay plan and construed the written plan liberally in favor of the employees. [Bellino v Schlumberger Technologies, Inc, 944 F 2d 26 (1st Cir 1991)] In contrast, the U.S. Court of Appeals for the Second Circuit upheld an employer's right to amend an ERISA severance plan to deny severance benefits to employees who would retain their positions in a division that was to be sold as a going concern. The appellate court expressly noted that nothing in ERISA creates a continuing obligation on the part of the employer to provide severance benefits and that, as welfare benefits, they do not become vested. Accordingly, the employer has the right at any time to amend or terminate a severance pay plan. [Reichelt v Emhart Corp, 921 F 2d 425 (2d Cir 1990)]

> **Planning Pointer**: In view of the above decisions, as well as numerous other decisions concerning whether an acquiring employer is obligated to pay severance benefits to employees who continue to work for a successor employer, an employer wishing to deny severance payments in such situations should adopt a formal plan setting out precisely what rules govern payment or nonpayment of severance benefits, particularly in the case of acquisitions or divestitures.

Q 14:23 Will an acquiring employer be required to give severance benefits based upon years of service with a prior employer?

At least one court, the U.S. Court of Appeals for the Eighth Circuit, has held that an employer's calculation of severance pay benefits must credit years of service with a prior employer, where the acquiring employer's severance pay plan did not define "service." [Jacobs v Pickands Mather & Co, 933 F 2d 652 (8th Cir 1991)]

> **Planning Pointer**. In addition to having a written severance pay plan, the employer will want to consider how its benefit formula will work under various scenarios and then add appropriate exclusions and clarifications. In addition, the prior service question could arise in another context: It is important for the acquiring employer to examine, before to signing the acquisition agreement,

its provisions relating to employee benefit plans to determine whether the acquiring employer will be bound to offer the same or comparable benefits to the acquired employees.

Q 14:24   What if state law mandates that employers provide severance pay?

It appears that state laws purporting to require employers to establish and maintain ongoing severance pay plans are preempted by ERISA. [Brunner v Sun Refining & Marketing Co, 86 C 20272 (ND Ill 1989)] However, a one-shot severance pay requirement is not preempted. [Fort Halifax Packing Co v Coyne, 482 US 1 (1987)]

Q 14:25   Is severance pay taxable income to the recipient?

Yes, severance pay is taxable and is subject to wage withholding. [IRC §§ 61, 3401; Treas Reg § 340l(a)-l(b)(4)] Severance pay is also subject to FICA and FUTA taxes. [IRC §§ 3121(a), 3306(b)]

Note. The tax treatment of settlements and judgments in employment termination lawsuits is beyond the scope of this book. For an excellent discussion, see C. K. Combe, *Employment Law Disputes: Law and Strategies for Representing the Employer* (Butterworth, 1993).

Q 14:26   May the employer deduct severance pay expense?

Yes, it may. Severance pay is generally deductible as reasonable compensation for prior services rendered. [IRC § 162; Treas Reg § 1.162-10]

"Golden Parachute" Payments

Q 14:27   What is a "golden parachute" agreement?

In a "golden parachute" agreement a corporate employer states that it will pay a key employee or a number of key employees an amount over and above other compensation in the event of a change in ownership or control of the corporation or in a substantial portion of the corporation's assets. A golden parachute agreement or arrangement generally is intended to serve two purposes: (1) to frighten off attempted hostile acquisition of the employer by an outside party, and (2) to provide a special layer of severance pay for managers and executives whose employment would be terminated following such an acquisition. It is important to note that the tax consequences applicable to golden parachute payments are triggered merely by the payment of the requisite amount of compensation, and a termination of employment is not literally required. As a practical matter, however, golden parachute payment provisions in an employment agreement or employer's benefit plan usually are designed to be triggered upon loss of employment within a designated period of time following the acquisition of the employer.

Q 14:28   Is a golden parachute agreement subject to ERISA?

One U.S. district court has held that a series of individual executive employment contracts providing for golden parachute payments upon a change in control constituted an ERISA severance pay plan. [Purser v Enron Corp, 10 EBC 1561 (WD Pa 1988)] However, if the arrangement is unfunded and clearly restricted to providing benefits for a select group of management or highly compensated employees only, the arrangement should be exempt from virtually all of the reporting and disclosure requirements of ERISA (see SQs 2:2.8, 2:9).

Q 14:29   Do golden parachute payments receive special federal income tax treatment?

Yes. To the extent the amount of the golden parachute payments (called "parachute payments") is deemed to be excessive (called "excess parachute payments"), there are adverse tax consequences to both the payer and the recipient of the excess parachute payments. The payor is denied a deduction for the excess parachute payments, and the recipient is subject to an excise tax of 20 percent of the amount of the excess parachute payment. [IRC §§ 280G, 4999]

A golden parachute payment was held not to be subject to these adverse tax provisions when the employment agreement was entered into before June 15, 1984, the effective date of these tax provisions, and the employment agreement was not renewed or amended in any significant way on or after that date. [Virgil L. Powell, 100 TC No. 6 (1993)]

Q 14:30 What is the federal income tax definition of a parachute payment?

The term "parachute payment" in general means any payment in the nature of compensation to or for the benefit of a "disqualified individual" (see Q 14:31) that:

- Is contingent on a change in the ownership or effective control of the corporation or in the ownership of a substantial portion of the corporation's assets; and

- Has an aggregate present value for all such payments to the disqualified individual of at least three times the individual's "base amount."

The term "parachute payment" also includes any payment in the nature of compensation to or for the benefit of a disqualified individual if the payment is made pursuant to an agreement that violates any generally enforced securities laws or regulations, whether state or federal. Special rules apply to such payments. [IRC § 280G(b)(2); Prop Treas Reg § 1.280G-1, Q&A 2]

Q 14:31 Who is a "disqualified individual"?

A "disqualified individual" is an employee, personal service corporation, or independent contractor performing services for the corporation, who is:

- A shareholder owning stock with a fair market value that exceeds the lesser of $1 million or 1 percent of the total fair market value of the outstanding stock of the corporation;

- An officer, limited to no more than 50 officers (or if less than 50 officers, the greater of three officers or 10 percent of the number of employees); or

- A highly compensated employee, that is, a member of the group consisting of the lesser of: (1) the highest paid 1 percent of the employees of the corporation, or (2) the highest paid 250 employees of the corporation, provided that the employee's annualized compensation is $75,000 or more.

[IRC § 280G(c); Prop Treas Reg § 1.280G-1, Q&As 15-21]

Q 14:32   Are there certain types of payments that are are not considered parachute payments?

Yes, the term "parachute payment" does not include:

- A payment with respect to a Subchapter S corporation;
- A payment with respect to a corporation whose stock is not readily tradable on an established security market or otherwise, and whose shareholders with more than 75 percent of the voting power of the corporate stock have approved the payment after full disclosure;
- A payment from a qualified plan (for example, pension, profit-sharing), including a simplified employee pension (SEP) plan; or
- A payment that the taxpayer can establish by clear and convincing evidence is reasonable compensation for personal services to be rendered by the disqualified individual on or after the date of the change of ownership or control.

[IRC §§ 280 G(b)(4), (5), (6); Prop Treas Reg § 1.280G-1, Q&As 5-9]

In Private Letter Ruling 93-14-034, the Internal Revenue Service considered the case of a bank merger in which the terminated employees received lump-sum payments conditioned upon the terminated employees' refraining from working for another bank in the same area for three years. The IRS held that the portion of the payments allocable to the "no-compete" requirement would be considered payment for services rendered after the date of the change of ownership or control, and thus would not be considered to be "excess parachute payments" subject to excise tax.

Q 14:33   Is the payer of the parachute payment necessarily the corporation for which the disqualified individual provides services?

No. The parachute payment may be paid directly or indirectly by the corporation, by the person acquiring ownership or effective control of the corporation or ownership of a substantial portion of the corporation's assets, or by any person whose relationship to the corporation or other person is such as to require attribution of stock ownership between the parties under Code Section 318(a). [Prop Treas Reg § 1.280G-1, Q&A 10]

Q 14:34   When is a payment contingent on a change in ownership or control?

In general, a payment is treated as contingent on a change in ownership or control if the payment would not have been made had no change in ownership or control taken place. If it is substantially certain, at the time of the change, that the payment would have been made whether or not the change occurred, the payment is not contingent.

However, a payment is treated as contingent in part on a change of ownership or control, even though it would have been made whether or not a change occurred, if the change accelerated the time of payment.

It is not necessary that the change result in termination of the disqualified individual's services for a payment to be considered contingent on the change. A payment made pursuant to an agreement or an amendment to an agreement entered into within a year of a change in ownership or control is presumed to be contingent on such change, unless there is clear and convincing evidence to the contrary. [IRC § 280G(2)(C); Prop Treas Reg § 1.280G-1, Q&As 22-26]

Q 14:35   What constitutes an "excess parachute payment," subject to a 20-percent excise tax imposed on the recipient and not deductible by the payer?

To constitute an "excess parachute payment," the total present value of the parachute payment to the disqualified individual must equal or exceed three times the individual's "base amount." The "base amount" for this purpose generally is the individual's average annual compensation from the corporation over the most recent five taxable years of the individual ending before the change in ownership or control, or the period of service for the corporation during the five-year period, if less. When the parachute payments are spread over more than one taxable year, the base amount is allocated based on the present value of each payment. [IRC §§ 280G(b)(2)(A)(ii), 280G(d)]

An excess parachute payment generally does not include any portion of the payment that the taxpayer establishes by clear and convincing evidence is reasonable compensation for personal services actually rendered by the disqualified individual before the date of the change in ownership or control. [IRC § 280G(b)(4); Prop Treas Reg § 1.280G-1, Q&As 3, 34, 35]

Q 14:36   When does a change in ownership of the corporation occur?

A change in ownership of the corporation occurs when any one person, or more than one person acting as a group, acquires stock ownership of more than 50 percent of the total fair market value or total voting power of the corporation's stock. [Prop Treas Reg § 1.280G-1, Q&A 27]

Q 14:37   When does a change in the effective control of the corporation occur?

A change in the effective control is presumed to occur on the date that either:

- Any one person, or more than one person acting as a group, acquires (or has acquired during the 12-month period preceding the most recent acquisition) ownership of stock possessing 20 percent or more of the total voting power of the corporate stock; or

- A majority of members of the board of directors is replaced during any 12-month period by directors whose appointment or election is not endorsed by a majority of the members of the prior board.

This presumption may be rebutted by a showing that there was not in fact a transfer of effective control. [Prop Treas Reg § 1.280G-1, Q&A 28]

Q 14:38 When does a change in the ownership of a substantial portion of the corporation's assets occur?

A change in the ownership of a substantial portion of the corporation's assets occurs on the date that any one person, or more than one person acting as a group, acquires (or has acquired within the 12-month period ending on the date of the most recent acquisition) assets from the corporation that have a total fair market value equal to or more than one-third of the total fair market value of all the assets of the corporation. [Prop Treas Reg § 1.280G-1, Q&A 29]

Q 14:39 Is the disqualified individual permitted to deduct the 20-percent excise tax he or she is required to pay on receipt of an excess parachute payment?

No, the 20-percent excise tax is not deductible on the individual's federal income tax return. [IRC § 275(a)(6)]

Q 14:40 Is the payment of an excess parachute payment to a disqualified individual subject to tax withholding?

If the disqualified individual is an employee, and not an independent contractor, an excess parachute payment is subject to income tax withholding and is also subject to withholding for the 20-percent excise tax. [IRC §§ 3401, 4999(c)(1)]

Q 14:41 Is the payment of an excess parachute payment subject to FICA and FUTA tax?

Yes, if paid to an employee. [IRC §§ 3121(a), 3121(v)(2), 3306(b)]

Chapter 15

Family and Medical Leave

This chapter covers the federal law requirements for family and medical leave under the Family and Medical Leave Act (FMLA) of 1993. It covers the details of the Act, including what is meant by "family leave" and "medical leave," under what conditions the leave must be granted, when it is discretionary, and when it can be denied; the length of required leave and whether it must be taken all at once or can be spread out; documentation requirements, and business necessity exceptions.

Basic Concepts

Q 15:1   What is the Family and Medical Leave Act of 1993?

The Family and Medical Leave Act of 1993 (FMLA) is a new federal law, signed into law by President Clinton on February 5, 1993, which will require many employers to permit their employees to take leaves of absence for up to 12 weeks in any 12-month period of employment for certain types of family or medical conditions or emergencies. [Pub Law 103-3, Feb 5, 1993, 107 Stat 6] The law is intended to allow employees to balance workplace and family needs by permitting them to attend to family emergencies and vital needs at home without being forced to quit their jobs. [29 CFR § 825.101]

Important. In evaluating their responsibilities to provide family or medical leave under the FMLA, employers must consult state law as well. This is because part or all of the leave might be considered to be an exempt "payroll practice" under the Employee Retirement Income Security Act (ERISA) rather than an ERISA-covered plan and, to the extent that exemption applies or the employer's family leave program fails to constitute an ERISA-covered plan, ERISA would not operate to preempt state laws requiring more generous family leave than is required under the FMLA. ERISA may possibly, however, preempt a state law requirement to extend ERISA-covered employee benefit plan coverage during periods of leave. See Chapter 2 for a discussion of ERISA's coverage and preemption provisions. (See also Q 15:34.)

Q 15:2   What is the effective date of the FMLA?

Generally, the new law becomes effective on August 5, 1993. However, in the case of a collective bargaining agreement in effect on August 5, 1993, the FMLA takes effect on the earlier of the date the collective bargaining agreement terminates or February 5, 1994. [FMLA § 405(b); 29 CFR § 825.700]

Covered Employers

Q 15:3 Which employers are subject to the FMLA?

Title I of the FMLA applies to employers engaged in commerce or in any industry or activity affecting commerce who employ 50 or more employees for each working day during each of 20 or more calendar workweeks in the current or preceding calendar year, regardless of whether the 20 calendar workweeks are consecutive. [29 CFR § 825.105(e)]

The FMLA applies to state and local government employers as well as to nongovernmental employers. [FMLA § 101(4)] Titles II and V of the FMLA provide for similar family and medical leave coverage for federal civil service employees and congressional employees. Public agencies and private elementary and secondary schools are also covered employers *regardless* of the number of employees they have. [29 CFR §§ 825.104, 825.108(d), 825.109, 825.600]

Employer. Under the FMLA, all of an employer's separate establishments or divisions are considered to be a single "employer." In addition, an "employer" also includes (1) any person acting, directly or indirectly, in the interest of a covered employer to any of the employees of the employer, (2) any successor in interest [defined at 29 CFR § 825.107] of a covered employer, and (3) any public agency. [29 CFR § 825.104] Employees of more than one employer will be treated as being employed by a single employer for purposes of the FMLA if the employers meet either an "integrated employer" test or "joint employment" test (see Q 15:4).

Q 15:4 When are two or more corporations treated as a single "employer" for purposes of the FMLA?

When one corporation has an ownership in a second corporation, the FMLA treats each as a separate employer unless they meet an "integrated employer" test or a "joint employment" test. If either of these tests is met, the employers will be treated as a single employer for all purposes of the FMLA, including employer coverage, employee eligibility, and employer liability under the FMLA's enforcement provisions.

Integrated Employer Test. This test is subjective rather than objective and appears deliberately designed to afford the Department of Labor (DOL) broad leeway to find that a single, "integrated employer" exists. According to the DOL's Interim Final Rule under the FMLA, "[a] determination of whether or not separate entities are an integrated employer is not determined by the application of any single criterion, but rather the entire relationship is to be reviewed in its totality." Several factors are to be considered, including, *but not limited to:*

- Common management
- Interrelation between operations
- Centralized control of labor relations and
- Degree of common ownership/financial control

[29 CFR § 825.104(c)(2)] The DOL has not specified any minimum percentage of common ownership or financial control for this purpose.

Joint Employment Test. This test operates to treat two or more businesses that exercise some control over the work or working conditions of the employee as joint employers for purposes of the FMLA. Under this test, even separate and distinct entities with separate owners, managers, and facilities could be deemed to be joint employers for purposes of the FMLA. If a joint employment relationship exists, then additional rules prescribe which of the joint employers has what FMLA duties with respect to shared, leased, and temporary employees and employees in various other employment arrangements (see Q 15:44). Like the "integrated employer" test described above, the determination of whether a joint employment relationship exists is subjectively determined by viewing the entire relationship in its totality, not by the application of any single criterion. The factors considered in determining whether a joint employment relationship exists include, *but are not limited to:*

- The nature and degree of control of the workers
- The degree of supervision, direct or indirect, of the work
- The power to determine the pay rates of, or the methods of paying, the workers

- The right, directly or indirectly, to hire, fire, or modify the workers' employment conditions and
- Preparation of the payroll and payment of wages.

[29 CFR § 825.106(a), (b)]

The DOL's Interim Final Rule notes that a joint employment relationship will often exist (1) if there is an arrangement between employers to share an employee's services or to interchange employees; (2) if one employer directly or indirectly acts in the interest of a second employer in relation to the employee; or (3) if the employers are "not completely disassociated" with respect to the employee's employment and may be treated as directly or indirectly sharing control of the employee because one employer controls, is controlled by, or is under common control with the other employer. [29 CFR 21 825.106(c)]

Q 15:5   For purposes of the 50-employee test, when is an individual deemed to be "employed" by the employer?

When counting whether the employer employs at least 50 employees for each working day during each of 20 or more calendar workweeks in the current or preceding calendar year, certain rules are to be applied to determine whether a particular employee is counted.

Listing on Payroll. If the employee's name appears on the employer's payroll, he or she must be counted as employed on each working day of the calendar week regardless of whether he or she receives any compensation for the week. [29 CFR 105(a)] This is true regardless of whether the employee actually performs work on each working day of the calendar week. [Preamble to 29 CFR § 825, Section III]

Part-Time Employees. For purposes of the 50-employee test, part-time employees are also considered as being employed on each working day of the calendar week, as long as they were maintained on the payroll.

Example. Big Supermarket has a seven-day workweek. Several of its employees are part-time and work three days per week. Under the above rule, they must be treated as employed on all seven days of the calendar week for purposes of the 50-employee test.

Leased or Temporary Employees. The DOL's Interim Final Rule under the FMLA indicates that, if a "joint employment" relationship exists, an employer who employs workers from a leasing or temporary help agency must count such individuals (regardless of whether they are maintained on the employer's payroll) when determining employer coverage and employee eligibility under the FMLA. In addition, the leasing or temporary help agency *also* must count such individuals. The various duties under the FMLA are then divided between the "primary" employer and the "secondary" employer (see Q 15:44). [29 CFR § 825.106]

Mid-Week Commencement or Termination of Employment. Employees who are hired after the first working day of the calendar week or who terminate employment before the last working day of the calendar week are not treated as employed on every working day of the calendar week. [29 CFR § 825.105(c)]

Paid or Unpaid Leave. Employees who are on paid or unpaid leave, including FMLA leave, leave of absence, or disciplinary suspension, must be counted for purposes of the 50-employee test if the employer has a reasonable expectation that the employee will later return to active employment. [29 CFR 825.105(a)]

Layoff. Employees on layoff are not counted for purposes of the 50-employee test, regardless of whether the layoff is temporary, long-term, or indefinite. [29 CFR 825.105(b)]

Eligible Employees

Q 15:6   Is an employer subject to the FMLA required to provide family or medical leave to all its employees?

No, only "eligible employees" of a covered employer are entitled to family or medical leave under the FMLA. Eligibility is determined based upon two factors: (1) service and (2) size of the employing unit. As a result of the FMLA's minimum service requirement, some short-time and part-time employees may be excluded from eligibility for family and medical leave, even though they are counted for the purpose of determining whether the employer is subject to the FMLA (see Q 15:5).

Service Requirement. An eligible employee means an employee who has been employed (1) for at least 12 months by the employer (the 12 months are not required to be consecutive), and (2) for at least 1,250 hours of service during the 12-month period immediately preceding the date the leave of absence begins. [FMLA § 101(2)(A); 29 CFR § 825.110] The period prior to the FMLA's effective date must be considered when determining eligibility. [29 CFR § 815.110(e)] An employer claiming that an employee is not "eligible" for FMLA leave must "clearly demonstrate" that the employee failed to work 1,250 hours during the previous 12 months. [29 CFR § 825.110(c)] "Hours of service" are determined according to principles established under the Fair Labor Standards Act (FLSA) for determining compensable hours of work. The employer may use any accurate accounting of actual hours worked under the FLSA's principles. If actual records of hours worked are not available, employees who are exempt from the FLSA's recordkeeping requirement (that is, bona fide executive, administrative, and professional employees) and any other employees who have worked for the employer for at least 12 months, are *presumed* to have met the FLSA's service requirement (special rules apply to teachers). [29 CFR §§ 825.110(b), (c), 825.500(d)(1)] If an employee notifies the employer of the need for FMLA leave prior to the date he or she has satisfied the service requirement, the employer may either advise the employee when the service requirement has been met or may confirm the employee's eligibility based upon a projection that the employee will be eligible on the date the leave would commence. Evidently, the employee may rely on the employer's projection regardless of whether it is correct, and the employer that makes such a projection may be barred from subsequently challenging the employee's eligibility due to failure to meet the service requirement. [29 CFR § 825.110(d)]

Size of Employing Unit. An employee who meets 1,250 hours of service within 12 months of employment described above nonetheless is not "eligible" under the FMLA if the number of employees employed at the worksite, plus the total number of employees employed by the employer within 75 miles of the worksite, is less than 50. [FMLA § 101(2)(B)(ii); see 29 CFR § 825.111 for the rather complex definition of what constitutes a "worksite" and for how to measure the 75-mile radius in road miles.] For example, if an employee works full-time for three years at a restaurant that employs 35 people, and the owner of the restaurant operates another restaurant 20 miles away which employs 25 people, the employee is eligible for family or medical leave.

Note that, if the employing unit drops below the minimum size requirement, FMLA benefits must continue to be provided to those employees already on FMLA leave. Additionally, FMLA benefits must be provided to any employee who both *requested and was determined eligible for* FMLA leave while the employing unit still met the minimum size requirement, even if the leave does not begin until after the employing unit has dropped below the minimum required size. [29 CFR 825.111(c)]

Family and Medical Leave

Q 15:7 What kinds of family or medical conditions or emergencies qualify for leave under the FMLA?

The new law requires that leave be permitted to an eligible employee in the following four circumstances:

1. Because of the birth of a son or daughter of the employee and in order to care for such son or daughter;
2. Because of the placement of a son or daughter with the employee for adoption or foster care [29 CFR § 825.112(e)];
3. In order to care of the spouse, or a son, daughter, or parent, of the employee, if such spouse, son, daughter, or parent has a *serious* health condition (see Q 15:8); or
4. Because of a *serious* health condition (see Q 15:8) that makes the employee "unable to perform the functions of his or her position" (see Q 15:9).

[FMLA § 102(1)]

The employee is entitled to FMLA leave for one of the above events even if it occurred prior to August 5, 1993 (the effective date of the FMLA), so long as any other requirements are satisfied. [29 CFR

825.105(c)] Whether the adopted child comes from a licensed placement agency or otherwise is irrelevant in determining eligibility for leave. Employers may not impose any maximum age limit on a child being adopted or placed for foster care for purposes of determining the employee's eligibility for FMLA leave. [29 CFR § 825.112(d)]

FMLA leave rights apply equally to male and female employees. Fathers, as well as mothers, can take family leave for the birth, placement for adoption or foster care of a child. [29 CFR 825.112(b)]

Son or Daughter. A "son or daughter" is defined to include a biological, adopted or foster child, a stepchild, a legal ward, or a child of a person standing in the position of a parent (in loco parentis), if the child is either under 18 years of age or 18 years of age or older but incapable of self-care because of a mental or physical disability. [FMLA § 101(12)] For this purpose, an individual is considered to be "incapable of self-care" if he or she requires either supervision or active assistance in providing daily self-care with regard to several "activities of daily living," including caring appropriately for one's grooming and hygiene, bathing, dressing, eating, cooking, cleaning, shopping, taking public transportation, paying bills, maintaining a residence, using telephones and directories, using a post office, and so forth. "Physical or mental disability" means a physical or mental impairment that substantially limits one or more of the major life activities of the individual, as defined in the Equal Employment Opportunity Commission (EEOC) regulations under the Americans with Disabilities Act (ADA) of 1990 (see Chapter 17). [29 CFR § 825.113(c)]

Parent. The definition of a "parent" is similarly very broad. A "parent" is defined as the biological parent of an employee, or an individual who stood in loco parentis to an employee when the employee was a child. [FMLA § 101(7); 29 CFR § 825.113(c)(3)] It does not include parents-in-law. [29 CFR § 825.113(b)]

Spouse. On the other hand, the definition of "spouse" is limited to a person who is a husband or wife, as the case may be. [FMLA § 101(13)] Thus, persons who live together but are not married pursuant to state law (including common-law marriage in states where it is recognized) would not qualify for spousal medical leave. [29 CFR § 825.113(a)]

Q 15:8   What is a "serious health condition" under the FMLA?

A "serious health condition" is defined as an illness, injury, impairment, or physical or mental condition that involves inpatient care in a hospital, hospice, or residential medical care facility, or continuing treatment by a health care provider. [FMLA § 101(11)] The DOL's Interim Final Rule greatly expands this definition to include the following:

- Any period of incapacity or treatment in connection with, or following, inpatient care (that is, an overnight stay) in one of the above entities;

- Any period of incapacity that requires an absence of more than calendar three days from work, school, or other regular daily activities, provided that the absence also involves continuing treatment by, or under the supervision of, a health care provider; or

- Continuing treatment by, or under the supervision of, a health care provider for (1) health care conditions that are chronic or long-term and either incurable or so serious that, if not treated, would likely result in a period of incapacity of more than three calendar days; or (2) prenatal care.

Provided that all of the other conditions of the DOL's Interim Final Rule are met, the following conditions are expressly recognized as "serious health conditions": restorative dental surgery after an accident, removal of cancerous growths, treatments for allergies or stress, treatments for substance abuse, prenatal care. Voluntary or cosmetic treatments (such as for acne or orthodontia) that are not medically necessary are considered serious health conditions only if inpatient hospital care is required. Routine preventive physical examinations are not "serious health conditions." [29 CFR § 825.114(c)]

Continuing Treatment by a Health Care Provider. For FMLA purposes, "continuing treatment by a health care provider" means that the employee or family member is:

- Treated two or more times for the injury or illness by a health care provider (including by a nurse or physician's assistance under the direct supervision of a health care provider, or by a provider of health care services (such as a physical therapist) under the orders of, or on referral by, a health care provider;

- Treated for the injury or illness at least once by a health care provider, resulting in a regimen of continuing treatment under the health care provider's supervision to resolve the health condition (for example, a course of medication or therapy); or

- Under the continuing supervision of, but not necessarily being actively treated by, a health care provider because of a serious long-term or chronic condition or disability that cannot be cured (such as Alzheimer's disease, severe stroke, or the terminal stages of a disease).

[29 CFR § 825.114(b)]

Health Care Provider. The term "health care provider" is defined as (1) a doctor of medicine or osteopathy who is authorized to practice medicine or surgery (as appropriate) by the state in which the doctor practices, or (2) any other person determined by the secretary of labor to be capable of providing health care services. [FMLA § 101(6)] This latter category, according to the DOL's Interim Final Rule, includes only Christian Science practitioners listed with the First Church of Christ, Scientist in Boston, Massachusetts, and the following individuals if authorized to practice under state law and performing within the scope of their practice under state law: nurse practitioners and nurse-midwives; podiatrists, dentists, clinical psychologists, optometrists, and chiropractors (limited to treatment consisting of manual manipulation of the spine to correct a subluxation shown by X-ray to exist). [29 CFR § 825.118]

Q 15:9 When is an employee "unable to perform the functions of the position of employee"?

For FMLA purposes, an employee is considered to be "unable to perform the functions of the position" when the health care provider finds that he or she (1) is unable to work at all, or (2) is unable to perform any of the essential functions of the employee's position within the meaning of the ADA and the regulations thereunder (see Question 17:3). [29 CFR § 825.115]

Q 15:10   How long a period of family or medical leave must an employer provide to an eligible employee?

An eligible employee is entitled to a total of 12 workweeks of family or medical leave during any 12-month period. [FMLA § 102(a)(1)] Leave taken prior to August 5, 1993 does not count for purposes of the FMLA. [29 CFR § 825.103(a)] The employer has several options for defining the 12-month period during which leave must be taken (see Q 15:11).

Commencement of Leave. For the birth of a child, expectant mothers may take FMLA leave before the delivery date for prenatal care or if the mother's condition makes her unable to work. [29 CFR § 825.112(c)] FMLA leave can also begin before actual placement or adoption of a child if the employee must be absent for the placement for adoption or foster care to proceed (for example, for required attendance at counselling sessions, court appearances, consultations with attorneys and doctors, and physical examinations). [29 CFR §§ 825.112(c), (d)]

Special Limit for Husband and Wife Working for Same Employer. If a husband and wife both work for the same employer and both are entitled to leave (1) for birth of a child, (2) for placement for adoption or foster care, or to care for the child after placement, or (3) care of a sick parent with a serious health condition, the aggregate leave taken by the husband and wife for the same event may be limited to 12 workweeks during any 12-month period (even if the husband and wife are employed at different worksites of the employer). Personal medical leave taken by one or both of the spouses is not subject to the aggregate limit. [FMLA § 102(f); 29 CFR § 825.202(b)]

Example. Bill and Mary Smith, who are married, work for the same employer. Mary gives birth to a child and requests a maternity leave. Bill applies for a family leave to care for the newborn child. The employer can limit the two leaves to a combined maximum of 12 workweeks because of the husband-wife relationship. Bill decides to take three workweeks and Mary takes nine workweeks. Neither is entitled to any further FMLA leave for this event.

However, each spouse is entitled to the difference between the leave he or she took and the 12-workweek limit for FMLA leave for any other purpose. Thus, in the above example, Mary could take an additional three workweeks for another type of FMLA leave (for example, to care for a parent having a serious medical condition), and Bill could take up to an additional nine workweeks for a separate FMLA event. [29 CFR § 825.202(c)] The DOL's Interim Final Rule also provides another way to stretch combined leave for the birth of a child; if the mother receives paid disability leave for the birth of a child, that is apparently treated as FMLA leave for a serious medical condition of the mother rather than as FMLA leave due to the birth of a child. [29 CFR § 825.207(c)(2)] See Questions 15:19 and 15:22 for a discussion of paid leave and FMLA leave.

Q 15:11 May the employer select the 12-month period in which the employee's 12-week leave entitlement occurs?

Yes, it may. The DOL's Interim Final Rule provides four different methods of selecting the 12-month period during which employees may take their FMLA leave. Whichever alternative the employer selects must be applied consistently and uniformly to all employees. If the employer wishes to switch to another method, it must give at least 60 days notice to all employees and transition to the new method must provide that employees will retain the full benefit of 12 workweeks of leave under whichever method affords the greatest benefit to the employee. Employers are prohibited from switching to a new method in a manner designed to avoid the FMLA's leave requirements. [29 CFR § 825.200(d)]

The four alternatives for determining the "12-month period" during which the 12 workweeks of leave entitlement occurs are as follows:

1. The calendar year: Under this method, employees would be entitled to their FMLA leave at any time during the calendar year.

2. Any fixed 12-month period (such as a fiscal year, a year starting on the yearly "anniversary" of the employee's date of hire, or a year required by state law): Under this method, employees would be entitled to take their FMLA leave at any time in the fixed 12-month period.

3. The 12-month period measured forward from the date the employee's first FMLA leave begins.

4. A "rolling" 12-month period measured backward from the date an employee uses any FMLA leave (except that leave taken prior to August 5, 1993 does not reduce available FMLA leave): Under this method, the employee's entitlement to FMLA leave is the balance of the 12 weeks that has *not* been taken during the immediately preceding 12 months. For example, if the employee has taken only three weeks of FMLA leave in the past 12 months, then the employee is entitled to up to 9 weeks of additional leave.

[29 CFR §§ 825.200(b), (c)]

Note that, under the fixed-year methods listed above, employees might be able to "bunch" two year's worth of FMLA leave together. For example, with a calendar year period, an employee could take 12 workweeks of FMLA leave in October, November, and December of one calendar year and then an additional 12 workweeks of FMLA leave in January, February, and March of the next calendar year (assuming all other FMLA requirements are satisfied). The "rolling" 12-month period would prevent such "bunching" of FMLA leave, but would be more administratively complex.

Q 15:12   Must a family or medical leave be taken on a continuous and full-time basis?

No, the FMLA does not require that family or medical leave always be taken on a continuous, full-time basis. Provided that certain conditions are met, an employee may take FMLA leave on an intermittent or reduced-leave (that is, part-time) basis. A "reduced-leave" schedule is a change in the employee's schedule for a period of time that reduces the employee's usual number of hours per workweek, or hours per workday (such as from full-time to part-time). "Intermittent leave" is leave, due to a single illness or injury, that is taken in separate blocks of time rather than one continuous period of time. Intermittent leave may include leave of periods from one hour or more to several weeks. The DOL's Interim Final Rule notes that permissible intermittent leave might include leave taken on an occasional basis for medical appointments or leave taken several days at a time spread over several months, such as for chemotherapy. [29 CFR §§ 825.203, 825.800]

Birth or Placement of Child for Adoption or Foster Care. If the leave is taken for the birth of a child or the placement of a child for adoption or foster care, the employee cannot take the leave intermittently or on a reduced-leave schedule unless both the employer and employee agree to such a leave schedule.

Example 1. Mary gives birth to a daughter. Mary requests that she be allowed to take her family leave in half-days, so that she can work part-time for 24 weeks rather than take full-time leave for 12 weeks. Her employer will not agree to this schedule. As a result, Mary may not take her leave in half-days.

Example 2. Joe and his wife are adopting a baby. Joe requests that he be allowed to take his family leave on Fridays to help out at home. His employer does not agree to this intermittent leave, so Joe may not take his family leave in that manner.

Example 3. Jeannette adopts a baby girl. She can get a baby-sitter for five days a week, but the baby-sitter cannot work Monday mornings. Jeannette requests that she be given family leave on Monday mornings only. Her employer agrees to this schedule, even though it is not obligated to do so; Jeannette therefore can take her family leave on an intermittent basis.

Note, however, that entitlement to FMLA leave for birth or placement for adoption or foster care expires at the end of the 12-month period beginning on the date of birth or placement; the balance of any leave available but not taken for this purpose will be forfeited (see Q 15:14). [29 CFR § 825.201]

Serious Health Conditions. If the leave is taken for care of a spouse, child, or parent with a serious health condition or because of the employee's own serious health condition, the leave may be taken intermittently or on a reduced-leave schedule when "medically necessary." For this purpose, there must be a medical need for leave (in contrast to voluntary treatments and procedures) and the medical need can be best accommodated through an intermittent or reduced leave schedule. [29 CFR § 825.117]

Example. John Miller works a 40-hour week, and takes a leave of four hours each week for chemotherapy treatment for a cancerous condition. Each four-hour absence by Mr. Miller is treated as one-tenth of a workweek in applying the 12-workweek leave limit.

Temporary Transfer to Another Job. If an employee requests leave that is foreseeable based on planned medical treatment and that would be intermittent leave or leave on a reduced-leave schedule, the employer can require the employee to transfer *temporarily* to an available alternative position for which the employee is qualified provided that the alternative position:

1. Has equivalent pay and benefits (but it need not have equivalent duties); and
2. Better accommodates recurring periods of leave than does the employee's regular position.

[FMLA § 102(b)(2); 29 CFR § 825.204]

In doing so, the employer may not eliminate benefits that are provided to full-time employees but not to part-time employees, although the FMLA does not bar an employer from proportionately reducing *earned* benefits (such as vacation leave) if such a reduction is normally made for its part-time employees. [29 CFR § 825.204(c)]

Determining Amount of Leave Used. For part-time or intermittent leave, only the time actually taken as leave may be charged against the 12-workweek maximum annual leave limitation. [FMLA § 102(b)(1)] Thus, an employee normally working a five-day work week who takes off one day would be treated as using 1/5 of a week of FMLA leave. If a full-time employee who normally works 8-hour days works four-hour days on a reduced-leave schedule, he or she is treated as using one-half week of FMLA leave each week. The amount of leave credited to an employee who normally works a part-time schedule or variable hours is determined on a pro rata or proportional basis. For example, if an employee who normally works 25 hours per week works 15 hours per week under a reduced-leave schedule, the employee's 15 hours of leave would constitute three-fifths of a week of FMLA leave for each week the employee works the reduced leave schedule. For variable hours (that is, when the number of hours worked by the employee varies from week to week), the employee's normal workweek is calculated by determining the weekly average of hours worked during the 12 weeks immediately prior to the beginning of the leave period, and the employer and employee must agree on the employee's normal schedule or average hours worked each week and reduce their agreement to a written record. [29 CFR §§ 825.205, 825.500(d)(2)]

Special Rules for Employees of Schools. Special rules apply to employees of schools whose intermittent or reduced-leave schedule would cause them to be on leave for more than 20 percent of the total number or working days during the period of the leave, or who begin leave close to the beginning or end of an academic term. Such employees may be required, under certain circumstances, to take leave for a particular duration (even if they are willing to return to work earlier) or to transfer to an available alternative position. [29 CFR §§ 825.600-824.604]

Q 15:13 Do salary deductions for unpaid FMLA leave cause an executive, administrative, or professional employee to lose such designation under the FLSA?

No, they do not. Deductions from such an employee's salary for any hours taken as intermittent or reduced-leave schedule within a workweek, provided that such leave is FMLA leave, have no effect on the employee's exempt status under the FLSA. [29 CFR § 825.206] However, if the employee's salary is reduced for any additional leave that does not qualify as FMLA leave (such as more generous leave required by state law or permitted under the employer's policy), the employee may possibly lose exempt status under the FLSA unless such salary reduction is permitted under 29 CFR Part 541. [29 CFR § 825.206(b)]

Q 15:14 Is there any lifetime maximum on the amount of FMLA leave that can be taken for a particular event or condition?

With one exception, there is no limit on the number of years that an employee can take FMLA leave for the same event or condition. The exception to this general rule occurs in the case of the birth of a child or a placement for adoption or foster care. Entitlement to FMLA leave for the birth of a child or placement for adoption or foster care expires at the end of the 12-month period beginning on the date of the birth or placement. Any unused FMLA leave as of that date relating to the birth, placement for adoption, or foster care of that particular child is forfeited. [FMLA § 102(a)(2); 29 CFR § 825.201]

Example 1. Joe's father has Alzheimer's disease. Assuming that Joe satisfies all of the requirements for FMLA leave, he may use his 12 workweeks of FMLA leave during each 12-month period to care for his father.

Example 2. Susan works for Big Company, which runs its FMLA leave program on a calendar year basis. In year 1, Susan has a baby on May 1 and uses her 12 workweeks of FMLA leave as maternity leave. In year 2, Susan takes no FMLA leave until June 1, when she wants to take additional leave to care for her baby (who does not have a serious health condition). Susan is entitled to up to 12 workweeks of FMLA leave in year 2, but her entitlement to FMLA leave *due to the birth of her child* expired on April 30 of year 2, which date was the end of the 12-month period beginning on the date of her child's birth. Although she could have used part or all of her FMLA leave in Year 2 to care for her baby provided that she took such leave prior to May 1 (that is, still within a year from the date her child was born), she failed to do so and now cannot take any further FMLA leave due to the birth of that particular baby. Susan may still take her 12 workweeks of FMLA leave in year 2 for any other event or condition for which FMLA leave must be granted (including, for example, if her baby develops a serious health condition or for the birth, placement for adoption, or foster care of another child).

Q 15:15 Can the employer require the employee to provide advance notice that a family or medical leave will be taken?

Yes, the employer can require the employee to provide advance notice in certain circumstances. Permissible methods of notice include in person or by telephone, telegraph, facsimile or other electronic means, and can be given by the employee's family member or other representative if the employee cannot do so personally. [29 CFR § 825.303]

Birth, Placement for Adoption, or Foster Care of a Child. In the case of the birth of a child or a placement of a child for adoption or foster care which is expected and foreseeable, the employee can be required to give at least 30 days notice before the leave is to begin.

Example. An employee's spouse gives birth to a child five weeks prematurely. Shortly after the birth, the employee requests a leave to care for the spouse and child and provides the required health care provider certificate. The notice requirement would appear to be satisfied.

Serious Medical Condition. If a leave is on account of a serious medical condition of the employee or a spouse, child, or parent and is foreseeable, based on planned medical treatment, then the employee is:

1. Required to make a reasonable effort to schedule the treatment so as not to disrupt unduly the operations of the employer, subject to the approval of the health care provider; and

2. Expected to provide the employer with at least 30 days notice, before the leave begins, of the employee's intention to take the leave, except that if the date of treatment requires leave to begin in less than 30 days, the employee is to provide notice as practicable.

[FMLA § 102(e)(2)]

When notice is given of the need for leave for medical treatment, the employer may, for justifiable cause, require the employee to attempt to reschedule treatment, subject to the health care provider's ability to reschedule and its approval as to any modification of the treatment schedule. If intermittent leave or a reduced-leave schedule is being requested, the employee must inform the employer of the reasons why this type of leave is necessary and of any applicable schedule of treatment. Both are to attempt to work out a schedule that meets the employee's needs without unduly disrupting the employer's operations, subject to the health care provider's approval. [29 CFR § 825.302]

Unforeseeable Event. If the event is not foreseeable, notice is to be given as soon as practicable, which ordinarily means at least verbal notification to the employer within one or two business days of when the need for leave becomes known to the employee, except in extraordinary circumstances. The employer may not require advance notice for FMLA leave in the case of a medical emergency requiring leave due to a serious health condition of the employee or a family member. [FMLA § 102(e)(1); 29 CFR §§ 825.302, 825.303]

Failure to Give Notice of Foreseeable Event. If the employee fails to provide notice for foreseeable leave with no reasonable excuse for the delay, the employer is permitted to deny the taking of FMLA leave for 30 or more days after the date the employee does provide notice of the need for the leave, under a policy that is uniformly applied in similar circumstances. To do this, it must be clear that the employee had actual notice of the FMLA notice requirements (which may be satisfied if the posting requirement is met; see Q 15:30) and that the leave clearly was foreseeable. [29 CFR § 825.304]

Q 15:16 What proof of entitlement to a family or medical leave on the basis of a serious medical condition may an employer require an employee to provide?

If the leave is requested on the basis of a serious medical condition (whether of the spouse, child, or parent of the employee, or the employee himself or herself), the employer can require the employee to provide the employer with a certification from a health care provider to substantiate that the leave is in fact due to the serious health condition of the employee or the employee's immediate family member. The certification may be required to be provided no sooner than 15 calendar days after the employer's request, and longer if it is not practicable under the particular circumstances to do so despite the employee's diligent, good faith efforts. At the time the employer requests the certification, it must also advise the employee of the anticipated consequences of the employee's failure to provide adequate certification. [29 CFR § 825.305]

The certification of the health care provider is required to include:

1. The date on which the serious health condition commenced;
2. The best medical judgement of the probable duration of the condition;
3. Diagnosis of the serious health condition;

4. A brief statement of the regimen of treatment that the health care provider prescribed for the condition (including estimated number of visits, nature, frequency and duration of treatment, including treatment by another provider of health services on referral by or order of the health care provider);

5. Whether inpatient hospitalization is required; and

6. A statement of the circumstances:

   a. In the case of a leave to care for a spouse, child, or parent, a statement that the employee is needed to care for the sick person because that patient requires assistance for basic medical, hygiene, nutritional needs, safety or transportation, or that the employee's presence would be beneficial or desirable for the care of the family member (including psychological comfort) and an estimate of the time that the employee is needed to provide care;

   b. In the case of a leave for the employee's own serious health condition, a statement that the employee is unable to perform work or any kind or that he or she is unable to perform the functions of his or her position;

   c. In the case of intermittent leave or leave on a reduced-leave schedule for planned medical treatment, the dates on which the treatment is expected to be given and the duration of the treatment;

   d. In the case of intermittent leave or leave on a reduced-leave schedule for the employee himself or herself, a statement of the medical necessity for such a leave and the expected duration; or

   e. In the case of intermittent leave or leave on a reduced-leave schedule for care of a spouse, child, or parent, a statement that the leave is necessary for the care of the spouse, child or parent, or that the leave will assist in the recovery, and the expected duration and schedule of the leave.

[FMLA § 103(b); 29 CFR § 825.306]

With regard to the employee' inability to perform the functions of the position, the employer may provide a statement of the essential functions of the employee's position for the health care provider to review [29 CFR 825.115]

If the employer has reason to doubt the validity of the health care provider's certification, the employer can require, at its own expense, that the employee obtain a second opinion of a health care provider designated or approved by the employer (but not a health care provider regularly employed by the employer or regularly utilized by the employer, with certain exceptions in rural areas). [FMLA § 103(c); 29 CFR § 825.307]

If there is a conflict between the first and second opinions, the employer may require, again at its own expense, the opinion of a third health care provider designated or approved jointly by the employee and the employer. The opinion of the third health care provider is final and binding on both the employer and employee. When, however, the employee fails to attempt in good faith to reach agreement, he or she will be bound by the second certification, and an employer failing to attempt in good faith to reach agreement will be bound by the first certification. [FMLA § 103(d); 29 CFR § 825.307]

The employer may require an eligible employee to obtain subsequent recertifications on a reasonable basis and no more frequently than every 30 days, unless the employee requests an extension of leave, or the circumstances described in the original certification have changed significantly, or the employer receives information casting doubt upon the continuing validity of the certification. [FMLA § 103(e); 29 CFR § 825.308]

(See also Q 15:25 and 15:27.)

Q 15:17 What proof of entitlement to a family or medical leave on the basis of the birth, placement for adoption, or foster care of a child may an employer require an employee to provide?

In the case of the birth of a child, or the placement of a child for adoption or foster care, presumably the employer can require the employee to provide reasonable proof that the event has in fact occurred.

Q 15:18   Can an employee be required to waive his or her rights under the FMLA?

No, they cannot. Employers are prohibited from including an employee to waive his or her FMLA rights. In addition, employers (or their collective bargaining representatives) are barred from "trading off" the right to take FMLA leave against another benefit offered by the employer. [29 CFR § 800.220]

Rights and Obligations of Employees on Leave

Q 15:19   Is the employee entitled to be paid by the employer while on a family or medical leave pursuant to the FMLA?

No, the employer is not required to pay the employee any wages or salary while the employee is on a family or medical leave pursuant to the FMLA. FMLA leave generally is unpaid. [FMLA § 102(c); 29 CFR § 825.207(a)]

If the employee is eligible for paid leave, such as for accrued vacation, the employer may require, or the employee may request, that such paid leave be taken before any unpaid leave. In such a case, the paid leave period counts toward the 12-workweek maximum leave period. [FMLA § 102(d)] (See Q 15:20, 15:21.)

Q 15:20   When can an employer require an employee to use his or her paid leave as all or a part of otherwise unpaid FMLA leave?

Employers may require employees to substitute paid leave (including earned or accrued leave), for all or a part of unpaid leave for purposes of the FMLA in several circumstances.

1. *Paid medical/sick leave.* Paid medical or sick leave provided under a plan covering temporary disabilities is automatically treated as FMLA leave if it is being provided in the particular case for a purpose that qualifies under the FMLA, such as for the employee's own serious health condition (and, only if the

employer's sick/medical plan would otherwise permit, for the serious health condition of a family member).

2. *Earned or accrued vacation and paid time off.* An employer may, at its option, require its employees to substitute earned or paid vacation and/or any paid time off for all or a part of any unpaid FMLA leave.

3. *Paid personal or family leave.* An employer may, at its option, require its employees to substitute paid personal leave for all or a part of unpaid FMLA leave. It may also require its employees to substitute paid family leave for unpaid FMLA leave relating to birth, placement of a child for adoption or foster care, or care for a family member.

[29 CFR § 825.207]

When an employee takes accrued paid leave such as vacation or personal leave, he or she may not always "spontaneously explain" the reasons for using the accrued leave; the employer may not have enough information to know whether the leave is for qualified FMLA purposes, so that the employer could require that it be counted toward the 12-week FMLA leave limit.

How and When Paid Leave Is Designated as FMLA Leave. Employers are permitted to designate paid leave as FMLA leave only based upon information provided by the employee to the employer, not on the basis of information provided or obtained from another party. The employer must immediately notify the employee that paid leave is being designated and will be counted as FMLA leave. Any disputes regarding such designation "should be resolved through discussions between the employee and the employer." [29 CFR § 825.208] The employer must make the determination to count paid leave as FMLA leave (1) before the leave starts, or (2) before an extension of current leave is granted, unless the employer does not receive sufficient information concerning the reason for the leave until the leave has already begun. Evidently in anticipation of employee attempts to take paid leave first and then take the full 12-weeks of unpaid FMLA leave, the DOL's Interim Final Rule expressly permits employers to count paid leave toward the employee's entitlement to unpaid FMLA leave if the employee attempts to extend the paid vacation or personal leave by "tacking on" unpaid FMLA leave, and it becomes apparent that the extension is being requested due to an event that occurred during the period of paid leave. [29 CFR § 208 (a)] Also, under certain circumstances, employers will be permitted to retroactively count paid leave toward FMLA leave when the facts come to light, but under no circumstances may an employer designate leave as FMLA leave after the leave has ended.

Planning Pointer. Because the employer cannot retroactively designate paid leave as FMLA leave after the leave has ended, an employer desiring to avoid expensive "double dipping" by employees will want to have sufficient procedures in place to extract the information necessary for it to make FMLA entitlement decisions. Additionally, the employer may wish to include an antifraud provision in each paid leave plan requiring employees to promptly disclose the anticipated or actual use of paid leave for FMLA purposes and to penalize those who fail to so disclose by, among other things, suspension from the plan or termination of employment.

See Question 15:21 for a discussion of when an employee has a right to take paid leave without having it count toward FMLA leave.

Q 15:21 When does the employee have the option to substitute paid leave for all or part of any otherwise unpaid FMLA leave?

The employee has the right to substitute paid leave under certain circumstances and may do so in other circumstances only if his or her employer agrees.

1. *Paid sick/medical leave.* If the paid medical/sick leave is provided under a plan covering temporary disabilities, it is already automatically treated as FMLA leave. The employee is entitled to substitute other paid medical/sick leave for all or a part of unpaid FMLA leave only if it does not cause the medical/sick leave to be used in a situation that the employer would not normally allow. The employer may, but is not required to, permit the employee to substitute paid sick or medical leave for unpaid FMLA leave in situations that the employer would not normally allow such paid leave.

2. *Earned or accrued vacation and paid time off.* The employee is entitled to substitute paid vacation and/or paid time off for any qualified FMLA leave. The employer may not limit the substitution of paid vacation for this purpose.

3. *Paid personal or family leave.* The employee is entitled to substitute paid personal leave for any qualified FMLA leave. The employer may not place any limits on the substitution of personal leave for these purposes. However, an employee is entitled to substitute paid family leave only under circumstances permitted by the employer's family leave plan. If the employer's family leave plan allows paid family leave to be used for a particular type of FMLA leave (for example, if the employer's paid family leave plan allows use of family leave to care for a child but not for a parent), the employer may, but is not required to, permit the employee to allow accrued paid family leave to be substituted for that purpose (in this example, to care for a parent).

[29 CFR § 825.207]

No "magic words" are necessary to assert substitution rights under the FMLA. However, if the employee requests to use paid leave for an FMLA qualifying event without explaining the reason for the leave, the employer may deny such request under an "established policy or practice" of requiring the employee to provide sufficient information to establish an FMLA qualifying event. If the employee provides the documentation, the employer will be aware that the leave may not be denied and can count the paid leave against the employee's 12-week unpaid FMLA leave requirement. [29 CFR § 825.208]

Q 15:22   When does the employee have a right to take paid leave without having it count toward unpaid FMLA leave?

The employee's use of his or her paid leave for non-FMLA purposes does not count against the 12 weeks of FMLA entitlement, and the employer cannot "dock" the employee an equivalent number of days of FMLA leave. Examples of non-FMLA purposes include using vacation days to go to Disney World or paid sick leave for a medical condition that is not a "serious health condition" under the FMLA. [29 CFR § 825.207(f)]

If the employer chooses not to require employees to substitute paid leave for unpaid FMLA leave as described above, then employees remain entitled to all paid leave that is earned or accrued under the terms of the employer's plan *as well as* up to an additional 12 workweeks of unpaid FMLA leave. [29 CFR § 825.207]

Additionally, if the employee uses paid leave for an FMLA purpose without disclosing the purpose to the employer, and the employer fails to find out the true purpose before the conclusion of the leave, the employer may not, after the leave has ended, retroactively redesignate the paid leave as substituting for unpaid FMLA leave and count it toward the employee's 12-week FMLA entitlement. [29 CFR § 825.208(a), (c)]

Q 15:23   Is the employee on a family or medical leave entitled to continued coverage under the employer's health benefit plans?

Yes, an employee on a family or medical leave authorized by the FMLA must continue to receive group health plan coverage for the duration of the leave at the level and under the conditions coverage would have been provided if the employee had continued in employment continuously for the duration of the leave. [FMLA § 104(e)(1); 29 CFR § 825.209] The class of coverage must be the same (for example, an employee who has family medical coverage must be permitted to maintain family medical coverage during the leave), and the benefit coverage must be maintained during the leave regardless of whether it is provided in a base medical plan, supplemental medical plan, a flexible spending account, or any other component of a cafeteria plan. All benefit increases (and, presumably, benefit decreases) as well as premium increases or decreases made under the plan must be provided to employees on FMLA leave. In addition, employees on FMLA leave retain the right, if available under the applicable group health plan provisions, to add or drop family members or to switch plan coverage options during the period of FMLA leave. Notices of any such opportunity must also be provided to employees on FMLA leave. [29 CFR §§ 825.209, 825.210(a)]

Required Employee Contributions. If the group health plan requires contributions by active employees, the employee on leave must continue to make the required contributions. The employer may not add any additional charge for administrative expenses. For *paid* leave being counted as FMLA leave, contributions must be made by the method normally used (such as by payroll deduction). For *unpaid* FMLA leave, the employer may require the employee contributions to be paid to it or directly to an insurance carrier (1) at the same time as it would be due if made by payroll deduction; (2) on the same schedule as COBRA payments; (3) by prepayment, at the employee's option, under a cafeteria plan; (4) under the employer's existing rules for payment by employees on "leave without pay" (except that prepayment cannot be required); or (5) any other method voluntarily agreed to between the employer and the employee (which may include prepayment of premiums through increased payroll deductions or otherwise when the need for FMLA leave is foreseeable). [29 CFR § 825.210] If the employee had been making contributions on a pre-tax basis under a cafeteria plan and does not choose to prepay them, the contributions during the unpaid leave may have to be made on an after-tax basis. [29 CFR § 825.210] The COBRA rate (which includes a charge for administrative expenses) may not be charged because the employee is treated as not having experienced a COBRA qualifying event until he or she notifies the employer of his or her intent not to return from the leave or actually fails to return from the leave. [29 CFR § 825.209]

Failure to Make Timely Premium Payments. If the employee's premium payment for health insurance coverage is more than 30 days late, the employer's obligation to maintain health insurance coverage during the FMLA leave ceases. [29 CFR § 825.212(a), (c)] If, on the other hand, the employer paid the employee's missed contribution in order to maintain his or her health coverage, the employer may recover such "makeup" payment from the employee. [29 CFR § 825.212(b)] In either case, the employer's other obligations under the FMLA continue, including the obligation to restore the employee's health insurance coverage upon his or her return from FMLA leave (see Q 15:24). [29 CFR § 825.212]

Failure to Maintain Group Health Plan Coverage. If the employee either chooses not to maintain health coverage during FMLA leave or loses health insurance coverage during FMLA leave due to failure to make timely premium payments, he or she nonetheless is entitled, upon return from FMLA leave, to be reinstated in the group health plan on the same terms as prior to taking the leave, without any qualifying period, physical examination, exclusion or preexisting conditions, and so forth. [29 CFR §§ 825.209(e), 825.212]

Special Rule for Multiemployer Health Plans. Employers are required to continue to make contributions on behalf of employees on FMLA leave as though they had continued to be employed, unless the multiemployer health plan expressly contains an alternate procedure for maintaining such coverage. Employees cannot be required to use "banked" hours or to pay greater premiums then they would have been required to had they been continuously employed. [29 CFR § 825.212]

Group Health Plan. The FMLA defines a "group health plan" by reference to Code Section 5000(b)(1). The DOL's Interim Final Rule states this definition as any plan of, or contributed to by, an employer (whether self-insured or otherwise) to provide health care, directly or indirectly, to the employer's employees, former employees, or the families of such employees or former employees; be aware that the Omnibus Budget Reconciliation Act of 1993 (OBRA '93) has amended the text of Code Section 5000(b)(1). [FMLA § 104(c)(1); 29 CFR §§ 825.209, 825.800; IRC § 5000, as amended by Section 13561 of OBRA '93] See Question 3:49 for a discussion of the Code Section 5000(b)(1) definition as amended after the DOL issued its Interim Final Rule.

Q 15:24 Is the employee on a family or medical leave entitled to continued coverage under the employer's other benefit plans?

No, the employee is not. Benefit coverage that has not accrued can be canceled or suspended during the leave period. Thus, group life insurance coverage, for example, apparently could be terminated without violating the FMLA.

However, an employee taking a family or medical leave authorized by the FMLA cannot lose any employment benefit that was accrued before the date on which the leave begins. [FMLA § 104(a)(2)] Employees are not entitled to accrue any seniority or employment benefits during the leave period. [FMLA § 104(a)(3)(A)] This means, for example, that the employee is not required to be given pension credits or vacation credits for the period of leave (although benefits such as paid vacation, sick or personal leave, accrued at the time the leave began must be available to the employee upon his or her return from the leave to the extent not substituted for FMLA leave). At the end of the employee's FMLA leave, the employee is entitled to be returned to the same position with the same benefits or to an equivalent position with equivalent benefits (see Q 15:23), including all benefits provided or made available to employees by the employer (regardless of whether provided via an ERISA plan), such as group life insurance health insurance, disability insurance, sick leave, annual leave, educational benefits, and pensions. Benefits must be resumed "in the same manner" and "at the same levels" as before the leave, except that benefit changes made during the period of leave and affecting the entire workforce also must be provided to the employee unless the changes are dependent upon seniority or accrual). In particular, employees returning from FMLA leave cannot be required to requalify for any benefits they enjoyed before the FMLA leave started. [29 CFR § 825.215]

> **Planning Pointer.** In view of the short leave period (maximum 12 workweeks), and the possible application of state insurance law requirements for continuance and conversion of group life insurance coverage during a family or medical leave, terminating coverage may not be desirable in most instances.

Employer Payment and Recovery of Premiums. Some employers may decide that it is easier to avoid a lapse of the employee's coverage (such as life or disability insurance) by simply paying the employee's share of premiums during the period of FMLA leave. If the employer does so, it may recover such payments in the same manner as its own contributions toward health insurance (see Q 15:27). [29 CFR § 824.213(f)]

Q 15:25   Once a health care provider has certified the need for leave due to a serious medical condition, must the employee provide additional certifications?

Yes, if additional certification(s) are requested by the employer. If the leave has been granted on the basis of a serious medical condition of the spouse, child, or parent of the employee, or of the employee himself or herself, the employer can require the eligible employee to obtain subsequent recertifications on a reasonable basis. The FMLA does not define what constitutes a "reasonable basis." [FMLA § 103(e)]

Q 15:26   Does an employee who has taken a family or medical leave authorized by the FMLA have a right to be reinstated when the leave period has expired?

Yes, generally, an employee on a family or medical leave who elects to return to work after the leave is over must be given back his or her former position or an equivalent position with equivalent benefits, pay, and other terms and conditions of employment. [FMLA § 104(a)(1); 29 CFR §§ 825.100(b), 825.214-825.216] If the leave was due to the employee's serious health condition, the employer may, pursuant to a uniformly applied policy, require that the individual first submit a certification of fitness to return to work that relates to the health condition that caused his or her absence (and also may refuse to restore to employment any individual who fails to submit such certification). [29 CFR §§ 825.100, 825.310, 825.311]

Exception. The employer may deny reinstatement to a salaried eligible employee (or "key employee") who is among the highest-paid 10 percent of the employees employed by the employer within 75 miles of the facility at which the employee is employed, if the following requirements are met:

1. The employer's denial of reinstatement is necessary to prevent substantial and grievous economic injury to the operations of the employer (as defined in 29 CFR Section 825.218);

2. The employer notifies the employee of the employer's intent to deny reinstatement on such basis at the time the employer determines that substantial and grievous economic injury will occur (in accordance with the procedure contained in 29 CFR Section 825.219); and

3. In any case in which leave has commenced, the employee elects not to return to work after receiving the notice.

[FMLA § 104(b)]

The methodology for determining the highest paid 10 percent of employees is set forth in 29 CFR Section 825.217.

If the employer invokes this exception and the highly paid employee elects, after receiving notice that reinstatement will be denied, to take or continue the leave, the employee is entitled to continuation of health benefits during the leave, and the employer can not recoup any of the cost of the coverage from the highly compensated employee. [29 CFR §§ 824.219, 825.213] (See Question 15:27 for a discussion of the employer's right generally to recoup its premium payments.)

Q 15:27 **If an employee on a family or medical leave does not return to work upon the expiration of the leave, can the employer recover from the employee the employer's cost of providing group health plan coverage during the leave?**

If an employee on family or medical leave fails to return to work (defined for this purpose as returning to work for at least 30 calendar days) after his or her leave entitlement expires or has been exhausted, the employer can, with two exceptions discussed below, attempt to recoup the employer's cost of group health plan coverage for the unpaid portion (if any) of the FMLA leave period. For self-insured plans, this amount is limited to the employer's share of allowable COBRA premiums, excluding the 2-percent administrative fee. [29 CFR § 825.213] The health premiums that are permitted to be recovered are treated as a debt owed by the nonreturning employee. The employer's responsibility to provide health coverage and, for self-insured plans, to pay claims incurred during the period of FMLA leave, does not change.

However, if the employee's failure to return to work is due to (1) the continuation, recurrence, or onset of a serious health condition of the employee, or of a spouse, child, or parent, or (2) other circumstances beyond the control of the employee, no recoupment of the employer's cost for group health plan coverage during the leave is permitted. [FMLA § 104(c)(2)]

Required Medical Certification. If the employee claims that he or she is unable to return to work because of a serious health condition affecting the employee or a family member, the employer is entitled to receive from the employee a certification by a health care provider. In the case of a serious health condition of the employee, the certification must state that a serious health condition prevents the employee from being able to perform the functions of the employee's position on the date the leave expires. In the case of a serious health condition of a spouse, child or parent of the employee, the certification must state that the employee is needed to care for the family member on the date the leave expires. [FMLA § 104(c)(3)] The employee must provide such certification within 30 days of the employer's request. If the employee fails to provide such certification within the 30-day time limit, the employer may recover the health benefit contributions paid by it during the period of *unpaid* FMLA leave. [29 CFR §§ 825.214(a)(1), (a)(3), (b)]

Other Circumstances Beyond the Employee's Control. The DOL's Interim Final Rule gives several examples of circumstances which, in its view, qualify as "other circumstances beyond the employee's control," including an unexpected transfer of the employee's spouse to a job location more than 75 miles from the employee's worksite; a need for the employee to provide care to a relative or other individual who is not an immediate family member who has a serious medical condition; the employee is laid off while on leave; or the employee is a "key employee" who, after having been notified of the employer's intention to deny restoration because of substantial and grievous economic injury to the employer's operations, decides not to return to work and is not reinstated. According to the DOL, "other circumstances beyond the employee's control" do not include an employee's desire to stay in a distant city with a parent who no longer require's the employee's care, or a mother's decision to stay home with a newborn child rather than return to work. [29 CFR § 825.213(b)]

Permitted Methods of Recovery. If recovery is allowed, the employer may do so by deducting its share of health insurance premiums from any sums due to the employee, such as wages, vacation pay, or profit sharing, provided that such deductions are otherwise permitted under applicable federal or state wage payment laws or other laws. Employers may also commence legal action to recover such amounts. [29 CFR § 825.213(e)]

Q 15:28   If the employer has paid the employee's portion of premiums for other coverage during an unpaid FMLA leave, may the employer recover the payments if the employee fails to return from the leave?

Yes, if the employer chooses to pay the employee's portion of premiums to maintain other coverage such as life insurance or disability insurance (or example, to avoid a lapse in coverage), the employer may recover the premium payments in the same manner, and upon the same basis, as it is permitted to do for its own contributions toward health coverage (see Q 15:27). [29 CFR § 825.213(f)]

Relationship to COBRA Continuation of Group Health Plan Rules

Q 15:29   Is the group health plan coverage during a leave considered to be continuation coverage for COBRA purposes?

No, it is not. Under the COBRA continuation of group health plan coverage rules, a leave of absence generally would be considered to be a reduction in hours. Thus, if the employee on leave of absence loses group health plan coverage at any time during the maximum applicable COBRA continuation period (see Chapter 6) because of that leave of absence, a qualifying event would occur and the maximum applicable COBRA period would be counted from the date the leave commenced. However, the legislative history of the FMLA indicates that *commencement* of a family or medical leave is not considered a qualifying event for COBRA purposes, since it does not result in a loss of coverage. Instead, the legislative history indicates that there may be a qualifying event for COBRA purposes *at the time it becomes known that the employee is not returning to employment and therefore ceases to be entitled to leave.* The qualifying event, in this instance, appears to be the employee's decision not to return from the leave of absence—in essence, a voluntary termination of employment. It appears that, in most cases, this date will coincide with the date of expiration of the leave period. [Sen Rpt No 103-3, 103rd Cong 1st Sess, at 32 (1993)]

Posting and Disclosure Requirements

Q 15:30   What posting requirement must employers satisfy under the FMLA?

All employers subject to the FMLA must post a notice, in conspicuous places on their premises where it can be readily seen by employees and applicants for employment, that explains the FMLA's provisions and provides information concerning the procedures for filing complaints of FMLA violations with the U.S. Department of Labor's Wage and Hour Division. In locations where a significant portion of the employer's workers are not literate in English, the employer must provide the information required by the FMLA's various notice provisions in a language in which the employees are literate. [29 CFR § 300] A sample form of notice has been published by the DOL for use by employers. [DOL Publication 1420, reprinted in 20 Pension & Benefits Reporter (BNA), No 30 at 1602 (July 26, 1993)]

If the employer fails to post the required notice, it cannot take any adverse action against an employee, including denying FMLA leave, for failing to furnish advance notice of a need to take FMLA leave. The employer also can be assessed a $100 penalty for each separate offence. [29 CFR § 825.300]

Q 15:31   How must an employer provide written guidance to employees concerning FMLA entitlements and employee obligations under the FMLA?

Employers must provide such information (1) in any written guidance to employees concerning benefits or leave rights (such as in employee handbooks or other documents), and (2) at the time an employee provides notice of the need for FMLA leave.

The information that employers must provide is very detailed and specific:

1. The leave will be counted against their annual FMLA entitlement;

2. Requirements (if any) for the employee to furnish medical certifications and the consequences of failing to do so;

3. The employee's right to substitute paid leave and whether the employer requires substitution of paid leave, as well as the conditions related to any substitution;

4. Requirements about any premium payments that must be made to maintain health benefits and the procedure for making the payments;

5. Any requirement for the employee to present a fitness-for-duty certificate in order to be restored to employment;

6. The employee's right to be restored to the same or an equivalent job;

7. The conditions under which restoration of employment might be denied; and

8. The employee's potential liability to refund group health plan contributions paid by the employer during the leave if he or she fails to return to work at the conclusion of the FMLA leave.

[29 CFR § 825.301]

Recordkeeping Requirements

Q 15:32 What records are employers required to maintain under the FMLA?

Employers are required to make, keep, and preserve records regarding their obligations under the FMLA in accordance with the recordkeeping requirements of both the FMLA and Section 11(c) of the FLSA.

Required Records. Under the FMLA, employers must keep the following records:

1. Basic payroll and employee data (including name, address, occupation, rate of pay and terms of compensation, daily and weekly hours worked per pay period, wage deductions and additions, and total compensation paid);

2. Dates FMLA leave is taken by employees (the employer's records must expressly designate FMLA leave as such);

3. The hours of leave, if taken in increments of less than one full day;

4. Copies of all general and specific notices provided to employees under the FMLA and copies of employee notices of leave given to the employer under the FMLA;

5. All documents, whether written or electronic, describing employee benefits or employer policies and practices concerning taking paid and unpaid leave;

6. Employee benefit premium payments; and

7. Records of any dispute over designation of leave and FMLA leave, including any written statement from the employer about the reasons for the designation and for the disagreement.

All records and documents relating to medical certifications, recertifications, or medical histories of employees or their family members must be maintained in separate files or records. They are to be treated as confidential medical records, although (1) supervisors and managers may be informed concerning any necessary restrictions on, and accommodations for, the employee's work or duties; (2) first aid and safety personnel may be informed (when appropriate) if the employee's physical or medical condition might require emergency treatment; and (3) government officials investigating FMLA compliance are to be provided relevant information upon request. [29 CFR §§ 825.500(c), (e)]

Q. 15:33   In what form are FMLA records required to be kept?

No particular order or form of records is required. Records must be kept for at least three years, and must be made available for inspection, copying, and transcription by representatives of DOL upon request. Records may be kept on microfilm or "other basic source document of an automated data processing memory" if adequate viewing equipment is kept available and the reproductions are clear and may be identified by date or pay period, and transcriptions or extensions are made available upon request. Computer records must be made available for copying or transcription. [29 CFR § 825.500(b)]

Relationship to State Laws

Q 15:34　Does the FMLA supersede all state and local laws requiring employers to provide family or medical leave?

No, the FMLA does not supersede any provision of any state or local law that provides greater family or medical leave rights than the rights under the FMLA. [FMLA § 401(b)]

> **Planning Pointer.** A number of state laws currently provide for greater rights in some respects and employers need to take state and local laws into effect in establishing a leave policy under the FMLA. ERISA might preempt the application of such state laws to a particular ERISA employee benefit plan (see Chapter 3). [Shaw v Delta Airlines, Inc, 463 US 85 (1983), footnote 22]

A discussion of the interplay between the FMLA and state family leave laws, which omits mention of the effect of ERISA preemption, is contained in 29 CFR Section 825.701.

Penalties and Enforcement

Q 15:35　Are employees who exercise their rights under the FMLA protected from discrimination by the employer?

Yes, they are. Under the FMLA, employers may not interfere with, restrain, or deny any exercise or attempted exercise of FMLA rights, or discharge or otherwise discriminate against any person for opposing or complaining about unlawful practices under the FMLA, or for filing any charge, commencing any proceeding, giving information regarding, or testifying in connection with any FMLA right. All individuals, not just employees, are protected from retaliation for opposing any unlawful practice under the FMLA or that they reasonably believe to be a violation. [29 CFR § 825.220]

Q 15:36 What federal agency is responsible for the interpretation and enforcement of the FMLA?

The DOL is the federal agency charged with implementation of the new law. [FMLA §§ 101(10), 106, 107, 404] The DOL is directed to prescribe regulations as are necessary to carry out the law by June 5, 1993. [FMLA § 404] In a notice published March 3, 1993, the DOL requested comments on a number of interpretation issues and indicated that interim final regulations would be issued by the June 5, 1993 deadline. [58 Fed Reg 13394]

The DOL also has broad investigative authority over employee compliance and the power to investigate and attempt to resolve complaints of violations of the FMLA. [FMLA §§ 106, 107(b)(1)]

Q 15:37 Can the DOL bring suit for violations of the FMLA?

Yes, the DOL has the authority to bring a suit for damages on behalf of one or more employees and to bring an action for injunctive relief and other equitable relief against the employer. [FMLA §§ 107(b)(2), 107(d)]

Q 15:38 Can an employee bring a lawsuit against an employer for violations of the FMLA?

Yes, except when the DOL already has such a lawsuit pending. An action may be brought in federal or state court for damages or equitable relief on behalf of the employee or employees suing or on behalf of the employees suing and other employees similarly situated. [FMLA § 107(a)]

Q 15:39 What damages and penalties can an employer be liable for if it violates the FMLA?

The employer is subject to a $100 penalty per violation of the FMLA notice posting requirement, as well as barred from taking adverse action against an employee or denying FMLA leave due to the employee's failure to furnish the employer with advance notice of a need to take FMLA leave (see Question 15:31).

In addition, the employer can be held liable for:

1. Any wages, salary, employment benefits, or other compensation denied or lost to the employee by reason of the violation, or in a case in which wages, salary, employment benefits, or other compensation have not been denied or lost to the employee (for example, the employee does not go on leave), any actual monetary losses sustained as a direct result of the violation, such as the cost of providing care for up to 12 weeks of wages or salary for the employee;

2. Interest on the above damages at the prevailing rate;

3. Liquidated damages equal to the actual damages above plus interest, unless the employer proves to the satisfaction of the court that the act or omission causing the violation was in good faith and that the employer had reasonable grounds for believing that the act or omission was not a violation; and

4. Such equitable relief as may be appropriate, including employment, reinstatement, and promotion.

[FMLA §§ 107(a)(1)(A), 107(b)(2); 29 CFR § 825.401]

Note. The term "employer" includes any person who acts directly or indirectly in the interest of an employer to any of the employer's employees. According to the DOL's Interim Final Rule under the FMLA [29 CFR § 815, effective August 5, 1993], individuals such as corporate officers who act in the interest of an employer would be individually liable for FMLA violations. [29 CFR § 825.104(d)]

Q 15:40   Can the employer be held liable for costs and fees in a successful lawsuit brought by an employee?

Yes, in addition to a judgment in favor of the plaintiff employee (or employees), the court may allow reasonable attorney and expert witness fees and other costs of the lawsuit to be paid by the employer. [FMLA § 107(a)(3)]

Q 15:41   What is the statute of limitations for a lawsuit claiming a violation of the FMLA?

In general, a lawsuit must be brought not later than two years after the date of the last event constituting the alleged violation for which the action is brought. [FMLA § 107(c)(1)]

However, in the case of a willful violation, the lawsuit may be brought within three years of the date of the last event constituting the alleged violation. [FMLA § 107(c)(2)]

Miscellaneous

Q 15:42   Is a family and medical leave policy conforming to the FMLA a welfare benefit plan subject to ERISA?

It appears not. Unpaid leave is not a type of welfare benefit described in Section 3(1) of ERISA or in DOL regulations. The continuation of group benefit health plan coverage during leave is, per the FMLA, now a federally mandated part of the group health plan and should not be deemed to create a separate ERISA plan. Likewise, any paid leave required to be taken before the unpaid leave would appear to be either an exempt payroll practice under DOL regulations or part of a separate ERISA plan. [DOL Reg § 2510.3-1]

Q 15:43   Are public and private primary and secondary schools and their employees subject to special rules under the FMLA?

Yes, they are. Congress apparently felt that without certain special rules modifying the general rules for employers and employees in other employment, the educational needs of children in school could be adversely affected. These special rules are contained in Section 108 of the FMLA. [Sen Rpt 103-3, 103rd Cong 1st Sess, at 36 (1993); see also 29 CFR § 825, Subpart F]

Q 15:44 What special rules apply to leased employees?

The DOL's Interim Final Rule contains special rules for determining whether a "joint employment" relationship exists. If so, the "primary" employer is responsible for giving the required notices to employees, providing leave, maintaining health benefits and restoring jobs. The "secondary employer" with 50 or more employees (including jointly employed employees) is responsible for compliance with the prohibited acts provisions with respect to its temporary and leased employees, including provisions barring discharge or discrimination for exercising, or attempting to exercise, rights under the FMLA. [29 CFR § 825.106]

Which employer is primary, and which is secondary, is a facts-and-circumstances determination based upon various factors listed in the regulations. [29 CFR § 825.196(e)]

Chapter 16

Age Discrimination in Employment Act (ADEA) of 1967

The federal Age Discrimination in Employment Act of 1967 (ADEA) places significant restrictions on the content of employee benefits plans. This chapter reviews the general requirements of the Act as well as the specific limitations which affect particular types of plans, including medical plans, disability insurance plans, group term life insurance plans, and severance pay plans.

Basic Concepts

Q 16:1   What is the federal law that prohibits employment discrimination on the basis of age?

The federal Age Discrimination in Employment Act of 1967, as amended (ADEA), prohibits discrimination by an employer against employees aged 40 or older in hiring and firing, in compensation, and in the terms, conditions, and privileges of employment. [ADEA § 4(a); 29 USC § 623(a) (1988)]

In 1990 Congress enacted major changes to the ADEA, under the Older Workers Benefit Protection Act (OWBPA), providing new age discrimination rules aimed specifically at employer-provided pension and welfare benefit plans. [Pub L No 101–433, 100 Stat 978 (1990), as amended by Pub L No 101–521, 104 Stat 2287 (1990)]

Covered Employers

Q 16:2   Which employers are subject to the ADEA?

An employer is subject to the ADEA if it is engaged in an industry affecting interstate commerce and has 20 or more employees for each working day in each of 20 or more weeks in the current or preceding calendar year. [ADEA § 11(b); 29 USC § 630(b) (1988)] State and local governments, agencies, and instrumentalities, as well as interstate agencies, are also covered employers. [ADEA § 11(b); 29 USC § 630(b) (1988)] Special provisions also apply to personnel actions affecting certain categories of federal employees. [ADEA § 15; 29 USC § 633(a) (1988)]

Covered Employees

Q 16:3   Does the ADEA apply to welfare benefits for retirees?

No, the ADEA currently applies only to older workers, that is, active employees. Once an older employee has retired or otherwise terminated employment, the employer may reduce or eliminate welfare benefits without violating the ADEA. [ADEA §§ 2, 4, 11(f); 29 USCA §§ 621, 623, 630(f) (1992 Supp); Equal Employment Opportunity Commission (EEOC) Reg § 1625.10(f)(1)(i)]

The legislative history of the OWBPA indicates that retiree benefits cannot be used as a means for discriminating against an active employee on the basis of age. This appears to mean, for example, that an employer could not provide that employees retiring at age 65 will receive group term life insurance coverage in retirement but that employees working past age 65 will receive no retiree group term life insurance coverage. [136 Cong Rec S13609 (Sept 24, 1990), H8618 (Oct 2, 1990)]

Providing Lesser Benefits to Older Workers

Q 16:4   Prior to the effective date of the OWBPA amendments to the ADEA, what rules governed whether employers could provide lesser welfare benefits to older workers as compared to younger workers?

For the period before the effective date of the OWBPA amendments (see Q 16:6), an employer generally could reduce or even eliminate welfare benefits for older employees without violating the ADEA. It previously was not a violation of the ADEA for an employer to observe the terms of a bona fide employee benefit plan that was not a subterfuge to evade the purposes of the ADEA, provided that no such employee benefit plan could be used to refuse to hire someone because of age, or to retire someone involuntarily on the basis of age (except for certain executive and high policy-making employees who may be required to retire at age 65). [ADEA §§ 4(f)(2), 12(c); 29 USC §§ 623(f)(2), 631(c) (1988)]

The U.S. Supreme Court held that this "bona fide employee benefits plan" exception under the ADEA permitted discriminatory reductions in benefits for older employees, unless the older employees claiming discrimination on the basis of age could show that the discriminatory benefits coverage was intended to serve the purpose of discriminating in some aspect of the employment relationship other than fringe benefits. [Public Employees Retirement System of Ohio v Betts, 492 US 158 (1989)] The Supreme Court also reaffirmed its position that an employee benefits plan that was adopted prior to the enactment of the ADEA could not be considered a subterfuge to evade the purposes of the Act.

On remand from the U.S. Supreme Court, the U.S. Court of Appeals for the Sixth Circuit held in the *Betts* case that because the employee was denied disability benefits because of age, she had been forced to choose between taking unpaid medical leave or taking retirement with a benefit substantially lower than what the disability benefit would have been. The court concluded (in a two-to-one decision) that the employee's choice of retirement was, in effect, forced upon her, and thus the bona fide employee benefit plan exemption did not apply. [Betts v Hamilton Co Board of Mental Retardation and Developmental Disabilities, (897 F 2d 1380 (6th Cir 1990); but see EEOC v Westinghouse Electric Corp, 907 F 2d 1354 (1990)]

Q 16:5 Can an employer still rely on the U.S. Supreme Court decision in *Betts* case to reduce or eliminate welfare benefits for older employees?

No. The OWBPA amendments to the ADEA legislatively over-turned the U.S. Supreme Court decision in the *Betts* case on a prospective basis. Now that the OWBPA amendments are effective with respect to plans (see Question 16:6 for effective dates):

1. Age discrimination in employee benefits and employee benefits plans is prohibited;

2. The employer is required to bear the burden of proof in order to justify a reduction in benefits for older employees on a cost-equivalency basis;

3. The "subterfuge" wording in the law has been eliminated and the ADEA applies to an employee benefits plan regardless of whether it, or any of its discriminatory provisions, predated the enactment of the ADEA; and

4. The circumstances under which employees can waive their rights under the ADEA are expressly restricted.

Q 16:6   What is the effective date of the OWBPA amendments to the ADEA?

In the case of any employee benefit established or modified on or after October 16, 1990, the OWBPA amendments apply as of the date of establishment or modification.

With respect to employee benefits that existed on October 16, 1990 and that have not been modified, the general effective date is the 181st day after the date of enactment, or April 15, 1991. In other words, plans must have been brought into compliance by no later than April 14, 1991.

However, in the case of a collective bargaining agreement that was in effect on October 16, 1990, the effective date for application of the OWBPA amendments is the *earlier* of (1) The date of termination of the collective bargaining agreement, or (2) June 1, 1992.

Where the employer is a state, a political subdivision of a state, or an agency or instrumentality of either, and the employer maintained an employee benefit plan at any time between June 23, 1989 and October 16, 1990 that can be modified only through a change in applicable state or local law, the effective date is October 16, 1992.

Series of Benefit Payments Commencing Prior to October 16, 1990. A series of benefit payments made to an individual or the individual's representative that began prior to October 16, 1990 and that continue after that date pursuant to an arrangement that was in effect on October 16, 1990 is not subject to the OWBPA amendments. However, no substantial modification to such an arrangement may be made after October 16, 1990 if the intent of the modification is to evade the purposes of the OWBPA. [Pub L No 101–433, 100 Stat 978 § 105 (Oct 16, 1990)]

Bona Fide Plan Requirements

Q 16:7   What initial requirements must a welfare benefits plan meet in order to qualify for the differences in cost or the latitude in benefit design permitted under the ADEA regulations?

To qualify for the differences in cost or the latitude in benefit design permitted by the ADEA, an employee benefits plan must be "bona fide": The plan's terms must have been accurately described in writing to all employees and the plan must actually provide benefits in accordance with the terms of the plan. In addition, employees must be notified promptly of the plan's provisions and any changes thereto so that they will know how the plan affects them. For this purpose, satisfaction of ERISA's disclosure requirements is sufficient. [ADEA § 4(f)(2); 29 USCA § 623(f)(2) (1992 Supp); EEOC Reg § 1625.10(b)] [See Chapter 2 for a discussion of Employee Retirement Income Security Act (ERISA) disclosure requirements.]

Cost-Equivalency Rule

Q 16:8 What is the "cost-equivalency" rule under the ADEA?

The EEOC regulations state that, in general, an employer violates the ADEA *unless*:

1. Older employees are provided with the same benefits as younger employees; or

2. Older employees are provided with benefits that are reduced only to the extent that the cost of the benefits for older employees is at least equal to the cost of the benefits for younger employees.

[EEOC Reg § 1625.10(a)]

Q 16:9 What is the rationale for the cost-equivalency rule under the ADEA?

The purpose of the cost-equivalency rule is to permit age-based reductions in bona fide employee benefit plans where such reductions are justified by significant cost considerations. If the benefits plan satisfies certain specified conditions, then benefit levels for older workers may be reduced to the extent necessary to achieve approximate equivalency in cost for older and younger workers. A benefits plan will be treated as complying with the ADEA where the actual amount of payment made (or cost incurred) on behalf of an older worker is equal to that made (or incurred) on behalf of a younger worker. [EEOC Reg § 1625.10(a)(1)]

Q 16:10   Under the ADEA's cost-equivalency rule, what methods of cost comparison and adjustment are permitted?

The EEOC regulations provide two methods for making cost comparisons and adjustments: the benefit-by-benefit approach and the benefit package approach (see Q 16:21).

Q 16:11   What is the benefit-by-benefit approach?

Under the benefit-by-benefit approach, an employer may adjust the amount or level of a specific form of benefit for a specific event or contingency.

For example, the employer can reduce the amount of group term life insurance for older workers, based on their ages, to reflect higher group term life insurance costs for older workers. However, under the benefit-by-benefit approach, an employer may not substitute one form of benefit for another, even if both forms of benefit are designed for the same contingency (for example, death). [EEOC Reg § 1625.10(d)(2)(i)] An employer may not reduce paid vacations and uninsured paid sick leave based on age, since reductions in these benefits would not be justified by significant cost considerations. [EEOC Reg § 1625.10(a)(1)]

Q 16:12   What kind of cost data may be used under ADEA to support a reduction in benefits?

Cost data that is used to justify a reduction in benefits for older employees must be valid and reasonable. This standard is met where an employer has cost data that show the actual cost to the employer of providing the particular benefit (or benefits) in question over a representative period of years. An employer may rely on:

1. Cost data for its own employees over such a period, or

2. Cost data for a larger group of similarly situated employees.

However, an employer may not rely on cost data for a similarly situated group of employees if:

1. Due to experience rating or other causes, the employer incurs costs that differ significantly from costs for a group of similarly situated employees; and

2. Such reliance would result in significantly lower benefits for its own older employees.

If reliable cost information is not available, reasonable projections made from existing cost data meeting the standards set forth above will be considered acceptable. [EEOC Reg § 1625.10(d)(1)]

Q 16:13 Must the cost of coverage for older workers be compared on a year-by-year age basis?

No, an employer is permitted to compare the increased cost of providing a benefit on the basis of age brackets encompassing up to five years. Thus, under the benefit-by-benefit approach, a particular benefit may be reduced for employees of any age within the ADEA's protected age group (age 40 and older) by an amount no greater than that which could be justified by the additional cost of providing them with the same level of benefit as younger employees within the five-year age group immediately preceding theirs.

Example. If the employer desires to reduce the amount of group term life insurance for employees beginning at age 60, the group term life insurance benefits provided to employees aged 60 to 64 can be reduced only to the extent necessary to achieve approximate equivalency in costs with employees aged 55 to 59. Similarly, if the employer also desires a further reduction in the benefit levels for employees aged 65 to 69, such a further reduction cannot exceed an amount that is proportional to the additional costs for that age group's coverage over that of the group aged 60 to 64.

[EEOC Reg § 1625.10(d)(3)]

Q 16:14 If an employer reduces benefits based on age, must it do so for all age brackets?

No, the employer remains free to offer level coverage up to a particular age and then begin reducing coverage. For example, the employer may decide to reduce coverage beginning at age 70. However, reductions at that or any later age cannot exceed the amount that is proportional to the additional costs for that five-year age bracket over that of the preceding five-year age bracket. [EEOC Reg § 1625.10(d)(3)]

Q 16:15 Can an older employee be required to make greater contributions to an employee benefit plan than a younger employee as a condition of employment?

No, such a requirement would be, in effect, a mandatory reduction in take-home pay based on age and would discourage employment of older employees. [EEOC Reg § 1625.10(d)(4)(i)]

Q 16:16 Can an older employee be required to make greater contributions than younger employees to a voluntary employee benefit plan as a condition of participation in such plan?

Yes. As long as participation in the plan is voluntary, no mandatory reduction in take-home pay based on age is being imposed. However, the older employee cannot be required to bear a greater proportion of the total premium cost (both employer-paid and employee-paid) than the younger employee. Requiring an older employee to bear a greater proportion of the premium cost would make compensation in the form of an employer contribution available on less favorable terms than for the younger employee and would have the effect of denying that compensation altogether to older employees unwilling or unable to meet the less favorable terms. [EEOC Reg § 1625.10(d)(4)(ii)]

Employer-Pay-All Plans. If younger employees are not required to contribute any portion of the premium cost, older employees may not be required to do so either. [EEOC Reg § 1625.10(d)(4)(ii)(B)]

Employee-Pay-All Plans. All employees, young and old alike, may be required to contribute as a condition of participation up to the full premium cost for their age. [EEOC Reg § 1625.10(d)(4)(ii)(A)]

Contributory Plans. If the employer and the participating employees share the premium costs, the required participant contributions may increase with age provided that the proportion of the total premium that participants are required to pay does not increase with age. For example, all participants could be required to bear 25 percent of the cost of the plan at each age bracket, but the employer could not require employees under age 60 to contribute 25 percent of the cost and require employees aged 60 and above to contribute 50 percent of the cost.

Q 16:17   Can the employer give older employees the option to pay more in order to receive full, unreduced benefits?

Yes, it may. If the employer's plan reduces coverage by age on a cost-justified basis in accordance with the EEOC regulations, the employer may voluntarily offer older employees the choice of paying extra to purchase full, unreduced coverage (but not more than such coverage actually costs at that age bracket). [EEOC Reg § 1625.10(d)(4)(iii)]

Q 16:18   How is the benefit-by-benefit approach applied to life insurance?

It is common practice for employer-provided life insurance to remain constant until a specified age, such as age 65 or 70, and then be reduced thereafter. This practice will not violate the ADEA as long as the reduction for an employee of a particular age is justified by the increased cost of coverage for that employee's specific age bracket encompassing no more than five years. [EEOC Reg § 1625.10(f)(1)(i)]

A total denial of life insurance at any age cannot be justified on a benefit-by-benefit basis. It is permissible, however, to cease life insurance coverage upon retirement or other separation from service. [EEOC Reg § 1625.10(f)(1)(i)]

Q 16:19   How is the benefit-by-benefit approach applied to long-term disability insurance?

Under the benefit-by-benefit approach, an employer providing long-term disability coverage to all employees may avoid any cost increases that such coverage for older employees would entail by reducing the level of benefits available to older employees. An employer may also avoid such cost increases by reducing the duration of the long-term disability benefits available to employees who become disabled at older ages, without reducing the level of benefits. (Any such reduction in the level or duration of benefits must be justified on the basis of the permitted age-based cost considerations set forth in Questions 16:8 through 16:17.)

The EEOC regulations restored by the OWBPA contain a safe harbor provision for long-term disability plan designs. No ADEA violation will be asserted by the EEOC if the level of benefits is not reduced and the duration of benefits is reduced according to the following:

1. For disabilities that occur at or before age 60, the long-term disability benefits may cease at age 65,
2. For disabilities that occur after age 60, the long-term disability benefits may cease five years after disablement. Cost data may be produced to support other patterns of reduction as well.

Of course, it is also permissible to cut off long-term disability benefits and coverage on the basis of recovery from disability or because of some other non-age factor. However, a total denial of long-term disability benefits at any age cannot be justified on a benefit-by-benefit basis. [EEOC Reg § 1625.10(f)(1)(ii)]

Note. If long-term disability payments began prior to October 16, 1990 under an arrangement in existence on that date, such an arrangement is grandfathered unless it is modified with the intent to evade the purposes of the OWBPA (see Q 16:6.)

Q 16:20   Can an employer's employee welfare benefit plan coordinate with government-provided benefits?

Yes, with the important exception noted in the following paragraph, an employer's plan can "wrap around" government-provided benefits as long as, taking the employer-provided and government-provided benefits together, an older employee is entitled to a benefit (including coverage for family and/or dependents) that is no less than that provided to a similarly situated younger employee. [EEOC Reg § 1625.10(e)]

One very important exception to this rule is coordination with Medicare benefits. The EEOC regulations restored by the OWBPA contain outdated language permitting employer group health plans for active employees to wrap around Medicare. Those regulations were never updated to reflect subsequent amendments to the ADEA that expressly prohibited reduction of group health benefits of an active employee or spouse due to attainment of age 65 (referred to as the "working aged" provisions). Furthermore, ADEA's working-aged provisions have since been legislatively deleted from the ADEA and moved to Section 5000 of the Internal Revenue Code (Code), which generally does not allow employer group health plans to wrap around Medicare benefits for active employees. (See Qs 3:57–3:61 for the rules on group health plan coordination with Medicare.)

Q 16:21   What is the benefit package approach?

As an alternative to the benefit-by-benefit approach, the restored EEOC regulations also permit employers to reduce the level or duration of benefits by using a second method, the benefit package approach. Under this second method, employer justifies the age-related cost reduction under one benefit by aggregating the costs of two or more benefits. Essentially, if the employer reduces a benefit more than is justified by a benefit-by-benefit approach, it must give an offsetting benefit so that the overall effect is not lesser benefits or greater cost to employees on the basis of age. No employees may be deprived of one benefit because of age unless an offsetting benefit is made available to them.

Example: Suppose an employer could make age-based, cost-justified reductions in benefits under benefit Plan A and benefit Plan B on a benefit-by-benefit basis. Assume that benefits under each plan could be reduced by 10 percent. If the reduction under both plans costs the same, the employer could, under the benefit package approach, leave benefits under Plan A at 100 percent and reduce benefits under Plan B by 20 percent instead. However, if the permitted reduction on a benefit-by-benefit basis under Plan A costs one half of the permitted reduction under Plan B, an employer using the benefit package approach could only reduce benefits under Plan B by 15 percent.

In other words, the benefit package approach consists of calculating the permissible age-based, cost-justified reductions on a benefit-by-benefit approach, totaling them, and applying them all to one plan or, by splitting them among plans, applying them on an aggregate basis. However, under the benefit package approach, employees cannot be deprived of one benefit because of age unless an offsetting benefit is made available to them. [EEOC Reg §§ 1625.10(d)(2)(ii), 1625.10(f)(2)(iv), 1625.10(f)(2)(v)]

Using Retirement Benefits to Reduce Other Benefits

Q 16:22   May the benefit package approach be used for any kind of employee benefits plan?

Under the restored EEOC regulations, pension or retirement benefits may not be used to justify reductions in other benefits such as employee welfare benefits. In addition, reductions in health benefits may be justified only on the basis of the health benefits standing alone; the cost of other coverage cannot be used to justify reductions in health benefits. On the other hand, health benefits may be included in a benefit package to justify age-based reductions in other benefits. [EEOC Reg §§ 1625.10(f)(2)(ii), 1625.10(f)(2)(iii)]

However, these restored EEOC regulations do not reflect the ADEA amendments added by the OWBPA. The OWBPA amendments contain two statutory exceptions to the rule that pension or retirement benefits may not be used to justify reductions in employee welfare benefits (see Qs 16:23 and 16:28).

Q 16:23   Does the ADEA permit retirement benefits to be used to reduce long-term disability benefits?

Yes, the OWBPA amendments to the ADEA provide that long-term disability benefits may be offset by pension benefits (other than those attributable to the individual's own contributions), provided that:

1. The individual has voluntarily elected to receive the pension benefits; or

2. The individual has attained the later of age 62 or normal retirement age and is eligible for pension benefits.

[ADEA § 4(1)(3), 29 USCA § 623(1)(3) (1992 Supp)]

This permitted integration of pension benefits with long-term disability benefits avoids "double-dipping" by employees while permitting the benefits to be integrated in such a way that the employee receives combined payments at the level of the greater of either pension or disability benefits. Accordingly, the income payments to the employee do not decrease, but the source of payments may shift. [136 Cong Rec S13606 (Sept 24, 1990)] (See Question 16:6 for the grandfather rule applicable to long-term disability payments commencing before October 16, 1990.)

> **Planning Pointer.** The statute does not discuss how the amount of pension benefits attributable to the employee's contributions is to be calculated. Presumably, until the EEOC promulgates regulations, it should be permissible to follow the pension accrual rules under ERISA and the IRC.

Q 16:24   What special ADEA rules apply to long-term disability plans of state and local governments?

Special transitional provisions apply to state long-term disability plans because of concerns about the cost of compliance with the OWBPA rules and possible conflict with state anti-cutback statutes or with contract clause restrictions in state constitutions.

A state or local government (or instrumentality of either) that had a long-term disability plan in existence at any time between June 23, 1989 and prior to October 16, 1990 may offer employees covered by such a plan a choice between (1) a new plan complying with the ADEA as amended by the OWBPA and (2) the old plan, regardless of whether the employees are currently disabled. The following conditions must be satisfied:

1. The offer to each employee must be made and "reasonable notice" be given to employees no later than October 16, 1992; and

2. Each employee must be given up to 180 days after the offer in which to make the election.

[OWBPA § 105(c)]

Note. The legislative history indicates that the election period must be "at least" 180 days. Thus, a technical correction to the statute appears to be necessary to clarify this point. [136 Cong Rec H8619 (Oct 2, 1990)]

Q 16:25 How does a state or local government satisfy the "reasonable notice" standard when offering employees an alternate long-term disability plan during the ADEA transition period?

To satisfy the requirements of the transitional rule under the ADEA as amended by the OWBPA, a state or local government offering an alternative long-term disability plan must give each employee notice that satisfies the following conditions:

1. It is sufficiently accurate and comprehensive to apprise the employee of the terms and conditions of the disability benefits, including whether the employee is immediately eligible for such benefits; and

2. It is written in a manner calculated to be understood by the average employee eligible to participate.

[OWBPA § 105(c)(4)(C)]

Q 16:26 If the state or local governmental employee elects the new long-term disability plan, does he or she retain any rights under the old plan?

No. If the employee of a state or local government elects coverage under the new plan offered as an alternative by the employer during the transitional period, he or she gives up all rights to receive existing disability benefits. However, the employee keeps all accumulated years of service for purposes of determining eligibility for the new benefits. [OWBPA § 105(c)(2)(C)]

Q 16:27 What if a state or local government provides long-term disability benefits through a pension plan?

The special transitional rules under the ADEA for state and local governmental long-term disability plans apply whether the long-term disability plan is freestanding or is part of a pension plan. [OWBPA § 105(c)(4)(B)]

Q 16:28 Can severance pay be denied or reduced because of eligibility for, or receipt of, retirement benefits?

In general, the ADEA, as amended by the OWBPA, prohibits an employer from reducing or eliminating severance pay solely because the employee is eligible for, or will receive, retirement plan benefits. However, a limited statutory exception exists.

Where the severance pay is payable as a result of a contingent event unrelated to the employee's age, such as a plant closing or layoff, the severance pay may be reduced by additional pension benefits (called "pension sweeteners") that are payable solely as a result of the contingent event, provided that the individual is eligible for an immediate and unreduced pension. [ADEA § 4(1)(2)(A)(ii); 29 USCA § 623(1)(2)(A)(ii) (1992 Supp)]

For this purpose, severance pay includes supplemental unemployment benefits under Code Section 501(c)(17) for up to 52 weeks, having the primary purpose and effect of continuing benefits until the individual becomes eligible for an immediate and unreduced pension and ceasing once the individual becomes eligible for the immediate and unreduced pension. [ADEA § 4(1)(2)(C); 29 USCA § 623(1)(2)(C) (1992 Supp)]

Q 16:29 May severance pay be denied or reduced because of receipt of retiree health benefits?

Generally, the ADEA, as amended by the OWBPA, also prohibits reduction or elimination of severance pay solely because the employee is eligible for, or receives, retiree health benefits. ADEA does, however, contain a carefully circumscribed exception to this general rule.

Where the severance pay is payable as a result of a contingent event unrelated to the employee's age, such as a plant shutdown or layoff, the value of retiree health benefits may be subtracted from severance benefits (including supplemental unemployment benefits, as described in Question 16:28) if the following conditions are satisfied:

1. The employee must be eligible for an immediate pension;

2. If the individual receives immediate pension benefits that are actuarially reduced, the value of retiree health benefits that may be subtracted is reduced by the same percentage as the reduction in pension benefits; and

3. Retiree health benefits must have a certain minimum value in order to be subtracted from severance pay benefits (see Question 16:30 to determine this minimum value).

[ADEA §§ 4(1)(2)(A)(i), 4(1)(2)(D); 29 USCA §§ 623(1)(2)(A)(i), 623(1)(2)(D) (1992 Supp)]

Q 16:30   For purposes of calculating the permitted reduction of severance pay by the value of retiree health benefits, how is the value of the retiree health benefits determined?

The OWBPA amendments to the ADEA contain explicit rules concerning the value of retiree health benefits which can be used to reduce severance pay that is payable as a result of a contingent event unrelated to the employee's age, as follows:

1. The retiree health benefits provided to retirees below age 65 must be at least "comparable" to Medicare benefits under Title XVIII of the Social Security Act. [ADEA § 4(1)(2)(D)(i); 29 USCA § 623(1)(2)(D)(i) (1992 Supp)]

2. The retiree health benefits provided to retirees aged 65 and above must be at least "comparable" to 25 percent of Medicare benefits under Title XVIII of the Social Security Act. [ADEA § 4(1)(2)(D)(ii), 29 USCA § 623(1)(2)(D)(ii) (1992 Supp)]

If the employer's obligation to provide retiree health benefits is of limited duration, the value for each individual is to be calculated at a rate of $3,000 per year for benefit years before age 65 and $750 per year for benefit years beginning at age 65 and above. [ADEA § 4(1)(2)(E)(i); 29 USCA § 623(1)(2)(E)(i) (1992 Supp)]

If the employer's obligation to provide retiree health benefits is of unlimited duration, the value for each individual is to be calculated at a rate of $48,000 for individuals below age 65 and $24,000 for individuals aged 65 and above. [ADEA § 4(1)(2)(E)(ii); 29 USCA § 623(1)(2)(E)(ii) (1992 Supp)]

The age of the individual that is used for this purpose is his or her age as of the date of the contingent event unrelated to age. For contingent events occurring in years following the year after enactment of the OWBPA amendments, the dollar values described in the preceding paragraphs will be adjusted annually based on the medical component of the Department of Labor's all-urban Consumers Price Index. [ADEA § 4(1)(2)(E)(iii); 29 USCA § 623(1)(2)(E)(iii) (1992 Supp)]

Contributory Plans. If the individual is required to pay a premium for the retiree health benefits, the value calculated under the rules in the preceding paragraphs must be reduced by whatever percentage of the overall premium the individual is required to pay. [ADEA § 4(1)(2)(E)(iv); 29 USCA § 623(1)(2)(E)(iv) (1992 Supp)]

Q 16:31 Must the employer make retiree health benefits available to all retirees regardless of age in order to be entitled under ADEA to use the value of such benefits to reduce severance pay?

No. A technical amendment to the OWBPA contained in Public Law Number 101-521 (November 5, 1990) clarified that point. The employer is not required to offer health benefits to retirees both above and below age 65 in order to offset severance pay by the value of retiree health benefits. An employer may offer health benefits only to retirees under age 65 and still make the offset described in the ADEA, as amended by the OWBPA. [ADEA § (4)(1)(2)(D)(iii); 29 USCA § 623(1)(2)(D)(iii) (1992 Supp)]

Q 16:32   Does the ADEA permit employers to reduce severance pay by the value of both pension benefits and retiree health benefits?

Yes; in the case of a contingent event unrelated to age, an employer having both pension sweeteners (see Q 16:28) and retiree health benefits (see Qs 16:28 and 16:29) may reduce the severance pay payable as a result of such contingent event by either or both. [ADEA § (4)(1)(2)(A); 29 USCA § 623(1)(2)(A) (1992 Supp)]

Q 16:33   If the employer reduces severance pay by the value of retiree medical benefits, as permitted under the ADEA, what recourse do retirees have in the event the employer fails to fulfill its obligation to provide retiree medical benefits?

If the employer has availed itself of the limited ADEA exemption allowing severance pay that is payable due to a contingent event unrelated to age to be reduced by the value of retiree health benefits, the employer is subject to an action for specific performance by any "aggrieved individual" for failing to fulfill its obligation to provide retiree health benefits. This relief is in addition to any other remedies provided under federal or state law. [ADEA § 4(1)(2)(F); 29 USCA § 623(1)(2)(F) (1992 Supp)]

Q 16:34   Prior to the OWBPA amendments to the ADEA, could an employer require an employee to waive his or her rights under the ADEA as a condition of receiving severance pay?

Yes, waivers occurring before October 16, 1990 are valid under the ADEA (as well as under other federal laws) in certain circumstances. In determining whether these pre-October 16, 1990 waivers are valid, courts look to such factors as the following:

1. The clarity of the release's language;

2. Whether the employee received additional substantial consideration, such as additional severance benefits beyond what the employee would otherwise receive;

3. Whether the employee received advice of legal counsel or, if not, whether he or she had an opportunity or was encouraged to do so;

4. Whether the employee had an opportunity to negotiate the terms of the release;

5. How much time the employee had to consider his or her options; and

6. The employee's level of education and experience.

If the court is satisfied, based on these factors, that the employee was fairly treated, then the pre-October 16, 1990 release will be enforceable. [Bormann v AT&T Comm, Inc, 875 F 2d 399 (2d Cir 1989), *cert denied,* 110 S Ct 292 (1989); see also Gormin v Brown-Forman Corp 963 F 2d 323 (11th Cir. 1992)]

Note. Under the OWBPA amendments to the ADEA, waivers occurring on or after October 16, 1990 must meet specified minimum statutory requirements in order to be treated as valid (see Qs 16:36-16:40). [OWBPA § 201, adding ADEA § 7(f); 29 USCA § 626(f) (1992 Supp)]

Providing Greater Benefits to Older Workers

Q 16:35   May an employee benefits plan provide greater benefits to older employees on the basis of age without violating the ADEA?

Yes, it appears so. A benefit plan that provided early retirement benefits only to employees 50 years old or older was held not to violate the ADEA. The court found that the ADEA does not prohibit reverse discrimination on the basis of age, but only discrimination against older employees. [Hamilton v Caterpillar Inc, 966 F 2d 1226 (7th Cir 1992)]

Waiver of ADEA Rights and Claims

Q 16:36   May an individual waive all rights and claims under the ADEA?

Yes, an individual may waive all of his or her rights and claims under the ADEA. However, any waiver made on or after October

16, 1990 must be "knowing and voluntary" under the ADEA, as amended by the OWBPA. [ADEA § 7(f)(1); 29 USCA § 626(f)(1) (1992 Supp)]

Q 16:37   What specific criteria must be met in order for a waiver to be considered "knowing and voluntary"?

A waiver of ADEA rights and claims that occurs on or after October 16, 1990 will not be considered to be knowing and voluntary *unless* the following conditions are met:

1. The waiver is part of a written agreement between the individual and the employer that is written in a manner calculated to be understood by such individual, or by the average individual eligible to participate;
2. The waiver specifically refers to rights or claims arising under the ADEA;
3. The individual does not waive rights or claims that may arise after the date the waiver is executed;
4. The individual waives rights or claims only in exchange for money or other consideration in addition to anything of value to which the individual already is entitled;
5. The individual is advised in writing to consult with an attorney prior to executing the agreement;
6. The individual is given a period of:
   — At least 21 days to consider the agreement, or
   — At least 45 days to consider the agreement in the case of an exit incentive or other employment termination program offered to a group or class of employees;
7. The agreement provides that, for a period of at least seven days after the date it is executed, the individual may revoke it and the agreement will not become effective or enforceable until the seven-day period has expired; and
8. If the waiver is requested in connection with an exit incentive or other employment termination program offered to a group or class of employees, the employer must satisfy the addi-

tional statutory disclosure requirements set forth in Question 16:48.

[ADEA § 7(f)(1); 29 USCA § 626(f)(1) (1992 Supp)]

Q 16:38 What disclosure must an employer make in connection with an exit incentive or other employment termination program offered to a group or class of employees?

If the employer offers an exit incentive or other employment termination program to a group or class of employees and, in connection with such a program, requests that the employee waive any right or claim under the ADEA, the employer must, as an additional condition of obtaining a knowing and voluntary waiver from the employee, also supply the following information to the eligible employees at the beginning of the 45-day election period described in Question 16:47:

- Any class, unit, or group of individuals covered by the program;
- Any eligibility factors for the program;
- Any time limits applicable to the program;
- The job titles and ages of all individuals eligible or selected for the program; and
- The ages of all individuals in the same job classification or organizational unit who are not eligible or selected for the program.

This information must be provided to the individual employees in writing, in a manner calculated to be understood by the average individual eligible to participate in such a program. [ADEA § 7(f)(1)(H); 29 USCA § 626(f)(1)(H) (1992 Supp)]

Q 16:39 Who must prove that a waiver under ADEA is knowing and voluntary—the employer or the employee?

The person asserting the validity of a waiver of rights and claims under the ADEA (usually, the employer) has the burden of proving that the waiver occurred under circumstances meeting the ADEA's requirements to be considered knowing and voluntary. [ADEA § 7(f)(3); 29 USCA § 626(f)(3) (1992 Supp)]

Q 16:40   Does a waiver that is knowing and voluntary under the ADEA restrict the EEOC's powers to investigate and enforce the ADEA?

No. Even if a waiver of all rights and claims under the ADEA meets all of the statutory requirements necessary to be considered knowing and voluntary, the EEOC remains free to pursue its rights and responsibilities to enforce the ADEA. In addition, no waiver may be used to justify interfering with the employee's protected right to file a charge or participate in an investigation or proceeding conducted by the EEOC. [ADEA § 7(f)(4); 29 USCA § 626(f)(4) (1992 Supp)]

Penalties

Q 16:41   What penalties apply if the ADEA is violated?

The ADEA incorporates by reference the remedies of the federal Fair Labor Standards Act of 1938 (FLSA). In general, complainants may obtain attorneys' fees, back pay, and either (1) equitable relief such as a judgment compelling employment, reinstatement, or promotion, or enforcing liabilities for amounts held to be owing or (2) "front pay" equal to the pay the plaintiff would have received from the date of judgment to the date he or she would have left the defendant's employ, had there been no discrimination. The employee must mitigate (that is, try to reduce) damages by seeking other employment. Liquidated damages equal to the back-pay liability are payable only in cases of a willful violation of the ADEA. [ADEA § 7; 29 USCA § 626 (1992 Supp)]

The OWBPA amendments to the ADEA also give an individual whose severance pay was offset by the value of retiree health benefits a right to compel specific performance of the employer's obligation to provide such retiree health benefits. [ADEA § (4)(1)(2)(F), 29 USCA § 623(1)(2)(F) (1992 Supp)]

Relationship to State Laws

Q 16:42　Does the ADEA preempt state age discrimination laws purporting to regulate welfare benefit plans?

No, state age discrimination laws generally are not preempted by the ADEA and often also protect young workers (for example, age 18 through 39) as well from discrimination on the basis of age. [ADEA § 14; 29 USC § 633 (1988)] However, ERISA preempts state age laws that affect benefit plans that are ERISA plans. [Shaw v Delta Airlines, Inc, 463 US 85 (1983), note 22]

Chapter 17

Americans with Disabilities Act of 1990

Basic Concepts

Q 17:1 What does the Americans with Disabilities Act of 1990 (ADA) cover?

The ADA prohibits covered employers from discriminating against a disabled individual in regard to any of the following aspects of employment:

- Recruitment, advertising, and job application procedures

- Hiring, advancement, or discharge (including upgrading, promotion, award of tenure, demotion, transfer, layoff, termination, right of return from layoff, and rehiring)
- Compensation (including rates of pay or any other form of compensation and changes in compensation)
- Job assignments, job classifications, organizational structures, position descriptions, lines of progression, and seniority lists
- Leaves of absence, sick leave, or any other leave
- Fringe benefits available by virtue of employment, whether or not administered by the covered employer
- Job training (including selection and financial support for training), such as apprenticeships, professional meetings, conferences, and other related activities and selection for leaves of absence to pursue training
- Activities sponsored by a covered employer (including social and recreational programs), and
- Any other term, condition, or privilege of employment

[ADA § 102(a); 42 USCA § 12112(a) (1992 Supp); EEOC Reg § 1630.4]

Covered Employers

Q 17:2   What employers are covered by the ADA?

An employer engaged in an industry affecting commerce, and any agent of such employer, will be covered under the ADA, effective on the following dates:

1. July 26, 1992, if the employer has 25 or more employees on each working day in each of 20 or more calendar weeks in the current or preceding calendar year; and
2. July 26, 1994, if the employer has 15 or more employees for each working day in each of 20 or more calendar weeks in the current or preceding calendar year.

[ADA § 101(5); 42 USCA § 12111(5) (1992 Supp); EEOC Reg. § 1630.2(e)(1)]

Covered employers include state and local governments (but not the United States or a corporation wholly owned by the United States, or an Indian tribe). [EEOC Reg § 1630.2(e)(2)]

Covered Disabilities

Q 17:3   What is a covered disability under the ADA?

A covered disability is any of the following:

- A physical or mental impairment that substantially limits one or more of the major life activities of such individual
- A record of such an impairment, or
- Being regarded as having such an impairment

[ADA § 3(2), 42 USCA § 12102(2) (1992 Supp)]

Physical or mental impairment: For purposes of the ADA, a "physical or mental impairment" is defined as:

- Any physiological disorder, or condition, cosmetic disfigurement, or anatomical loss affecting one or more specified body systems: neurological, musculoskeletal, special sense organs, respiratory (including speech organs), cardiovascular, reproductive, digestive, genito-urinary, hemic and lymphatic, skin, and endocrine systems, or
- Any mental or psychological disorder, such as mental retardation, organic brain syndrome, emotional or mental illness, and specific learning disabilities

[EEOC Reg. § 1630.2(h)]

Major life activities: For purposes of the ADA, "major life activities" include caring for oneself, performing manual tasks, walking, seeing, hearing, speaking, breathing, learning, and working. [EEOC Reg § 1630.2(i)]

Substantially limits: The EEOC regulations define "substantially limits" in both work and non-work contexts. In general, the term means that an individual is (1) unable to perform a major life activity that can be performed by the average person in the general population, or (2) significantly restricted as to the condition, manner, or duration in which he or she can perform a major life activity compared to the average person in the general population. Factors to be considered in making a determination of "substantially limited" include the nature and severity of the impairment, the duration or expected duration of the impairment, and the actual or expected permanent or long-term impact of, the impairment. (However, either one of the limits described above or a perceived limit could form the basis of an employment discrimination charge.)

For the major life activity of "working," substantially limited means significantly restricted, as compared to the average person having comparable training, skills, and abilities, in the ability to perform within a class of jobs or within a broad range of jobs in various classes. However, an inability to perform a single, particular job is not a substantial limitation in the major life activity of working. In addition to the factors listed previously, the EEOC regulations state that certain additional factors should be considered when evaluating whether an individual is substantially limited in the major life activity of working. These factors include the following:

1. The geographical area to which the individual has reasonable access;

2. The job from which the impairment disqualifies the individual and the number and types of other jobs within the geographic area that use similar training, knowledge, skills, or abilities, from which the individual also is disqualified because of the impairment (a class of jobs); and

3. The job from which the impairment disqualifies the individual and the number and types of other jobs within that geographic area that do not use similar training, knowledge, skills, or abilities, from which the individual is also disqualified because of the impairment (a broad range of jobs in various classes).

[EEOC Reg § 1630.2(j)(3)(ii)]

Q 17:4 Are there physical or medical conditions that do not constitute impairments protected by the ADA?

Yes. The term impairment does not include physical characteristics such as eye color, hair color, left-handedness, or height, weight, or muscle tone that are within normal range and are not the result of a physiological disorder.

Characteristic predisposition to illness or disease is not an impairment. Other conditions, such as pregnancy, that are not the result of a physiological disorder are not impairments, either.

Common personality traits such as poor judgment or a quick temper, which are not symptoms of a mental or psychological disorder, are not protected, nor are environmental, cultural, or economic disadvantages such as poverty, lack of education, or a prison record.

Advanced age, in and of itself, is not an impairment, but medical conditions commonly associated with advanced age, such as hearing loss, osteoporosis, or arthritis would be protected impairments. [Appendix to EEOC Reg Part 1630—Interpretive Guidance on § 1630.2(h)]

Q 17:5 What conditions are excluded from coverage under the ADA?

Homosexuality and bisexuality are not considered to be impairments and are not disabilities for purposes of the ADA. [ADA § 511(a); 42 USC § 12211(a); EEOC Reg § 1630.3(e)]

In addition, covered disabilities under the ADA do not include transvestism, transsexualism, pedophilia, exhibitionism, voyeurism, gender identity disorders not resulting from physical impairments, or other sexual behavior disorders, compulsive gambling, kleptomania, or pyromania, or psychoactive substance use disorders resulting from current illegal use of drugs. [ADA § 511(b); 42 USC § 12211(b); EEOC Reg § 1630.3(d)]

The ADA generally does not protect persons engaging in the illegal use of drugs, but it does cover individuals who are erroneously regarded as engaging in the illegal use of drugs or who are participating in a supervised rehabilitation program (or have in the past or were otherwise rehabilitated successfully) and are no longer engaging in such use. [ADA § 510; 42 USC § 12210; EEOC Reg §§ 1630.3(a), (b)]

Effect on Welfare Benefit Plan Design

Q 17:6　Is a benefit plan discriminatory under the ADA if it adversely affects individuals with disabilities?

Not necessarily. An employer's uniformly applied leave policies or benefit plans will not be considered to violate the EEOC's ADA regulations merely because they do not address the special needs of every individual with a disability. Thus, for example, an employer may reduce the number of paid sick days that it provides to all employees, or reduce the amount of medical coverage that it provides to all employees, without violating the EEOC's regulations even if the reduction has an impact on employees with disabilities in need of greater sick leave and medical coverage. However, if the benefit reduction is adopted for discriminatory reasons, it will violate the EEOC's regulations. [Appendix to EEOC Reg Part 1630—Interpretive Guidance on Regulation § 1630.5]

Q 17:7　Does the ADA prohibit an employer from including a preexisting condition clauses in its health insurance plan?

No, the ADA's prohibition against limiting, segregating, and classifying employees on the basis of disability does not bar an employer from including a preexisting condition clause in its health insurance plan, so long as the clause applies uniformly to all employees and is not used as a subterfuge to evade the purposes of the ADA (regardless of whether the provision was adopted before the ADA became effective with respect to the plan). The intent of the EEOC regulations is that employees with disabilities should be accorded equal access to whatever health insurance coverage the employer provides to other employees. The regulations state that they are not intended to affect preexisting condition clauses in employer-provided health insurance policies. A blanket preexisting condition clause that excludes coverage for treatment of conditions which arose prior to the individual's eligibility for plan benefits is not a disability-based distinction and does not violate the ADA. Accordingly, employers may continue to include such clauses in their plans, even if such clauses would adversely affect individuals with disabilities. [Appendix to EEOC Reg Part 1630—Interpretive Guidance on Regulation § 1630.5; EEOC Interim Guidance on Application of ADA to Health Insurance, reprinted at 109 *Daily Labor Rept* (BNA) E-1 (June 9, 1993)]

Q 17:8 Does the ADA prohibit an employer from limiting plan coverage on a uniform basis for certain treatments or procedures?

No, it does not. An employer's welfare benefit plan may include one or more limits on covered benefits if such limits apply equally to all insured employees, regardless of whether they have a protected disability. The EEOC regulations also permit employer-provided health insurance plans to limit coverage for certain procedures or treatments to a specified number per year. The appendix to the EEOC regulations gives the following example of a permissible way to limit health plan coverage:

> If a health insurance plan provided coverage for five blood transfusions a year to all covered employees, it would not be discriminatory to offer this plan simply because a hemophiliac employee may require more than five blood transfusions annually. However, it would not be permissible to limit or deny the hemophiliac employee coverage for other procedures, such as heart surgery or the setting of a broken leg, even though the plan would not have to provide coverage for the additional blood transfusions that may be involved in these procedures. Likewise, limits may be placed on reimbursements for certain procedures or on the types of drugs or procedures covered (for example, limits on the number of permitted X-rays or noncoverage of experimental drugs or procedures), but that limitation must be applied equally to individuals with and without disabilities.

[Appendix to EEOC Reg Part 1630—Interpretive Guidance on Regulation § 1630.5]

The EEOC's Interim Guidance issued in June 1993 provides further examples of plan limits that pass muster under the ADA because they apply to all individuals on a uniform basis. Any universal limit or broad distinction, which applies to individuals both with and without disabilities, is not a disability-based distinction under the ADA. Additionally, a coverage limit on medical procedures that are not exclusively, or nearly exclusively, utilized for the treatment of a particular disability is not considered to be disability-based distinction under the ADA.

The Interim Guidance also gives several examples of common health plan limits which it does not consider to be disability-based distinctions because they apply to numerous conditions that affect individuals with and without disabilities: universal limits on, or universal exclusions for, treatment for mental/nervous conditions, eye care, experimental drugs, experimental treatments, elective surgery, or the number of blood transfusions or X-rays. Even though such distinctions may have a greater impact on certain individuals with disabilities, the EEOC has stated that such provisions do not intentionally discriminate on the basis of disability and, consequently, do not violate the ADA. [EEOC Interim Guidance on Application of ADA to Health Insurance, reprinted at 109 *Daily Labor Rept* (BNA) E-1 (June 9, 1993)]

In contrast, a health-related insurance distinction that is disability-based (see Question 17:9) will violate the ADA unless it falls under one of the ADA's exceptions (see Qs 17:10, 17:11).

Q 17:9   What is a disability-based distinction?

According to the EEOC, a disability-based distinction is one which:

1. Singles out a particular disability (such as AIDS, deafness, or schizophrenia);

2. Singles out a discrete group of disabilities (such as cancers, muscular dystrophies, or kidney diseases); or

3. Singles out disability in general (for example, all conditions that substantially limit a major life activity).

[EEOC Interim Guidance on Application of ADA to Health Insurance, reprinted at 109 *Daily Labor Rept* (BNA) E-1 (June 9, 1993)]

Q 17:10   Does the ADA prohibit an employer from excluding or limiting coverage for a particular disability (such as AIDS) or group of disabilities?

Such discrimination generally is prohibited. However, provided that such provisions are not a subterfuge to evade the purposes of the ADA, the ADA does not prohibit or restrict:

1. An insurer, hospital, medical service company, health maintenance organization, any agent or entity that administers benefit plans, or similar organizations from underwriting risks, classifying risks, or administering such risks that are based on, or not inconsistent with, state law regulating insurance;

2. A covered employer from establishing, sponsoring, observing, or administering the terms of a bona fide benefit plan that are based on underwriting risks, classifying risks, or administering such risks that are based on, or not inconsistent with, state laws that regulate insurance; or

3. A covered employer from establishing, sponsoring, observing, or administering the terms of a bona fide benefit plan that is not subject to state laws that regulate insurance.

[ADA § 501(c); 42 USC § 12201(c); EEOC Reg § 1630.16(f)]

The burden will be on the employer to demonstrate that a disability-based provision complies with the ADA. [EEOC Interim Guidance on Application of ADA to Health Insurance, reprinted at 109 *Daily Labor Rept* (BNA) E-1 (June 9, 1993)]

The Appendix to the EEOC regulations notes that the purpose of the above provisions is to permit the development and administration of benefit plans in accordance with accepted principles of risk assessment. These provisions are not intended to disrupt the current regulatory structure for self-insured employers, nor, according to the Appendix to the EEOC regulations, are they intended to disrupt the current nature of insurance underwriting or current insurance industry practices in sales, underwriting, pricing, administrative and other services, claims, and similar insurance-related activities based upon classification of risks as regulated by the states. The permitted activities do not violate the EEOC regulations even if they result in limitations on individuals with disabilities, unless used as a subterfuge to evade the purposes of the regulations. The question of subterfuge will be determined without regard to the date the insurance plan or employee benefit plan was adopted. (See Q 17:11)

However, the Appendix to the EEOC regulations cautions (without distinguishing the different treatment accorded self-insured plans under the ADA) that an employer or other covered entity cannot deny a qualified individual with a disability equal access to insurance or subject a qualified individual with a disability to different terms or conditions of insurance based on disability alone, unless the disability poses increased risks. Decisions not based on risk classification must conform to nondiscrimination requirements. [Appendix to EEOC Reg Part 1630—Interpretive Guidance on § 1630.16(f)]

The Interim Guidance issued by the EEOC in June 1993 expands upon the above explanation and clarifies what will be required to demonstrate that a challenged disability-based health plan provision complies with the ADA.

Insured Plans. If the disability-based provision is contained in an insured health plan, the respondent must show that (1) the provision is not a subterfuge to evade the purposes of the ADA (see Q 17:11), and (2) the plan is a bona fide insured health insurance plan that is not inconsistent with state law. The plan will be treated as bona fide if it exists and pays benefits and its terms have been accurately communicated to eligible employees. It will be treated as consistent with state law if it is not inconsistent with state law as interpreted by the appropriate state authorities.

Self-Insured Plans. Self-insured health plans need only prove that the plan is bona fide (that is, it exists and pays benefits and its terms have been accurately communicated to covered employees) and that the disability-based provision is not being used as a subterfuge to evade the purposes of the ADA (see Q 17:11).

[EEOC Interim Guidance on Application of ADA to Health Insurance, reprinted at 109 *Daily Labor Rept* (BNA) E-1 (June 9, 1993)]

Q 17:11   When is a disability-based distinction in a health insurance plan considered to be a subterfuge to evade the purposes of the ADA?

A disability-based provision contained in a health insurance plan (regardless of whether the plan is insured or self-insured), might be viewed as a subterfuge to evade the purposes of the ADA. It is irrelevant whether the provision was adopted prior to the effective date of the ADA, as the ADA does not contain a "safe harbor" for preexisting plans.

For purposes of the ADA, a "subterfuge" exists when the disability-based disparate treatment is not justified by the risks or costs associated with the disability. This will be determined on a case-by-case basis, taking into account the totality of the circumstances.

The employer bears the burden of proving that a challenged disability-based distinction contained in a health insurance plan is not a subterfuge to evade the purposes of the ADA. The EEOC's Interim Guidance on Application of ADA to Health Insurance provides five possible business/insurance justifications for health plan provisions and states that other methods also may be used. The five methods relating to health plans are:

1. Prove that the provision actually is not disability-based (for example, an annual dollar limit on benefits that applies to all conditions in the same way);

2. Prove that the provision is justified by legitimate actuarial data or by actual or reasonably anticipated experience *and* that conditions with comparable actuarial data are treated in the same fashion. In other words, prove that such disparate treatment results from the application of legitimate risk classification and underwriting procedures to the increased risks of the disability (with increased cost to the health plan) and is not a result of the disability *per se*. For this purpose, seriously outdated and/or inaccurate actuarial data does not suffice. The respondent may not rely on actuarial data about a disability that is based upon myths, fears, stereotypes, or false assumptions (or assumptions that are no longer true) about a disability.

3. Prove that the disparate treatment is necessary to ensure that the plan satisfies commonly accepted or legally required

standards for the fiscal soundness of the plan. (However, the Interim Guidance narrowly defines "necessary" to mean that there is *no* nondisability-based health insurance plan change that could be made.)

4. Prove that the provision is necessary (again, "necessary" is used to mean that there is *no* nondisability-based change that could be made) to prevent an unacceptable change in the coverage of the health insurance plan or an unacceptable change in the premiums charged for such coverage. For this purpose, an "unacceptable" change means a drastic increase in premium payments, co-payments or deductibles, or a drastic alteration to the scope of coverage or level of benefits provided, that would make the health insurance plan effectively unavailable to a significant number of other employees, or so unattractive as to result in significant adverse selection, or so unattractive that the employer cannot compete with other employers in the community in recruiting and maintaining qualified workers due to the superiority of their health insurance plans.

5. If a denial, under the disability-based provision, of coverage for a particular treatment is being challenged, the employer may prove by reliable scientific evidence that the particular treatment has no medical value (that is, that it does not cure the condition, slow the degeneration/deterioration or harm resulting from the condition, alleviate the condition's symptoms, or maintain the disabled individual's current health status).

[EEOC Interim Guidance on Application of ADA to Health Insurance, reprinted at 109 *Daily Labor Rept* (BNA) E-1 (June 9, 1993)]

Q 17:12   Does the ADA prohibit an employer from excluding or limiting coverage under a health insurance plan because of concerns about the impact on the plan of the disability of someone else with whom the employee has a relationship?

Yes, it does. The ADA prohibits employers, or others acting on their behalf, from denying employment opportunities to job applicants or employees who are otherwise qualified individuals with a disability because of the known disability of an individual with whom he or she is known to have a relationship or association. The EEOC, in Interim Guidance issued in June 1993, has taken the position that this provision of the ADA prohibits making employment decisions about any person, *whether or not that person has a disability,* because of concerns about the impact on the employer's health insurance plan of the disability of someone else with whom that person has a relationship.

The EEOC apparently means that if a person with whom the employee has a relationship has a disability (such as AIDS), coverage for the employee cannot be denied or limited on the basis of a suspicion or worry that the employee may have it as well and incur significant expenses under the employee's health insurance plan. This is because the ADA's broad definition of disabled individuals also includes any employee who is *perceived* as having a disability even if he or she actually does not. [ADA §§ 3(2)(C) and 102(4); 42 USC §§ 12102(2)(C) and 12112(4); EEOC Interim Guidance on Application of ADA to Health Insurance, reprinted at 109 *Daily Labor Rept* (BNA) E-1 (June 9, 1993)]

Q 17:13   Does the ADA require that dependent coverage under a health insurance plan be the same as employee coverage?

No, the ADA does not require that dependent coverage under a health insurance plan be the same in scope as employee coverage. Thus, for example, a plan could limit a particular benefit to $100,000 for employees and $50,000 for dependents or could cover prescription drugs for employees only. However, the EEOC takes the position that dependent coverage is a benefit available to the employee by virtue of employment, so all insurance terms, provisions, and conditions concerning dependent coverage are subject to the same ADA standards (including standards regarding disability-based distinctions) that apply to employee coverage (see Qs 17:10–17:12).

Penalties

Q 17:14   What sanctions apply to an employer that violates the ADA?

The remedies under the ADA are the same as those under Title VII of the Civil Rights Act of 1964 (see Q 18:28). [ADA § 107(a)]

Q 17:15   Is an employer liable under the ADA for discrimination by an insurance company, third party administrator, HMO, or other entity with which it has a contract?

Yes, it can be. The EEOC Interim Guidance on Application of ADA to Health Insurance expressly puts employers on notice of this potential liability and explains how it could occur in the health insurance context.

The Interim Guidance explains that the ADA also prohibits employers from *indirectly* discriminating on the basis of disability in the provision of health insurance. Any contractual or other arrangement or relationship, including a contractual or other relationship with an organization that provides fringe benefits to employees, will violate the ADA if the contract or relationship has the effect of discriminating against the employer's own qualified applicants or employees with disabilities. If prohibited discrimination results from a contract or agreement with an insurance company, health maintenance organization, third party administrator, stop-loss carrier, or other organization to provide or administer a health insurance plan on behalf of its employees, the employer will be liable under the ADA. [EEOC Interim Guidance on Application of ADA to Health Insurance, reprinted at 109 *Daily Labor Rept* (BNA) E-1 (June 9, 1993)]

Effect of State Laws

Q 17:16   Does the ADA preempt state laws or other federal laws?

No, it does not. Thus, if a state or local government has a nondiscrimination law providing greater protections for individuals with disabilities, that law is not invalidated. [ADA § 501(b)] The law directs the agencies with enforcement authority under the ADA and the Rehabilitation Act of 1973 to develop procedures to avoid duplication of effort and inconsistent standards for the same requirements under each Act. [ADA § l07(b), 42 USC § 12117(b)]

It should be noted that ERISA, on the other hand, does preempt the application of most state laws to ERISA-covered employee benefit plans. Although ERISA does not preempt other *federal* laws, the fact that the ADA (which does not preempt state nondiscrimination laws) also applies to ERISA plans does not nullify ERISA's preemption of state wage and labor laws. ERISA preemption generally cannot be evaded by attempting to characterize a state nondiscrimination law as part of the "federal scheme" under another federal law. The Supreme Court previously has rejected an attempt to "bootstrap" state nondiscrimination laws into the "federal scheme" of Title VII of the Civil Rights Act of 1964 in an attempt to avoid ERISA's state law preemption provisions. [Shaw v Delta Air Lines, 463 US 85 (1983)]

Chapter 18

Other Federal Laws

Various other federal laws can directly or indirectly affect the content of employee welfare benefit plans. This chapter briefly highlights some of those laws.

Labor Laws and Collective Bargaining

Q 18:1 Must an employer bargain with a labor union representing its employees concerning welfare benefits?

Yes, an employer is generally required to bargain in good faith with a union representing its employees regarding "wages, hours, and other terms and conditions of employment." [National Labor Relations Act of 1935, as amended (NLRA) § 8(d); 29 USC § 158(d) (1988)] Employee pension and welfare benefits are within the scope of this requirement. [Inland Steel Co v NLRB, 170 F 2d 247 (7th Cir 1948), *cert denied* 336 US 960 (1949)] Note that the subject of when a union represents the employees is beyond the scope of this book.

Q 18:2   Must an employer bargain with respect to welfare benefits for retired employees?

No, retirees are not considered to be "employees" under the NLRA and, therefore, an employer need not bargain over their welfare benefits, although it may agree to do so. [Allied Chemical & Alkali Workers of America Local Union No 1 v Pittsburgh Plate Glass Co Chemical Div, 404 US 157 (1971)] However, an employer is required to bargain with a union about the benefits active employees will receive when they retire.

Q 18:3   May an employer contribute to a welfare benefit fund administered by a labor union?

Generally, no, it cannot. It is unlawful for an employer to contribute to a union-administered plan unless the plan is jointly administered by the employer and the union and satisfies the conditions listed in Question 18:4. [Labor Management Relations Act of 1947 (LMRA) § 302(c); 29 USC § 186 (1988)]

Q 18:4   May an employer contribute to a trust fund it does not control that provides welfare benefits to employees in a collective bargaining unit?

Yes, it may, provided the following conditions are met:

1. A written agreement specifies in detail the basis upon which payments are to be made to the employees.

2. The employer and employees are equally represented in the administration of the plan, that is, each must appoint an equal number of trustees. The parties may also agree on the appointment of additional, neutral trustees.

3. The agreement provides that, in the event of a deadlock among the trustees, the two sides will agree on an impartial umpire or a federal court will appoint one.

4. The agreement provides for an annual audit of the trust fund, the results of which will be available for inspection by interested persons.

[LMRA § 302; 29 USC § 186(c) (1988)]

Q 18:5 May the employer unilaterally change welfare benefits for employees covered by a collective bargaining agreement?

No; generally, it may not. Even if the changes are improvements in benefits, the employer must notify, and bargain the changes with, the union. An employer was found to have violated the NLRA by unilaterally increasing union employees' contributions for health benefits coverage, and was required to reimburse the union employees for the additional contributions made. [North Star Steel Co v NLRB, 974 F 2d 68 (8th Cir 1992]

Q 18:6 Must the employer bargain over a change in insurance carriers or other change in the method of funding the plan?

At least one federal appeals court has held that a mere change in insurance carriers does not substantially affect the terms and conditions of employment and that, therefore, the employer could change insurance carriers without union consultation or approval. [Connecticut Light & Power Co v NLRB, 476 F 2d 1079 (2d Cir 1973)] However, if the terms of the agreement specify a particular carrier, the employer might have to consult with the union.

Additionally, an employer under a contributory plan should not unilaterally switch from an insured to a self-insured arrangement or modify the plan benefits. [Bastian-Blessing, Div of Golconda Corp v NLRB, 474 F 2d 49 (6th Cir 1973)]

Q 18:7   May an employer terminate welfare benefit plan coverage for striking employees?

Generally, yes, it may. [International Union of Electrical and Machine Workers v General Electric Co, 337 F Supp 817 (SD NY 1972)] However, if the contract is ambiguous, the issue is one for arbitration. [Viggiano v Shenango China Div of Anchor Hocking Corp, 750 F 2d 276 (3d Cir 1984)] Additionally, the striking employees would have COBRA continuation of coverage rights regarding their health coverage. (See Chapter 6 for a discussion of COBRA.)

Q 18:8   May an employer terminate welfare benefit plan coverage for union employees when a collective bargaining agreement expires?

Generally, no; the employer must bargain with the union and cannot drop the benefits unilaterally unless and until the two sides reach an impasse or the employer can demonstrate that the union no longer represents a majority of the employees in the collective bargaining unit. [Stone Boat Yard v NLRB, 715 F 2d 441 (9th Cir 1983)]

Q 18:9   May an employer offer or provide welfare plan benefits as an inducement to discourage union activity?

Ordinarily no, it may not. The employer's action may constitute an unfair labor practice if the employer's motivation is to discourage a vote in favor of unionization, to reward employees who vote against unionization, to penalize employees who have joined a union, or the like. [NLRB v Great Dane Trailers, Inc, 388 US 26 (1967); NLRB v Exchange Parts Co, 375 US 405 (1964)]

Q 18:10   May an employer terminate coverage of health or life insurance benefits for retirees required under a collective bargaining agreement once the collective bargaining agreement expires?

It depends on the terms of the collective bargaining agreement. If the agreement clearly provides that the obligation to provide the retiree coverage is limited to the period of the agreement, the courts will recognize it. However, if the collective bargaining agreement does not clearly limit the employer's obligation to the period of the agreement, a number of courts have found the employer to be obligated to continue the retiree coverage for the lifetimes of the retirees. [UAW Local 134 v Yard-Man, Inc, 716 F 2d 1476 (6th Cir 1983), *cert denied* 104 S Ct 1002 (1984); UAW Local 784 v Cadillac Malleable Iron Co, Inc, 728 F 2d 807 (6th Cir 1984); Weimer v Kurz-Kasch, Inc, 773 F 2d 669 (6th Cir 1985); Policy v Powell Pressed Steel Co, 770 F 2d 609 (6th Cir 1985), *cert denied* 106 S Ct 1202 (1986)]

Title VII of the Civil Rights Act of 1964

Q 18:11   What does Title VII of the Civil Rights Act of 1964 provide?

Title VII prohibits discrimination in employment practices based on race, color, religion, sex, or national origin. [42 USC §§ 2000e–2000e-17 (1982)]

Q 18:12   Which employers are subject to Title VII?

Title VII applies to employers in industries affecting commerce with 15 or more employees in at least 20 weeks in the current or preceding year. State and local government employers, but not the federal government or corporations wholly owned by the federal government, are also covered. [42 USC § 2000e(b) (1982)]

Q 18:13   Does discrimination on the basis of sex include discrimination based on pregnancy disability?

Yes, it does. The Pregnancy Discrimination Act of 1978 amended Title VII to also specifically prohibit employment discrimination based on pregnancy. [42 USC § 2000e (1982)]

Q 18:14   What is pregnancy disability under Title VII?

A pregnancy disability protected under Title VII is a disability caused or contributed to by pregnancy, childbirth, or related medical conditions. This includes disability related to abortion where the life of the mother would be endangered if the fetus were carried to term and medical complications arising from abortion. [42 USC § 2000e(k) (1982); EEOC Reg § 1604.10, 29 CFR § 1604.10]

Q 18:15 What employment benefits are affected by the pregnancy disability provisions of Title VII?

Formal and informal health or disability insurance and sick leave plans must cover disabilities caused or contributed to by pregnancy, childbirth, or related medical conditions in the same manner as disabilities caused or contributed to by other medical conditions. [EEOC Reg § 1604.10(b)]

Q 18:16 Does Title VII require that welfare benefits be provided for abortion?

With the exception of health insurance benefits, all other fringe benefits (including sick leave) provided for other medical conditions must also be provided for abortions. Health insurance benefits must be provided only when the life of the woman would be endangered if the fetus were carried to term and for medical complications arising from abortion, such as excessive hemorrhaging. Employers are not precluded from providing benefits for abortion either directly or through a collective bargaining agreement; but if they do so, then it must be done in the same manner and to the same degree as other medical conditions are covered. [EEOC Reg, Pt 1604, App Q&As 35–37]

Q 18:17 Must an employer provide the same benefits to an employee on leave for pregnancy-related conditions as it does for employees on leave for other reasons?

Yes. This would include installment purchase disability insurance, payment of premiums for health, life, or other insurance, and continued payments into pension, saving, or profit-sharing plans. [EEOC Reg, Pt 1604 App, Q&A 17]

Q 18:18   May employees who are absent due to pregnancy-related disabilities be required to exhaust vacation benefits prior to receiving sick pay or disability benefits?

No, not unless employees who are absent because of other disabilities are also required to first exhaust vacation benefits. [EEOC Reg, Pt 1604 App, Q&A 18]

Q 18:19   May time spent on leave for pregnancy-related reasons be treated differently from time spent on leave for other reasons when calculating credit toward vacations and pay increases?

No. Leave for pregnancy-related reasons cannot be treated less favorably than leave for other disabilities. Accordingly, the time spent on pregnancy-related leave would count on the same basis as other disabilities toward accrual of vacation pay and toward pay increases, which would affect the level of pay-related welfare benefits such as group term life insurance, accidental death and dismemberment benefits, and long-term disability benefits. [EEOC Reg, Pt 1604 App, Q&A 11]

Q 18:20   If the employer provides benefits for long-term or permanent disabilities, must such benefits be provided for pregnancy-related conditions?

Yes, they must. [EEOC Reg, Pt 1604 App, Q&A 16]

Q 18:21   Can the employer limit pregnancy disability benefits to married employees?

No, it cannot. [EEOC Reg, Pt 1604 App, Q&A 13]

Q 18:22   Can pregnancy disability benefits be limited to employees only?

If the employer's plan does not cover dependents, Title VII does not require that pregnancy disability benefits for dependents be offered. Similarly, the employer need not provide pregnancy-related benefits to dependents other than spouses, so long as both male and female dependents other than spouses are equally excluded. If the employer's insurance program covers medical expenses of the spouses of female employees, then it cannot exclude medical expenses for spouses of male employees, including those arising from pregnancy-related conditions. [EEOC Reg, Pt 1604 App, Q&A 21] However, if the employer's plan distinguishes between the level of benefits available to employees and spouses (for example, employees get 100 percent reimbursement and spouses, both male and female, get 50 percent reimbursement), then female spouses of male employees may be reimbursed for pregnancy-related benefits at the level applicable to spouses (in this example, at 50 percent). [EEOC Guidelines, Q&A 29]

Q 18:23 Can a female employee be required to purchase dependent or family coverage in order to receive coverage for her own pregnancy-related condition?

No. A female employee with single coverage cannot be forced to pay for more expensive dependent or family coverage in order to have her own pregnancy-related condition covered. A female employee is entitled to personal coverage, regardless of marital status. [EEOC Reg, Pt 1604 App, Q&A 24]

Q 18:24 Can the employer offer an employee-pay-all optional coverage which excludes pregnancy-related conditions or provides less coverage for them than for other medical conditions?

No. Regardless of who pays the premiums, pregnancy-related conditions must be treated the same as all other medical conditions under any sick leave plan, health insurance, or disability insurance available in connection with employment. [EEOC Reg, Pt 1604 App, Q&A 23]

Q 18:25 May an employer exclude pregnancy-related conditions from one or more health insurance plans or options so long as it offers such coverage under at least one plan or option?

No. If employees have a choice among several health insurance plans or options, pregnancy-related conditions must be covered in all of them on the same basis as other medical conditions. [EEOC Reg, Pt 1604 App, Q&A 24]

Q 18:26 On what basis must pregnancy-related conditions be reimbursed?

The EEOC guidelines contain the following rules for reimbursement of pregnancy-related conditions:

1. Deductible amounts must be the same for both pregnancy-related and nonpregnancy-related conditions. Employers may not impose a separate deductible on pregnancy-related conditions nor may they impose a higher deductible applicable only to pregnancy-related conditions.

2. Maximum recoverable amounts, such as annual limits or lifetime limits, must be the same for both pregnancy-related and nonpregnancy-related conditions.

3. Pregnancy-related expenses must be reimbursed in the same manner (for example, through a fixed dollar amount or a percentage of the reasonable and customary charge) as non-pregnancy-related expenses.

4. The percentage of reimbursement (for example, 80 percent after a uniform annual deductible amount) for pregnancy-related conditions must be the same as for nonpregnancy-related conditions, so that the plan pays the same proportion of actual costs.

5. Pregnancy-related expenses must be eligible under any otherwise covered benefits. For example, a plan must cover the cost of a private hospital room for pregnancy-related conditions if a private room is covered for other expenses. Similarly, if the plan covers physician office visits, prenatal and postnatal office visits must be covered.

6. Preexisting condition limitations, which exclude conditions existing at the time the insured's coverage becomes effective, may exclude benefits for preexisting pregnancies as well if other preexisting conditions are excluded in the same manner.

7. If the plan provides an extension of benefits after coverage stops (usually due to termination of employment), pregnancy-related benefits cannot be treated less favorably than benefits for other medical conditions.

[EEOC Reg, Pt 1604 App, Q&As 24 through 30]

Q 18:27   May an employer impose a "head of household" requirement for medical plan eligibility?

Yes, an employer may impose a head of household requirement for medical plan eligibility under certain circumstances. A "head of household" is defined as the principle (or highest-paid) wage earner. Such a rule would prevent an employee from enrolling his or her spouse unless the spouse earns less than the employee. An employment practice does not violate Title VII if the employment practice satisfies any one of the four affirmative defenses to the Equal Pay Act of 1963, which were incorporated by reference into Title VII. One of these defenses is payment made pursuant to a differential based on any factor other than sex. A recent U.S. Court of Appeals case upheld a head of household eligibility requirement where the employer desired to provide the greatest benefits for the people who needed coverage (that is, employees who did not have a more highly paid spouse) and wished to avoid covering spouses likely to have coverage from their own employers. The court found that the employer adopted the provision because it "wanted the biggest 'bang' for the buck with its benefit package," a reason the court found to be a legitimate business reason. [EEOC v JC Penney Co, Inc, 843 F 2d 249 (6th Cir 1988)]

Q 18:28   What penalties apply if Title VII is violated?

Under Title VII, an employer may be liable for back benefits for a period of not more than two years prior to filing a discrimination charge with the EEOC and for attorneys' fees, plus injunctive relief. [42 USC § 2000e-5 (1982)]

Title VI of the Civil Rights Act of 1964

Q 18:29 What does Title VI of the Civil Rights Act of 1964 provide?

Title VI of the Civil Rights Act of 1964, unlike Title VII of the same Act, applies only to recipients of federal financial aid where the primary purpose of the federal financial aid is to provide employment. Such employers cannot discriminate on the basis of race, color, or national origin. [42 USC §§ 2000d–2000d-6 (1982)]

Q 18:30 What penalties apply if an employer violates Title VI?

If an employer violates Title VI, its federal funds may be withdrawn. In addition, individual employees have a private right of action for intentional acts of discrimination and may obtain prospective relief. [42 USC § 2000d (1982)]

Equal Pay Act of 1963

Q 18:31 What does the Equal Pay Act provide?

The Equal Pay Act of 1963 prohibits employers from discriminating on the basis of sex, by paying lower wages to employees of one sex than to employees of the opposite sex for equal work on jobs in the same facility, performed under similar circumstances, and which require equal skill, effort, and responsibility. Exceptions are provided for pay practices based on a seniority system, merit system, or system which measures earnings by quantity or quality of production, or a wage differential based on factors other than sex. [29 USC § 206(d) (1988)]

For this purpose, wages include all remuneration for employment, including fringe benefits such as medical, hospital, accident, life insurance, and retirement benefits; profit-sharing and bonus plans; and leave practices. Additionally, differences in the application of fringe benefit plans which are derived from sex-based actuarial studies are not considered to be based on a factor other than sex. [EEOC Reg § 1620.11]

Q 18:32   Which employers are subject to the Equal Pay Act?

All employers engaged in interstate commerce or in the production of goods for interstate commerce are subject to the Equal Pay Act, as are state and local governments (with certain exceptions). [29 USC § 206(d) (1988); EEOC Reg § 1620.1]

Q 18:33   What penalties apply if the Equal Pay Act is violated?

If the employer violates the Equal Pay Act, it can be liable for back pay (including any wrongfully denied benefits), liquidated damages equal to the back pay, and attorneys' fees. Complainants may also obtain injunctive relief against the employer. In addition, the Equal Pay Act contains criminal penalties for willful violations. Employers may be subject to a fine of up to $10,000 or imprisonment for up to six months, or both. [29 USC § 216(1988)]

Rehabilitation Act of 1973

Q 18:34   What does the Rehabilitation Act of 1973 provide?

The Rehabilitation Act provides that a covered employer cannot exclude an otherwise qualified individual with handicaps from participation in, or deny the individual the benefits of, or subject the individual to discrimination under the federally funded program or activity. [Rehabilitation Act § 504, 29 USC § 794 (1988)]

Q 18:35   Which employers are covered by the Rehabilitation Act?

Section 504 of the Rehabilitation Act covers any program or activity receiving federal financial assistance. This is not limited to the particular branch or department of the employer covered by the financial assistance; rather, the Act's protections apply on an employer-wide basis. [29 USC § 794 (1988); Civil Rights Restoration Act of 1988, Pub L No 100–259, 102 Stat 29 (1988)]

Q 18:36 Who is a handicapped individual under the Rehabilitation Act?

A handicapped individual under the Rehabilitation Act is one who:

- Has a physical or mental impairment which substantially limits one or more of the individual's major life activities;
- Has a record of such impairment; or
- Is regarded as having such an impairment.

However, this definition does not include an individual who has a currently contagious disease or infection and who, by reason of such infection, would constitute a direct threat to the health or safety of other individuals or who, because of it, is unable to perform his or her job duties. [29 USC § 706(8)(B) (1988)] In addition, under some circumstances detailed at length in the statute, a handicapped individual does not include an individual who is currently engaging in the illegal use of drugs, when a covered employer acts on the basis of such use. [29 USC § 706(8) (1988), as amended by the Americans with Disabilities Act of 1990 (ADA) § 512]

Q 18:37 To qualify for coverage under the Rehabilitation Act, must the employee's handicap be so severe as to render the employee unable to perform his or her job?

No, an individual can be qualified as handicapped under the Act if he or she:

- Actually suffers from a disabling handicap;
- Has recovered from a previous such condition;
- Was previously misclassified as having the condition; or
- Is thought to have the condition regardless of whether or not he or she actually has the condition.

In other words, the Rehabilitation Act protects individuals with present, past, or perceived handicaps. [Memorandum from Arthur B Culvahouse, Jr, counsel to the President (Sept 27, 1988), *reprinted in* BNA Daily Labor Rpt No 195 (Oct 7, 1988), at D-1]

Q 18:38   Is Acquired Immune Deficiency Syndrome (AIDS) a covered handicap under the Rehabilitation Act?

Yes, AIDS is a covered handicap until the individual is no longer able to perform the duties of the job or until the individual constitutes a direct threat to the health or safety of other individuals. An HIV-positive individual will be covered regardless of whether or not he or she exhibits symptoms of AIDS.

Q 18:39   Does the Rehabilitation Act permit an employer to exclude or limit coverage of AIDS under an employee welfare benefit plan?

The Rehabilitation Act calls into question the validity of exclusions for handicaps such as AIDS from a covered employer's medical plan.

Worker Adjustment and Retraining Notification Act of 1988 (WARN)

Q 18:40   What does the Worker Adjustment and Retraining Notification Act (WARN) provide?

WARN requires that an employer cannot order a plant closing or mass layoff that would result in at least 50 full-time employees at a single employment site losing employment during any 30-day period, unless the employer gives at least 60 days' advance notice to affected employees or to their representatives plus the state dislocated worker unit and the chief elected local governmental official. In other words, compensation and employee benefits must be continued during the 60-day period. Smaller employment losses over a 90-day period will be aggregated for purposes of determining whether this 50-employee threshold has been reached unless the employer can demonstrate that they result from separate and distinct actions and causes and are not an attempt to evade the WARN requirements. [29 USC §§ 2102(a), 2102(d) (1988)]

The first and each subsequent group of terminated employees are entitled to a full 60 days' notice. [Department of Labor (DOL) Reg § 639.5(a)]

Notice may be given less than 60 days from the plant closing or mass layoff in the case of a faltering company, unforeseeable business circumstances, natural disaster or when a layoff of six months or less is extended beyond six months as a result of business circumstances which were not reasonably foreseeable at the time of the initial layoff. [29 USC § 2102(b) (1988); DOL Reg §§ 639.4(b), 639.9]

Q 18:41 Which employers are subject to the requirements of WARN?

WARN covers any employer having:

- 100 or more employees, excluding part-time employees; or
- 100 or more employees, including part-time employees, who in the aggregate work at least 4,000 hours per week (not including overtime).

[29 USC § 2101(a)(1) (1988)]

For purposes of determining whether the employer is covered by WARN, workers on temporary layoff or on leave who have a reasonable expectation of recall are counted as employees. [DOL Reg § 630.3(a)(1)]

Q 18:42 What is a covered "plant closing"?

Under WARN, a covered plant closing is a permanent or temporary shutdown of:

- A single employment site, or
- One or more facilities or operating units within a single employment site,

provided that the shutdown results in employment loss at such site for at least 50 full-time employees during a 30-day period. [29 USC § 2101(a)(2) (1988)]

Q 18:43   What is a covered "mass layoff"?

Under WARN, a mass layoff is a reduction in force that does not result from a plant closing and which causes, during any 30-day period, employment loss at that employment site for either:

- 33 percent of the full-time employees, which must be at least 50 employees; or
- 500 full-time employees.

[29 USC § 2101(a)(3) (1988)]

Q 18:44   What constitutes employment loss under WARN?

For purposes of triggering the employer's obligation to provide the WARN notice, employment loss means the following:

- Termination of employment for reasons other than discharge for cause, voluntary departure, or retirement;
- A layoff exceeding six months; or
- A greater-than-50-percent reduction in the employee's hours of work for each month of any six-month period.

[29 § USC 2101(a)(6) (1988)]

However, an employee is not considered to have experienced an employment loss if the closing or layoff results from relocation or consolidation of all or a part of the employer's business and, prior to the closing or layoff, the employer offers either of the following:

1. To transfer the employee to a different site of employment within a reasonable commuting distance with no more than a six-month break in employment; or
2. To transfer the employee to any other site of employment regardless of distance, and the employee accepts within 30 days of the offer or of the closing or layoff, whichever is later.

[29 USC § 2101(b)(2) (1988)]

Q 18:45   Who is responsible for providing the WARN notice?

The employer is responsible for giving the WARN notice. The employer is permitted to decide who is the most appropriate person within the employer's organization to prepare and deliver the notice. This may be the local site plant manager, the local personnel director, or a labor relations officer. [DOL Reg § 639.4(a)]

In the case of the sale of a part or all of the business, the seller is responsible for providing notice of any plant closing or mass layoff that takes place up to and including the effective date of the sale. Thereafter, the buyer is responsible for providing notice of any plant closing or mass layoff that takes place after the date of the sale. [29 USC § 2101(b) (1988)]

Q 18:46   To whom must the WARN notice be given?

The 60-day advance notice of a plant closing or a mass layoff must be given to:

- All affected employees;
- The state dislocated worker unit; and
- The chief elected local governmental official.

[29 USC § 2902(a) (1988)]

Affected Employees. Affected employees who must receive the WARN notice are those who may reasonably be expected to experience an employment loss, including employees who are likely to lose their jobs because of "bumping" rights or other factors if such factors can be identified at that time. Part-time employees, who are not counted in determining whether plant closing or mass layoff trigger points have been reached, are nonetheless required to be given the WARN notice. For union employees, the notice is to be given to the chief elected officer of the exclusive representative(s) or bargaining agent(s) of the employees. [DOL Reg § 639.6(a)]

Q 18:47   Are there any exceptions to the WARN notice requirement?

Yes, there are. WARN does not require notice to be given if a temporary facility is being closed, or if the closing or layoff results from the completion of a particular project or undertaking and the affected employees were hired with the clear understanding that their employment was limited to the duration of the facility, project, or undertaking. [DOL Reg § 639.5(c)]

Notice also is not required in certain cases involving employment transfers and for strikes and lockouts that are not intended to evade the requirements of WARN. [DOL Reg §§ 639.5(b), 639.5(d)]

Q 18:48   What penalties apply to WARN violations?

An employer that fails to comply with the WARN notice requirements will be liable for back pay and benefits for up to 60 days. Such liability includes the cost of medical expenses incurred during the employment loss which otherwise would have been covered under an employee benefit plan. In addition, failure to give notice to the chief elected official of the local governmental unit is punishable by a penalty of up to $500 per day. [29 USC § 2104 (1988)]

Retiree Benefits of Bankrupt Companies

Q 18:49   Can bankrupt companies avoid the obligation to pay benefits to retirees and their dependents?

No, they cannot. The federal Retiree Benefits Bankruptcy Protection Act of 1988 does not permit companies that have filed for Title 11 bankruptcy protection to cut back or terminate certain benefits for retirees, their spouses, and dependents, except under specified circumstances. [Retiree Benefits Bankruptcy Protection Act of 1988, Pub L No 100-334, adding 11 USC § 1114 (1988)] It appears that in order for the Retiree Benefits Bankruptcy Protection Act to apply, there must be a legally binding obligation on the employer to provide the retiree benefits, absent the Title 11 reorganization filing.

In a decision by the U.S. Court of Appeals for the Second Circuit, it was held that a debtor-employer in a Title 11 reorganization was not required to continue collectively bargained retiree health benefits after the wage agreement expired, since it no longer had any legal obligation to continue the benefits. [In re Chateaugay Corp, 945 F 2d 1205 (2d Cir 1991)]

In a U.S. bankruptcy court decision, a debtor-employer in a Title 11 reorganization was held not to be subject to the requirements of the Retiree Benefits Bankruptcy Protection Act with respect to future reduction or elimination of salaried retiree health and life insurance coverage, because the salaried plan documents gave the employer the right to amend, modify, or terminate the retirees' coverage at any time on a prospective basis. [In re Doskocil Companies, Inc, 14 Employee Benefits Cas. 1132 (Bankr Ct D Kan 1991)]

Q 18:50   Which benefits are protected?

The Retiree Benefits Bankruptcy Protection Act covers medical, surgical, and hospital benefits. It also covers benefits provided in the event of sickness, accident, disability, or death. [11 USC § 1114(a) (1988)]

Q 18:51   Which plans are covered by the bankruptcy restrictions?

Any plan established before filing of the bankruptcy petition is covered. [11 USC § 1114(a) (1988)]

Q 18:52   Are all retirees protected?

No, retirees are not protected if their gross income for the 12 months preceding the filing of the bankruptcy petition exceeded $250,000, unless the retiree demonstrates to the bankruptcy court's satisfaction that he or she is unable to obtain insurance coverage comparable to that provided by the employer on the day before the bankruptcy petition was filed. When retirees are excluded from the Act's protection, so are their spouses and dependents. [11 USC § 1114(l) (1988)]

Q 18:53   May retiree benefits covered under the Act be modified or terminated while the bankruptcy case is pending?

Yes, the employer, or trustee if one has been appointed, may do this by negotiating with the authorized representative of the retirees. The employer or trustee must propose modifications needed to permit the reorganization and at the same time assure that all parties are treated fairly and equitably. Then the employer or trustee must engage in good-faith negotiations. Retiree benefits must continue to be paid during the negotiation period. [11 USC §§ 1114(e), 1114(i) (1988)]

Q 18:54   Who is authorized to represent the retirees in negotiations about discontinuance?

The union is the authorized representative of unionized retirees receiving benefits covered by a collective bargaining agreement, unless the union refuses to serve or the bankruptcy court appoints a committee of retirees. The bankruptcy court always appoints such a committee to represent nonunion retirees. [11 USC § 1114(b)–1114(d) (1988)]

Q 18:55   What happens if the negotiations do not lead to a resolution?

The bankruptcy court has the power to approve a modification of the retiree benefits if:

1. The authorized representative of the retirees refuses the proposal without good cause;

2. The modification is necessary to permit the company to be reorganized; and

3. The modification is clearly favored by the balance of the equities and treats all affected parties fairly and equitably.

[11 USC § 1114(g) (1988)]

Q 18:56 Can the bankruptcy court later make further modifications of the retiree health benefits?

Yes, it can. The bankruptcy court may approve additional modifications, including restoring benefits to their prebankruptcy level. [11 USC § 1114(g) (1988)]

Q 18:57 Can the employer stop paying benefits once the reorganization plan is approved?

Not necessarily; all reorganization plans must include a provision to the effect that the employer must continue the retiree benefits, at the level established during the bankruptcy proceeding for the duration of the period the employer has obligated itself to pay such benefits. [11 USC § 1129(a)(13) (1988)] Note, however, the recent case law indicating that a bankruptcy court is apparently powerless to affect retiree benefits which the employer has no binding legal obligation to provide (see Q 18:49).

Veterans Health Care Amendments of 1986

Q 18:58 How do the Veterans' Health Care Amendments of 1986 affect health plan contracts?

The Veterans' Health Care Amendments of 1986 [Pub L No 99–272, 100 Stat 382 (1986)] provide that exclusions in a "health plan contract" for expenses incurred for care furnished by a department or agency of the United States, such as for treatment in a Veterans Administration (VA) hospital or nursing home related to treatment of a veteran's non-service-connected disability are inapplicable. They also authorize the VA to recover the reasonable cost of such care from any "third-party payer," if the health plan contract would otherwise cover the care or services had they not been furnished by a department or agency of the United States. [38 USC § 629 (1988)]

Q 18:59 Who is a third-party payer from whom the Administrator of Veterans Affairs may recover expenses?

A third-party payer for these purposes generally includes:

- Employers;
- The employer's insurance carrier; and
- Persons obligated to provide or pay expenses of health services under a health plan contract.

[38 USC § 629(i)(3)(1988)]

Q 18:60 What health plan contracts are covered?

A covered health plan contract generally includes insurance policies or contracts, medical or hospital service agreements, membership or subscription contracts, or similar arrangements under which the expenses for health services incurred by individuals are paid or under which the services are provided to individuals. [38 USC § 629(i)(1)(A)(1988)]

Q 18:61 What are the health services for which the VA may recover expenses?

Expenses for health care and services which are incurred for a military veteran's non-service-related disabilities can be recovered under covered health plan contracts, regardless of any exclusion under the contract concerning care or services furnished by a department or agency of the United States, if the care or services would otherwise be covered under the health care contract. [38 USC § 629(a)(1988)]

Q 18:62 How much is the VA authorized to recover?

The VA may recover an amount which shall be the reasonable cost of such services determined pursuant to regulations to be issued by the Administrator of Veterans Affairs reduced by any applicable plan deductible and copayment amounts. This amount cannot exceed the amount which the third party demonstrates to the Administrator's satisfaction would be payable under a comparable health plan contract to a nongovernmental facility. [38 USC § 629(c)(2)(B) (1988)]

Military Retirees

Q 18:63   How does Title II of COBRA affect health plan contracts?

Title II of COBRA provides that exclusions in health plan contracts for inpatient care received by military retirees and their dependents from military hospitals are inapplicable if the contract would otherwise cover such care and authorizes the Secretary of Defense to recover the reasonable cost of such services from third-party payers. [Pub L No 99–272 § 2001(a)(1); 10 USC § 1095 (1988)]

The legislative history clarifies that this provision is to apply to both insurance underwriters and private employers that offer health insurance plans which are either self-insured or partially self-insured and partially underwritten. [HR Rpt No 300, 99th Cong, 1st Sess 1985 at 8]

Q 18:64   What is a covered health plan contract?

A covered health plan contract generally includes insurance policies or contracts, medical or hospital service agreements, membership or subscription contracts, or similar arrangements under which the expenses for health services for individuals are paid or under which the services are provided to individuals. [10 USC 1095(b) (1988)]

Q 18:65   What are the health services for which the Secretary of Defense may recover expenses?

Expenses for health care and services which are incurred for inpatient care received by military retirees and their dependents from military hospitals can be recovered, regardless of any exclusion under the health care contract concerning care or services furnished by a department or agency of the United States, if the care or services would otherwise be covered under the health care contract. [10 USC § 1095(a)(1) (1988)]

Veterans' Re-employment Rights

Q 18:66   What does the Vietnam Era Veterans Readjustment Assistance Act of 1974 provide?

This Act, which incorporates prior laws dealing with veterans' re-employment rights, provides that, for veterans generally, an employee who, during employment, was inducted into service in the U.S. military and promptly applies for re-employment after completion of military service, must be restored to his or her former employment with like seniority, status, and pay. Such an employee is also entitled to coverage under employee welfare benefit plans on the same basis as an individual who is not a veteran. [38 USC § 2021 (1988)]

Similar rights must be provided to employees who, during employment, enlist in the U.S. armed forces for limited periods, or who are members of the Reserve or the National Guard and are called to active duty. [38 USC § 2024 (1988)]

Q 18:67   If an employee welfare benefit plan provides benefits based on length of service, is an employee who returns from military service entitled to have such military service counted for purposes of the benefit?

Yes, when the benefit is dependent upon length of service, credit must be given for military service covered by the Act. [38 USC § 2021 (1988); Alabama Power Company v Davis, 97 S Ct 2002 (1977)] It was held that an employee could not waive, before entering military service, his or her right to participate in the employer's pension plan upon his or her return and to be given credit for military service. [Leonard v United Air Lines, 972 F 2d 155 (7th Cir 1992)]

Q 18:68   If an employee returns from military service, can health plan waiting periods and preexisting condition limitations be imposed?

No, they cannot. Individuals covered by the Vietnam Era Veterans Readjustment Assistance Act of 1974 who reapply for employment within the time limits and under the conditions required by such law must be offered employer-provided health insurance without the imposition of any exclusions or waiting periods on the individual or his or her family members if the following circumstances apply:

1. The condition at issue arose before or during the employee's period of training or service in the armed forces;
2. The exclusion or waiting period would not have been imposed had the individual been participating in the plan; and
3. The Secretary of Veterans Affairs has not determined the individual's condition to be service-related.

[38 USC § 2021(b)(1) (1991), as amended by the Soldiers' and Sailors' Relief Act Amendments of 1991, 105 Stat 34, 36 (1991)]

Q 18:69 What penalties apply if a veteran's re-employment rights are violated?

The veteran may bring an action in U.S. District Court to require the employer to comply with the law and to compensate the veteran for any loss of wages or benefits. No fees or court costs are payable by the veteran. Also, no state or other statute of limitation applies to the action. Thus, a World War II veteran could bring a current action for failure to take his or her service during World War II into account for welfare benefits which are dependent upon service. [38 USC § 2022 (1988)]

Miscellaneous

Q 18:70 Do any other federal laws regulate employee welfare benefit plans?

Yes, they do. The other primary federal laws affecting employee welfare benefits are discussed in Chapter 2 (ERISA), Chapter 15 (Family and Medical Leave Act of 1993), Chapter 16 (ADEA), and Chapter 17 (ADA). In addition, several other federal laws concerning governmental contracts directly or indirectly affect welfare benefit plans. These laws may be specific, such as the Davis-Bacon Act, which is concerned with federal contracts to construct, alter, or repair federal public buildings or public works [40 USC § 276(a) (1988)], or general in nature, such as the Walsh-Healey Public Contracts Act, which governs federal contracts in amounts exceeding $10,000. [41 USC § 35 (1988)] Employers with federal contracts should be aware that various federal labor laws applicable to federal contractors may affect their welfare benefit plans.

Chapter 19

Funding and Financing Welfare Benefits

This chapter discusses many of the rules that can come into play in benefit funding and financing, as well as some related considerations such as tax rules that apply if the funding method chosen is a voluntary employees' beneficiary association (VEBA) or other welfare benefit fund and the requirements and limitations involved in funding postretirement medical benefits under a pension plan or annuity. It also covers the use of corporate-owned life insurance (COLI) as a method of financing welfare benefits.

Overview of Funding Alternatives

Q 19:1 Does the Employee Retirement Income Security Act (ERISA) of 1974 require that all welfare benefit plans be funded?

No, ERISA only imposes advance funding requirements on pension plans. Accordingly, employers are permitted to pay for the benefits under a welfare benefit plan out of their general assets.

Q 19:2 What funding alternatives does an employer have for a welfare benefit plan?

An employer may choose among the following funding alternatives:

- Fully insure the benefits by purchasing an insurance policy;
- Self-insure the benefits under the plan by paying for them out of its general assets;
- Self-insure and fund the benefits by setting aside money in trust to pay benefits (sometimes referred to as "self-funding"); or
- Partially insure the benefits, by self-insuring or self-funding them up to a certain point and insuring them above that point under either a minimum premium or stop-loss arrangement.

A single plan may also use a combination of these funding methods. See Questions 2:68 through 2:72 for a discussion of the ERISA trust requirement as it relates to employee contributions.

Q 19:3 What is full insurance coverage?

Under a fully insured plan, the promised benefits are paid pursuant to the terms of an insurance contract between the insurance carrier and the policyholder (the employer or trust), which provides insurance coverage for employees and their eligible dependents as third-party beneficiaries of the contract. The insurance company promises to pay for the benefits described in the contract and is "at risk" for the degree to which the benefits are used; that is, the annual premiums paid for the insurance may or may not be sufficient to pay for the cost of covered benefits incurred by the insured employees together with administrative costs. Usually, the insurance company also performs the claims paying function under the insurance contract.

Q 19:4   What are the advantages of the purchase of full insurance coverage?

By purchasing full insurance coverage, the employer can protect itself during the policy year against a higher than expected overall rate of claims and against individual claims that are extremely expensive. The employer's liability under full insurance is generally limited to the premiums paid to the insurer, and the insurer is liable for all plan benefits, within the plan's limits, regardless of the volume of claims or the amounts of such claims.

Another advantage of insurance is that the employer can budget its costs by paying regular premiums; however, the employer may be subject to increased premiums for future periods to cover expected utilization based on historical patterns of utilization in the insured population or in a population of similar size or makeup. In some cases, the contract may provide for a "retrospective" premium to offset a portion of the prior adverse experience. The insurance policy typically provides for a dividend or experience-rating credit if premiums paid exceed benefit payments plus the insurer's charge for expenses and profit.

In addition, the employer has the assurance that the plan's claims (and often also claim appeals) will be handled by insurance company professionals. Furthermore, the insurer provides an impartial buffer between the employer and its employees in the handling of the claims (and claim appeals, if applicable).

Tax Benefits. The premiums for an insured plan, which include amounts needed to cover incurred but unpaid claims, are generally deductible by the employer when paid or accrued. [IRC §§ 162(a), 461(h)] Additionally, because life insurance death benefit proceeds are taxed more favorably than self-insured death benefit proceeds, plans providing substantial amounts of death benefits are usually fully insured. See Chapter 12 for a discussion of death benefit proceeds. [IRC § 101(a)] Finally, an insured medical plan is not subject to any nondiscrimination rules (unless the policy is held in a VEBA, in which case Code Section 505 would apply), whereas a self-insured medical plan must meet the nondiscrimination requirements of Code Section 105(h) to obtain fully favorable tax treatment for all participants (see Qs 3:81–3:91). Note that medical plans within cafeteria plans are subject to additional cafeteria plan rules.

Q 19:5   Are there any disadvantages to purchasing full insurance for a plan?

Yes, there are. The disadvantages of a fully insured plan include the extra costs attributable to the insurer's profit margins built into the premium rates as well as the cost attributable to state premium taxes. State premium taxes are taxes imposed by all states on insurance companies; they are measured by the insurance premiums the insurance companies receive (for example, a tax of 2 percent of life or health insurance premiums). Typically the insurer passes on the cost of the premium tax to the employer or trustee purchasing the insurance.

Also, the portion of the investment earnings the insurer earns on monies received under the policy that it passes through to the employer under the policy through dividends or experience-rating credits may be less than what the employer could earn by investing the monies directly or in trust.

Finally, an insured plan is subject to state insurance laws, including those mandating certain types of benefits, whereas a self-insured or trusteed plan is not. [Metropolitan Life Ins Co v Massachusetts, 471 US 724 (1985)] See Chapter 2 for a discussion of ERISA preemption.

Q 19:6   What is self-insurance?

Under self-insurance, the employer obligates itself to pay for all of the covered plan benefits incurred by participants during the plan year. Although the plan may contain maximum limits on the frequency or cost of particular benefits, the employer is fully at risk for the benefits that are represented as being covered under the plan. In other words, within the plan's limits, the employer bears the full brunt of higher-than-expected utilization of benefits or of individual claims that turn out to be very expensive.

Self-insured plans usually are unfunded, that is, benefits are paid out of the employer's general assets. Self-insured plans can, however, be funded (sometimes referred to as self-funded). This means that the employer sets aside monies in trust to pay for all or a part of the benefits under the plan.

In some cases, the employer may also require employee contributions to help defray the cost of benefits and associated administrative costs. A trust may be required to hold such employee contributions (see Q 2:70).

Q 19:7 What are the advantages of unfunded self-insurance?

There are four main advantages associated with unfunded self-insurance:

1. The employer need satisfy benefit claims only as they actually become payable. Thus, amounts needed for future benefits, which would be collected as premiums and held by an insurance company under an insured plan, can be kept in the employer's business, perhaps earning more than they would if such amounts were turned over to an insurer or trust.
2. A self-insured plan does not incur the state premium tax cost (see Q 19:5) that an insured plan would incur.
3. An unfunded self-insured plan may also lead to savings in administrative costs and expenses.
4. A self-insured plan is also exempt under ERISA from a variety of state insurance laws mandating types of benefits, as well as from state laws generally. See Chapter 2 for a discussion of ERISA preemption.

Q 19:8 Are there any disadvantages to self-insurance?

Yes, there are several major disadvantages associated with self-insurance:

1. The employer bears the full brunt of the economic risk that benefit costs may substantially exceed the employer's estimates.

2. Benefit payments may vary greatly during the plan year, making budgeting difficult.

3. The employer may find it difficult to maintain a claims administration operation that functions smoothly and objectively.

4. The employer can deduct only amounts actually used to pay benefits under a self-insured plan in the taxable year. No deduction is allowed for claims incurred but unreported, and perhaps not for claims reported but unpaid.

Because of these difficulties, smaller employers generally do not find self-insurance attractive. They usually prefer to purchase full insurance, which limits the economic risk of liability for excessive claims and permits the budgeting of costs through periodic and regular premium payments. Larger employers, on the other hand, are better able to handle these problems and are attracted to self-insurance because of the cost savings features and because of the advantages of preemption of varying state laws by ERISA.

Tax Disadvantages. A death benefit under a self-insured death benefit plan is exempt from income tax up to a maximum of $5,000, whereas a fully insured death benefit plan provides a full death benefit exclusion regardless of amount. [IRC §§ 101(a), 101(b)] In addition, a self-insured medical plan must meet the nondiscrimination requirements of Code Section 105(h), while a fully insured medical plan is not subject to any nondiscrimination rules.

Q 19:9   How is a trust used to self-fund benefits under a welfare benefit plan?

Under a self-insured plan that is also funded, the employer contributes monies to a trust to be used for the payment of plan benefits and, if the trust document permits, for the payment of related administrative expenses. Generally, the trust will be set up as a tax-exempt irrevocable trust under Code Section 501(c)(9) (that is, a VEBA trust). (see Qs 19:52–19:69.) Once the monies are held irrevocably in trust, they are segregated from the general assets of the employer and are not subject to the claims of the employer's creditors. They are also protected in the event of an employer's insolvency or bankruptcy.

Investment earnings on the monies in trust are also used to pay benefits and, if authorized, administrative costs. A trust may be required in any event, if the employer requires employee contributions toward the cost of coverage (see Qs 2:70–2:72).

Q 19:10   What is the difference between self-insurance and self-funding?

With self-insurance, the full economic risk for payment of benefits under the plan lies with the employer, and the employer pays such amounts out of its general assets.

Under self-funding, the economic risk for payment of benefits still lies with the employer, but in this latter case the employer sets aside funds in trust to meet its obligation under the plan. Sometimes, the employer includes a statement in the plan document and employee communications that, regardless of the benefits described as covered, the employer's liability is limited to the amount in the trust. Practically speaking, however, an employer with an ongoing plan often simply will contribute more to the trust to make up any shortfall rather than incur employee dissatisfaction.

Both self-insurance and self-funding usually are referred to generically as "self-insurance" whenever the key issue is whether or not the employer bears the economic risk (such as when determining whether ERISA preempts state insurance laws).

Q 19:11   What are the advantages of self-funding a plan using a trust?

If a trust is used to fund benefits payable under a self-insured plan, plan costs can be budgeted through regular contributions to the trust.

In addition, since funded and unfunded self-insured plans are not considered to be in the business of insurance (see Qs 2:138–2:141), state insurance laws relating to premium taxes and other state laws mandating the inclusion of particular benefits are, for such plans, preempted by ERISA. (However, it may not always be possible to avoid state insurance law regulation if the trust is part of a multiple employer welfare arrangement (MEWA) (see Q 2:149).

The trust can be established on a tax-free basis, and tax deductions can be taken for contributions for both incurred and paid claims.

Still another advantage of using a trust to fund a plan is that the plan gets the benefit of investment earnings on trust funds held for future claims.

Q 19:12   Are there any disadvantages to funding a self-insured plan using a trust?

Yes, there are four major disadvantages, as follows:

1. Once funds are contributed to the trust, they generally cannot be recovered by the employer.
2. Trustees' fees, legal fees, and other administrative costs of maintaining the trust may be substantial.
3. Compliance by the trust with Internal Revenue Service (IRS) VEBA requirements and ERISA fiduciary responsibility requirements may prove difficult.
4. Although the trust approach can limit the employer's liability for higher than anticipated benefits to the amount of funds in the trust, as a practical matter an employer with an ongoing plan voluntarily will provide the trust with the money needed to pay for all of the benefits due under the terms of the plan.

Q 19:13   What is a minimum premium insurance arrangement?

This is an arrangement under which the employer self-insures plan benefits up to a specified amount, the trigger point, and the insurer agrees to be liable to employees and their beneficiaries for all benefits in excess of the trigger point. The trigger point frequently is set at the level of expected claims under the plan but it can be a negotiated amount that is higher or lower than the level of expected claims.

Typically, the insurance company performs the administrative services relating to claims payment for the plan as a whole, drawing funds for payment of the self-insured portion of the arrangement out of a checking account set up by the employer specifically to cover benefit payments. The employer is responsible for keeping sufficient monies in the checking account to cover its obligation under the self-insured portion of the minimum premium arrangement. Usually, the employer has only a very short grace period in which to remedy any underfunding of the checking account, such as two or three business days, or the arrangement will abruptly terminate.

In many (but not in all) cases, the minimum premium contract provides that, in the event of termination of the arrangement, the insurer then becomes liable to pay all claims incurred but unpaid prior to the effective date of the termination. Thus, unlike stop-loss insurance (see Q 19:14), the insurance under the traditional type of minimum premium arrangement may "drop-down" and assume the employer's portion of the economic risk if the employer reneges on its obligation under the arrangement. At that point, the employer usually must pay an additional premium to the insurer for this additional protection. Also at that time, under the traditional method of setting up a minimum premium arrangement, such arrangement would then revert to full insurance and the employer would be required to pay premiums for the full insurance coverage. This happens because, under the traditional method, the minimum premium arrangement is created by a rider to an insurance policy which makes the policy an excess risk policy (with a correspondingly smaller premium, hence the name "minimum premium") rather than a full insurance policy. The rider self-destructs if the employer fails to keep up the funding on its share of the economic risk, leaving the underlying insurance policy in full force.

However, in some cases, the minimum premium setup may not revert to full insurance or obligate the insurance company to drop down and cover the employer's liability for claims incurred but unpaid prior to the date the minimum premium arrangement terminates.

State Premium Tax Costs. Minimum premium plans generally are not subject to state premium taxes on the self-insured portion of the plans—that is, amounts below the trigger point—but only on the actual premiums received by the insurance carrier. However, the state of California imposes premium taxes on amounts below the trigger point under certain employer-maintained minimum premium plans, and it has been held that ERISA does not preempt California's taxation of such amounts. [Metropolitan Life Ins Co v State Bd of Equalization, 32 Cal. 3d 649 (1982); General Motors Corp v California State Bd of Equalization, 815 F 2d 1305 (9th Cir 1987), *cert denied,* 108 S Ct 1122 (1988)]

However, in a recent California appellate court decision involving a minimum premium plan, the court found that the facts in the *Metropolitan Life* case were distinguishable and therefore the earlier case was not controlling. Under the minimum premium plan involved in the later case, the insurer had no contractual obligation to pay pre-trigger point claims the employer failed to pay, the coverage did not revert to full insurance coverage if the employer failed to pay pre-trigger point claims, and there was no obligation to pay an additional premium to the insurer upon termination. The fact that the insurer was obligated to pay plan benefits in excess of the agreed-upon trigger point was held to be not enough to justify the imposition of state premium tax based upon the amount of pre-trigger point benefits paid by the employer. [Aetna Life Ins Co v State Bd of Equalization, 15 Cal Rptr 2nd 26 (Ct App 1992)]

Q 19:14　What is a stop-loss insurance arrangement?

Under a stop-loss insurance arrangement, the employer fully self-insures the plan benefits. However, the insurer agrees to reimburse the employer (but not the employees) to the extent that plan benefits paid or incurred by the employer exceed a specified level (for example, 120 percent of expected claims). If the policy proceeds are payable to the employer, they become part of the employer's general assets and are not specifically earmarked for payment of benefits under the particular plan. Accordingly, stop-loss insurance payable to the employer can be viewed as a hedging technique against potential adverse impact of plan costs on the employer's cash flow.

Occasionally, the plan trustee purchases stop-loss insurance under which the policy proceeds are payable to the plan or trust. In this latter case, the proceeds payable to the trust become plan assets.

State Premium Costs. Stop-loss insurance plans generally are not subject to state premium taxes except with respect to the actual stop-loss premium paid to the insurer. California does not extend its taxation of benefits paid under certain minimum premium plans to benefits paid under plans with stop-loss coverage.

Q 19:15 Are minimum premium and stop-loss arrangements ever considered to be insured?

The characterization of these "in-between" arrangements as insurance depends on the particular statute at issue.

ERISA Preemption. If these in-between arrangements are characterized as insured, then ERISA will not preempt attempted state regulation of the content of the plan. The ability of multistate employers to maintain a single, uniform benefit plan for all of their geographic locations thus hinges on how the plan is characterized.

The federal common-law cases under ERISA are presently unsettled, evidently due to confusion, in some instances, over which of these two types of arrangements is at issue. Stop-loss arrangements generally have been held to be self-insured for ERISA purposes. [United Food & Commercial Workers v Pacyga, 801 F 2d 1157 (9th Cir 1986); see also Moore v Provident Life & Accident Ins Co, 786 F 2d 922 (9th Cir 1986); and Rasmussen v Metropolitan Life Ins Co, 675 F Supp 1497 (WD La 1987)] The latter two cases involve plans characterized as stop-loss insurance arrangements that actually appear to be minimum premium plans. However, a US District Court case concluded that, for ERISA purposes, the type of minimum premium arrangement at issue in that case was more analogous to an insured plan with a large deductible. [Hall v Pennwalt Group Comprehensive Medical Expense Benefits Plan, Civil Action No 88-7672 (ED Pa 1989); see also Michigan United Food and Commercial Workers Unions v Baerwaldt, 767 F 2d 308 (6th Cir 1985), *cert denied,* 474 US 1059 (1986), stating that ERISA did not preempt the application of state insurance law to a stop-loss arrangement that actually appeared to be a minimum premium arrangement.] Note that, if stop-loss policy proceeds are payable to the employer rather than to employees or to the plan, the arrangement should not be characterized as insured for ERISA purposes, because the payment of policy proceeds is merely triggered by a particular benefit expense level under the plan but the proceeds themselves are not committed for the payment of such benefit expenses. The case law does not follow this theory so neatly, however.

State Insurance Law. Whether such an in-between arrangement is considered to be insured for state law purposes initially depends on the individual state's law and the state law regulator's interpretation, and is then subject to court decisions on ERISA preemption.

Federal Tax Law. For purposes of determining whether a plan is self-insured under Code Section 105(h), ERISA and state insurance law characterizations are not controlling. The regulations under Code Section 105(h) do not take an all-or-nothing approach, but rather recognize that a plan may be both partially insured and partially self-insured. In other words, for tax purposes, it appears that the portion of a minimum premium arrangement for which the employer bears the economic risk is treated as self-insured (and thus subject to the nondiscrimination tests of Code Section 105(h)) and the portion for which the insurance carrier bears the economic risk is treated as insured (and thus exempt from nondiscrimination testing under Code Section 105(h)). [Treas Reg § 1.105-11(b)(2)] In the case of stop-loss arrangements where the policy proceeds are payable into the general assets of the employer, it appears that the plan would be considered to be fully self-insured under Code Section 105(h) because the employer is fully liable for plan benefits.

Q 19:16   What is an administrative-services-only (ASO) arrangement?

Under an administrative-services-only arrangement, the employer fully self-insures the plan benefits. However, an insurance company or other third-party administrator agrees to administer claims and provide other administrative services for a fee. Administrative-services-only arrangements are not subject to state premium taxes.

Q 19:17   What are some other funding alternatives?

Other funding alternatives for the provision of health benefits include the use of health maintenance organizations (HMOs) and preferred provider organizations (PPOs) (see Qs 3:16–3:17). (See Chapter 5.) Special arrangements are also available for restricted funding of postretirement life insurance and health benefits (see Qs 19:39–19:42).

Q 19:18   Does the method of funding affect the amount of the employer's tax deduction for welfare benefit plan contributions?

Yes, it does. First, the employer's contributions will be deductible only to the extent that they constitute ordinary and necessary business expenses of the employer under Code Section 162(a).

Note. Deductibility is also effective for hospital services provided after February 2, 1993 and on or before May 12, 1995, conditioned upon the plan reimbursing hospitals in New York at a specified rate. See Q 3:51, which discusses new Code Section 162(n).

Second, if the contributions are made to a welfare benefit fund, the contributions to the fund (1) must be within the deductible limits specifically applicable to welfare benefit funds, and (2) actually must be paid, regardless of whether the employer is on an accrual or a cash basis of tax accounting. [IRC § 419(a)]

The amount of an excess contribution by the employer in one taxable year may be treated as "carried over" for tax deduction purposes and deemed paid by the employer to the fund in the succeeding taxable year (subject, of course, to the deduction limits for that succeeding year). [IRC § 419(d)]

Special rules, applicable to VEBAs and Code Section 401(h) medical accounts in pension and annuity plans, are discussed later in this chapter.

Q 19:19   How do these deduction limits apply to insured and self-insured plans?

These rules apply as follows:

- *Insured plans.* If the plan is insured, the welfare benefit fund limits generally do not apply. (The temporary regulations apply the welfare benefit rules only to certain narrow categories of employer arrangements with insurance companies; see Qs 19:21–19:25.) The employer can generally deduct the actual premiums charged by the insurer, including the portion of the premiums that the insurer needs to establish reserves for incurred but unpaid claims. [IRC § 162(a); Rev Rul 56-632, 1956-2 CB 101]

- *Self-insured plans that are unfunded.* If the self-insured plan is unfunded, the welfare benefit fund limits on deductibility do not apply. The employer can deduct amounts actually used to pay benefits in the taxable year. However, no deduction is allowed for claims incurred but unreported, and perhaps not for claims reported but unpaid. [IRC § 461(h); United States v General Dynamics Corp, 107 S Ct 1732 (1987)]

- *Self-insured plans that are funded.* If a self-insured plan is funded through a welfare benefit trust, the limits on the deductibility of an employer's contributions to a welfare benefit fund apply (see Q 19:20–19:51). The employer generally can deduct amounts contributed to the trust, except to the extent they exceed the maximum deductible amounts applicable to welfare benefit funds. [IRC § 419 and 419A]

Welfare Benefit Fund Rules

This section describes the rules that limit an employer's tax deduction to a welfare benefit plan when a fund exists, or is considered to exist. Questions 19:20 through 19:28 describe what a *welfare benefit fund* is; Questions 19:29 and 19:30 discuss *qualified cost*; Question 19:31 discusses *qualified direct cost*; Questions 19:32 through 19:38 discuss the *qualified asset account limits;* Questions 19:39 through 19:42 discuss special limits on *reserves for postretirement medical and life insurance*; Question 19:43 discusses the calculation of the *after-tax income* of the fund; and Questions 19:44 through 19:51 discuss *taxes* applicable to welfare benefit funds.

Q 19:20   What is a welfare benefit fund under the Internal Revenue Code (IRC)?

A welfare benefit fund is any "fund" that is part of a plan through which the employer provides welfare benefits to employees or their beneficiaries. [IRC § 419(e)(1)] If a welfare benefit fund exists, then the employer's tax deduction for the amount it contributes to the welfare benefit fund cannot exceed the limits contained in Code Sections 419 and 419A.

A fund is defined as:

- A tax-exempt trust or other tax-exempt organization described in Code Sections 501(c)(7), 501(c)(9), 501(c)(17), or 501(c)(20). This encompasses a nonprofit social club [IRC § 501(c)(7)]; a voluntary employees' beneficiary association (VEBA) providing life, sickness, accident, or other benefits [IRC § 501(c)(9)]; a trust providing supplemental unemployment compensation benefits [IRC § 501(c)(17)]; and a trust or other organization that is part of a group legal services plan [IRC § 501(c)(20)]. Most welfare benefit funds are formed as trusts pursuant to Code Section 501(c)(9) and are commonly referred to as 501(c)(9) trusts or VEBAs.

- Any trust, corporation, or other organization not exempt from tax. Thus, a taxable trust or taxable corporation that is maintained for the purpose of providing welfare benefits is a welfare benefit fund.

- To the extent provided in regulations, any account held for an employer by any person.

[IRC § 419(e)(3); Temp Treas Reg § 1.419-1T, Q&A 3]

Q 19:21   Do any employer arrangements with insurance companies constitute welfare benefit funds?

Under temporary regulations issued by the Treasury and supplemented by IRS Announcement 86-45 (1986-15 IRB 52), only the following employer arrangements with insurance companies are considered funds:

1. Certain retired lives reserves held for postretirement life insurance or medical benefits. The reference to "certain" reserves
   suggests that retired lives reserves established from employee
   contributions only are not funds.

2. Certain administrative-services-only arrangements. Again,
   the reference to "certain" arrangements suggests that some
   administrative-services-only arrangements are not funds for
   this purpose. In most administrative-services-only arrangements, the insurer holds no plan funds, and benefits are paid
   from the employer's or trustee's bank account.

3. Certain arrangements under which the employer (a) makes deductible contributions and (b) has, on or before the later of the
   end of the policy year to which such contributions relate or the
   time such contracts are made, a *contractual right* to a dividend,
   refund, credit, or additional benefit based on the benefit or claims
   experience, administrative cost experience, or investment experience attributable *solely* to the employer. Most group experience-rated policies do not contain a contractual right to a
   dividend or refund, and do not base the dividend or refund solely
   on the single employer's plan experience. Instead, the contract
   typically provides for a dividend or refund at the insurance
   company's discretion. Any such dividend or refund generally is
   reduced to reflect risk charges and pooling charges under the policy
   and, thus, is not based solely on that particular employer's plan
   experience. (A risk charge generally is an across-the-board charge
   made by the insurance carrier to all of its group policyholders. A
   pooling charge is an additional charge the insurance company makes
   for high amounts of insurance coverage or extraordinary risks which
   are pooled rather than charged to that particular employer's experience, so that they do not skew the premiums on the group.)

Possible Future Expansion of the Term "Fund". The Treasury has
indicated that, at some time in the future, it may issue additional
regulations expanding the types of insurance company arrangements that
will be treated as funds. However, any such regulations will not have
retroactive effect. Moreover, Congress has provided that, except for the
arrangements described in paragraphs (1) and (3) of the preceding list,
any regulations expanding the definition of fund will not become effective
until six months after final regulations are issued. [Temp Treas Reg

§ 1.419-1T, Q&A 3, as modified by Ann 86-45, 1986-15 IRB 52; TRA '86 § 185(a)(8)(B)]

Q 19:22   Are experience-rated group insurance contracts treated as welfare benefit funds?

Generally no, they are not. The temporary Treasury regulations, as modified by IRS Announcement 86-45, include a narrow group of insurance company arrangements within the Code Section 419 definition of welfare benefit fund. Congress subsequently indicated that typical group insurance arrangements should not be subject to the welfare benefit fund rules because the economic risk of benefit payments is transferred to the insurance company. [Ann 86-45, 1986-15 IRB 52; Conf Rpt to TRA '86, HR Rpt No 841, 99th Cong, 2d Sess, Vol II, at 850 (1986)]

Q 19:23   Are insurance contracts paid for solely by employee contributions considered welfare benefit funds?

Under the temporary regulations (see Q 19:21), only certain insurance arrangements involving employer contributions (and related tax deductions) are treated as funds. Therefore, unless future regulations further expand the term "fund," insurance contracts paid for solely by employee contributions are not welfare benefit funds.

Q 19:24   What other types of employer arrangements with insurance companies are not welfare benefit funds?

The IRC definition of fund also excludes a life insurance contract under which the employer is directly or indirectly the beneficiary. Thus, corporate-owned life insurance and insurance used to fund split-dollar plans do not constitute a fund subject to the deduction limits of Code Sections 419 and 419A. [IRC § 419(e)(4)(A)(i)] (Split-dollar insurance as a benefit is discussed at Questions 12:47 through 12:54.)

In addition, the IRC definition of fund specifically excludes from fund status a "qualified nonguaranteed contract." [IRC § 419(e)(4)(A)(ii)]

Q 19:25   What is a qualified nonguaranteed contract?

Under an exclusion from fund status contained in Code Section 419, a qualified nonguaranteed contract is any insurance contract (including a reasonable reserve held thereunder to cover higher than expected future costs, called a "premium stabilization reserve") if:

- There is no guarantee of a renewal of the contract (at guaranteed renewal rates); and
- The only payments (other than those for insurance protection) to which the employer or employees are entitled are experience-rated refunds or policy dividends that are not guaranteed and that are determined by factors (such as risk charges and pooling charges) other than the amount of welfare benefits paid to or on behalf of the employees or their beneficiaries.

In addition, in order to have the exclusion apply, the employer must treat any experience-rated refund or policy dividend attributable to a policy year as received or accrued for tax purposes in the taxable year in which the policy year to which it relates ends. [IRC § 419(e)(4)(B)]

> **Planning Pointer.** The legislative history to the TRA '86 amendments expresses Congress's intent that the definition of fund avoid encompassing true insurance arrangements. Accordingly, an employer with an experience-rated group policy that does not fit the definition of fund in the temporary regulations and the IRS Announcement 86-45 apparently does not have to attempt to fit within the statutory exclusion for qualified nonguaranteed contracts in order to avoid welfare benefit fund tax treatment. (Note that this situation may change if further regulations are issued expanding the classes of insurance contract arrangements that are to be treated as funds. Any such expansion of the definition of fund will be applied on a prospective basis only.)

Q 19:26   Is a fund maintained for more than one employer a welfare benefit fund?

Generally, yes, it is. However, the welfare benefit fund rules do not apply to a 10-or-more-employer plan. This is a plan under which:

- No employer normally contributes more than 10 percent of the total contributions to the plan, and

- The experience rating, if any, does not apply to individual employers, that is, the experience of the group is pooled.

[IRC § 419A(f)(6)]

Q 19:27   Must there be a formal welfare benefit plan in order for the welfare benefit fund rules to apply?

No; if there is no plan as such, but there is a method or arrangement of employer contributions or benefits that has the effect of a plan, the welfare benefit fund rules will apply to a fund maintained under the informal arrangement. [IRC § 419(f)]

Q 19:28   Must there be an employer-employee relationship for the welfare benefit fund rules to come into play?

No, an employer-employee relationship is not necessary. If the arrangement would be a welfare benefit fund, except that the person providing services is an independent contractor and not an employee, the welfare benefit fund rules apply. [IRC § 419(g)]

Q 19:29   What are the limits on the employer's tax deduction for contributions to a welfare benefit fund?

If a welfare benefit fund exists, the employer's deduction for a taxable year is limited to the fund's "qualified cost" for the year. [IRC § 419(b)]

Q 19:30   What is the fund's qualified cost?

The welfare benefit fund's qualified cost is:

- The sum of the "qualified direct cost" (see Q 19:31) plus permitted additions (within limits) to a "qualified asset account" (see Qs 19:32–19:42) for the taxable year;
- Reduced by the fund's after-tax income for the taxable year (see Q 19:43).

[IRC § 419(c)]

Q 19:31 What is the fund's qualified direct cost?

When calculating the qualified cost that the employer can deduct, the first element is the fund's qualified direct cost. The fund's qualified direct cost is the aggregate amount of cash expenses for benefits and administrative expenses that would have been allowed as a deduction under Code Section 162 by a cash-basis employer if they had been provided directly by the employer rather than through a fund.

Note: The Code Section 162 deduction is unavailable unless new Code Section 162(n) is satisfied. See Question 3:51.

A benefit is treated as provided when it would be includible in the employee's gross income (if there were no statutory exclusion). Special rules are provided for amortization of the cost of a child care facility. [IRC § 419(c)(3)]

Q 19:32 What is a qualified asset account?

The second element that needs to be known when calculating the amount of the employer's qualified cost is the permitted amount under the qualified asset account. A qualified asset account is an account consisting of assets set aside to provide for the payment of the following benefits:

- Disability
- Medical
- Supplemental unemployment compensation or severance pay
- Life insurance

[IRC § 419A(a)]

Q 19:33   What limits apply to the qualified asset account?

The overall account limit is the amount reasonably and actuarially necessary to fund benefit claims incurred and unpaid as of the end of the taxable year, together with related administrative costs. [IRC § 419A(c)(1)]

Disability Benefits. The qualified asset account may not, in any event, include disability benefits to the extent that they are payable at an annual rate exceeding the lower of:

- 75 percent of the employee's average compensation for his or her three most highly compensated years; or
- The amount of the Code Section 415 limit applicable to benefits payable under defined-benefit pension plans (in 1993, this limit is $115,641).

Supplemental Unemployment Compensation or Severance Pay Benefits. The qualified asset account also may not, in any event, include supplemental unemployment compensation or severance pay benefits to the extent that they are payable at an annual rate in excess of 150 percent of the Code Section 415 dollar limitation in effect for defined-contribution retirement plans (in 1993, this limit is 150 percent of $30,000, or $45,000). [IRC § 419A(c)(4)]

Reserve for Postretirement Medical or Life Insurance Benefits. The account limit may, however, include contributions to an additional reserve for postretirement medical or life insurance benefits, if certain conditions are satisfied (see Qs 19:39–19:42). [IRC § 419A(c)(2)]

Q 19:34   How does the employer establish that the amount it contributes to a qualified asset account is reasonably and actuarially necessary, and thus deductible?

Two alternatives are available for a taxable year:

1. If the employer chooses not to get an actuarial certification, the employer must be able to justify that the reserve for incurred

but unpaid claims is reasonable, and the account limit cannot exceed safe-harbor limits set forth in the IRC or to be set forth in Treasury regulations; or

2. The employer may obtain a certification from an actuary that the entire amount of the account (not just the amount exceeding the safe-harbor limits) is actuarially justified.

[IRC § 419A(c)(5); Conf Rpt 861, 98th Cong, 2d Sess, at 1158 (1984)]

Q 19:35 What are the safe-harbor limits for qualified asset accounts?

The safe-harbor limits vary according to the type of benefit being funded, as follows:

- *Medical benefits.* 35 percent of qualified direct costs (other than insurance premiums) for the immediately preceding taxable year;
- *Life insurance and death benefits.* To be prescribed in Treasury regulations;
- *Short-term (up to 12 months) disability benefits.* 17.5 percent of qualified direct costs (other than insurance premiums) for the immediately preceding taxable year;
- *Long-term disability.* To be prescribed in Treasury regulations;
- *Supplemental unemployment compensation and severance pay benefits.* 75 percent of the average annual qualified direct costs for any two of the immediately preceding seven taxable years.

[IRC § 419A(c)(5)]

Planning Pointer. The use of the term "safe harbor" in the law is somewhat misleading, since the legislative history indicates that the reserve also must meet a requirement that the reserve be reasonable in amount. Thus, if in a particular case a reasonable incurred claims reserve for medical benefits would be only 20 percent of qualified direct costs for the preceding year, it appears that a reserve equal to the 35-percent-safe harbor would exceed the permissible limit.

Q 19:36   Can a qualified asset account include a premium or cost stabilization reserve?

No. A premium or cost stabilization reserve is not a reserve held to pay claims incurred but unpaid and thus is not an allowable reserve. In a technical advice memorandum (Priv Ltr Rul 91-45-003, June 18, 1991), the IRS indicated that reserves set aside to pay level dividends or to stabilize premium rates are not allowable reserves and thus can trigger an unrelated business income tax if maintained by a VEBA.

> **Planning Pointer.** If a VEBA is being used by an employer to provide group term life insurance coverage through an insurance carrier, and a premium stabilization reserve is desired, it generally is preferable for the insurance company to hold the premium stabilization reserve because the group policy ordinarily will not be subject to the welfare benefit fund limitations (see Qs 19:21–19:25). If a VEBA is being used to fund a collectively bargained plan or an employee-pay-all plan, the VEBA is not subject to the qualified asset account limits (see Q 19:37) and thus can hold a premium or cost stabilization reserve without triggering an unrelated business income tax.

Q 19:37   Are all welfare benefit funds subject to the qualified asset account limits?

No, they are not. The account limits do not apply to a collectively bargained plan. The account limits also do not apply to an employee-pay-all plan funded through a Code Section 501(c)(9) trust (VEBA) if (1) the plan has at least 50 employees (determined without relying on the plan aggregation rules) and (2) no employee in the plan is entitled to a refund other than one based on the experience of the entire fund. [IRC § 419A(f)(5)] In addition, special transitional relief from the account limits was provided for funds that had excess reserves on hand at the time of enactment in 1984 of the account limit rules. [IRC § 419A(f)(7)]

Q 19:38   If an employer has more than one welfare benefit fund, may the funds be aggregated in applying the limits?

Yes; the employer generally may elect to treat two or more welfare benefit funds as a single fund. [IRC § 419A(h)(1)] Furthermore, the tax rules in the pension plan area treating related employers as a single employer also apply to welfare benefit funds. [IRC § 419A(h)(2)]

Q 19:39   Can the fund's qualified asset account also include a reserve for postretirement medical and life insurance benefits for future retirees?

Yes, the fund's qualified asset account limit can include a reserve for postretirement medical or life insurance benefits. This means that the employer can make advance, deductible contributions to build up a reserve fund to pay for retiree medical or life insurance benefits in future years. The reserve must be funded over the working lives of the covered employees and be actuarially determined on a level basis using assumptions that are reasonable in the aggregate.

Postretirement Medical Benefits. In funding for postretirement medical benefits, no increase in current medical costs can be assumed, even if some assumption of future increases in medical costs could be actuarially justified. In other words, the amount that the employer contributes to the reserve cannot include any amount to cover anticipated inflation in medical costs. [IRC § 419A(c)(2)]

Postretirement Life Insurance Benefits. Postretirement life insurance (including uninsured death benefits) may be funded only for amounts not in excess of $50,000, except in the case of "grandfathered" employees and retirees who continue to enjoy the full exclusion from income for group term life insurance coverage following actual retirement and attainment of retirement age as long as they retain grandfather group status. (See Question 11:48 for a discussion of who is a grandfathered individual.) For those individuals, the full amount of their postretirement group term life insurance may be prefunded. [IRC § 419A(e)(2); TRA '86 § 1851(a)(3)(B)]

Q 19:40 Can an employer also fund postretirement medical or life insurance benefits for individuals who have already retired?

According to the legislative history of the welfare benefit fund rules, no advance deduction is allowed with respect to a plan providing benefits exclusively for retirees, because such a plan is considered a plan of deferred compensation subject to the rules of Code Section 404. [Conf Rpt to TRA '84, HR Rpt No 861, 98th Cong, 2d Sess, at 1157 (1984)] However, if the retiree plan is a continuation of a plan covering active employees, the welfare benefit fund rules do apply.

In a private letter ruling, IRS considered the case of an employer with three separate medical plans, one plan for active employees and the other two plans for retirees. Both of the retiree plans required, as a condition of eligibility, prior coverage under the active plan for a period of up to 10 years immediately prior to retirement. The IRS held that the benefits under the retiree plans were a continuation of the active plan benefits, and therefore the employer's deductions were governed by Secton 419 of the Code rather than by Code Section 404. [Priv Ltr Rul 91-51-027, Sept 23, 1991]

Funding Limits for Postretirement Benefits of Existing Retirees. In the absence of regulations, it is uncertain what the permissible limits are for funding the postretirement benefits of existing retirees, since they obviously have no remaining working lives over which the benefits can be funded. One possibility is that the full amount of the liability for postretirement coverage for existing retirees can be funded in a lump sum. [Priv Ltr Rul 78-29-054, Apr 20, 1978] The other extreme would be that, since existing retirees have a zero working life, their benefits cannot be prefunded at all. Another possibility is to come up with an approach somewhere between these two extremes, such as amortizing the cost over a reasonable period (for example, over the anticipated remaining average lifetime of the retiree group or over a fixed period such as ten years, similar to what is done in the pension area for past service costs).

Q 19:41 Do any nondiscrimination rules apply to the funding of postretirement medical and life insurance benefits for employees?

Yes, the employer may not deduct its contributions to a reserve for postretirement life insurance or medical benefits unless the plan, under which the reserve is maintained, does not discriminate in favor of the highly compensated. For this purpose, the nondiscrimination tests of Code Section 79 apply to group term life insurance (see Qs 11:40–11:48), the nondiscrimination rules of Code Section 105(h) apply to self-insured medical benefit plans (see Qs 3:81–3:91), and the nondiscrimination rules of Code Section 505(b) apply to insured medical benefits. However, the nondiscrimination rules do not apply to a collectively bargained plan if the retiree benefits were the subject of good-faith bargaining. [IRC §§ 419A(e)(1), 505(b)(3)]

Q 19:42 What other special rules apply to funding postretirement medical and life insurance benefits?

If the reserve for postretirement medical and life insurance benefits is maintained for the benefit of one or more key employees, a separate account must be established for each key employee so covered, and such postretirement benefits for the key employee may be paid only from his or her separate account. [IRC § 419A(d)(1)]

For this purpose, a key employee is defined as any employee who, during the plan year or any preceding plan year, was a key employee as defined under the rules for top-heavy qualified retirement plan purposes. [IRC §§ 416(i), 419A(d)(3)]

How a Separate Account Is to Be Charged. In the absence of regulations, it is not clear how the key employee-retiree's separate account is to be charged. It appears that the separate account perhaps should be charged with the term cost of life insurance and insured postretirement medical benefit coverage during retirement. In the case of uninsured medical or death benefits, the separate account probably should be charged with the actual benefits when paid.

Effect on Tax-Qualified Retirement Plans. Any amount to be used for postretirement medical benefits that is allocated to a key employee's separate account is treated as an annual addition to a defined-contribution plan, for purposes of the dollar limitation on contributions to defined contribution plans under Code Section 415. [IRC § 419A(d)(2)] The effect of this rule is to discourage funding of retiree medical benefits for key employees because it can reduce their retirement plan benefits.

Q 19:43   How is the fund's after-tax income determined?

The last element that needs to be known when calculating the employer's deductible amount of qualified cost is the amount of the fund's after-tax income for the taxable year. This after-tax income is subtracted from the sum of the qualified direct cost and the permitted additions to the qualified asset account in order to arrive at the employer's qualified cost.

When calculating the amount of the fund's after-tax income, the starting point is the fund's gross income for income tax purposes. Employee contributions, if any, then are added to the gross income, but employer contributions are not. Gross income (including employee contributions) then is reduced by expenses directly connected with the production of the gross income and by any income or unrelated business income taxes imposed on the fund. [IRC § 419(c)(4)]

Q 19:44   What are the tax consequences if the employer contributes more to a welfare benefit plan than can be deducted under the welfare benefit fund rules?

The employer cannot take a current deduction for contribution amounts made (or deemed to be made) to the extent that they collectively exceed the qualified cost limit of Code Section 419, although the excess can be carried over to a later tax year. [IRC § 419A(b)]

In addition, the net investment income of the fund will be taxed as so-called unrelated business taxable income (if a VEBA or other tax-exempt trust is involved) or taxed as "deemed unrelated income" (if a taxable trust or fund held by an insurance company is involved) to the extent that the fund exceeds the Code Section 419A qualified asset account limit. [IRC §§ 419A(g), 512(a)(3)]

Q 19:45   Does investment income on a reserve for postretirement medical benefits accumulate tax-free?

No, generally it does not. The net investment income from a reserve for postretirement medical benefits is not be treated as part of the qualified asset account when applying the unrelated business income or deemed unrelated income tax rules. The Code provides that net investment income earned on reserves held for postretirement medical benefits accumulates on an after-tax basis. [IRC § 512(a)(3)(E)(i)]

An exception is provided for a retired lives reserve that was in existence at the time of enactment of these welfare benefit fund rules in 1984. Such a reserve is exempt from the unrelated business income or deemed unrelated income tax rules, provided that all payments during plan years ending on or after the date of enactment (July 18, 1984) are charged against the existing retired lives reserve until it is used up. [IRC § 512(a)(3)(E)(ii)]

If the welfare benefit fund is a separate fund established under a collective bargaining agreement, no account limits apply to the qualified asset account of the fund, and therefore it should have no tax on its postretirement medical benefits reserve. [IRC § 419A(f)(5)(A)]

In addition, no account limits apply to the qualified asset account of a separate fund that is an employee-pay-all plan established under Code Section 501(c)(9) (that is, a VEBA), if:

- The plan has at least 50 employees (determined without relying on the plan aggregation rules); and
- No employee in the plan is entitled to a refund other than one based on the experience of the entire fund.

Since there are no account limits in such a case, the postretirement medical benefits reserve can earn income tax-free. [IRC § 419A(f)(5)(B)]

It should also be noted that the unrelated business income tax does not apply to a welfare fund where substantially all of the contributions to the fund are made by employers who were tax-exempt organizations throughout the five-taxable-year period ending with the taxable year in which the contributions are made. Thus, such employers can fund a postretirement medical benefits reserve free of tax. [IRC § 512(a)(3)(E)(iii)]

Q 19:46 Are there any other circumstances where the income on a reserve held for postretirement medical benefits is not subject to tax?

Yes, if the income itself is not gross income under the IRC. For example, if a VEBA maintains a reserve for postretirement medical benefits and invests the funds in tax-exempt municipal obligations, it will have no gross income and thus no unrelated business income. [IRC § 521(a)(3)] Of course, it will generally receive a lower return on tax-exempt obligations than it would pre-tax on fully taxable obligations.

A VEBA apparently can avoid the unrelated business income tax by purchasing life insurance on the lives of the employees covered with the VEBA as owner and beneficiary and maintaining the insurance coverage until the employee's death. Some insurers have developed a group universal life insurance policy (fixed or variable) specifically for this market. This type of product is commonly referred to as trust-owned life insurance (TOLI). One potential issue raised by this product is whether the VEBA will be considered to have an insurable interest in the lives of the employees involved. A number of state laws defining insurable interest have been liberalized in recent years to cover this and similar situations (see the discussion of insurable interest under corporate-owned life insurance policies in Question 19:101).

Q 19:47 Are reserves established to fund postretirement medical and life insurance benefits required to be maintained separately from other benefit funds?

Yes, it appears so, as a condition to receiving favorable tax treatment of the funding.

Some practitioners have contended that a retiree medical or life insurance reserve could be established within a VEBA and that the amounts, once set aside, could be used at any time thereafter for any benefits the VEBA was authorized to provide (for example, medical benefits for active employees). However, a recent private letter ruling strongly suggests that IRS will require that the retiree reserve be used solely for its intended purpose, at least as long as there are employees and retirees in the covered group still alive.

In Private Letter Ruling 92-06-030 (November 13, 1991), IRS considered the proposed transfer of retiree group term life insurance reserves from three life insurance companies to a VEBA. The reserves were held by the insurers under contractual arrangements that met the requirements of Revenue Ruling 69-382 (1969-2 CB 28), the ruling that spelled out the requirements for favorable tax treatment on retired lines reserves prior to the enactment of the statuatory provisions governing such reserves in the Deficit Reduction Act of 1984.

The private letter ruling held that the reserves could be transferred from the insurers to the VEBA without resulting in gross income to the employer or triggering a 100-percent excise tax under Code Section 4976, if both the VEBA trust agreement and the plan document were amended to provide that the amounts transferred are to be credited to a separate account for postretirement life insurance benefits and that the funds in the separate account will be used exclusively for the payment of postretirement life insurance benefits.

It seems probable that when Treasury regulations are issued under Code Section 419A (a regulations project is pending), the regulations will require that the retired lives reserves be maintained in a separate account and used exclusively for retiree benefits. The separate account presumably will be a bookkeeping account and will not require a physical segregation of assets; it will most likely have rules similar to the rules governing Code Section 401(h) separate accounts (see Q 19:75).

In addition, if the employer wishes to take the amount of the retired lives reserve into account as a reduction in its FAS 106 postretirement benefit liabilities, it appears necessary to maintain a separate account, to be used exclusively to provide postretirement benefits (see Q 20:14).

Q 19:48   Who pays the applicable taxes, if any, on the welfare benefit fund's investment income?

If a VEBA or other tax-exempt trust holds the fund, the trust pays the unrelated business income tax at trust income tax rates. If the tax-exempt entity is organized in corporate form, the corporate entity pays the tax at corporate income tax rates. If the fund is held by a taxable trust or other entity or by an insurance company, the fund's deemed unrelated income is taxable to the employer; it is taxed at whatever corporate income tax rates apply to the employer. [IRC §§ 511, 419A(g)]

If a trust pays the unrelated business income tax, the monies in the trust are reduced, possibly enabling further deductible employer contributions before the applicable limit is reached. To achieve an equivalent result, the tax paid by the employer on any deemed unrelated income is treated as an employer contribution to the fund on the last day of the taxable year when calculating the employer deduction and, in determining the fund's after-tax income, the tax paid is treated as if it were imposed on the fund. [IRC § 419A(g)(3)]

Q 19:49   What federal excise taxes can apply to an employer maintaining a welfare benefit fund?

If the employer maintains a welfare benefit fund and "disqualified benefits" are provided, a whopping excise tax of 100 percent of the disqualified benefit is imposed on the employer. [IRC § 4976]

Q 19:50   What disqualified benefits trigger the 100 percent excise tax?

A disqualified benefit is defined as:

- Any postretirement medical benefit or life insurance benefit provided by a welfare benefit fund with respect to a key employee if a separate account is required to be established for the key employee but the payment is not made from the separate account;
- Any postretirement medical benefit or life insurance benefit that a discriminatory plan provides with respect to an individual in

whose favor discrimination is prohibited (this provision does not apply to a collectively bargained plan in which the postretirement benefits were the subject of good-faith bargaining); or

- Any portion of a welfare benefit fund reverting to the benefit of the employer (this provision does not apply to a return of contributions that were not deductible for the current taxable year or any prior year).

[IRC § 4976(b)]

Q 19:51   How can the 100-percent excise tax triggered by a disqualified benefit be avoided?

The answer depends on why the benefit is disqualified.

Failure to Pay from a Separate Account When Required. In order to avoid a possible penalty, the need to establish separate accounts for key employees, and the necessity of taking additions to separate accounts into consideration when applying the dollar limitation for defined-contribution plans, some employers have excluded key employees from coverage under retired lives reserves arrangements. In such cases, the separate account requirement does not apply, and the retiree benefits for key employees can be paid out of current employer funds during the period of retirement.

In addition, it should be noted that the excise tax provisions do not apply to grandfathered retired lives reserves that were in existence in 1984. [IRC § 4976(b)(4)]

Discriminatory Plan. There is no way to avoid the excise tax, other than to maintain a nondiscriminatory plan. However, the grandfathered portion of the reserve will not be subject to the nondiscrimination rules and, hence, the excise tax.

Surplus Funds Reverting to the Employer. A direct return of deductible contributions or fund earnings to the employer apparently would trigger the 100-percent excise tax plus regular income tax, even if all liabilities to employees and retirees under the plan had been fully satisfied. Presumably, any surplus remaining in the fund must be used to provide additional employee benefits, distributed in cash to the participants in a nondis-criminatory manner, or donated to charity. Additionally, applica-tion of such a surplus to employer contributions under another existing welfare benefit plan should not be viewed as an indirect reversion. [GCM 39774 (Aug 1, 1988)] For example, if there is a surplus remaining in a retired lives reserve held under a medical benefit plan after all plan obligations have been fully satisfied, the employer should be able to use the surplus to pay for the benefits under a disability plan. It may be desirable to apply for an IRS private letter ruling in such a case.

Voluntary Employees' Beneficiary Associations (VEBAs)

Q 19:52   What is a VEBA?

A VEBA is a tax-exempt organization, described in Code Section 501(c)(9), that provides for the payment of life, sickness, accident, or other benefits to its members or their dependents or designated beneficiaries. No part of the VEBA's net earnings may inure (other than through benefit payments) to the benefit of any private shareholder or individual.

Q 19:53   Why are VEBAs useful?

VEBAs can provide several advantages:

- A VEBA trust may be used to satisfy the employer's obligation to hold employee contributions under an ERISA plan in trust (see Qs 2:68–2:72 for a discussion of the ERISA trust require-ment);
- Some employers try, in the plan document and trust, to limit their economic risk for payment of plan benefits to the monies held by the trust;
- The investment income on funds set aside in the VEBA trust (other than reserves for postretirement medical benefits) generally can accumulate tax-free, within limits;

- Disability income payments made from a VEBA can avoid mandatory income tax withholding requirements if the risk of payment is shifted from the employer to a third-party payer (the VEBA trust); and

- In the case of employee-pay-all group term life insurance, imputed income under Code Section 79 may be avoided entirely because the coverage is not carried directly or indirectly by the employer (see Qs 11:33–11:37).

Q 19:54   How is a VEBA organized?

A VEBA may be organized in the legal form of a trust or a nonprofit corporation. In practice, the trust form is almost always used. The trust may be established by the employer or by the employees themselves. In most cases, however, the employer establishes the VEBA.

Q 19:55   Who can join a VEBA?

Membership must consist of individuals who become entitled to participate by reason of their being employees and whose eligibility for membership is defined by reference to objective standards that constitute an employment-related common bond. The employment-related common bond can include a common employer or affiliated employers, coverage under the same collective bargaining agreement or agreements, membership in a labor union, or membership in one or more locals of a national or international union.

The regulations consider employees of one or more employers engaged in the same lines of business in the same geographic locale to share an employment-related bond. [Treas Reg § 1.501(c)(9)-2(a)(1)] In administering this requirement, the IRS took the position that the same geographic locale requirement covered only a single state or a single standard metropolitan statistical area (SMSA) as defined by the Bureau of the Census. However, a federal appeals court has held this same geographic locale requirement of the regulations invalid. [Water Quality Assn Employees' Benefit Corp v United States, 795 F 2d 1303 (7th Cir 1986)]

The IRS has now proposed a regulatory definition of a single geographic locale as one which cannot exceed the boundaries of three contiguous states, that is, three states each of which shares a land or river border with at least one of the others. In addition, Alaska and Hawaii are deemed to be contiguous with each other and with the states of Washington, Oregon, and California. [IRS Prop Reg § 1.501(c)(9)-2(d)(1)]

Also, the proposed regulation would give the IRS discretionary authority to recognize an even larger geographic area as a single geographic area if:

- It would not be economically feasible to cover employees of employers engaged in that line of business in that area under two or more separate VEBAs each extending over fewer states, and

- Employment characteristics in that line of business, population characteristics, or other regional factors support the particular states included (this requirement is deemed satisfied if the states included are contiguous).

[Prop Treas Reg § 1.501(c)(9)-2(d)(2)]

Q 19:56 Do all of the members of the VEBA have to be employees?

No; however, Treasury regulations stipulate that, at a minimum, 90 percent of the total membership of the association must be employees on one day of each quarter of the association's taxable year. [Treas Reg § 1.501(c)(9)-2(a)(1)]

Q 19:57 Can non-employees be VEBA members?

Yes; some non-employees, that is, independent contractors, may be members, as long as 90 percent of the members are employees. [Treas Reg § 1.501(c)(9)-2(a)(1); Water Quality Assn Employees' Benefit Corp v United States, 795 F 2d 1303 (7th Cir 1986)]

Q 19:58 Can retirees and other former employees be VEBA members?

Yes, retirees and other former employees can be members of the VEBA and count as employees for purposes of the requirement that 90 percent of the total membership of the association must be employees. [Treas. Reg. § 1.501(c)(9)-2(b)(2)]

Q 19:59 Can spouses and dependents be VEBA members?

Spouses and dependents of active employees cannot be VEBA members, although they can participate in the VEBA's employee benefit plans. However, surviving spouses and dependents of deceased participants can be treated as employees for purposes of the 90-percent rule. [Treas Reg § 1.501(c)(9)-2(b)(3)]

Q 19:60 How is the requirement that VEBA membership must be voluntary met?

Membership is voluntary if an affirmative act on the part of an employee to become a member is necessary. However, membership will be *treated* as voluntary (even if no affirmative act by the employees is necessary) if the employees do not incur a detriment, such as a deduction from pay, as a result of membership. [Treas Reg § 1.501(c)(9)-2(c)(2)]

Q 19:61 May the employer control the VEBA?

No; Treasury regulations provide that a VEBA must be controlled by:

- Its membership;
- An independent trustee (or trustees) such as a bank; or
- Trustees or other fiduciaries, at least some of whom are designated by cr on behalf of the membership.

However, the tax requirement of control by an independent trustee is deemed satisfied if the VEBA is an employee welfare benefit plan subject to ERISA. [Treas Reg § 1.501(c)(9)-2(c)(3)] It was widely assumed that, as long as the VEBA was a welfare benefit plan subject to ERISA, the employer could exercise substantial control, as a fiduciary, over the VEBA. However, a U.S. Claims Court decision suggests that substantial employer control over the VEBA could jeopardize its tax-exempt status. [Lima Surgical Assoc Inc Voluntary Employees' Beneficiary Assn v United States, 12 EBC 1641, 20 Cl Ct 674 (1990), *affd* on other grounds, 14 EBC 1346 (Fed Cir 1991)]

Q 19:62   What benefits may a VEBA provide?

A VEBA may provide the following benefits:

1. Life benefits, payable on the death of a member or dependent. The death benefit may be provided directly or through insurance. Pensions, annuities, and similar benefits are not included, except for a death benefit payable in the form of an annuity.
2. Sickness and accident benefits, which include medical benefits and disability income benefits, whether insured or uninsured. This category also contains benefits in noncash form, such as clinical care by visiting nurses and medical care transportation.
3. Other benefits, which are intended to safeguard or improve the health of a member or his or her dependents or to protect against a contingency that interrupts or impairs a member's earning power. These may consist of vacation and recreational benefits, child care facilities, supplemental unemployment compensation benefits, severance benefits, disaster loans and grants, and legal services benefits.

[Treas Reg § 1.501(c)(9)-3]

Exclusions. Not included in the category of "other benefits" provided by VEBAs are commuting expenses, property insurance (for example, auto or homeowner's), loans other than disaster loans, savings facilities, and pensions and other deferred-compensation-type benefits. Where a severance plan provided benefits for termination of employment for any reason (other than death), including retirement, the benefits were held to be pension-type benefits rather than severance benefits and the VEBA was held not to be tax-exempt. [Lima Surgical Assoc, Inc Voluntary Employees' Beneficiary Assn v United States, 12 EBC 1641, 20 Cl Ct 674 (1990), *affd* on other grounds, 14 EBC 1346 (Fed Cir 1991)]

The IRS took the position that income maintenance benefits payable when an employee's monthly compensation dropped below 80 percent of the average over a three-year period for any reason did not qualify as a VEBA benefit because the payments were not the result of an unanticipated event similar in nature to death, sickness, or accident, and the payments could result from the employee's own decision to work less hours. [GCM 39879 (January 6, 1986)]

Q 19:63 What is prohibited inurement to a private shareholder or individual?

No part of the VEBA's net earnings may inure (other than through benefits payments) to the benefit of any private shareholder or individual. Prohibited inurement is defined by regulations to include the following:

- Disposition of VEBA property to, or performance of services for, a person for less than adequate consideration (other than as benefits);
- Payment of unreasonable compensation to the trustees or employees of the VEBA; and
- The purchase of insurance or services at more than fair market value from a company in which one or more of the VEBA's trustees, officers, or fiduciaries have an interest.

[Treas Reg § 1.501 (c)(9)-4(a)]

Also, payment to highly compensated employees of benefits that are disproportionately high in relation to the benefits of other members may constitute prohibited inurement, unless the benefits are based on objective and reasonable standards. A VEBA plan that based termination benefits on a formula that took into account both compensation and length of service, and under which 95 percent of the benefits were attributable to the highly compensated stockholder-employees, was held to violate the prohibited inurement restriction. [Treas Reg § 1.501(c)(9)-4(b); Lima Surgical Assocs, Inc Voluntary Employees' Beneficiary Assn v United States, 12 EBC 1641, 20 Cl Ct 674 (1990), *affd* on other grounds, 14 EBC 1346 (Fed Cir 1991]

Rebates of Premiums. Rebates of excess insurance premiums, based on the mortality or morbidity experience of the insurer, to the person or persons who paid the premiums, is not prohibited inurement. Thus, if the employer pays the premiums on an insurance policy owned by the VEBA, the employer can receive dividends or experience-rating credits from the insurer without violating the prohibited inurement restriction. [Treas Reg § 1.501 (c)(9)-4(c)]

Q 19:64 Do any special restrictions apply to the disposition of VEBA assets on termination?

Yes, the prohibited inurement rule affects how VEBA assets may be disbursed when a plan maintained by the VEBA, or the VEBA itself, terminates.

On termination of a plan maintained by the VEBA, the prohibited inurement rule will not be violated if any assets remaining after satisfaction of all liabilities are used to provide additional life, sickness, accident, or other benefits to employees using criteria that avoid disproportionate benefits to officers, shareholders, or highly compensated employees of the employer.

Similarly, the prohibited inurement rule is not violated if, on termination of the VEBA, the assets are distributed to members on the basis of objective and reasonable standards which do not result in either unequal payments to similarly situated members or disproportionate payments to officers, shareholders, or highly compensated employees. If the VEBA's governing document or applicable state law provides that any assets remaining will be returned to the employer or employers that contributed to it, the VEBA will fail to qualify for tax exemption under Code Section 501(c)(9). [Treas Reg § 1.501(c)(9)-4]

Q 19:65   What is the tax status of a VEBA?

A tax-qualified VEBA is exempt from regular income tax but is subject to the deductible contribution limits under Code Sections 419 and 419A, discussed previously. However, as discussed in connection with the welfare benefit fund rules (see Qs 19:44, 19:45), the VEBA may be subject to unrelated business income tax on some or all of its income if:

- It holds reserves in excess of the limits permitted by Code Sections 419 and 419A, or
- It holds a reserve for postretirement medical benefits.

[IRC § 512(a)(3)(E)(i)] (See Q 19:48.)

Q 19:66   May a VEBA provide benefits that discriminate in favor of highly compensated employees?

Generally, if a VEBA discriminates in favor of highly compensated employees, it will lose its tax qualification. [IRC §§ 505(a)(1), 505(b)] However, the nondiscrimination rules do not apply in the case of collectively bargained plans where there was good-faith bargaining. [IRC § 505(a)(2)]

Q 19:67   What are the nondiscrimination requirements for a VEBA?

The general rules are as follows:

- Each class of benefits under the plan must be provided under a classification of employees set forth in the plan that does not discriminate in favor of highly compensated individuals; and
- No class of benefits can discriminate in favor of highly compensated individuals.

Life insurance, disability benefits, severance pay, and supplemental unemployment compensation benefits do not violate the second requirement merely because the benefits bear a uniform relationship to total compensation or to a basic or regular rate of compensation. [IRC § 505(b)] In applying the Code Section 505(b) nondiscrimination requirements, the employer may disregard employees with less than three years of service, employees under age 21, seasonal employees, less-than-half-time employees, employees covered by a collective bargaining agreement, and nonresident aliens with no U.S.-source earned income.

However, if the benefit is subject to nondiscrimination rules contained in some other provision of the IRC, those other nondiscrimination rules supersede these general rules in Code Section 505(b)(1). [IRC § 505(b)(3)] Thus, if the nondiscrimination rules of Code Sections 79 (group term life insurance), 105(h) (self-insured medical plans), 125 (cafeteria plans), and 129 (dependent care assistance) apply, the nondiscrimination rules of Code Section 505(b)(l) do not apply.

Q 19:68 Is there a limit on the amount of compensation that may be used as a base for VEBA benefits?

Yes, compensation is defined in the same manner as for qualified retirement plan purposes. For years before 1994, compensation taken into account cannot exceed $200,000, indexed to the cost of living. (For 1993, the indexed amount is $235,840.) [IRC §§ 414(s), 505(b)(6), 505(b)(7)] For 1994 and later, the compensation limit is set at $150,000, indexed to the cost of living starting in 1995. [OBRA '93 § 13212(c)] In the case of a plan maintained pursuant to one or more collective bargaining agreements in effect on August 10, 1993, the new compensation limit takes effect on the later of January 1, 1994 or the date the last collective bargaining agreement terminates (without regard to any extension, amendment, or modification after August 10, 1993). [OBRA '93 § 13212(d)] The compensation limit does not apply to a group term life insurance plan subject to Code Section 79. [IRC § 505(b)(7)] If the VEBA bases benefits on compensation in excess of the limit, and the plan is not governed by Section 79 (for example, it is a disability income plan or an employee-pay-all group term life insurance plan not subject to Code Section 79), the limit *does* apply to the plan. If the plan fails to comply with this compensation limit, it appears that the VEBA will lose its tax exemption.

Q 19:69   Must a VEBA file a notice with the IRS in order to be tax-exempt?

Yes. A VEBA should file an application for exemption on IRS Form 1024, generally within 15 months of the month of its organization. [IRC § 505(c); Temp Treas Reg § 1.505(c)-1T]

Funding Postretirement Medical Benefits under a Pension Plan

Q 19:70   How may postretirement medical benefits be funded other than through a welfare benefit fund (including a VEBA or a retired lives reserve)?

A pension or annuity plan may provide for the payment of benefits for sickness, accident, hospitalization, and medical expenses of retired employees and their spouses and dependents, provided that certain requirements are met. [IRC § 401(h)]

Q 19:71   What requirements apply to the funding of retirement medical benefits through a pension plan or annuity plan?

The following seven requirements must be satisfied:

1. The benefits must be subordinate to the retirement benefits under the plan (see Q 19:72);
2. A separate postretirement medical benefit account separate from the pension account, must be established and maintained for the benefits;
3. The employer's contributions to the separate account must be reasonable and ascertainable;
4. Before all liabilities for the postretirement medical benefits are satisfied, it must be impossible to use the separate account funds for any other purpose;
5. The plan must require, by its terms, that once all liabilities for postretirement medical benefits are satisfied, any surplus will be returned to the employer;

6. Individual separate accounts (within the overall retiree medical benefit separate account) must be established for retiree medical benefits payable to each key employee covered for medical benefits; and

7. Retiree medical benefits for the key employee and his or her spouse and dependents may be paid only from the key employee's individual separate account.

[IRC § 401(h)]

These accounts are not subject to the Code Section 419 welfare benefit fund rules.

Q 19:72 When do the retiree medical benefits qualify as subordinate to the retirement benefits under the pension or annuity plan?

Retiree medical benefits are considered subordinate to the pension benefits if at all times the total contributions for retiree medical benefits (plus any contributions for life insurance protection)—that are made after the date on which the plan first provides retiree medical benefits—do not exceed 25 percent of the total contributions (for pensions and retiree medical and any life insurance) made after that date (excluding contributions made to fund past service pension credits). [Treas Reg § 1.401-14(c)(1)] This limit translates to one third of the cumulative current service pension contributions since the date the Code Section 401(h) account was established under the pension plan. For example, if an employer establishes a Code Section 401(h) retiree medical separate account on January 1 of a taxable year and the employer's current service pension contribution for the year is $3 million, the employer can contribute $1 million to the Code Section 401(h) account for that year.

This regulatory interpretation of the statutory "subordinate" test was widely criticized, since it meant that, in the case of a well-funded pension plan, little or no contribution could be made to a Code Section 401(h) medical benefit separate account to fund retiree medical benefits.

For a brief time in 1989, the IRS permitted employers with a pension plan that was fully funded or close to fully funded to use the cost of pension benefit accruals for current service, rather than actual contributions, in applying the subordinate test in the regulations. [GCM 39785 (Mar 23,1989)] However, Congress, concerned over the revenue loss implications of the liberalized IRS position, reinstated the more restrictive test, applicable generally to contributions after October 3, 1989. [IRC § 401(h); OBRA '89 § 7311]

Q 19:73 May a Code Section 401(h) account be maintained under a defined-contribution money purchase pension plan?

Yes, it appears that it can. Traditionally, Code Section 401(h) accounts have been maintained in connection with defined benefit plans. However, the Code provision merely refers to a "pension or annuity plan." Since a defined-contribution money purchase plan is a type of pension plan, such a plan should be able to establish a Code Section 401(h) account.

Q 19:74 May a Code Section 401(h) account be maintained under a profit-sharing plan?

No. A profit-sharing plan is not a "pension or annuity plan" under the IRC, and thus a profit-sharing plan cannot have a Code Section 401(h) account associated with it. [IRC §§ 401(a), 403(a)(1)]

Q 19:75 Does the Code Section 401(h) separate account requirement require a physical segregation of assets?

No; the separation between pension and medical benefits is required for record-keeping purposes only. The funds attributable to the medical benefit separate account need not be invested separately from the pension funds. If the investment properties are not allocated separately, the earnings on the plan investments must be allocated between the pension and medical benefits account in a reasonable manner. [Treas Reg § 1.401-14(c)(2)] It appears that the individual separate accounts required for key employees covered for the retiree medical benefits are also record-keeping accounts only, with no physical separation of plan assets required.

Q 19:76 What deductibility limits apply to employer contributions to fund retiree medical benefits under Code Section 401(h)?

The employer must, when making a contribution to the plan, designate the portion of the contribution allocable to the retiree medical benefit account.

The amounts of deductible contributions that are made to fund the retiree medical benefit account cannot exceed the total cost of providing the medical benefits. The total cost of providing the medical benefits is to be determined in accordance with any generally accepted actuarial method that is reasonable in view of the provisions and coverage of the plan, the funding medium, and other applicable considerations.

The amount deductible for any taxable year cannot exceed the greater of:

- An amount determined by distributing the remaining unfunded costs of past and current service credits as a level amount, or as a level percentage of compensation, over the remaining future service of each employee (assuming future service of at least one year); or
- 10 percent of the cost that would be necessary to completely fund or purchase the retiree medical benefits.

Carryovers. Contributions in excess of the amount deductible can be carried over and deducted in later years, subject to the limits applicable in those years. However, making a nondeductible contribution will subject the employer to a 10-percent excise tax. [IRC § 4972; Treas Reg §§ 1.401-14(c)(3), 1.404(a)-3(f)]

Q 19:77 How must a Code Section 401(h) account deal with employee forfeitures of retiree medical benefit accounts?

The pension plan must expressly provide that, in the event an individual's interest in the Code Section 401(h) medical benefit account is forfeited, the amount of the forfeiture must be applied as soon as possible to reduce employer contributions to fund the medical benefits. [Treas Reg § 1.401-14(c)(6)]

Q 19:78　May the funds in the Code Section 401(h) account be used to pay pension benefits under the plan?

No. The prohibition against diversion of the retiree medical benefit funds for any other purpose includes using the funds for pension objectives. Conversely, excess assets under the pension portion of the plan generally cannot be transferred to the retiree medical benefit account without causing the plan to lose its tax-qualified status. [Treas Reg § 1.401-14(c)(4); IRS Tech Assist Mem (Jan 9, 1987)] However, under Code Section 420, added by the Omnibus Budget Reconciliation Act of 1990 (OBRA '90), "qualified transfers" of excess pension assets to a Code Section 401(h) account are permitted. (See Qs 19:80–19:94.)

Q 19:79　Are payments from a Code Section 401(h) account used to pay for retiree health coverage costs or benefits subject to income tax?

No. If the amounts are withdrawn from the Code Section 401(h) account to pay for the costs of medical care coverage for a retiree (for example, to pay premiums for medical care insurance), the amounts are excluded from the retiree's income under Code Section 106. If amounts are withdrawn from the Code Section 401(h) account to provide retiree medical care benefits directly, the amounts are excludable from the retiree's income under Code Section 105(b), or under Code Section 104(a)(3) if the payments are attributable to employee contributions to the Code Section 401(h) account.

Q 19:80　Under what types of plans can a qualified transfer of excess pension assets be made to a Code Section 401(h) account?

The plan must be a defined benefit pension plan. Thus, a qualified transfer cannot be made under a defined-contribution money purchase pension plan. Also, a defined benefit plan that is a multiemployer plan is not eligible for a qualified transfer. [IRC § 420(a)]

Q 19:81   How does an employer determine the amount of excess pension assets that can be transferred in a qualified transfer to a Code Section 401(h) account?

The amount of the excess pension assets is determined pursuant to the full funding limitation rules of Code Section 412(c)(7)). The term "excess pension assets" (if any) is equal to:

- The value of the plan's assets (determined under Code Section 412(c)(7)(A)(ii)); minus
- The greater of (1) the lesser of 150 percent of current liability or the accrued liability (including normal cost); or (2) 125 percent of current liability.

The determination of the amount of excess pension assets generally is to be made as of the most recent plan valuation date preceding the date of the qualified transfer. [IRC § 420(e)(2)]

Q 19:82   What is a qualified transfer of excess pension assets of a Code Section 401(h) account?

In order to be considered a qualified transfer, a transfer of excess pension assets to a Code Section 401(h) account must satisfy the following six requirements:

1. A transfer to a Code Section 401(h) account may be made only once in any taxable year of the employer and may be made only in taxable years beginning after 1990 and before 1996. (See an exception for 1990 expenses in Question 19:87.)

2. The assets transferred (and the income of such assets) must be used to pay qualified current retiree health liabilities other than liabilities of key employees as defined in Code Section 416(i)(1) (see Q 19:83).

3. Certain vesting requirements under the pension plan must be satisfied (see Q 19:84).

4. The employer must meet a minimum cost requirement for retiree health benefits in the year of transfer and in the following four years (see Q 19:85).

5. The amount transferred cannot exceed specified limits. (see Q 19:86).

6. The transfer cannot contravene any other provision of law (see Q 19:88).

Q 19:83   What are qualified current retiree health liabilities?

A transfer of excess pension assets can be used only for qualified current retiree health liabilities.

The term "qualified current retiree health liabilities" means, with respect to any taxable year, the aggregate amounts (including administrative expenses) that would have been allowable as a deduction to the employer for the taxable year with respect to health benefits for existing retirees entitled to the health benefits as well as to pension benefits under the plan, and health benefits for their spouses and dependents, if:

- The health benefits were provided directly by the employer; and
- The employer was a cash-basis taxpayer.

The amount of qualified retiree health liabilities must be reduced by any amount previously contributed to a Code Section 401(h) account or to a Code Section 419 welfare benefit fund to pay for the qualified current retiree health liabilities. The portion of any such reserves remaining as of the end of 1990 are to be allocated to qualified current retiree health liabilities on a pro rata basis. Key employees (as defined in Code Section 416(i)(1)) cannot be taken into account in calculating qualified current retiree health liabilities. [IRC § 420(e)(1)]

Q 19:84   What vesting requirements apply in order to have a qualified transfer to a Code Section 401(h) account?

In order to have a qualified transfer, the pension plan must provide that the accrued benefits of any plan participant or beneficiary become nonforfeitable as if the plan had terminated immediately before the qualified transfer. For a participant who separated during the one-year period ending on the date of the qualified transfer, his or her benefits must become nonforfeitable as if the plan had terminated immediately before the separation from service. [IRC § 420(c)(2)]

Planning Pointer. Because of the substantial cost impact on the employer of full vesting of accrued benefits, an employer with an overfunded defined benefit pension plan should carefully consider the pros and cons before entering into a qualified transfer.

Q 19:85 What is the minimum cost requirement for retiree health benefits that an employer must satisfy in order to have a qualified transfer?

This requirement is met if each group health plan or arrangement under which retiree health benefits are furnished provides that the "applicable employer cost" for each taxable year during the cost maintenance period (the taxable year of the qualified transfer and the succeeding four taxable years) cannot be lower than the higher of the applicable employer costs in each of the two taxable years immediately preceding the taxable year of the qualified transfer.

In applying the minimum cost requirements, the term applicable employer cost means, for any taxable year, the amount determined by dividing:

- The qualified current retiree health liabilities of the employer for the taxable year (determined by excluding any reduction for prior contributions to the Code Section 401(h) account or to a Code Section 419 welfare benefit fund (and, if there was no qualified transfer in the taxable year, by assuming that such a transfer occurred at year-end)), by
- The number of individuals (retirees, spouses, and dependents) to whom retiree health coverage was provided during the taxable year.

The employer may elect to determine the applicable employer cost separately for Medicare-eligible individuals and for individuals who are not eligible for Medicare. [IRC § 420(c)(3)]

Planning Pointer. Assuming a continuation of ever-increasing medical cost inflation, an employer continuing to provide the same level of retiree health coverage should have no problem with this requirement.

Q 19:86 What are the limits on the amount of excess pension assets that can be transferred in a qualified transfer?

The amount of excess pension assets that may be transferred in a qualified transfer cannot exceed the amount reasonably estimated to be what the employer will pay (directly or through reimbursement out of the Code Section 401(h) account) during the taxable year of the transfer for qualified current retiree health liabilities. [IRC § 420(b)(3)] Therefore, qualified transfers cannot be used to pre-fund future retiree health liabilities.

Q 19:87 What is the special rule that applies to a qualified transfer for the taxable year beginning in 1990?

A qualified transfer for a taxable year beginning in 1990 may be made after the close of the taxable year if

- It is made by the earlier of the due date (including extensions) of the employer's tax return or the date of actual filing of the return; and
- The amount transferred does not exceed the amount of the expenditures by the employer for qualified current retiree health liabilities for such 1990 taxable year.

[IRC § 420(b)(4)]

Q 19:88 What is the significance of the provision that a transfer of excess pension assets to a Code Section 401(h) account cannot contravene any other provision of law?

The legislative history indicates that the amendments made to the Code and to ERISA to authorize such transfers do not supersede any legal restrictions that may prevent an employer from using pension benefits to satisfy pre-existing corporate retiree health benefit liabilities. As one example, such a transfer might be in violation of a collective bargaining agreement. Also, a transfer might violate laws dealing with government contractors. [IRC § 420(b)(1)(B); Conf Rpt 101-964, 101st Cong, 2d Sess, at 1147 (1990)]

Q 19:89 What limits apply to employer contributions where a qualified transfer is made?

An employer may not contribute any amount to a Code Section 401(h) account or Code Section 419 welfare benefit fund with regard to qualified current retiree health liabilities for which transferred assets are required to be used. Any amount paid out of a Code Section 401(h) account is treated as paid first out of the transferred assets and the income thereon. [IRC § 420(d)(2)]

Q 19:90 What limits apply to employee tax deductions where a qualified transfer is made?

No employer deduction is allowed for the amount of any qualified transfer, or for any qualified current retiree health liabilities paid out of the transferred assets (and the income thereon). [IRC § 420(d)(1)] In the case of a qualified transfer made for the 1990 taxable year, the employer's otherwise allowable tax deduction for the 1990 tax year is reduced by the amount of the qualified transfer. [IRC § 420(b)(4)(B)]

Q 19:91 What happens if the amount of the qualified transfer exceeds the qualified current retiree health benefits?

If there is an amount left over, it must be transferred back to the pension portion of the plan from the Code Section 401(h) account. In such cases, the amount transferred is not includable in the employer's income, but is treated as an employer reversion for purposes of the 20-percent excise tax under Code Section 4980(a) on pension plan reversions (but not for purposes of the 50-percent tax on certain reversions under Code Section 4980 (d)). [IRC § 420(c)(1)(B)]

Q 19:92   If a qualified transfer is planned, are there special notice requirements under ERISA that must be followed?

Yes. Under an amendment to ERISA in OBRA '90, the pension plan administrator must notify each participant and beneficiary under the plan of a qualified transfer at least 60 days before the date of the transfer. The notice is to include information regarding the amount of excess pension assets, the portion to be transferred, the amount of retiree health benefits expected to be provided by the transferred assets, and the amount of pension benefits of the participant that will be nonforfeitable following the transfer.

In addition, the statute requires that employer notice is required to be given to the Department of Labor, IRS, the pension plan administrator, and each employee organization representing participants in the plan at least 60 days prior to the date of the transfer. By agreement between IRS and the DOL, the employer's filing with the DOL will be considered to satisfy the IRS filing requirement as well. Accordingly, the employer need not make a separate filing with IRS. [ERISA Tech Rel 91-1, 56 FR 10927 (Mar 14, 1991); IRS Ann 92-54, 13 IRB 35 (Mar. 30 1992)] This notice must identify (1) the plan from which the qualified transfer is being made, (2) the amount of the transfer, (3) a detailed accounting of assets projected to be held by the plan immediately before and immediately after the transfer, and (4) the current liabilities under the plan at the time of the transfer. [ERISA § 101(e), 29 USC § 1021(e), as added by OBRA '90 § 12012]

Q 19:93   What effect does a qualified transfer have on the minimum funding rules for the pension plan?

For purposes of the minimum funding rules, the assets transferred in a plan year on or before the valuation date for the year (and any income allocable thereto) are treated as assets in the plan as of the valuation date, and the plan is treated as having a net experience loss in the amount of the transfer, amortizable over 10 years. [IRC § 420(e)(4); ERISA § 302(g)]

Q 19:94 Does a qualified transfer violate the exclusive benefit requirement or the prohibited transaction and prohibited reversion rules of ERISA and the Code?

No. ERISA and the IRC, as amended by OBRA '90, provide that a qualified transfer does not violate the exclusive benefit rule or give rise to a prohibited transaction or a reversion to the employer. [IRC § 420(a); ERISA §§ 403(c)(1), 408(b)(13)] The procedure for requesting a determination letter on the pension plan's tax-qualified status, where the plan document is amended to incorporate plan language designed to comply with Code Section 420, is set forth in Revenue Procedure 92-24 [1992-1 CB 739]

Q 19:95 Is the investment income of the Code Section 401(h) account subject to tax?

No; as part of a tax-exempt pension or annuity plan, the earnings on the Code Section 401(h) account are tax-free. In this respect, funding postretirement medical benefits through a Code Section 401(h) account has a major advantage over funding retiree medical benefits through a VEBA or a retired lives reserve held by an insurance company. In those cases the investment earnings are subject to unrelated business income tax (or deemed unrelated income tax) (see Q 19:45).

Financing Welfare Benefits with Life Insurance

Q 19:96 How can the employer's cost of welfare benefits be financed through the purchase of life insurance?

It is fairly common for employers who wish to minimize the cost of employee welfare benefits, particularly benefits that are not prefunded (such as uninsured death benefit plans, retiree health benefits, and executive plans of various types), to consider the purchase of life insurance as a financing mechanism for meeting the cost of such benefits. These arrangements generally are referred to as corporate-owned life insurance (COLI).

Q 19:97 How does COLI operate?

Under COLI, the employer is the owner and beneficiary of life insurance policies on the lives of certain of its employees. COLI does not constitute a funding method for the welfare plan, since the policy is wholly owned by the employer and is subject to the claims of its creditors. The employees have no rights or interest in the insurance policies on their lives.

The COLI policy is purchased to cover the employer's liability for benefits under the plan, but the policy proceeds are not committed to pay any particular plan's benefits. The technique is designed to ensure adequate cash flow and, if leveraged COLI is used, tax advantages as well. The employer generally will compare a prospective COLI purchase to what it could earn after-tax by retaining the funds to be used to pay premiums in its business or by investing in other alternatives.

The attractiveness of COLI as a financing mechanism is related in large part to the special tax treatment that life insurance policies receive under current federal income tax law.

Q 19:98 How is a COLI policy treated for income tax purposes?

A COLI policy generally receives the same income tax treatment as other types of life insurance. Thus, if the employer keeps the coverage in force until the employee's death, the policy proceeds are received free of income tax. [IRC § 101(a)] However, if the employer is subject to the corporate alternative minimum tax, that tax may apply to earnings on the cash value and to a portion of the death proceeds.

Under a COLI policy, the employer also can take a loan against the policy on a tax-free basis, as long as the employer takes care to avoid having the policy treated as a modified endowment contract. (See Questions 12:34 through 12:39 for a discussion of when a policy becomes a modified endowment contract.) Interest on the policy loan may also be tax deductible to the employer, subject to the limits described in Question 19:100 discussing leveraged COLI. [IRC § 72(e)(10)]

The employer also can make tax-free withdrawals from the COLI policy up to the extent of its tax basis in the policy, provided modified endowment contract status is not triggered. [IRC § 72(e)(10)]

Q 19:99   Can the employer obtain an income tax deduction for the premiums it pays on COLI policies?

No, since the employer is the owner and beneficiary of the policies, it cannot take an income tax deduction for the premiums it pays. [IRC § 264(a)(1)]

Q 19:100   What limitations apply to COLI policy loans in order for the interest to be deductible?

There are three major limitations:

1. No interest deduction is allowed if the policy is a single premium policy [IRC § 264(a)(2)];
2. No interest deduction generally is allowed unless at least four out of the first seven years' premiums are paid other than by means of indebtedness [IRC §§ 264(a)(3), 264(c)(1)]; and
3. An interest deduction is not allowable to the extent that the sum of all policy loans on all COLI policies of the employer on the life of the individual employee exceeds $50,000. [IRC § 264(a)(4)]

Q 19:101   Can an employer take out COLI policies on any or all of its employees?

In order for a COLI policy to receive favorable tax treatment as a life insurance policy, it must meet the definition of a life insurance contract under Code Section 7702. One of the requirements of that section is that the policy must be a life insurance contract under applicable law (that is, state law). [IRC § 7702(a)]

State law requires that the employer have an "insurable interest" in the life of the insured employee. Traditionally, an employer has been considered to have an insurable interest in its key employees (that is, senior management) and other employees critical to the success of the business. However, it is not clear to what extent lower-level employees can be considered to be employees in whom the employer has an insurable interest.

In one case an employer was held not to have an insurable interest in its truck drivers, and therefore was taxed on the death proceeds of a COLI policy it owned on a driver. [Atlantic Oil Co v Patterson, 331 F 2d 516 (5th Cir 1964)]

Because of the $50,000 loan limit per employee under leveraged COLI, it frequently is desirable for financial purposes to insure a large group of employees. A number of states have amended their insurance laws in recent years to provide that an employer has an insurable interest in a broader class of employees than in key employees only.

Once insurable interest is satisfied at the issue of the COLI policy, it generally is not lost thereafter, even if the employee terminates employment.

Q 19:102   If COLI is used to finance the benefits payable under an ERISA plan, is the COLI policy a plan asset for ERISA purposes?

No, if the arrangement is structured properly, a COLI policy remains an employer asset rather than a plan asset. The Department of Labor concluded that a COLI policy purchased to finance a noncontributory death benefit plan for employees, where the corporation owned the policy and proceeds were payable directly to the corporation as beneficiary, was not a plan asset. [DOL Op 81-11A (Jan 16, 1981)]

Chapter 20

Financial Accounting Rules for Nonpension Retiree and Postemployment Benefits

Statement of Financial Accounting Standards No. 106, Employers' Accounting for Postretirement Benefits Other Than Pensions (FAS 106), has affected the redesign of retiree medical plans as much as, and perhaps more than, any recent legal development. As such, its requirements regarding recognition of unfunded future liability for retiree benefits should be borne in mind when reviewing or redesigning retiree benefit programs. This special chapter on accounting issues also includes a brief explanation of Statement of Financial Accounting Standards No. 112, Employers' Accounting for Postemployment Benefits (FAS 112), which established accounting standards for employers who provide benefits to former or inactive employees after termination of employment but before retirement.

Postretirement Welfare Benefits

Q 20:1   What financial accounting considerations apply to postretirement welfare benefits?

The Financial Accounting Standards Board (FASB), the body responsible for setting financial accounting standards, has been concerned for some time that employers were not adequately accounting for their postretirement health care, life insurance, and other retiree benefit liabilities. In particular, the FASB has been concerned about investor ability to gauge the effect of anticipated retiree medical benefits on the financial viability of a company. However, until recently, no useful disclosure has been required that would permit investors to compare information on retiree medical benefits based upon uniform presentation of such financial information. In the past, employers had simply accounted for retiree medical benefits on a "pay-as-you-go" basis (that is, showing them as an expense when paid). Because of this, many employers truly had no idea of the magnitude of liability for promised future benefits under their retiree medical plans (which in some cases was shockingly high). Similarly, investors were largely in the dark about the extent of such liability.

In December 1990, the FASB released its Statement of Financial Accounting Standards No. 106, Employers' Accounting for Postretirement Benefits Other Than Pensions (FAS 106). FAS 106 requires employers to disclose on their financial statements the unfunded liability for future retiree medical benefits using specified assumptions and methodology. The new accounting treatment specified by FAS 106 forces an awareness of the true cost of retiree benefit promises and a disclosure of the substantial future financial impact that they can have.

Financial Accounting Series Report No. 129-B, "A Guide to Implementation of Statement 106 on Employers' Accounting for Postretirement Benefits Other than Pensions: Questions and Answers" (August 1993), provides further details about applying FAS 106, and guidance about whether FAS 106 or FAS 112 (also discussed in this chapter) applies.

Q 20:2   When does FAS 106 become effective?

Generally, FAS 106 is applicable for accounting fiscal years begin-ning after December 15, 1992. However, in the case of small, non-public employers with no more than 500 participants in the aggregate and non-U.S. plans, the effective date is two years later (fiscal years beginning after December 15, 1994). An employer can elect to apply FAS 106 earlier than the effective date if it chooses, and the FASB encourages such action. [FAS 106, ¶ 108] Also, for publicly traded companies, Security and Exchange Commission (SEC) rules require employers to disclose the impact of FAS 106 on current financial statements.

FAS 106 does not apply to governmental plans. [FAS 106, ¶ 108]

Q 20:3   What is the FASB's position on how postretirement nonpension benefits should be treated for accounting purposes?

The FASB views a postretirement benefit plan as a deferred compensation arrangement. In the FASB's view, the employer promises to exchange future benefits for an employee's current services, and the benefit obligation accrues as employees render the services necessary to earn benefits according to the plan's terms. Even though a legal liability to provide retiree medical benefits may not exist, an accounting liability nonetheless may exist. [FAS 106, Appen-dix A, Basis for Conclusions, ¶¶ 154 and 155]

Case law has not been unequivocal about the legal enforceability or lack thereof of promises to provide postretirement benefits, al-though legal enforceability of certain claims has been demonstrated. However, the Board has looked beyond the legal status of the promise to consider whether the liability is effectively binding on the employer because of past practices, social or moral sanctions, or customs.

Q 20:4   What benefits are subject to the new accounting rules in FAS 106?

All postretirement benefits expected to be provided by the employer to current and former employees and their beneficiaries and dependents, other than pensions and life insurance provided through a pension plan, are covered. Postretirement benefits include health care, life insurance (outside a pension plan), and other welfare benefits such as tuition assistance, day care, legal services, and housing subsidies provided after retirement. [FAS 106, ¶¶ 6, 11]

For purposes of FAS 106, these benefits are divided into two general types of retiree welfare benefit plans, namely:

- Defined contribution plans; and
- Defined benefit plans.

[FAS 106, ¶¶ 10, 16]

Note. Postemployment benefits other than retirement benefits are the subject of a separate accounting standard issued by the FASB (FAS 112) (see Qs 20:24-20:27).

Q 20:5   Does FAS 106 apply if the employer is not legally obligated to provide retiree benefits?

Yes, it does. [FAS 106, Appendix A, Basis for Conclusions, ¶ 156]

Under FAS 106, no legally enforceable obligation is required. The statement applies to any arrangement that is in substance a postretirement benefit plan, regardless of its form or the means or timing of its funding. FAS 106 applies to written plans and to unwritten plans whose existence is based on a practice of paying postretirement benefits or on oral representations made to current or former employees. In the absence of evidence to the contrary, it is presumed that an employer that has provided postretirement benefits in the past or is currently promising such benefits to employees will continue to provide retiree benefits in the future. [FAS 106, ¶ 8]

FAS 106 also applies to funded and unfunded retiree welfare benefits. [FAS 106, ¶ 8]

Q 20:6   What does FAS 106 require for retiree medical plans?

FAS 106 requires that the employer's liability for postretirement medical benefits be shown on the employer's balance sheet and profit and loss statement. The liability must be accounted for on an accrual basis rather than on a cash (pay-as-you-go) basis. However, FAS 106 does not require that the liability for postretirement medical benefits be funded.

For calculating the amount of the employer's postretirement liability, FAS 106 divides retiree medical plans into two broad categories: defined contribution plans and defined benefit plans (see Qs 20:7–20:10). The main impact of FAS 106's provisions is on employers' maintenance of defined benefit plans—plans that list specific covered benefits and limits thereon—because the ultimate cost of the plan will depend upon factors such as future utilization, longevity of participants, and medical cost inflation. FAS 106 specifies uniform assumptions to be used when calculating the cost effect of these and other factors. The cost of such future benefits is then allocated to the employee's service period (generally, the employee's date of hire to his or her date of initial eligibility for retiree medical benefits, whether or not he or she elects early retirement) and must be accrued by the employer and shown on its financial statements during those years.

Q 20:7   What is a "defined contribution postretirement plan"?

Under FAS 106, a "defined contribution postretirement plan" is a plan that provides postretirement benefits in return for service rendered, establishes an individual account for each participant, and has terms that specify how contributions to the individual's account are determined (rather than the amount of postretirement benefits to be received). Under such a plan, the individual's postretirement benefits are limited by the amounts in the individual's account (derived from contributions, investment earnings, and allocation of forfeitures by other employees, if any). [FAS 106, ¶ 104]

Planning Pointer. In the past, defined contribution welfare benefit plans for retirees were relatively rare. However, in order to control costs and to limit the amount of the FAS 106 liabilities, many employers are giving increased consideration to switching from a defined benefit plan approach to a defined contribution plan approach.

Q 20:8   What are the FAS 106 accounting requirements for a defined contribution postretirement plan?

To the extent that the defined contributions are to be made to an employee's account during the periods in which the employee is providing services, the contribution required for a period is the cost to be charged as an expense for that period. If the plan provides for contributions for periods after the employee retires or terminates, the estimated cost is to be accrued during the employee's service period. [FAS 106, ¶ 105]

Q 20:9   What is a "defined benefit postretirement plan"?

Under FAS 106, a "defined benefit postretirement plan" is a plan that defines the postretirement benefits in terms of:

- Monetary amounts (for example, $100,000 of life insurance); or
- Benefit coverage to be provided (for example, up to $200 per day for hospitalization, or 80 percent of surgical fees).

Such a plan will be treated as a defined benefit plan even if the employer limits its obligation through an individual or aggregate cap on the employer's cost or benefit obligation. [FAS 106, ¶¶ 16, 17]

Q 20:10   What are the FAS 106 accounting requirements for a defined benefit postretirement plan?

In the case of a defined benefit postretirement plan, FAS 106 requires accounting on an actuarial cost basis similar to the accounting standards required and in use for defined benefit pension plans, as set forth in FAS 87, Employers' Accounting for Pensions. The FAS 106 computations must take into account the following components:

- Service cost;
- Interest cost;
- Actual return on plan assets (if any);
- Amortization of prior service cost;

- Recognized gain or loss (including changes in assumptions); and
- Amortization of any transitional obligation or asset existing at the date that FAS 106 is first applied.

[FAS 106, ¶¶ 19-22]

Q 20:11 Is the FAS 106 liability determined based solely on the written terms of the postretirement plan?

Generally, yes. However, if the employer has a cost-sharing policy, the written plan may be modified to take into account the employer's cost-sharing policy, if the cost-sharing policy meets either of the following conditions:

1. The employer has a past practice of (a) maintaining a consistent level of cost-sharing between itself and its retirees through changes in deductibles, coinsurance provisions, or retiree contributions, or (b) consistently increasing or reducing the employer's share of the cost of covered benefits through changes in retired or active plan participants' contributions toward their retiree health care benefits, deductibles, coinsurance provisions, out-of-pocket limitations, and so forth, in accordance with the employer's established cost-sharing policy; or

2. The employer has the ability to institute different cost-sharing provisions at a specified time or when certain conditions exist (for example, when health care cost increases exceed a certain level) and has communicated its intent to do so to affected plan participants.

[FAS 106, ¶¶ 23-28]

Q 20:12 What special actuarial assumptions does FAS 106 require in the case of postretirement health care benefits?

FAS 106 requires the use of several assumptions unique to health care benefits. These assumptions include:

- Consideration of historical per capita claims cost by age (and perhaps also by sex and geographical location);
- Health care cost trend rates, if the plan provides benefits-in-kind; and
- Medical coverage to be paid by governmental authorities (for example, Medicare) and other providers of health care benefits.

[FAS 106, ¶¶ 34-42]

Q 20:13 Does FAS 106 require an employer to fund its postretirement welfare benefits?

No, FAS 106 only requires the employer to recognize its liability for postretirement benefits on its financial statements. The FASB has no authority to require funding of benefits.

Q 20:14 If the employer has funded its postretirement benefits, do the fund assets offset the employer's FAS 106 liabilities?

Yes, they do, provided the assets are segregated in a trust, or otherwise effectively restricted (such as in a retired lives reserve held by an insurance company) so that they can be used to provide postretirement benefits only. [FAS 106, ¶¶ 63-66]

> **Planning Pointer.** Some employers have purchased corporate-owned life insurance (COLI) policies on their employees, with the intention of using the policy proceeds to pay for postretirement benefit costs. Since these policies are general assets of the employer and subject to the claims of the employer's creditors, the policies cannot be considered plan assets and cannot be used to offset the employer's liabilities for postretirement benefits.

Q 20:15 How are postretirement benefits that are insured under an insurance contract treated for FAS 106 purposes?

To the extent that postretirement benefits are covered by insurance contracts, the benefits are excluded from the employer's postretirement benefit obligation. For this purpose, an insurance contract is a contract in which an insurance company undertakes an unconditional legal obligation to provide specified benefits to specific individuals in return for a fixed consideration or premium. (As a practical matter, insurance coverage that guarantees payment of *all* postretirement medical benefits is generally unavailable except at a cost the employer finds unacceptable. However, an insurer may be willing to insure a portion of the benefits, such as benefits not exceeding a specified cap.) The contract must be irrevocable and involve the transfer of significant risk from the employer or plan to the insurance company. If the insurer does business primarily with the employer and related parties (that is, is a captive insurer) or if there is any reasonable doubt that the insurer will meet its obligations, the contract is not treated as an insurance contract.

Insurance contracts that qualify as such are not treated as plan assets, except when if the insurance contract is a participating contract that shares in the experience of the insurer, the participation right is considered a plan asset. [FAS 106, ¶¶ 67-71]

Disclosure Requirements

Q 20:16   Does FAS 106 impose disclosure requirements for postretirement benefits that must be included in financial statements?

Yes, defined benefit postretirement plans and defined contribution postretirement plans must satisfy FAS 106 disclosure requirements. The disclosures must be presented separately for the following plans:

- Plans that provide postretirement health care benefits and plans that primarily provide other postretirement benefits (if the obligations are significant); and

- Plans inside and plans outside the United States (if the obligations for non-U.S. plans are significant).

[FAS 106, ¶¶ 74-78]

Q 20:17   What disclosure requirements under FAS 106 apply to defined benefit postretirement plans?

An employer sponsoring one or more defined benefit postretirement plans must disclose (to the extent applicable) the following information about the plans:

1. A description of the plan, including such items as the nature of the plan, the groups of employees covered, company policy for funding, and commitment to increase benefits;

2. The amount of the plan expense for the accounting period involved, broken down into the components of service cost, interest cost, actual return on plan assets, amortization of the transition obligation or asset, and the net total of other components;

3. A schedule reconciling the funded status of the plan with the postretirement balance sheet liability, showing separately:

   —The fair value of plan assets (if any),

   —The postretirement benefit obligation, broken down among retirees, fully eligible participants, and other participants,

   —Prior service cost,

   —Net gain or loss,

   —Remaining transition obligation or asset, and

   —The net postretirement balance sheet amount;

4. The assumed health care cost trend rates, and the impact of a one-percentage-point increase in the trend rates;

5. Weighted average rates for assumed discount rates, rates of compensation increase (for pay-related plans), and expected long-term rates of return on plan assets (including estimated income tax rates if any);

6. The amount and type of employer (and related party) securities included in plan assets and the amount of plan benefits covered by insurance contracts issued by the employer (and related parties);

7. Alternative amortization methods;

8. Gain or loss recognized during the period of a settlement or curtailment and a description of the nature of the event; and

9. The cost of providing special or contractual termination benefits recognized during the accounting period and a description of the nature of the event.

[FAS 106,¶ 74]

Q 20:18   What disclosure requirements under FAS 106 apply to defined contribution postretirement welfare plans?

An employer sponsoring one or more defined contribution postretirement plans is required to disclose separately from any defined benefit plan disclosures the following information:

1. A description of the defined contribution plans, including:
   —Employee groups covered,
   —The basis for determining contributions, and
   —The nature and effect of significant matters affecting comparability of information for all periods presented; and
2. The amount of expense recognized during the period.

[FAS 106, ¶ 106]

Q 20:19   What impact will the FAS 106 requirements have on employers' financial statements?

In almost all cases, employers will be required to show greater expenses on the profit and loss statement and greater liabilities on the balance sheet. The effect will depend upon the age of the employer's workforce and the comparative size of its current retiree population. Although there are several combinations, two examples are given below for illustrative purposes:

Example 1. Employer A is an employer with a mature workforce (average age 50) and a very large retiree population. It will have a large FAS 106 liability in absolute dollar terms. Note, however, that since it has already been paying a high amount on a pay-as-you-go basis for its substantial retiree population, the increase in accrued benefits that FAS 106 will require it to disclose may be smaller, as a percentage of what it was recording on its financial statements as a pay-as-you-go expense, than an increase of an employer such as the one in Example 2 below.

Example 2. Employer B, with the same number of employees, has a very young workforce (average age 27) and only one retiree to date. Its current retiree medical expense, on a pay-as-you-go basis, is insignificant. This employer will have a relatively small FAS 106 liability in absolute dollar terms as compared to Employer A, because the required accruals are spread out over the service period (date of hire to date of first eligibility for retiree medical benefits) and the yearly increments for prefunding at such young ages are small. In percentage terms, however, its retiree medical expense liability will be huge—many times what its retiree medical expense had been previously.

Employers who were able to substantially prefund their postretirement welfare benefits will be less affected than similarly situated employers who did no prefunding.

Q 20:20   How does the FAS 106 liability affect the employer's ability to conduct its business?

The FAS 106 liability could affect a company in a number of ways, including the following:

1. The requirement that employers accrue the cost of postretirement medical coverage over the working lives of employees and disclose how much of this obligation is unfunded can affect the financial ratios required to be maintained under the terms of the company's existing loans.

2. A company's ability to obtain short-term and long-term financing is affected by the amount of liability shown on the company's balance sheet. Banks scrutinize a company's cash flow picture over the anticipated period of the loan to gauge the company's ability to repay the loan. The state of a company's finances (including its cash flow obligations for future benefit payments under a retiree medical plan) will affect whether loans will be obtainable and, if so, how favorable the terms (for example, repayment period, interest rate, and points) will be.

3. The company's annual benefit payment obligation and balance sheet liability could also be a factor in assessing the value of the company in a merger, acquisition, or divestiture situation.

4. The FAS 106 liability could affect the value of the company's stock, since it affects the earnings of the company as well as its surplus.

Reducing or Eliminating FAS 106 Liability

Q 20:21 What steps can an employer take to limit or reduce its FAS 106 liability?

There are a number of steps that an employer may wish to consider in order to control its FAS 106 liability. They may include:

- Capping the amount of the plan benefits;
- Instituting or increasing employee and/or retiree contributions;
- Switching from a defined benefit plan to a defined contribution plan approach;
- Increasing deductible and/or copayment levels;
- Extending a cafeteria plan to include retirees;
- Replacing one form of benefit with another (for example, dropping postretirement medical coverage and increasing pension benefits);
- Prefunding retiree benefits;
- Incorporating managed care features;
- Basing the level of retiree benefits on length of service (for example, full benefits after 30 years of service, half benefits after 15 years of service); and
- Integration of the retiree plan with other benefits (for example, Medicare)

Q 20:22 How will funding the employer's liability for retiree medical benefits affect the employer's FAS 106 liability?

The amount of a "plan asset" reduces the liability that must be shown on the employer's balance sheet. Additionally, the income on plan assets reduces the expense that is shown on the profit and loss statement.

To be a "plan asset" for this purpose, the asset must be segregated and restricted (usually in a trust) to be used for postretirement benefits. Plan assets ordinarily cannot be withdrawn by the employer except under specified limited circumstances. However, assets not segregated in a trust, or otherwise effectively restricted so that they cannot be used by the employer for other purposes, are not "plan assets" for FAS 106 purposes. Under certain circumstances, an insurance contract is not treated as a plan asset. [FAS 106, ¶¶ 63-66]

Q 20:23   How will retiree medical plan cutbacks affect the employer's FAS 106 liability?

The FAS 106 accounting liability required to be disclosed by an employer can be reduced, sometimes significantly, by cutting back the employer's retiree medical plan on a prospective basis. For many employers, the accounting liability will be so large that taking steps to reduce it is imperative. (See the discussion of cost containment through plan redesign contained in Questions 20:21.)

Employers with a large retiree population and a mature workforce will be affected greatly, whereas employers with few retirees and a young work force will be impacted much less severely.

Postemployment Benefits

Q 20:24   What is the difference between postemployment benefits and postretirement benefits?

Postemployment benefits are benefits provided by an employer to former or inactive employees (and their beneficiaries and covered dependents, if applicable) after employment but *before* retirement.

Inactive employees. For this purpose, inactive employees are those who are not currently rendering service to the employer and who have not been terminated. This category includes those who have been laid off and those on disability leave, regardless of whether they are expected to return to active status.

Q 20:25   What postemployment benefits are subject to FAS 112?

FAS 112 governs all types of benefits provided to former or inactive employees, their beneficiaries and covered dependents, including but not limited to salary continuation, supplemental unemployment benefits, severance benefits, disability-related benefits (including workers' compensation), job training and counseling, and continuation of benefits such as health care benefits and life insurance coverage. [FAS 112, ¶ 1] Financial Accounting Series Report No. 129-B, "A Guide to Implementation of Statement 106 on Employers' Accounting for Postretirement Benefits Other than Pensions: Questions and Answers" provides guidance on whether FAS 106 or FAS 112 applies.

Q 20:26   What is the FASB's position on how postemployment benefits should be treated for accounting purposes?

The FASB takes the position that, for accounting purposes, postemployment benefits are part of the compensation provided to an employee in exchange for services. As such, it requires that the cost of postemployment benefits be recognized on an accrual basis in accordance with FAS 5, Accounting for Contingencies, or FAS 43, Accounting for Compensated Absences, depending upon the particular type of postemployment benefit at issue.

Q 20:27   When is FAS 112 effective?

FAS 112 is effective for fiscal years beginning after December 15, 1993.

Appendix A—President Clinton's Proposed Health Plan

On October 27, 1993, the Clinton Administration released its proposed health bill, the "Health Security Act." Although competing legislative schemes will undoubtedly be introduced and the Clinton Health Plan proposal will undergo further refinements in Congress, a summary of the bill as introduced is included below for your reference.

THE HEALTH SECURITY ACT (PROPOSED OCTOBER 27, 1993)

PART I—THE OVERALL SCHEME

1. Eligible Individuals

Eligible individuals would include all individuals residing in the United States who are citizens or U.S. nationals, aliens who are permanently residing in the United States, and "certain long-term nonimmigrants." Undocumented aliens would not be eligible. Medicare-eligible individuals generally would be covered under Medicare rather than under the Health Care Security Program.

An individual would qualify as a spouse if married according to state law. Unmarried children under age 18, or unmarried full-time students to age 24, who are dependents of an eligible individual (as determined under state law) also would be eligible. Unmarried dependent children of any age who are incapable of self-support because of mental or physical disability that existed before age 21 also would be eligible. In addition, grandchildren would be covered if the parent of the child is a child himself or herself and both the child and the grandchild are living with the grandparent.

A new National Health Board would promulgate rules for families in which members are not residing in the same area and other special circumstances.

2. Health Alliances

Health care would be delivered throughout regional alliances established by states. Each state would be responsible for establishing one or more regional alliances. Regional alliances would not be permitted to overlap geographically. They would also have to encompass a population large enough to enable the alliance to negotiate effectively with health plans that provide comprehensive benefit packages to eligible individuals residing in the alliance's geographic area.

The health alliances would be governed by a board of directors consisting of equal number of employers and members or their representatives (none of whom could be a health care provider or have a substantial ownership in, or income from, a health care provider, health plan, pharmaceutical company, or supplier of medical equipment or supplies or an immediate family member of the same). Each health alliance also would be required to establish a provider advisory board consisting of representatives of providers and professionals who provide covered services throughout the health plans offered by the alliance.

The regional alliances would select the health plans that would be permitted to offer the Act's required comprehensive benefit package to eligible individuals. Health plans would be required to meet standards regarding such matters as quality, financial stability, and capacity to deliver health care services in order to be certified as a participating health plan by the regional alliance. At least one of the health plans offered by the regional alliance would be required to be a fee-for-service plan.

If a participating health plan were to fail or become insolvent, eligible individuals would be assured continuity of coverage for the comprehensive benefit package. Health care providers would be paid from a state guaranty fund and would not have a legal right to seek payment (other than for deductibles, copayments, and coinsurance amounts) for covered items and services from eligible individuals. The affected health care providers also would be required by law to continue caring for such individuals until they are enrolled in a new health plan.

3. Corporate Health Alliances

As an alternative to participating in a regional alliance, certain large employers and certain sponsors of multiemployer plans would be permitted a one-time election to sponsor a corporate alliance. Notice of the election would be required to be provided to the Secretary of Labor, and the sponsor would be required to file a document prescribed by the Secretary detailing how the corporate alliance would carry out its activities.

Large Employers: For this purpose, a large employer is one that has more than 5,000 full-time employees in the United States. All full-time employees would be eligible to enroll in the corporate alliance's health plans. A large employer could, when electing to be a corporate alliance, simultaneously elect to exempt any location at which it has fewer than 100 full-time employees, as long as the number of full-time United States employees in the locations covered by the corporate alliance still exceeds 5,000. If the number of full-time employees drops below 4,800, the employer would cease to qualify as an eligible sponsor of a corporate alliance.

Sponsor of a Multiemployer Plan: For this purpose, the multi-employer group health plan had to be in effect on September 1, 1993 and, on *both* September 1, 1993 and January 1, 1996, either (i) had to have more than 5,000 active participants or (ii) be affiliated with a national labor agreement covering more than 5,000 employees. If the plan drops below 4,800 active participants, the sponsor would cease to qualify as an eligible sponsor of a corporate alliance.

Excluded Employers: Employers whose primary business is employee leasing, the federal government (other than the United States Postal Service), and state and local governments would not be permitted to establish corporate health alliances.

Required Benefits: Corporate alliances must offer at least one fee-for-service plan and two health plans that are not fee-for-service. The plans offered by the corporate alliance may either be self-insured or state-certified health plans.

Corporate Alliance Insolvency Fund: The Secretary of Labor would establish a corporate alliance health plan insolvency fund. The Act provides a mechanism for borrowing to provide monies for the fund and for assessments against corporate alliances in an amount up to 2 percent of the aggregate annual premiums paid to self-insured plans of the corporate alliance, if necessary to repay monies borrowed to maintain the insolvency fund.

4. Single-Payer System

As an alternative to health alliances, a state may establish a single-payer system on either an alliancewide or statewide basis. Under a single-payer system, a state would pay health care providers directly and assume the financial risk of such payments. However, health care providers could agree to receive payments from the plan on a capitated (that is, a per-individual or per-head) basis under which the provider assumes the risk of the actual cost of treatment. At the state's option, corporate alliances could be required to participate in the single-payer system.

5. Enrollment

Regional alliances would hold annual open enrollment periods, during which eligible individuals would have the opportunity to choose among the health plans offered by the regional alliance. If the eligible individual fails to enroll in a participating health plan, he or she would automatically be enrolled at the time he or she first seeks treatment from a participating health plan. Enrollment in a particular health plan could be limited if it is oversubscribed.

Multiple Employment: If one spouse is a qualifying employee of a regional alliance employer and the other spouse is a qualifying employee of a corporate alliance employer (or each spouse has a different corporate alliance employer), the spouses would select which health alliance they want.

Health Security Card: All eligible individuals will be entitled to a "health security card" from a health alliance.

Disenrollment: No eligible individual can be disenrolled form a health plan until he or she is enrolled under another one or becomes eligible for Medicare.

6. Required Benefit Package

Each health alliance and corporate alliance would be required to offer the minimum comprehensive benefit package, which would include, subject to various limits, coverage for hospitalization, services from physicians, and other health professionals, emergency care, family planning services, hospice and home health care services, extended care, outpatient diagnostic and laboratory services, prescription drugs, vision and dental care, mental health and substance abuse series, and preventive care. Preventive evaluations, tests, and immunizations would be covered based upon an age-based schedule (the groupings initially proposed are individuals under age three, ages three to five, six to 19, 20 to 39, 40 to 49, and 50 to 65) detailing the services covered and how frequently they may be obtained. Benefits would not be permitted to be subject to any duration or scope limitation or any deductible, copayment, or coinsurance amount except those specifically authorized under the Act. However, a health professional or health facility would not be required to provide items or services covered under the comprehensive health package if it objects to doing so on the basis of a religious belief or moral conviction.

No Health Restrictions: Health plans would not be permitted to exclude any individual because of existing medical conditions, impose waiting periods before coverage begins or otherwise discriminate based upon health status or anticipated need for health services.

Materials: The health alliance would be responsible for providing enrollment materials (including costs, information concerning participating providers and health care institutions, and any restrictions on access to providers and services under the plan) in easily understood and useful form. The National Health Board may require the inclusion of additional information.

Claims: Each regional alliance would be required to establish and maintain a grievance procedure, plus an office of an ombudsman to assist members in dealing with problems that arise with health plans or with the alliance.

7. Cost-Sharing

The Act would require individuals enrolled under the plan to share costs through annual deductibles, copayments, and coinsurance, but individuals would be protected by an annual out-of-pocket expense limit. Each of these limits would be indexed under a formula that takes into account the rate of health care inflation. Plans would be permitted to charge a higher coinsurance rate for out-of-network items and services, subject to the maximum statutory coinsurance rate or any higher limit permitted by the National Health Board.

8. National Health Board

A new National Health Board would establish uniform standards regarding medical necessity, update the frequency schedules for age-appropriate immunizations, tests and clinician visits, and adopt other rules and regulations to effectuate the health program.

9. Effective Date

The Program is scheduled to become effective on January 1, 1998.

PART II—FINANCING AND EMPLOYER CONTRIBUTIONS

The proposed Clinton Health Plan, as embodied in the Health Security Act introduced in October 1993, would be financed through several sources.

Revenue would be generated from, among other things:

1. An increase on the tax on tobacco products;

2. Premiums paid jointly by employers (at least 80% of the average cost of premiums of health plans in the alliance) and employees (the difference between the employer contribution and the cost of the particular health plan chosen by the worker). Premiums charged to employers would be based upon a percent of payroll, capped at 7.9 percent and with lower caps on employers with 75 employees or less based upon the size of the employer (under 25 employees, 25 to 50 employees, and 50 to 75 employees) and graduated based upon the average wage paid by the employer;

3. A temporary assessment (payable in years 1998 through 2000) on employers who had retiree health benefit costs during 1991, 1992, and 1993 for individuals aged 55 to 64; and

4. A requirement that part of the cost of the program be borne by covered individuals directly, through the imposition of annual deductibles, copayments, and coinsurance amounts on the receipt of benefits (these cost-shifting techniques are discussed in Chapter 3).

Another factor in paying for the program is an attempt to make the cost of health care itself decrease, including by forcing a reduction in health-related litigation. This cost reduction would be sought to be achieved through a combination of various methods, including:

1. Taking advantage of efficiencies generated by bulk purchasing through alliances;

2. Reducing paperwork through the use of standardized forms;

3. Emphasizing the use of health maintenance organizations (which have the capability to control more cost variables) and the use of "gatekeepers" in preferred provider arrangements to shift individuals to more cost-effective treatment;

4. Avoiding duplicative medical determinations by incorporating workers' compensation and auto insurance medical benefits into the health plan;

5. Requiring adherence to a detailed review procedure for health claim grievances;

6. Limiting the jurisdiction of courts to hear health and medical malpractice claims;

7. Requiring plaintiffs to obtain a certificate of merit from a qualified medical specialist before proceeding with health care litigation; and

8. Limiting recovery of attorneys' fees in medical malpractice cases brought on a contingency fee basis to one-third of the award or recovery.

PART III—EFFECT ON OTHER WELFARE BENEFITS

If the broad-ranging scheme for health insurance reform contained in President Clinton's proposed Health Security Act were to be enacted, a number of corollary changes would be made to other welfare benefits. In addition, other long-overdue changes have simply been incorporated into the Health Security Act as a convenient vehicle to get everything accomplished all at once. This section describes some of the major changes that would occur under the proposed Health Security Act. The proposed Health Security Act, as first introduced, also included various transition rules for many of the changes described below.

Transition Period Restrictions

Of particular note are a few of the requirements that would be in effect during a transition period prior to full implementation of the program embodied in the Health Security Act.

Most importantly, during the transition period self-insured plan sponsors would be prohibited from cutting back, limiting, or reducing coverage for any medical condition or course of treatment for which the anticipated cost is likely to exceed $5,000 in any 12-month period. This would include terminating the plan and adopting a new plan with lesser benefits. Any such attempted modifications or cutbacks would be null and void and a civil penalty of up to $25,000 would apply to each violation. Individual health insurance plans could not be terminated except for very limited circumstances. Premium increases for individual insurance, insurance for groups with fewer than

100 covered lives, and insurance for groups with at least 100 lives would be restricted and closely regulated during the transition period.

Preexisting condition exclusions would be permitted in health plans during the transition period, but such exclusions could not exceed six months and could apply only to conditions that had been diagnosed or treated during the six-month period ending on the day before the first date of coverage. Further, the permitted six month exclusion would be required to be reduced month-for-month by the period the individual has been in "continuous coverage" (that is, covered by another group or individual health plan, Medicare, Medicaid, or other arrangement, without a three-month break in coverage).

Waiting periods evidently could still be imposed during the transition period, but not due to the employee's (or his or her dependent's) health status, claims experience, receipt of health care, medical history, or lack of evidence of insurability.

Code Section 106 Exclusion for Employer-Provided Health Coverage

Effective January 1, 2003, the Code Section 106 exclusion for employer-provided accident and health insurance would be restricted to the Health Security Act's comprehensive benefit package and other coverage that is expressly defined as "permitted coverage." Permitted coverage is limited to:

1. Wage replacement for absences from work due to sickness or injury (which presumably includes long-term disability insurance coverage);
2. Current Code Section 105(c) payments unrelated to absences from work for the permanent loss, or loss of the use, of a member or function of the body or permanent disfigurement;
3. Coverage provided to employees and former employees aged 65 or older (except coverage due to current employment);
4. "Qualified long-term care insurance"; and
5. Certain coverage for members of the armed services, veterans, and others to be determined.

Flexible spending arrangements would be excluded from Code Section 106 effective January 1, 1997.

COBRA

The Health Security Act would repeal the COBRA continuation of coverage requirements on January 1, 1988 or any earlier date on which all states have their health alliance programs in effect. Since eligible individuals would be permitted to enroll in a regional health alliance or (if they become reemployed) another corporate health alliance without the imposition of waiting periods or preexisting condition limitations, "bridging" of coverage evidently would not be necessary. Regardless of whether the individual loses employment, becomes divorced, or ceases to be a dependent, he or she would be eligible to become a member in the same or another regional health alliance immediately. (A limited group of individuals would not be able to receive coverage through a health alliance, including unemployed individuals age 65 or older who are eligible for Medicare, since Medicare initially would remain a separate system unless a state exercises its option to integrate Medicare with its regional health alliances.)

Cafeteria Plans

Effective January 1, 1997, neither employer-provided health benefits nor health care flexible spending accounts would be permitted under cafeteria plans. The definition of "qualified benefit" contained in Code Section 125 would be amended to exclude all coverage under accident and health insurance plans except for coverage providing wages or payments in lieu of wages for periods during which the employee is absent from work on account of sickness or injury. As a result, long-term care insurance and accidental death and dismemberment insurance also would not be qualified benefits and could not be offered on an employer-paid or salary-reduction basis under cafeteria plans.

Long-Term Care Insurance

The Health Security Act would amend the Code Section 213 definition of "medical care" to include qualified "long-term care services." This would include necessary diagnostic, curing, mitigating, treating, preventive, therapeutic, and rehabilitative services, and maintenance and personal care services (performed in either a residential or nonresidential setting) performed during a period when the individual is "incapacitated." For this purpose, an incapacitated individual would be one who is unable to perform at least two activities of daily living (defined as eating, toileting, transferring, bathing, or dressing) without substantial assistance from another individual or who has a severe cognitive impairment as defined by the Secretary of Labor. The primary purpose of the qualified long-term care services must be (i) to provide needed assistance with one or more of the activities of daily living or to protect the incapacitated individual from threats to health and safety due to severe cognitive impairment and (2) provided pursuant to a continuing plan of care prescribed by a licensed professional. Policy benefits would not be permitted to overlap the comprehensive health coverage required to be offered by health alliances or Medicare.

A new Code Section 7702B would expand the definition of "accident and health insurance contract" for tax purposes to include a "qualified long-term care insurance policy." A long-term care insurance policy would be required to satisfy certain standards in order to be treated as "qualified," including a maximum daily benefit limit of $150 (indexed to a new cost index for nursing homes and similar facilities) and nondiscriminatory eligibility and benefits requirements. All employees (other than those with less than three years of service, or who have not attained age 25, part-time or seasonal employees, and nonresident aliens with no U.S.-source income) must be allowed to participate, and the benefits provided under the plan must be identical for all employees who elect to participate.

Beginning January 1, 2003, the Code Section 106 exclusion for employer-provided accident and health insurance would be expanded to include such qualified long-term care insurance policies. As a result, employees would not be taxed either on the monthly value of coverage, or on benefit payments received under, qualified long-term care insurance policies paid for by the employer. This change would greatly facilitate the development of employer-paid long-term care insurance plans.

However, the revised definition of "qualified benefit" under Code Section 125 discussed above would prohibit the inclusion of employer-provided qualified long-term care insurance in cafeteria plans.

Accelerated Death Benefits Under Life Insurance Contracts

Accelerated death benefits under life insurance contracts would be treated as death benefits that are excluded from gross income under Code Section 101(a), and insurance contracts offering "qualified accelerated death benefit riders" for terminally ill in- dividuals would be treated as life insurance for tax purposes, provided that the insured is expected to die within 12 months of the accelerated death benefit payment.

Funding Retiree Health and Life Insurance Benefits

The Code Section 419A provisions regarding permissible reserves for postretirement medical and life insurance would be amended to require that such reserves be funded over a minimum working-lives figure of ten years. Prefunding would not be permitted for any benefits that are reasonably expected to be taxable when received. In addition, such reserves would be required to be maintained in a separate account.

No further contributions to Code Section 401(h) accounts under pension or annuity plans would be allowed after December 31, 1994. For plans maintained pursuant to one or more collective bargaining agreements ratified on or before October 29, 1993, contributions would not be permitted after the earliest of the date on which the last of such agreements terminates (disregarding extensions after such date), or January 1, 1995 (if later than that), or January 1, 1998.

Code Section 420 transfers would still be permitted but would be required to take into account cost savings under the Health Security Act to the extent required by the Secretary of the Treasury.

Prepayment of Medical Insurance Premiums

Beginning in 1997, a taxpayer's ability to prepay and deduct medical insurance premiums would be limited. Code Section 213 would be amended to provide that any prepayment of coverage to be provided more than 12 months after the month in which the premium payment is made would be required to be treated as paid ratably over the period during which the insurance coverage or care is provided.

Workers' Compensation

Health plans that participate in health alliances would be required to provide workers' compensation services (other than emergency services) through the health plan (even if such services are not a part of the comprehensive benefit package) and to use a case manager for such services. (Case management is discussed in Chapter 3.) States would have the option of designating specialized workers' compensation providers for certain geographic areas to provide coverage for one or more types of injuries or illnesses. In addition, the worker and a workers' compensation carrier may agree to the provision of care outside of the health plan. State laws restricting choice of workers' compensation providers or payment of them would be preempted, although the determination of whether an individual is injured and entitled to workers' compensation medical benefits and the scope of items and services available to such injured workers would continue to be determined under state law.

Delivery of auto insurance medical benefits also would be coordinated with the health alliances.

ERISA

ERISA would be amended to provide that its reporting and disclosure provisions and its fiduciary responsibility provisions would not apply to state-certified health plans. For those health plans to which the ERISA reporting and disclosure and fiduciary responsibility provisions continue to apply (including self-insured plans of corporate health alliances), the Secretary of Labor would be authorized to require more frequent reports and disclosures to the government and to participants and beneficiaries. Benefit claim procedures would be coordinated with those mandated by the Health Security Act. ERISA preemption rules also would not apply to state-certified health plans.

Glossary of Terms

The following is a list of terms (arranged in alphabetical order) that is intended to provide the reader with an additional guide to understanding the complex concepts that apply to employee welfare benefit plans.

Account limit: The maximum addition to a qualified asset account of a welfare benefit fund that an employer is permitted to deduct. It equals the amount reasonably and actuarially necessary to fund benefit claims incurred but unpaid as of the end of the taxable year, plus administrative costs and certain contributions to an additional reserve for postretirement medical or life insurance benefits; these limits do not apply to employee-pay-all voluntary employees' beneficiary associations (VEBAs) covering more than 50 employees, none of whom is entitled to a refund that is not based on the experience of the entire fund.

ADA: The Americans with Disabilities Act of 1990.

ADEA: The Age Discrimination in Employment Act (29 USC §§ 621 et seq. [1967]). This statute protects workers over 40 from compulsory retirement at any age as long as they are capable of performing their jobs adequately; it also protects them from adverse job actions based on age (e.g., refusal to hire; discriminatory layoff) and against benefits discrimination. Employers are subject to ADEA if they engage in an industry affecting interstate commerce and had 20 or more employees in each working day of 20 or more weeks in the current or preceding calendar year.

Age Discrimination in Employment Act: See ADEA.

Aggregation: The process of considering separate plans together to see whether they satisfy requirements under ERISA and/or the Internal Revenue Code. Aggregation can be either permissive or mandatory.

ASO arrangement: Administrative-services-only arrangement. A system under which an employer self-insures its welfare benefit plan, but contracts with a third-party administrator such as an insurance company that provides claims administration and related services.

Cafeteria plans: Plans allowing employees to choose from a "menu" of one or more qualified benefits and cash (including nontaxable benefits). Under Code Section 125, benefits from a properly drafted cafeteria plan are not taxed to the employee who selects them—unless the employee actually chooses taxable benefits (and is not merely entitled to do so).

Capitation fee: The set fee that an employer pays an HMO to provide care for each member employee, regardless of the actual cost of the care.

Captive insurance company: An insurance company that is partially or wholly owned by an employer.

COB: Coordination of benefits. A group health insurance plan's COB provisions deal with the situation in which more than one plan covers a particular medical expense, in order to cut costs and prevent windfalls to employees. The general rule is that if a person is covered under one plan as an employee and under another as a dependent, the employment-related plan is the primary payor.

COBRA: The Consolidated Omnibus Budget Reconciliation Act of 1985 (Pub. L. No. 99-272). This statute (signed in 1986) requires employers to offer the option of purchasing continuation coverage to qualified beneficiaries who would otherwise lose group health insurance coverage as the result of a qualifying event (such as termination of employment or divorce from an employee).

Code: The Internal Revenue Code of 1986 (26 USC § 1 et seq.), as adopted by TRA 1986 (Pub. L. No. 99-514). ("Former Code" refers to repealed provisions, including those in the previous Internal Revenue Code of 1954.)

Coinsurance: A cost-sharing mechanism under which the employee is required to pay a percentage (e.g., 10 percent) of medical expenses arising after the deductible has been satisfied; the plan pays the balance.

Collectively bargained plan: Plans whose terms have been the subject of good-faith bargaining between an employer or group of employers and employee representative(s) (e.g., union(s)). For COBRA purposes, an employer whose group health plan covers both union and nonunion employees and their families is considered to have two separate plans, only one of which is collectively bargained.

Common-law employee: A person who performs service(s) for an employer, if the employer has the right to direct both the objective of the services and the manner in which they are performed.

Continuation coverage: Health insurance that employees can purchase when they cease to be covered under the employer's plan as a result of a "qualifying event" such as retirement or divorce. Continuation coverage is regulated by COBRA.

Coordination of benefits: See COB.

Deductible: A cost-sharing method under which employees are required to assume part of the cost of health care (e.g. $500 per person per year) before direct payment or reimbursement is available from the plan.

Deemed death benefit: See DDB.

Dependent care assistance plan: A plan under which an employer provides assistance for an employee's employment-related expenses of caring for a child, parent, or other dependent—either directly in the form of dependent care centers or through cash reimbursements for dependent care expenses. Benefits of up to $5,000 ($2,500 for a married employer filing a separate return) from such a plan are not taxable income for the employee, subject to certain income limitations.

Dependent care assistance program: See dependent care assistance plan.

Determination period: Under COBRA, a period of 12 consecutive months that is used to calculate the premiums for continuation coverage.

Disability plan: A plan that provides benefits to employees who are unable to work because of illness or accident. As a general rule. benefits under these plans are taxable to employees who receive them. State workers' compensation laws compel employers to provide coverage for job-related disabilities. Disability plans include wage continuation (sick pay) plans and plans paying temporary or long-term disability benefits.

Disqualified benefit: In a welfare benefit fund context: (1) a portion of the fund that reverts to the benefit of the employer or (2) a postretirement medical or life insurance benefit provided either (a) under a discriminatory plan or (b) with respect to a key employee but not made from the mandatory separate account. The employer is subject to an excise tax equal to 100 percent of the disqualified benefit.

Diversification rule: An ERISA rule mandating that fiduciaries diversify plan investments to avoid the risk of large losses—unless circumstances make it imprudent to diversify.

DOL: Department of Labor. The U.S. Department of Labor has enforcement authority over the regulatory and administrative (i.e., nontax) provisions of ERISA.

Educational assistance program: A program under which employers provide tuition assistance for employees' continuing education. Benefits under such programs are taxable to the employee receiving them (unless certain income exclusions available through 1989 are restored).

EEOC: Equal Employment Opportunity Commission; the federal agency that enforces ADA, ADEA, and Title VII of the Civil Rights Act of 1964.

Employee-pay-all plans: Plans that are paid for entirely by the employees, with no financial input from the employer.

Employee welfare benefit plan: Any plan, fund, or program that is established or maintained by an employer and/or an employee organization to provide benefits (e.g., medical, sick pay, and vacation benefits) to plan participants or their beneficiaries. Under Department of Labor regulations, certain severance pay arrangements and supplemental retirement income payments may be treated as welfare plans rather than pension plans.

Employer-provided benefit: A benefit that is provided, directly or via employer contributions, by an employer.

ERISA: Employee Retirement Income Security Act of 1974 (Pub. L. No. 93-406). ERISA is the basic law designed to protect the rights of beneficiaries of employee benefit plans offered by employers, unions, and the like. ERISA imposes various qualification standards and fiduciary responsibilities on both welfare benefit and retirement plans, and provides enforcement procedures as well.

Exclusive benefit rule: The ERISA requirement that plans, by their terms and operations, be maintained for the exclusive benefit of employees who are plan participants. Under ERISA, fiduciaries have a duty to administer plans solely in the interest of participants and beneficiaries and are not permitted to allow plan assets to inure to the benefit of the employer.

FASB: Financial Accounting Standards Board; the body that sets uniform standards for treatment of accounting items. In the employee benefits context, FASB has prepared an exposure draft concerning disclosure of unfunded retiree welfare benefit liabilities.

Federally qualified HMO: An HMO that meets the standards set forth in the HMO Act and can "mandate" an employer to provide HMO coverage to employees in the HMO's service area.

Flexible benefit account: A type of medical or dependent care expense reimbursement option under a cafeteria plan or which is a cafeteria plan standing alone. Coverage is paid for by employer contributions, or salary reduction contributions, or both.

FICA: Federal Insurance Contribution Act; the statute that requires employers and employees to pay Social Security taxes.

Fiduciary: Any person (in the legal sense of an individual, corporation, etc.) that exercises discretionary authority or control over the administration of the plan or the management or disposition of plan assets or that gives investment advice to the plan for a fee or other compensation.

Flexible spending account (FSA): A cafeteria plan benefit option (most commonly used for medical expense reimbursement and dependent care costs) that reimburses employees for certain expenses they incur.

FMLA: The Family and Medical Leave Act of 1993.

401(k) plan: An arrangement (defined by IRC Section 401(k)) under which a covered employee can elect to defer income by making pretax contributions to a profit-sharing or stock bonus plan. A cafeteria plan may provide a 401(k) plan as a qualified benefit option.

FSA: See Flexible Spending Account.

Funding: Accumulating money or other assets that can be used to pay for plan benefits—e.g., by creating a welfare benefit trust or other welfare benefit fund.

General death benefit: A benefit payable under a group term life insurance plan on the death of an employee, without special conditions (e.g., double indemnity for accidental death). This is the type of benefit that can qualify for special tax treatment under an IRC Section 79 group term life insurance policy.

Group enrollment period: An annual period of at least 10 working days during which employees must be given the option of enrolling in one or more federally qualified HMOs or switching from an HMO to another health plan option offered by the employer.

Group health plan: Under ERISA, an employee welfare benefit plan providing medical care to participants and beneficiaries, either directly or indirectly (e.g., through insurance or otherwise). Under the Internal Revenue Code, a plan maintained by an employer to provide medical care, directly or indirectly, to employees, ex-employees, and their families.

Group legal services plan: An employer-funded program that provides personal legal services to employees and their spouses and dependents. Benefits received under a group legal services plan are taxable to the employee (unless certain income exclusions available through 1989 are restored).

Group term life insurance plan: A plan qualifying under Code Section 79 to provide employees with employer-paid life insurance coverage at little or no tax cost. Employees have taxable income only to the extent that (1) the cost of insurance providing a group term general death benefit exceeds the cost of providing $50,000 of coverage or (2) the plan contains nonqualifying features. Special rules may apply to highly compensated employees or key employees.

Group universal life insurance: A program (usually on an employee-pay-all basis) that provides employees with universal life insurance, giving them a choice between a fixed death benefit or a death benefit that is a multiple of compensation plus the policy's cash value at the time of death. Group universal life insurance does not qualify for special tax treatment under Code Section 79.

HCFA: Health Care Financing Administration. The agency of the U.S. Department of Health and Human Services that is responsible for administering the Medicare and Medicaid programs.

HHS: The U.S. Department of Health and Human Services, which promulgates the regulations issued under the HMO Act.

Highly compensated employee: An employee who is paid over $75,000 a year (or over $50,000 if that places the employee in the top 20 percent of earnings paid by the employer); a 5 percent owner; or an officer paid more than 50 percent of the defined-benefit limit set by Code Section 415(b)(1)(A). Code Section 89, and various other Code provisions, prohibit benefit plan discrimination in favor of highly compensated employees.

HMO: Health maintenance organization; an organization of medical care providers that provides a specified range of medical care in return for a set "capitation fee," without regard to the actual cost of providing medical care for each HMO member.

HMO Act: The Health Maintenance Organization Act of 1973. This federal statute, as amended, sets the standard for federally qualified HMOs that can mandate employees and regulates other HMO matters.

Incidents of ownership: Rights that will result in the inclusion of life insurance policy proceeds in the policyholder's estate for federal estate tax purposes.

Independent contractor: A person who performs services for another, but who is not a common-law employee because he or she is a member of a traditionally independent profession or exercises such control over the services as to preclude the existence of an employment relationship.

Insured plan: A welfare benefit plan that is funded by the employer's purchase of policies from commercial insurers.

Internal Revenue Code: See Code.

Investment Manager: Under ERISA, the registered investment advisor, insurance company, or bank and trust company to which a plan's named fiduciary delegates investment authority over plan assets pursuant to an express authorization in the plan documents. Investment managers must acknowledge in writing that they are fiduciaries with respect to a plan.

IPA: Independent practice association; a type of HMO consisting of coordinated groups of physicians practicing out of individual offices.

IRC: See Code.

IRS: Internal Revenue Service; the federal agency, which is part of the U.S. Department of the Treasury, that is charged with primary responsibility for administering, interpreting, and enforcing the Code. (Note, however, that the Secretary of the Treasury—and not the IRS—issues regulations under the Code.)

Key employee: Under the pre-TRA '86 rules governing group term life insurance plans, an officer of the employer earns more than 150 percent of the defined-benefit limit; a 5 percent direct or indirect owner of the employer; a 1 percent direct or indirect owner of the employer receiving compensation over $150,000 from the employer; or a ½ percent owner of the employer (if this is one of the 10 largest holdings) who earns more than the defined-contribution limit under IRC Section 415. A person who was a key employee at retirement or separation from service retains that status.

Medical care: Under the IRC definition, diagnosis, cure, mitigation, treatment, or prevention of disease or affecting any structure or function of the body; also traveling for or incidental to medical care.

Insurance for medical care is treated as medical care; so is the cost of prescription drugs and insulin.

Medical plan: An arrangement sponsored by an employer that reimburses employees for costs of personal injuries or illness.

Medicare and Medicaid coverage data bank: A data bank to be established by the U.S. Department of Health and Human Services to receive information required to be reported regarding group health plan participants.

MEWA: Multiple employer welfare arrangement; a noncollectively bargained arrangement or plan maintained to benefit employees of two or more employers that are not under common control. ERISA generally does not preempt state law with regard to MEWAs. Small employers participating in MEWAs may be exempt from COBRA's continuation-coverage requirement, and other special rules apply under COBRA.

Minimum-premium insurance arrangement: A method of funding welfare benefit plans under which benefits are self-insured by an employer or trustee up to a set trigger point; a commercial insurer is liable for all benefits above the trigger point.

NAIC: National Association of Insurance Commissioners.

Named fiduciary: For ERISA purposes, a fiduciary to which the ERISA plan document gives express authority to control plan operations and administration.

Net single premium: The premium for one dollar of paid-up whole life insurance. This amount is used; e.g., in calculating the cost of nonqualifying permanent benefits for an employee that are provided under a Code Section 79 group term life insurance plan.

Noncompliance period: Under COBRA, the period beginning on the date a violation first occurs. The period is used to compute the penalty excise tax imposed on employers that violate COBRA rules.

Nondiscrimination rules: Rules that deny the employer, the employee, or both, certain tax benefits if plans discriminate in favor of certain employees, such as highly compensated employees or key employees.

OBRA '93: The Omnibus Budget Reconciliation Act of 1993.

Open enrollment period: See group enrollment period.

Party in interest: A person who stands in a relationship to a plan (e.g., sponsor, fiduciary, provider of services) that is close enough to result in the prohibition of certain transactions (e.g., sales, loans, leases, exchange of property).

Plan administrator: Under ERISA, the plan sponsor (e.g., employer) or person that the plan instrument designates as the plan administrator.

Plan sponsor: The employer or employee organization that establishes or maintains a plan; the association, committee, joint board of trustees, or similar group if the plan is established or maintained by two or more employers and/or employee organizations.

PPO: Preferred provider organization; a network of medical care providers organized by an employer or insurer to provide various medical care services to covered employees for specified fees. The covered employees are required or encouraged to go to these preferred providers when they need medical care, on the assumption that the preferred providers will charge less than other providers.

Pregnancy disability: Disability that is caused, or contributed to, by pregnancy, childbirth, or related medical conditions. Under Title VII of the Civil Rights Act of 1964, employers must treat such disabilities on a parity with other, nonpregnancy-related conditions.

Prohibited transaction: Specified transactions (e.g., sales and exchanges, leases, and loans) between the plan and a party in interest that are forbidden by ERISA. The Department of Labor has the power to exempt individual transactions or classes of transactions from the restriction.

Prudent man rule: Under ERISA, the standard of care to which fiduciaries are held—i.e., the care, skill, diligence, and prudence that a prudent man, acting in a like capacity and familiar with such matters would use in conducting an enterprise of the same character and aims under similar circumstances.

QMCSO: A Qualified Medical Child Support Order.

Qualified asset account: An account consisting of assets set aside for future payment of benefits by a welfare benefit fund. The Internal Revenue Code sets limits on the deduction employers may take for additions to a qualified asset account.

Qualified beneficiary: A person entitled to COBRA continuation coverage because of his or her status on the day before a qualifying event occurs. Covered employees under a group health plan can be qualified beneficiaries; so can their covered spouses and covered children.

Qualified benefit: A noncash benefit that a cafeteria plan is permitted to offer.

Qualified cash-or-deferred arrangement: See 401(k) plan.

Qualified cost: The limit on an employer's tax deduction for contribution to a welfare benefit fund. It equals the fund's qualified direct cost and permitted additions to a qualified asset account, minus the fund's after-tax income for the taxable year.

Qualified direct cost: The aggregate benefits and administrative expenses of a welfare benefit fund that a cash-basis employer would be entitled to deduct if it paid the expenses directly.

Qualified Medical Child Support Order: A court order satisfying certain form and content requirements, under which the group health plan must pay plan benefits to the child or children listed as alternate payee(s).

Qualified nonguaranteed contract: An insurance contract that is excluded from the Internal Revenue Code's definition of a welfare benefit fund. All insurance contracts are treated as qualified nonguaranteed contracts unless they provide a guarantee of renewal at set rates and do not provide only insurance protection and nonguaranteed policy dividends or experience-rated refunds determined by factors other than the level of welfare benefits paid.

Qualifying event: An event that entitles a person to elect continuation coverage under COBRA—e.g., termination of employment for reasons other than gross misconduct, or separation or divorce from a covered employee. The nature of the qualifying event determines whether continuation coverage will be available for 18, 29, or 36 months.

Retiree medical account: A separate account that is contained in a pension or annuity plan, providing health benefits subordinate to the plan's retirement benefits.

Rollout: Termination of a split-dollar life insurance plan by giving the employee complete ownership and control of the life insurance policy.

Salary reduction contribution: A contribution (also called an elective contribution) made to purchase a cafeteria plan benefit under an agreement between employer and employee. Such a contribution is a pretax contribution, which is not included in the employee's taxable income.

Self-dealing: Under ERISA, prohibited activities by a plan fiduciary such as using plan assets for personal profit, accepting bribes or kickbacks from anyone dealing with the plan, or acting on behalf of a party whose interests are adverse to those of the plan.

Self-insurance: An employer's practice of paying benefits out of its own assets or funds (without involvement of a commercial insurer) to pay benefits.

Self-insured medical reimbursement plan: A plan that reimburses employees for their medical expenses but does not use accident and health insurance policies or prepaid health care plans (e.g., HMOs) for this purpose.

Service area: The geographic area within which an HMO provides health care.

Severance pay plan: A plan that pays benefits (usually proportionate to length of employment) to employees undergoing a voluntary or involuntary separation from service.

Split-dollar plan: A life insurance plan that gives both the employer and the employee an interest in a cash-value life insurance policy on the employee's life. Either (1) the employer owns the policy, and the policy is endorsed to show the employee's beneficial interest (endorsement method) or (2) the employee owns the policy and makes a collateral assignment to the employer to evidence the employer's beneficial interest. The employee has taxable income equal to the value of death benefit coverage paid for by the employer.

SPD: The summary plan description required by ERISA that is distributed to plan participants. It explains the material terms of the plan and contains required technical information and a notice of ERISA rights.

Stop-loss insurance arrangement: A funding mechanism for welfare benefit plans under which an employer self-insures the plan benefits but arranges to have an insurance company pay for claims above a specified level, such as 120 percent of expected claims.

Table I: A table, found in the Treasury Regulations under IRC Section 79, that gives the monthly cost of providing $1,000 of insurance coverage, based on the employee's age. Table I is used to value coverage under IRC 79.

TAMRA: The Technical and Miscellaneous Revenue Act of 1988 (Pub. L. No. 100-647).

Term life insurance: Insurance that provides death benefit coverage for a specified period, without permanent policy benefits such as cash or loan value.

Title VII: The portion of the Civil Rights Act of 1964 that deals with discrimination in employment. Title VII forbids employment discrimination (e.g., in hiring, firing, and promotion) based on suspect criteria such as race, sex, religion, and national origin.

TRA '84: The Tax Reform Act of 1984, enacted as part of the Deficit Reduction Act of 1984 (Pub. L. No. 98-369).

TRA '86: The Tax Reform Act of 1986 (Pub. L. No. 99-514), the statute that enacted the comprehensive changes that led to the redesignation of the Internal Revenue Code as the Tax Code of 1986 rather than 1954.

Treasury regulations (Treas. Reg.): Regulations promulgated by the U.S. Department of the Treasury. IRS is a part of the Treasury Department, and regulations interpreting the Internal Revenue Code are technically Treasury Regulations.

Use-it-or-lose-it rule: A rule forbidding cafeteria plans to let participants defer receipt (and taxation) of compensation from year to year by carrying over unused pretax contributions or plan benefits.

Vacation pay plan: An employee plan that compensates employees for holidays and vacation (including vacation time that has been earned but not taken).

VEBA: Voluntary employees' beneficiary association; a tax-exempt welfare benefit fund regulated by Code Section 501(c)(9) that pays death, sickness, accident, or other benefits to members, their dependents, and/or beneficiaries.

Welfare benefit fund: A fund created by an employer to pay welfare benefits to employees or their beneficiaries pursuant to an employee benefit plan.

Welfare benefit plan: See Employee Welfare Benefit Plan.

Written plan: A plan all of whose material terms are set forth in a single written document and/or incorporated by reference to another document. ERISA and various sections of the IRC impose separate single-written-plan requirements.

ZEBRAs: Zero balance cafeteria plan accounts, under which participants purchase medical expense reimbursement coverage by making salary reduction contributions only in the amount to be reimbursed. Such arrangements are specifically forbidden in cafeteria plans.

Index

[References are to question numbers.]

Index

[*References are to question numbers.*]